International Asset Transfer
An Overview of the Main Jurisdictions

International Asset Transfer
An Overview of the Main Jurisdictions

A Practitioner's Handbook

Edited by

Gero Pfeiffer, Sven Timmerbeil, Frederik Johannesdotter

in collaboration with

Kay L. Tidwell

De Gruyter Recht · Berlin 2010

♾ Printed on acid-free paper that falls within the guidelines of the ANSI
to ensure permanence and durability.

ISBN 978-3-89949-482-2

Bibliografische Information der Deutschen Nationalbibliothek

Die Deutsche Nationalbibliothek verzeichnet diese Publikation in der Deutschen Nationalbibliografie; detaillierte bibliografische Daten sind im Internet über http://dnb.d-nb.de abrufbar.

Printed in Germany
Data Conversion: jürgen ullrich typosatz, Nördlingen
Printing and Binding: Hubert & Co., Göttingen

Preface

Business transactions do not stop at national borders. The objective of this handbook is to explain the basic legal issues that must be considered when acquiring a business by way of an asset deal in any of thirty-two major jurisdictions around the world. The authors of the chapters are all local lawyers working in international law firms or enterprises, well-reputed local firms, associations or academic institutions. All of them have practiced mergers and acquisitions in the field of corporate law for a number of years in their respective jurisdictions.

Publishing a handbook with authors from so many countries is challenging not only from a substantive perspective but also in terms of coordination and process management. The editors have tried to ensure that the chapters – which were contributed to by sixty-nine authors in total (including several co-authors in a number of countries) – are as uniform in language and presentation as possible, so as to emphasize the substantive differences among the laws of the various jurisdictions. Special thanks in this regard goes to our American colleague Kay Tidwell, who reviewed from a native-speaker perspective all of the chapters in this tome and provided comments to improve fluency and readability.

We hope that this handbook may serve as helpful guidance to the reader when considering an acquisition of assets in any of the jurisdictions covered here. Should you need any individual local legal advice, the authors are happy to assist you. Their contact details are set forth in the Directory of Authors following the Table of Contents.

Many thanks to the publisher Walter de Gruyter, and in particular to Michael Schremmer, who was very patient with us during the entire project. Particular appreciation is due also to all the authors for their participation in the publication of this handbook and all the other individuals who supported us, including but not limited to Nina Siegfried, Ronny Duckstein and Jacqueline Killian.

Gero Pfeiffer Sven Timmerbeil Frederik Johannesdotter

Frankfurt am Main/Germany, July 2009

Table of Contents

Directory of Authors

Introduction

Kay L. Tidwell
Tel.: +1 (213) 891 8419
Fax: +1 (213) 891 8763
kay.tidwell@lw.com

Latham & Watkins LLP
355 South Grand Avenue
Los Angeles CA, 90071-1560
USA
www.lw.com

Argentina

Christian Krüger
Tel.: +54 (11) 4114 3000
Fax: +54 (11) 4114 3001/2
ck@pagbam.com.ar

Juan Pedeflous
Tel.: +54 (11) 4114 3000
Fax: +54 (11) 4114 3001/2
jp@pagbam.com.ar

Pérez Alati, Grondona, Benites, Arntsen & Martínez de Hoz (h)
Suipacha 1111, piso 18
1008 – Buenos Aires
Argentina
www.pagbam.com.ar

Australia

John Mollard
Tel.: +61 (3) 9617 4450
Fax: +61 (3) 9614 2103
john.mollard@bakernet.com

Baker & McKenzie
Level 19
181 Williams Street
Melbourne, Victoria 3000
Australia
www.bakernet.com

Jason Cornwall-Jones
Tel.: +61 3 9679 3000
Fax: +61 3 9679 3111
jason.cornwall-jones@blakedawson.com

Blake Dawson
Level 26
181 Williams Street
Melbourne, Victoria 3000
Australia
www.blakedawson.com

Austria

Andreas Zahradnik
Tel.: +43 (1) 5334795 42
Fax: +43 (1) 5334795 5042
andreas.zahradnik@dbj.at

Co-Author:
Barbara Cervenka

DORDRA BRUGGER JORDIS Rechtsanwälte GmbH
Dr. Karl Lueger-Ring 10
1010 Vienna
Austria
www.dbj.at

Belarus

Maksim Salahub
Tel.: +375 (17) 306 2102
Fax: +370 (17) 306 2079
sorainen@sorainen.com

Co-Authors:
Kiryl Apanasevich,
Ann Valchok,
Iryna Mitsianiova

Sorainen
Pobediteley Ave. 23/3
220004 Minsk
Belarus
www.sorainen.com

Brasil

Marcelo Takeyama
Tel.: +55 (11) 3065 4480
Fax.: +55 (11) 3064 6049
marcelo.takeyama@baschrameh.com.br

Roberta Marques de Camargo Vianna Godoy
Tel: + 55 (11) 3065 4469
Fax: + 55 (11) 3064 6049
roberta.vianna@baschrameh.com.br

Basch & Rameh
Rua da Consolação, 3741-13o
01416-001 – São Paulo, SP
Brasil
www.baschrameh.com.br

Bulgaria

Plamen Marintchov Borissov
Tel.: +359 (2) 811 7751
Fax: +359 (2) 811 7752
office@borissov-law.com

Borissov Law
NDK Administrative Building
1 Bulgaria Sq., P.O. Box 246
1463 Sofia
Bulgaria
www.borissov-law.com

Canada

Stephen Rigby
Tel.: +1 (416) 865 7793
Fax: +1 (416) 865 7048
stephen.rigby@mcmillan.ca

Bruce Chapple
Tel.: +1 (416) 865 7024
Fax: +1 (416) 865 7048
bruce.chapple@ mcmillan.ca

McMillan LLP
Brookfield Place, Suite 4400
Bay Wellington Tower
181 Bay Street
Toronto, Ontario M5J 2T3
Canada
www.mcmillan.ca

China (PRC)

Audry (Hong) Li
Tel.: +86 (21) 5037 2011
Fax: +86 (21) 5037 2678
audryli@zhonglun.com

Lefan Gong
Tel.: +86 (21) 5037 2668
Fax: +86 (21) 5037 2678
lefangong@zhonglun.com

Zhong Lun Law Firm
200 Yin Cheng Road Central
11th Floor, Bank of China Tower
Pudong, Shanghai, 200120
China
www.zhonglun.com

Colombia

Andrés Téllez-Núñez
Tel.: +57 (1) 2749901
Fax: +57 (1) 2749901
tellez.andres@gmail.com

Pontificia Universidad Javeriana
Facultad de Ciencias Jurídicas
Calle 40 No. 6-23
Colombia
www.javeriana.edu.co

Denmark

Nils Kjellegaard Jensen
Tel.: +45 (36) 944 113
Fax: +45 (36) 944 010
nils@nkj-legal.com

Law Firm Kjellegaard Jensen
Tuborg Boulevard 12, 3rd Floor
2900 Hellerup (Copenhagen)
Denmark
www.nkj-legal.com

England & Wales

Andrew Gillen
Tel.: +44 (207) 295 3000
Fax: +44 (207) 295 3500
andrew.gillen@traverssmith.com

Co-Author:
Fay Anthony

Travers Smith
10 Snow Hill
London
EC1A 2AL
UK
www.traverssmith.com

Estonia

Paul Künnap
Tel.: +372 (6) 400 900
Fax: +372 (6) 400 901
paul.kunnap@sorainen.ee

Toomas Prangli
Tel.: +372 (6) 400 900
Fax: +372 (6) 400 901
toomas.prangli@sorainen.ee

Sorainen
Pärnu mnt 15
10141 Tallinn
Estonia
www.sorainen.com

France

Bénédicte Bremond
Tel.: +33 (1) 4062 2080
Fax: +33 (1) 4062 2062
benedicte.bremond@lw.com

Latham & Watkins AARPI
53, quai d'Orsay
75007 Paris
France
www.lw.com

Germany

Sven Timmerbeil
Tel.: +49 (176) 2079 1408
Fax: +49 (69) 6062 6700
sut@georgetown.edu

Gero Pfeiffer
Tel.: +49 (69) 6062 6560
Fax: +49 (69) 6062 6700
gero.pfeiffer@lw.com

Frederik Johannesdotter
Tel.: +49 (69) 6062 6000
Fax: +49 (69) 6062 6700
frederik.johannesdotter@lw.com

Latham & Watkins LLP
Reuterweg 20
60323 Frankfurt am Main
Germany
www.lw.com

Hungary

Péter Berethalmi
Tel.: +36 (1) 487 8712
Fax: +36 (1) 487 8701
berethalmi.peter@nt.hu

Nagy és Trócsányi Ügyvédi Iroda
Ugocsa utca 4/B
1126 Budapest
Hungary
www.nt.hu

India

Shourya Mandal
Tel.: +91 (33) 40056000
Fax: +91 (33) 40056016
shourya.mandal@foxmandal.com

Orijit Chatterjee
Tel.: +91 (33) 40056000
Fax: +91 (33) 40056016
orijit.chatterjee@foxmandal.com

Fox Mandal
6, Church Lane
Kolkata - 700001
India
www.foxmandal.com

Italy

Carlo Pianese
Tel.: +971 (4) 4267 125
Fax: +971 (4) 4267 199
carlo.pianese@allenovery.com

Co-Author:
Elia Ferdinando Clarizia

Allen & Overy
Suite 101/202, Level 1&2
The Gate Village Building GV08
Dubai International Finance Centre
PO Box 506678,
Dubai
United Arab Emirates
www.allenovery.com

Japan

Kengo Nishigaki
Tel.: +81 (3) 5157 2790
Fax: +81 (3) 5157-2903
kengo.nishigaki@bakernet.com

Co-Author:
Rodell Molina

Baker & McKenzie
The Prudential Tower 2-13-10
Nagatacho Chiyoda-ku
Tokyo 100-0014
Japan
www.taalo-bakernet.com

Latvia

Agris Repšs
Tel.: +371 (6) 736 5000
Fax: +371 (6) 736 5001
agris.repss@sorainen.lv

Co-Authors:
Eva Berlaus-Gulbe
Lauma Bērziņa
Ūve Zosārs

Sorainen
Kr. Valdemāra 21
1010 Riga
Latvia
www.sorainen.com

Lithuania

Mantas Petkevičius
Tel.: +370 (5) 268 5040
Fax: +370 (5) 268 5041
mantas.petkevicius@sorainen.lt

Co-Author:
Laimonas Skibarka

Sorainen
Jogailos g. 4
01116 Vilnius
Lithuania
www.sorainen.com

Malaysia

Ang Siak Keng
Tel.: +604 227 0888
Fax: +604 228 6755
siak.keng.ang@zaidibrahim.com.my

Co-Authors:
Chew See Khee
Tan Lay Choo
Gooi Kathleen
Teoh Pei Pei

Zaid Ibrahim & Co.
No. 51-22-B&C
Menara BHL
Jalan Sultan Ahmad Shah
10050 Penang
Malaysia
www.zaidibrahim.com

Mexico

Eugenio Bernal
Tel.: +52 (55) 5540 9629
Fax: +52 (55) 5540 9699
ebernal@whitecase.com

Lizette Neme Bechara
Tel.: +52 (55) 5540 9656
Fax: +52 (55) 5540 9699
lneme@whitecase.com

White & Case, S.C.
Blvd. Manuel Ávila Camacho 24 - PH
Lomas de Chapultepec
Mexico City, 11000
Mexico
www.whitecase.com

Netherlands

Kim F. Tan
Tel.: +31 (20) 551 7906
Fax: +31 (20) 626 7949
kim.tan@bakernet.com

Baker & McKenzie Amsterdam N.V.
Claude Debussylaan 54
1082 MD Amsterdam
The Netherlands
www.bakernet.com

Russia

Alexander Kalinov
Tel.: +7 (812) 332 9300
Fax: +7 (812) 332 9341
akalinov@chadbourne.com

Co-Author:
Nadezhda Drobilko

Chadbourne and Parke LLP
Stroganovsky Business Centre
19A Nevsky Prospect
St. Petersburg 191186
Russian Federation
www.chadbourne.com

Singapore

Colin Ong Pang Huan
Tel.: +(65) 6416 8004
Fax: +(65) 6532 5711
colin.ong@wongpartnership.com

WongPartnership LLP
One George Street 20-01
Singapore 049145
Republic of Singapore
www.wongpartnership.com.sg

South Africa

Madelein Burger-van der Walt
Tel.: +27 (11) 530 5278
Fax: +27 (11) 530 6278
madelein.burger-vanderwalt@webberwentzel.com

Co-Authors
Brian Dennehy
Bernadette Heever
Claire Gaul

Webber Wentzel
10 Fricker Road
Illovo Boulevard
Johannesburg 2107
South Africa
www.webberwentzel.com

Spain

Juan Manuel De Remedios
Tel.: +34 (917) 915 016
Fax: +34 (902) 882 228
juanmanuel.deremedios@lw.com

Paco Iso
Tel.: +34 (917) 915 011
Fax: +34 (902) 882 228
mariano.francisco@lw.com

Xavier Pujol
Tel.: +34 (917) 915 018
Fax: +34 (902) 882 228
xavier.pujol@lw.com

Manuel Deó
Tel.: +34 (917) 915 013
Fax: +34 (902) 882 228
manuel.deo@lw.com

Latham & Watkins LLP
Marìa de Molina 6, 4th Floor
28006 Madrid
Spain
www.lw.com

Switzerland	**Eva-Maria Strobel** Tel.: +41 (44) 384 1411 Fax: +41 (44) 384 1214 eva-maria.strobel@bakernet.com **Co-Author:** Matthias Maurer	**Baker & McKenzie** Zollikerstrasse 225 8034 Zurich Switzerland www.bakernet.com
Taiwan (ROC)	**Jackie S.J. Lin** Tel.: +886 (2) 2781 4111 Fax: +886 (2) 2721 3834 jackielin@tsartsai.com.tw **Yvonne C.Y. Liu** Tel.: +886 (2) 2781 4111 Fax: +886 (2) 2721 3834 yvonneliu@tsartsai.com.tw	**Tsar & Tsai Law Firm** 8th Fl., 245 DunHua S. Rd., Sec. 1 Taipei 106 Taiwan R.O.C. www.tsartsai.com.tw
United Arab Emirates	**Florian Amereller** Tel.: +971 (4) 332 9686 Fax: +971 (4) 332 9687 fa@amereller.com **Jochen Murach** Tel.: +971 (4) 332 9686 Fax: +971 (4) 332 9687 murach@amereller.com	**Amereller Legal Consultants** P.O. Box 97706 Dubai United Arab Emirates www.amereller.com
United States of America	**Marcel Valenta** Tel.: +1 (650) 857 3710 Fax: +1 (650) 857 6238 marcel.valenta@hp.com	**Hewlett-Packard Company** 3000 Hanover Street Palo Alto, CA 94304 USA www.hp.com
Vietnam	**Matthias Dühn** Tel.: +84 (8) 38 239 772 Fax: +84 (8) 38 230 909 duehn@gba-vietnam.org	**German Business Association (GBA)** 5th Floor Somerset Chancellor Court 21–23 Nguyen Thi Minh Khai Street, District 1 Ho Chi Minh City Vietnam www.gba-vietnam.org
	Christoph Angerbauer Tel.: +84 (8) 38244 225 Fax: +84 (8) 38244 226 christoph.angerbauer@roedlasia.com	**Rödl & Partner Vietnam Legal Ltd.** 5th Floor Somerset Chancellor Court 21–23 Nguyen Thi Minh Khai Street District 1 Ho Chi Minh City Vietnam www.roedl.com

Introduction

By *Kay L. Tidwell*

A. International M&A

Long gone is the time when deals were confined within the borders of nations. Even now, as the global economy contracts in the wake of one of the worst recessions in history, the trend of globalization remains remarkably strong. Capital, labor and products are becoming increasingly mobile, and as they are moved across borders causing markets to converge, they generate greater competition and new opportunities for strategic cross-border acquisitions and dispositions. In many ways, mergers and acquisitions (M&A) are as much a cause as an effect of economic globalization; M&A is both a means of integrating global economies and a natural consequence of that integration. The advent of the cross-border M&A transaction is perhaps the strongest evidence of this. In 2007, for the first time history, the value of cross-border M&A deals rivaled the value of domestic M&A deals. According to the United Nations World Investment Report 2008, despite the languishing liquidity crisis and altered lending behavior, cross-border M&A activity in the second half of 2007 grew USD 879 billion to a record high, mostly owing to mega deals that were on an unparalleled scale.

There are many strategic reasons why international M&A makes sense, even in times like the present. Not least among them is the ability to access the wealth of opportunities presented by the expansion of global markets and to effectively compete with foreign firms to maximize market power. Acquiring a foreign firm may be the most direct way to tap a foreign market, and it is certainly easier than starting from scratch and creating a "greenfield" subsidiary. Macroeconomic differences between countries and the potential for substantial synergies also drive firms to consider cross-border deals. The relatively low cost of transportation and communication, coupled with an overall trend in market deregulation, have helped make cross-border transactions more attractive, and have facilitated the meeting of expanding demand in developing and Third World countries.

Although the acquisition of a business organization is perhaps one of the most complex legal transactions that can be undertaken, the process always begins with the basic question of how to structure the transaction, and this is true whether it involves a foreign entity or not. Similarly, the possibilities are no different: the transaction can either be structured as an acquisition of individual assets (asset deal) or an acquisition of shares or interests in the company operating the business (share deal). The many issues that must be considered in order to arrive at the fundamental and significant decision of which method to choose, 'why' and, in an even larger sense, 'where' are the primary subject of this book. Obviously, the decision as between the alternatives depends on a multitude of considerations, which include, among many others, tax treatment and liability issues under the laws of a particular country. The treatment of these issues may – and often does – vary from one jurisdiction to another. It is this book's aim to provide helpful guidance on the most significant structural considerations in an acquisition of assets and the distinctions and characteristics among them in major jurisdictions around the world.

B. The Asset Deal

What should be immediately apparent to the reader in the following chapters is that, despite the variations as among legal regimes, there is a typical and familiar set of transfer issues that arise in any asset deal, anywhere. These issues are the principal structural concerns that every lawyer doing a deal will have to address. First and foremost, it is self-evident that there are problems associated with the sheer variety of assets that may be the subject of an acquisition. Tangible assets demand different treatment than intangible assets, such as intellectual property rights. The transfer of real property, contracts, receivables, employment relationships and even liabilities also often require particular treatment. In most jurisdictions, these assets can be transferred, but not without special consideration being given to the technical complexities that each brings to the table. This is to say nothing of the variances among the different transfer concepts, which may have different legal requirements to facilitate a valid transfer.

Tax considerations, which are at once complex and crucial, are emphasized throughout this text, as is the accompanying caveat that any serious questions about tax matters should always be brought to competent tax counsel early in the game before the conversations on structuring the deal even commence. It cannot be said enough: the tax treatment of an acquisition is assuredly a highly technical area of the law nearly everywhere in the world, and its consequences shape the course of the transaction at the most essential level. After-tax consequences vary dramatically depending how a deal is structured, and could mean the difference between a share deal or an asset deal, or *no* deal. Its varied application to certain assets may determine everything from purchase price to the relative bargaining postures of the respective parties. State and local sales taxes, taxes on real estate conveyances and stock transfers are among the key forms of tax that have to be addressed.

Other issues that the reader will find discussed in each chapter include the degree to which assets must be specified (for identification purposes) to ensure that the transfer will be valid in the respective jurisdiction; liability issues, including insolvency, environmental hazard and contamination (in some countries, the purchaser may be liable for contamination caused by the seller); labor and employment considerations (and how they influence and are influenced by unions, works councils, as well as the rudimentary question of whether employees will be transferred automatically with the other assets of the target), employee objection rights regarding the transfer, and company pension schemes.

The subject of permits and approvals – in all forms and from all authorities – is of course also discussed here. Of particular interest in the context of any cross-border transaction is whether the transaction can happen *at all*, since at least some governments impose strict limitations on the acquirer if it is a foreign entity, depending on the asset in question or its value, and almost all require some sort of government approval for such an acquisition. In addition to regulatory approvals that may have to be obtained by a foreign acquirer to consummate the acquisition, there may also be certain state or local authorizations required for the operation of the business, which could be related to the personnel employed or the facility used to run the business. Lastly, due consideration is given to the subject of corporate authorization and internal approval requirements, such as the need to obtain board or other approvals, which is also often tied to the nature of the assets or the value of the transaction.

There are a number of other relevant considerations that are touched upon in this book, such as encumbrances (mortgages and liens), the form and language of the agreement, choice of law and the availability of arbitration (to settle any disputes under the purchase agreement), as well as any special protocol (such as notarization, registration or filings) that must be followed to make the agreement effective.

The menu of topics here is by no means exhaustive, and there are certainly a few things that are not covered in this text, such as the integration process, cultural resistance, post-merger activities and (in many chapters) anti-trust issues, all of which are not unimportant to the average deal. But it is our hope that we have covered the essentials in each chapter of this book in order to give the practicing M&A lawyer an adequate sense of what to expect in an acquisition in each jurisdiction, as well as how to be prepared for it. And as the adage goes, "knowing is half the battle."

C. The Purpose of this Book

If it has not yet become evident, the purpose of this book is singular: to provide the kind of practical guidance any transactional lawyer might seek in the context of selecting whether to structure a transaction as a share purchase or asset purchase, where the entities involved are not domestic and the lay of the law is, at best, unfamiliar. The essays comprising the book canvass thirty-two major jurisdictions to draw on the most valuable and highly-regarded commodity a legal practitioner can possess – raw experience, acquired over time and iterations of transactions – and seek to present, in a brief and palatable fashion, the kind of wisdom one might desire when making a decision that could have far-reaching consequences in an area with which one has very little familiarity. There are no theoretical detours into the rationale of why and how the law in each jurisdiction may have evolved into its current state or reflections on how it could be improved, as this kind of philosophical debate is about as useful for our purposes as a solar-powered flashlight. Instead, the focus here is strictly on articulating and analyzing the experiences of transactional lawyers in each of these thirty-two countries in order to enable an informed decision on how to structure a transaction that might implicate the laws of any of these jurisdictions.

As is often the case today, transactions involve a variety of assets, some of which may be subject to unconventional treatment in various lands. These essays highlight those areas, with a particular eye towards anticipating potential problems and recommending viable solutions. The practical considerations include an understanding of how the transaction works from a timing perspective, what certain protocol are required for validity and enforceability of agreements under the law of the jurisdiction, and how to improve project management for optimal efficiency in getting the deal done. Considerations such as confidentiality (and how to preserve it in light of certain reporting and filing requirements in the respective jurisdiction), the extent to which local counsel must be engaged, and the best approach to coordinating with local counsel (providing specific instructions based on more than a rudimentary understanding of potential issues) are discussed. The substantive aspects of the law and basic acquisition principles, while necessarily informing the practical advice given here, are beyond the scope of this book, which treats solely those considerations that are relevant to *doing deals*. That said, it should not be construed as merely of potential interest to lawyers; investment bankers, accountants, entrepreneurs and anyone else who contributes to and is engaged in the art of deal-making will find the content of this book useful, especially when contemplating a cross-border transaction.

D. How to Use this Book

The chapters of this book are designed to be as user-friendly as possible for the practicing attorney, who, more often than not, may have one or two specific questions in mind about an aspect of law in a particular jurisdiction and, more often than not, little time to waste looking for the answer in a dense academic treatise. To that end, each chapter is devoted to the laws of single jurisdiction, and is organized identically under the same headings applicable to all jurisdictions. Treatment of each subject is terse, relevant and formulaic. The editors (myself included) have done their utmost to streamline the vocabulary and legal terms of art, while recognizing fully that some subtleties of the individual languages may necessarily force us to sacrifice accuracy for the sake of simplicity. We hope that the underlying meaning is nevertheless conveyed.

Finally, no text on a legal subject would be complete without the usual set of disclaimers. Obviously, while the authors of these texts have endeavored to provide practical guidance on the most important aspects that should be considered in an acquisition of assets or shares in their respective jurisdictions, this guidance should not be construed as – and is by no means a substitute for – the advice of legal counsel familiar with the particular facts and circumstances of a situation. The authors of the following essays offer, at best, only general observations and recommendations based on their experiences. They (and we) make no representation as to the validity, completeness or accuracy of any of their statements, which should be read as reflecting the legal situation in each respective jurisdiction as of June 1, 2009. It goes without saying, further, that each author is only responsible for the essay concerning his or her particular jurisdiction.

Although whole books on the subject of M&A have been written about many of these jurisdictions (and we commend them to you), our objective here is to bring together in a single volume the wealth of knowledge and experience of practicing M&A attorneys in each of these jurisdictions. We hope that the wisdom collected here will serve you well in the many cross-border transactions that are sure to come your way.

Argentina

By *Christian Krüger* and *Juan Pedeflous*

A. General Aspects

1. Asset Deal vs. Share Deal: Essential Considerations

There are various considerations that have to be taken into account when deciding whether a transaction should be structured as a share purchase and transfer or as an asset purchase and transfer, but normally the purchase of shares is the preferred method.

Probably the most important aspect is tax considerations. Neither value added tax nor income tax (provided the seller is a natural individual domiciled in or outside Argentina who is not engaged in the trade of stock as his or her profession or a legal entity domiciled outside Argentina) are applicable to the sale of shares.

On the other hand, as a general rule, income tax and value added tax are applicable to the transfer of assets; however, value added tax is generally not applicable to the transfer of real estate.

The purchaser of a business normally deducts the acquisition costs as operating expenses. Thus, there is a preference to structure the transaction as a purchase and acquisition of assets so that the purchaser can increase the depreciation basis, i.e. the net book value of the depreciable assets, by the difference between the purchase price paid and the book value of the assets (so-called "step-up").

Usually, the accomplishment of the transfer of a business by way of a transfer of its assets is more complex since it requires that one identify the assets belonging to such business and ensure that all such assets are validly transferred. In a purchase and acquisition of assets, the purchaser may choose the assets to be purchased and acquired, while in a purchase and acquisition of shares the purchaser has to accept all assets and liabilities owned by the respective entity, regardless of whether he is aware of such assets and liabilities. Thus, a share deal bears the risk of assuming undisclosed liabilities.

Another aspect that might be relevant in determining the structure of the transaction is related to permits. Some businesses require permits that are either tied to the business itself or to its owner. While the ones tied to the business usually are transferred together with the assets of the business, the permits tied to the owner are not transferred in such case. Thus, the purchaser will have to apply for new permit(s). This issue does not arise in a purchase of shares since the owner of the business, i.e. the entity owning the assets forming the business, does not change.

If the purchase and transfer of assets qualifies as the transfer of a "Going Concern" (*"Fondo de Comercio"*), Argentine Law provides for a procedure addressed to limit the liabilities assumed by the purchaser of the Going Concern.

Although the legislation does not explicitly define a Going Concern, it describes the following elements as comprising a "Going Concern": installations, inventory, leaseholds, name and commercial logos, patronage, patents, trademarks, drawings and industrial models, honorary distinctions; and all others rights derived from the commercial and industrial or artistic property. In other words, the Law is applicable when (i) the assets transferred will enable the purchaser to continue carrying out, substantially in the same manner, the same business that was carried out by the seller, and (ii) due to the transfer the seller will not be able to continue performing its business in substantially the same manner that was carried out prior to the transfer.

Since the description above is admittedly vague, Argentine scholars and case law have interpreted that the list of features that comprise a Going Concern is not exhaustive, and may comprise any other assets that are part of the business unit that is subject to the transfer. There are, however, certain exceptions that are considered to be excluded from the scope of the Law such as in rem rights on real estate and agreements, which have specific procedures that must be followed in order for them to be transferred (e.g., a public deed and the appropriate registration in the cases of real estate, etc.).

The legislation applicable to the transfer of a Going Concern (i) provides the seller's creditors with the opportunity to obtain a judicial attachment for a certain limited period of time, and (ii) entitles the purchaser to receive the assets included in the Going Concern, limiting the purchaser's liability in connection with the transferred assets with respect to hidden liabilities or contingencies, except for the ones related to the transfer of the personnel.

Although there is joint and several liability as between purchaser and seller for the fiscal debts that have been determined prior to the moment of the transfer, it is possible to limit such liability with respect to the fiscal debt that remains to be determined, as described in more detail below.

The transfer of the assets composing the Going Concern should be executed according to a specific procedure established under the law in order to have effect vis-à-vis third parties, as well as to limit the purchaser's liabilities, as will be described further. Such procedure consists of the following steps:

(i) the seller shall provide the purchaser with a letter indicating the outstanding debt, names and addresses of the creditors, and debt amounts and respective due dates, if any;

(ii) the transfer of the Going Concern should be published for five days in the Official Gazette and in a well known newspaper in the area in which the Going Concern is located;

(iii) during the ten days following the last publication, the creditors that consider themselves to be affected by the transfer of the Going Concern are required to notify their claims to the address indicated by the seller in the above-referenced publications. The seller's creditors may claim the retention of the amounts of their credits and require the deposit of the corresponding amounts in a special account. These rights could be exercised by creditors identified in the letter mentioned in i) above, as well as by any omitted creditor holding an outstanding credit against the seller;

(iv) the purchaser shall retain the sums necessary for the payment of the credits and shall deposit those amounts in a special account opened for this purpose. The amounts deposited should be retained for a 20-day period, during which the creditors need to obtain a judicial attachment;

(v) in no event may the price of the transfer be lower than the amount of the outstanding debt declared by the seller plus the amount resulting from the credits not declared by the seller but notified by the seller's creditors according to iii) above;

(vi) the definitive sale document for implementing the transfer of the Going Concern shall be executed upon expiration of the term granted to the creditors to challenge the transfer, or once the 20-day period has elapsed with respect to such amounts that have not been subject to a judicial attachment. Within ten days following the execution of the definitive transaction document, such document shall be registered before the Public Registry of Commerce; and

(vii) additionally, the provisions and special formalities required by applicable law for the transfer of certain assets (e.g., the transfer of real estate requires a public deed, and the transfer of trademarks requires the filing of certain documents before the Office of Trademarks, etc.) should also be complied with.

It is important to point out that in the event the entire procedure described above is not followed, the purchaser shall be jointly and severally liable with the seller for any liabilities of the seller in connection with the transferred assets, up to the price of the transfer.

2. Distinction between Sale and Transfer in Rem

Argentine Law distinguishes between the sale of assets (i.e. obligation to transfer) and the perfection of the transfer of ownership, as the transfer of ownership generally requires delivery of the assets and/or registration of the transfer with an oficial register. However, an invalid or null agreement creating the obligation to transfer assets may not be validly cured by registration.

If assets are to be sold and transferred in multiple jurisdictions, it is possible to address the sale in a single master purchase agreement while transferring the assets in the respective jurisdictions.

3. Regional Differences

Since the essential rules applicable to the sale and transfer of assets are part of Argentine federal law, there are no regional differences as regards the legal requirements applicable to an asset transfer within Argentina.

4. Acquisition by Foreigners

As a general rule, foreigners receive the same legal treatment as locals. However, special requirements have to be met in certain industries, such as the armament industry. In addition, purchase of land located next to the international border or acquisition of a controlling stake in a company that owns land located therein requires a special permit from the federal government. Last, the Province of Corrientes has recently enacted an amendment to its Constitution providing for certain restrictions on the purchase of land by foreign nationals or companies.

5. Public Registers, Records and Databases

In Argentina, no central institution maintains all relevant information in connection with an asset transfer. Each Province has a register of real property. Information as to real property, including ownership and encumbrances, can be obtained from these registries. An inspection of the Real Property Register does not require the declaration of a qualified interest by the interested party.

In addition, there are various registries for certain movable assets, such as automobiles, machinery, etc. and for intellectual property and utility and design patents.

6. Purchase Price Requirements

The parties are free to determine the purchase price, provided it is not substantially below market value. The price may be stated in any currency; however, the ability to perform obligations payable in non-Argentine currency will be subject to the exchange and transfer regulations and interpretation of such regulations in effect at the time of payment. The same will apply to the ability of any person to remit out of Argentina the proceeds of sale and transfer of assets.

An allocation of the purchase price to individual assets or groups of assets is recommendable for tax and accounting purposes.

B. Tangible/Movable Assets

1. Characteristics as to:

a) Language of Documentation. The sale and transfer documents regarding tangible assets may be drafted in any language. Bilingual documents are permitted. A translation will be required if the transfer must be filed with public authorities. However, if transfer of the assets needs to be registered with a public register (for example, if it qualifies as the transfer of a Going Concern), a translation into Spanish may be required as well as a special registration form filled out in Spanish. Granting of rights concerning real estate always requires a Spanish document.

b) Form of Documentation. As a general rule, the transfer of tangible assets must be memorialized in writing. Notarization of the sale and purchase agreement might be required for certain assets or if the transfer qualifies as the transfer of a Going Concern.

The sale and transfer documents may be executed outside Argentina. Signing in counterparts is permissible, provided (i) there are as many counterparts as parties, and (ii) each party is furnished with a counterpart executed by the other parties.

c) Specification of Assets. As a general rule, the assets to be transferred must be described in detail in the transfer agreement to such an extent that a third party would be able to distinguish the assets from any other non-transferred assets (principle of identification). In order to comply with this, the use of asset lists (or schedules) is advisable but not mandatory. A specification by category or location is sufficient, provided that identification is possible without recourse to any legal evaluation.

If and to the extent that the asset specification is insufficient, the assets will not be transferred and will remain with the seller.

2. Administrative, Corporate and Other Approvals

As a general rule, the transfer of tangible assets does not require special governmental or administrative approvals. However, exceptions might apply with regard to special categories of assets (e.g., certain weapons, dangerous substances). In addition, certain transfers may require the approval of the Antitrust Authority. Non-compliance will invalidate the transfer.

Please note that Argentine Law requires that certain transactions that exceed a specified threshold must be submitted for prior review and approval of the Antitrust Authority as a condition for the transaction to be effective.

The transactions subject to review and approval include the transfer of assets when the business volume of the target company and the purchaser, on an annual basis, exceeds ARS 200 million in aggregate (approximately USD 68 million). However, certain exceptions apply.

The transactions subject to review will only be recognized as valid transactions among the parties and vis-a-vis third parties upon their review and approval by the Antitrust Authority.

Notice of any of the transactions subject to prior review and approval must be filed with the Antitrust Authority (i) prior to consummation of the transaction; or (ii) within "one week" from the earlier of the execution of the respective agreement, the publication of a tender offer or exchange offer, or the actual acquisition of a controlling interest.

The failure to notify the Antitrust Authority of any transaction subject to review and approval within the specified periods is punishable by fines of up to ARS 1 million (approximately USD 340,000) per each day notice is delayed.

As a general rule, the approval of any corporate body is not required, unless otherwise provided for in seller's and/or purchaser's articles of association or partnership agreement. If the seller is a stock corporation or a limited liability company, the approval of its shareholders' meeting might be required if the assets to be transferred form a substantial part of seller's core business, even if not expressly required in the articles of association or partnership. Non-compliance may invalidate the transfer.

The transfer of encumbered assets or of assets used as collateral does not require the security holder's approval per se, but all liens and rights will be transferred ipso facto to the purchaser. However, agreements creating liens typically specify the need for security holder approval to transfer the collateral. In all cases, transferor has the legal duty to inform the purchaser of all existing liens and rights on the assets to be transferred.

3. Filing Requirements

As a general rule, transfer of tangible assets does not require special filings. However, (i) certain types of tangible assets (such as automobiles) require a filing with public authorities or registrations, and (ii) if the transfer qualifies as the transfer of a Going Concern, registration is required.

4. Automatic Transfer of Encumbrances

As a general rule, encumbrances regarding tangible assets automatically transfer to the purchaser. In particular, pledged assets remain pledged. However, this rule does not apply where the purchaser acquires the assets in good faith, has paid the purchase price, and the related encumbrance is not registered with the public register (bona fide principle).

C. Real Property

1. Characteristics as to:

a) Language of Documentation. As a general rule, the sale and transfer documents regarding real property must be drafted in Spanish since they must be filed with the real property register. However, a certified translation into a foreign language may be attached to the Spanish documents. Documents that do not need to be registered with the real property register (such as a preliminary sales agreement) may be drafted in any language.

b) Form of Documentation. Regarding transfer of title to real property, a public deed in the Spanish language executed by the parties and a public notary is mandatory. The public deed may be executed overseas but a transcription of the deed by an Argentine public notary is required in order for the public deed to be registered with the real property register. In all cases, in order for a public deed executed overseas to be valid in Argentina, local requirements concerning a real property transfer must be complied with.

Signing in counterparts is not permissible.

c) Specification of Assets. A detailed description of the real estate as provided by the real property register is mandatory to effect the transfer of real property.

2. Administrative, Corporate and Other Approvals

As a general rule, the transfer of real property does not require special governmental or administrative approvals. However, transfer of a piece of real property located next to the international border requires prior authorization from the federal government. Please refer to B, 2 in connection with the Antitrust Authority's approval.

As a general rule, the approval of any corporate body is not required, unless otherwise provided for in seller's and/or purchaser's articles of association or partnership agreement (such provisions are customary with respect to real property). If the seller is a stock corporation or a limited liability company, the approval of its shareholders' meeting might be required if the assets form a substantial part of the seller's core business, even if not expressly mentioned in the articles of association or partnership. Failure to comply with this provision may invalidate the transfer.

In the event the real property is encumbered with mortgages, land charges or usufruct rights, the transfer will generally not be subject to the approval of the security holders who continue to be secured following the transfer, due to the fact that all encumbrances and liens automatically transfer to the purchaser. However, usually agreements creating mortgages or liens specify the need for security holder approval to transfer the real estate. In this case, if the security holders' approval is withheld, then the transfer will not be effective vis-à-vis the non-consenting security holder. Should this be the case, in some jurisdictions within Argentina, the purchaser will be liable to the security holder for the total amount secured, even if it exceeds the value of the collateral.

3. Filing Requirements

The transfer of real property must be registered with the Real Property Register and is not valid until such registration takes place. The relevant filings must be made by the public notary in charge. In addition, the public notary is obliged to provide the tax authorities with information regarding the transfer.

4. Automatic Transfer of Encumbrances

All registered encumbrances on real property remain valid after the transfer of the real estate. The waiver of encumbrances requires a notarized form (public deed).

5. Automatic Transfer of Lease Agreements

Lease agreements are automatically transferred to the purchaser upon purchase of the real property. Neither the seller nor the purchaser may terminate the lease agreement in a sale of real property. However, the tenant may terminate the lease if the first six months have elapsed and the tenant pays a penalty amounting to one and a half month's rent (if termination is effective before the first year has elapsed) or one month's rent (if termination is effective after the first year has elapsed).

D. Contracts

1. Characteristics as to:

a) Language of Documentation. As a general rule, the transfer of contracts may be memorialized in any language. Bilingual documents are permitted. Since such documents do not need to be filed with public authorities, a translation into Spanish is not required. However, if the contract to be transferred has been executed by means of a public deed, then a public deed will be required to transfer the said contract, which must be drafted in Spanish. In addition, if the transfer qualifies as the transfer of a Going Concern, certain documents involved in the transaction will have to be drafted in Spanish.

b) Form of Documentation. As a general rule, the written form is required to transfer contracts. In addition, delivery of the document assigned to the purchaser is necessary for the transfer to be effective. If the contract to be transferred has been executed by means of a public deed, then a public deed will be required to transfer the said contract. In addition, if the transfer qualifies as the transfer of a Going Concern, certain documents involved in the transaction will have to be notarized.

The transfer documents may be executed outside Argentina. Execution in counterparts is permissible.

c) Specification of Contracts. A general or generic description is sufficient to transfer the contracts, provided the original counterpart of the agreements is delivered to the purchaser.

2. Administrative, Corporate and Other Approvals

As a general rule, the transfer of contracts does not require special governmental or administrative approvals, except (i) if the government or any of its agencies is party to the related agreement and (ii) execution of the contract requires a special governmental or administrative approval. Please refer to B, 2 in connection with the Antitrust Authority's approval.

The approval of any corporate body is basically not required unless otherwise provided for in seller's articles of association or partnership agreement. For further details, please refer to B, 2 above.

As a general rule, the counterparty's consent is not required for the transfer to be effective, except if specifically required in the contract to be transferred. If the counterparty's consent is required and is withheld, then the transfer will be void. In addition, if the counterparty's consent is not required as a condition of validity of the transfer but is nevertheless given, this will imply that the counterparty has waived his right to oppose to the transfer before the seller. Last, if the counterparty's consent is not required for the transfer to be valid but is not given, then the seller will remain obliged vis-à-vis his counterparty according to the contract transferred.

In addition, consent of the other parties will be required if the nature of the contract requires so (agreements intuitu personae).

3. Automatic Transfer of Contracts (Other than Lease and Employment Agreements)

There are there no other contracts that automatically transfer to the purchaser in the event of an asset deal other than lease and employment agreements.

4. Filing Requirements

As a general rule, the transfer of contracts does not require a filing or registration with public authorities or registers or databases. However, if the transferred contract has been filed with any public authority or registered with any public register or database, then filing and/or registration will be required.

5. Treatment of Existing Contractual Claims and Obligations

Claims and obligations arising from the transferred contract automatically transfer to the purchaser. It is customary to agree upon indemnification clauses.

6. Warranty Claims Resulting from Events prior to Transfer

As a general rule, the transfer of a contract also includes the transfer of any claims and obligations related to such contract. Please refer to A, 1 for further details regarding the transfer of a Going Concern; the potential exposure resulting from such a transfer is customarily covered by representations and warranties and/or indemnifications.

E. IP Rights

1. Characteristics of Intellectual Property Rights (e.g., Trademarks, Patents, Utility Models, Domain Names,) ("*IP Rights*") as to:

a) Language of Documentation. As a general rule, the sale and transfer documents regarding IP Rights may be drafted in every language. In case of registered IP Rights (e.g., trade marks, patents, design patents, domain names) a translation into Spanish may be needed for filing purposes; bilingual documents are permitted. However, the required registration form must be in Spanish.

b) Form of Documentation. As a general rule, the transfer of IP Rights is required to be in writing.

The sale and transfer documents may be executed outside Argentina. Signing in counterparts is permissible, provided (i) there are as many counterparts as parties, and (ii) each party is furnished with a counterpart executed by the other parties.

For registration purposes of IP Rights, a special form must be filed in Spanish and the signatures therein must be notarized.

c) Specification of IP Rights. The principle of identification (see B, 1, c above) also applies to the transfer of IP Rights, which means they must be specified sufficiently. In order to comply with these requirements the use of lists (or schedules) is advisable but not mandatory.

2. Administrative, Corporate and Other Approvals

As a general rule, the transfer of IP Rights does not require special governmental or administrative approvals. Please refer to B, 2 in connection with the Antitrust Authority's approval.

The approval of any corporate bodies is basically not required unless otherwise provided for in seller's and/or purchaser's articles of association or partnership agreement. For further details, please refer to B, 2 above.

The transfer of encumbered IP Rights without the security holder's consent is not effective vis-à-vis the security holder.

3. Filing Requirements

If and to the extent the IP Rights to be transferred are registered in public registers, the change of ownership requires the filing with the relevant public registers to be effective vis-à-vis third parties. However, such registration is merely of a declaratory nature and does not affect the validity of the transfer. In addition, if the transfer qualifies as the transfer of a Going Concern, the filing procedure detailed in C, 1 will have to be followed.

4. Applicable International (Multilateral) Agreements or Treaties

Argentina participates in the TRIPS Agreement and in the Paris Convention for the Protection of Industrial Property. In addition, Argentina and Germany signed the Treaty of Rome, the Berne Convention and the Universal Convention.

F. Receivables

1. Characteristics as to:

a) Language of Documentation. As a general rule, the transfer of receivables may be drafted in every language. Bilingual documents are permitted. Since there is no need for filing such documents with public authorities, a translation into Spanish is not required. However, if the underlying document is a public deed, then a public deed (in Spanish) will be required to transfer the related receivables. In addition, if the transfer qualifies as a transfer of a Going Concern, certain documents will have to be drafted in Spanish.

b) Form of Documentation. As a general rule, the written form is required to transfer receivables. If the underlying document is a public deed, then a public deed will be required to transfer the receivables. In addition, if the transfer qualifies as the transfer of a Going Concern, certain documents will have to be notarized.

The transfer documents may be executed outside Argentina. Execution in counterparts is permissible.

c) Specification of Receivables. The principle of identification (see B, 1, c above) also applies to the transfer of receivables, which must be specified sufficiently. In order to comply with such requirements it is recommendable to list the receivables to be transferred in schedules to the asset transfer agreement, specifying the underlying legal relationships and the outstanding amount of the relevant receivables.

2. Administrative, Corporate and Other Approvals

As a general rule, the transfer of receivables does not require special governmental or administrative approvals. Please refer to B, 2 in connection with the Antitrust Authority's approval.

Approval of any corporate body is generally not required unless otherwise provided for in seller's and/or purchaser's articles of association or partnership agreement. For further details, please refer to B, 2 above.

The validity of the transfer is not subject to the approval of the debtors, provided that the underlying agreement does not state otherwise.

3. Filing Requirements

Regarding the transfer of receivables, no filings with public authorities or registrations into public registers or databases are required. The notification of the transfer to the debtors is required, since as long as the debtors are not aware of the transfer, payments on the receivables would still be made to the former owner of the receivables.

G. Liabilities

1. Characteristics as to:

a) Language of Documentation. As a general rule, the sale and transfer documents regarding the transfer of liabilities may be drafted in every language. Bilingual documents are permitted. However, if the underlying document is a public deed, then a public deed (in Spanish) will be required to transfer liability. In addition, if the transfer qualifies as the transfer of a Going Concern, certain documents will have to be drafted in Spanish.

b) Form of Documentation. As a general rule, the written form is required to transfer liabilities. If the underlying document is a public deed, then a public deed will be required to transfer the said liability. In addition, if the transfer qualifies as the transfer of a Going Concern, certain documents must be notarized.

The transfer documents may be executed outside Argentina. Execution in counterparts is permissible.

c) Specification of Liabilities. The principle of identification (see B, 1, c above) also applies to the transfer of liabilities, which must be specified sufficiently. In order to comply with such requirements, it is recommendable to list the liabilities to be transferred in schedules to the asset transfer agreement, specifying the underlying legal relationships and the outstanding amount of the relevant liabilities.

2. Administrative, Corporate and Other Approvals

As a general rule, the transfer of liabilities does not require special governmental or administrative approvals. Please refer to B, 2 in connection with the Antitrust Authority's approval.

The approval of corporate bodies is basically not required unless otherwise provided for in seller's and/or purchaser's articles of association or partnership agreement. For further details, please refer to B, 2 above.

As a general rule, creditor's consent is not required for the transfer to be effective, except if specifically required in the underlying document. If the creditor's consent is required and withheld, then the transfer will be void. In addition, if the creditor's consent is not required for the transfer to be valid but is nevertheless given, this will imply that the creditor has given up his right to make any claim against the seller in connection with the liability transferred. Finally, if the creditor's consent is not required for the transfer to be valid but is not given, then the seller will remain obliged vis-à-vis his counterparty in connection with the liability transferred.

In addition, consent of the other parties will be required if the nature of the liability requires so (obligations intuitu personae).

3. Filing Requirements

In addition, if the transfer of liabilities qualifies as the transfer of a Going Concern, the filing procedure detailed in C, 1 must be complied with.

4. Purchaser's Liability for:

a) Tax Obligations. Although there is joint and several liability between purchaser and seller for the tax liability that has been determined at the moment of the transfer, it is possible to limit such liability with respect to the taxes accrued but not assessed, provided a notice to the Argentine Tax Authority with respect to the transfer is sent at least 15 days before the transfer takes place. Therefore, it is highly advisable to send such notice within the 15-day period in order to limit the purchaser's liability.

The tax liability shall be considered assessed when:

(i) it has been determined by the taxpayer by filing a tax return; or

(ii) it has been determined by the tax authorities on the basis of information provided by the taxpayer or by an assessment procedure ending in a notice of deficiency.

According to the Tax Procedure Law, the purchaser of assets and liabilities of a company shall be personally and jointly liable with the seller with regard to the tax liability already assessed at the time of the transfer, in the event the seller fails to pay it.

With regard to the tax liability arising from provincial taxes, in general, regulations similar to the federal regulation have been adopted by the provincial tax codes.

b) Environmental Contamination. All environmental liabilities (even those arising from periods prior to the acquisition) are transferred to the purchaser, who will be jointly and severally liable with the seller.

c) Products Sold or Services Rendered by the Seller to Third Parties. Please refer to A, 1 regarding the liability arising from the transfer of a Going Concern.

5. Automatic Transfer of Other Liabilities

No other liability transfers automatically due to the acquisition of assets.

6. Contractual Protection as to 4 and 5 above

It is customary to include indemnification clauses in favor of the purchaser of assets in connection with (i) tax and environmental liabilities, and (ii) products sold or services rendered by the seller to third parties prior to the acquisition.

H. Employees

1. Transfer of Employees

According to mandatory Argentine law, all existing employment agreements pertaining to a business automatically transfer to the purchaser by operation of law. This does not apply if the transaction only involves selected assets that collectively do not form a distinct business unit.

As a consequence of the transfer, the purchaser becomes part of the employment agreement and is bound to its terms and conditions, as well as to any arrangements stipulated between the seller and the affected employee.

The seller will remain liable vis-à-vis the employees as regards obligations arising from the employment relationships that were incurred prior to the date the transfer is effective. On the other hand, the purchaser will be liable vis-à-vis the employees as regards obligations arising from the employment relationships that were incurred both prior to and after the effective date of the transfer.

As a general rule, the transfer does not require the employees' consent and therefore employees cannot claim to have been dismissed as a consequence of the transfer. However, if the transfer affects the working/economic conditions of the employees, the employees may put themselves in a situation of a constructive dismissal and may have a claim for severance.

2. Approval of Works Council, Trade Union or Other Institutions

The transfer of a business by way of transfer of the individual assets does not trigger co-determination rights of the works council.

3. Contractual Protection as to Labor Issues

As a general rule, the transferor of the assets is liable for labor obligations until the transfer is effective or the purchaser takes control of the assets.

I. Tax Implications

1. Value Added Tax

Transfer of assets triggers the obligation to pay VAT. The regular VAT rate in Argentina amounts to 21%.

2. Real Property Transfer Tax

The transfer of real estate in Argentina does not trigger any real estate tax. However, if the seller of a real property is a natural person, then a 1.5% tax calculated on the purchase price is applicable.

3. Other Tax Issues

As a general rule, stamp tax is applicable to the asset transfer agreements. The stamp tax rate varies according to the jurisdiction; as a general rule we may state that the current rate is not higher than 4% of the purchase price.

J. Bankruptcy Law

1. Challenge of Asset Transfer in Case of Insolvency

Creditors of a bankrupted seller or purchaser may challenge the transfer provided that:

(i) the transfer had taken place within a two-year period before the bankruptcy is declared by a court;

(ii) insolvency of the seller or the purchaser is public by the time the transfer takes place; and

(iii) the transfer implies a damage to the purchaser's or seller's economic capability.

2. Acquisition of Assets that are Subject to Insolvency Proceedings

If the seller has been declared bankrupt by a court, then the court's approval is required in order to execute any kind of transfer of assets.

If the seller has been declared to be under '*concurso preventivo*' (similar to Chapter 11 bankruptcy under U.S. law) the court's approval will be required only in order to execute any kind of contract, among which the transfer of a Going Concern is included.

K. Timing and Costs

1. Timeframe of Asset Transfer

As a general rule, it may be said that registration of the transfer of assets may require up to seven months.

2. Costs of Asset Transfer

The stamp tax rate varies according to the jurisdiction; as a general rule, the current rate does not exceed 4% of the purchase price.

Notarization costs may amount to up to 3% of the transfer price.

L. Miscellaneous

1. Choice of Foreign Law

As a general rule, the sale of assets may be subject to foreign law. However, the formalities to transfer assets located in Argentina are always subject to Argentine law.

2. (International) Arbitration, Choice of Venue

International arbitration is always possible.

3. Other Distinctions, Characteristics

If the seller is an individual person and if he/she is married, the consent of his/her spouse is required for the transfer of assets whose transfer is registered. Without such consent, the transfer of the assets may be challenged by the non-consenting spouse.

M. Literature

Jorge Osvaldo Zunino, Fondo de Comercio, 2nd Edition, 2000

Jorge Adolfo Stegmann, Transferencia de Fondo de Comercio, 1st Edition, 2000

Orlando Taleva Salvat, Cómo hacer una transferencia de Fondo de Comercio, 2nd Edition, 1998

Australia

By *John Mollard* and *Jason Cornwall-Jones*

A. General Aspects

1. Asset Deal vs. Share Deal: Essential Considerations

There are a number of factors to consider when deciding whether to structure a sale of business transaction in Australia to be by way of an asset transfer or a share transfer. The key considerations for the parties are briefly set out below (and described in more detail later in this chapter).

Stamp Duty

In some jurisdictions of Australia there is stamp duty on the sale of unquoted securities (New South Wales, South Australia and the Australian Capital Territory). The duty has been abolished in all other jurisdictions.

In all jurisdictions there is (a) land rich duty payable on the transfer of 50% or more of the shares in a company whose land assets exceed a threshold percentage of total assets (except in Western Australia where a 90% level applies), and (b) stamp duty on the sale of certain assets.

Goods and Services Tax (GST)

GST (10%) is generally not chargeable on the sale of shares or the sale of a business if the business is sold as a going concern.

The sale of shares is an input taxed financial supply. Hence, no amount in respect of GST should be charged on the sale of shares. However, any GST amounts incurred on costs that relate to the sale of shares cannot be claimed back as input tax credits.

The sale of all of an entities' business assets can be treated as a GST-free supply of a going concern. If the relevant requirements (described below) are met, no amount of GST should be charged on the sale of the business assets, but any amounts of GST incurred on costs that relate to the sale of the business assets can still be claimed back as input tax credits.

For a sale of business assets to meet the requirements of a GST-free supply of a going concern:

- the supplier must supply to the recipient all of the things that are necessary for the continued operation of the enterprise; and

- the supplier must carry on, or will carry on, the enterprise until the day of the supply.
- The recipient of the supply must also be registered or required to be registered for GST and the supplier and the recipient must agree in writing that the supply is of a going concern.
- If the sale of business assets do not meet the requirements of a GST-free supply of a going concern, the supply will generally be a taxable supply and be subject to GST.
- It should be noted that if the asset being supplied as a taxable supply is a freehold interest in land, the margin scheme could be applied in calculating the GST amount payable on this taxable supply.
- Ordinarily, the amount of GST on a taxable supply is 10% of the value of the taxable supply. If the margin scheme applies, the amount of GST on the supply is 1/11 of the margin for the supply.
- The margin for the supply is the amount by which the total consideration for the supply exceeds the consideration for the acquisition of the freehold interest in the land in question. If the interest in the land was held prior to July 1, 2000, instead of using the consideration for the acquisition of the land, a margin scheme valuation, determined at July 1, 2000, may be substituted for this amount in calculating the margin.
- The margin scheme may only be applied in certain circumstances, e.g., the land was acquired by applying the margin scheme, and both the purchaser and the seller must agree in writing that the margin scheme is to apply to the supply of the land.

Roll Over of Tax Losses, Capital Gains and Depreciation and Other Tax Treatment

A sale of shares will generally be subject to capital gains tax for any gain realized by the seller.

If all of the shares in a company are purchased, the purchaser will usually acquire the historic tax assets and liabilities of the company. This means that the purchaser may benefit from tax attributes of the company (such as franking credits and tax losses), but may suffer the burden of prior period under-payments of income tax. Accordingly the purchaser will usually seek comprehensive tax warranties and a specific tax indemnity.

The ability to do this is dependent on whether a company is a subsidiary member of a consolidated group for income tax purposes. If so, the tax attributes of the company will remain with the "head entity" of the income tax consolidated group. The acquisition of a company (as opposed to assets) by a purchaser who is itself a member of an income tax consolidated group will allow for the value of the underlying assets to be "reset", based on the purchase price of the shares, adjusted for inherited liabilities and other characteristics.

A purchaser who is not a member of an income tax consolidated group may prefer an asset acquisition, as this will permit the purchaser to establish the value of such assets going forward. Otherwise, the purchaser will inherit the tax value of the assets to the seller as at the time of acquisition. As the seller would typically retain the historic tax attributes, assets and liabilities of the company, a purchaser will also seek a less comprehensive range of tax warranties and indemnities.

In contrast, in broad terms a seller may prefer a share sale rather than an asset sale where the seller has available capital gains tax relief (such as a 50% capital gains tax discount or ability to "rollover" the shares).

Ability to "Cherry Pick" Assets and Liabilities

A purchaser may not require all of the assets of a seller due to its key objectives, or following due diligence a purchaser may identify certain assets which it does not which to purchase. This is to be balanced with the desire of a seller to sell all of its business or be left with certain assets (which may be unsaleable in the future as separate assets, not forming part of a business).

Material Contracts

Certain key contracts may require the consent of the counter parties for a direct transfer. If those counter parties do not wish to provide that consent, and the relevant contracts do not contain change of control clauses, a transfer of shares may be the practical solution.

Preservation of Material Licenses or Authorizations

Depending on the nature of the operations of the business being acquired, it may possess certain governmental licenses or authorizations which relate to the entity, rather than the assets. Generally governmental licenses and authorizations are not transferable and therefore the purchaser of assets would have to make new applications. A purchaser of shares may or may not need to make a new application depending on the terms of issue of the license (i.e. change of control).

Deemed Redundancy of Employees

A transfer of employees from the seller to a purchaser where the employee does not receive "equivalent" terms of employment may trigger certain redundancy or severance payment obligations for the seller.

Usually a transfer of business undertaken as an asset transfer will involve greater detail in the documentation (to describe the assets being purchased and the allocation of a value to those assets for tax purposes) and potentially more complex formalities to register different types of assets transferred. A share transfer on the other hand can be easily documented by a single share transfer.

In Australia, the acquisition of a business by way of the transfer of shares is more common, but it will depend on the objectives of the purchaser and seller.

2. Distinction between Sale and Transfer in Rem

Conceptually, the jurisdictions within Australia do not generally distinguish between the sale (obligation to transfer) and the transfer in rem (fulfillment of the obligation to transfer).

Parties are able to contractually agree to the sale of the relevant business and provide separately for the actual mechanics of the transfer, but the agreement on sale must be sufficiently clear and certain to allow a court to objectively determine what the transfer process ought to be.

If desired, one can draft a master agreement regarding the sale/purchase and separate local agreements regarding the transfer of particular individual or groups of assets (including those in different jurisdictions).

3. Regional Differences

Generally the essential rules applicable to the sale and transfer of assets are the same across the different States and Territories as they are covered by the common law principles.

Different legislation, however, applies in different States and Territories with respect to certain aspects of the transfer of assets, such as with respect to the transfer of real property, land rich and general stamp duty and the sale of goods. But this different legislation operates on similar general legal principles and there are generally only minor differences in its application across the various jurisdictions (for example, different stamp duty rates apply in different States and Territories in Australia).

4. Acquisition by Foreigners

The acquisition of interests in Australian shares or businesses by foreign entities is regulated primarily through a regime established under the Foreign Acquisitions and Takeovers Act 1975 (FATA), as supplemented by Australian government policy. That regime is administered by the Australian Treasurer. In practice, the Treasurer acts through the Foreign Investment Review Board (FIRB).

Under the FATA, acquisitions of a business above a certain monetary threshold by foreign persons, acquisitions by foreign governments or those in certain sensitive industries are required to be notified to FIRB on a compulsory basis.

For non-US investors, FIRB notification and approval is required for a foreign persons to acquire a substantial interest in an Australian business (shares or assets) where the investment values the gross assets of the target at more than AUD 100 million. For US investors, the threshold is AUD 913 million, however a lower threshold of AUD 105 million applies where the US acquisition is involved in a prescribed sensitive sector or where the acquiring entity is controlled by the US government. Please note that these thresholds change from time to time. The above thresholds are current as of January 1, 2008.

The prescribed sensitive sectors include business activity in any of the following areas:

- media;
- telecommunications;
- transport (including airports, port facilities, rail infrastructure, international and domestic aviation and shipping services provided within, or to or from, Australia);
- the supply of training or human resources, or the manufacture or supply of military goods or equipment or technology, to the Australian Defense Force or other defense forces;
- the manufacture or supply of goods, equipment or technology able to be used for a military purpose;
- the development, manufacture or supply of, or the provision of services relating to, encryption and security technologies and communications systems; and
- the extraction of (or the holding of rights to extract) uranium or plutonium or the operation of nuclear facilities.

For these purposes:

- a 'foreign person' is a person who is not ordinarily resident in Australia or a corporation where persons who are not normally resident in Australia control that corporation;
- a person holds a 'substantial interest' if they alone (or together with their associates) is in a position to control not less than 15% of the voting power of the corporation or holds interests in not less than 15% of the issued shares in the corporation; and
- two or more persons hold a 'substantial interest' if they (together with their associates) are in a position to control not less than 40% of the voting power of the corporation or hold interests in not less than 40% of the issued shares in the corporation.

Subject to certain exceptions, the acquisition of an interest in urban land in Australia by foreign persons is caught by the FATA. Urban land is generally described as any land in Australia other than land that is used wholly and exclusively for carrying on a business of primary production. There is no minimum monetary threshold in relation to the transfer of urban land to a foreign person. Any transfer will require notification to and the approval of the Treasurer unless exemptions apply. Some of the main exempted acquisitions are over:

- developed commercial property valued at less than AUD 100 million where it is non-heritage listed, or less than AUD 913 million (for US investors); and
- developed commercial property where the property is to be used immediately and in its present state for industrial or non-residential commercial purposes.

FIRB has wide powers to prohibit foreign investment proposals and to order divestiture or unwinding of foreign investment arrangements in respect of Australian companies and businesses if they are considered contrary to the national interest.

An agreement in respect of a proposed acquisition which requires FIRB clearance will contravene the FATA unless FIRB clearance has been obtained prior to execution of the agreement or the agreement is expressed to be conditional on FIRB clearance.

5. Public Registers, Records and Databases

There is no central register containing information on all aspects of a business. Different government departments are mandated to regulate various aspects of business in Australia. Save in respect of certain information that must be filed with the Australian Securities and Investments Commission (ASIC), there is generally no obligation on parties to register with the various authorities, but it is typically useful to ensure priority. The main public registers are as follows:

ASIC

Corporate information concerning a seller (if it is a company) can be obtained from ASIC through company searches which show basic details such as (i) a company's share capital structure (ii) the directors and shareholders (iii) a company's registered business address and (iv) any registered charges over the company's assets.

<http://www.asic.gov.au>

Land Titles

Information concerning real property can be obtained from the land titles office, or through online title searches. The property title searches will reveal the ownership of the property and any registered encumbrances over the property, including any registered caveats, easements or covenants over the property.

Environmental Information

Each State in Australia has a register of contaminated sites maintained by its respective Environment Protection Authority (EPA). Information regarding environmental licenses, clean up and enforcement orders is also available from the EPAs and online registers where available.

There is an online National Pollutant Inventory that contains information regarding emission estimates for 93 toxic substances from 4,000 facilities.

<http://www.npi.gov.au>

Planning

Planning certificates in relation to land can be obtained in Australia from the relevant local government and/or state Planning Department. Planning certificates typically identify the zoning of the land, the environmental planning instruments which apply to the land and in some States also specify whether there are development permits and ongoing conditions regarding the use of the land.

IP Australia

Information concerning registerable intellectual property rights such as patents, designs, plant breeder's rights and trade marks are publicly available on the website of IP Australia. <http://www.ipaustralia.gov.au>

Other Permits and Licenses

Other public registers exist for certain licenses and permits issued by the governmental departments, including those as relating to mining tenements, water licenses, indigenous sites/objects, non indigenous heritage sites, Australian financial services licenses and NEMMCO registrations.

6. Purchase Price Requirements

The parties are free to determine the purchase price to be paid in connection with an asset deal. There is no prescribed minimum price or currency in which the purchase price must be paid.

There is no general requirement to allocate the purchase price to groups of assets or individual assets, save that where stamp duty applies the parties must be able to provide evidence of the value of the relevant assets the subject of the duty by an allocation of the purchase price (expressed in the contract or otherwise).

For income tax purposes, where a "lump sum" is paid in consideration for the acquisition of a number of assets, any subsequent allocation must be "reasonable", having regard to market values, contemporaneous documentation and other information relevant to the acquisition process. In general, a purchaser will usually prefer to allocate the purchase price to assets whose cost is either immediately deductible or depreciable, whereas a seller may prefer to allocate the price to assets that are subject to capital gains tax (particularly where capital gains tax relief, as above, is available).

As mentioned in A, 4 above FIRB or the Australian Competition and Consumer Commission (ACCC) may impose undertakings on a seller or purchaser in relation to the sale of assets or shares that they review. Compliance with those undertakings will be necessary in order to obtain the relevant approval or consent from these government bodies. This is discussed further at B, 2 below.

B. Tangible/Movable Assets

1. Characteristics as to:

a) Language of Documentation. The sale documents regarding tangible assets may be drafted in any language. English is the usual language, but it is not mandatory.

The documents can be executed in two languages, preferably with a nominated language prevailing in case of any inconsistency.

b) Form of Documentation. In New South Wales, Queensland, South Australia, Victoria and the Australian Capital Territory, there are no special formalities for the enforcement of a contract of sale of goods.

In Tasmania, Western Australia and the Northern Territory there is a formal requirement that a contract for the sale of goods of a certain value shall not be enforceable by action unless the purchaser accepts part of the goods sold and actually receives them, gives something in earnest to bind the contract or in a part payment, or a note or memorandum in writing of the contract is made and signed by the party to be charged or that party's agent (compare Sale of Goods Act 1923 (Tas), ss 8, 9; Sale of Goods Act 1896 (WA), ss 3, 4; Sale of Goods Act 1895 (NT), s 8). A contract for the sale of assets would constitute a sufficient written note or memorandum.

Non-compliance with the relevant statutory provisions would not render a contract void, but would make it unenforceable at the suit of a party seeking to enforce it. Accordingly, it is strongly advisable that all sale of assets be recorded in the form of written contract. But the contracts do not need to be notarized.

Documents recording the transfer of tangible assets can be executed outside Australia. The parties can agree to execute counterparts, and should clearly specify in the contract that this is permitted.

c) Specification of Assets. The tangible assets being transferred may be generally described such as "all tangible assets relating to the [Business]" (as long as the business is clearly identifiable) or they may be identified by reference to certain categories or location, but in each case the tangible assets to be transferred must be clearly described to allow them to be objectively identified.

There is no requirement for the parties to list assets being transferred in separate schedules. In practice, parties will usually identify each material tangible asset, where capable of specific identification.

2. Administrative, Corporate and Other Approvals

The transfer of tangible assets normally do not require any special governmental or administrative approvals, unless they are subject to notification to FIRB (referred to in A, 4 above) or involve any anti-competitive issues under the Trade Practices Act 1974 (Cth) in which case the ACCC's clearance may be required. In addition, certain restricted assets (e.g., weapons or dangerous substances) may also be subject to special rules in relation to their transfer. The ACCC may impose undertakings on a seller or purchaser in relation to the sale of a business if it would lead to a substantially lessening of competition in a market. Compliance with those undertakings will be necessary in order to obtain the relevant approval or consent from these government bodies.

The constitution or articles of association of the seller and purchaser will usually set out the corporate actions required of the seller or purchaser for the proposed transaction.

The transfer of assets may require the approval of shareholders of a listed company in certain circumstances.

Whether approval of a security holder is required will depend on the terms of the agreement creating the encumbrance. If under the terms of the agreement the seller must obtain prior approval of the security holder before being able to deal with the assets, then such consent should be obtained.

3. Filing Requirements

The transfer of tangible assets generally does not require any special filings with public authorities or databases.

4. Automatic Transfer of Encumbrances

Generally, encumbrances relating to tangible assets automatically transfer to the purchaser if the purchaser has notice of the same. This means that the assets pledged will remain pledged and assets which are subject to retention of title clauses will remain subject to such clauses.

However, bona fide purchasers for value may have a superior title to these tangible assets as compared with the encumbrancer if the encumbrance is unregistered and the bona fide purchaser did not have knowledge of the encumbrance.

C. Real Property

1. Characteristics as to:

a) Language of Documentation. Documentation regarding the transfer of real property is generally drafted in English. Many documents regarding the transfer of real property will need to be lodged at the applicable State or Territory revenue office for stamp duty purposes and at the land titles office for registration. Such documents will often need to be presented in a prescribed form and may not be accepted in languages other than English.

b) Form of Documentation. Each Australian State and Territory has legislation which provides that no interest in land can be created or disposed of except by writing signed by the transferring party or by its authorized agent (compare Conveyancing Act 1919 (New South Wales), s 54A; Property Law Act 1974 (Queensland), s 59; Law of Property Act 1936 (South Australia), s 26; Conveyancing and Law of Property Act 1884 (Tasmania), s 36; Instruments Act 1958 (Victoria) s 126; Property Law Act 1969 (Western Australia), s 34(1) Civil Law (Property) Act 2006 (Australian Capital Territory), s 201 (1)(a); Law of Property Act 2000 (Northern Territory), s 10(1)(a).

Such instruments must generally be in the form of a deed. There are some exceptions to the requirement for a deed. For example, short term leases and instruments which are registered on title (which instruments are deemed to take the form of a deed on registration).

Documents recording the transfer of real property can be executed outside Australia, but may need to be brought into Australia for stamping and registration at the applicable revenue office and land titles office respectively.

The parties can agree to execute counterparts, and if so, should clearly specify in the contract that this is permitted. If executing counterparts, ideally the contract should address at what point the agreement becomes binding, whether on execution or exchange.

c) Specification of Assets. Where real property is the subject matter of a contract, the real property must be described with sufficient particularity so that the intention of the parties may be objectively discerned with certainty. The degree of detail that is required to achieve this objective may range from a broad description of particular real property owned by a party at any given time, to the inclusion of detailed schedules of documents, title details or plans. For the avoidance of doubt, it may be preferable to err on the side of providing more rather than less detail. Instruments that are required to be registered on title will need to describe the relevant property by reference to its title details and possibly a properly surveyed plan.

2. Administrative, Corporate and Other Approvals

The transfer of real property does not generally require governmental or administrative approval. However, there are some important exceptions. Such exceptions include transfers of land to foreign persons covered by FATA (see Section A, 4 above). Land may also be reserved for certain purposes or use by specific entities. Approval for the transfer of such land, or rights relating to such land, may be required. There are also some types of property rights, including some types of easement, that can only be held by authorized entities. Failure to obtain the necessary approvals or authorizations may render a transfer of the land or interests in land described above void, or cause the property right to fail or revert to the Crown.

In the case of a transfer of a real property interest other than the freehold (such as a lease), it may be necessary to obtain the consent of the owner of the freehold (i.e. the lessor) to such transfer. Leases in Australia commonly include a restriction on assigning the lease without the consent of the lessor. It is also not uncommon for a lease to restrict a change in control in the shareholding of a lessee. This means that when acquiring a business, it is important to the check the provisions of relevant leases, whether acquiring the assets of a company or acquiring the shares. Failure to obtain required consents to an assignment of a lease or a change in control of the lessee may constitute a breach of the lease entitling the lessor to terminate the lease.

In the case of a transfer of a lease or other interest in real property, if the freehold is subject to a mortgage, it may be necessary to obtain the consent of the freehold mortgagee, particularly if the transfer is required to be registered on title. If the lease itself is subject to a leasehold mortgage, whether approval of the security holder is required will depend on the terms of the agreement creating the encumbrance. If under the terms of the agreement the seller must obtain prior approval of the security holder before being able to deal with the assets, then such consent should be obtained.

3. Filing Requirements

Transfers of real property generally need to be registered with the land titles office in the applicable State or Territory. There are some types of interest in land that do not need to be registered on title, meaning a transfer of such interest need not be registered. For example, in Victoria, the interest of a tenant in possession is often not registered on title.

4. Automatic Transfer of Encumbrances

If real property in Australia is subject to an encumbrance, that encumbrance will survive the transfer unless the right in question is only personal in nature (as opposed to an interest that touches and concerns the land in question), or is expressed to terminate on transfer. However, a transferee of freehold property will usually require any freehold mortgage of the transferor to be discharged at or prior to settlement of the transfer.

5. Automatic Transfer of Lease Agreements

A leasehold interest is considered to "run with the land" subject to the lease, which means the lease is binding on successive owners of the freehold. This means a transferee of a freehold interest in real property will be subject to the leasehold interest without the need for any documentation. However, on the basis that a lease may include rights and obligations that are personal in nature that do not "run with the land", it is not uncommon for a transferee of a freehold interest in real property to enter into a deed with a lessee under which each party covenants to comply and perform with their respective obligations under the lease.

A lessee would not ordinarily be entitled to terminate a lease following a transfer of the freehold unless specifically provided for in the lease, which would be uncommon.

D. Contracts

1. Characteristics as to:

a) Language of Documentation. The sale documents regarding the transfer of contracts may be drafted in any language. English is the usual language, but it is not mandatory.

The documents can be executed in two languages, preferably with a nominated language prevailing in case of any inconsistency.

b) Form of Documentation. The transfer of contracts does not require a special form of documentation. However, the requirements for it to be in written form or other procedural formalities may be contained in the original contracts. For example, there may be provisions requiring any amendments, assignments or novation of the contracts to be in writing. In addition, there may be a requirement to obtain consent from the other parties to the contracts for the assignment or transfer of the contract.

Documents recording the transfer of contracts can be executed outside Australia. The parties can agree to execute counterparts, and should clearly specify in the contract that this is permitted.

c) Specification of Contracts. The contracts being transferred may be generally described such as "all contracts entered into by [Party X] relating to the [Business]" (as long as the business is clearly identifiable and/or defined) or they may be identified by reference to certain categories or location, but in each case the contracts to be transferred must be clearly described to allow them to be objectively identified.

There is no requirement for the parties to list the contracts being transferred in separate schedules. In practice, parties will usually agree a schedule listing the material contracts to be transferred with specific details such as date of the contract, title of the contract, and parties to the contract.

2. Administrative, Corporate and Other Approvals

Generally, the transfer of contracts does not require any special governmental or administrative approvals. The transfer of contracts relating to certain industries may require government or industry authority approval, such as a contract for the transfer of an interest in a licensed (and non exempt) electricity generator.

The constitution or articles of association of the seller and purchaser will usually set out the corporate actions required of the seller or purchaser for the proposed transaction.

Approval from counter parties and other third parties may be required if it is so stated in the contracts to be transferred. If the other parties refuse to grant approval, there may be an argument that the other parties to the contract cannot unreasonably withhold their consent or approval. If the approvals or consent from the other parties are not given, the transfer of the contracts may be invalid.

3. Automatic Transfer of Contracts (Other than Lease and Employment Agreements)

Some examples of contracts which may be automatically transferred to the purchaser in the event of an asset deal are hire purchase agreements and some asset related insurance contracts, but this will depend on their terms on a case by case basis.

4. Filing Requirements

Generally, the transfer of contracts does not require special filings with public authorities or registrations.

5. Treatment of Existing Contractual Claims and Obligations

If the counter party consented to the transfer of the contract, then any unperformed obligations or unfulfilled liabilities under the contracts will automatically transfer to the purchaser upon transfer of the contracts.

If the seller has previously disclosed to the purchaser the extent of the unperformed obligations or liabilities under these contracts, the parties may agree to adjust the purchase price to take them into consideration. Alternatively, it is also usual for the purchaser to require some form of indemnity from the seller in relation to unperformed obligations in the asset transfer agreement.

6. Warranty Claims Resulting from Events prior to Transfer

Since the transfer of contracts also involves the transfer of claims and obligations relating to the contracts, the purchaser upon assuming the obligations of the seller under the contracts will also become liable for warranty claims resulting from events prior to the transfer of the assets being affected. The purchaser can seek to protect its interest by specifically contracting out of that liability (such as entering onto a deed of novation with the counter parties clarifying the same) or by including indemnity provisions in the asset transfer agreement.

E. IP Rights

1. Characteristics of Intellectual Property Rights (e.g., Trademarks, Patents, Utility Models, Domain Names) ("*IP Rights*") as to:

a) Language of Documentation. The sale documents regarding the transfer of IP Rights may be drafted in any language. English is the usual language, but it is not mandatory. An English translation should be prepared so that the transfer of any registered IP Rights can be recorded on the relevant Register. The transfer documentation must be lodged with the relevant office within IP Australia for the transfer to be recorded.

The documents can be executed in two languages, preferably with a nominated language prevailing in case of any inconsistency.

b) Form of Documentation. Documents recording the transfer of tangible assets can be executed outside Australia. The parties can agree to execute counterparts, and should clearly specify in the contract that this is permitted.

c) Specification of IP Rights. The intellectual property rights being transferred may be generally described such as "all intellectual property rights relating to the [Business]" (as long as the business is clearly identifiable and/or defined), but the intellectual property rights to be transferred must be clearly described to allow them to be objectively identified. Typically, a definition of what constitutes intellectual property rights will be included.

There is no requirement for the parties to list the intellectual property rights being transferred in separate schedules. However, in practice, parties will usually identify each registerable intellectual property right with relevant registration numbers to allow ease of recordal of the transfer of ownership. Without each registrable IP Right specified, the document will not be able to be relied upon to have the transfer recorded on the relevant Register.

2. Administrative, Corporate and Other Approvals

Transfer of intellectual property normally does not require any special governmental or administrative approvals.

The constitution or articles of association of the seller and purchaser will usually set out the corporate actions required of the seller or purchaser for the proposed transaction.

Whether approval of a security holder is required will depend on the terms of the agreement creating the encumbrance. If under the terms of the agreement the seller must obtain prior approval of the security holder before being able to deal with the assets, then such consent should be obtained. If the security interest is recorded on the Register for the relevant IP Right, the relevant office at IP Australia will notify the security holder before taking any action in relation to the IP Right.

3. Filing Requirements

When registerable IP Rights are transferred, the transfer of those rights should be notified to the relevant office of IP Australia so that the transfer is recorded on the relevant Register (for example, the transfer of a patent must be notified to the Patents Office so that the transfer can be recorded on the Patents Register). This requires lodgment of the relevant transfer documents. The recordal of the transfer is declaratory only, and it is not necessary to effect the transfer of the relevant IP Right.

4. Applicable International (Multilateral) Agreements or Treaties

Australia is a party to, and has ratified, the TRIPS Agreement and the Paris Convention for the Protection of Industrial Property.

Australia is a party to, and has ratified, the Madrid Agreement and the Madrid Protocol regarding Trade Marks.

F. Receivables

1. Characteristics as to:

a) Language of Documentation. The sale documents regarding the transfer of receivables may be drafted in any language. English is the usual language, but it is not mandatory.

The documents can be executed in two languages, preferably with a nominated language prevailing in case of any inconsistency.

b) Form of Documentation. The transfer of receivables does not require any special form of documentation. It is usually provided for in the asset sale or transfer agreement.

Documents recording the transfer of receivables can be executed outside Australia. The parties can agree to execute counterparts, and should clearly specify in the contract that this is permitted.

c) Specification of Receivables. The receivables being transferred may be generally described such as "all accounts receivable relating to the [Business]" (as long as the business is clearly identifiable and/or defined) or they may be identified by reference to certain categories, but in each case the receivables to be transferred must be clearly described to allow them to be objectively identified.

There is no requirement for the parties to list the receivables being transferred in separate schedules.

2. Administrative, Corporate and Other Approvals

The transfer of receivables does not require special governmental or administrative approvals.

Whether or not corporate approvals are required depends on the constitutional documents of the seller and purchaser.

Notification of the transfer to the debtors is generally not required unless the underlying debt agreements provide otherwise. However, for practical reasons, the purchaser should inform the debtor of the transfer. If the debtor is not notified then they may continue to make payments to the seller on the receivables transferred.

3. Filing Requirements

The transfer of receivables does not require special filing with any public authorities or registration with registers or (online) databases.

G. Liabilities

1. Characteristics as to:

a) Language of Documentation. The sale documents regarding the transfer of contracts may be drafted in any language. English is the usual language, but it is not mandatory.

The documents can be executed in two languages, preferably with a nominated language prevailing in case of any inconsistency.

b) Form of Documentation. The transfer of liabilities does not require special form of documentation. It is usually included in the asset sale or transfer agreements.

Documents recording the transfer of liabilities can be executed outside Australia. The parties can agree to execute counterparts, and should clearly specify in the contract that this is permitted.

c) Specification of Liabilities. The liabilities being transferred may be generally described such as "all liabilities relating to the [Business]" (as long as the business is clearly identifiable and/or defined) or they may be identified by reference to certain categories, but in each case the liabilities to be transferred must be clearly described to allow them to be objectively identified.

There is no requirement for the parties to list the liabilities being transferred in separate schedules. Typically the parties will define the parameters of the nature of the liabilities being transferred.

2. Administrative, Corporate and Other Approvals

The transfer of liabilities does not require special governmental or administrative approvals.

Whether corporate approvals are required, and at what level, depends on the constitutional documents of the seller and purchaser.

Generally at law, a liability cannot be transferred without the consent of the creditor. Typically, the provisions of the underlying agreement will stipulate that the creditor's consent is required.

3. Filing Requirements

The transfer of liabilities does not require any special filings with public authorities or registration with registers or (online) databases.

4. Purchaser's Liability for:

a) Tax Obligations. A wide range of different income tax rules may apply (depending on the nature of the asset involved) to impose income tax on a seller disposing of assets. In broad terms these rules will impose liability for and responsibility for any tax obligations up to the date of disposal on the seller. While the seller will usually be liable for unpaid taxes, to the extent that a purchaser may be impacted by historical tax obligations relating to assets acquired as part of a business acquisition, a purchaser will usually seek to factor such obligations into the purchase price, and seek to accompany the acquisition with appropriate tax warranties and indemnities.

b) Environmental Contamination. In Australia contaminated land laws are on a state-by-state basis, and range between a strict "polluter pays" policy and the "leave it to the occupier" approach. National policies favor the polluter pays principle if the polluter is solvent and identifiable. Liability otherwise extends to the person in control of the site, irrespective of whether the person is the owner or the current occupier. In some instances an occupier is deemed to have caused pollution on commercial or industrial premises. The legislative regimes in most states established a hierarchy of clean-up liability.

State environmental regulators have the ability to serve a clean up order on the occupiers of premises or the person who caused or permitted the pollution to occur. The hierarchy of assigning responsibility for the clean up varies from state to state. Generally, the occupier has a statutory right to recover reasonable costs from the polluter, but where the polluter is no longer solvent the costs may be borne by the occupier.

In both asset transfers and share transfer transactions it may be appropriate to obtain environmental indemnities for environmental contamination occurring prior to the date of sale. If there is significant contamination which is likely to continue, it is usual practice to obtain an environmental consultant's assessment of the pollution at the date of sale. The consultant's report will then set a baseline from which calculations regarding liability may be made. The agreement can then be amended or a price reduction sought to reflect clean up costs or other liabilities.

c) Products Sold or Services Rendered by the Seller to Third Parties. This depends on if the liabilities for these products sold or services rendered were included as the list of liabilities to be assumed by the purchaser. If the past products are sold or services rendered by the seller as a company (without connection to any assets), then on an asset sale, the purchaser should not be responsible for any liabilities arising from the products sold or services rendered by the seller to third parties for the period prior to the acquisition. The consumer of the products or services should only have a cause of action against the seller. Typically a purchaser would seek indemnification or warranty protection against any potential product recall or liability.

5. Automatic Transfer of Other Liabilities

Unless required by law, a purchaser will generally only assume those liabilities of a business that it agrees to accept, however, certain liabilities attaching to the assets may automatically transfer to the purchaser on an asset sale such as any outstanding payments for insurance premiums and liabilities under hire and purchase agreements.

From an income tax perspective, other liabilities (such as provisions for employee entitlements and provisions for bad or doubtful debts) may also be transferred to a purchaser depending on the nature of the assets (or business) acquired. Specific income tax rules will apply to determine the treatment of such items.

For example, in broad terms, a purchaser will not be able to claim a deduction for income tax purposes in respect of debts purchased from a seller that are subsequently written off as "bad". In these circumstances, again to the extent that a purchaser may be impacted by such items, a purchaser will usually seek to factor these into the purchase price in an endeavor to make the acquisition as "tax-neutral" as possible.

From a GST perspective, the view taken by the Australian Taxation Office is that there are no additional GST consequences arising if the purchaser assumes any liabilities attaching to the assets that automatically transfer to the purchaser by virtue of statue. However, if the liabilities do not transfer by virtue of statute, but are transferred under an agreement between the purchaser and the seller, the amount of the assumed liabilities is viewed as being part of the consideration paid for the supply.

6. Contractual Protection as to 4 and 5 above

It is usual for the purchaser to protect itself by obtaining a broad range of representations and warranties from the seller relating to the business.

Indemnity provisions for tax and environmental concerns are more common in share transfer agreements, but may be negotiated in asset transfer agreements depending on the nature of the business being sold.

H. Employees

1. Transfer of Employees

Under an asset sale, the employees of the seller do not automatically transfer to the purchaser.

Typically, at completion of the acquisition the current employment contracts will be brought to an end and the employees would simultaneously be re-employed by the purchaser, on substantially identical terms. This requires offers of employment to be made and individually accepted.

The purchaser usually recognizes prior service and accrued service based entitlements, such as annual leave, for transferring employees. Superannuation (pension) entitlements typically continue with the purchaser taking responsibility for future contributions. It is sometimes the case that employees will no longer be eligible for membership of the fund sponsored by the seller. In that situation, either employees are invited to transfer to a new fund into which contributions can be made, or arrangements are made for a compulsory transfer to a successor fund.

Redundancy entitlements are capable of being triggered because the employment will terminate for the reason that the seller no longer requires the job the employee has been doing to be done by anyone. Whether or not an employee has severance pay entitlements upon redundancy will depend on the terms of the employee's employment. It is usual for a seller to avoid severance pay liability arising by requiring that the purchaser make offers of acceptable alternative employment which reflect the current employment terms and recognize prior service and accrued leave entitlements. This needs attention and planning in each case.

There are limited statutory transfer of business undertaking provisions which make some industrial instruments and employment entitlements binding upon the transmitee of a business.

2. Approval of Works Council, Trade Union or Other Institutions

No approvals, as such, are required from any works council, labor agency, trade union or other institution.

There are specific notification requirements under the Workplace Relations Act 1996 (Cth) where a business has been transmitted and an employee of the transmittor becomes an employee of the transmitee.

It is common for collective agreements and other industrial instruments to contain requirements to notify and consult relevant trade unions where a decision is made about changes to a business (such as the sale of the business) and which will result in terminations of employment. There are similar requirements under the Workplace Relations Act 1996 in the case of an anticipated termination of 15 or more employees.

A failure to comply with these requirements would not invalidate the asset transfer but could attract penalties and other adverse practical consequences.

3. Contractual Protection as to Labor Issues

Depending on the number of employees being transferred and the complexity of the employment arrangements in relation to them, it is customary to provide (a) indemnities from the purchaser to the seller against claims from transferring employees relating to the period of employment following completion and (b) indemnities from the seller to the purchaser against claims from non-transferring employees and for the period of employment prior to completion.

I. Tax Implications

1. Value Added Tax

The relevant tax that is equivalent to the VAT in Australia is the Goods and Services Tax or the GST. The GST Law is provided for under the A New Tax System (Goods and Services Tax) Act 1999 (Cth).

Typically, a supply of assets is treated as a taxable supply. The GST amount payable on a taxable supply is 10% of the value of the taxable supply.

However, if the assets are being transferred as part of a going concern which meets the requirements of a GST-free supply of a going concern, there may not be any GST payable on the supply. Please refer to Section A, 1 above for further information in this regard.

2. Real Property Transfer Tax

Different States and Territories in Australia apply different rates of stamp duty to the transfer of dutiable property, including land. Duty rates for the transfer of an interest in land apply on a rising scale. The table below outlines which property is dutiable on their transfer in each State and Territory and the highest rate of duty.

State/Territory	Dutiable Property	Highest Rate of Duty
New South Wales	Includes land and an option to purchase land. Transfer of a lease for a premium also dutiable.	AUS 40,490, plus 5.5% over AUD 1,000,000
South Australia	Includes conveyance of any real or personal property.	AUD 21,330, plus 5.5% over AUD 500,000
Queensland	Includes land or an option to purchase dutiable property.	AUD 23,975, plus 4.5% over AUD 700,000
Western Australia	Includes land and leases.	AUD 20,700, plus 5.4% over AUD 500,000
Northern Territory	Includes land or an option to purchase dutiable property.	5.4% over AUD 500,000
Tasmania	Includes land, a mineral tenement or fixtures thereon, or an option to purchase dutiable property.	AUD 6,550, plus 4.0% over AUD 225,000
Victoria	Includes interests in land (an estate in fee simple, a life estate/estate in remainder, Crown lease, granting of a lease for a premium with a covenant for future transfer of fee simple).	5.5% over AUD 870,000
Australian Capital Territory	Includes land, Crown lease, long term lease, or an option to purchase land or a Crown lease.	AUD 49,250, plus 6.75% over AUD 1,000,000

3. Other Tax Issues

A wide range of different income tax rules will apply to the disposal of an asset, depending on the nature of the asset involved. For example, sellers should be aware that a disposal of trading stock will ordinarily be deemed to take place at market value for income tax purposes.

Purchasers should also be aware that the ability to claim depreciation deductions in respect of certain types of assets (such as eligible construction expenditure incurred in connection with buildings) may be restricted to the quantum of any undeducted/undepreciated amount of the seller, irrespective of the purchase price allocated to such assets. Again in these circumstances, the purchaser will usually seek to adjust the purchase price to reflect the tax status of the particular assets after acquisition.

While not usually as "onerous" in terms of obligations when compared to share sales, asset disposals nevertheless still require appropriate and due attention to relevant issues required to be considered, including income tax, GST and stamp duty implications.

J. Bankruptcy Law

1. Challenge of Asset Transfer in Case of Insolvency

A transaction which is an uncommercial transaction may be set aside by a court in Australia under the Corporations Act 2001 (Cth). A transaction will be an uncommercial transaction if:

(i) it may be expected that a reasonable person in the company's circumstances would not have entered into the transaction having regard to the benefits (if any) and detriment accruing to the company, and the benefits accruing to other parties, as a result of the transaction (Section 588FB of the Act);

(ii) the company was insolvent at the time the transaction was entered into or became insolvent as a result of the transaction (Section 588FC); and

(iii) the transaction was entered into during the two years ending on the date the company entered liquidation (or in the case of a transaction with a "related entity party", four years) (Section 588FE).

In addition, a transfer may be deemed an unfair preference for the purposes of Section 588FA of the Corporations Act 2001 (Cth) if it constitutes the repayment of an unsecured debt, ahead of other creditors.

2. Acquisition of Assets that are Subject to Insolvency Proceedings

An officially appointed liquidator is an officer of the court and has the power to sell the business (including individual assets) of the company in liquidation. If the seller is in liquidation, it is the liquidator, and not the board of directors of the company, which has the power to sell the business. Certain obligations are imposed on the liquidator in relation to its conduct in obtaining the best price possible.

K. Timing and Costs

1. Timeframe of Asset Transfer

If the transaction requires approval from FIRB, according to the FATA the Treasurer must make a decision within 30 days of the date of receipt of the application. The Treasurer may ask for an extension/further information extending such 30 day period by a further period of time.

If the transfer is referred to the ACCC, the ACCC must decide on such applications within 40 business days (which may be extended in certain circumstances, for example where further information is required). Clearance is deemed to be refused if the ACCC does not make a decision within the required timeframe.

If the ACCC refuses to grant a clearance, or grants it subject to conditions, the person who applied for clearance may seek a review by the Australian Competition Tribunal.

Most registrations may be undertaken simultaneously with completion.

2. Costs of Asset Transfer

There are no requirements for notarization or legalization for any asset transfer contracts in Australia.

Registration costs with ASIC and other government departments is nominal.

Each Australian State and Territory has different legislation prescribing the different rates applicable for the calculation of stamp duty as set out in the table at I, 2 above.

L. Miscellaneous

1. Choice of Foreign Law

It is open to the parties to specify their choice of governing law in the contract. If the parties do not choose a law an Australian court may accept jurisdiction and deem that an Australian state's law will apply if that law has the closet nexus to the subject matter of the contract and to the parties.

2. (International) Arbitration, Choice of Venue

The parties are free to choose dispute resolution by way of court or arbitration (or other means). International arbitration is possible and the parties can specify the agreed arbitration procedures in the contract. There are no restrictions as to the choice of venue, for example, the parties can chose to have their disputes heard by specialized arbitration bodies overseas.

3. Other Distinctions, Characteristics

There are no other noteworthy distinctions or characteristics as to the transfer of assets in Australia.

M. Literature

S. A. Christensen and *W. D. Duncan*, Sale of Business in Australia, 1st Edition, 1997

Austria

By *Andreas Zahradnik* and *Barbara Cervenka*

A. General Aspects

1. Asset Deal vs. Share Deal: Essential Considerations

Generally speaking, a share deal is easier to implement and can be effected more quickly than an asset deal. Asset deals are more complex since each asset that is sold needs to be transferred and "handed-over" individually in the required form from the seller to the purchaser. Therefore, asset deals are only used in constellations in which only a few specific assets, rather than all of the operating business, shall be acquired.

Under Austrian law, tax, liability, administrative, regulatory and employee issues commonly form the main points to be considered in the decision regarding whether the transaction will be structured as an asset or a share deal.

Tax Issues

A very important criterion in deciding between an asset deal and a share deal is taxes. Tax implications will mainly depend on the legal form as well as the nationality of the entities that sell and purchase the business.

The main tax advantages of an asset deal for the purchaser are the following: The purchaser gets a step-up of the value of the assets and may depreciate the fair value of the assets instead of the previous book value. Thus, his taxable profit will be reduced in the years following the asset deal. Moreover, the purchaser may depreciate the "goodwill," which is the part of the purchase price that exceeds the value of the assets. In some rare cases, the purchaser may even depreciate more than 100% of the purchase price.

The disadvantage of an asset deal for the seller is the full taxation of the profit derived from the assets. This is especially true for corporations that sell assets. Only natural persons as sellers may, in some cases, enjoy tax advantages from an asset deal: Their profit may be left tax exempt provided that they acquire other assets instead. If a natural person sells his/her entire business due to his or her retirement, the profit is also taxed at a lower rate. In any other case, the asset deal is not favourable for the seller from a tax point of view.

Takeover Act

The Austrian Takeover Act of 2006, which implements the EU Takeover Directive, must only be followed for share deals. It regulates both mandatory and voluntary takeover bids of shares in a joint stock company that are listed on the Viennese Stock Exchange for official trading or regulated unofficial trading.

Administrative Permits and Regulatory Issues

Legal consequences regarding administrative permits and regulatory law are quite different for share and asset deals. Administrative permits are required in order to operate certain business plants, facilities and machinery (facility permit, building permit). Additionally, certain businesses require administrative approval in the form of a trade license under the Trade Commerce and Industry Regulation Act or a banking or other license in order to be permitted to operate. In share deals, licenses and permits usually remain unaffected, with the exception that some permits contain change of control clauses. However, in asset deals, all administrative permits, licenses and authorizations that are not issued with respect to physical objects ("in rem" permits) must be newly obtained. Public permits relating to a certain asset, rather than to the owner of the respective asset, will regularly remain unaffected in the case of transfer of ownership.

Liability Issues

Liabilities constitute a very decisive factor when weighing benefits and risks of an asset or a share deal. Both the Austrian Civil Code (*ABGB*) and the Business Entrepreneur Act (*UGB*) contain liability provisions. Share deals have the advantage that neither of the below-outlined statutory liability provisions applies. Share deals might only be affected by the provision contained in Section 1409 of the Austrian Civil Code, where the shares essentially form the only asset of the seller.

- Section 1409 of the ABGB stipulates the compulsive liability of the purchaser of an undertaking or a significant portion of the seller's assets. The purchaser becomes liable for all business-related debts of the seller that the purchaser was aware of or should have been aware of when taking over the business. "Debts" are defined quite simply as pecuniary obligations that comprise, inter alia, contractual and tortious claims for damages as well as statutory debts. Under Section 1409 of the ABGB, compulsive liability of the purchaser means that the purchaser can be held liable by a creditor to pay the debt of the seller if the creditor chooses so. However, the extent of liability of the purchaser is limited by the net value of the received assets. Furthermore, the purchaser will not be held liable pursuant to Section 1409 ABGB if it uses the purchase price (which must correspond to the value of the acquired business) to actually satisfy the seller's creditors on the seller's behalf or if the seller itself uses the purchase price to liquidate the company's liabilities.
- Section 38 of the UGB sets forth that the purchaser of an undertaking, by law, enters into all legal relationships of the seller related to said undertaking. Other than the liability according to Section 1409 ABGB, the liability according to Section 38 UGB can either be excluded by registering the "exclusion of liability" with the Company Register or by directly informing the affected third parties of such liability exclusion. As previously mentioned, the liability imposed by Section 38 UGB does not apply to share deals. In addition, Section 38 UGB requires that the other party to any transferred legal relationship is informed of the transfer. Such third

party may object to the transfer within three months of receipt of the respective notice. In such case, the contractual relationship is not transferred and remains in place between the seller and the third party.

2. Distinction between Sale and Transfer in Rem

According to the Austrian Civil Code, the sale (obligation to transfer) and the transfer in rem (fulfilment of the obligation to transfer) are strictly distinguished. The sale contract itself only represents the legal title and entitles the purchaser to take possession of property; however, it does not automatically transfer the ownership. The purchaser only becomes owner by physically taking over the sold goods. A valid transfer in rem can (under certain circumstances) be effected even if the sale and purchase agreement is invalid. However, the seller might claim a re-transfer of assets in the absence of a valid title.

In Austria, an asset deal requires that each asset be individually transferred; therefore, an asset deal cannot be handled via universal succession. Movable physical assets must either be taken into possession by the purchaser or the purchaser must instruct a third person to take possession of the goods for its benefit. In cases where the actual taking of possession is impossible, it is possible to acquire possession through symbolic delivery. The Civil Code mentions the following three forms of symbolic delivery: delivery through documents (e.g., share certificates), tools (e.g., keys to a warehouse) and marks (e.g., branding of wood). Receivables and claims must be assigned, and contractual relationships must be taken over by assumption of the contract subject to approval of the other parties involved. In cases where the registration of a right has constitutive effect (e.g., real property), the transfer will only become effective upon registration of the new owner in the respective register. Various federal acts contain exceptions for labor contracts, tenancy contracts, property insurance contracts, patent license agreements, trademark license agreements, semi-conductor license agreements and license agreements for property protected by copyright.

If multiple jurisdictions are implicated in an asset deal, it is advisable to effect the sale by way of a single master purchase agreement, while the asset transfer can be conducted on the basis of various local transfer agreements. The benefit of such an approach is that local transfer requirements can be fulfilled by the local transfer agreement without affecting the master purchase agreement. This approach also avoids the disclosure of the entire asset transfer where the transfer has to be filed with authorities for the purpose of registration.

3. Regional Differences

Austria is a Federal Republic that is divided into nine states (*Bundesländer*). Most applicable laws such as the Civil Code or the Business Entrepreneurs Act are federal laws and are therefore uniform for all states. Nevertheless, some laws, such as laws regulating the transfer of property (*GrundverkehrsG*), are state laws and vary from state to state. States are, inter alia, also competent in deciding which types of real estate construction are permitted and which conditions apply to construction.

4. Acquisition by Foreigners

The respective state laws governing real estate property transfers usually require foreigners or foreign entities to request prior approval for the purchase. EU and EEA citizens are exempted from such approval requirements. Additionally, some state laws contain special rules concerning the acquisition of farm land and forests.

5. Public Registers, Records and Databases

Austria does not have a general database recording ownership. The following registers can either be accessed over the internet (where applicable, the relevant World Wide Web (www) address is specified) or by an attorney at law, notary and the courts and administrative authorities:

Land Register

The Land Register contains information relating to real property ownership and encumbrances. Please note that for information retrieval from the Land Register, either the land property number, the number of the Land Register or an exact address of the property is required. Inquiries using the name of the owner are only permitted in exceptional cases.

Company Register

Information related to companies can be retrieved from the Company Register. All excerpts contain information on the date of establishment, the legal form, power of representation, amount of registered share capital, capital increases and mergers, as well as information regarding the general assembly/meeting. Additionally, the Company Register contains an electronic catalog of documents from which annual financial statements and shareholder's resolutions can be extracted. It is also possible to retrieve historical company register excerpts that indicate all past changes. Other than in the Land Register, the registration of ownership is not binding and not required for a valid share transfer.

Trademark and Patent Register

The Trademark and Patent Register is publicly accessible from the homepage "www.patentamt.at". Some information may be acquired free of charge. The register has information regarding ownership, the scope of protection and duration of the rights concerned.

Insolvency and Bankruptcy Register

Austria also has a public Insolvency and Bankruptcy Register. In this register, which can be accessed free of charge from the homepage "www.edikte.justiz.gv.at", private persons and companies are registered directly after the initiation of an insolvency or bankruptcy proceeding.

Other Registers

Further, the Austrian Air Traffic Management keeps an Aircraft Register for the registration of ownership of aircraft, and the courts maintain a Maritime Register where the ownership of vessels must be registered. The law differentiates between inland navigation vessels and seagoing vessels, whereby only the ownership registration of seagoing vessels has constitutive effect for the acquisition of ownership.

6. Purchase Price Requirements

There are no special rules regarding the purchase price or the currency in which the purchase price must be paid, apart from the obligation to be precise. The condition of a precise price is met whenever the price is either explicitly fixed in the contract or when it is expressed as a formula by reference to which a price can be determined. If the agreement is too imprecise to allow the price to be determined, the contract will fail to create a binding legal obligation.

Though advisable for tax reasons, it is not necessary to allocate the purchase price to certain assets. Additionally, the purchase price should always explicitly state whether VAT is included or excluded in order to avoid disputes. It is advisable to allocate the purchase price in case only certain portions of it are subject to VAT or stamp duties.

B. Tangible/Movable Assets

1. Characteristics as to:

a) Language of Documentation. Documents concerning the sale and transfer of tangible assets may be drafted in any language. Usually bilingual documents are permitted, but not required by law. If the document is required for public use (e.g., registration), bilingual documents can be executed if they are also in German, which is the official language in Austria; otherwise, a certified translation will be required. In any case, the prevailing language (in the event of discrepancy) should be clearly indicated.

b) Form of Documentation. The documentation for the sale and transfer of tangible assets – other than shares in a company with limited liability (*GmbH*) – does not require a specific form. As described above, it is necessary, however, to distinguish between the obligation to transfer a legal title such as, e.g., a sales contract and the transfer itself, by taking possession of the tangible asset. Tangible assets can only be transferred by taking possession of them (which is possible in various ways). Sale and transfer documents may be executed outside of Austria. Signing in counterparts is also permissible. For the transfer of shares in a company with limited liability (*GmbH*), an Austrian notarial deed is required.

c) Specification of Assets. As a basic principle, tangible assets require a physical transfer, thus each object, in theory, must be transferred by itself. In the case of "common tangible assets" (*Gesamtsache*), the law also provides for the transfer by deed, therefore, a physical transfer of each single object is not required. Nonetheless, sufficient specification of the respective assets is required to identify the acquired assets.

2. Administrative, Corporate and Other Approvals

The transfer of tangible assets typically does not require any governmental or administrative approvals. However, approvals may be required in specific cases, such as the transfer of shares in regulated entities, pieces of art or other items of cultural value, weapons, equipment subject to embargo, etc. A transfer without such a required permit could be void.

The approval of corporate bodies is only required if the parties' articles of association or partnership agreements contain corresponding provisions. This is usually the case if all, or substantially all, or material assets are sold. However, failure to procure internal approval typically would not render the sale void.

In cases where tangible assets are subject to encumbrances and similar securities, the approval of the respective security holder is required for a valid transfer of the asset.

3. Filing Requirements

The transfer of tangible assets neither requires special filings with public authorities nor registration in public registers or databases. Exceptions apply to the transfer of shares in listed or regulated entities as they may trigger filing requirements. Additionally, the transfer of seagoing vessels requires the registration of ownership with the Maritime Register, as such a registration has constitutive effect for the acquisition of ownership.

4. Automatic Transfer of Encumbrances

Under Austrian law, pledges and transfers of title for security purposes are subject to strict publicity requirements. Where the assets are pledged or transferred by way of security, all encumbrances will automatically transfer to the purchaser in connection with the asset transfer. However, the bona fide acquisition of encumbered assets (i.e. an unencumbered acquisition) may be possible in cases where publicity requirements are not met, and, therefore, the purchaser may have no knowledge of the encumbrance. In this context, please note that tangible assets usually must be handed over for publicity requirements to be effective. In situations where the actual transfer is impossible, a sign or notification on the asset may indicate encumbrances.

Since the retention of title is not subject to strict publicity requirements, it is possible that a retention of title may not be apparent. Usually, it is possible to determine retention of title from the account documents.

C. Real Property

1. Characteristics as to:

a) Language of Documentation. In theory, documents for the transfer of real property may be drafted in every applicable language or bilingually. Since the Land Register will only accept transfer deeds in German, it is advisable to at least use a bilingual version (stipulating that the German version prevails). The sale and transfer deeds are registered in the electronic document register, which forms part of the Land Register.

b) Form of Documentation. The sale and purchase agreement for real property must be submitted to the Land Register; therefore, the agreements must be drafted in written form. Additionally, all documents must be notarized either by an Austrian notary public or a foreign public notary (in which case an Apostille is required). Real property sale and purchase agreements may be executed in counterparts, if all parties have their signatures notarized.

c) Specification of Assets. A transfer of real property requires a very precise and detailed description and should correspond with the data at the Land Register. Austrian land register authorities are very accurate, and small deviations can lead to a dismissal of the registration request.

2. Administrative, Corporate and Other Approvals

To transfer real property, foreigners from non-EU or non-EEA countries might require an administrative approval in accordance with the land transfer laws that differ from state to state. Additionally, the transfer of certain kinds of real property (agriculture, forest) requires special approval.

Documents regarding the transfer of real property are only valid if the rules on power of representation are met. Many company statutes/articles of association contain special provisions that need to be met for the real property sale and purchase agreement.

Since encumbrances automatically transfer to the purchaser, encumbered real property can be transferred without the prior approval of security holders.

3. Filing Requirements

The transfer of real property needs to be registered in the Land Register and is not effective before such registration. The Land Register is publicly accessible and also contains an electronic document register.

4. Automatic Transfer of Encumbrances

Encumbrances such as mortgages, usufruct rights, easements, real burdens, construction rights and the right of pre-emption are registered as encumbrances in Schedule C of the relevant entry in the Land Register. Since the principle of accuracy applies to the Austrian Land Register, everyone can rely on the registered information as correct and valid.

All registered encumbrances attach to the real property to which they are registered and generally follow the ownership of the property. Therefore, encumbrances usually transfer to the purchaser automatically.

It is possible and very common that several mortgages are registered on the same property. According to the principle of priority, the ranking of a mortgage depends on the date of the application for registration. A waiver of encumbrances can be obtained; however, such waivers must be notarized in order to be admitted as a document with which the deletion of the encumbrance can be requested from the Land Register.

Personal easements commonly only cease with the death of the beneficiary. Easements are very common for public utilities such as water supply and electricity pipes.

Caution is advised whenever the Land Register indicates a right of pre-emption. In such cases, the seller of the real property must advise the pre-emptor of the terms and conditions of a sale and purchase. The pre-emptor then has the right to acquire the property in question under the same conditions under which the purchaser wishes to buy. If the pre-emptor wishes to acquire the property under the described conditions, the seller is obliged to enter into the contract. If the pre-emptor does not make use of his right, the Land Register will demand a written confirmation that the pre-emptor will not make use of his right. The right of pre-emption is not transferable.

In certain cases, the transfer of land within a family may be subject to approval by other family members if this requirement is recorded in the Land Register.

5. Automatic Transfer of Lease Agreements

The transfer of lease agreements and the right of termination of such agreements depends on the rules that apply to such lease agreement. Under Austrian law, there are various possibilities: Some lease agreements are subject to the Austrian Lease Act (*Mietrechtsgesetz*, MRG), in other cases, the MRG only applies partially, and finally there are lease agreements that are simply regulated by the Austrian Civil Code (ABGB). Moreover, under Austrian law it is possible to register lease contracts in Schedule C of the relevant entry in the Land Register. As a consequence, the acquirer of the lease object must assume the lease agreement under the terms and conditions under which it was concluded.

Lease Agreements Subject to the MRG

The MRG also differentiates with respect to whether the transfer of lease agreements takes place by itself or in the context of a transfer of a business. Whenever a business is transferred, the following applies: Under the application of the MRG, lease agreements transfer to the purchaser of a business by operation of law, provided that the business activities are not modified. It is possible that the transfer of a lease agreement by law also applies to an asset deal, since assets are sometimes considered to be a business under the MRG's business definition. Thus, an assessment of each individual asset deal is recommended. Section 12a of the MRG only stipulates that the landlord must be informed immediately by the seller and the purchaser. The landlord may demand an increase in the rent to an amount that corresponds to a fair market value within a six-month period after notification of the lease transfer. The fair market value must take the exercised business activity into account. This provision contained in Section 12a might be of importance in situations where the seller has a minimal amount of rent due to the conclusion of the lease agreement in the past. The right of the landlord to increase the rent also applies in situations where a share deal is used in order to bypass the mandatory provision, which allows the landlord to increase the rent. In such a case, the tenant must establish that the share deal structure was not used for the purpose of evading Section 12a of the MRG.

Lease Agreements Partially Subject to the MRG or Subject to the Civil Code

If a lease agreement only falls under the partial application of the MRG or in cases where the Civil Code (ABGB) applies, the lease agreement will transfer automatically to the business purchaser in accordance with Section 38 UGB and the lessor will only be able to object to the transfer of the agreement within a three-month period.

Transfer of a Leased Piece of Real Property

The legal consequence of the sale and transfer of a leased piece of real property depends on whether the MRG or the Civil Code applies. Under the application of the MRG, the real property owner will be bound to existing lease contracts since the MRG does not contain provisions that allow the termination of a lease contract due to the acquisition of ownership. However, if the Civil Code applies to the lease contract, it will be possible for the acquirer to terminate existing lease contracts under the terms and provisions provided for by law (usually within 14 days, if not agreed upon otherwise). In such cases, the seller will be obligated to compensate the lessee.

The transfer of a lease contract by the lessee to a new lessee is usually possible only by way of sublease or where the lease contract contains provisions that allow such a transfer. However, the MRG contains various special provisions and it is therefore recommended to review each case individually.

D. Contracts

1. Characteristics as to:

a) Language of Documentation. The sale and transfer documents regarding contracts may be drafted in any language (bilingual documents are permitted). German translations are not required (unless they are used as evidence in court).

b) Form of Documentation. The transfer of contracts does not require a special form unless the conclusion of the contract to be transferred is subject to certain formal requirements. Nevertheless, the written form is advisable for evidentiary purposes. The documents may be executed outside of Austria. Signing in counterparts is permissible.

c) Specification of Contracts. The principle of determination, which applies to all contracts in Austria, requires the parties to specifically describe contracts that form part of the sale and purchase agreement. However, as described above, whenever an entire business is transferred, all contracts that are business-related will transfer automatically. According to Section 38 of the Austrian Entrepreneurs Act, contractual parties have the right to object to the transfer of a contract. In such case, the contractual relationship with the seller will remain unaffected.

2. Administrative, Corporate and Other Approvals

The transfer of contracts generally does not require special governmental or administrative approvals. The approval of any corporate body is not required either, unless otherwise provided in the articles of association of the seller and/or purchaser. In case of a stock corporation (or a limited liability company with a supervisory board), the applicable Austrian provisions stipulate that the purchase or sale of a business or a plant requires the prior approval of the supervisory board. However, the transfer would usually be valid without such approval.

In any case, under Austrian law, the transfer of contracts (besides certain exceptions, e.g., employment contracts, certain insurance contracts, etc.) generally requires the consent of all parties to the agreement if not agreed otherwise or if Section 38 of the Austrian Entrepreneurs Act does not apply (see D, 1, c above). Failure to comply with this provision will invalidate the transfer.

3. Automatic Transfer of Contracts (Other than Lease and Employment Agreements)

Austrian insurance contract law provides for an automatic transfer of asset-related insurance agreements such as certain property insurances. The insurer is not bound to such transfers unless it is notified of them. Please note that the transfer of assets must be immediately reported to the insurer. In the event such notification is neither effected by the purchaser nor by the seller, the insurer is generally not obliged to effect payment for an insured event that occurs a month after the date the insurer should have been notified of the transfer.

The insurer is entitled to terminate the insurance contract within a period of one month after the insurer has been notified of the transfer. Furthermore, the purchaser is entitled to terminate the insurance contract with immediate effect or with effect as to the end of the current period of insurance. Such termination right is limited to a period of one month after the transfer or after the purchaser has been notified of the existence of the insurance contract.

4. Filing Requirements

Generally, no filings with public authorities or registrations with registers (or databases) are required with regard to the transfer of contracts.

5. Treatment of Existing Contractual Claims and Obligations

Under Austrian law, as pointed out above, the transfer of contracts generally requires the consent of all parties to the agreement. If and to the extent that the contractual parties consent to the transfer of a contract, the respective rights and/or obligations arising from the contract transfer to the purchaser. This also applies to incomplete or partially fulfilled contracts unless otherwise stipulated in the transfer agreement. The issue of incomplete or partially fulfilled contracts is typically dealt with in the purchase agreement and influences the purchase price (purchase price adjustment). A respective indemnification clause can also be included in the transfer agreement. Moreover, the transfer agreement can be closed under the condition precedent that the parties to a transferred contract waive their rights to extraordinary termination arising from a change-of-control clause.

6. Warranty Claims Resulting from Events prior to Transfer

In general, the transfer of a contract also includes the transfer of any rights and obligations arising from such contract due to the fact that the required consent of all contractual parties commonly also covers such rights and obligations. This also applies to warranty claims resulting from events prior to the transfer of the affected assets, unless provided otherwise in the transfer agreement. The resulting potential exposure is typically covered by warranties, representations and/or indemnifications.

E. IP Rights

1. Characteristics of Intellectual Property Rights (e.g., Trademarks, Patents, Utility Models, Domain Names) ("*IP Rights*") as to:

a) Language of Documentation. Documents concerning the sale and transfer of intellectual property rights may be drafted in any language. Bilingual documents are permitted.

b) Form of Documentation. According to Section 11 of the Austrian Trademark Protection Act (*Markenschutzgesetz, MaSchG*), trademarks that belong to a business will only automatically transfer to the purchaser if the entire business is transferred. The parties may agree otherwise. If only a part of a business is transferred, the Austrian Trademark Protection Act does not provide for an automatic transfer of trademarks by law. In such cases, the transfer of trademarks must explicitly be agreed upon by the parties.

Since the purchaser of a trademark must apply for registration with the Patent and Trademark Register in order to have the trademarks and patents assigned, the application for registration of the new ownership will require a written document that must be notarized, indicating that the seller disposes of his right. The registration with the Trademark Register only has declarative effect. Caution is advised in regard to pledged trademarks, as such pledges do not have to be registered with the Trademark Register in order to be effective.

Patents are regulated by the Austrian Patent Act, which distinguishes between patents and patent licenses. According to Section 33 of the Austrian Patent Act (*Patentgesetz, PatG*), patents can be transferred by contract. Patents and patent licenses can also be pledged. Since registration with the Patent Register has constitutive effect, all rights related to patents, including pledges, must be registered in order to become effective. For the purpose of registration, the patent office will require an application for registration and a notarized sale and purchase agreement. In cases where patent licenses are not transferred with the business undertaking that they form a part of, the consent of the patent owner will also be required in notarized form (Section 36 of the Austrian Patent Act). Since encumbrances of patents must be registered with the patent office in order to become valid, the Austrian Patent Act requires the transfer of all encumbrances to the new patent owner by law.

Utility models are regulated in the Austrian Utility Models Act (*Musterschutzgesetz, MuSchG*) and can be transferred either wholly or in imaginary shares. The mandatory registration of the new owner in the Utility Models Register is required for a transfer to be effective. The registration has constitutive effect.

The transfer of domain names is usually regulated by private contract. Consequently, no general rules apply.

All documents can be executed outside of Austria; however, whenever a notarized document is required by law, foreign documents might additionally require an Apostille. Signing in counterparts is permitted.

c) Specification of IP Rights. The principle of determination, which applies to all contracts in Austria, requires the parties to specifically describe all IP rights that will form part of the sale and purchase agreement. However, as described above, whenever an entire business is transferred, trademarks will transfer automatically and a written confirmation will only be required for the registration of the new owner with the Trademark Register.

In practice, it is common to append schedules or lists of all IP rights that are to be transferred to the sale and purchase agreement.

2. Administrative, Corporate and Other Approvals

In Austria, the transfer of IP rights does not require special governmental or administrative approvals. However, the registration of patents and utility models in the respective registers has constitutive effect. Without registration, the transfer will therefore not become effective.

Approvals of the corporate bodies of the seller or the purchaser in connection with the transfer of IP rights are only required in cases where the statutes or the articles of association contain special provisions.

The Austrian Business Enterprise Code stipulates in Section 38 that contracts transfer automatically to the purchaser of a business, and third parties shall have the right to object to the transfer. With respect to encumbered IP rights directly relating to the sold business, all encumbrances such as pledges remain in force.

3. Filing Requirements

The transfer of IP rights such as trademarks, patents and utility models should be registered with the corresponding registers. The registration with the Trademark Register only has declarative effect. However, registration with the Patent and the Utility Models Registers has constitutive effect (see E, 1, b above); the transfer, therefore, only becomes effective with such registration.

4. Applicable International (Multilateral) Agreements or Treaties

Austria participates in the TRIPS Agreement and in the Paris Convention for the Protection of Industrial Property. Additionally, Austria signed the Madrid Agreement, the Madrid Protocol regarding trademarks and the Council Regulation on the Community Trademark of the European Community.

F. Receivables

1. Characteristics as to:

a) Language of Documentation. Austria does not have mandatory rules regarding the language of documentation for the sale and transfer of receivables. Documents may be therefore drafted in English or bilingually. In the event the relevant documents are required in connection with a legal dispute, Austrian courts may demand a certified translation.

The transfer of receivables is effected by the execution of the deed of assignment and by either giving notice of the assignment to the debtor or by an entry into the books of the assignor. Section 1395 of the Civil Code provides that the debtor may discharge his liability with payment to the assignor as long as it did not receive notice regarding the assignment. The law holds the assignor liable for the correctness and collectability (unless agreed otherwise). Liability is limited to the amount that the assignor received from the assignee; furthermore, liability is excluded for receivables that, according to the Insolvency and Bankruptcy Register and the Land Register, were uncollectible at the time of assignment.

Contracts occasionally prohibit the assignment of receivables. Such prohibition might be invalid if the terms were not negotiated but were in the form of general terms and conditions.

b) Form of Documentation. As a basic principle, the transfer of receivables does not require any kind of form apart from the above-mentioned disclosure acts. Including a schedule of all receivables in the sale contract is recommended. Documents may be executed outside of Austria, and signing in counterparts is permissible.

c) Specification of Receivables. The principle of identification also applies to the transfer of receivables. It is therefore advisable to give an exact description of all receivables that will be transferred. Under Austrian law, it is also possible to transfer future receivables; however, the receivables must be sufficiently described.

2. Administrative, Corporate and Other Approvals

The transfer of receivables neither requires governmental nor administrative approval.

Approvals of the corporate bodies of the seller or the purchaser are only required in cases where the statutes or the articles of association contain special provisions.

Generally, the transfer of receivables is not subject to the debtor's approval. In certain cases, the assignor and the debtor may have agreed upon a prohibition of assignment; thus, the debtor's approval might be required.

3. Filing Requirements

The assignment and transfer of receivables does not require any special filings with the Austrian authorities or any registrations into registers.

The notification of the debtor is not required by law but advisable. As long as the debtor has not been notified regarding the assignment, the debtor may discharge his liability by payment to the assignor.

G. Liabilities

1. Characteristics as to:

a) Language of Documentation. The documents concerning the transfer of liabilities may be drafted in any language. Bilingual documents are permitted, but are not required by law. Note, however, that certain liabilities transfer automatically (see G, 4, 5 below).

If the exclusion of liabilities according to Section 38 of the Austrian Business Entrepreneurs Act is to be registered with the Company Register, the corresponding document must be drafted in German, or a certified translation of the foreign contract will be required.

b) Form of Documentation. The transfer of liabilities does not require a special form, thus oral agreements are valid. For proof of evidence, written form is nonetheless recommendable. The sale and transfer documents may be executed outside Austria and may be signed in counterparts.

c) Specification of Liabilities. Due to the principle of identification, it is advisable to specify all liabilities and guarantees in the sale and transfer agreements. Contracts occasionally stipulate that all liabilities will be transferred to the purchaser; however, in order to avoid potential disputes over liabilities (especially in tax matters), it is highly recommended to contractually regulate the scope of liabilities as precisely as possible. Where liabilities cannot be regulated by contract because they are regulated by law, the parties will frequently make use of guarantees. The use of schedules is an option but is not mandatory.

Austrian law contains numerous provisions that provide for partial/general succession in an asset deal. As a result, considerable liability risks might arise in an asset deal in relation to liabilities incurred by the seller. Apart from the above-described binding liability provisions (see A, 1 above), please find a brief overview regarding selected provisions under Austrian law which could result in liability claims against the purchaser of certain assets, in particular, if undertakings or businesses are acquired:

(i) Tax obligations (Section 14 of the Federal Fiscal Code): Liability under this provision is essentially related to all tax obligations imposed on or otherwise tied to the acquired undertaking/business that arise from the beginning of the calendar year preceding the year of the acquisition, provided that the purchaser actually knows or should know of such obligations. This liability is limited to the value of the acquired undertaking/business (not taking into account any obligations also acquired in the course of the respective transaction by deducting these from the value of the acquired assets).

(ii) Social security obligations (among others, Section 67 of the General Social Insurance Act): In general, the purchaser is liable for all social security obligations related to the last twelve months before the day of the acquisition of the business, unless the purchaser has obtained a special certificate (*Rückstandsausweis*) of the competent social security institution; in the latter case, said liability is limited to the obligations indicated in this certificate.

(iii) Employee relationships and obligations (Section 6 para. 1 of the Employment Law Harmonization Act): The purchaser is liable for claims arising from employment relationships that have been established prior to the time of transfer. This liability is limited to the value of the assets transferred and to the claims "known or culpably unknown" to the purchaser.

2. Administrative, Corporate and Other Approvals

The transfer of liabilities neither requires governmental nor administrative approval. If the exclusion of liability according to Section 38 of the Austrian Business Entrepreneurs Act will be registered with the Company Register, a written document is required.

Approvals of the seller's or the purchaser's corporate bodies are only required in cases where the statutes or the articles of association contain special provisions.

The transfer of liabilities generally is only possible with participation of the creditor. Therefore, checking whether the creditors consent can be obtained beforehand is recommended. If such an approval cannot be obtained, a similar result can be achieved by way of vicarious performance ("*Schuldübernahme*"). In such case, the purchaser commits himself, vis-à-vis the seller, to perform in the transferor's place. As a result, the seller can sue the purchaser to ensure performance to the creditor. The creditor does not obtain any rights vis-à-vis the purchaser; nevertheless, the creditor must accept the purchaser's performance. However, prior to such performance the seller remains liable.

3. Filing Requirements

The transfer of liabilities does not require filings with the public authorities. In cases where the liability-exclusion according to Section 38 of the Austrian Entrepreneurs Act shall become effective, registration with the Company Register is required. Since the transfer of liabilities generally is subject to the creditor's consent, additional notifications are not required.

4. Purchaser's Liability for:

a) Tax Obligations. According to Section 14 BAO (Federal Fiscal Code), the purchaser of a company is liable for tax debts that concern the last calendar year prior to the asset transfer. The liability is limited to debts that the purchaser knew of, or should have known of, at the time of acquisition. The liability is, furthermore, limited to the value of the acquired assets including the outstanding transferred debts.

b) Environmental Contamination. Austria had planned to implement the European Directive on environmental liability 2004/35/CE by April 30, 2007; however, due to various political discussions, the implementation was postponed. At the moment, liability for environmental contamination is therefore regulated by the above outlined general liability provision of Section 1409 of the Austrian Civil Code. Additionally, some environmental laws such as the Water Act (*Wasserrechtsgesetz*) contain special liability provisions.

c) Products Sold or Services Rendered by the Seller to Third Parties. Austrian law regulates product liability in the Austrian Product Liability Act (*Produkthaftungsgesetz*) and warranty in Section 918 et seq. of the Civil Code. The term "product liability" encompasses the liability for the production and the placement on the market (import) of products, whereby the producer is held liable for certain damages to objects and persons. The liability of the producer is limited to a three-year period after the injured person obtained knowledge of the damage and the person causing the damage; for imported goods, the Austrian Product Liability Act provides that the importer cannot be held liable ten years after importing the concerned goods. Whether the purchaser of assets will be held liable for product defects depends on the type of asset deal completed. In line-ups where an entire business is acquired, the purchaser will most commonly take the position of the former producer or importer.

Warranties are regulated by Section 918 et seq. of the Austrian Civil Code. The seller of goods can be held liable within three years following the transfer of the goods. Within the first six months, the law presumes that the goods were defective upon delivery. Warranty obligations may transfer to the purchaser if the contract containing the warranty is transferred. As described above, such transfer must be agreed upon.

5. Automatic Transfer of Other Liabilities

As described above, according to Section 38 of the Austrian Business Entrepreneurs Act, the purchaser of an undertaking, by law, enters into all legal relationships of the seller related to such undertaking. The liability as per Section 38 of the Federal Entrepreneurs Act can be excluded by either registering the "exclusion of liability" with the Company Register or by directly communicating such liability exclusion to the affected third parties.

Additionally, the Federal Fiscal Code, the General Social Insurance Act and the Employment Law Harmonization Act contain mandatory liability provisions (see G, 1, c).

6. Contractual Protection as to 4 and 5 above

It is very common that certain indemnifications and warranties as to the issues mentioned under 4 and 5 above are included in the asset purchase agreement.

H. Employees

1. Transfer of Employees

In cases where a company, a plant or a part thereof is transferred, the purchaser, by law, enters into all employment contracts in force at the time of the transfer, and all individual rights and obligations of such employees are maintained (please note that it is disputed whether this entry also applies to employment contracts with executive directors). Such automatic entry into existing employment contracts cannot be modified by means of bilateral agreements. The transfer of employment relationships inevitably takes place at the time of the transfer of the company and cannot be shifted to a later time. The definition of a transfer of a part of a company, for instance the transfer of a certain part of the workforce, applies only to transfers where economic units are passed over and the transfer includes various factors that permit dependable continuation of previous activities with the new employer. According to the Austrian Supreme Court, there is no transfer (of a part) of a company in the event that only the workforce is transferred without the functional and economical unit in which the relevant employees were integrated. In the event that the transfer of business does not qualify as a transfer of a company, the employee, the previous employer and the new employer must all agree on a transfer of the employment relationship. Any modifications to the employment contract must be mutually agreed upon.

By statute, collective bargaining agreements (*Kollektivverträge*) and plant agreements (*Betriebsvereinbarungen*) are generally not transferred to the new employer. In the event that the transfer of a company leads to the implementation of a different collective bargaining agreement, the "new" collective bargaining agreement is usually applicable to the transferred employment relationships. Please note that there are certain exceptions to this rule; for example, minimum wages granted by the previous collective bargaining agreement cannot be reduced under the "new" applicable collective bargaining agreement.

A transfer of an undertaking is not a valid reason for the termination of an employment relationship without a term. A mutually-agreed upon termination of the contract in connection with a transfer of an undertaking is permitted. However, termination of an employment relationship that occurs in the timeframe of the transfer of an undertaking can be justified by economical, technical, functional or personal reasons and, thus, can be legally effective. The employee is entitled to terminate the employment relationship if the transfer of the company leads to a major deterioration of working conditions.

The employee is entitled to object to the transfer of the employment relationship in the event that the change as regards the applicable collective bargaining agreement results in the loss of special protection of termination and the new employer refuses to grant the same protection. The same applies to cases in which the new employer refuses to uphold existing individual pension entitlements. The employee can object to the transfer of the employment relationship within one month after the new employer refuses to grant the same special protection against termination as provided by the previous bargaining agreement or to uphold the employee's individual pension entitlements, or one month after the actual transfer of business, in the event that the new employer did not comment on whether it will uphold the employee's entitlements.

In the event that individual pension entitlements have been granted by the seller, the purchaser is not obliged to uphold these entitlements unless the purchaser can be qualified as a universal successor. In the course of the transfer negotiations or within a deadline set by the employee, the purchaser must declare whether it will uphold the individual pension entitlements. If the purchaser refuses to uphold the relevant entitlements or in the case of a lapse of claims granted by a collective bargaining agreement or plant agreement, the employee may claim his/her already acquired entitlements from the transferor.

2. Approval of Works Council, Trade Union or Other Institutions

Please note that there are no provisions that require the approval of the asset transfer by the works council or any other institution/authority.

However, in the case of a transfer of business, the employer is obligated to inform the works council (if any) in writing regarding the intended changes as soon as possible, and at least early enough to make it possible for the works council to participate in the negotiations regarding the terms of the transfer. The writing must contain information regarding the reasons for the restructuring, the legal, economic and social consequences for the employees and the planned arrangements for the employees. The participation of the works council includes the right to advise the employer on the intended measures. It is prohibited to present the works council with a *fait accompli*; the works council must be informed well enough in advance (one or two months prior to the actual measure is considered insufficient) to respond to the planned measures. However, the violation of the provision to inform the works council has practically no adverse consequences. In particular, failure to notify the works council will not make the transfer void, but in cases where a special plant agreement ("social plan") has been enforced, the failure to inform the works council may be considered in the plant agreement. There is no requirement to inform individual employees before the transfer takes place.

3. Contractual Protection as to Labor Issues

Generally, the existing employment contracts or other terms of employment related to the transferred business are specified in an annex to the sale and/or transfer agreement and the seller guarantees the correctness and completeness of such enumeration.

With regard to liabilities arising from employment contracts, the following applies: The seller and the purchaser are jointly liable for liabilities resulting from employment contracts existing prior to the transfer. However, the purchaser's liability is limited to obligations that the purchaser knew or should have known about at the time of transfer and that do not exceed the value of the transferred assets. The seller is liable for entitlements regarding statutory severance payments and pension payments that exist after the transfer for a period of five years. The seller is only liable for claims until the time of the transfer. If backup bonds or other backup resources concerning pension claims are transferred, the seller is only liable for the difference between the value of the transferred backups and the actual entitlement at the time of the transfer. Furthermore, the seller is liable for the pro rata share of regularly granted payments, even if the entitlement becomes due after the actual transfer. The same applies to compensatory allowances. Such seller's liability is limited to one year. The purchaser is obligated to keep the backups in his property for a period of five years and to use them only in connection with possible claims regarding severance payments or pensions. Up to twelve months prior to the transfer, the purchaser is liable for all contributions to the social insurance that the seller was obliged to pay.

I. Tax Implications

1. Value Added Tax

The regular VAT rate in Austria is 20%. The transfer of certain assets such as animals, vegetables and comestibles is taxed at a lower rate of 10%.

An asset deal triggers VAT unless the transfer of this specific asset is tax exempt. The VAT is calculated on the taxable base. The taxable base is the purchase price plus the amount of liabilities assumed together with the assets. The taxable base then must be allocated to the different assets accordingly due to different VAT rates and exemptions for certain assets.

Once the taxable base has been allocated to (i) assets taxed at 20%, (ii) assets taxed at 10% and (iii) tax exempt assets, the total VAT can be determined. Thus, by allocating the taxable base, the VAT can be optimized.

Usually, however, the purchaser – if it is a taxable person – may deduct the VAT charged to him: To the extent the goods and services are used for the purposes of his taxable transactions, a taxable person is entitled to deduct VAT due or paid with respect to goods supplied or services rendered to him by another taxable person from his tax liability.

The transfer of real estate is tax exempt from VAT, but the seller may opt for the taxation of the transfer. This may be very important for the seller: If it does not opt for taxation and the transfer would be tax exempt, it could be bound to repay the input tax deducted earlier by the seller when the real estate was purchased by the seller itself.

2. Real Property Transfer Tax

The transfer of real property triggers real estate transfer tax. The real estate transfer tax amounts to 3.5% of the taxable base. The taxable base is the purchase price for the real property (including VAT, if any). The purchase price for the building and the furniture is also part of the taxable base, but not the purchase price for any machinery and other substantial assets, which are not part of the real estate.

Regarding the transfer of real property among family members, a reduced tax rate of 2% applies.

The registration of the new owner of the real property in the Land Register triggers a registration fee of another 1% of the taxable base. This is a court fee. The taxable base is the same as the one for the real estate transfer tax.

3. Other Tax Issues

In Austria, stamp duty and its avoidance is always an issue. Particularly in an asset deal, the assignment of receivables could very well be subject to stamp duty. The stamp duty for the assignment of receivables amounts to 0.8% of the taxable base. The taxable base is the purchase price for the receivables. Stamp duty, however, will only be triggered if a written document giving evidence for the assignment of receivables is executed. There are ways to avoid stamp duty (in particular by not executing such a document), but it has become more and more difficult due to an increasingly rigid approach of tax authorities with regard to these structures.

Stamp duty is also due on the execution of written documents for lease contracts and credit and loan agreements. Therefore, if in the course of an asset deal the purchaser needs to make a new lease agreement with the owner of the real property, stamp duty could also be due on the execution of this new lease agreement. In this case, the taxable base is a multiple of the annual rent, and the tax rate is 1%.

Stamp duty issues may be a decisive criterion in the choice between an asset deal and a share deal, in particular if many receivables must be transferred.

J. Bankruptcy Law

1. Challenge of Asset Transfer in Case of Insolvency

Whether an asset transfer can be challenged due to the bankruptcy or insolvency of the seller depends on the time of conclusion of the agreement containing the transfer obligation. If such an agreement is concluded before the registration of insolvency or bankruptcy with the Insolvency and Bankruptcy Register, the Austrian Bankruptcy

Act (*KO*) will apply. If the agreement was concluded after the opening of bankruptcy or insolvency proceedings, such agreement would be void without the consent of the administrator appointed by the bankruptcy court. The KO also entitles third parties to challenge contracts, whenever such contracts disadvantage creditors or in cases where the seller squanders its assets, if the agreement was concluded within a certain time period before the opening of insolvency procedures and the other party should have known or knew about the insolvency.

2. Acquisition of Assets that are Subject to Insolvency Proceedings

Austria does not have specific rules regarding the acquisition of assets that are subject to insolvency or bankruptcy proceedings; however, if real property is pledged or subject to public sale, this information can be retrieved from the Land Register or the Insolvency Register. Furthermore, all pending insolvency and bankruptcy proceedings are publicly accessible on the homepage of the Austrian Federal Ministry of Justice (www.edikte.justiz.gv.at).

Section 1409a of the Austrian Civil Code stipulates that the liability decreed in Section 1409 of the Austrian Civil Code (for more details as to such provision, please refer to A, 1 above) does not apply to the acquisition of businesses in an insolvency, bankruptcy or settlement proceeding.

If an agreement was concluded prior to the opening of insolvency procedures regarding the seller, but the assets are not yet transferred (e.g., handed over or in case of real property registered) and the purchase price is not yet paid, the administrator may decide whether he enters into the contract or not. If the purchase price was already paid, the purchaser can only claim the quota paid out in the insolvency and is not entitled to receive the assets.

K. Timing and Costs

1. Timeframe of Asset Transfer

The time necessary for the sale and acquisition of a business by way of an asset deal depends mainly on the size of the deal and the kind of assets acquired. Usually, an asset deal will take between one to six months, depending on registration requirements. The registration with the Land Register typically takes between four to sixteen weeks. Notarial deeds are usually quickly obtainable.

2. Costs of Asset Transfer

Regarding stamp duties, please see I, 3 above. With respect to a real property transfer, the parties will have to calculate an additional 4.5% of the real property value for tax and registration costs (see I above).

L. Miscellaneous

1. Choice of Foreign Law

Sale and/or transfer agreements generally can be made subject to foreign law; however, certain rules, e.g., the real property registration rules and transfer of property, cannot be waived.

2. (International) Arbitration, Choice of Venue

The parties to a sale and/or transfer agreement may agree upon an international or national arbitration clause. Whenever an international arbitration clause is chosen, it is important to ensure that an arbitration award can actually be executed.

In general, Austrian law does not have restrictions regarding the choice of venue; however, certain legal venues such as those regarding real property or lease disputes cannot be modified upon agreement.

3. Other Distinctions, Characteristics

Generally, Austrian law does not provide for other distinctions or unusual characteristics noteworthy in connection with a customary asset deal. Regarding the stamp duty issue see K, 2 above.

M. Literature

Walter Brugger, Acquisition of Business Enterprises in Austria, 4th Edition, 1990

Walter Brugger, Unternehmenserwerb – Acquisition of Business Enterprises, (German/ English), 1st Edition, 1990

Belarus

By *Maksim Salahub*, *Kiryl Apanasevich*, *Ann Valchok* and *Iryna Mitsianiova*

A. General Aspects

In light of the effective Belarusian laws one can distinguish between two types of transactions that could be regarded as asset deals: transfer of enterprise as an asset complex (hereinafter referred to as "sale of enterprise") and piece-by-piece asset transfer.

According to the Belarusian Civil Code, an enterprise as the object of rights is an asset complex used for performance of entrepreneurial activity. This asset complex includes assets of all kinds that are used for the enterprise's operations, including land plots, buildings, construction, equipment, inventory, raw material, ready-made goods, claims, debts, as well as trademarks, service marks, etc. and other exclusive rights. The enterprise in its entirety may be an object of sale, pledge, lease and other transactions connected with the establishment, alteration and termination of the property rights.

According to the Belarusian Civil Code, under the agreement on the sale of an enterprise, the seller undertakes to transfer into the purchaser's property the whole enterprise as the asset complex, except for rights and obligations that the seller may not transfer to the other persons. Based on this concept of the object of the agreement on sale of enterprise, it is understood by certain scholars and also confirmed by special rules of law that, in a sale of a part (even a substantial part) of the enterprise rather than the enterprise as a whole, additional requirements set by the Belarusian Civil Code with regard to the procedure of sale of enterprise do not apply.

This research mostly addresses piece-by-piece asset transfers, and comments contained herein concern piece-by-piece transfers unless specific reference is made to transfer of enterprise as an asset complex.

1. Asset Deal vs. Share Deal: Essential Considerations

With regard to businesses of certain organizational and legal forms, a share deal cannot be executed. Out of commercial companies, these are the companies established in the form of a unitary enterprise. According to the Belarusian Civil Code, a unitary enterprise is a commercial organization not holding the right of property in the assets allocated thereto by the owner of the unitary enterprise. Assets of the unitary enterprise are indivisible, i.e. they may not be distributed in proportion to shares, pays, etc. Statutory fund of a unitary enterprise may not be divided into shares. Therefore, with regard to a unitary enterprise, an asset deal (whether sale of enterprise as an asset complex or piece-by-piece asset deal) is the only option for the acquisition.

Asset deals are, as a rule, more complex than share purchase deals. In principle, in a share transfer, the procedural requirements mainly relate to the exercise of the preemption rights by the shareholders (in the limited liability companies (**"LLC"**), added liability companies (**"ALC"**), and closed joint stock companies (**"CJSC"**), notarization of the transaction (which may be required with regard to transfer of LLC, ALC shares), and registration of the transaction (which is required with regard to transfer of CJSC shares). A share purchase agreement should be executed in writing.

In case of a transfer of assets in the form of sale of the enterprise, the asset complex is subject to appraisal by professional appraisers and registration. These procedures precede the sale and normally require significant time and monetary expenditures.

In a transfer of assets in the form of piece-by-piece acquisition, general requirements of the Belarusian Civil Code applicable to the form of particular agreements should be followed (for example, by default, transactions between legal entities require simple written form. Certain conditions for executing a transaction are also provided by laws (e.g., in a transfer of real estate, the agreement is subject to registration). As to procedure, the general requirements of the Civil Code are applicable as well, e.g., generally, a party may transfer its obligations under a contract concluded with a third party only upon written consent of that third party.

As regards transfer of enterprise, the agreement on transfer of enterprise should be verified and certified by a notary or a registrar of the National Cadastral Agency. In addition, extensive formal requirements, especially related to the protection of creditors' rights (notification of the creditors, appointment of a third party (a bank, other credit institution or an insurance company) to settle with creditors, appointment of an independent auditor to evaluate the assets of the company) are applicable. Furthermore, as already mentioned above, the concept of a transfer of an enterprise is relatively new and fragmentary in Belarus and there is no reliable court practice. All this makes the procedure for a transfer of an enterprise rather complicated and burdensome, as well as somewhat uncertain.

2. Distinction between Sale and Transfer in Rem

Pursuant to the Belarusian Civil Code, by default, right of property in transferred assets passes to the purchaser at the moment of delivery of the assets to the purchaser, unless otherwise provided by the agreement of the parties. In case the agreement on transfer of the assets is subject to state registration, the purchaser acquires the right of property in the assets from the moment of such registration.

According to the Belarusian Civil Code, the agreement on the sale of the enterprise should be executed in writing by means of production of a single document signed by the parties. This document should always be supplemented with the act of inventory taking, balance sheet, auditors' report on composition and value of the enterprise, as well as a list of all debts (liabilities) included in the composition of the enterprise, with details of all creditors, nature, amount of their claims and terms within which the claims are effective. The law does not stipulate that the agreement on the sale of the enterprise should be supplemented by agreements regarding the transfer of individual assets or groups of assets.

In the case of a piece-by-piece asset acquisition, no master agreement is required by law and no such agreement is produced in practice; this type of asset deal is formalized by a series of sale-purchase agreements executed with regard to individual assets.

3. Regional Differences

Belarus is a unitary state, so effect of the laws establishing legal requirements concerning transfer of assets is the same in every part of the country. There may be minor differences in technical procedures in the practice of different local government bodies concerning registration of assets and transactions, etc.

4. Acquisition by Foreigners

Acquisition of assets by foreigners or foreign entities is regarded as one of the forms of investment activity defined by Belarusian laws. A national regime was established for overseeing the activity of the foreign investors, which may not be less favorable than the regime established for property, property rights, and conditions for investment activity enjoyed by Belarusian legal entities and individuals.

However, there are several restrictions on investments in certain areas. Foreign investors may not invest

(i) in the defense and security of the Republic of Belarus unless they receive a special permit from the President; or

(ii) in the production of narcotic, virulent, and poisonous substances included on the list produced by the Ministry of Healthcare.

There are also restrictions in the area of antitrust law. Foreign investments in the property of legal entities that hold monopolist positions in the Belarusian market require special approval from the Ministry of Economy.

There are also objects that cannot be owned by foreign entities, such as land plots. Therefore, when purchasing real property (e.g., a building) a foreign entity may only be granted a lease right to the land plot.

Foreign investments in the banking and insurance sectors of Belarus are limited by general quotas. In this regard, an increase of statutory capital of banks and insurance companies at the expense of contributions made by non-residents, as well as sale of shares to non-residents, requires permission from the regulator, the National Bank of Belarus. In September 2008, the National Bank approved a 50% quota for foreign capital in the banking sector. For the insurance sector, the current quota for foreign capital is 30%.

5. Public Registers, Records and Databases

Information related to the asset transfer can be found in a number of registers.

Unified State Register of Legal Entities and Individual Entrepreneurs contains corporate details of the seller, purchaser and target company, including name, registration number, and official legal seat of the legal entity; incorporation details; status of the legal entity (e.g., operating company, company in liquidation stage, reorganized company, liquidated company), information on management. However, information about shareholders and owners of the inquired company can be accessed only on the grounds of a request made by a judge, controlling authorities or law enforcement authorities.

Information on transferred real property can be found in the Unified State Register of Real Property, Rights thereto and Transactions therewith, which is maintained by the National Cadastral Agency. The Register contains data both on land plots and on other real property objects (e.g., buildings and structures). Registration data is open for public use. The data includes not only identifying information with regard to the object, but also details regarding the owner and ownership, information about actual rights and encumbrances concerning the asset, and data about rights holders. At the same time, it is impossible to get a list of all real estate objects that belong to a particular individual or legal entity, as access to such data is given only to the rights holders, their successors and government authorities. Access to data on conditions of specific transactions concerning real property is provided only to the parties to such transactions. The history of the real property objects (previous rights holders, deals, encumbrances, court decisions) is also not available to the public.

A database of patents, utility models and patterns as well as a database of trademarks can be accessed freely at the website of the National Center of Intellectual Property (www.belgospatent.org.by).

Register of the domain BY contains data on domain names in the BY zone. There are no specific rules regarding access to this Register.

6. Purchase Price Requirements

The purchase price is a material condition of every agreement on the transfer of assets (whether a sale of the enterprise or a piece-by-piece acquisition). By default, the parties establish the price of the transaction freely. One of the main considerations when establishing price is the tax burden.

Special rules regarding a minimum price apply to government-owned assets. There are special provisions regulating the procedure for the evaluation of such assets for the purposes of further sale, lease, mortgage, etc.

In settlements between foreign purchasers and Belarusian sellers foreign currency may be used if its exchange rate towards the Belarusian rouble is officially established by the National Bank of Belarus. Other rules can be provided by bilateral agreements between the National Bank of Belarus and the central bank of the foreign purchaser's country allowing usage of national currencies in a transaction between residents of the two countries.

Under a general rule, only the Belarusian national currency may be used in settlements between Belarusian sellers and Belarusian purchasers.

The purchase price should be allocated to each asset that is subject to a sale-purchase agreement in a piece-by-piece acquisition.

B. Tangible/Movable Assets

1. Characteristics as to:

a) Language of Documentation. The language of documentation may be chosen freely, and production of the documents in a local language is not obligatory. Bilingual documents are permitted. With regard to an export-import transaction, from a practical standpoint it is advisable to produce a bilingual version of the contract in order to pass various formalities related to customs clearance, foreign trade and currency flow control, money transfers, etc. Agreements should be verified by the Belarusian resident's servicing bank, which may request translation of any documents executed in foreign languages into the local language (Russian or Belarusian).

b) Form of Documentation. The sale and transfer of tangible assets requires simple written form of the agreement; notarization is voluntary (if so provided by agreement of the parties). Sale and transfer of tangible assets may be executed outside Belarus, provided that a written form of documents is observed. An agreement may be concluded by way of producing one document signed by the parties, and also by way of exchange of documents by means of fax, e-mail or other means of communication whereby it may be established that the document comes from a party under the agreement.

c) Specification of Assets. Tangible assets transferred under the agreement on the sale of the enterprise should be listed in the act of inventory taking attached to the agreement.

With regard to each agreement comprising a piece-by-piece acquisition, the condition of the agreement on the purchased assets is recognized as agreed upon by the parties if the name and quantity of the assets can be determined from the agreement.

In practice, a detailed description of the assets is typically contained in specifications or schedules attached to the given sale-purchase agreement.

2. Administrative, Corporate and Other Approvals

The transfer of tangible assets generally does not require special governmental or administrative approvals. However, in certain cases such approvals are needed, in particular when assets are related to the defense and security of the state or the manufacturing of narcotic, virulent, or poisonous substances. If approvals are not granted, the transaction may be recognized as invalid based on failure to comply with the law.

When the assets of a legal entity are owned by the state, the legal entity may transfer these assets only subject to consent of the supervising government authority.

If the transfer of tangible assets comprises a large-scale transaction of a commercial company (ALC, LLC, JSC; unitary enterprises are outside of the scope of these regulations), such transactions may be executed upon approval of the company's general meeting of the shareholders, or board of directors, or supervisory board (as established by the company's articles).

A large-scale transaction is a transaction or several interconnected transactions resulting in direct or indirect transfer or possibility of transfer by the company of assets, the value of which constitutes 25% or more of the balance sheet value of the company's assets. Furthermore, the constituent documents may contain corporate rules and provide for such approval if the total cost of a transaction exceeds a certain amount, even if such transaction does not comprise 25% of the balance sheet value of the company's assets. Constituent documents of the unitary enterprise may also provide for necessity of approval by the founder if the total cost of the transaction exceeds a certain amount.

Transactions with regard to tangible assets in which the company's affiliated persons are interested may be executed only upon resolution taken by the majority of the votes of the company's shareholders not interested in execution of the transaction.

The company's affiliated persons are defined as legal entities and individuals capable of determining, directly or indirectly, decisions of the company (including influencing adoption of the decisions by the company), as well as legal entities whose decisions are influenced by the company.

Resolutions of the general meeting of the company's shareholders concerning the transaction in which its affiliated persons are interested may not be required in case the terms and conditions of such transactions do not differ materially from terms and conditions of similar transactions executed by the company in the regular course of business.

Transactions executed in breach of the regulations concerning large-scale transactions and transactions in which the company's affiliated persons are interested may be recognized as invalid by the court. As regulations with regard to large scale transactions and transactions in which company's affiliated persons are interested were introduced by the new Law on Commercial Companies in 2006, there is comparatively limited practical application of these regulations (also by courts).

The transfer of encumbered tangible assets generally requires the written consent of security holders.

3. Filing Requirements

As a rule, the transfer of tangible assets does not require filings with public authorities or registrations into public registers or databases, with the exception of certain types of assets.

4. Automatic Transfer of Encumbrances

In case of transfer of encumbered assets, the encumbrance remains effective and is transferred to the purchaser automatically if not otherwise agreed by the seller and the security holder.

C. Real Property

1. Characteristics as to:

a) Language of Documentation. Local language is mandatory as documents (e.g., sale and purchase agreement) should be filed for state registration. Bilingual contracts in a local language are acceptable.

b) Form of Documentation. The agreement on the sale and purchase of real property should be concluded in written form by way of producing one document signed by all parties. The agreement may be executed outside Belarus, provided that the form and contents of the agreement comply with Belarusian laws. Notarization is not required (if the parties are legal entities) but may be required in compliance with the agreement of the parties. As soon as the agreement is signed, the transfer of real property should be performed by means of signing of the act on transfer. The agreement itself and transfer of title to the real property are subject to state registration with the respective territorial agency on state registration and land cadastre.

c) Specification of Assets. The agreement regarding the sale and purchase of the real property must contain all essential details enabling one to define the real property subject of the transfer. In practice, exact location, cadastral number, and other details are to be provided.

2. Administrative, Corporate and Other Approvals

The local executive authority has a priority right to purchase real property objects located within its jurisdiction, and, therefore, the seller must obtain a waiver of the priority right from that authority prior to transferring the real property to the purchaser.

Also, approval procedures and restrictions listed in B, 2 above apply to the transfer of real property. Any transfer of real property without obtaining the respective approvals or observance of the procedures is considered invalid or can be found invalid by court subject to nature of approval.

3. Filing Requirements

Transfer of real property is subject to state registration in the Unified State Register of Real Property, Rights thereto and Transactions therewith, in the State Register of Vessels or in the State Register of Marine Vessels. In the first case the filing is to be made with the respective territorial agency on state registration and land cadastre. For river and marine vessels the filing is to be made with the Belarusian River Navigation Inspection or to the Ministry of Transport and Communication, respectively.

Failure to comply with the requirement on state registration of the agreement results in the transaction being invalid.

4. Automatic Transfer of Encumbrances

In the case of a transfer of encumbered real property, the encumbrance remains effective if not otherwise agreed by the seller and the security holder. Waiver of the encumbrance should be made in the same form as the respective agreement that constitutes the ground for this encumbrance (at least in written form). Waiver of encumbrance is subject to state registration, as well as other rights to real property and termination thereof.

5. Automatic Transfer of Lease Agreements

Lease agreements pertaining to real property are subject to automatic transfer to the purchaser, who assumes all rights and obligations under such lease agreements vis-à-vis the tenant. Neither of the parties has an extraordinary right to terminate a lease agreement on the grounds of the transfer, unless otherwise provided for in the lease agreement.

D. Contracts

Belarusian laws do not provide for the transfer of contracts. Pursuant to the Belarusian Civil Code, substitution of the parties to a contract is possible either via agreement on cession of rights or an agreement on assignment of debt.

1. Characteristics as to:

a) Language of Documentation. Agreements on cession of rights and agreements on assignment of debt may be drafted in any language. Bilingual documents are permitted. Bilingual documents or a certified translation into Belarusian/Russian language may be required if certain formalities need to be performed with the government authorities. For example, if the right (the debt) to be ceded (assigned) is based on an agreement that was subject to state registration in the public register, the agreement on cession of rights (assignment of debt) should be registered as well. Some loan agreements may be executed with special permission from the National Bank of Belarus, and special permissions may be required in case rights (debt) under the loan agreement are ceded (assigned).

b) Form of Documentation. Cession of rights, assignment of debt under the agreement executed in writing or in a notarized form should be effected in the same form. Cession of rights, assignment of debt under the agreement subject to state registration should, as a rule, be registered under the same procedure as the agreement itself.

The documents may be executed outside the Republic of Belarus, provided that a written form of documents is observed. Signing in counterparts is permissible.

c) Specification of Contracts. Different rules apply with respect to a sale of the enterprise as a complex of assets and in a piece-by-piece acquisition.

As discussed above, enterprise as a complex of assets includes, inter alia, rights of claim and debts. Certain obligations may not be transferred by the seller by virtue of law. Composition of the enterprise intended for sale should be confirmed in the agreement on the sale of the enterprise. One of the documents that should be produced and approved by the parties prior to the execution of the agreement is a list of all debts (obligations) of the enterprise, including details about the creditors, and the nature, amounts and maturity dates of their claims.

In a piece-by-piece acquisition, agreements on cession of rights and assignment of debt need to have a specific subject-matter, i.e. rights ceded and debts assigned should be identified sufficiently, such that at least the amount of the right/debt and the grounds on which right/debt is based should be provided, and the parties should be identified.

There is no requirement that schedules or lists of contracts be attached to the agreement formalizing the transfer.

2. Administrative, Corporate and Other Approvals

(i) Administrative Approvals

Under a general rule, the cession of rights and assignment of debt does not require any special governmental or administrative approvals.

However, in certain cases such approvals may become necessary. Thus, transactions that include settlements under obligations undertaken by a Belarusian company on the grounds of the agreement on cession of rights/assignment of debt with a foreign company may be executed only on the grounds of the respective permission issued by the National Bank of Belarus.

(ii) Corporate Approvals

Approval of cession of rights and the assignment of debt by corporate bodies regarding the seller and/or the purchaser may be required if such transaction constitutes a large-scale transaction, or a transaction in which the seller's or purchaser's affiliated persons are interested parties as defined in B, 1, b above.

Transactions executed in breach of the regulations concerning large scale transactions and transactions in which the company's affiliated persons are interested may be recognized as invalid by the court.

(iii) Other Approvals

Again, different rules apply in the sale of an enterprise as a complex of assets and in case of a piece-by-piece acquisition of assets.

In a sale of the enterprise, creditors with respect to the obligations included in the composition of the enterprise should be notified of the sale in writing by either party to the agreement on sale of the enterprise prior to transfer of the enterprise to the purchaser.

A creditor that has not notified seller or purchaser of his consent to the assignment of debt may, within three months after receiving the notification of sale of the enterprise, claim termination or immediate performance of the respective obligation and claim damages caused by such assignment from the seller.

A creditor that was not notified of the sale as described above may file claims described above within one year after the day on which he learned or should have learned about the transfer of the enterprise by the seller to the purchaser.

After the enterprise is transferred to the purchaser, seller and purchaser bear joint liability with regard to the debts that were included in the composition of the enterprise and transferred to the purchaser without the creditor's consent.

In a piece-by-piece acquisition of assets, general rules concerning consents/notification of the parties apply; i.e. by default, cession of rights does not require consent of the debtor if not otherwise provided by the agreement of the parties; assignment of debt by a debtor requires consent of the creditor. Failure to comply with these requirements may result in the transfer being invalid.

3. Automatic Transfer of Contracts (Other than Lease and Employment Agreements)

In a sale of the insured assets, rights and duties under the insurance agreement automatically transfer to the purchaser. The purchaser only needs to notify the insurer of the transfer without delay.

4. Filing Requirements

The cession of rights and assignment of debts under the transactions that are subject to state registration are subject to state registration under the same procedure as the main transaction.

5. Treatment of Existing Contractual Claims and Obligations

In the event sold contracts are not or not completely fulfilled, the respective claims and/or obligations automatically transfer to the purchaser.

In the sale of the enterprise, all claims and obligations included in the composition of the enterprise should be listed in a special supplement to the agreement regarding the sale of the enterprise.

In the cession of a claim and assignment of debt in a piece-by-piece acquisition, transferred claims or obligations need to be sufficiently identified in the agreements formalizing the transfer.

It is not a common practice to include special provisions (e.g., indemnifications) in the asset sale and/or transfer agreement.

6. Warranty Claims Resulting from Events prior to Transfer

If otherwise not provided for by the law or by agreement of the parties, the right of the initial creditor passes to the new creditor to the same extent and on the same conditions that existed as of the moment of transfer of the right. The new creditor acquires, inter alia, the rights securing performance of the main obligation, as well as other rights connected with the claim, including the right to unpaid interest.

As a general rule, the transfer of assets also comprises the transfer of any claims and any obligations related to such asset. This also applies to warranty claims resulting from events prior to the transfer, unless otherwise provided for in the asset sale and/or transfer agreement.

It is not a common practice to include special provisions (e.g., indemnifications) in the asset sale and/or transfer agreement.

E. IP Rights

1. Characteristics of Intellectual Property Rights (e.g., Trademarks, Patents, Utility Models, Domain Names) ("*IP Rights*") as to:

a) Language of Documentation. The documents can be drafted in any language. However, since the agreement on the transfer of IP Rights must be registered in the public register, the agreement should be translated into Russian or Belarusian. The translation should be certified either by the patent holder or a patent attorney. A bilingual version of the documents is also permissible.

b) Form of Documentation. The transfer of IP Rights must be in writing. The documents may be executed outside the Republic of Belarus, provided that a written form of documents is observed. Signing in counterparts is permissible.

c) Specification of IP Rights. The sale of an enterprise as a property complex, the rights to firm name, trademark, service mark, and other means of individualization of the seller and its goods, work, or services, and also the right to use such means of individualization belonging to it on the basis of a license, automatically transfer to the purchaser unless otherwise agreed upon by the parties.

In a piece-by-piece transfer of assets, the agreement with respect to the transfer of IP rights should refer to specific intellectual properties as well as contain the description of specific rights with regard to each IP Right transferred. IP Rights that are not specified in the agreement are considered as not having been transferred.

2. Administrative, Corporate and Other Approvals

The transfer of IP Rights does not require special governmental or administrative approvals. Issues of approval of the agreements on transfer of IP Rights by corporate bodies, as well as the consequences if such approvals are not granted, are the same as described in B, 2 above.

The transfer of encumbered IP Rights requires a written consent of the security holders. Non-compliance will invalidate the transfer.

3. Filing Requirements

The transfer of IP Rights requires a registration in the relevant public register. Transfer of IP Rights without registration is considered invalid.

4. Applicable International (Multilateral) Agreements or Treaties

The Republic of Belarus is a party to the following agreements or treaties:

- Paris Convention for the Protection of Industrial Property,
- Madrid Agreement Concerning the International Registration of Marks and the Protocol Thereto,
- Strasbourg Agreement Concerning the International Patent Classification,
- Nice Agreement Concerning the International Classification of Goods and Services for the Purposes of the Registration of Marks,
- Locarno Agreement Establishing an International Classification for Industrial Designs,
- International Convention for the Protection of New Varieties of Plants, and
- Eurasian Patent Convention and the Patent Cooperation Treaty.

Moreover, the Republic of Belarus has concluded a number of bilateral agreements on cooperation in the field of industrial property protection.

F. Receivables

Belarusian laws do not provide for special regulations with regard to the transfer of receivables. The transfer of receivables may be effected by means of the agreements on cession of rights. Therefore, general rules set out in D above apply.

1. Characteristics as to:

a) Language of Documentation. General rules set out in D, 1, a above apply to language of documentation.

b) Form of Documentation. General rules set out in D, 1, b above apply to the form of documentation.

c) Specification of Receivables. General rules set out in D, 1, c above apply to the description of receivables.

2. Administrative, Corporate and Other Approvals.

General rules set out in D, 2 above apply to approvals required with respect to the transfer of receivables.

3. Filing Requirements

General rules set out in D, 3 above apply to filings required with respect to the transfer of receivables.

G. Liabilities

1. Regarding the transfer of liabilities, are there any characteristics as to:

Belarusian laws do not provide for special regulations with regard to the transfer of liabilities. The transfer of liabilities may be effected by means of the agreements on assignment of debt. Therefore, the general rules set out in D above apply.

a) Language of Documentation. General rules set out in D, 1, a above apply to the language of documentation.

b) Form of Documentation. General rules set out in D, 1, b above apply to the form of documentation.

c) Specification of Liabilities. General rules set out in D, 1, c above apply to the description of liabilities.

2. Administrative, Corporate and Other Approvals

General rules pertaining to the assignment of debt set out in D, 2 above apply.

3. Filing Requirements

General rules pertaining to the assignment of debt set out in D, 2 above apply.

4. Purchaser's Liability for:

a) Tax Obligations. Under a general rule, all tax liabilities of the purchaser arise after the acquisition of the assets. For instance, the purchaser should not be liable for the payment of the immovable property tax for periods prior to the acquisition of the immovable property, since under Belarusian laws, the immovable property tax should be calculated as of the month when the title to the immovable property is acquired, the immovable property starts to be used for economic activities or is assumed by the company. Therefore, the seller of the assets should be liable for the tax obligations related to the periods prior to the transfer of the asset. Issues of tax liability cannot be circumvented by the asset (enterprise) purchase agreement.

However, laws may provide exclusions from this rule (e.g., in cases of reorganization), and the decree of the President and a decision of local authorities may grant to another person the right to pay for the debts of the initial payer.

b) Environmental Contamination. In general, violation of environmental laws of Belarus (environmental contamination is one of the possible violations) may result in subjecting the person that committed the violation to disciplinary, administrative, and criminal liability.

It follows from the language of the laws that liability for environmental contamination may be imposed on the person responsible for the contamination and does not pass with the respective assets. However, as legal regulations on this matter are scarce and varying interpretations are possible, and there is no consistent court practice related to this issue, in certain situations responsible government authorities may attempt to hold the purchaser of the assets liable for environmental contamination, especially if the purchaser was aware of the fact of such contamination at the time of purchase of the assets.

c) Products Sold or Services Rendered by the Seller to Third Parties. Belarusian laws do not specifically regulate issues related to the liability of the purchaser for products sold or services rendered by the seller to third parties prior to the acquisition.

Pursuant to the Belarusian Civil Code, the seller should deliver the goods to the purchaser free of any rights of third persons, unless the purchaser agrees to accept the goods encumbered with the rights of third persons.

Also, pursuant to provisions of the Civil Code, damage caused to the person or property of an individual, as well as damage caused to the property of a legal entity, should be compensated fully by the person who caused the damage. The law may impose the obligation to compensate the damage on the other persons.

When acquiring assets, purchasers should be careful to avoid being jointly liable for any damage caused, which is a possibility provided for under the law.

5. Automatic Transfer of Other Liabilities

As a general rule, piece-by-piece acquisition of assets should not result in the purchaser's liability towards third parties. However, each case should be analyzed separately.

In a sale of an enterprise, under the general rule, the purchaser will assume all the rights and obligations related to the acquired assets complex.

6. Contractual Protection as to 4 and 5 above

It is not customary to include special provisions, including indemnifications as to the issues mentioned under 4 and 5 above, either in the agreement on sale of the enterprise or in agreements formalizing the piece-by-piece acquisition.

H. Employees

1. Transfer of Employees

Under Belarusian laws, both in the sale of enterprise as a complex of assets and a piece-by-piece acquisition, employees are considered as independent subjects of the law and not assets subject to transfer.

According to the Labor Code of Belarus, if the owner of the company's assets changes, the labor relations continue subject to employee's consent; if the employee refuses to continue to work, the labor contract is terminated. Special regulations apply to the company's director, his deputies, and chief accountant, whereby the purchaser may terminate labor contracts with these employees at any time during three months after acquiring the right of property to the assets. It follows from the language of these provisions that they apply to the sale of an enterprise as a complex of assets.

In a piece-by-piece acquisition, general provisions of labor laws apply. The most feasible option for the seller and purchaser normally is termination of labor contracts with the seller (old employer) by agreement of the parties (no severance pays, no special notification periods in this case) and conclusion of the new labor contracts with the purchaser (the new employer).

2. Approval of Works Council, Trade Union or Other Institutions

The asset transfer per se does not require approval of any works council, labor agency, trade union, or other institution. However, internal regulations of the seller need to be confirmed in each particular case.

3. Contractual Protection as to Labor Issues

In the light of the foregoing, inclusion of such special provisions as to employees in the agreements formalizing the transfer of assets is not customary.

I. Tax Implications

1. Value Added Tax

The transfer of assets is generally treated as a sale of goods for VAT purposes. Thus, if a seller is subject to VAT and the assets are located in the territory of Belarus, the Belarusian VAT of 18% shall be applied. However, the Belarusian Law on VAT contains many exceptions as to the particular type of assets and, therefore, each case should be analyzed separately. Lower VAT rates may apply to certain assets, and in case of export of the assets 0% VAT applies.

2. Real Property Transfer Tax

In Belarus, legal entities presently may not acquire and hold property rights to land, yet they are not subject to transfer tax like real property. Normally, certain rights to land (lease, permanent or temporary use rights) are transferred along with the real property. No transfer taxes are established by Belarusian laws.

3. Other Tax Issues

In addition to issues related to VAT (discussed above in I, 1), corporate tax should be taken into account. Profit tax is paid at the rate of 24% of the taxable profit. Profit tax is levied on gross profit and the taxable base is determined as income reduced by deductible expenses, value added tax, turnover tax, real estate tax, and tax benefits. Furthermore, if the seller of the assets is a non-resident, the purchaser of the assets is obliged to withhold income tax at the source of payment. By default, the rate of the withholding income tax is 15%.

J. Bankruptcy Law

1. Challenge of Asset Transfer in Case of Insolvency

As discussed above in D, 2, (iii), the sale of the enterprise is subject to special regulations concerning protection of the creditors.

Creditors that have not given their consent to the transfer of the liabilities included in the composition of the enterprise may claim termination or early performance of the respective obligations, and compensation of damages caused by the transfer by the seller.

Creditors that were not notified of the transfer may file the same claims in court within one year after they learn or should have learned about the transfer of the enterprise.

Also, creditors that have not given their consent to the transfer of the respective debts may hold seller and purchaser of the enterprise jointly liable with regard to these debts after transfer of the enterprise.

Under the Belarusian Law on Economic Insolvency (Bankruptcy) of 2000 (hereinafter – the "**Law on Bankruptcy**"), the following regulations apply both to the sale of the enterprise as a complex of assets and the piece-by-piece acquisition.

Transactions executed by the debtor in the bankruptcy case, including those executed prior to opening the bankruptcy proceedings, may be recognized as null and void by a commercial court upon the claim filed by the receiver in the following cases:

(i) such transactions were executed during the last six months preceding commencement of the bankruptcy case or after the commercial court has opened the bankruptcy case, if such transactions result in preferential satisfaction of the claims of certain creditors as compared to other creditors, or in case these transactions are connected with extraction of a share in the debtor company's assets (proprietary/monetary equivalent thereof) in favor of a shareholder in connection with his exit from the debtor company;

(ii) such transactions were executed during the last year preceding commencement of the bankruptcy case or after the commercial court has opened the bankruptcy case, if by execution of these transactions the debtor willfully injured interests of the creditors, and the other parties to the transactions knew or should have known about it;

(iii) such transactions were executed during the last three years preceding commencement of the bankruptcy case or after the commercial court has opened the bankruptcy case, if the debtor caused his insolvency by a penal act proved by a court verdict, and the other parties to the transactions knew or should have known about it, or the debtor, by executing such transactions, willfully injured the interests of the creditors, and the other parties to the transactions were persons interested in relation to the debtor (as defined by the Law on Bankruptcy), and, presumably, were aware the debtor willfully injured the interests of the creditors by execution of these transactions.

Upon proposal of the receiver, public prosecutor, or on its own initiative, the commercial court may decide that actions of certain individuals who are interested persons in relation to the debtor company (as defined by the Law on Bankruptcy) may be equated to the above described actions of the debtor company itself.

Transactions executed by the debtor may be recognized as null and void on other grounds provided by civil law.

Certain gifts/donations made by the debtor, and transactions contradictory to the interests of the state, may also be recognized as null and void by a commercial court.

If it is obvious from the inequality of the parties to the transaction that a sale-purchase agreement, exchange agreement, or other transaction was fully or partially executed not in favor of the debtor at a price significantly lower or higher than the price normally collected for similar goods, work, services (by their nature constitute a donation), the commercial court should recognize such transactions as null and void.

Pursuant to the Belarusian Civil Code, the general consequence of recognition of a transaction as null and void is a bilateral restitution, whereby the parties return to each other any assets or consideration they have received under the transaction; where assets cannot be returned, monetary equivalent thereof is returned.

2. Acquisition of Assets that are Subject to Insolvency Proceedings

The Law on Bankruptcy provides for special rules with regard to the acquisition of assets subject to bankruptcy proceedings.

These rules differ with regard to the two main bankruptcy procedures established by the Law, economic sanitation and liquidation. Also, different rules apply in the sale of the enterprise and the piece-by-piece sale of assets of the insolvent debtor.

Sale of the enterprise may be provided for by the plan of economic sanitation if it allows most effectively, in comparison to other measures, the achievement of the goals of sanitation and does not contradict public or government interest. The decision regarding the sale of the enterprise may be taken after expert examination ordered by the commercial court. Such expert examination should focus on the financial condition of the debtor and possible consequences of the sale of the enterprise.

In such a sale, the payment obligations of the debtor that existed on the date of acceptance of the debtor's application for bankruptcy by the commercial court are not included in the composition of the enterprise.

Sale of the enterprise is carried out at a public auction, although certain exceptions from this rule may be provided for by law. The auction is organized by the receiver or by a special organization.

The Law on Bankruptcy establishes a special procedure of organization and conduct of the public auction. Where only one order to purchase the enterprise is filed, the auction may not be conducted. The enterprise that was not sold at the first auction may be offered for sale at a second auction; in this case, the initial price may be lowered by the commercial court upon proposal of the creditors' meeting or the creditors' committee. The enterprise may be sold without conducting the second auction, subject to the consent of the creditors' meeting or the creditors' committee.

On the day of the auction, the winner of the auction and the organizer of the auction should sign special minutes that will be effective as a contract.

The transaction on sale of the enterprise may be recognized as null and void upon demand of the public prosecutor or other specially authorized government bodies in cases where:

(i) the sale of the enterprise resulted in the impossibility for the debtor to carry on his activities;

(ii) the price of the enterprise was set too low due to unlawful deliberate actions of the creditors, receiver, persons assisting the receiver, or specialized organization that conducted the auction;

(iii) the transaction does not allow achievement of the purposes of the sanitation for certain reasons;

(iv) there are some other grounds for recognition of the transaction as null and void.

Where only a part of the debtor's assets is sold rather than the whole assets complex (enterprise), the receiver may commence the sale of these assets at the auction after decision on sanitation is issued by the commercial court.

Certain assets that are restricted in the commercial turnover may be sold only at a closed auction (with limited range of participants).

The receiver may act as organizer of the auction or, upon decision of the commercial court, delegate this function to a specialized organization.

The initial price of the assets put up for sale at the auction is established by the commercial court upon request of the receiver. The winner of the auction should pay for the purchased assets within the term stipulated by the minutes or sale-purchase agreements executed based on the outcomes of the auction, and in any event not later than one month after completion of the auction.

Assets that were not sold at the first auction may be offered at the second auction unless otherwise provided for by the plan of economic sanitation. The initial price may be lowered by the commercial court upon proposal of the receiver (if by more than ten per cent, then subject to consent of the creditors' meeting or the creditors' committee).

Assets that were not sold at the second auction may be sold by the receiver without an auction on the grounds of a sale and purchase agreement subject to consent of the creditors' meeting or the creditors' committee.

The following rules apply in the case of liquidation. After opening of the liquidation proceedings, the receiver sells the debtor's assets at the auction if another procedure of the sale of the assets is not established by the commercial court, creditors' meeting, or creditors' committee.

The procedure and term for the sale of the assets should be in any event approved by the creditors' meeting or by the creditors' committee.

Assets which were not sold at the first auction should be offered for sale at the second auction, or sold by the receiver based on the concluded sale-purchase agreement, without conducting an auction.

Sale of the enterprise is effected under the same procedure as in case of economic sanitation of the insolvent debtor (as described above).

A receiver may also offer for sale at an auction claims belonging to the insolvent debtor, if another procedure of sale (assignment) of the claims is not established by the creditors' meeting or the creditors' assembly.

K. Timing and Costs

1. Timeframe of Asset Transfer

There are no particular timeframes applicable by virtue of law to asset deals. Timelines usually depend on the type of the transaction (piece-by-piece sale or sale of enterprise) as well as peculiarities of a particular transaction.

Peculiarities of timing in the course of sale of the enterprise include time necessary for inventorying of assets as well as production of the auditing report. Furthermore, the enterprise itself, the seller's rights thereto, transaction therewith and right thereto of the purchaser are subject to state registration under the same procedure as real property. Provided that the documents are in good standing, each registration procedure usually takes no more than seven business days. However, if the transaction is complex, this term may be prolonged to 14 business days. The registration procedure may also be suspended for the period of one month for the purposes of verification of the documents.

2. Costs of Asset Transfer

Costs related to the transaction depend greatly on the peculiarities of the particular transaction.

However, the state fees for notarization of contracts as well as for the certification of contract by registrars of the National Cadastral Agency are always fixed. The state fee for notarization (certification) of agreements on the sale of the enterprise comprises the equivalent of about EUR 225. Notarization of other agreements (including agreements on sale of real property) normally amounts to EUR 45. It makes no difference whether the parties to the contract are natural persons or legal entities, residents or foreigners. State fees for registration of all types of objects are also fixed.

L. Miscellaneous

1. Choice of Foreign Law

As a rule, the parties to the sale agreement, at the conclusion of the agreement or later, may choose any law that may apply to their rights and duties under this agreement. However, if the subject of the sale agreement is any kind of real property the law of the country, where this property is located, shall be applied. With regard to the property registered in the Republic of Belarus, the application of the laws of the Republic of Belarus is mandatory.

2. (International) Arbitration, Choice of Venue

As a general rule, an international arbitration is permissible and the parties may, by the agreement between them, choose the venue of the arbitration. However, there are exceptions to this rule; in particular, disputes relating to real property located within the territory of the Republic of Belarus must be submitted to the commercial court of the Republic of Belarus.

3. Other Distinctions, Characteristics

Regulation of the sale of an enterprise is relatively new and fragmentary in Belarus, and there is no reliable court practice. Due to the fact that the established procedure is rather burdensome and somewhat uncertain, parties usually perform asset transfers as piece-by-piece acquisitions rather than transfer of enterprise.

M. Literature

A. Karavai, Sale of the Enterprise, Industrial and Trade Law, No. 2, 1st Edition, 2001

Y. Founk, Sale of the Enterprise of a Joint-Stock Company, 1st Edition, 2007

Brazil

By *Marcelo Takeyama* and *Roberta Marques de Camargo Vianna Godoy*

A. General Aspects

1. Asset Deal vs. Share Deal: Essential Considerations

The essential considerations for the choice between asset deal and share deal are: a) the existing liabilities of the seller (i.e. tax, environmental, labor, contracts, litigation, corporate, real property, assets and so on); b) tax issues: depending on the applicable taxes on the transaction, which are calculated in accordance with its value and the income generated, the seller or purchaser may prefer an asset deal instead of a share deal; c) certain rights: sometimes the rights of the seller entity are more important for the purchaser than the seller's assets, e. g., a long-term contract with a third party provider of raw material.

2. Distinction between Sale and Transfer in Rem

The distinction between sale and transfer in rem exists in Brazil, and it is possible to provide for the sale and the transfer/conveyance in separate documents.

3. Regional Differences

Considering that the Civil Code, the Commercial Code and the law applicable to notaries are federal laws, there are no regional differences as regards the legal requirements in connection with the transfer of assets. However, matters related to the amount charged by state and municipal tax authorities are not included in the above conclusion.

4. Acquisition by Foreigners

In principle, foreigners and foreign entities are free to purchase other assets in Brazil and no prior approval is required. However, there may apply restrictions for foreigners or foreign entities which may purchase real properties located within the Brazilian territory but, in certain situations, restrictions may apply and/or authorizations may be necessary (for properties not located in urban areas or for properties located in areas that may be considered relevant due to national security reasons, for instance). Therefore, in principle, foreigners and foreign entities are free to purchase assets in Brazil and no prior approval is required but in certain specific situations restrictions and authorizations may apply.

5. Public Registers, Records and Databases

Real property, aircraft, and automobiles are registered in specific public registers where information (such as ownership and encumbrances) may be obtained. All of the notaries of real property have a limited jurisdiction and information may be obtained by the public directly at the applicable notary with jurisdiction over the asset through the request of certificates. Online information regarding real property is not available in Brazil.

In relation to aircraft, there is only one Register, which is currently located in the city of Rio de Janeiro and commonly known as RAB (*Registro Aeronáutico Brasileiro*). Again, online information cannot be obtained, but any person may obtain information through the request of certificates.

Automobiles are registered with the state authority (each State of the Federative Republic of Brazil is by its authority responsible for the registration of automobiles). Online information is available on a restricted basis because usually only the owner has all the required information to obtain access to the online database and it is not clear whether the available information on liens is actually reliable.

There is no public register or online database where one can obtain all of the information to assess the financial standing of an entity. Usually, this type of information must be compiled from several searches, such as research at the notary of unpaid credit documents (promissory notes, for instance) (each city has a certain number of these notaries), research at the database of private credit protection entities (which requires a subscription for access), research at the applicable courts (to locate the filling of lawsuits such as bankruptcy proceedings).

6. Purchase Price Requirements

The only special rule with regard to the purchase price concerns currency. Note that one is not allowed to make payments in the Brazilian territory in a currency other than the Brazilian official currency (*Reais*). However, parties may stipulate that payments be made abroad in a foreign currency.

B. Tangible/Movable Assets

1. Characteristics as to:

a) Language of Documentation. Documents may be executed in English, but for the purposes of judicial enforcement these documents shall be translated into Portuguese by a sworn translator. The document and its sworn translation then must be registered by a notary of documents before its filing with the applicable court. This procedure may be avoided by having bilingual execution of the documentation.

b) Form of Documentation. Usually, the written form is required. Notarization may be required for certain types of assets (aircraft, for instance) and it is recommended that a verification be performed in each case. Other formalities may be necessary if the document is executed in another jurisdiction. Thus, execution in foreign jurisdictions is allowed but this may necessitate additional formalities for the purposes of registering the documents in Brazil or for judicial enforcement in Brazil. In principle, joint signing is not mandatory.

c) Specification of Assets. Usually it is not necessary to describe the assets in detail. However, if litigation originates from such transaction, there may be controversies in relation to the assets that are included in the transaction. This may be avoided or mitigated by attaching a list of assets.

2. Administrative, Corporate and Other Approvals

The transfer of tangible assets usually does not require any special governmental or administrative approvals. The approval of corporate bodies may be necessary if the articles of association or by-laws of the purchaser/seller require this type of approval, which is usually verified in each transaction. If the assets are encumbered, approval of security holders may be necessary depending on the type of encumbrance, which is also analyzed in each specific situation.

3. Filing Requirements

As mentioned earlier, there are specific public registers for real properties, aircraft and automobiles. Other than that, the transfer of tangible assets does not require special filings with public authorities. However, in certain specific situations the registration of the transaction in a general register of documents may be recommendable when the knowledge of third parties is a relevant matter.

4. Automatic Transfer of Encumbrances

In case the assets are subject to encumbrances (e.g., pledges, retention of title), such encumbrances automatically transfer to the purchaser.

C. Real Property

1. Characteristics as to:

a) Language of Documentation. Documents regarding the transfer of real property must be in Portuguese, which is the local language in Brazil.

b) Form of Documentation. Written public form is required for documents regarding the transfer of real property. Documents cannot be executed outside the Brazilian jurisdiction and joint signing before the representative of a notary is mandatory.

c) Specification of Assets. The real properties to be transferred must be described in detail.

2. Administrative, Corporate and Other Approvals

In general, special governmental approvals or administrative approvals are not required. Approval of corporate bodies in transactions involving real properties is usually required in the articles of association/by-laws of Brazilian legal entities. The approval of the security holders may be necessary depending on the type of security and its form of execution.

3. Filing Requirements

With regard to the transfer of real property, registration with the applicable Real Property Notary is necessary. Registration with the local municipal authority that is responsible for charging the municipal tax related to real properties is also necessary.

4. Automatic Transfer of Encumbrances

Encumbrances would follow the real property and therefore affect the purchaser. Any waiver as regards such encumbrances should be obtained in written form in a public document executed before a notary's representative.

5. Automatic Transfer of Lease Agreements

An automatic transfer of lease agreements in connection with the transfer of the respective real property depends on the terms and conditions of the lease agreement. Usually, lease agreements may be terminated and there may be clauses providing for compensation in the event of early termination.

D. Contracts

1. Characteristics as to:

a) Language of Documentation. As a general rule, the local language should be used in order to enforce the contract. Documents can be drafted in English, or be executed bilingually, if they are not going to be registered with public authorities. If executed overseas, the contract will need to be notarized, legalized (by a Brazilian Consulate with jurisdiction over said Notary) and translated into Portuguese by a certified translator for purposes of registration and validity with respect to third parties or judicial enforcement by a Brazilian Court.

b) Form of Documentation. The written form is required to transfer contracts. Documents can be signed in counterparts, but a joint signing on the same document is required.

c) Specification of Contracts. A general or generic description can be used. It is recommendable that a schedule or list of contracts and documents related to the master transfer agreement be attached to avoid controversies in an eventual legal dispute.

2. Administrative, Corporate and Other Approvals

Normally, a transfer of contracts does not require special governmental approval. Of course, it depends on the nature of the contract. If in the original execution a special governmental or administrative approval was not required, the transfer of such contract shall not required said type of approval.

The approval of corporate bodies regarding the seller and/or the purchaser should be required if so provided by their articles of incorporation/by laws. Finally, the approval of other parties of the contract shall be required if it is a condition for the transfer to be effective. This is usually defined in the contract because in the Brazilian Civil Code, the parties are free to determine restrictions in the transfer of a contract.

3. Automatic Transfer of Contracts (Other than Lease and Employment Agreements)

There are no other kinds of contracts that automatically transfer to the purchaser in the asset deal.

4. Filing Requirements

Any required filings with public authorities or registrations into registers or (online) databases depend upon the specific rights or assets covered by the contract.

5. Treatment of Existing Contractual Claims and Obligations

Claims and/or obligations are transferred to the purchaser once the contract is executed. It is customary to include special provisions in the asset sale and/or transfer agreement.

6. Warranty Claims Resulting from Events prior to Transfer

Normally, the seller is held liable for events prior to the transfer of the assets affected, but once the transfer of a contract is completed, any claims and/or obligations of such contract are transferred to the purchaser. Therefore, it is customary to include special provisions in the asset sale and/or transfer agreement covering eventual prior claims and/or obligations.

E. IP Rights

1. Characteristics of Intellectual Property Rights (e.g., Trademarks, Patents, Utility Models, Domain Names) ("*IP Rights*") as to:

a) Language of Documentation. The same comments made under item D, 1, a above apply. In case of registered IP Rights, use of local language is mandatory.

b) Form of Documentation. The written form is required. Documents can be signed in counterparts, but a joint signing on the same document is required.

c) Specification of IP Rights. Comments made under item D, 1, c above also apply.

2. Administrative, Corporate and Other Approvals

(See comments to item D, 2 above).

3. Filing Requirements

Because IP Rights are registered in public registers, the transfer of these rights requires the filing with the relevant public authorities in order to be effective (INPI-National Institute of Industrial Property). In this sense, the transfer only becomes effective with the registration.

4. Applicable International (Multilateral) Agreements or Treaties

Brazil participates in several Treaties regarding Intellectual Property Rights, such as:

- The Paris Convention (ratified by the Brazilian Decree n. 9233, of June 28, 1884);
- The Rome Convention (ratified by the Brazilian Decree n. 57.125 of September 19, 1965);
- The Berne Convention (ratified by the Brazilian Decree n. 75.699 of May 6, 1975);
- The Universal Convention on Authors' Rights (ratified by the Brazilian Decree n. 76.905 of December 24, 1975);
- Cooperation Treaty in Patents Issues (PCT) (ratified by the Brazilian Decree n. 81.742 of May 31, 1978); and
- TRIPS Agreement – Annex 1C of Marrakesh Treaty (ratified by the Brazilian Decree n. 1.355 of December 30, 1994).

F. Receivables

1. Characteristics as to:

a) Language of Documentation. Similar comments made regarding previous items apply here.

b) Form of Documentation. The written form and a joint signing are required. Execution in a foreign jurisdiction is allowed.

c) Specification of Receivables. Receivables should be sufficiently described. It is recommendable to attach schedules or lists of receivables to the transfer agreement.

2. Administrative, Corporate and Other Approvals

Similar comments made regarding previous items apply here.

3. Filing Requirements

The debtor must be notified and the contract that originates the receivables must be reviewed, as the debtor's approval for assignment of rights is typically included. Registration is usually not required.

G. Liabilities

1. Characteristics as to:

a) Language of Documentation. Again, the local language should be used in order to enforce the contract. Documents can be drafted in English, or executed bilingually if they are not going to be registered with public authorities. If executed overseas, the contract will need to be notarized, legalized (by a Brazilian Consulate with jurisdiction over said Notary) and translated into Portuguese by a certified translator for purposes of registration and validity upon third parties and for the purposes of submission before Brazilian Courts.

b) Form of Documentation. Generally, the written form is required. Notarization and other procedural formalities (i.e, legalization) may be required if the documents were executed abroad and in a foreign language. Documents can be signed in counterparts, but a joint signing on the same document is required.

c) Specification of Liabilities. The same rule specified in previously applies to the transfer of liabilities: a general or generic description can be used, and it is recommendable to attach a schedule or list of contracts and documents related to the transfer agreement in order to avoid controversies in an eventual legal dispute.

2. Administrative, Corporate and Other Approvals

As a general rule, special approvals are not required to transfer liabilities. Depending on its terms or nature of the contract, a special governmental or administrative approvals may be required (e.g., the Antitrust Authority's approval); or an approval of corporate bodies (if so provided by the seller's and/or purchaser's articles of incorporation); or an approval of the creditors, if required in the contract or by the nature of the liability (e.g., personal obligations).

3. Filing Requirements

Normally, the transfer of liabilities doe not require special filings, notifications or registrations. However, this rule has several exceptions that must be analyzed individually. Some examples refer to liabilities connected to real properties. Again, a case by case analysis is recommended.

4. Purchaser's Liability for:

a) Tax Obligations. As a general rule, all tax obligations are transferred to the purchaser, that will be jointly and several liable with the seller. It is possible, in the contract, to limit such liability to determine that the seller should be responsible for taxes prior to the acquisition and up to the transfer of the asset and for taxes accrued but not assessed in that opportunity.

b) Environmental Contamination. Environmental responsibilities related to the acquired assets for periods prior to the acquisition are transferred to the purchaser, which will be joint and several liable with the seller.

c) Products Sold or Services Rendered by the Seller to Third Parties. The purchaser's liability regarding products sold or services rendered by the seller to third parties depends on how the acquisition was structured. However, as a general rule, the consumers of services or goods are strongly protected in the Brazilian territory and are considered as a weaker party in any transaction.

5. Automatic Transfer of Other Liabilities

No other liabilities automatically transfer to the purchaser due to the acquisition of assets.

6. Contractual Protection as to 4 and 5 above

It is customary to include special provisions (representations and warranties) as to the issues mentioned under items 4 and 5 above into the asset sale and/or transfer agreement.

H. Employees

1. Transfer of Employees

In an asset transfer deal, employees of the seller are not automatically transferred to the purchaser. On the other hand, in a share deal, employees are automatically transferred to purchaser. Usually, in an asset deal, seller terminates all of the employment agreements and pays all of the termination fees.

2. Approval of Works Council, Trade Union or Other Institutions

As a general rule, the asset transfer does not require the approval of any labor organization. Depending on the size of the company and/or importance of its segment, the trade union or works council may intervene to guaranty that the employees' rights are being respected.

3. Contractual Protection as to Labor Issues

As a general rule, the seller is liable for labor obligations until the transfer of the asset is completed. In this sense, it is common to include a provision that the seller is liable for any labor obligations incurred until the effective transfer of the asset to the purchaser.

I. Tax Implications

1. Value Added Tax

The asset transfer triggers the obligation to pay VAT. The standard VAT rate in Brazil (*ICMS*) ranges from 7% to 25%, with average rate of 17% (e.g., rate in Sao Paulo is 18%, while in Rio de Janeiro the rate is 19%).

2. Real Property Transfer Tax

The transfer of real estate triggers the obligation to pay tax in Brazil.

- Real Estate Transfer Tax: The tax is imposed on the purchaser of real property. The tax rates are 2%–6% of the sale value;
- Real Estate Property Tax: The annual tax is imposed by the local authority, and the rates vary from State to State. The rates are 0.3%–1% of the market value;
- Rural Property Tax: The annual tax is imposed on rural property. The tax rates are 0.03%–20% depending on the location and use of the property.

3. Other Tax Issues

Issues related to income tax and/or capital gain may arise and must be checked if applicable on a case-by-case perspective.

J. Bankruptcy Law

1. Challenge of Asset Transfer in Case of Insolvency

Creditors may challenge the asset transfer 1) if the transfer has taken place within 90-days prior to when the bankruptcy is declared by a court affecting the company's assets and rights and 2) and if insolvency of any of the parties is public at the time of the asset transfer.

2. Acquisition of Assets that are Subject to Insolvency Proceedings

If, at the time of transfer, the seller has been declared bankrupt by a court, then the court's approval is necessary to transfer the assets.

K. Timing and Costs

1. Timeframe of Asset Transfer

The applicable timeframes for an asset transfer may vary depending on the manner of execution of the sale/acquisition instruments and depending upon the type of assets that are acquired. If the sale/acquisition instruments are executed outside the Brazilian territory, it is necessary to notarize the signatures and legalize the transaction documents in the Brazilian Embassy with jurisdiction over the place of signing. This procedure may take up to 15 (fifteen) days. In addition to that, if the document is executed in a language other than Portuguese, such document must be translated into Portuguese by a sworn translator and registered in a general notary of documents before submitting its registration in the applicable register place (real property register, aircraft register, automobile register and so on). This step (i.e., sworn translation and registration before a general notary of documents) may take up to approximately 10 (ten) days. Obviously, these 2 (two) prior estimates (15 and 10 days) may vary depending on the applicable Embassy and depending upon the length of documents.

Thus, any estimate depends on the manner of execution of the transaction documents. In addition to that, the assets involved may have an impact on the estimate. For instance, registration of a real property or an aircraft may take longer than the registration of an automobile. On the other hand, certain assets do not need to be registered (property of ordinary equipment in general does not need to be registered).

In conclusion, even a rough estimate is not possible and must be obtained individually considering the manner of execution of documents, assets involved and their legal status (for instance, if the aircraft or real property have liens, the registration may take longer).

2. Costs of Asset Transfer

These costs for an asset transfer may vary depending on the value of assets involved. There is no general percentage because the costs (notarization or registration) vary from notary to notary. In addition to that, stamp duties may also vary, depending on the location of the applicable notary. This overview can only be provided on a case-by-case situation.

L. Miscellaneous

1. Choice of Foreign Law

In principle, a sale and/or transfer agreement can be made subject to foreign law.

2. (International) Arbitration, Choice of Venue

In principle, international arbitration is possible and choice of venue can be agreed by the parties. However, certain restrictions may apply depending on the type of matter being arbitrated. For instance, if there is any discussion involving a real property or the rights of a minor, the matter/discussion should be submitted before Brazilian courts. In the majority of matters, (international) arbitration is possible and there are no restrictions as to the choice of venue.

3. Other Distinctions, Characteristics

Normally, if the seller is married, it is recommendable to check his/her marital property regime and obtain the consent of the seller's spouse regarding the transfer of registered assets. This consent is required to avoid any challenge in the future by the non-consenting spouse.

M. Literature

Orlando Gomes, Contratos (Contracts), 17th Edition, 1997

Silvio de Salvo Venosa, Direito Civil (Civil Law), 4th Edition, 2004

Maria Helena Diniz, Tratatado Teórico e Prático dos Contratos (Theoretical and Practical Treatise about Contracts), 5th Edition, 2003

Bulgaria

By *Plamen Marintchov Borissov*

A. General Aspects

1. Asset Deal vs. Share Deal: Essential Considerations

There are various considerations that have to be taken into account when deciding whether the transaction should be structured as a share purchase and transfer or as an asset purchase and transfer.

Probably the most important aspects are tax considerations. The purchaser of a business is interested in deducting the acquisition costs as operating expenses. Thus, he prefers to structure the transaction as a purchase and acquisition of assets, so that he is able to increase the depreciation basis, i.e. the book value of the depreciable assets, by the difference between the purchase price paid and the book value of the assets (so-called "step-up"). On the other hand, however, seller's gain (which is calculated as the positive difference between the acquisition price and the sales price) is taxable irrespective of whether the deal is structured as an asset or share transfer. There are some special regimes of tax relief, but they are not applied by the tax authorities in practice.

Usually the accomplishment of the transfer of a business by way of a transfer of its assets is more complex since one has to identify the assets belonging to such business and has to make sure that all such assets are validly transferred. On the other hand, however, in the case of a purchase and acquisition of assets, the purchaser may choose the assets and liabilities that it wants to purchase and acquire, while in the case of a purchase and acquisition of shares, the purchaser has to take all assets and liabilities owned by the respective entity regardless of whether it is aware of such assets and liabilities. Thus, a share deal bears the risk of the assumption of undisclosed liabilities.

Another aspect that might be relevant in determining the structure of the transaction is permits. Some businesses require permits that are either tied to the business itself or to its owner. While permits tied to the business usually are transferred together with the assets of the business, permits tied to the owner do not transfer. Thus, the purchaser has to apply for new permit(s). On the other hand, in the case of a purchase and acquisition of shares, such issue does not arise since the owner of the business, i.e. the entity owning the assets and forming the business, does not change.

An asset deal may further serve as a way of avoiding the application of the provisions regarding the takeover of public companies.

In Bulgaria, the acquisition of a business by way of purchasing and acquiring the shares of the entity operating the respective business is more common than an asset acquisition since it is less complex and often less expensive.

2. Distinction between Sale and Transfer in Rem

Bulgarian law does not distinguish between the sale of assets (i.e. obligation to transfer) on the one hand and the transfer in rem as the fulfillment of the transfer obligation on the other hand. The contracts for sale and purchase have automatic in rem effect, i.e. the assets are transferred by virtue of the sale and purchase agreement.

Nevertheless, if assets are to be sold and transferred in multiple jurisdictions, it might be advisable to execute the sale through a single master purchase agreement while the assets can be transferred in the respective jurisdictions on the basis of local transfer agreements. The benefit of such an approach is that local transfer requirements can be fulfilled by the local transfer agreement without affecting the master purchase agreement (for instance, notarial form for transfer of immovable assets or endorsements of share certificates). This also avoids the disclosure of the entire asset transfer (including the master purchase agreement) if the transfer has to be filed with any authorities. However, where a special form is required by Bulgarian law (for example, in the transfer of real property), the transfer of ownership rights will take effect after execution of the local transfer agreement and compliance with all legal requirements.

3. Regional Differences

There are no regional differences as regards the legal requirements in connection with the transfer of assets applicable to an asset transfer within Bulgaria. However, there may be differences in the amount of taxes paid in connection with the transfer of certain assets.

4. Acquisition by Foreigners

As to distinctions regarding the acquisition of assets by foreigners or foreign entities, it is a principal of Bulgarian law that all economic operators are equal and have equal rights to do business unless the contrary is explicitly provided for by the law. Presently, foreign individuals and foreign legal entities may not directly acquire land.

5. Public Registers, Records and Databases

In Bulgaria, no central institution retaining all relevant information in connection with an asset transfer is in existence.

Corporate details about the seller and the purchaser can be obtained from the public Commercial Register with the Registration Agency (*Търговски регистър*) which contains basic details as to (i) legal form, (ii) powers of representation, (iii) registered share capital, (iv) pledges over certain type of shares (most common shares in limited liability companies) and (v) certain corporate events such as capital increases, mergers, insolvency or liquidation. Information from the Commercial Register is available on-line on http://www.brra.bg. These resources are available to everyone.

In Bulgaria, transfer of de-materialized (book-entry form) shares of a joint stock company is effected by registration in the Central Depository. Pledges of de-materialized shares are made by registration in the same body.

Information as to certain types of encumbrances (non-possessory pledges, receivables pledges, etc.) can be obtained from the Central Register of Special Pledges. It is a central body that provides information about all special pledges in the country.

Information as to real property, including ownership and encumbrances, can be obtained from the Real Estate Registers with the different Regional Courts in the country. There is no one single institution retaining all relevant information in connection with real property, which may sometimes make the transfer of assets more difficult and time consuming. The Registers are public and any interested party may view them.

Information as to intellectual property rights such as trademarks, patents, industrial designs, etc. can be obtained from the Bulgarian Patent Office (www.bpo.bg). Some information (about trade marks) is available online. Regarding copyrights, however, no such information is available, since a general copyright register does not exist in Bulgaria.

Information as to vessels, including ownership and encumbrances, can be obtained from the Register with the Executive Agency "Sea Administration."

Finally, information as to the ownership of internet domains can be obtained from the incumbent authority Register.BG (www.register.bg).

6. Purchase Price Requirements

There are special rules with regard to the purchase price to be paid in connection with a real property deal. The law provides for a minimal price for tax purposes, i.e. the parties may agree on a lower transfer price but the tax paid in connection with the property transfer will be calculated on the basis of the tax value of the property established by the law.

Furthermore, for tax and accounting purposes, an allocation of the purchase price to individual assets or groups of assets may be advisable.

B. Tangible/Movable Assets

1. Characteristics as to:

a) Language of Documentation. We would like to make a note that Bulgarian law divides property assets into two general categories, i.e. movable property (tangible assets) and immovable property (real property).

Principally, the sale and transfer documents regarding tangible assets may be drafted in every language. Bilingual documents are permitted. Since there is no need for filing such documents with public authorities, a Bulgarian translation is not required.

However, it should be pointed out that there is a special form for transfer of some tangible assets (for instance, automobiles or vessels are also regarded by the Bulgarian law as tangible (movable) assets). Where a special form and registration with a Bulgarian authority is required, the documents must be executed in Bulgarian as well or a certified translation must be provided. Bilingual forms are admissible and if the signatories do not know Bulgarian, a sworn translator must verify the translation.

b) Form of Documentation. The transfer of most tangible assets does not require a special form; oral agreements are valid. For evidentiary purposes, the written form is nonetheless advisable. In the event the assets are sold as part of a transfer of an entire enterprise of the seller, notarization of the sale and purchase agreement (i.e. the transfer obligation) is required. Also, as noted above, certain assets are transferred with notarial certified signatures of the seller and purchaser.

The sale and transfer documents may be executed outside Bulgaria. Signing in counterparts is permissible, but where notarial certification is required this is in fact impracticable.

c) Specification of Assets. In theory, a general description of the assets is possible where assets are transferred as part of the whole enterprise of the seller. However, it is advisable that the assets subject to the transfer are specified in the transfer agreement to such an extent that any third party would be able to distinguish the assets from any other non-transferred assets. In order to comply with this so-called identification principle, the use of asset lists (or schedules) is advisable but not mandatory. Specification by category or location is sufficient provided that identification is possible without recourse to any legal valuation or discretion. The transfer of "all assets" located at a certain place (e.g., a warehouse) meets these requirements.

If and to the extent that the asset specification is insufficient (for instance, references the sale of generic goods) the assets will not be transferred but will instead remain with the seller. Once the assets are individualized, the title is transferred to the purchaser.

2. Administrative, Corporate and Other Approvals

The transfer of tangible assets generally does not require special governmental or administrative approvals. However, exceptions might apply with regard to special categories of assets (e.g., certain weapons or dangerous substances). Failure to comply will invalidate the transfer.

The approval of any corporate bodies is basically not required unless otherwise provided for in seller's and/or purchaser's articles of association or partnership agreement. If the seller is a joint stock corporation, the approval of its shareholders' meeting might be required in the event the sold assets form a substantial part of seller's business, regardless of whether such provision is expressly mentioned in the articles. Non-compliance does not affect the validity of the transfer.

In case the assets are encumbered or used as collateral, the following applies: If the seller is the owner of the sold assets (e.g., in case the assets are pledged), no such approval is required. If a third party is the owner of the assets (e.g., in case of retention of title, security assignment), the transfer is basically invalid unless purchaser acquired the assets in good faith (the bona fide purchaser principle).

3. Filing Requirements

In principle, the transfer of tangible assets requires no filings with public authorities or registrations in public registers or databases. There are a few exceptions that concern automobiles, vessels, etc.

4. Automatic Transfer of Encumbrances

In case the assets are subject to encumbrances (e.g., pledges, retention of title), the general rule is that encumbrances regarding tangible assets are automatically transferred to the purchaser. In particular, pledged assets remain pledged, and assets that are subject to retention of title clauses in favor of suppliers remain in the ownership of such suppliers. However, this does not apply in case the purchaser acquires the assets in good faith (the bona fide purchaser principle).

C. Real Property

1. Characteristics as to:

a) Language of Documentation. The contract for sale and purchase regarding the transfer of real property must be drafted in Bulgarian only. Bilingual versions are not acceptable. Some of the supporting documentation, such as powers of attorney, declarations, etc. may be drafted in bilingual parts, but in this case they must be accompanied by a certified and legalized translation in Bulgarian.

b) Form of Documentation. The sale and transfer of real property in Bulgaria is done by way of execution of a written notarial deed, which, after execution, is registered with the Real Estate Register with the respective Regional Court. The sale and purchase agreement itself may not be executed outside Bulgaria. What is more, it must be certified by a notary public with authority to execute deeds in the respective region where the real property is located. Signing in counterparts is not permissible; joint signing of the same document is mandatory.

c) Specification of Assets. The principle of identification applies to the transfer of real property. The property thus has to be specified in detail; a general description is not permissible. In order to comply with this requirement it is necessary to refer to the relevant sections in the title document of the seller that is on record with the relevant Real Estate Register, and which contains a detailed description of the property.

2. Administrative, Corporate and Other Approvals

The transfer of real property does not require special governmental or administrative approvals.

For limited liability companies, the approval of the shareholders' meeting is necessary for the sale or purchase of real property; this is a condition precedent for the transaction and the notary public will not certify the deed without such approval. The approval of any corporate bodies of joint stock companies is basically not required unless otherwise provided for in seller's and/or purchaser's by-laws. For further details, please refer to B, 2 above.

In the event the real property is encumbered with mortgages, land charges or usufruct rights, the transfer is not subject to the approval of the security holders, who continue to be secured following the transfer due to the fact that the encumbrances automatically transfer to the purchaser (see C, 4 below).

3. Filing Requirements

The transfer of any real property must be registered in the Real Estate Register of the respective regional court, which registration must be carried out on the same day as the execution of the notarial deed. If registration is not executed, the transfer will still be valid but the purchaser cannot exercise his rights against third parties who may have acquired title and registered the transfer before him. The relevant filings must be made by the notary in charge. Within two months of the date of transfer, the purchaser must register the real property with the tax authorities with copies of the executed and notarized transfer documents. Foreigners purchasing real property for the first time must also be registered for statistical purposes (the so-called Bulstat registration).

4. Automatic Transfer of Encumbrances

Any encumbrances on the real estate that are registered in the Real Estate Register remain valid after the transfer of the real estate. Similar to the granting of encumbrances, the waiver of encumbrances requires notarial form (notarial certified consent of the secured creditor).

5. Automatic Transfer of Lease Agreements

Lease agreements entered into by the seller remain valid for the purchaser for the full term of the lease if the lease agreements are registered in the Real Estate Register. If the lease agreements are not registered but have an authentic date, they are obligatory for the purchaser for the term of the lease but not for more than one year from the date of the transfer of the real property. In the event the lease agreements have no authentic date, they are obligatory for the purchaser as lease agreements with indefinite term (which in fact means that the purchaser may terminate them with one-month notice to the tenant, or one-day notice if the lease is concluded for a number of days).

D. Contracts

1. Characteristics as to:

a) Language of Documentation. The sale and transfer documents regarding contracts may be drafted in any language. Bilingual documents are permitted. Since there is no need for filing such documents with public authorities, a Bulgarian translation is not required.

b) Form of Documentation. The transfer of contracts generally does not require a special form unless the conclusion of the contract to be transferred required a specific form. For evidentiary purposes, the written form is nonetheless recommendable. The seller must confirm to the purchaser the transfer in written form. He also must notify the other party (debtor) to the contract about the transfer. In case the contracts are sold as part of the whole commercial enterprise of the seller, notarization of the sale and purchase agreement is required.

The sale and transfer documents may be executed outside Bulgaria. If no special form is required, signing in counterparts is permissible but rare.

c) Specification of Contracts. The principle of identification (see B, 1, c above) also applies to the transfer of contracts. The contracts thus have to be sufficiently specified. In order to comply with this requirement it is advisable to list the contracts to be transferred in schedules appended to the asset transfer agreement, specifying subject, parties and date of the relevant agreements.

2. Administrative, Corporate and Other Approvals

The transfer of contracts does not require special governmental or administrative approvals.

The approval of any corporate body is basically not required unless otherwise provided for in seller's and/or purchaser's statutes. For further details, please refer to B, 2 above.

Under Bulgarian law, the transfer of contracts requires the consent of the other party to the contract to be transferred. For certain types of contracts (e.g., employment agreements, lease agreements, and certain types of insurance agreements) exceptions apply (see D, 3 and H, 1 below as well as C, 5 above). Failure to comply will invalidate the transfer.

3. Automatic Transfer of Contracts (Other than Lease and Employment Agreements)

Besides lease and employment agreements (see H, 1 and C, 5), Bulgarian law provides for the automatic transfer of certain types of asset-related insurance agreements, such as certain property insurances. The rationale behind such rule is to avoid insurance gaps in case the insured assets are transferred. However, the insurer and the purchaser have special termination rights following the completion of the transfer.

4. Filing Requirements

Regarding the transfer of contracts, no filings with public authorities or registrations in public registers or databases are required.

5. Treatment of Existing Contractual Claims and Obligations

If and to the extent the other party to a contract consents to the transfer of such contract, the respective claims and/or obligations arising from such contract do automatically transfer to the purchaser. This also applies to contracts not or not completely fulfilled unless otherwise provided for in the transfer agreement. The issue of contracts that are not or not completely fulfilled is usually dealt with in the purchase price adjustment mechanism. An alternative treatment of such issues would be to include a respective indemnification clause in the asset sale and/or transfer agreement.

6. Warranty Claims Resulting from Events prior to Transfer

As a general rule, the transfer of a contract also comprises the transfer of any claims and any obligations related to such contract since the required consent of the other contractual party usually also covers such claims and obligations. This also applies to warranty claims resulting from events prior to the transfer of such contract if not otherwise provided for in the asset sale and/or transfer agreement. The potential exposure resulting thereof is customarily covered by representations and warranties and/or indemnifications.

E. IP Rights

1. Characteristics of Intellectual Property Rights (e.g., Trademarks, Patents, Utility Models, Domain Names) ("*IP Rights*"), as to:

a) Language of Documentation. The sale and transfer documents regarding IP Rights may be drafted in any language. In the case of registered IP Rights (e.g., trademarks, patents, design patents, domain names), a Bulgarian translation is necessary for filing purposes; bilingual documents are permitted.

Please note that, according to Bulgarian law, copyrights cannot be transferred. Only a license can be granted.

b) Form of Documentation. The transfer of IP Rights must be in writing due to the fact that a filing with the Bulgarian Patent Office is necessary. In case the IP Rights are sold as part of the whole commercial enterprise of the seller, notarization of the sale and purchase agreement is required.

The sale and transfer documents may be executed outside Bulgaria. Signing in counterparts is permissible but not customary.

c) Specification of IP Rights. The principle of identification (see B, 1, c above) also applies to the transfer of IP Rights. The IP Rights thus have to be specified sufficiently.

In order to comply with such requirements the use of lists (or schedules) is recommendable but not mandatory.

2. Administrative, Corporate and Other Approvals

The transfer must be filed with the state register maintained at the Patent Office. The Chair of the Patent Office issues a special administrative act for the proposed transfer. The transfer of trademarks, for instance, may be rejected if it can mislead the consumers. In such cases, the transfer is invalid with respect to third parties.

The approval of any corporate bodies is basically not required unless otherwise provided for in seller's and/or purchaser's statutes. For further details, please refer to B, 2 above.

In case the IP Rights are encumbered or used as collateral the following applies: If the seller is the owner of the IP Rights (e.g., in case the IP Rights are pledged), no such approval is required. If a third party is the owner of the assets (e.g., in case of security assignment), the transfer is invalid.

3. Filing Requirements

If and to the extent the IP Rights to be transferred are registered in public registers (such as patents, utility models, trademarks and domain names), the change of ownership requires the filing with the relevant public registers. Such registration is merely of a declaratory nature and does not affect the validity of the transfer. However, the transfer will have effect in respect of third parties only after registration.

4. Applicable International (Multilateral) Agreements or Treaties

Bulgaria participates in the TRIPS Agreement and in the Paris Convention for the Protection of Industrial Property. In addition, Bulgaria signed the Madrid Agreement and the Madrid Protocol regarding trademarks. Finally, Bulgaria is subject to the Council Regulation on the Community Trademark of the European Community.

F. Receivables

1. Characteristics as to:

a) Language of Documentation. The sale and transfer documents regarding receivables may be drafted in any language. Bilingual documents are permitted. Since there is no need for filing such documents with public authorities, a Bulgarian translation is not required.

b) Form of Documentation. The transfer of receivables does not require a special form; oral agreements are valid. For evidentiary purposes, the written form is nonetheless advisable. In case the receivables are sold as part of the whole commercial enterprise of the seller, notarization of the sale and purchase agreement is required.

The sale and transfer documents may be executed outside Bulgaria. Signing in counterparts is permissible.

c) Specification of Receivables. The principle of identification (see B, 1, c above) also applies to the transfer of receivables. The receivables thus have to be sufficiently specified. In order to comply with this requirement, it is advisable to list the receivables to be transferred in schedules to the asset transfer agreement, specifying the underlying legal relationships and the outstanding amount of the relevant receivables.

2. Administrative, Corporate and Other Approvals

The transfer of receivables does not require special governmental or administrative approvals. The approval of any corporate body is basically not required unless otherwise provided for in seller's and/or purchaser's statutes. For further details, please refer to B, 2 above.

The validity of the transfer is not subject to the approval of the debtor, provided that the underlying agreement does not state otherwise. However, the transfer of the receivables will have effect with respect to the debtor and third parties after the transfer is notified to the debtor by the seller.

3. Filing Requirements

Regarding the transfer of receivables, no filings with public authorities or registrations in public registers or databases are required. As noted above, the notification of the transfer to the debtors is required. As long as the debtors are not aware of the transfer, payments on the receivables can still be made to the former owner of the receivables.

G. Liabilities

1. Characteristics as to:

a) Language of Documentation. The sale and transfer documents regarding liabilities may be drafted in every language. Bilingual documents are permitted. Since there is no need for filing such documents with public authorities, a Bulgarian translation is not required.

b) Form of Documentation. The transfer of liabilities does not require a special form; oral agreements are valid. For evidentiary purposes, the written form is nonetheless advisable. The sale and transfer documents may be executed outside Bulgaria. Signing in counterparts is permissible.

c) Specification of Liabilities. The principle of identification (see B, 1, c above) also applies to the transfer of liabilities. The liabilities thus have to be specified sufficiently. In order to comply with such requirements it is advisable to list the liabilities to be transferred in schedules appended to the asset transfer agreement, specifying the underlying legal relationships and the outstanding amount of the relevant liabilities.

2. Administrative, Corporate and Other Approvals

The transfer of liabilities does not require special governmental or administrative approvals. The approval of any corporate bodies is basically not required unless otherwise provided for in seller's and/or purchaser's statutes. For further details, please refer to B, 2 above.

Under Bulgarian law, the transfer of liabilities requires the consent of the creditors. Failure to comply will invalidate the transfer.

3. Filing Requirements

Regarding the transfer of liabilities, no filings with public authorities or registrations in public registers or databases are required. Due to the fact that the transfer is subject to the creditors' consent, a separate notification to the creditors is not necessary.

4. Purchaser's Liability for:

a) Tax Obligations. Where assets are acquired, normally the purchaser is liable for taxes from the acquisition date onwards. The potential exposure resulting from this is customarily covered by representations and warranties and/or indemnifications.

b) Environmental Contamination. The same principle applies as outlined in G, 4, a above.

c) Products Sold or Services Rendered by the Seller to Third Parties. The same principle applies as outlined in G, 4, a above. The purchaser, however, may undertake warranty service after transfer upon separate agreement.

5. Automatic Transfer of Other Liabilities

If an acquisition of assets is carried out as part of a purchase of the whole commercial enterprise of the seller, the purchaser generally assumes all liabilities of the seller. The potential exposure resulting thereof is customarily covered by representations and warranties and/or indemnifications. For employment issues see H below.

6. Contractual Protection as to 4 and 5 above

Since it cannot always be established clearly which assets are subject to a sale (especially in the case of a transfer of the whole enterprise), it is customary to include special provisions (e.g., indemnifications) as to the issues mentioned under 4 and 5 in the asset sale and/or transfer agreement.

H. Employees

1. Transfer of Employees

According to mandatory Bulgarian law, all existing employment agreements pertaining to the sold business automatically transfer to the purchaser by operation of law. This does not apply if the transaction only involves selected assets that do not form a distinct business unit or separate activity of the enterprise. As a general rule, service agreements with board members or managing directors are not subject to such transfers.

As a consequence of the transfer, the purchaser becomes part of the employment agreement and is bound to its terms and conditions as well as to any arrangements stipulated between the seller and the affected employee. The seller, jointly with the purchaser, remains liable vis-à-vis the employees as regards all obligations arising from the employment relationships that were incurred prior to the transfer.

At least two months prior to a transfer of business, the seller or the purchaser has to inform the affected employees on, inter alia, the planned change and the transfer date, the reason for the transfer, the legal, economic and social impact of the sale on the employees as well as the planned measures in respect of the employees, including for the fulfillment of the obligations incurred prior to the transfer.

As a general rule, termination by the seller or the purchaser of an employment agreement merely due to the transfer of business is void. However, termination due to other reasons, if any, is possible. The employee has the right to terminate the employment relationship without notice if, as a result of the transfer, the working conditions provided by the new employer have significantly deteriorated.

2. Approval of Works Council, Trade Union or Other Institutions

In general, the transfer of a business by way of transferring the individual assets does not trigger co-determination rights of the works council, if any. However, if the transfer is accompanied by substantial redundancies or reorganization measures, the employer is obliged to commence consultation with the trade unions prior to the transfer and to make every effort to reach an agreement. There is an obligation to commence consultation, but not an obligation to reach a definitive agreement.

3. Contractual Protection as to Labor Issues

It is customary to include special provisions (e.g., guarantees, indemnifications) as to employees in the asset sale and/or transfer agreement where the asset transfer triggers transfer of employment contracts.

I. Tax Implications

1. Value Added Tax

The regular VAT rate in Bulgaria amounts to 20%. However, the transfer of assets is exempt from VAT if it constitutes a transfer of an entire enterprise of the seller as provided for in the Commercial Act. The basis for calculating the VAT is the combined total value of the assets, i.e. in most cases the purchase price. Where VAT is due, it should be added to the purchase price in the seller's invoice and is payable by the purchaser together with the purchase price. Where the purchaser is VAT-registered, it can normally recover the VAT input on the asset acquisition.

2. Real Property Transfer Tax

The transfer of real estate in Bulgaria triggers a local transfer tax in an amount that varies between 2% and 3% of the purchase price depending on the region of the location of the property. The tax base shall not be below the tax value of the real estate (i.e. if the declared purchase price is lower than the tax value of the property, the local tax will be established as a percentage of the tax value). The real estate transfer tax is due upon the transfer of the real estate.

3. Other Tax Issues

If there is a positive difference between tax net book value and accounting book value of the asset, such positive difference shall become taxable for the seller in the year of the transfer. Revaluation reserve, if any, attached to transferred land in the year of the transfer is taxable.

J. Bankruptcy Law

1. Challenge of Asset Transfer in Case of Insolvency

The general rules of the Bulgarian bankruptcy law provide for the following:

Certain transactions are considered void with respect to the bankruptcy creditors if effected after the date of the judgment for institution of bankruptcy proceedings and if not in compliance with the established procedure (e.g., fulfillment of obligation that has occurred prior to the date of the judgment for institution of bankruptcy proceedings; pledging or mortgaging rights or chattels included in the bankruptcy estate; transactions with rights or chattels included in the bankruptcy estate). Furthermore, certain actions and transactions carried out by the debtor after the initial date of the bankruptcy, respectively the over-indebtedness, are void regarding the creditors (e.g., fulfillment of pecuniary obligations regardless of the way of fulfillment; gratuitous transaction with proprietary right from the bankruptcy estate; pledging, mortgaging or establishment of other security on proprietary right of the bankruptcy estate; value transaction with proprietary right of the bankruptcy estate where the value of the delivered considerably exceeds the value of the received).

In addition, certain transactions carried out by the debtor may be voidable with respect to the bankruptcy creditors (e.g., gratuitous transactions, except ordinary donations, in favor of a person related to the debtor effected within three years prior to the institution of bankruptcy proceedings; gratuitous transactions in favor of third parties effected within two years prior to the institution of bankruptcy proceedings; value transaction where the value of the delivered considerably exceeds the value of the received effected within two years prior to the institution of bankruptcy proceedings; fulfillment of pecuniary obligations by way of transfer of property effected within three months prior to the initial date of the bankruptcy if the return of the property could result in an increase in the amount to be received by the creditors; mortgaging, pledging or establishment of another security over unsecured receivables effected within one year prior to the institution of bankruptcy proceedings; mortgaging, pledging or providing another security over unsecured receivable of a partner or shareholder effected within two years prior to the institution of bankruptcy proceedings; transaction effected within two years prior to the institution of bankruptcy proceedings which is detrimental to the creditors if one of the parties thereto is a person related to the debtor).

2. Acquisition of Assets that are Subject to Insolvency Proceedings

There are specific rules for transactions with assets that form part of the bankruptcy estate. Such transactions must be effected by the syndic appointed by the court following special procedure and restricted by special rules. For more information see J, 1 above.

K. Timing and Costs

1. Timeframe of Asset Transfer

Acquisition of a business will require notarial certification of the signatures of the seller and purchaser, which can be executed in one day. If real property is transferred, a notarial deed and registration in the real estate register must be executed. By law it is mandatory that both proceedings are accomplished in the same day. If other filings are required, they certainly can be executed in one day. Of course, this term does not include the time for doing due diligence and drafting the transaction documents.

2. Costs of Asset Transfer

Notary fees in Bulgaria are set in a progressive table and depend on the interest certified, i.e. the higher the interest, the higher the fee. In any case, the notary fee may not exceed BGN 6,000 (approximately EUR 3,070). In case of transfer of real property, there is also a local transfer tax ranging between 2% and 3% of the purchase price, depending on the region in which the property is located and the registration fee in the amount 0.1% of the purchase price. The costs of other filings are insignificant.

L. Miscellaneous

1. Choice of Foreign Law

For most assets, the sale and/or transfer agreement may be made subject to foreign law, provided that the mandatory provisions of the Bulgarian law are complied with. In certain cases, Bulgarian law provides for special form and/or orders for the transfer (e.g., notary certification, etc.) that must be followed by the parties. Acquisition of real property located in Bulgaria, however, may not be subject to foreign law; Bulgarian law must apply.

2. (International) Arbitration, Choice of Venue

The Bulgarian law allows certain proprietary disputes to be referred to arbitration instead of to ordinary state court unless they concern rights of real property, alimony or employment rights. If the residence/seat of one of the parties is abroad, the dispute may be referred to international arbitration. There are no specific restrictions as regards the choice of venue.

There are certain cases, however, where the Bulgarian courts have exclusive authority (e.g., disputes on IP Rights originating from Bulgaria, etc.)

3. Other Distinctions, Characteristics

The Bulgarian Family Code introduces the so called "matrimonial proprietary community". This concept means that the properties (movable and immovable) and the rights to properties, as well as the bank deposits acquired by spouses during their marriage as a result of a joint contribution (excluding assets acquired by inheritance, donation and some other special ways of acquisition) belong jointly to both spouses notwithstanding the name in which they have been acquired. The joint contributions of the spouses can be expressed in investing resources and work, in care for the children and work in the household. The joint contribution is presumed until proven otherwise.

If the seller is an individual person rather than a legal entity and if he/she is married, the consent of his/her spouse is required regarding the transfer of the assets that constitute the matrimonial proprietary community. The disposition of a common immovable property or a right thereto carried out only by one of the spouses will be valid in respect of the other spouse if the latter does not dispute it by way of court claim within six months from learning about the transfer. As a rule, notaries confirm this issue in advance and would not execute the notary deed if the other spouse does not consent to it. The same rule applies in case of gratuitous disposition of movable property. However, if the disposition of the chattel is executed by way of value transaction, the transfer will not be valid in respect of the other spouse provided the third person has known or, according to the circumstances, could have known that the consent of the other spouse is missing.

Canada

By *Stephen Rigby* and *Bruce Chapple*

A. General Aspects

1. Asset Deal vs. Share Deal: Essential Considerations

There are numerous considerations for the parties to address in assessing whether to structure a transaction as an "asset deal" or as a "share deal". We have grouped the most common considerations into two loose categories that we have labeled "Business Considerations" and "Tax Considerations".

Business Considerations

An asset deal allows the parties to designate the specific assets and liabilities to be transferred. This may be a significant consideration where the transaction involves only a portion of the seller's business operations or where specific assets or liabilities of the seller are not to be transferred to the purchaser. By comparison, a share transaction involves the purchaser acquiring a corporation which may have unknown or undisclosed liabilities.

The third party consents required to transfer shares rather than assets are often less burdensome, particularly in relation to contracts. However, some contracts, in particular real property leases, may contain "change of control" restrictions that, in practice, require similar consents to those that may be required in connection with an asset deal. Since most business permits are non-transferable, a share deal may be preferred where the application for new permits on the completion of an asset transfer would be cumbersome. Similarly, share purchase transactions may be more simple where employees, pension plans and/or benefit plans are also to be transferred to the purchaser.

Finally, the parties to an asset transaction may be required to comply with the Bulk Sales Act in Ontario which requires compliance with a complicated payment methodology that makes provision for the payment of a seller's unsecured creditors.

Tax Considerations

In an asset sale, any "recapture" of capital cost allowance (depreciation for tax purposes) on a sale of depreciable property and any gain on the sale of inventory would normally be treated as ordinary income of the seller for income tax purposes. Any gains on the sale of most assets above the "recaptured" capital cost allowance would normally be treated as a capital gain of the seller. One half of capital gains are included in income for Canadian tax purposes. Typically, any gain realized by a seller of shares would be treated as a capital gain. In addition, where the seller is an individual, up to CAD 500,000 of the gain may be sheltered under the lifetime capital gains exemption, provided the shares constitute "qualified property". Thus, a typical seller may prefer a share transaction to an asset transaction from an income tax perspective.

A purchaser of assets would generally be entitled to use the full amount of the purchase price allocated to each class of asset as the basis for calculating capital cost allowance for future taxation years. Following a share sale, the tax cost of assets held by a corporation will normally not change and the purchaser will, in effect, inherit the seller's depreciated tax cost of the assets. Thus, a typical purchaser may prefer an asset transaction to a share transaction from an income tax perspective. However, there are some circumstances where the tax cost of certain assets may be "bumped" following a share transaction, eroding the principal advantage to the purchaser of an asset sale. In addition, if the target corporation has "loss carry forwards", those may be more easily accessed by a purchaser following a share sale.

2. Distinction between Sale and Transfer in Rem

A typical purchase agreement includes an obligation of the seller to sell and an obligation of the purchaser to buy the assets, subject to the satisfaction of any conditions set out in the purchase agreement. The transfer of title to the purchased assets may be completed by a separate bill of sale or similar instrument in respect of most of the purchased assets. The conveyance of real property requires the execution, delivery and registration of title conveyance documents in registrable form. Similarly, certain other assets (including certain intellectual property, aircraft, ships and motor vehicles) may require registrable conveyance instruments.

3. Regional Differences

Property rights are a matter of provincial jurisdiction. Accordingly, the legal requirements to implement a transfer of assets may vary from province to province. However, the laws relating to asset transfers are, in general, very similar particularly in the common law provincial jurisdictions (i.e., all provinces, outside of Québec). While Québec is a civil law jurisdiction, as a practical matter, there are few significant differences. These differences include the use of notaries public in the transfers of immovable (real) property and the rules relating to the use of the French language.

Certain categories of assets are regulated by the federal government (including intellectual property, aircraft and ships). Federal registrations may be required to complete transfers of such assets.

4. Acquisition by Foreigners

Investment Canada Act

When foreign investors acquire assets of an existing Canadian business (whether from a Canadian or a non-Canadian), they are subject to the Investment Canada Act (ICA). Although this document addresses the ICA only in its application to corporations, the Act also covers partnerships, trusts and joint ventures. Under the ICA, a "non-Canadian corporation" exists whenever individuals who are neither Canadian citizens nor members of specified classes of Canadian permanent residents hold ultimate control, through ownership of voting shares.

Reviewable and Notifiable Transactions

The book value of the acquired business' assets, the industry in which that business operates, and the investor's nationality together determine whether the non-Canadian investor must simply notify the Investment Review Division of Industry Canada (the Division) or file a more onerous application for review with the Division. Consequently, it is important to recognize the distinction between a reviewable transaction and a notifiable transaction.

Until newly amended provisions are proclaimed into force, a transaction subject to the ICA is a reviewable transaction if the acquired Canadian business' book value, as seen in its most recent financial statements, exceeds the applicable threshold. If the investor is a "WTO Investor", direct acquisitions of a Canadian business are reviewable only if the book value of the acquired business' assets exceeds an annually adjusted threshold (currently CAD 312 million). A WTO Investor is defined as an investor ultimately controlled by nationals of World Trade Organization member states.

A lower review threshold of CAD 5 million is applicable for acquisitions in the so-called "cultural" sector. Moreover, the Federal Cabinet, at its discretion, may initiate review of investments even below these thresholds in the cultural sector. The Cabinet frequently does exercise this right to review cultural sector transactions. Any review in this sector is conducted by the Department of Canadian Heritage instead of the Division.

If the book value of the acquired Canadian business' assets exceeds the applicable threshold for review, the investor must file an application for review and obtain the approval of the Minister of Industry before implementing the transaction. In deciding whether to approve the reviewable transaction, the Minister considers whether the investment "is likely to be of net benefit to Canada". This determination is made on the basis of economic and policy criteria included in the ICA. Often, the investor must be prepared to meet with government officials and give undertakings concerning the acquired business.

The approval process begins with an initial review period of 45 days from the date the completed application is received. However, the Minister of Industry has authority to extend the review period unilaterally for 30 more days.

Notifiable transactions involve a far less onerous process. A notifiable transaction exists where the book value of the acquired Canadian business' assets falls below the applicable thresholds described above. Such acquisitions are not subject to review and the investor need only notify the Division of the transaction either before or within 30 days of its completion. To meet the notification requirement, the investor files a simple two-page form.

As noted, recent legislative amendments will, when proclaimed into force, amend the Investment Canada Act to reduce barriers to foreign investment by increasing review thresholds. The review threshold will be raised from a book value of CAD 312 million to an “enterpise value” of CAD 600 million during the two years after the amendments come into force; to CAD 800 million for investments made during the third and fourth years after the amendments come into force; and finally to CAD 1 billion for investments made between the fifth year after the amendments come into force and December 31 of the sixth year. The threshold will be indexed thereafter.

The amended Investment Canada Act allows the Federal Cabinet to review and ultimately block any investment it considers “could be injurious to national security”.

Specific Industry Legislation

In addition to the ICA, other statutes contain ownership and investment restrictions with respect to specified industries, such as financial services, airlines, broadcasting and telecommunications. Any proposed investment or acquisition in these sectors therefore must be assessed in light of the specific regulatory regime to which that industry is subject.

5. Public Registers, Records and Databases

There is no central register maintained in respect of asset transfers in Canada.

Title to and encumbrances affecting real property are publicly recorded in provincially administered land registry offices. In some jurisdictions, real property title and encumbrances may be searched on line. All information in the land registry offices is publicly available.

There is no central register for title to personal property. Title to certain intellectual property including trademarks, patents and industrial designs are publicly registered and searchable online.

Security interests in personal property are registered in a public registry, searchable by debtor and, in respect of certain assets, by the serial number of the asset. Outside Québec, all jurisdictions have enacted similar personal property security legislation governing the creation, perfection and priority of security interests in personal property. Such legislation resembles Article 9 of the United States Uniform Commercial Code (UCC). Within Québec, Canada’s only civil law jurisdiction, the Civil Code codifies a personal or “movable” property security registration system that contemplates the use of a hypothec as the most common form of security in that province.

Corporation information concerning Canadian reporting issuers (public companies) is publicly available from the databases maintained by the provincial securities regulators. Limited information is available in respect of non-reporting issuers (private companies) including articles of incorporation, location of head office and names and contact information for directors and officers. Financial information and information regarding shareholders of private companies is generally not publicly available in Canada.

6. Purchase Price Requirements

The parties to an asset purchase transaction are free to set the purchase price and select the currency in which it is stated. The parties will typically agree on the allocation of the purchase price among the classes of purchased assets and agree to file all tax returns, etc. in accordance with such allocation. In general, where the parties are at arm's length, the Canadian tax authorities will accept the parties' allocation of the purchase price. Allocation of the purchase price to each parcel of real property is also required in connection with the calculation of land transfer tax (discussed in I, 2 below).

B. Tangible/Movable Assets

1. Characteristics as to:

a) Language of Documentation. Canada is officially bilingual and the two national languages are English and French. French is the primary language in the province of Québec and English is the primary language in the rest of the country, although the province of New Brunswick is officially bilingual.

Sale documents regarding tangible assets may be drafted in any language. Bilingual documents are permitted. Documents do not need to be translated into English or French. However, there is legislation in the province of Québec relating to the protection of the French language. Accordingly, where a language other than French is used for a legal document that is governed by the laws of Québec, the parties should include a provision in the language of the document and in French stating that it is their express wish that the document be drawn up in the applicable language.

b) Form of Documentation. The transfer of tangible assets does not require a special form. Oral agreements are valid. For the sake of provability, written form is nonetheless recommended and is usual practice.

Sale documents may be executed outside Canada. Signing in counterparts is permissible.

c) Specification of Assets. As a general rule, the assets to be transferred must be described and determined or determinable in the transfer agreement with sufficient particularity that a third party will be able to distinguish the assets from any other non-transferred assets. In order to accomplish this, the use of asset lists (or schedules) is recommended but not mandatory. Description by category or location is sufficient. The transfer of "all assets" located at a certain place (e.g., a warehouse) is typically a sufficient description; however, there is the risk of proving what assets were present at such location at the applicable time.

2. Administrative, Corporate and Other Approvals

The transfer of tangible assets generally does not require special governmental or administrative approval. However, exceptions might apply with regard to special categories of assets: see the discussion of the Investment Canada Act and of Specific Industry Legislation in A, 4 above. Also, see the discussion of the Competition Act in K, 1 below.

In order to determine required corporate approvals, it is necessary to review the constating documents, by-laws and applicable resolutions for the applicable corporation. In transactions, it is common practice for the purchaser and the vendor to each deliver a certificate of a senior officer of the applicable corporation which certifies copies of such constating documents, by-laws and applicable resolutions. Note that analogous documents should also be certified, delivered and reviewed for non-corporate entities such as trusts or partnerships. Historically, for larger transactions in Canada, it has also been customary for each of the seller and the purchaser to deliver an opinion of respective counsel that all corporate approvals have been obtained (or analogous approvals for non-corporate entities). The scope of such opinions is a matter of negotiation and the practice in each province. Constating documents may include, as applicable, articles of incorporation, articles of amendment, articles of amalgamation and/or a unanimous shareholder agreement. Analogous documents for a trust and/or partnership may include a trust indenture, a declaration of trust and/or a partnership agreement, as applicable. With respect to corporate sellers, if the seller will be selling all or substantially all of its assets, the approval of its shareholders by special resolution is required by statute in most Canadian jurisdictions. There is often an analogous requirement for trusts and partnerships; however the requirement derives from the analogous documents and not from statute. While non-compliance may affect the validity of the transfer for corporations, most Canadian statutes provide that no act of a corporation including any transfer of property to or by the corporation is invalid by reason only that the act or transfer is contrary to its constating documents, by-laws or the applicable statute. The counterparty may rely on the act of the corporation unless such counterparty knew or ought to have known of a failure to comply with the constating documents, by-laws or statute.

Where assets are encumbered or used as collateral, the seller may not have the right to sell the assets to the purchaser and the purchaser must proceed with extreme caution. Outside Québec, all jurisdictions have enacted similar personal property security legislation governing the creation, perfection and priority of security interests in personal property. Such legislation resembles Article 9 of the United States Uniform Commercial Code (UCC). In most cases, the security interest itself is created under a general security agreement or other instrument and the creditor perfects its security interest by registering a financing statement. Where a security interest in assets is validly created, attached and perfected, the purchaser of these assets will acquire title to the assets subject to the security interest.

Québec, Canada's only civil law jurisdiction, has a European-style Civil Code that codifies the province's general principles of law. The hypothec, Québec's main form of security, may be granted by a debtor to secure any obligation, and may create a charge on existing and after-acquired movable or immovable property. The seller's ability to sell assets, and the title in the assets to be acquired by the purchaser, will be subject to the terms of the foregoing.

3. Filing Requirements

No filings with public authorities or registrations into public registers or databases are required in respect of the transfer of most tangible assets. Certain tangible assets are subject to specific registration requirements including aircraft, ships and motor vehicles.

4. Automatic Transfer of Encumbrances

As a general rule, if encumbrances on tangible assets are validly created, attached and perfected, such encumbrances would defeat the interest of the purchaser in the sold assets. Accordingly, it is important that such encumbrances are released or that the transaction has the consent of the secured party. A bona fide purchaser of assets for value without notice of an unperfected security interest would generally take title to those assets without the encumbrance.

C. Real Property

1. Characteristics as to:

a) Language of Documentation. Canada is officially bilingual and the two national languages are English and French. French is the primary language in the province of Québec and English is the primary language in the rest of the country, although the province of New Brunswick is officially bilingual.

Generally, the sale and transfer documents regarding real property may be drafted in any language. Bilingual documents are permitted. Documents do not need to be translated into English or French. However, there is legislation in the province of Québec relating to the protection of the French language. Accordingly, where a language other than French is used for a legal document, the parties should include a provision in the language of the document and in French stating that it is their express wish that the document be drawn up in the applicable language. Typically the form of transfer document to be registered on title to the real property will be a prescribed form and therefore the language will be dictated by such prescribed form.

b) Form of Documentation. Each province has unique requirements for documenting the transfer of real property. In many provinces the transfer document to be registered against title to the real property will need to be originals. Counterparts will not be permitted. In provinces that have moved to the electronic registration systems, these requirements are becoming unnecessary. In addition, in Québec, the transfer documentation must be signed before a Québec notary.

c) Specification of Assets. A precise legal description and/or registry identification number and not merely a municipal address is required by the transfer documentation for real property in each province.

2. Administrative, Corporate and Other Approvals

The transfer of real property generally does not require special governmental or administrative approvals. However, exceptions might apply with regard to special categories of assets: see the discussion of the Investment Canada Act in A, 4 above. Also, see the discussion of the Competition Act in K, 1 below.

In order to determine required corporate approvals, it is necessary to review the constating documents, by-laws and applicable resolutions for the applicable corporation. In transactions, it is common practice for the purchaser and the vendor to each deliver a certificate of a senior officer of the applicable corporation which certifies copies of such constating documents, by-laws and applicable resolutions. Note that analogous documents should also be certified, delivered and reviewed for non-corporate entities such as trusts or partnerships. Historically, for larger transactions in Canada, it has also been customary for each of the seller and the purchaser to deliver an opinion of respective counsel that all corporate approvals have been obtained (or analogous approvals for non-corporate entities). The scope of such opinions is a matter of negotiation and the practice in each province. Constating documents may include, as applicable, articles of incorporation, articles of amendment, articles of amalgamation and/or a unanimous shareholder agreement. Analogous documents for a trust and/or partnership may include a trust indenture, a declaration of trust and/or a partnership agreement, as applicable. With respect to corporate sellers, if the seller will be selling all or substantially all of its assets, the approval of its shareholders by special resolution is required by statute in most Canadian jurisdictions. There is often an analogous requirement for trusts and partnerships; however the requirement derives from the analogous documents and not from statute. While non-compliance may affect the validity of the transfer for corporations, most Canadian statutes provide that any act of the corporation including any transfer of property, to or by a corporation is invalid by reason only that the act or transfer is contrary to its articles or the applicable statute and the counterparty may rely on the act of the corporation unless such counterparty knew or ought to have known of a failure to comply with the constating documents or by-laws.

Where real property is encumbered or used as collateral, the seller may not have the right to sell the assets to the purchaser and the purchaser must proceed with extreme caution. Generally, the rule in Canada is "first in time, first in line". This refers to the order in which registrations are made in the applicable real property registry. The seller's ability to sell the real property, and the title in the real property to be acquired by the purchaser, will be subject to the terms of the encumbrances registered before the transfer. One encumbrance of particular concern is a mortgage. Most mortgages state that it is an event of default to transfer the real property without the consent of the secured party. So, where the real property is subject to a mortgage it is important to obtain a discharge or the consent of the secured party.

3. Filing Requirements

While transfer documentation for the purchased real property may be valid as between a seller and a purchaser, generally, it will not be valid as against third parties unless registered in the applicable government registry. Accordingly, almost universally in Canada, purchasers of real property require that the transfer be registered in the applicable government registry and such registration may be a requirement of the lender for funding the closing. If, however, the purchaser is obtaining title insurance in respect of the purchased real property, it may be possible to obtain "gap coverage" which would insure the purchaser's interest in the real property and, if applicable, the lender, for the period from delivery of the transfer documentation until the time of registration and certification.

4. Automatic Transfer of Encumbrances

As a general rule, if encumbrances on real property are validly created and perfected, such encumbrances follow the land and would defeat the interest of the purchaser in the real property. Accordingly, it is important that such encumbrances are released or that the transaction has the consent of the secured party.

5. Automatic Transfer of Lease Agreements

In Ontario, if the purchaser has notice of a real property tenancy either by registered notice of lease, information in a purchase agreement or gained through due diligence or a site inspection, then the purchaser's rights will be subject to the rights of the tenant. Whether the lease is assignable or whether there are termination rights would be governed by the terms of the lease. Many leases contain a provision that assignment without consent gives rise to a right to terminate but again these rights would be contained in the lease. In Quebec, if the lease is not registered against title to the real property and the purchaser has not assumed the lease, the purchaser may be able to terminate a tenancy that is in excess of 12 months, at the end of the 12 month period after acquisition upon 6 months' notice to such tenant.

D. Contracts

1. Characteristics as to:

a) Language of Documentation. Canada is officially bilingual and the two national languages are English and French. French is the primary language in the province of Québec and English is the primary language in the rest of the country, although the province of New Brunswick is officially bilingual.

Sale documents regarding contracts may be drafted in any language. Bilingual documents are permitted. Documents do not need to be translated into English or French. However, there is legislation in the province of Québec relating to the protection of the French language. Accordingly, where a language other than French is used for a legal document that is governed by the laws of Québec, the parties should include a provision in the language of the document and in French stating that it is their express wish that the document be drawn up in the applicable language.

b) Form of Documentation. The transfer of contracts does not generally require a special form. Oral agreements are valid. For the sake of provability, written form is nonetheless recommended and is usual practice.

Sale documents may be executed outside Canada. Signing in counterparts is permissible.

The foregoing notwithstanding, it is always important to consult the terms of the contract to be assigned. The contract may mandate requirements with regard to the form of an effective transfer.

c) Specification of Contracts. Transferring contracts has two elements: (a) an assignment of the benefits under the contract by the seller and (b) an assumption of the obligations under the contract by the purchaser. Generally, subject to the terms of the contract, the benefits of a contract may be assigned to a third party, however, the obligations under a contract may not be assigned. Therefore, unless a release is obtained from the counterparty to the contract, a seller will continue to be liable for the obligations under an assigned contract, notwithstanding an assumption by the purchaser of such obligations. Accordingly, the seller must consider whether it wishes to require that a release be obtained from the counterparty as condition of closing the transaction of purchase and sale.

In considering the form of transfer documentation, it is important to consult the terms of the contract to be transferred. The contract may limit or prohibit transfer or provide that consent to transfer must be obtained from the counterparty as discussed below. Accordingly, the delivery of such consents to transfer is, where required, typically a condition of closing the transaction of purchase and sale.

As a general rule, the contracts to be transferred must be described and determined or determinable in the transfer agreement with sufficient particularity that a third party will be able to distinguish the transferred contracts from any other non-transferred assets. To accomplish this, the use of contract lists (or schedules) is recommended but not mandatory. Such lists may also enumerate any required consents to transfer. General (e.g., "all contracts related to the business") or generic descriptions (e.g., "all customer contracts") are sufficient; however, because contracts include obligations as well as entitlements, parties generally try to be as specific as possible in their descriptions. A purchaser is typically careful not to become obliged for unwanted or unknown contractual obligations.

2. Administrative, Corporate and Other Approvals

The transfer of contracts generally does not require special governmental or administrative approvals. However, exceptions might apply with regard to special categories of contracts: see the discussion of the Investment Canada Act and Specific Industry Legislation in A, 4 above. Also, see the discussion of the Competition Act in K, 1 below.

In order to determine required corporate approvals, it is necessary to review the constating documents, by-laws and applicable resolutions for the applicable corporation. In transactions, it is common practice for the purchaser and the vendor to each deliver a certificate of a senior officer of the applicable corporation which certifies copies of such constating documents, by-laws and applicable resolutions. Note that analogous documents should also be certified, delivered and reviewed for non-corporate entities such as trusts or partnerships. Historically, for larger transactions in Canada, it has also been customary for each of the seller and the purchaser to deliver an opinion of respective counsel that all corporate approvals have been obtained (or analogous approvals for non-corporate entities). The scope of such opinions is a matter of negotiation and the practice in each province. Constating documents may include, as applicable, articles of incorporation, articles of amendment, articles of amalgamation and/or a unanimous shareholder agreement. Analogous documents for a trust and/or partnership may include a trust indenture, a declaration of trust and/or a partnership agreement, as applicable. With respect to corporate sellers, if the seller will be selling all or substantially all of its assets, the approval of its shareholders by special resolution is required by statute in most Canadian jurisdictions. There is often an analogous requirement for trusts and partnerships; however, the requirement derives from the analogous documents and not from statute. While non-compliance may affect the validity of the transfer for corporations, most Canadian statutes provide that no act of a corporation including any transfer of property to or by the corporation is invalid by reason only that the act or transfer is contrary to its constating documents, by-laws or the applicable statute. The counterparty may rely on the act of the corporation unless such counterparty knew or ought to have known of a failure to comply with the constating documents, by-laws or statute.

Generally, contracts may be transferred without consent of the counterparty unless either (a) the terms of the contract prohibit transfer or state that consent to transfer is required or (b) the contract is a personal service contract that contemplates services that can only be provided by specific individuals. However, unless a release is obtained from the counterparty to the contract, the seller will continue to be liable to the counterparty for the obligations under the contract notwithstanding an assumption by the purchaser of such obligations. Accordingly, the seller must consider whether it wishes to require that a release be obtained from the counterparty as condition of closing the transaction of purchase and sale.

3. Automatic Transfer of Contracts (Other than Lease and Employment Agreements)

Contracts do not generally automatically transfer to the purchaser in the event of an asset deal, unless the terms of the contract have a specific provision to such effect.

4. Filing Requirements

Regarding the transfer of contracts, no filings with public authorities or registrations into public registers or databases are required. However, if the contract is a security contract (i.e., it grants a security interest in favour of the seller against a third party) or the seller has otherwise registered against the third party under applicable personal property security legislation, the purchaser may wish to update the related filing to describe the transfer.

5. Treatment of Existing Contractual Claims and Obligations

It is customary for the purchaser to indemnify the seller in respect of the contractual obligations assumed by the purchaser.

6. Warranty Claims Resulting from Events prior to Transfer

The purchaser is not generally liable for warranty claims resulting from events prior to the transfer of the assets affected. However, in many asset transactions, the seller is no longer in a position to handle warranty claims post-closing and, accordingly, bargains for an assumption of such claims by the purchaser. Also, it may be difficult to distinguish whether events are prior to or after the transfer of the assets. For example, when the purchaser uses packaging acquired from the seller or sells products produced by the seller prior to closing. Accordingly, where the risk of warranty claims is high (for example, where the applicable business sells consumer goods), it is customary to clearly delineate warranty claims which are excluded and those which are assumed. It is also customary to have cross indemnities to protect the seller and the purchaser from the respective claims.

E. IP Rights

1. Characteristics of Intellectual Property Rights (e. g., Trade Marks, Patents, Utility Models, Domain Names) ("*IP Rights*") as to:

a) Language of Documentation. Intellectual property in Canada is subject to the jurisdiction of the federal government. The Canadian Intellectual Property Office administers Canada's IP laws and regulations and grants or registers ownership of the following five types of intellectual property: copyright, trade marks, patents, industrial designs and integrated circuit board topographies. Each of these types of intellectual property rights has a separate registry where ownership, transfers and encumbrances are registered.

Canada is officially bilingual and the two national languages are English and French. French is the primary language in the province of Québec and English is the primary language in the rest of the country, although the province of New Brunswick is officially bilingual.

Since they must be registered, sale documents regarding IP Rights should be in English or French. However, there is legislation in the province of Québec relating to the protection of the French language. Accordingly, where a language other than French is used for a legal document that is governed by the laws of Québec, the parties should include a provision in the language of the document and in French stating that it is their express wish that the document be drawn up in the applicable language.

b) Form of Documentation. The transfer of intellectual property assets does not require a special form, however, transfers must be in writing and signed by the owner of the intellectual property. The sale and transfer documents may be executed outside Canada. Signing in counterparts is permissible.

Often the parties to an asset purchase agreement that involves intellectual property will execute one or more intellectual property transfer instruments that evidence the transfer of title to the intellectual property, subject to the terms of the asset purchase agreement. This intellectual property transfer instrument may be registered with the Canadian Intellectual Property Office as discussed below and is typically a short form that does not contain many provisions normally found within an asset purchase agreement. This way, the parties are able to register the transfers of intellectual property without disclosing confidential terms of the asset purchase arrangements. In order to be registered, an asset purchase agreement or an intellectual property transfer instrument must be in English or French.

c) Specification of IP Rights. The intellectual property to be transferred must be described and determined or determinable in the transfer agreement with sufficient particularity that a third party will be able to identify the transferred intellectual property. In addition, sufficient particularity must be included in the transfer instrument to allow for registration. Typically, a list of intellectual property (including the relevant registration numbers) is attached as a schedule to the transfer instrument.

2. Administrative, Corporate and Other Approvals

Copyrights, trade marks, patents, industrial designs and circuit board topography rights may all be transferred without special governmental or administrative approvals. Moral rights, the author or creator's personal rights over the integrity of the work and the right to be associated with the work by name, may not be transferred but may be waived.

In order to determine required corporate approvals, it is necessary to review the constating documents, by-laws and applicable resolutions for the applicable corporation. In transactions, it is common practice for the purchaser and the vendor to each deliver a certificate of a senior officer of the applicable corporation which certifies copies of such constating documents, by-laws and applicable resolutions. Note that analogous documents should also be certified, delivered and reviewed for non-corporate entities such as trusts or partnerships. Historically, for larger transactions in Canada, it has also been customary for each of the seller and the purchaser to deliver an opinion of respective counsel that all corporate approvals have been obtained (or analogous approvals for non-corporate entities). The scope of such opinions is a matter of negotiation and the practice in each province. Constating documents may include, as applicable, articles of incorporation, articles of amendment, articles of amalgamation and/or a unanimous shareholder agreement. Analogous documents for a trust and/or partnership may include a trust indenture, a declaration of trust and/or a partnership agreement, as applicable. With respect to corporate sellers, if the seller will be selling all or substantially all of its assets, the approval of its shareholders by special resolution is required by statute in most Canadian jurisdictions. There is often an analogous requirement for trusts and partnerships; however, the requirement derives from the analogous documents and not from statute. While non-compliance may affect the validity of the transfer for corporations, most Canadian statutes provide that no act of a corporation including any transfer of property to or by the corporation is invalid by reason only that the act or transfer is contrary to its constating documents, by-laws or the applicable statute. The counterparty may rely on the act of the corporation unless such counterparty knew or ought to have known of a failure to comply with the constating documents, by-laws or statute.

Encumbrances of intellectual property may be registered under the applicable provincial personal property security regime and also in the intellectual property registries maintained by the Canadian Intellectual Property Office. Both federal and provincial registries have jurisdiction over the granting of security of other encumbrances in intellectual property. Under the doctrine of Federal paramountcy, Federal laws will govern to the extent that they address the particular issue. Therefore, with regard to encumbrances over copyright and patents, Federal law will govern as it specifically addresses the registration of transfers. For trade-marks and industrial designs, the law is less clear but the recommended action is to register the encumbrance in both provincial and federal registries. Therefore, prior to completion of an asset transfer including intellectual property, a purchaser will wish to search both provincial and federal registries for encumbrances and deal with such encumbrances as a condition of closing.

3. Filing Requirements

In order to protect its interests in the transferred intellectual property, the purchaser must register the transfer in the applicable registry maintained by the Canadian Intellectual Property Office. These registrations are declaratory in nature and, as between the parties, a transfer of intellectual property is generally effective without registration.

4. Applicable International (Multilateral) Agreements or Treaties

Canada is a party to all major treaties relating to intellectual property rights such as the Paris Convention for Trademarks, Industrial Designs and Patents, the Patent Cooperation Treaty signed in Washington, the Berne Convention and the Rome Convention for copyrights and the Agreement of Trade-Related Aspects of Intellectual Property Rights, including trade in counterfeit goods (TRIPs). However, Canada is not a member of the Madrid Protocol or the Nice Agreement concerning international classification of goods and services.

F. Receivables

1. Characteristics as to:

a) Language of Documentation. Canada is officially bilingual and the two national languages are English and French. French is the primary language in the province of Québec and English is the primary language in the rest of the country, although the province of New Brunswick is officially bilingual.

Sale documents regarding receivables may be drafted in any language. Bilingual documents are permitted. Documents do not need to be translated into English or French. However, there is legislation in the province of Québec relating to the protection of the French language. Accordingly, where a language other than French is used for a legal document that is governed by the laws of Québec, the parties should include a provision in the language of the document and in French stating that it is their express wish that the document be drawn up in the applicable language.

b) Form of Documentation. The transfer of receivables does not generally require a special form. Oral agreements are valid. For the sake of provability, written form is nonetheless recommended and is usual practice.

Sale documents may be executed outside Canada. Signing in counterparts is permissible.

The foregoing notwithstanding, it is always important to consult the terms of the contract under which the assigned receivables arose. The contract may mandate requirements for a particular form of transfer.

c) Specification of Receivables. In considering the form of transfer documentation, it is important to consult the terms of the contract under which the assigned receivable arose. The contract may limit or prohibit transfer or provide for consent to transfer to be obtained from the counterparty as discussed below. Accordingly, the delivery of such consents to transfer is, where required, a typical condition of closing the transaction of purchase and sale.

As a general rule, receivables to be transferred must be described and determined or determinable in the transfer agreement with sufficient particularity that a third party will be able to distinguish the receivables from any other non-transferred receivables. To accomplish this, the use of receivable lists (or schedules) is recommended but not mandatory. Such lists may also enumerate any required consents to transfer. General (e.g., "all receivables related to the business") or generic descriptions (e.g., "all receivables from customers") are sufficient.

2. Administrative, Corporate and Other Approvals

The transfer of receivables generally does not require special governmental or administrative approvals. However, exceptions might apply with regard to special categories of receivables: see the discussion of the Investment Canada Act and Specific Industry Legislation in A, 4 above. Also, see the discussion of the Competition Act in K, 1 below.

In order to determine required corporate approvals, it is necessary to review the constating documents, by-laws and applicable resolutions for the applicable corporation. In transactions, it is common practice for the purchaser and the vendor to each deliver a certificate of a senior officer of the applicable corporation which certifies copies of such constating documents, by-laws and applicable resolutions. Note that analogous documents should also be certified, delivered and reviewed for non-corporate entities such as trusts or partnerships. Historically, for larger transactions in Canada, it has also been customary for each of the seller and the purchaser to deliver an opinion of respective counsel that all corporate approvals have been obtained (or analogous approvals for non-corporate entities). The scope of such opinions is a matter of negotiation and the practice in each province. Constating documents may include, as applicable, articles of incorporation, articles of amendment, articles of amalgamation and/or a unanimous shareholder agreement. Analogous documents for a trust and/or partnership may include a trust indenture, a declaration of trust and/or a partnership agreement, as applicable. With respect to corporate sellers, if the seller will be selling all or substantially all of its assets, the approval of its shareholders by special resolution is required by statute in most Canadian jurisdictions. There is often an analogous requirement for trusts and partnerships; however the requirement derives from the analogous documents and not from statute. While non-compliance may affect the validity of the transfer for corporations, most Canadian statutes provide that no act of a corporation including any transfer of property to or by the corporation is invalid by reason only that the act or transfer is contrary to its constating documents, by-laws or the applicable statute. The counterparty may rely on the act of the corporation unless such counterparty knew or ought to have known of a failure to comply with the constating documents, by-laws or statute.

There are specific rules regarding the assignment of consumer receivables. The right of set-off and other defences that may be available to a consumer against the seller of a receivable are, in some circumstances, preserved as against an assignee of that receivable. In addition, as part of its due diligence, a purchaser may wish to ensure that the transactions that generated consumer receivables were completed in accordance with applicable consumer protection legislation.

Generally, receivables may be transferred without consent of the debtor unless either the terms of the contract under which the debt arose prohibits transfer or state that consent to transfer is required. In the event that such prohibition exists or consent to assignment is required, generally the transfer will be valid as between the purchaser and the seller, however, there will be a breach of contract which may entitle the debtor to terminate such contract and/or claim damages.

3. Filing Requirements

Regarding the transfer of receivables, no filings with public authorities or registrations into public registers or databases are required. However, it is possible for the purchaser to better protect its entitlement to the receivables by making a filing under applicable personal property security legislation.

While the transfer of the receivables is valid as between the seller and the purchaser when the applicable transfer documentation is executed and delivered, an assignment or transfer of a receivable is not binding as against the debtor under the receivable until the debtor has received notice of the assignment or transfer. Thus, until notice is delivered, a debtor may continue to make payments to an assignor of a receivable and any such payment validly discharges the debtor's obligations to the extent of such payment. Therefore, a typical asset purchase agreement: (a) provides that any payment received by the seller/assignor of a receivable is received in trust by the seller for the purchaser and be paid over to the purchaser promptly, and (b) includes as a condition to closing that significant account debtors are notified of the sale of receivables directed to make future payments to the purchaser and acknowledge receipt of such notice and direction.

G. Liabilities

1. Characteristics as to:

a) Language of Documentation. Canada is officially bilingual and the two national languages are English and French. French is the primary language in the province of Québec and English is the primary language in the rest of the country, although the province of New Brunswick is officially bilingual.

Sale documents regarding liabilities may be drafted in any language. Bilingual documents are permitted. Documents do not need to be translated into English or French. However, there is legislation in the province of Québec relating to the protection of the French language. Accordingly, where a language other than French is used for a legal document that is governed by the laws of Québec, the parties should include a provision in the language of the document and in French stating that it is their express wish that the document be drawn up in the applicable language.

b) Form of Documentation. The transfer of liabilities does not generally require a special form. Oral agreements are valid. For the sake of provability, written form is nonetheless recommended and is usual practice.

Assignment documents may be executed outside Canada. Signing in counterparts is permissible.

The foregoing notwithstanding, it is always important to consult the terms of the contract under which the liability arose. The contract may mandate requirements for a particular form of assignment.

c) Specification of Liabilities. Unless a release is obtained from the creditor or obligee of a liability, a seller will continue to be liable for the obligations under an assigned liability, notwithstanding an assumption by the purchaser of such obligations. Accordingly, the seller must consider whether it wishes to require that a release be obtained from the creditor or obligee as condition of closing the transaction of purchase and sale.

As a general rule, the liabilities to be transferred must be identified in the assignment instrument with sufficient particularity that a third party will be able to distinguish transferred liabilities from any other liabilities of the Seller. To accomplish this, the use of a list (or schedule) of liabilities is recommended but not mandatory. General (e.g., "all liabilities related to the business") or generic description (e.g., "all accounts payable") are sufficient, however, a purchaser typically tries to be as specific as possible in the description of the liabilities to be assigned in order to ensure that it does not become obliged for unwanted or unknown liabilities.

2. Administrative, Corporate and Other Approvals

The transfer of liabilities generally does not require special governmental or administrative approval. The approval of any corporate bodies is not generally required unless otherwise provided for in seller's and/or purchaser's constating documents or partnership agreement.

A transfer of liabilities without the consent of a creditor or obligee may be effective as between the purchaser and the seller, but will not be effective against the creditor or obligee who will retain its rights against the seller. However, unless a release is obtained from the creditor or obligee, the seller will continue to be liable to the creditor or obligee for the liabilities notwithstanding an assumption by the purchaser of such obligations. Accordingly, the seller must consider whether it wishes to require that a release be obtained from the creditor or obligee as condition of closing the transaction of purchase and sale.

3. Filing Requirements

The transfer of liabilities does not require special filings with public authorities or registrations into registers or databases. Where a liability is transferred with the consent of the creditor or obligee and such liability is secured by a registered security interest against assets to be transferred to the Purchaser, the creditor or obligee may require the registration of a financing change statement pursuant to a relevant provincial Personal Property Security Act in respect of the transfer.

4. Purchaser's Liability for:

a) Tax Obligations. Except in a situation involving bankruptcy of a transferor, taxing authorities are, in general, in the same position as other creditors of a seller and a bona fide purchaser will not become liable for tax liabilities generated by the seller prior to the acquisition. However, in the provinces that impose provincial retail sales tax (PST)

(Ontario, Manitoba, Saskatchewan, British Columbia and Prince Edward Island), a purchaser of assets may in some circumstances become liable for PST collectible by the seller prior to the acquisition unless the purchaser obtains, as a condition of closing, a certificate from the applicable province(s) certifying that no PST is owing by the seller.

b) Environmental Contamination. Any person or entity in possession or control of real property that is affected by environmental contamination may be responsible for liabilities relating to environmental remediation. Typically, a purchaser of real property would conduct an environmental assessment of the real property and other environmental due diligence prior to completion of the purchase in order to assess any potential liability for environmental contamination.

c) Products Sold or Services Rendered by the Seller to Third Parties. A purchaser would not become liable for product liability claims arising prior to a purchase of assets. In some circumstances, a purchaser may wish to assume these obligations from the seller in order to control all product liability claims following closing, however, there is not automatic transfer of liability for these claims.

5. Automatic Transfer of Other Liabilities

In general, liabilities of a seller do not automatically pass to a purchaser. However, in Ontario, the parties must comply with the provisions of the Bulk Sales Act or the sale may be declared void on the application of an unpaid creditor of the seller. The Bulk Sales Act requires that the parties comply with a cumbersome payment methodology that makes provision for the payment of the seller's unsecured creditors or otherwise make adequate provision for the payment of these creditors. In some circumstances, the parties may obtain a court order exempting a transaction from the application of the Bulk Sales Act. Where a purchaser is satisfied of a seller's credit worthiness, the parties may agree to not comply with the Bulk Sales Act and in these circumstances the seller would typically provide an indemnity to the purchaser in respect of the non-compliance. Where transferred assets (other than inventory transferred in the ordinary course of business) are encumbered by a validly created, attached and perfected (registered) security interest in favour of a third party, the purchaser takes such assets subject to the security interest. Accordingly, a personal property security search is typically conducted as part of due diligence and the interests of any secured parties are dealt with prior to the completion of the purchase.

6. Contractual Protection as to 4 and 5 above

An asset purchase agreement typically contains representations and warranties to the effect that there are no liens for the seller's unpaid taxes that affect the purchased assets. Similarly, an asset purchase agreement typically contains representations and warranties regarding the environmental condition of any properties to be transferred, including leasehold interests. Many asset purchase agreements contain indemnity provisions for misrepresentations and breaches of warranties.

Many asset purchase agreements contain provisions regarding the respective responsibilities of the purchaser and seller regarding past and future product liability claims and indemnity provisions in respect of any failure to comply with the agreed division of responsibility.

As noted above in G, 5, an indemnity for failure to comply with the Bulk Sales Act (Ontario) may be included in an agreement of purchase and sale.

H. Employees

1. Transfer of Employees

Employment law is, for most part, a matter of provincial jurisdiction. There are many differences among the laws of the various provinces, some of which are substantial. This section focuses on the laws of Ontario. Somewhat different results may arise under the laws of other provinces. Local counsel should always be consulted in connection with employment matters.

In considering the position of a purchaser relative to employees of the seller in a purchase and sale of assets, it is useful to distinguish between non-unionized employees and unionized employees.

Non-Unionized Employees

Non-unionized employees do not automatically transfer to the purchaser as a result of an asset sale. Rather, such employees are generally considered to have been dismissed by the seller upon closing the transaction of purchase and sale. However, if the purchaser offers employment to employees of the seller, then the employment of any employee who accepts such offer is deemed not to be terminated or severed for the purposes of employment standards legislation.

Customarily, the seller negotiates for offers of employment to be made by the purchaser to those employees to be transferred to the purchaser on substantially similar (or substantially the same) terms as those that the employees had with the seller. If any employee chooses not to accept an offer on substantially similar terms, the employee's ability to recover damages for wrongful dismissal against the seller will typically be limited by his/her failure to appropriately mitigate his/her losses (particularly with respect to common law as opposed to statutory damages). Employees who reject the purchaser's offer of employment will nonetheless be entitled to statutory notice of termination (or pay in lieu thereof) and statutory severance pay (if applicable).

Often, however, the purchaser does not want to hire all of the employees of the seller. Accordingly, the purchaser may negotiate for the termination of applicable employees pre-closing (and hence the cost of termination would be paid by the seller). On the other hand, the seller will negotiate for the purchaser to make offers to all employees so that the purchaser would be forced to pay any termination obligations following the closing. It is important to note that, in such circumstances, the purchaser will be responsible for termination pay based on the period of employment with the purchaser and the seller and not only for the period of employment with the purchaser. In such circumstances, the purchaser may negotiate for some reimbursement by the seller of the costs of termination attributable to the employees' period of service with the seller. Further, the purchaser may try to limit its liability for termination costs by including termination provisions in its offer letters to employees and providing that employees' service with the seller will only be recognized for the purposes of, and to the extent required by, applicable employment standards legislation. However, this would need to be negotiated with the seller and reflected in the purchase agreement.

Unionized Employees

Whether or not the purchaser offers employment to unionized employees of the seller, the purchaser of a business is bound by any collective agreement binding on the seller which relates to that business. In addition, if there is a pending application for certification or termination of bargaining rights to the Ontario Labour Relations Board (or similar bodies in other provinces), the purchaser becomes the employer for the purposes of such an application. Further, if a trade union or council of trade unions is certified as a bargaining agent for the employees of the seller, such bargaining agent continues to represent the applicable bargaining unit in negotiations and relations with the purchaser.

Canada Pension Plan and Employment Insurance

For employees hired by the purchaser immediately upon the acquisition of all or part of a business, the purchaser may take into account the statutory contributions of the seller under the Employment Insurance Act and the Canada Pension Plan (**"CPP"**), for the transferred employees in the year of the transaction, as if those contributions had been made by the purchaser. If the purchaser takes the seller's contributions into account in determining the employer contributions, it must also take into account the employees' Employment Insurance and CPP contributions for the year.

Private Pension Plans and Other Benefit Plans

Customarily, in order to offer employment to employees on substantially similar terms as their existing employment, the purchaser will need to offer the same or substantially similar pension benefits and other benefits.

With respect to pension benefits, the purchaser typically will want to avoid any funding shortfalls in any existing defined benefits plan and so will want to establish a new mirror plan which applies to the period of employment from and after the closing date. However, the benefits received by employees may be affected by the "mirror plan" approach (as opposed to a purchaser taking over an existing pension plan). This is typically a heavily negotiated provision of the purchase agreement.

With respect to other benefits, if the seller has no other employees who participate in the benefit plan(s), the seller may be willing to transfer such plan(s) to the purchaser. Such plans are generally a contract with a benefits provider. If a plan is to be transferred, it would be prudent for the purchaser to confirm whether there are any outstanding amounts owing by the seller to the provider. The parties should also review applicable contracts to determine if consent to assignment is required. If the seller continues to have employees and requires ongoing benefits plans, the purchaser may establish substantially similar plans.

The purchaser may also negotiate with the seller to include the transferred employees in its own pension and benefit plans.

WSIB

The Workplace Safety and Insurance Act, 1997 (Ontario) (the "**WSIA**") is a government insurance scheme mandated in some industries and optional in others. It is closely replicated in other Canadian jurisdictions. The purchaser will be liable for any amounts owing by the seller under the WSIA and similar legislation in other provinces. Therefore, the purchaser will generally require a Purchase Certificate from the seller verifying that the seller has workplace safety and insurance coverage (where applicable) and that there are no outstanding debts on the account.

2. Approval of Works Council, Trade Union or Other Institutions

With respect to non-unionized employees, an asset transfer generally does not require the approval of any works council, labor agency, trade union or other institution. With respect to unionized employees, it is important to review the collective agreement in order to determine whether there are any restrictions or requirements related to the transfer of assets.

3. Contractual Protection as to Labor Issues

Customarily, an asset sale agreement includes an indemnification by the seller in favour of the purchaser for all liabilities to or in respect of employees, which relate to the period prior to the closing date.

I. Tax Implications

1. Value Added Tax

Federal Goods and Services Tax (GST) and Harmonized Sales Tax (HST)

The GST is a 5% multi-stage value-added tax that generally applies to domestic supplies of most types of property and services within Canada but outside the provinces of Nova Scotia, New Brunswick and Newfoundland and Labrador. Within Nova Scotia, New Brunswick and Newfoundland and Labrador, the 13% HST rate comprises an 8% provincial sales tax component and a 5% federal GST component. GST and HST are not generally intended to be costs of doing business and registered businesses can generally claim input tax credits (ITCs) to recover GST or HST paid by them. GST and HST do apply to asset sales transactions, however, there is an exception where the assets transferred constitute all of the assets of a business. Where available, this exemption may be beneficial to reduce the cash flow impact of GST or HST.

Provincial Sales Tax

Québec levies a 7.5% multi-state value-added Québec sales tax (QST) that generally mirrors the GST/HST. The 7.5% QST is imposed on the 5% GST for an effective combined rate of 12.88% within Québec. The same exemption for a transfer of all assets of a business is available with regard to QST as for GST/HST.

The provinces of Ontario, Manitoba, Saskatchewan, British Columbia and Price Edward Island impose a single stage retail sales tax (tax is paid only by the final consumer, business, institution or individual). The rate of this tax varies from province to province, with the current rate in Ontario being 8%. This tax generally applies to tangible assets transferred on the sale of a business subject to exceptions in some circumstances for goods held for resale (inventory), real property and, in some jurisdictions, manufacturing equipment. Unlike GST/HST and QST, where this tax applies, it represents a real transaction cost to the parties. The province of Ontario has, however, announced that it will eliminate its retail sales tax effective as of July 1, 2010 and it will introduce a replacement 8% multi stage value-added tax harmonized with the GST so that there will be a 13% harmonized tax comprised of an 8% provincial sales tax component and a 5% federal GST component.

2. Real Property Transfer Tax

A buyer of real property in any Canadian province must pay land transfer tax levied by that province based on the value of the consideration paid. The rates of tax vary among the provinces, often increasing with the amount of the consideration.

3. Other Tax Issues

See A, 1 and G, 4, a above.

J. Bankruptcy Law

1. Challenge of Asset Transfer in Case of Insolvency

The Bankruptcy and Insolvency Act (Canada) (the "**BIA**") and the Winding-up and Restructuring Act (Canada) as well as various provincial statutes contain provisions for setting aside asset transfers made prior to insolvency or bankruptcy proceedings. Depending upon the circumstances, these provisions can be used by trustees in bankruptcy, receivers, or creditors in court proceedings to set aside an asset transfer. The statutory provisions are complex and have been subject to much litigation. However, generally, transactions may be set aside by a court in the following circumstances:

- a transaction entered into by an insolvent debtor with the intention of giving any of its creditors a preference over its other creditors;

- a transfer of property made with the intention of defeating, hindering, delaying, defrauding or prejudicing creditors or others of their claims against the transferor;
- a settlement of property where the settlor subsequently becomes bankrupt; and
- a transfer of property made by an insolvent debtor at any time during the thirty (30) day period prior to the commencement of the winding-up of the debtor or thereafter with a person unaware of the debtor's insolvency, which transfer has the effect of injuring or obstructing creditors.

In addition, a transaction entered into by a person who becomes bankrupt within twelve months of the transaction may be reviewed by a court pursuant to the BIA upon the application of the trustee in bankruptcy where the transaction was not at arm's length and the consideration given or received by the bankrupt person was conspicuously greater or less than the fair market value of the property or services concerned in the transaction, and a judgment may be given by the court against the other party to the transaction for the difference between such consideration and such fair market value.

2. Acquisition of Assets that are Subject to Insolvency Proceedings

Both the Bankruptcy and Insolvency Act (Canada) (BIA) and the Companies' Creditors Arrangement Act (Canada) (CCAA) allow debtors to reorganize their affairs. In addition, the BIA contains provisions for the assets of a bankrupt or insolvent debtor to be sold by a trustee or receiver. In CCAA proceedings, assets may be sold to facilitate the reorganization of the debtor.

The specific rules regarding the acquisition of assets which are subject to insolvency proceedings depend on whether the transferor is subject to a proceeding under the BIA or the CCAA. In addition, such rules depend on who is transferring the assets: e. g., the debtor, a secured creditor realizing on its security, or a trustee in bankruptcy. In most cases, approval of the applicable court will be required in order to effect a transfer of the assets.

Generally, the onus will be upon the vendor to satisfy the court that the terms of sale are commercially reasonable and that appropriate efforts were made to canvass the market for purchasers in a fair and transparent sales process.

K. Timing and Costs

1. Timeframe of Asset Transfer

Except where transaction approval is required under the Investment Canada Act or notification is required under the Competition Act, there are few outside constraints on the time frames applicable to the acquisition of a business by way of an asset sale and the parties are free to establish their own timetable.

The Investment Canada Act approval process is discussed in A, 4 above.

The Competition Act applies to any merger, regardless of size, that either occurs in Canada or causes a substantial lessening of competition in Canada. Mergers that stifle competition are regulated by discretionary administrative and civil laws rather than by criminal prohibitions.

Size-of-person and size-of-transaction tests determine pre-merger notification filing requirements in Canada. Parties who, together with their affiliates, do not have Canadian assets or annual gross revenues from sales in, from or into Canada exceeding CAD 400 million are exempt. Pre-merger notification is necessary only if the value of the Canadian assets to be acquired, or annual gross revenues from sales generated by those assets, exceeds CAD 70 million.

Where Competition Act pre-merger notification is required, the parties may not close the transaction until the mandatory waiting period expires. This 30 day period commences when the completed filing is delivered to the Commissioner of Competition (the Commissioner). If during the 30 day waiting period, the Commissioner issues a request for additional information, there is a further no-close waiting period which runs until 30 days after the Commissioner's requirements have been fully satisfied (subject to early termination by the Commissioner).

The Competition Act does not provide for mandatory extension of waiting periods by the Commissioner. In practice, however, the statutory waiting periods are invariably extended by consent in cases where any competitive impact is anticipated. If the parties refuse to grant an extension, the Commissioner may seek early injunctive relief, to prevent closing, or costly post-closure divestiture proceedings.

2. Costs of Asset Transfer

Where Competition Act pre-merger notification is required, the parties are required to submit a fee (currently CAD 50,000) with their application.

Search and registration fees under the various Personal Property Security Acts and intellectual property search and transfer registration fees are nominal.

L. Miscellaneous

1. Choice of Foreign Law

Commercial parties are free to make any agreement between them subject to foreign law and this choice will, in general, be respected by Canadian courts provided that the choice of law is bona fide (in the sense that it was not made with a view to avoiding the consequences of the laws of any other jurisdiction) and is not contrary to public policy as applied by a Canadian court.

2. (International) Arbitration, Choice of Venue

The parties to an asset transaction are free to select whether disputes will be subject to arbitration, choose the rules applicable to any such arbitration (domestic or foreign) and the venue of any such arbitration.

M. Literature

Jennifer E. Babe, Sale of a Business, 6th Edition, 2006

John Swan (et al.), Business Acquisition Agreements: An Annotated Guide, 1st Edition, 1992

China (PRC)

By *Audry (Hong) Li* and *Lefan Gong*

A. General Aspects

1. Asset Deal vs. Share Deal: Essential Considerations

As compared to a share deal, an asset deal in China could mean increased tax obligations and added procedural steps. Often a primary driver behind an asset deal is the uncertainty over the target company's liabilities, including those that are hidden and contingent, which outweighs the taxes and practical hassles that would have otherwise been avoided in a share deal structure. Another benefit to an asset deal is that it allows the purchaser to "cherry pick" certain assets and leaves those "unwanted" assets behind with the seller, whereas an asset and/or obligation carve-out would not otherwise be viable in a share deal. These considerations could become compelling in situations where the target company has an untold amount of liabilities, an unclean history of privatization, or various legacy issues such as a large size of aged work force and unpaid pension plans.

In an asset deal, depending on the assets being sold and acquired, a host of transfer taxes could apply, including business tax, VAT, land appreciation tax (also known as land VAT), stamp duties, and deed tax. Also, the acquirer usually cannot inherit or otherwise take over any government-issued licenses or permits that the target company has. Employees cannot be transferred automatically; the purchaser will have to enter into new employment agreements for those employees transferred from the target company.

In an asset deal, the approaches and procedures of transfer applicable to the various assets would certainly have a bearing on the overall timing of the transaction. For instance, the transfer of land, patents and trademarks will not take effect until the relevant registrations have been made with the relevant government agencies.

If the asset acquisition transaction is subject to the Regulations for Foreign Investors to Merge and Acquire Domestic Enterprises (2006, as last amended in 2009) (the "**M&A Regulations**"), certain statutory procedures will apply and the process could take a few months more before it can close, including time needed for public notification to creditors, arrangement for the target company's employees, and governmental approval of the transaction.

2. Distinction between Sale and Transfer in Rem

Chinese law does not distinguish between the sale of assets and the transfer in rem as the fulfillment of the transfer obligation. In the event a sales and purchase agreement is determined as invalid, the seller may request to have the transaction unwound and assets returned, unless such assets have already been sold to third parties.

3. Regional Differences

In general, there are no regional differences within Mainland China as regards the legal requirements applicable to an asset transfer. However, procedural matters might vary from locale to locale, such as the requirement to use notarization and government boilerplate forms in connection with certain documentation.

4. Acquisition by Foreigners

Without first establishing a business entity and obtaining government approval, no foreigner or foreign entities may acquire assets in order to engage in businesses in China. Therefore, a foreigner or foreign entity would either have to first establish a new entity, or acquire or use an existing one as a vehicle to purchase assets for purposes of business operations. Such entity will usually take the form of Sino-foreign joint venture ("**JV**") or wholly-foreign owned enterprise ("**WFOE**"), both of which require government approval for establishment and are subject to restrictions on foreign investment in the relevant industries and sectors. Such restrictions are generally set out in the Catalogue for Foreign Investment Industries; its latest version was issued by the State Development and Reform Commission ("**SDRC**") and the Ministry of Commerce ("**MOFCOM**") on October 31, 2007.

If a JV or WFOE is to be established solely for purposes of acquiring Chinese assets, such establishment and the proposed assets acquisition will be governed by the M&A Regulations and subject to government approval.

Under the M&A Regulations, the Chinese seller and the foreign purchaser will go through a regulatory process, including asset appraisal, notification to creditors, public announcement in newspapers, and application for the establishment of the acquisition vehicle (i.e., the WFOE or JV to be formed) and the subsequent asset acquisition by such vehicle.

However, if the JV or WFOE has already been established, the foreign investor may use such existing entity to acquire Chinese assets, without triggering the application of the M&A Regulations. The law is not clear as to "how long" a newly-formed JV or WFOE must wait before it can engage in acquisition activities without approval. In other words, an established JV or WFOE is considered as a Chinese company whose acquisition activities are usually not subject to governmental approval. Thus, if the foreign investor separates or staggers the process of "vehicle formation" and "asset acquisition", it could potentially avoid the application of the M&A Regulations and the government's scrutiny of the asset acquisition.

5. Public Registers, Records and Databases

In China, there is no single or central institution or database that maintains all information that may be relevant to an asset transfer. Basic company information and records may be obtained from the local Administration of Industry and Commerce where the target company is registered, which normally include (i) copies of the company's business license and, if applicable, some other permits or certificates that may be required for its operation, (ii) documents and records relating to company formation, (iii) documents and records of any registration change such as change of shareholder, registered capital, company name, scope of business, address, and (iv) basic information of the company's shareholders.

Records of real estate including information about the title and encumbrances can be obtained at the local Administrative Bureau of Land and Building, or Property Exchange, an agency of the land bureau.

Registration information of intellectual property rights can be found at various government agencies, depending on the nature of the particular IP Right: (i) patent related information is available on the website of State Intellectual Property Office (www.sipo.gov.cn), (ii) trademark registration information is available on the website of Trademark Office of State Administration of Industry and Commerce (sbj.saic.gov.cn), (iii) ownership to Internet domain names can be found on the website of China Internet Network Information Center (www.cnnic.net.cn), (iv) registration information since 2003 of software products is available on the website of www.chinasoftware.com.cn, sponsored by the Department of Electronics and Information Products Administration under Ministry of Information Industry.

In addition, starting from October 1, 2007, information on pledges of accounts receivables may be found in the "Account Receivables Pledge Registration System" at the Credit Reference Center under the People's Bank of China.

6. Purchase Price Requirements

If the purchaser is a foreign investor and the proposed asset deal is governed by the M&A Regulations, the purchase price as agreed by the parties should be based on the appraisal results of the assets. If the seller is a state-owned enterprise selling substantial assets of its own, the sale could be subject to a public bidding or auction process to ensure fair price and approval at the local Asset and Equity Exchange and State-owned Assets Supervision and Administration Commission in charge of transfer of state-owned property rights, and the final purchase price normally should not be less than 90% of the appraisal value.

Under the M&A Regulations, there are two forms of purchase by a foreign investor of Chinese assets. First, the foreign investor purchases the assets in its own name, which assets will then be injected into a "foreign-invested enterprise" (**"FIE"**) that such foreign investor will immediately form to hold the assets and engage in business operations. A foreign entity itself cannot hold Chinese assets to engage in business activities; rather, it must set up an onshore Chinese company (FIE) for business operation. In such scenario, the M&A Regulations require that purchase price be paid in full within three months from the issuance of the business license of the new FIE. An extension may be available upon approval, but no less than 60% of the purchase price must nevertheless be paid within six months from the issuance of the new business license and the balance within one year.

Second, the foreign investor can form a FIE and then immediately have such FIE acquire Chinese assets; it would be the FIE that will pay for the acquired assets. Pursuant to the M&A Regulations, the foreign investor must make its capital infusion into the new FIE first such that the FIE can have the cash to make the payment. The capital contribution made by the foreign investor to the FIE can be in the form of any convertible currency, and it will be converted into RMB for the payment of purchase price.

B. Tangible/Movable Assets

1. Characteristics as to:

a) Language of Documentation. The law is generally silent on what language must be used for documenting a transfer of assets. However, in practice, all Chinese government agencies would normally only accept Chinese agreements and documents for filing and approval purposes, except for those documents originally prepared in English or another language from a different jurisdiction, such as the foreign investor's certificate of incorporation. For instance, if the transfer of tangible assets is part of an asset transfer transaction that is subject to the M&A Regulations, the documents will have to be submitted for government approval and the Chinese version must be filed with the government authorities.

If the documents do not have to be submitted for government filing or approval, the sale and transfer documents may be drafted in every language. Bilingual documents are permitted.

b) Form of Documentation. In general, there is no legal requirement for agreements to be in writing or other procedural formalities in respect of the transfer of tangible assets. But if such transfer is part of an asset acquisition under the M&A Regulations, and the documents need to be submitted to the authorities for approval, the agreement must be in writing and signed by both seller and purchaser, but generally it does not have to be notarized.

The sale and transfer documents may be executed outside China but should be governed by the laws of the People's Republic of China (PRC) if all assets concerned are in China. Signing in counterparts is generally permissible.

c) Specification of Assets. The law does not specifically require that the tangible assets to be transferred must be specified in the transfer agreement to such an extent that any third party will be able to distinguish the tangible assets from any other non-transferred tangible assets. But for practical considerations, a checklist or schedule of tangible assets with sufficient details would always be helpful for parties in the process of stocktaking and closing.

2. Administrative, Corporate and Other Approvals

If the transfer of tangible assets is regarded as an asset acquisition under the M&A Regulations, it must be approved by the MOFCOM or its local counterpart. If the seller is a state-owned enterprise selling substantial assets of its own, such sale will be subject to asset appraisal and approval and/or filing process applicable to transfer of state-owned assets with the local Assets and Equity Exchange. Transfer of tangible assets that have been subject to preferential tax treatment and are therefore under the Customs' supervision must be approved by the Customs. Non-compliance would not necessarily affect the validity of the asset transfer per se, but may trigger administrative or even criminal liabilities to the seller.

Whether the transfer of tangible assets is subject to approval of any corporate bodies basically depends on the constitutional documents (such as articles of association) of the relevant parties to the transaction. However, if the transfer of tangible assets is subject to the M&A Regulations, resolutions by the seller's corporate body approving the transfer must be submitted to the approval authority.

In addition, if the sale or purchase is made by a Chinese public company, and the assets account for more than 30% of its total assets (for the same year), such a transaction must be approved by no less than two-thirds of the shareholders present in a shareholders' meeting.

Without the above required approvals the transfer of tangible assets is voidable.

If a seller's assets are subject to encumbrances or have been used as collateral (e.g., the assets are mortgaged), the mortgagee's consent to the transfer is required for the transfer of the assets, unless the purchaser causes such mortgage to be removed by repaying the debt. If the assets are owned by a third party instead of the seller (e.g., in case of retention of title, security assignment), the transfer by the seller may be held invalid without the owner's consent, unless the purchaser has acquired the assets in good faith (bona fide principle).

3. Filing Requirements

Regarding the transfer of tangible assets, generally no filings with public authorities or registrations into public registers or databases are required. However, if the assets are automobiles or ships, the transfer and ownership change both need to be registered and updated with the relevant authorities or registers.

4. Automatic Transfer of Encumbrances

The law does not provide for an automatic transfer of encumbrances at the time of the assets transfer, as such transfer would not be valid without the mortgagee's consent unless the debt has been paid off by the purchaser or seller. If the mortgagee does not provide such consent, then the purchaser must pay off the debt or cause it to be repaid in order to make the asset transfer valid and effective. Thus, if the mortgagee consents to the asset transfer and the debt is not to be immediately repaid, the mortgagee would need to enter into a new mortgage agreement with the purchaser.

C. Real Property

1. Characteristics as to:

a) Language of Documentation. In practice, registration is required for the transfer of real property, and the registration authorities require those submitted documents to be in Chinese. Depending on the individual registration authority, bilingual documents may be accepted.

b) Form of Documentation. The documentation for the real property transfer must be in written form. In general, notarization is not required to effect acquisitions of real property. In practice, local real property authorities usually provide boilerplate real property sale and purchase agreements for the parties to use, with all the additional provisions and amendments included in a schedule attached to such form agreement.

The law does not require the sale and purchase agreement to be executed within China. Although there is no express legal requirement to sign on the same pages, the real property registration authority, depending on its location, may challenge signing in counterparts when they handle the property registration.

c) Specification of Assets. Sufficient information, including detailed addresses, purposes of use and an accompanying map must be provided so that purchaser, third parties and registration authorities will be able to find the relevant information and check the same against the public records (similar to B, 1, c above).

2. Administrative, Corporate and Other Approvals

The transfer of real property shall be registered with the local real property authority. The ownership transfer of the real property may not be effectuated without a registration change with the local real property authority.

Particularly, if the land use right to be transferred is an "allocated land use right", a right normally given by the state to state-owned enterprises for free or at a nominal cost, it cannot be transferred, sold or leased until first being converted into "granted land use right". Such conversion will require governmental approval, a public bidding process, and payment of land premiums.

Whether the transfer of real property is subject to approval of any corporate bodies basically depends on the constitutional documents (such as articles of association) of the relevant parties to the transaction. However, if the transfer of the real property is subject to the M&A Regulations, resolutions by the seller's corporate body approving the transfer must be submitted to the authorities for approval.

In addition, if the sale or purchase is made by a Chinese public company and if the assets account for more than 30% of its total assets (for the same year), such a transaction must be approved by no less than two-thirds of the shareholders present in a shareholders' meeting.

Without the above required approvals the transfer of real property may be invalid.

In the event that the real property is mortgaged, the mortgagee's consent will be required to effect the transfer, unless the purchaser has such mortgage removed by repaying the debt.

3. Filing Requirements

To effectively complete a transfer of real property, it must be properly registered with the local real property authority (registry).

4. Automatic Transfer of Encumbrances

As a general rule, the mortgage is not allowed to be transferred along with the real property unless the consent of mortgagee is given. In practice, some real property registration authorities do not accept registration of transfer if the real property is subject to mortgages or unless consents have been obtained from all relevant parties. Under such circumstances, mortgages would need to be cleared first before registration of the property transfer.

As the transfer of real property shall be registered with the local real property authority, the waiver of encumbrances is required to be made in writing.

5. Automatic Transfer of Lease Agreements

Unless a lease agreement provides otherwise, pursuant to PRC Contract Law, lease agreements on the real property are subject to automatic transfer to the purchaser who will assume all rights and obligations under such lease agreements as landlord. Neither the purchaser nor the tenant has an extraordinary termination right due to the transfer.

D. Contracts

1. Characteristics as to:

a) Language of Documentation. Usually the contracts to be transferred do not require governmental approval; therefore, the documentation related to contract transfer may be drafted in every language, including in English or bilingual, subject to the agreement of the parties.

As a cautionary note, assigning contracts that originally were approved by or registered with government authorities, such as a technology license agreement, would likely trigger same approval or registration process, and, therefore, in such circumstance a Chinese version or Chinese translation will be required.

b) Form of Documentation. Generally, no specific form is required under the law for transfer of contracts, unless it is otherwise required (i) under the contracts to be transferred or (ii) by the relevant local authorities, in their discretion, in connection with formalities, such as notarization. For good measure, however, parties should always consider putting everything in writing to avoid any future disputes.

In the same vein, there is no requirement under the law that the transfer documents must be executed in China. Signing in counterparts is allowed in China but joint signing (on the same signature page) may be a safer approach to reduce risks of future disputes over the authenticity and genuineness of the document's signatures.

c) Specification of Contracts. Although the law is silent on this, as good measure, the contracts to be transferred should be specified in the asset transfer agreement such that any third party will be able to distinguish the contracts from those that are not to be transferred.

2. Administrative, Corporate and Other Approvals

Usually the transfer of contracts does not require special governmental approvals. However, if the contracts to be transferred were originally approved by or registered with government authorities, such as a technology license agreement, it would likely trigger the same approval or registration process.

Whether the transfer is subject to approval of any corporate bodies depends on the constitutional documents (such as articles of association) of the relevant parties to the transaction. However, if the transfer of contracts is subject to the M&A Regulations, resolutions by seller's corporate body approving the transfer must be submitted to the authority for approval. Without such approval, if required, the transfer may be deemed as invalid.

Unless the contract to be transferred provides otherwise, according to the PRC Contract Law, assigning rights and benefits under a contract would require notice to, but not the consent of, the other party of the contract; assigning obligations and duties under a contract, however, would require consent from the other party to the contract. Without such consent, the transfer is voidable.

3. Automatic Transfer of Contracts (Other than Lease and Employment Agreements)

In terms of automatic transfer, property and casualty insurance policies typically may be transferred by default in an asset deal without consent, unless the insurance policy expressly provides otherwise.

4. Filing Requirements

In general, with respect to the transfer of contracts, there is no requirement for filings with public authorities or registrations in registers or (online) databases. Exceptions may apply. If the contracts are required under the law for approval or registration, special filings with public authorities or registrars may apply.

5. Treatment of Existing Contractual Claims and Obligations

Assuming the transfer of the contracts is not flawed, the respective claims and/or obligations under the transferred contracts will automatically transfer to the purchaser.

This applies to contracts not or not completely fulfilled unless otherwise provided for in the transfer agreement. If the transfer is flawed, however, the transfer may be considered as ineffective or void, the purchaser may assert its claims against the assignor.

In practice, one should always include special provisions in the purchase agreement, such as purchase price adjustment and indemnifications, to deal with issues of unfulfilled contracts and allocate the risks appropriately among the parties.

6. Warranty Claims Resulting from Events prior to Transfer

It is customary that the transfer of a contract usually comprises the transfer of any claims and any obligations related to such contract, since the required consent of the other party to this contract covers such claims and obligations. This also applies to warranty claims resulting from events prior to the transfer of such contract if not otherwise provided for in the asset sale and/or transfer agreement. The potential exposure is customarily covered by representations and warranties, covenants and/or indemnifications.

E. IP Rights

1. Characteristics of Intellectual Property Rights (e.g., Trademarks, Patents, Utility Models, Domain Names) ("*IP Rights*") as to:

a) Language of Documentation. To the extent the IP Rights are those registered with government agencies, such as trademarks and patents, transfer documentation must be in Chinese for filing and processing at the Trademark Office and Patent Office.

If the document does not have to be submitted for government filing or approval, the sale and transfer documents may be drafted in any language. Bilingual documents are permitted.

b) Form of Documentation. Transfer of patent, registered trademark, software, domain name and (registered) copyright, to the extent it needs to be filed with the relevant government agencies, usually has to comply with the official forms suggested by the respective government agencies. The transfer of other IP Rights normally does not require a special form. The sale and transfer documents may be executed outside China. Usually, signing in counterparts is permissible.

c) Specification of IP Rights. Although not required, it would be helpful, in practice, to specify the assets to be transferred in the transfer agreement to such an extent that a third party will be able to distinguish the assets from any other non-transferred assets. Specification by category is sufficient for the description of assets and usually lists of IP Rights are needed.

2. Administrative, Corporate and Other Approvals

As stated above, if the IP Rights involve registered trademarks and patents, the transfer can only be effectuated by registration with the Trademark Office and Patent Office.

Whether the transfer is subject to the approval of any corporate bodies depends on constitutional documents (such as articles of association) of the relevant parties to the transaction. However, if the transfer of IP Rights is subject to the M&A Regulations, resolutions by the seller's corporate body approving the transfer must be submitted to the approval authority.

The approval of security holders would be required prior to the transfer of IP Rights. Without any such approvals, if required, the transfer may be deemed invalid.

3. Filing Requirements

If the IP Rights to be transferred are registered in government agencies, the change of ownership would require filing or registration with such relevant agencies. For patents, the transfer goes into effect upon registration with the Patent Office. For trademarks, the transfer goes into effect upon the Trademark Office's publication of the updated registration. For registered software and domain names, although the law is unclear on exactly when the transfer is effective, it is likely that registration is the benchmark for an effective transfer.

4. Applicable International (Multilateral) Agreements or Treaties

China is member to the following international conventions and treaties on IP Rights: TRIPS Agreement, the Berne Convention for the Protection of Literary and Artistic Works, the Universal Copyright Convention, the Paris Convention for the Protection of Industrial Property, the Patent Cooperation Treaty, the Budapest Treaty on the International Recognition of the Deposit of Microorganisms for the Purposes of Patent Procedure, Locarno Agreement on Establishing an International Classification for Industrial Design, and Madrid Agreement Concerning the International Registration of Marks.

F. Receivables

1. Characteristics as to:

a) Language of Documentation. To the extent the document does not have to be submitted for government filing or approval, the sale and transfer documents may be drafted in any language. Bilingual documents are permitted. However, if the transfer of receivables is part of an asset transfer transaction under the M&A Regulations, the documents need to be submitted for approval, and a Chinese version or translation will be required.

b) Form of Documentation. Generally, no specific form is required under the law for a transfer of receivables, although in practice and for good measure, the transfer should be memorialized in writing. There is no requirement under the law that the transfer documents be executed in China. Signing in counterparts is allowed in China but joint signing (on the same signature page) may be a safer approach to reduce risks of future disputes over the authenticity and genuineness of the document's signatures.

c) Specification of Receivables. Although the law is silent on this, for good measure, the contracts to be transferred should be specified in the assets transfer agreement such that any third party will be able to distinguish the receivable from any other non-transferred receivables (same as B, 1, c above). The receivables thus need to be specified sufficiently. It is recommendable to list the receivables to be transferred in schedules to the asset transfer agreement, specifying the underlying legal relationships and the outstanding amount of the relevant receivables.

2. Administrative, Corporate and other Approvals

If the seller is a state-owned enterprise selling substantial assets of its own, such sale could be subject to asset appraisal and approval and/or filing process applicable to transfer of state-owned assets with the local Asset and Equity Exchange and approval of State-owned Assets Supervision and Administration Commission.

Whether the transfer of receivables is subject to the approval of any corporate bodies basically depends on the constitutional documents (such as articles of association) of the relevant parties to the transaction. However, if the transfer of receivables is subject to the M&A Regulations, resolutions by the seller's corporate body approving the transfer must be submitted to the authority for approval.

In addition, if the sale or purchase is made by a Chinese public company, and the assets account for more than 30% of its total assets (for the same year), such a transaction must be approved by no fewer than two-thirds of the shareholders present in a shareholders' meeting.

Without the above required approvals the transfer of receivables may be invalid.

If the receivables are subject to encumbrances or have been used as collateral (e.g., the receivables are pledged), the pledgee's consent to the transfer is required for the transfer of the receivables, unless the purchaser causes such pledge to be removed by repaying the debt.

The validity of the transfer is not subject to the approval of the debtors provided that the underlying agreement does not state otherwise. If the receivable is pledged to a third party, it cannot be transferred without prior consent by the pledgee. Information on the pledge of receivables, if recorded, may be found in the "Account Receivables Pledge Registration System" of the Credit Reference Centre (http://www.pbccrc.org.cn) under the People's Bank of China.

Without the above required approvals the transfer of receivables may be voidable.

3. Filing Requirements

In order for the transfer of receivables to take effect, notification to the debtors of the transfer is required. No special filings are required with any public authorities or registrars for the transfer of receivables.

G. Liabilities

1. Characteristics as to:

a) Language of Documentation. To the extent the document does not have to be submitted for government filing or approval, the sale and transfer documents may be drafted in any language. Bilingual documents are permitted.

b) Form of Documentation. Generally, no specific form is required under the law for transfer of liabilities, although in practice, for good measure, written form is recommendable. There is no requirement under the law that the transfer documents must be executed in China. Signing in counterparts is allowed in China but joint signing (on the same signature page) may be a safer approach to reduce risks of future disputes over the authenticity and genuineness of the signing of the document.

c) Specification of Liabilities. Although the law is silent on this, for good measure, the liabilities to be transferred should be specified in the assets transfer agreement such that a third party will be able to distinguish the liabilities from any other non-transferred liabilities (same as B, 1, c above). The liabilities thus have to be specified sufficiently. In order to comply with such requirements it is recommendable to list the liabilities to be transferred in schedules to the asset transfer agreement, specifying the underlying legal relationships and the outstanding amount of the relevant liabilities.

2. Administrative, Corporate and Other Approvals

If the transfer of liabilities is regarded as part of an asset acquisition under the M&A Regulations, the asset acquisition must be approved by the MOFCOM or its local counterpart. There is no statutory or regulatory requirement of approval by any corporate bodies of a proposed assets transfer.

Under the PRC law, transfer of liabilities requires the consent of the creditors. However, if the creditor in practice has accepted any performance by the assignee or transferee of such transferred liabilities, it is deemed that consent to such transfer has been granted by the creditor. Although no specific form of creditors' consent is required, written consent is recommendable.

3. Filing Requirements

In order for the transfer of liabilities to be effective, consent of the creditors is required. Practically, notification must first be sent to the creditors in order to obtain such consent. No special filings are required with any public authorities or registrars for the transfer of liabilities.

4. Purchaser's Liability for:

a) Tax Obligations. Unless otherwise provided in the asset transfer agreement, the purchaser will not be subject to tax obligations of the seller relating to the assets prior to the transfer.

b) Environmental Contamination. There are no express provisions under the law that impose liabilities on the purchaser of assets for environmental contamination prior to the transfer of the acquired assets. However, for good measure, it would be recommendable to make this clear and include an indemnification clause in the asset transfer agreement.

c) Products Sold or Services Rendered by the Seller to Third Parties. Unlike a share deal, in an asset deal, purchaser is not responsible for products sold or services rendered by the seller to third parties prior to the acquisition, unless otherwise provided in the asset purchase agreement.

5. Automatic Transfer of Other Liabilities

In an asset deal, normally there would not be any liabilities that would be automatically transferred from seller to purchaser due to the acquisition of assets.

6. Contractual Protection as to 4 and 5 above

To provide clarity, it would always be helpful for the purchaser to include special provisions in the asset transfer agreement, such as representations and warranties, covenants and indemnification.

H. Employees

1. Transfer of Employees

The law does not expressly provide for the automatic transfer of employees in an asset transfer unless the seller goes through a merger, division, or process of similar nature. The legislative intent seems to imply that if an entity merges out of existence, the employees of such entity must be carried over to the new entity automatically, but the law does not provide details on the procedures, conditions and consequences of such transfer. There are few legislative or regulatory interpretations on what may constitute such a process of a similar nature.

In general, an asset transfer in itself will not trigger the automatic transfer of employees. Therefore, in practice the transfer of employees is subject to negotiation and agreement of the parties to the transaction. If the purchaser wants to have employees transferred from the seller as part of an asset transfer deal, seller and purchaser can agree to do so in the asset purchase agreement. The seller will then notify those employees of such transfer, and those employees have the right to decide whether they want to work for the purchaser. If any of them decide to "opt out," the seller will have to pay those employees severance for the termination of the employment relationship.

For those employees willing to accept the transfer, they will need to enter into new employment agreements with the purchaser (or whichever entity that is going to hold the acquired assets). Since the employment relationship between those employees and the seller may be terminated earlier than its term, those employees can claim severance payment from the seller. In practice, however, if the service years of those employees are recognized and credited by the purchaser and their wages and benefits largely remain the same, judges and labor arbitrators generally will not rule that the seller should pay severance or other compensations to those employees.

2. Approval of Works Council, Trade Union and Other Institutions

In general, the approval of a workers council or labor organization is not required for an asset transfer. To the extent the M&A Regulations will apply, one of the required application documents is an "employee settlement plan" of the seller, providing information of the proposed arrangement of the employees after the transfer, such as termination, severance pay, and transfer of social benefits. The M&A Regulations do not require that such plan be approved by any labor organization or labor authority. However, if substantial assets of a state-owned entity are being transferred, such "employee settlement plan" must be approved by the seller's "employee representative assembly" and then filed for record with the local labor administrative authority. Without this step, the transaction may not be approved by the government authority. It is still unclear whether a transaction can be deemed invalid and then be forced to unwind if this process was either not complete or otherwise flawed.

3. Contractual Protection as to Labor Issues

In practice, it is customary to include special provisions as to employees in the asset sale and/or transfer agreement. It is important for the purchaser to ensure that it will not become jointly liable for any employee liabilities due to the asset transfer, regardless whether there is any transfer of employees. To the extent there is any employee transfer, the purchaser should take special care to avoiding assuming any liabilities for the seller's non-compliance with labor laws, such as seller's failure to make full contributions for employees' social security and other benefits. As the transferred employees might claim severance and other payments due to reasons of termination of the prior employee relationship, it would be in the purchaser's interest to include an indemnification clause to cover such risk.

I. Tax Implications

1. Value Added Tax

In an asset acquisition, the applicable VAT rate in China is normally either 13% or 17%, depending on the asset, which is calculated based on the difference between the "output VAT" for the current period and the "input VAT" for the current period. Output VAT is sales revenue or revenue from the provision of labor services for the period multiplied by the applicable VAT rate, and input VAT is the VAT paid or borne by the taxpayer with respect to its purchases of goods or labor services. Under the new Implementation Rules of the Provisional Regulations on Value Added Tax that took effect on January 1, 2009, the 13% VAT rate applies to food, food oil, tap water, heating, air conditioning, hot water, gas, natural gas, methane, books, newspaper, magazines, feedstuff, fertilizer, pesticide, agriculture-use equipment, agriculture-use film, and such other goods as prescribed by the State Council.

Under the new VAT regulations that took effect in 2009, sale of fixed assets that have been "self-used" will be subject to different VAT rates depending on the circumstances: (i) sale of "self-used" assets purchased or self-manufactured after January 1, 2009, the normal rate of VAT will apply; and (ii) sale of "self-used" assets that were purchased or self-manufactured prior to December 31, 2008, the applicable rate shall be 2%.

Second, if an asset transfer deal comprises of all assets, accounts receivable, accounts payable together with the labor force, the deal may be VAT exempt, as the tax authorities would deem such transaction as a share deal to which VAT does not apply. It is unclear under the law whether all liabilities (including hidden and contingent liabilities) must be assumed by the purchaser in order to qualify for such treatment, but it would be recommendable to discuss and negotiate with the local tax authority in order to seek such VAT exemption. It is occasionally the case that if all assets and labor force are to be transferred, the local tax authorities might exercise discretion and give such exemption without being too strict regarding the allocation of liabilities between seller and purchaser.

2. Real Property Transfer Tax

Transfer of real property would trigger land-value appreciation tax, deed tax and stamp duty. Land-value appreciation tax is payable by the seller, assessed at the progressive rates of 30%, 40%, 50% and 60% depending on the amount of the land value appreciation. Deed tax is payable by the purchaser with the going rate of 3% to 5% of the amount of the real property transfer. There may be an exemption of deed tax available if certain requirements are met: (i) sale of assets by either a state-owned enterprise or a "collective enterprise"; (ii) such enterprise will be de-registered; and (iii) the purchaser has undertaken the proper placement of all workers. If the purchaser signs employment agreement with no less than 30% of those employees each with a term of no less than three years, 50% of the deed tax will be exempted. If the purchaser signs employment agreement with all of the employees with a term of no less than three years, all deed tax will be exempted (see Circular on Applying Certain Policy on Deed Tax in Enterprise Restructuring, No. 175, 2008). In an asset transfer, sale of inventory and fixed assets is subject to 0.03% stamp duty, while immovable and intangible assets are subject to 0.05% stamp duty, payable by each of the seller and purchaser.

3. Other Tax Issues

The chart below summarizes all taxes that may be applicable in an asset transfer.

Business Tax	5%	Transfer of immovable or intangible assets	Seller
Deed Tax	3%–5%	Purchase of land-use rights or real estate property	Purchaser
Land Value Appreciation Tax	30%–60%	Gain on disposal of land-use rights and buildings	Seller
Value Added Tax (VAT)	13% or 17%	Transfer of inventory	Seller
	2%	Transfer of self-used fixed assets that were purchased or self-manufactured prior to December 31, 2008	Seller
Claw-back of Customs and Import Value Added Tax	To be determined by the Customs	Disposal of imported tax/duty-free equipment within the 5-year customs supervision period	Seller
Stamp Duty	0.03% to 0.05%	Execution of contractual document	Seller and Purchaser

J. Bankruptcy Law

1. Challenge of Asset Transfer in Case of Insolvency

The court in a bankruptcy proceeding has the power to decide whether to allow to continued performance of the agreements or to otherwise terminate agreements that have been entered into but have yet to be fully performed prior to the date on which the court accepted the bankruptcy case. Thus, if the asset purchase transaction is not closed by such date, the judge (or bankruptcy administrator) may decide to rescind the asset purchase agreement.

If the assets are being transferred for free or at clearly unreasonable prices within one year prior to the date the court accepted the bankruptcy case, the asset transfer transaction could become voidable and the receiver may apply to the court to rescind the transaction. If the transaction involves fraud, such as attempted concealing or (fraudulent) transfer of assets, the transaction will be deemed as void.

2. Acquisition of Assets that are Subject to Insolvency Proceedings

If the assets to be acquired are subject to insolvency proceedings, certain special rules will apply. First, the bankruptcy administrator will propose a plan of sale for insolvent assets at a reduced price, and submit it to the creditor's meeting for adoption. Once such plan is adopted by the creditors' meeting, the administrator will submit it to the court for approval. The administrator will then carry out the approved plan and proceed with the sale of assets through auction or such other means as approved by the creditors' meeting.

K. Timing and Costs

1. Timeframe of Asset Transfer

The timeline of a transaction will depend on many factors, including the complexity, size and required legal and regulatory procedures of the transaction. From the legal and regulatory perspective, the timeframe of a typical asset deal will largely depend on the following factors: (i) whether and how the M&A Regulations apply; and (ii) whether any state-owned assets transfer rules will apply.

If a foreign investor intends to set up a FIE to acquire substantial assets from a Chinese entity, the M&A Regulations will likely apply and the transaction will be subject to governmental approval. However, if the foreign investor already has an onshore entity formed and such formed entity will be used to acquire Chinese assets, the M&A Regulations will not apply, in which case the asset transfer will not be subject to governmental approval unless state-owned assets are involved.

When an asset transfer deal is subject to the M&A Regulations, the Chinese seller and the foreign purchaser will go through a regulatory process, including asset appraisal, notification to creditors, public announcement in newspapers, and application for the establishment of the acquisition vehicle (i.e., the WFOE or JV to be formed) and the subsequent asset acquisition by such vehicle. The process of the notification to creditors will normally take three months. The government approval will take approximately one month after receipt of the application package from the purchaser.

If the purchaser, regardless whether foreign or Chinese, intends to acquire substantial assets of a state-owned enterprise, transfer may be subject to a special process applicable to state-owned asset transfer, including asset appraisal, public bidding or auction process to ensure fair price. Such process could take two months and more.

2. Costs of Asset Transfer

The costs vary among locations in China. In Shanghai, for example, notarization charges on legal documents like lease, purchase agreement, articles of association, are usually RMB 500 per copy.

The amounts of stamp duties also vary depending on the contracts, ranging from 0.03% to 0.05% of the transaction value.

L. Miscellaneous

1. Choice of Foreign Law

If the asset acquisition is subject to the M&A Regulations, the PRC law should be the governing law. In other circumstances, although the law does not prohibit parties from selecting non-PRC law as governing law, it is somewhat impractical to select foreign law to govern transfer of land, buildings, patent, trademarks, where separate agreements need to be entered into for filing with governmental authorities for record or registration.

2. (International) Arbitration, Choice of Venue

To the extent the asset transfer involves a foreign element, parties may select international arbitration for dispute resolution purposes. In general, a clause electing a foreign arbitration tribunal to resolve disputes in a purely domestic transaction with no foreign element at all could be challenged by court and deemed voidable. As long as the arbitration clause is valid, the law does not have restrictions on the venue of the arbitration. However, if parties instead agree to use a court to adjudicate disputes, they may only select venues among the following: defendant's domicile, plaintiff's domicile, location where the contract was signed or performed, and the place where the subject matter of the contract is located.

3. Other Distinctions, Characteristics

Our jurisdiction does not provide for any other distinctions or unusual characteristics noteworthy in connection with a customary asset deal.

M. Literature

Ye Jun and *Bao Zhi*, An Anatomy of Merger and Acquisitions of Domestic Enterprises by Foreign Investors From Legal Perspective (Revised Edition 2008), 2nd Edition, 2008

Xiao Jinquan, *Guan Jingxin* and *Zhang Ting*, Control of Legal Risks on Merger and Acquisitions of Enterprises, 1st Edition, 2007

Wang Dong and *Zhang Qiusheng*, Case Studies on Merger and Acquisitions of Enterprises, 1st Edition, 2004

Colombia

By *Andrés Téllez-Núñez*

A. General Aspects

1. Asset Deal vs. Share Deal: Essential Considerations

In Colombia, there is no definitive distinction between an asset deal and a share deal. In fact, whenever a business unit is to be sold or purchased, and depending on the type of entity that is making the sale (either a corporation, a limited liability company, a partnership, etc.), the purchaser will acquire not only the shares (in the case of a corporation) or the interests (in the case of companies other than corporations), but also rights to the assets of the entity. Selling shares does not necessarily entail the selling of assets and the selling of assets does not necessarily entail the selling of shares. On some occasions, both types of transfers coincide, resulting in the transfer of shares and assets. There is, however, one special institution under Colombian commercial law denominated *establecimiento de comercio* that seeks to facilitate for any given entrepreneur the carrying out of his or her business whereby determined features of a business are encompassed in one single unit. In fact, Article 515 of the Colombian Commerce Code defines commercial unit (*establecimiento de comercio*) as "(...) estate configured and set by the entrepreneur in order to carry out the purposes of the company/enterprise. One person may be the owner of several commercial units, and in turn, one single commercial unit may belong to several people, and be devoted to the carrying out of several commercial activities." Article 516 of the Colombian Commercial Code states the following: "Except where there is an agreement to the contrary, a commercial unit is composed of: 1. Commercial names and products and services trademarks; 2. Rights of the entrepreneur over inventions or artistic or industrial creations being used for the activities of the commercial unit; 3. Merchandise deposited in storage units or being manufactured; credits and remaining similar securities; 4. Movables and premises; 5. Lease agreements, and in case of transfer, the lease rights of premises where the commercial units are operated if they are owned by the entrepreneur, and indemnifications that, according to the law, the tenant is entitled to; 6. The right to impede client-deviation mechanisms and the protection of good-will, and 7. Commercial rights and obligations derived from activities of the commercial unit, as long as they do not arise under contracts subscribed and executed by only the owner of that establishment." Article 525 of the Colombian Commercial Code in turn states that "the transfer of an '*establecimiento de comercio*' is presumed to take place as a whole, without need to specify in detail the elements it is composed of."

2. Distinction between Sale and Transfer in Rem

Colombian law distinguishes between the sale (obligation to transfer) and the transfer in rem (fulfillment of the obligation to transfer) of assets. It is worth noting that in the case of real estate transfer of property, contracts have always to be executed through a public deed. In theory, a master agreement could provide for the obligations of transfer, while a separate agreement could provide for the transfer, and both agreements would have to be contained in a public deed – in the case of real estate – and subsequently registered in a special registry office, which is tantamount to the transfer in rem. However, that is not practical and parties in Colombia prefer to set all obligations (obligation to transfer and fulfillment thereof) in one single document. For goods that are movable, the general rule is that the transfer in rem does not have to take place in the form of a public deed, but Colombian commercial law states that with respect to some special and particular types of goods, a registration in a special registry office (which is normally a sectional chamber of commerce or specially designated public registration offices) has to be evidenced in order for the property to be transferred.

3. Regional Differences

There are no regional differences as regards the legal requirements in connection with the transfer of assets. Since Colombia is a unitary state (not a federal one), the legal requirements throughout the Colombian jurisdiction are the same. The offices entrusted with the mission and task of registering deeds and contracts are the same throughout the Colombian territory and jurisdiction, and they are disseminated throughout the country.

4. Acquisition by Foreigners

There are no distinctions under Colombian law between the acquisition of assets by foreigners or foreign entities. However, due to exchange regulations in force, any acquisition of shares made by a foreigner under the form of investment has to be registered before the Central Bank of Colombia. Failure to register will result in a fine of up to 200% of the amount to be invested and the joint liability of the legal representatives of the company in Colombia as well as its legal counsel. In fact, exchange regulations in Colombia provide for obligations of registration both for the investor and the receptor of the investment. The investor shall channel its investment through means recognized by the Central Bank of Colombia and it has the duty and obligation to proceed with the registration of the investment. Normally, it is the investment receptor counsel who carries out the proceedings of registration before the Central Bank, which is a fair and easy online process whereby the identification of parties (investor and receptor of the investment), the amount of the investment, the purpose thereof, the economic sector, etc. are indicated. There are strict legal timeframes for execution of the registration and regulations also provide for time extensions that must be duly requested.

5. Public Registers, Records and Databases

There are two types of offices for public registers. One is called *Oficina de Registro de Instrumentos Públicos* in which all public deeds are registered and filed. Upon request, this office processes registration of all real estate in Colombia where encumbrances, limitations of property and alike can be verified by interested parties. The other office is entrusted to a separate chamber of commerce, which keep, the denominated *Matrícula Mercantil* and which issues, upon request, (Certificates of Existence and Legal Representation) *Certificados de Existencia y Representación Legal* where all companies of any nature, either civil or commercial, are registered and all their legal features are outlined and presented. As to the financial standing of seller and/or purchaser, there is a data base called *CIFIN* where the financial record of individuals and companies is kept (as to compliance of financial obligations or delinquency rates, etc.) and it is also issued upon request. As mentioned above, those types of certificates are issued throughout all the Colombian territory. Therefore, regional offices of chambers of commerce and of public instruments are disseminated throughout the country. However, it is most likely the case that contracts where property is limited are registered at a public office or a registry office where the transaction takes place.

6. Purchase Price Requirements

No special rules exist regarding the price to be paid in asset deal. However, civil rules in Colombia state that in no case may a price that is less than one-half of the fair value be paid to the seller, as that would nullity the contract. In fact, the Civil Code sets forth in Article 1947 the following: "Seller suffers a loss whenever the price received is less than half of the just or fair price of the good being sold; and purchaser suffers a loss whenever the just or fair price being purchased is less than half of the price being paid for it. Fair or just prices are determined upon the time of the transaction [contract]."

B. Tangible/Movable Assets

1. Characteristics as to:

a) Language of Documentation. Documents can be drafted in either Spanish or English. Normally, if foreign entities are involved, documents will be drafted in English. Documents can be executed bilingually, but must include a provision stating what version prevails, and normally documents have to be revised and reviewed by sworn translators, duly notarized and if necessary, legalized.

b) Form of documentation. If real estate is involved, notarization is always mandatory to the extent that the contract is not deemed perfected or completed if no granting of a public deed takes place. If no real estate is involved, notarization is not always required, but registration with special registration offices normally is. Documents can be signed separately. There is no special rule mandating that documents to be signed jointly. This depends on the autonomy of parties and the reach and scope of their agreement. Documents can be executed outside the jurisdiction of Colombia but if they are to have effects in Colombia they need to be duly legalized, and the inclusion of a provision dealing with choice of law and choice of forum is advisable. Once documents have been legalized, they have the same effect throughout the entire Colombian territory, which has only one jurisdiction as a unitary state.

c) Specification of Assets. There are legal requirements both under civil and commercial laws requiring that assets be listed and identified in a detailed fashion. Normally schedules and annexes are used for those types of contracts. In fact, civil and commercial laws in Colombia require that every time assets (movable or not) are to be transferred a clear description thereof has to be made. The legal requirements set out by civil laws establish that anything sold has to be present or expected to exist, determined or subject to determination. Also, commercial law rules establish some exceptions related to commercial units where the rule of identifying goods to be sold is not applicable. In no case, however, can a person sell all of its property as a set of goods, as the goods must be listed and numbered separately.

2. Administrative, Corporate and Other Approvals

Normally, no administrative or governmental permission is required for the transfer of assets. However, if the property is being administered or is state-owned, the respective governmental agency would have to issue the respective authorization, or the official representing the entity has to be duly authorized to enter into the sale agreement. Failure to adhere to this will result in the nullity of the contract; as to public procurement, the main regulations and guidelines can be found both in the Administrative Law Code (*Código Contencioso Administrativo*) and in the public contracting set of rules (*estatuto de contratación*) contained in Law 80 of 1993.

When state-owned entities or official parties are not involved, normally contracts have to state that persons executing the contract are duly authorized to do so; failure to mention this usually does not result in the invalidity or nullity of the contract. However, recently, contracts in Colombia are drafted more carefully and such provisions are normally included; mention also has to be made of the fact that commercial law regulations set forth a very stringent set of norms dealing with the responsibility and liability of directors and administrative officials of companies to the extent that, if by-laws are breached or fraudulent operations take place in detriment of the interests of the company, a wide array of legal actions can be filed both by partners, shareholders, public entities and third parties. If assets are to be encumbered, usually the approval and express authorization of directors (administrators) is sought and included in the respective contract; if the amount surpasses certain limits, shareholders have to be consulted and have to approve any operation related thereto. Usually, the top limits for encumbrances are indicated in the so-called Certificate of Existence and Legal Representation (*Certificado de Existencia y Representación Legal*) so third parties can know in advance whether they can or cannot subject property to encumbrances without the authorization of the Board of Directors. However, normally it is needed. Also, in the *Certificado de Tradición y Libertad* encumbrances already existing are indicated.

3. Filing Requirements

The transfer of tangible assets requires special filings with public authorities or registrations public registers. Every time assets are to be transferred a registration must take place, both before the *Oficina de Registro de Instrumentos Públicos* and the chamber of commerce of the respective jurisdiction. Public deeds related to transfer of real estate are granted before a Notary Public office selected by the parties. After the public deed has been granted (a process that may well take just one day or half a day), the Public Deed needs to be registered at the *Oficina de Registro de Instrumentos Público*. The process of registration normally takes about three days. Failure to register the public deed is not tantamount to the contract being deemed as an incomplete one (because the law requires that the transfer of real estate only needs to be contained in a public deed) but will prelude the transfer of property in Colombia; transfer of property only takes place by virtue of the registration of the Public Deed at the *Oficina de Registro de Instrumentos Públicos*.

4. Automatic Transfer of Encumbrances

In case the assets are subject to encumbrances, normally such encumbrances would be transferred to the purchaser. However, it will depend on the intention of the parties, and on the scope and reach of the agreement. The purchaser may require that any encumbrance be cancelled first prior to purchasing the property. A cancellation of an encumbrance on real estate will need to be formalized and legalized before a Notary Public office and duly registered in the *Oficina de Registro de Instrumentos Públicos* for it becoming effective.

C. Real Property

1. Characteristics as to:

a) Language of Documentation. Documents can be drafted in either Spanish or English, but a special provision must be included as to which version governs. Normally, documents and contracts are drafted in English only if a foreign entity is party or prospective party to the contract. The documents can be executed bilingually. It is usual for attorneys at law and counsel to be assisted by sworn translators, and when foreign entities are involved it is usually the English version that governs. It is also usual that versions of contracts and documents be furnished by investors abroad for revision by local counsel.

b) Form of Documentation. Documents regarding real property located in Colombia cannot be executed outside Colombia. The execution of documents by means of a Public Deed must take place before a Notary Public office located in Colombia. Normally, the Public Deed contains the sale agreement. But nothing impedes that separate agreements be reached. However, that is rare and it hardly ever takes place as it ends being not practical in terms of time management and business efficiency.

c) Specification of Assets. Colombian laws always require a detailed description of the property to be transferred. Failure to include a detailed description may result in the contract being voided or even declared as non-existent. However, as mentioned above, civil law rules state that for a real estate (real property) contract to be deemed as perfected and complete, an agreement on price and assets to be transferred has to be clear. But as to the property to be transferred, the law only requires that the property exists or that it is expected to exist, that it is determined or subject to determination and of course that is not owned by the purchaser. Civil law does not allow natural persons to sell all their property as a single unit. Property therefore has to be identified. As mentioned above, Colombian commercial law has established the so-called commercial unit, *establecimiento de comercio*, which is a true configuration of movable and non-movable goods and property devoted by any entrepreneur to achieve the corporate purpose of the entity (company in the form of partnership or corporation) and goods and property contained therein may be sold as a whole without identifying or listing goods and property separately.

2. Administrative, Corporate and Other Approvals

(i) The transfer of real property does not require special or administrative approval as long as the property to be transferred is not owned by the state or any governmental agency in any way, shape or form; however, as mentioned above, there are stringent laws and regulations in Colombia dealing with government procurement. Those regulations are contained in the Colombian Administrative Law Code and in Law 80 of 1993, which is the Public Contracting Statute;

(ii) this always requires the approval of the directors of any company interested in selling real property and if certain amounts are surpassed, the authorization of the proprietors and owners of the Company is also needed – by means of a duly legalized decision made by the shareholders or partners – and

(iii) this always requires the approval of property owners if property and real estate are to be encumbered. The encumbrance of property is regulated both by specific rules of civil laws and commercial laws and partners and shareholders usually outline particular rules in the corresponding by-laws.

3. Filing Requirements

The transfer of real property requires that the public deed be granted before a notary public and registered in the *Oficina de Registro de Instrumentos Públicos*. As mentioned above, any transfer of real property has to be made through the granting of a public deed; otherwise the contract is deemed as non-existent or incomplete. On the other hand, in order to carry out the transfer of property, the registration of the corresponding public deed needs to take place at the office mentioned above. Otherwise, legal transfer will not be deemed as verified and evidenced. Colombian laws establish a clear difference between the completion of a contract to sell real property, which, as noted, must be in the form of a public deed, and the transfer itself of property, which, is divided into two phases: the "legal" transfer that is evidenced when the public deed is registered, and the "actual" or "factual" transfer, which is the delivery itself of the real property to the purchaser.

4. Automatic Transfer of Encumbrances

Encumbrances on the real property are automatically transferred to the purchaser. If a waiver were to operate, then a cancellation of the encumbrance has to take place by means of a notarized public deed, and its corresponding registration must be evidenced before the *Oficina de Registro de Instrumentos Públicos*. As mentioned above, however, the transfer of encumbrances that does not occur automatically will depend on the scope and reach of the agreement executed by the parties and their specific intent which means that the parties should agree on whether the encumbrances are automatically transferred and the reach of obligations derived therefrom.

5. Automatic Transfer of Lease Agreements

In case the real property is subject to lease agreements, Colombian law distinguishes between two cases. If parties are not merchants, usually the termination of the lease or its continuation will depend upon the will of the parties and on the contract stipulations themselves, provided that the owner gives adequate and timely notification to the tenant for it to leave the property or to continue as tenant of the purchaser. Civil laws also provide for some sort of indemnification to be paid to the tenant in those legal cases in which the new owner "is not obligated to respect the lease agreement." If parties are both merchants, or one of them is a merchant, then special rights are given to both the tenant and the purchaser in some specific cases, considering special commercial purposes of the tenant and the purchaser. In fact, commercial regulations state that the tenant is entitled to the automatic renewal of a lease agreement devoted to his/her corporate interests but that automatic renewal or extension does not occur in the following cases (Article 518 of the Colombian Commercial Code): 1. When the tenant has breached or violated the lease agreement; 2. When the owner of the property uses the property for his own living or dwelling or for a commercial unit substantially different from that of the tenant; and 3. When the real property needs to be renewed or rebuilt with necessary works that may not be carried out without returning it or vacating it, or if it is to be demolished due to its dilapidated state or for the construction of a new edifice or building.

D. Contracts

1. Characteristics as to:

a) Language of Documentation. There is no special requirement as to the language of the agreement. Usually, if foreign parties are involved in the transaction, English will be the governing language. The documents can be executed bilingually and normally they will be translated by a sworn translator, and if necessary, duly legalized. As mentioned above, in Colombia (and perhaps in other developing countries) usually contracts in English are furnished by foreign counsel to be revised locally both by attorneys (those bilingual) and sworn translators.

b) Form of Documentation. Contracts can be assigned outside Colombia. Assignment of contracts can take place either in one single document or in a joint document. It is worth noting that Colombian civil and commercial laws make a pivotal distinction regarding the assignment of contracts. In that sense, the assignment of contracts may be regarded from the position of creditor or debtor (in this case, the contract will be assigned as a whole and with respect to all or part of the obligations) or it may be regarded as transfer of debt or of credit. The second case is governed generally by the rules of the first case. As to the first case, Colombian civil law distinguishes between contracts (a) intuitu personae, (b) contracts of successive performance and (c) contracts of instantaneous performance. In (a), the acceptance of the subsisting assignor is always required; in (b), the acceptance of the subsisting assignor is not required and in (c), the acceptance of the subsisting assignor is always required. The form under which the assignment operates depends on the underlying form of the contract being assigned. Therefore, if the contract to be transferred or assigned is a solemn one (for example, the sale of real property), then the assignment or transfer will have to operate through the granting of a Public Deed; if the underlying contract is not a solemn one, then normally, the assignment will be without formalities, too. Colombian civil law rules also distinguish the effects as between assignors and assignees. As to effects between assignors and assignees themselves, the one assigning the contract is liable for the existence and validity of the contract being assigned as well as of its guarantees and warranties. To that effect, if the contract never existed, the assignor will have to pay the assignee damages. If the contract did exist, but it was not a valid one, the following may apply: (i) it may be agreed that the assignor could not be held liable for certain nullity causes (an exception is made in cases where the purpose of the contract is an illegal or illicit one); (ii) the assignor may not be held liable if the other assignor (the one subsisting) does not comply with the obligations to the assignee. However, a stipulation to the contrary can be included. As to effects between the assignor who subsists in the contract and the assignee, the effects are of course those of the contract being assigned and the assignor subsisting in the contract may present legal exceptions that are not expressly related to the contract being assigned. Finally, as to the relations between assignors themselves, the assignor subsisting in the contract may not fulfill obligations in favor of the assignor who leaves the contract and likewise, the subsisting assignor may state that it does not deem the leaving assignor as exonerated of its responsibility. The effects of the assignment start upon the acceptance of the subsisting assignor; however, between the leaving assignor and the assignee all effects will be realized without their acceptance. When a contract assignment takes place, all elements of the contract are transferred and assigned, except the particular and personal conditions of the assignor, which cannot be assigned or transferred.

c) Specification of Contracts. Usually, a detailed description of the contracts to be assigned or transferred is needed. Failure to provide such description normally will not invalidate the transaction, but it will generate conflict and may result in the process being a lengthier one. The mention made in the case of commercial units as to identification of goods to be transferred cannot be made here to the extent that contracts cannot be entered into by *establecimientos de comercio* themselves but by juridical persons and *establecimientos de comercio* are not juridical persons but rather a special configuration of property and goods organized by merchants.

2. Administrative, Corporate and Other Approvals

(i) If state-owned companies are parties to the assignment or transfer of contracts, administrative and governmental approvals are always required;

(ii) corporate bodies are always entitled to approve the transfer and assignment of contracts and they usually do so. Failure to have the authorization of corporate bodies such as the board of directors or the shareholders themselves will normally result in invalidity of the transaction; however, particular provisions of the by-laws will require revision and confirmation because they usually provide for significant amounts involved that require authorizations; the same analysis can be applied to the contracts to be assigned that usually state how assignment has to operate and whether the authorization of directors is needed or not;

(iii) commercial and civil rules in Colombia are very stringent as to the notifications and acceptances of parties potentially involved in the assignment or transfer of a contract. The acceptance of the assignee is always required in the case of *intuitu personae* and instantaneous execution contracts. Acceptance in the case of successive execution contracts is not always required. The form of acceptance, however, differs depending on the nature and type of the contract.

3. Automatic Transfer of Contracts (Other than Lease and Employment Agreements)

The transfer of contracts is not always automatic. In Colombia, the transfer or assignment of certain contracts is semi-automatic. In the case of insurance policies, they are typically transferred but by means of an endorsement, and in that sense it could be said that transfer or assignment is a semi-automatic process.

4. Filing Requirements

Usually, the transfer or assignment of commercial contracts does not require registration. However, if an encumbrance is to be transferred, then the respective contract has to be notarized and registered before the *Oficina de Registro de Instrumentos Públicos*. Failure to register may result in the encumbrance not having any effect whatsoever.

5. Treatment of Existing Contractual Claims and Obligations

In the event sold contracts are not or not completely fulfilled, it depends on the type of obligations transferred and on the provisions of the contract themselves as to whether the respective claims and/or obligations automatically transfer to the purchaser. There are some obligations that are automatically transferred to the purchaser of the contract but Colombian law allows parties to agree to the contrary, and to that extent, negotiating entities are usually advised to include provisions to diminish or even eliminate the possibility of being held liable for non-compliance or the entitlement to make claims. A reference here has to be made as to the following: As to effects between assignors and assignees themselves, the one assigning the contract is liable for the existence and validity of the contract being assigned as well as for its guarantees and warranties. To that effect, if the contract never existed, the assignor will have to pay the assignee damages. If the contract did exist but was not valid, the following may apply: (i) it may be agreed that the assignor could not be held liable for certain nullity causes (exception made for cases where the purpose of the contract is an illegal or illicit one); (ii) assignor may not be held liable if the other assignor (the one subsisting) does not comply with the obligations to the assignee. However, a stipulation to the contrary can be included. As to effects between the assignor who subsists in the contract and the assignee, the effects are of course those of the contract being assigned and the assignor subsisting in the contract may present legal exceptions that are not expressly related to the contract being assigned. Finally, as to the relations between assignors themselves, the assignor subsisting in the contract may not fulfill obligations in favor of the assignor who leaves the contract and likewise, the subsisting assignor may state that it does not deem the leaving assignor as exonerated of responsibility. The effects of the assignment start upon the acceptance of the subsisting assignor; however, between the leaving assignor and the assignee, all effects will be realized without their acceptance. When a contract assignment takes place, all elements of the contract are transferred and assigned, except for particular and personal conditions of the assignor that cannot be assigned or transferred.

6. Warranty Claims Resulting from Events prior to Transfer

Whether the purchaser is liable for warranty claims resulting from events prior to the transfer of the assets depends on the contract provisions themselves. Usually, negotiating individuals are advised to include special provisions to eliminate their liability for warranties. This depends on the nature of the contract and the intent of the parties. For example, as to the effects between assignor and assignee, the assignor does not respond or can be held liable if the subsisting assignor does not comply with its obligations vis-à-vis the assignee. This may be agreed to the contrary and the assignee has to notify the assignor within ten days following the compliance of delay or the breach; failure to do so will normally result in the assignor being exonerated from the guarantee or warranty obligations. There is no joint liability between assignors (the leaving one and the subsisting one). If eventually the leaving assignor is the one complying with the obligations, he/she may be subrogated to exert rights against the subsisting assignor.

E. IP Rights

1. Characteristics of Intellectual Property Rights (e. g., Trademarks, Patents, Utility Models, Domain Names) ("*IP Rights*") as to:

a) Language of Documentation. Documents can be drafted either in Spanish or in English. Usually, if foreign entities are involved, documents are executed bilingually and a sworn translation is provided. As mentioned above, when foreign parties are involved, usually the executed versions of documents in English are provided and they are annexed to the official forms furnished by the Colombian Trademark and Patent Office (*Superintendencia de Industria y Comercio*).

b) Form of Documentation. No notarization is required to transfer IP Rights. However, the transfer has to be verified before the *Superintendencia de Industria y Comercio* or the *Dirección Nacional de Derechos de Autor*, the first being the office in charge of regulating and enforcing industrial property rights, and the second being entrusted with the mission of maintaining copyrights registrations and protecting them. Documents can be executed outside the jurisdiction (usually they are) but registration and local procedures need to take place in Colombia before the Colombian Trademark and Patent Office located in Bogotá. Lately and due to some legal reforms introduced in Colombia, regional Colombian chambers of commerce have been entrusted with the mission of managing trademark registrations and IP related rights, which has eased the corresponding proceedings.

c) Specification of IP Rights. The Trade Superintendent Office of Colombia (Trademark and Patent Office) requires IP Rights to be listed in a detailed fashion. Usually, lists of IP Rights are provided. However, reference is made to what has been mentioned regarding the commercial units. To that respect, it is useful to revisit the above cited Article 515 of the Colombian Commerce Code, which defines commercial unit as "(...) an estate configured and set by the entrepreneur in order to carry out the purposes of the company/enterprise. One person may be the owner of several commercial units, and in turn, one single commercial unit may belong to several people, and may be devoted to the carrying out of several commercial activities," Article 516 of the same Colombian Commercial Code states that the following: "Except agreement to the contrary, a commercial unit is composed of: 1. Commercial names and products and services trademarks (emphasis added); 2. Rights of the entrepreneur over inventions or artistic or industrial creations being used for the activities of the commercial unit; 3. Merchandise deposited in storage units or being manufactured; 4. Credits and remaining similar securities; 5. Movables and premises; 6. Lease agreements, and in case of transfer, the lease rights of premises where the commercial units function if they are owned by the entrepreneur, and indemnifications that according to the law the tenant is entitled to; 7. The right to impede client-deviation mechanisms and the protection of good-will; and 8. Commercial rights and obligations derived from activities of the commercial unit, as long as they do not arise under contracts subscribed and executed by only considering the owner of that establishment." Article 525 of the Colombian Commercial Code in turn states that "the transfer of an commercial unit is presumed to take place as a whole, without need to specify in detail the elements it is composed of" (emphasis added).

2. Administrative, Corporate and Other Approvals

(i) If IP Rights are owned by the state they require the corresponding administrative approvals; in fact, both the Colombian Administrative Law Code as well as Law 80 of 1993, which is the main statute governing governmental procurement, require administrative entities to have all permissions and licenses in place in order to transfer any type of property, including IP Rights;

(ii) corporate bodies have to authorize any transfer of IP Rights, and the absence thereof normally will result in the invalidity or nullity of the transfer; however, particular consideration and attention has to be paid to the particular conditions of the by-laws and of the IP assignment contracts themselves;

(iii) if IP Rights are to encumbered, approval of owners is always needed.

3. Filing Requirements

Registration of transfers of IP Rights is always needed. It shall take place before the Trademark and Patent Office or the Copyright Office (*Dirección Nacional de Derechos de Autor*). A distinction has to be made, however, regarding the granting of registration of trademarks and patents and the process of assignment of the registration and the process of copyright registration. Under Colombian law, the registration of trademarks and patents must take place before the Colombian Trademark and Patent Office (*Superintendencia de Industria y Comercio*). Assignment of trademarks and patents shall also be processed before that same Colombian Trademark and Patent Office (*Superintendencia de Industria y Comercio*). In turn, copyrights are the author's property at the time of creation of any work under the scope of copyright protection, but registration needs to take place in order to enhance legal protections granted.

4. Applicable International (Multilateral) Agreements or Treaties

Colombia participates in all international agreements related to IP protection, including TRIPS; the Paris Convention for the Protection of Industrial Property, and at the inter-American level in some treaties and special agreements. The scope of the Andean Community of Nations is worth noting. Currently the Andean Community of Nations, to which Colombia, Ecuador, Bolivia and Peru belong, is a customs union with a wide range of regulations dealing with foreign trade and IP Rights. The main custom is dealing with IP rights is "Decisión 486," by means of which those nations operate under the same laws regarding trademarks and patents. Therefore, if a person files a trademark application in Bolivia, it will also have automatic effects in Colombia or in any other nation participating in the Andean Community of Nations.

F. Receivables

1. Characteristics as to:

a) Language of Documentation. Documentation is normally executed bilingually when foreign entities are involved. A sworn translation is usually provided. As noted above, usually when foreign parties are involved, an English version of documents and documentation is generally provided and furnished by the foreign entity and revised and reviewed by Colombian local counsel.

b) Form of Documentation. Notarization is not needed and documents can be executed outside the Colombian jurisdiction. Documents can be signed separately or jointly. Despite the fact that documentation can be executed outside Colombia, foreign entities and foreign counsel are normally advised as to the compliance of certain accounting and corporate rules entailed by the transfer of receivables and that need to be taken into account. In this case, documents are prepared by local counsel both in Spanish and English and perused and reviewed by foreign counsel.

c) Specification of Receivables. Receivables have to be listed in a detailed fashion. Otherwise the transaction can be voided or result in a more lengthy process. The mention made as to commercial units cannot be made here, as commercial units are not juridical persons and do not have the authority to enter into contracts.

2. Administrative, Corporate and Other Approvals

(i) If governmental agencies are involved, official authorizations are always needed; in that sense the provisions contained in the Colombian Administrative Law Code as well as the ones contained in Law 80 of 1993 (Colombian Public Contracting Statute) have to be carefully followed;

(ii) authorizations of corporate bodies are always needed; failure to have the corporate body authorization will result in the contract being void;

(iii) no approval of debtors is needed as a general rule. Civil law rules establish that acceptance may be a tacit one (such as when debtor pays) or express (such as when a conflict arises between the assignee and the debtor).

3. Filing Requirements

(i) No special filings with public authorities are needed; however, particular registration in the accounting books, which in turn are registered with the chamber of commerce, is always required; and

(ii) notifications to debtors are normally required and the certificates or bonds evidencing the transfer of receivables are needed.

G. Liabilities

1. Characteristics as to:

a) Language of Documentation. Documents are usually drafted in Spanish and English (sworn translations provided thereto) when foreign entities are parties to the transaction. Usually, English is the governing language, and documents or versions are provided in English by the foreign entities for the review and revision thereof by local counsel.

b) Form of Documentation. A notarization is not needed, although parties may in effect demand so by means of a provision included in the corresponding contract. Documents can always be executed outside the jurisdiction of Colombia but legalization has to follow if contracts are to have effects inside Colombia. Documents can be signed jointly or separately. Usually they are signed in a joint fashion. It is rare for documents to be signed separately. However, foreign entities are usually and strongly advised by local counsel to follow the main rules governing the assignment of debt and liabilities, in particular regarding accounting technical rules and aspects and dealing with civil contractual liability

c) Specification of Liabilities. Liabilities have to be listed in a detailed fashion. Failure to do so will result either in the invalidity of the transaction or in it being a lengthier one. The same reference made about commercial units regarding the transfer of receivables can be made here. *Establecimientos de comercio* as such cannot assign or transfer debt because they lack juridical personality, so as a general rule, liabilities to be transferred need to be clearly identified and listed.

2. Administrative, Corporate and Other Approvals

(i) The transfer of liabilities does not require official approval unless a state-owned company or a governmental agency is party to the transfer of liabilities; particular attention has to be paid to the regulations contained and set out in the Colombian Administrative Law Code and in Law 80 of 1993, which is the Colombian government procurement and public contracting statute;

(ii) the authorization of corporate bodies is always required and needed;

(iii) approval of creditors is always required to the extent that a new juridical relationship is established between the new debtor and the old creditor. Failure to have creditors' authorization will result in the invalidity of the transaction.

3. Filing Requirements

No special filings are needed and creditors' notifications are always required.

4. Purchaser's Liability for:

a) Tax Obligations. Usually, sale agreements provide that sellers transfer property with all tax obligations having been complied with in a way that the purchaser does not have to be held liable for any tax item whatsoever. However, this all depends on how the contract is drafted and on the stipulations of the parties as to the tax implications of the operation.

b) Environmental Contamination. The inclusion of environmental provisions usually depends on the nature of the contract, its purpose and of the parties involved in the transaction. For some type of operations there are administrative laws and rules in place that require parties to comply with certain requirements. Failure to do so will normally result in fines imposed by environmental protection agencies.

c) Products Sold or Services Rendered by the Seller to Third Parties. Contracts usually have some conditions precedent that establish the rules contractors have to observe when transferring property and their previous relationships with other parties.

Particular consideration has to be made as to entities listed by the U.S. Government as terrorist supporters or money-laundering subjects. Likewise, in large operations taking place in Colombia (such as project finance operations and derived contracts) due diligence tasks usually take place allowing the verification of personal and corporate records in the way of a background check.

5. Automatic Transfer of Other Liabilities

No other liabilities of the seller automatically transfer to the purchaser due to the acquisition of assets, but particular conditions are usually set out in the contracts that reduce or modify the liability regime.

6. Contractual Protection as to 4 and 5 above

It is customary in mega-contracts where environmental impact or project finance operations are involved to include special provisions (e.g., indemnifications) as to the issues mentioned under 4 and 5 into the asset sale and/or transfer agreement.

H. Employees

1. Transfer of Employees

There is a labor law institution called *Sustitución Patronal* defined by Article 67 of the Colombian Labor Law Code as follows: "Employers substitution operates when a change of employers take place, as long as the identity of the entity subsists which means that no radical change in its corporate purpose is verified or evidenced." There is a legal regime for the *Sustitución Patronal* to operate: 1. Former and new employer are jointly liable for obligations that are at the date of substitution enforceable against the former employer, but if the new employer paid the obligations, then he may file recoup actions against the former employer; 2. The new employer is liable for all obligations arising after the substitution takes place; 3. In the case of retirement, which rights have been originated before the substitution, monthly pensions demandable after the substitution takes place shall be covered and paid by the new employer, but he may file subrogation actions against the former one; 4. The former employer may agree with one or all of the workers as to the definitive payment of all services rendered and time served up to the time of substitution, as if it were voluntary retirement, without the employment agreement being deemed as terminated; 5. If the mentioned agreement had not been subscribed, the former employer shall deliver to the new the amount of employment benefits in the amount the obligation is enforceable in the event that the contracts should be extinguished due to voluntary retirement at the date of substitution; hereafter it is the exclusive responsibility of the new employer to effect payment of employment benefits being caused thereon, even if the former employer does not comply with what is mandated in this provision; 6. The new employer may agree that all of the workers be paid their employment benefits for all time served in the same form and with all the same effects clause 4 of this Article 69 of the Colombian Labor Law Code refers to.

2. Approval of Works Council, Trade Union and Other Institutions

The asset transfer does not require any labor agency or trade union approval. An approval on the part of the Ministry of Labor is not needed either. No approval of the trade union is needed. However, and due to the particular conditions of Colombia and its economic environment, specific attention has to be paid to the influence of trade unions inside companies and corporations in Colombia and assess the impact of a possible asset transfer. Also, labor agreements subscribed with labor unions and labor unions leaders need to be revised carefully and thoroughly.

3. Contractual Protection as to Labor Issues

It is not customary to include special provisions (e.g., guarantees, indemnifications) as to employees in the asset sale and/or transfer agreement.

I. Tax Implications

1. Value Added Tax

The current VAT rate in Colombia is 16%. The asset transfer does not result in VAT.

2. Real Property Transfer Tax

The current land transfer tax rate is associated with the registration of the Public Deed transferring real property. There may also be income tax associated (35% average). Transfer of property of land always results in a land tax being paid in equal parts by the purchaser and by the seller.

3. Other Tax Issues

There are no other tax issues in connection with an asset transfer.

J. Bankruptcy Law

1. Challenge of Asset Transfer in Case of Insolvency

There is no way to challenge an asset transfer. However, particular consideration has to be paid as to the legal and contractual requisites referred to sale or transfer of assets as to liability of seller and purchaser. The commercial and civil rules in Colombia are particularly detailed as to that regard to the extent that an operation involving the transfer of assets may be reversed when certain conditions precedent, representations or warranties are not complied with or when fraudulent means or deceit took place. Criminal considerations may play a role here, too.

2. Acquisition of Assets that are Subject to Insolvency Proceedings

If the company or entity that is to make the transfer is a bankrupt one, there are special regulations in place to proceed with the transfer and it normally supervised by the Colombian Companies Superintendent Office (*Superintendencia de Sociedades*). If the company becomes bankrupt after the transfer has been made, there is no way to return things to the state before the transfer took place, unless a cause of nullity or invalidity is verified. A mention shall be made as to the fact that certain companies are not under the direct supervision of the Colombian Companies Superintendent Office (*Superintendencia de Sociedades*), but the largest and biggest ones are always subject to its supervision and oversight.

K. Timing and Costs

1. Timeframe of Asset Transfer

The sale/acquisition of a business by way of an asset deal normally takes at the most between six and eight months.

2. Costs of Asset Transfer

No estimate can be given as to the cost of an asset transfer because this is always related to the price of property and the time involved in the operation, which can be extraordinarily short or long depending on the parties involved and the sophistication or difficulty of property and entities.

L. Miscellaneous

1. Choice of Foreign Law

The sale and/or transfer agreement can be subject to foreign law and this is usually the case when there is a foreign party to the agreement. Advice is always given as to the essential inclusion of choice of law and choice of forum provisions.

2. (International) Arbitration, Choice of Venue

International arbitration is always possible. In fact, in Colombia, international and local arbitration has become more and more popular.

3. Other Distinctions, Characteristics

Our jurisdiction does not provide for any other distinctions or unusual characteristics noteworthy in connection with a customary asset deal.

M. Literature

José Alejandro Bonivento Fernandez, Los Principales Contratos Civiles y su Paralelo con los Comerciales, 11th Edition, 1995

Cesar Gómez Estrada, De los Principales Contratos Civiles, 3rd Edition, 1996

Denmark

By *Nils Kjellegaard Jensen*

A. General Aspects

1. Asset Deal vs. Share Deal: Essential Considerations

A seller and a purchaser may structure a transaction by way of an asset deal or a share deal. Opting for an asset deal as opposed to a share deal is, at least for the average purchaser, often driven by two essential considerations. First, there is no full assumption of liability for unknown or potential claims or obligations of the target company vis-à-vis the creditors, and, secondly, the buyer obtains a basis for depreciations for corporate income tax purposes (i.e. depreciations on the acquired assets and on the goodwill amount paid) on a going forward basis. Opting for a share deal may often be driven by the fact that most (customer or supplier) contracts automatically follow the target company (i.e. no change in contracting party and thus no re-negotiations), such that obtaining the consent of any such third parties is not legally required.

2. Distinction between Sale and Transfer in Rem

Danish law does not distinguish between the sale (obligation to transfer) and the transfer in rem (fulfillment of the obligation to transfer). If, however, an asset deal includes a transfer of title and ownership to land and/or buildings (real property), the registration of a deed of transfer in the Land Register (*Tingbogen*) is required, and it advised that – in addition to the sale and purchase agreement – a separate transfer deed be prepared and executed. The latter may be deemed as the transfer in rem.

3. Regional Differences

Danish law is geographically uniform in the sense that there are no regional differences within the jurisdiction as regards the legal requirements in connection with the transfers of assets. However, different rules may apply with respect to Greenland and Faroe Islands, which are not covered herein.

4. Acquisition by Foreigners

Outside of regulated or strategic industries such as the military, energy and nuclear industries or sectors such as banking, insurance and finance, there are no distinctions, restrictions, special approvals or verification requirements applicable to transfer of assets due to the nationality of the acquirer. With respect to transfers of real estate, restrictions apply if the acquirer is not resident in Denmark or a Danish legal entity. Please refer to C, 2 below in this respect.

5. Public Registers, Records and Databases

In connection with an asset transfer, relevant information on the selling entity and the assets/business to be acquired may be found and obtained via the following web-based public registers:

www.cvr.dk (data on business entities, identity of signatories, financial statements, and data on number of employees)

www.dkpto.dk (patents, trademarks)

With respect to information on real property, information may be found at:

www.ois.dk or www.tinglysningsretten.dk

or by calling the regional Land Register registrars (*Tingbogen*) organized at the regional city courts (note that effective as of September 8, 2009, one centralized digital Land Register covering all real property in Denmark will become available and operational; Tinglysningsretten (Land Registration Court), Majsmarken 5, DK-9500 Hobro, Phone +45 99 68 58 00).

Information on non-possessory pledges, including negative pledges, floating charges or certain other collateral rights on tangible assets, IP Rights and account receivables may be found by phone call to the Personal Book (*Personbogen*) or the Automotive Vehicles Book (*Bilbogen*), which since May 2009 are under the auspices of Tinglysningsretten (Land Registration Court), Majsmarken 5, DK-9500 Hobro, Phone +45 99 68 58 00.

6. Purchase Price Requirements

There are no special rules with regard to the purchase price (requiring a minimum or maximum price or use of the domestic DKK (*Danish kroner*) or only specific foreign currencies). For income tax and accounting purposes, it is advisable for (a domestic) seller or purchaser to agree on an allocation of the total purchase price on individual groups of assets.

B. Tangible/Movable Assets

1. Characteristics as to:

a) Language of Documentation. There is no mandatory language for legal contracts. All documents may be drafted in English or any other language with or without a Danish bilingual version.

b) Form of Documentation. There are no requirements for written form or notarization or other procedural formalities. In principle, oral agreements on transfer of tangible assets are legally valid as well. Practically speaking, however, only written form agreements are used. Legal agreements and documents regarding the transfer of tangible assets may be validly executed in counterparts. Furthermore, the transfer documents can be executed outside of Denmark.

c) Specification of Assets. General descriptions (e.g., "all tangible assets related to the business or to a certain unit of an entity") or a generic description (e.g., "all inventories located in ") are in principle sufficient for legal purposes. Inter partes exhaustive or exemplary schedules or lists of either included or excluded assets (if needed or recommended to avoid doubt in case of transfers of one of more divisions/business units) are often attached as appendices to the agreement.

2. Administrative, Corporate and Other Approvals

A transfer of tangible assets does not require general governmental or administrative approval except where Danish merger control laws may apply.

If a Danish corporate entity ("ApS" or "A/S") transfers (or acquires) a business unit or assets, it does not require approval by a particular corporate body in order to validate the transfer, as long as the formal rule of execution for the particular corporate entity is observed. If a transfer of assets comprises all or a substantial part of a legal entity's assets/business, a shareholder approval may be required internally, but as long as the formal rule of execution is observed, the transfer is legally valid also without such approval.

Holders of security rights to tangible assets (including negative pledges (i.e. a registered document, according to which the owner covenants not to pledge the real property without the prior consent of the third party, to whom the covenant is made) must consent to a transfer of the tangible asset in question. If such consent is not given, the asset remains subject to the security right and consequently the enforcement right, provided that the security holder has complied with the perfection (i.e. registration of his security right in the Personal Register (*Personbogen*)) acts and requirements applicable for the particular type of security interest and asset in question. If the security right holder has not met the perfection requirements, the purchaser may extinguish the security right, if purchaser is a good faith, bona fide purchaser. If the security right is "retention of title" in tangible assets other than automotive vehicles registered in Denmark, the purchaser does not extinguish the conflicting right, regardless whether purchaser was in good faith (bona fide). Retention of title in automotive vehicles registered in Denmark must be registered in the Automotive Vehicles Register (in Danish *Bilbogen*) in order to be protected against purchasers in good faith.

3. Filing Requirements

A transfer of tangible assets (except from exports of weapons, military equipment, ammunition, certain chemical substances, and other similar items) does not as such require special filings or registrations with public agencies in order to be valid inter partes.

4. Automatic Transfer of Encumbrances

If the tangible assets are subject to encumbrances, the holders of the security right must give their consent to the transfer of the tangible assets in question. If such consent is not given, the title transfers are valid inter partes (i.e. as between seller and purchaser), but the assets remain subject to the security rights and, consequently, the inherent enforcement rights, provided the security holders have complied with the perfection acts and requirements applicable for the particular types of assets in question. For further details, please refer to B, 2 above.

C. Real Property

1. Characteristics as to:

a) Language of Documentation. There is no mandatory language for legal contracts contemplating transfers of real property. All documents may be drafted in English or any other language with or without a Danish bilingual version. If a transfer deed for real estate property is to be registered in the Land Register (which is always recommended but not required), a signed version or a signed extract in the Danish language must be executed on special format paper. A Danish translation may suffice as long as it is executed by both seller and purchaser.

b) Form of Documentation. There are no requirements for notarization or other procedural formalities. In principle, oral agreements regarding transfer of real property are legally valid. In practice only written form agreements are used. It is often the case that preceding legal agreements and documents regarding details of the transfer are executed and signed, and the principle terms and conditions thereof are repeated in a separate deed of transfer (in special format and in Danish language) for the purpose of Land Register registration). The deed of transfer of real estate property, which is required in order to have purchaser's title registered in the Land Register (*Tingbogen*) must be in writing and cannot be executed in counterparts, and the signature(s) of the seller must be witnessed by two unrelated persons. The legal agreement regarding the obligation to transfer real property may, however, validly be signed in counterparts. In addition, all legal documents pertaining to real property – and also the deed of title transfer – may be signed outside of Denmark.

Effective as of September 8, 2009, all ownership and limited rights to real property are registered by use of digital filing/registration only. The traditional deed of transfer of real estate property, required in order to have purchaser's title registered in the Land Register (*Tingbogen*), will be replaced by a digital document and filing (by a Danish lawyer with authorized digital signature) on the basis of a digital or written power-of-attorney by the seller, the signature(s) of which must be witnessed by two unrelated persons. After September 8, 2009, hard copy deeds of transfer cannot form basis for registration in the Land Register.

c) Specification of Assets. General descriptions (e.g., "all real property related to the business or to a certain unit of an entity") or generic or geographically defined descriptions (e.g., "all real property located in, ...") are in principle sufficient for legal purposes. Inter partes exhaustive or exemplary schedules or lists of either included or excluded real property (if needed or recommended to avoid doubt in case of transfers of one of more divisions/business units) are often attached as appendices to the agreement, and in order to obtain registration of purchaser's title in the Land Registration a precise description of each separate piece of real property (by cadastral unit no., etc., address/zip code) is required.

2. Administrative, Corporate and Other Approvals

Transfers of title and ownership to real property to permanent Danish residents or to persons who in the preceding five years have had permanent residence in Denmark (a determination for which citizenship is irrelevant) and to legal entities incorporated in Denmark (regardless of the residence of the owners/members/shareholders) do not require special government or administrative approvals, except where the land is situated in recreational or agricultural/forest zones.

Transfers of title and ownership to real property to non-residents (another determination for which citizenship is irrelevant) and legal entities incorporated outside of Denmark do require special government approval from the Ministry of Justice. Applications must be filed not later than six months after conclusion of the binding agreement, and if approval is not applied for or not granted, the transfer is not legally invalid, but the purchaser is under both an administrative and criminally-sanctioned obligation to re-dispose of the real property.

Transfers of title and ownership to real property to EU/EFTA citizens (without residence in Denmark) and legal entities incorporated in EU/EFTA member states do not require special government or administrative approvals, except where the land is situated in recreational or agricultural/forest zones, provided the real property is to be used as a primary permanent residence (in connection with the free movement of workers in EU) or is a pre-condition for carrying out a trade or providing services.

If the land is situated in recreational or agricultural/forest zones, special legislation is applicable, which in certain circumstances requires additional special governmental approval in case of transfers to legal entities.

The Land Register registrars (i.e. at present the de-central regional city courts) observe compliance with all these rules in connection with filings of the deed of transfer for registration of change of title and ownership to purchaser in the Land Register.

If a Danish corporate entity ("ApS" or "A/S") transfers (or acquires) real property, it does not require approval by a particular corporate body in order to make the transfer valid, as long as the formal rule of execution for the particular corporate entity is observed. If a transfer of assets comprises all or a substantial part of a legal entity's assets/business, shareholder approval (and not merely a board approval) may be required internally, but as long as the formal rule on execution is observed, the transfer is legally valid and binding upon the legal entity without such shareholder or board approval.

Holders of security rights over real property must grant their consent to a transfer of the real property in question. If such consent is not granted, the real property remains subject to the security right and consequently the enforcement right, provided the security holder has complied with the applicable perfection acts and requirements (i.e. registration of the mortgage in the Land Register). If the security right holder has not met the perfection requirements (which is a rather unusual circumstance), the purchaser may extinguish the security right, if purchaser is a good faith, bona fide purchaser.

3. Filing Requirements

Certain data about each and any transfer of title of real property in Denmark must be reported to local tax agencies for statistical and municipal tax administration purposes prior to filing the deed of transfer for registration in the Land Register. Effective as of September 8, 2009, a digital filing/registration process for transfer of title to real property will become applicable, and the (separate) reporting to local tax agencies will occur automatically.

Except as outlined above under C, 1, b, transfer of title and ownership to real property does not, as such, require registration in the Land Register to be legally valid inter partes, but in order to protect purchaser against seller's creditors and third parties' junior conflicting rights, a special format deed of transfer must be executed and registered in the Land Register (*Tingbogen*). Effective as of September 8, 2009, only digital documents and filings (by a Danish lawyer with authorized digital signature) on the basis of a digital or written power-of-attorney by the seller, the signature(s) of which must be witnessed by two unrelated persons, can form basis for a registration in the Land Register.

4. Automatic Transfer of Encumbrances

If the real property is subject to mortgages, encumbrances, etc., the holder of the security right must grant its consent to the transfer of the real property in question. If such consent is not granted, the title transfer is valid inter partes (i.e. as between seller and purchaser), but the real property remains subject to the security right and consequently the inherent enforcement rights, provided the security holder has complied with the perfection acts and requirements applicable (registration in Land Register (*Tingbogen*)). Thus, in this sense the security right automatically transfers to or must be respected by the purchaser. If the security right holder has not met the perfection requirements, the purchaser extinguishes the security right, if purchaser is a good faith, bona fide purchaser.

If the real property is subject to easements, usufruct rights or lease agreements, the holder of the easement or usufruct right or the lessee, as appropriate, is not required to grant its consent to the transfer of the real property in question. The rights (and obligations) of the easements and usufruct rights or of the lease agreement, etc. will automatically transfer to purchaser and shall be respected by purchaser, provided that the easements, usufructs or lease agreements are registered in the Land Register (*Tingbogen*).

5. Automatic Transfer of Lease Agreements

If the real property is subject to commercial or residential lease agreements (in most cases regardless whether the agreements are registered in the Land Register (*Tingbogen*) or not), the tenants are not required to grant their consent to the transfer of the real property in question, and all rights and obligations under the lease agreements will automatically transfer to purchaser and must be respected by purchaser. A transfer of the real property does not, by operation of law, trigger an extraordinary right for purchaser to terminate the lease agreements or to terminate them with shorter or no notice.

A transfer of the real property also does not, by operation of law, trigger an extraordinary right for the tenant to terminate the lease agreement. If the real property is leased for residential purposes, the tenants as a collective unit often enjoy statutory and inalienable rights of first refusal to acquire the real property, if the lessor wishes to sell the property.

D. Contracts

1. Characteristics:

a) Language of Documentation. There is no mandatory language for legal contracts. All documents may be drafted in English or any other language with or without a Danish version (bilingual).

b) Form of Documentation. There are no requirements for notarization or other procedural formalities for agreements on transfer and assignment of contracts. In principle, oral agreements are legally valid, also. However, in practice, only written form agreements are used. Legal agreements and documents regarding transfer and assignment of contracts may validly be executed in counterparts and outside of Denmark.

c) Specification of Contracts. General descriptions (e.g., “all contracts related to the business or to a certain unit of an entity” or “all customer contracts”) are in principle sufficient for legal purposes. Inter partes exhaustive or exemplary schedules or lists identifying, e.g., all included customers or all excluded customers (if needed or recommended to avoid doubt in case of transfers of one of more divisions/business units) are often attached to the agreement.

2. Administrative, Corporate and Other Approvals

The transfer and assignment of contracts does not require any special governmental or administrative approval. Particular rules, however, apply in the banking and insurance industry, where the transfer of contracts on deposits and insurance contracts from one bank/insurance company to another require observance of a special administrative procedure and approval from the Financial Supervisory Agency (in Danish *Finanstilsynet*).

If a Danish corporate entity ("ApS" or "A/S") transfers (or acquires) contracts (as part a business transfer), it does not require approval by a particular corporate body in order to make the transfer valid, as long as the formal rule of signature for the particular corporate entity is observed. If a transfer of assets comprises all or a substantial part of a legal entity's assets/business, shareholder approval may be required internally, but as long as the formal rule on signature is observed, the transfer is also legally valid without such approval.

The transfer and assignment of contracts requires the consent of the other contracting party, unless the contract itself states that it may be assigned by the relevant party without the consent of the other party. If consent is required but not obtained, the assignment and transfer is not legally invalid inter partes, but the other contracting party may refuse to deliver to, or accept delivery by, or payment to the assignee.

3. Automatic Transfer of Contracts (Other than Lease and Employment Agreements)

Other than with respect to certain lease agreements for lease of real property and with respect to employment contracts, no contracts are transferred by operation of law from seller to purchaser. As regards certain asset or property insurance (damage to property), the relevant interest is insured to the benefit of the party who is concerned (i.e. including successors and assignees), and some property insurance contemplates a certain limited period of continued insurance coverage (the same as the seller enjoyed) in the event of transfer of ownership to the property insured (automotive vehicle damage insurance).

4. Filing Requirements

The transfer of contracts does not require filings be made to public authorities, except, e.g., in the banking and insurance industry.

5. Treatment of Existing Contractual Claims and Obligations

The rights and obligations/claims under a contract, which is not or not completely fulfilled, will automatically pass to the purchaser, provided and to the extent that the other contracting party has consented to the transfer of the contract from seller to purchaser. Often, the asset sale and purchase agreement will include provisions as to allocate the risks of earlier or subsequent bad performance of the contract by means of representations and warranties and corresponding indemnifications, or, if appropriate, by adjustment of the purchase price due to impact on the working capital.

6. Warranty Claims Resulting from Events prior to Transfer

If the rights and obligations/claims under a contract that is not fulfilled automatically pass to the purchaser because the other contracting party has consented to the transfer of the contract from seller to purchaser, it very often implies that all claims and obligations – even those that have arisen or were caused by events that occurred prior to the takeover date – pass to purchaser. As mentioned, the asset sale and purchase agreement will often include provisions to allocate such risks or exposure by stipulating various representations and warranties and respective indemnifications to the benefit of purchaser.

E. IP Rights

1. Characteristics of Intellectual Property Rights (e. g., Trade Marks, Patents, Utility Models, Domain Names) ("*IP Rights*"), as to:

a) Language of Documentation. There is no mandatory language for legal contracts regarding transfer of Danish IP Rights (patents, utility models, registered and unregistered trademarks, domain names, copyrights). All documents may be drafted in English or any other language with or without a Danish version (bilingual).

b) Form of Documentation. There are no requirements for notarization or other procedural formalities for agreements on transfer of Danish IP Rights. In principle, oral agreements on transfer of Danish IP Rights are legally valid. In practice, only written form agreements are used. Legal agreements and documents regarding transfer of Danish IP Rights may validly be signed in counterparts. In addition, the legal documents may be signed outside of Denmark. However, in order to have the transfer of ownership registered (in the case of trademarks, this only applies to registered trademarks) a special form in Danish and English must be signed by both seller and purchaser (not in counterparts) and submitted to the Patent and Trademark Office.

c) Specification of IP Rights. General descriptions of the respective IP Rights (e. g., "all IP Rights related to the business") or a generic description (e. g., "all trademarks related to the logistic division") are in principle sufficient for legal purposes. Inter partes exhaustive or exemplary schedules or lists of either included or excluded IP Rights (if needed or recommended to avoid doubt in case of transfers of one of more divisions/business units) are often attached to the agreement. Both registered and unregistered trademarks are by law presumed to be transferred if the business they relate to is transferred. However, in order to have the transfer of ownership registered (in case of trademarks, only registered trademarks) a special form in Danish and English must be signed by both seller and purchaser (not in counterparts) and submitted (post-closing) to the Patent and Trademark Office. For that purpose, an individual identification (by e. g., patent no., trademark no. etc.) of each IP Right is required.

2. Administrative, Corporate and Other Approvals

A transfer of IP Rights does not require general governmental or administrative approval.

If a Danish corporate entity ("ApS" or "A/S") transfers (or acquires) IP Rights, approval from a particular corporate body is not required in order for the transfer to be valid, as long as the formal rule of execution for the particular corporate entity is observed. If a transfer of IP Rights comprises all or a substantial part of a legal entity's assets/ business value, shareholder approval may be required internally. As long as the formal rule on execution is observed, the transfer is however legally valid also without such shareholder approval.

Holders of security rights to IP Rights must grant consent to a transfer of the tangible asset in question. If such consent is not granted, the asset remains subject to the security right and consequently the enforcement right, provided the security holder has complied with the perfection acts and requirements applicable to the particular type of asset in question (i.e. registration in the Personal Register (*Personbogen*)). If the security right holder has not met the perfection requirements, the purchaser may extinguish the security right, if purchaser is a good faith, bona fide purchaser.

3. Filing Requirements

Transfers of Danish registered patents, trademarks, and utility models must be filed with the Danish Patent and Trademark Office for changes in the registers. However, the filing/registration of the new owner is of declaratory nature (but of course highly recommendable on the side of purchaser) and the transfer is legally valid from the time of the execution of the asset sale and purchase agreement even if the filing/ registration is not made. The same applies for Danish domain names (".dk"). The full or partial transfer of ownership to copyrights (exclusive of the "droit moral" of the author, which cannot be transferred) or of unregistered trademarks does not require any filings and cannot be registered in any public database or register.

4. Applicable International (Multilateral) Agreements or Treaties

Denmark participates in the TRIPS Agreement ("Agreement on Trade-related aspects of Intellectual Property Rights") and the Paris Convention for the Protection of Industrial Property (and the PCT) and in the European Patent Convention (EPC), and, with respect to trademarks, the Madrid Agreement and Madrid Protocol. As EU-member state, Denmark is also subject to the EU-regulations on community trademarks and community design.

F. Receivables

1. Characteristics as to:

a) Language of Documentation. There is no mandatory language for legal contracts regarding transfer of receivables (account receivables). All documents may be drafted in English or any other language with or without a Danish version (bilingual).

b) Form of Documentation. There are no requirements for notarization or other procedural formalities for agreements on transfers of receivables. In principle, oral agreements on transfer of receivables are legally valid. In practice, only written form agreements are used. Legal agreements and documents regarding transfer of receivables may validly be signed in counterparts. In addition, the legal documents may be signed outside of Denmark.

c) Specification of Receivables. General descriptions of the receivables (e.g., "all receivables related to the business" or "all customer receivables related to the division X") are in principle sufficient for legal purposes. Inter partes exhaustive or exemplary schedules or lists of either included or excluded receivables (if needed or recommended to avoid doubt in case of transfers of one of more divisions/business units) are often attached to the agreement.

2. Administrative, Corporate and Other Approvals

A transfer of receivables does not require general governmental or administrative approval.

If a Danish corporate entity ("ApS" or "A/S") transfers (or acquires) receivables, approval from a particular corporate body is not required in order to make the transfer valid, as long as the formal rule of execution for the particular corporate entity is observed. If a transfer of receivables comprises all or a substantial part of a legal entity's assets/business value, shareholder approval may be required internally, but as long as the formal rule on execution is observed, the transfer is legally valid without such approval.

Holders of security rights to receivables must grant consent to a transfer of the tangible asset in question. If such consent is not granted, the asset remains subject to the security right and, consequently, the enforcement right, provided the security holder has complied with the perfection acts and requirements applicable to the particular type of security in question (e.g., in the event of a floating charge registration in the Personal Register (*Personbogen*) or notification to the individual debtor). If the security right holder has not sufficed the perfection requirements, the purchaser may extinguish the security right, if purchaser is a good faith, bona fide purchaser.

3. Filing Requirements

A transfer of ownership to receivables does not require filings with public authorities, but requires notification to the debtors in order to be valid against third parties and the creditors' of seller. A transfer of receivables is legally valid inter partes also without notification to the debtor. A debtor notification (executed by the seller, at minimum) is typically given in order to disallow debtor to pay to the seller (i.e. the previous creditor) in discharge of the payment obligation.

G. Liabilities

1. Characteristics:

a) Language of Documentation. There is no mandatory language for legal contracts regarding transfer of liabilities. All documents may be drafted in English or any other language with or without a Danish bilingual version. The only exceptions are if the liability is secured by a registered mortgage on real property or tangible assets, etc. In such event, a Danish-language assignment deed (with a bilingual English version, if desired), is required.

b) Form of Documentation. There are no requirements for notarization or other procedural formalities for agreements on the transfer of liabilities. In principle, oral agreements on transfer of liabilities are legally valid. In practice, only written form agreements are used. Legal agreements and documents regarding transfers of liabilities may validly be executed in counterparts. In addition, all agreements and documents on transfers of liabilities may be signed outside of Denmark.

If the liability is secured by registered mortgage in real property or tangible assets, etc., the written form is required and the documents (i.e. an assignment deed) cannot be signed in counterparts. In addition, the signature(s) of the purchaser (new obligee/debtor) must be witnessed by two unrelated persons.

Effective as of September 8, 2009, all (ownership and) limited rights to real property (such as e.g. mortgages) are registered by use of digital filing/registration only. The traditional assignment deed, required in order to have the transferee registered as new mortgagee in the Land Register (*Tingbogen*), will be replaced by a digital document and filing (by e.g. a Danish lawyer with authorized digital signature) on the basis of a digital or written power-of-attorney by the transferor, the signature(s) of which must be witnessed by two unrelated persons. After September 6, 2009, hard copy assignment deeds cannot form basis for registration (of change of mortgagee) in the Land Register.

c) Specification of Liabilities. General descriptions of the liabilities (e.g., "all liabilities related to the business" or "all liabilities towards suppliers") are in principle sufficient for legal purposes. Inter partes exhaustive or exemplary schedules or lists of either included or excluded liabilities (if needed or recommended to avoid doubt in case of transfers of one of more divisions/business units) are often attached to the agreement. If the liability is secured by registered mortgage in real property or tangible assets, etc. identification and specification of each mortgage is required.

2. Administrative, Corporate and Other Approvals

A transfer of liabilities does not require general governmental or administrative approval.

If a Danish corporate entity ("ApS" or "A/S") transfers (or acquires) liabilities, approval from a particular corporate body is not required in order to make the transfer valid, as long as the formal rule of execution for the particular corporate entity is observed.

A transfer of liabilities does not as such require the approval of the creditor to have legal effect as between the seller and purchaser. However, the creditor is not obliged to accept a new debtor (purchaser) and to release or discharge the previous debtor (seller), and is even legally entitled to refuse to accept payment by the new debtor unless the creditor approved the transfer of the liability.

3. Filing Requirements

A transfer of liabilities does not require filings with public authorities, but in each case notification of and approval by the creditors is required to validly release and discharge seller as debtor vis-à-vis the creditors.

4. Purchaser's Liability for:

a) Tax Obligations. The purchaser is not, by operation of law, liable for the tax obligations of seller relating to periods prior to the acquisition of the assets except for real property. Real property continues to provide security for the full payment of certain state or municipal real property taxes related to the real property also prior to the acquisition. Without express agreement between seller and purchaser, seller remains and purchaser does not become liable to, e.g., report/repay inbound VAT on investment goods acquired by seller prior to the acquisition, which later may be used and applied for private purposes.

b) Environmental Contamination. The purchaser, and, therefore, the new owner and operator of plants in Denmark that cause contamination, or of real property in Denmark that contains soil contamination or from which soil contamination may emanate), may be held liable to conduct investigations and to undertake the necessary clean-up measures at his own costs, provided the contamination occurred on or after January 1, 2001, or substantially increased or deteriorated after that date. If the contamination in fact only occurred during the time when the seller owned/operated the plant/real property, the purchaser (new operator/owner) cannot be held liable for the costs required to determine the contamination and to clean up ("polluter pays principle"). However, even in these cases, a purchaser who continues to carry on the same type of industry or production at the same location may be held liable to conduct certain investigative measures or clean-up activities if the environmental agency had already issued concrete decrees, instructions or warnings (to seller) prior to the acquisition and purchaser knew or had knowledge thereof. In such events, purchaser may not claim indemnification by seller, unless seller has given purchaser specific representations or warranties, the relevance of which was perhaps established during the due diligence investigations conducted by purchaser.

c) Products Sold or Services Rendered by the Seller to Third Parties. The purchaser is not – by operation of law – liable for defect or default claims from third parties for products sold or services rendered by the seller prior to the acquisition.

5. Automatic Transfer of Other Liabilities

Except as set forth in D, 4 E, 4 and F, 5 above and in J, 1 below, no other liabilities of the seller automatically transfer to the purchaser due to the acquisition of assets, as long as the transfer of assets/liabilities is not an integral part of a regulated domestic or cross-border merger or demerger under the Danish Act on Companies (*Aktieselskabsloven*) or the Danish Act on Limited Liability Companies (*Anpartsselskabsloven*). If the transfer of assets/liabilities is an integral part of a regulated domestic or cross-border merger or demerger under the Danish Act on Companies or the Danish Act on Limited Liability Companies, the new or the continuing entity automatically assumes sole and full liability for each and any of the known or unknown obligations of the prior entity.

6. Contractual Protection as to 4 and 5 above

In asset sale and purchase agreements it is customary to include special provisions (e.g., representations, warranties and indemnifications) regarding purchaser's potential risk of being faced with claims and liabilities due to environmental contamination that seller may have caused earlier or due to assumption of pending customer contracts, the delivery of which had begun prior to the acquisition. It is customary to include such special provisions to address purchaser's potential risk of being faced with claims and liabilities (e.g., for accrued vacation allowance, special severance agreements) of the employees that are assumed as part of the business transfer.

H. Employees

1. Transfer of Employees

If an asset transfer comprises the transfer of a business undertaking or a part thereof, all the affected employees' rights and claims (and obligations) arising from the employment relationships automatically transfer to the purchaser (releasing the seller), provided that the employment relationships were in force at the time of the acquisition. Rights and claims that pass to purchaser may be based on the individual employment contracts and on local shop or industry-/nationwide collective bargaining agreements and include rights to salary, vacation, fringe benefits, potential severance payments, etc. The transfer of rights for old age pension entitlements that are separately insured in a special company pension fund are regulated separately; purchaser must continue to honor employees' rights to receive employer's pension contributions in the existing or in a new pension insurance company. In short, the purchaser must honor and respect all rights of all employees in the transferred business whose employment relationship at the time of the acquisition has not yet expired or who is not on "garden leave." Registered general managers who do not qualify as employees are not covered by these statutory rules.

The business transfer itself neither justifies termination of the employment contract by either side nor the introduction of changes of employment terms and conditions by employer. Termination for other (fair) reasons is as always permitted. Outside of collective bargaining agreements, an unfair termination is still legally valid, but may result in an obligation to pay monetary compensation to the employee(s) in question.

If the employees at the relevant business or business unit have been covered by collective bargaining agreements, the purchaser is, however, entitled to terminate the collective bargaining agreement with the opposite labor market party (i.e. a union), if the notice of termination is effected not later than three weeks after the acquisition. Termination of the collective bargaining agreement as such does not affect the purchaser's obligation to comply with and honor the individual employees' rights that are deprived by the collective bargaining agreement.

Both seller and purchaser have certain duties of information and negotiations. The seller and purchaser must, a reasonable time prior to the transfer, inform their respective employees or their representatives about the contemplated transfer, the timing of the transfer, and the legal, social and occupational consequences thereof. If required, negotiations must be commenced, if, e.g., redundancies or the like are contemplated as a result of the business transfer. Failure to comply with these obligations will not render the business transfer invalid, but may lead to criminal fines being imposed on seller and/or purchaser. In practice, a 'reasonable time prior to the transfer' means one to two weeks.

2. Approval of Works Council, Trade Union or Other Institutions

In business undertakings, whether covered by collective bargaining agreements or not, with more than 35 employees, post-closing information to and hearing of a works council (*Samarbejdsudvalg*) or other bodies by purchaser may be applicable if substantial changes or impacts on the staffing, working conditions or production are contemplated or become apparent after closing of the business transfer. Failure to comply with this will not affect the legal validity of the business transfer, but the purchaser may be subject to contract penalties owed to the contracting partner under the collective bargaining agreement or criminal fines.

If, as a result of the business transfer, mass redundancies (i.e. at least ten redundancies out of 20–100 employees, redundancies of 10% as among 100–300 employees, or at least 30 redundancies out of at least 300 employees in any 30-day period) are contemplated, regulatory filings and involvement of regional labor agencies are mandatory. In the event of no or late filings, the redundancies may still be effected, but the applicable notice periods will be prolonged.

3. Contractual Protection as to Labor Issues

It is customary to include special provisions (e.g., representations, warranties and indemnifications) regarding purchaser's potential risk of being faced with claims and liabilities (e.g., for holiday allowance, special severance agreements) of the employees who are assumed as part of the business transfer and of employees who purchaser believed did not automatically transfer, but by operation of law did in fact transfer.

I. Tax Implications

1. Value Added Tax

The VAT rate in Denmark is 25%. Transfers of assets are exempt from VAT if the transfer constitutes a transfer of a business or business unit and if purchaser is or becomes registered for VAT. If not exempt, the basis for calculation of the VAT is the total value of the assets, i.e. the purchase price of the assets (but not the goodwill, if separately stated and agreed upon).

Due to potential uncertainty as to whether a transfer in question will or will not qualify as a business transfer, it is often recommended to include an explicit provision clarifying which party bears the VAT, if the transaction is deemed to be VAT liable. If it is agreed that purchaser will bear the VAT, seller shall be obliged by express clause in the sale and purchase agreement to send an invoice with the VAT amount in order to enable purchaser to enforce the inbound VAT refund claim. Either seller or purchaser must make a report to the local tax agency about the business transfer etc. within eight days after completion of the business transfer.

2. Real Property Transfer Tax

A transfer of real property in Denmark does not trigger any Danish real property transfer tax or stamp duty. However, in order to register the separate (digital) deed of transfer in the Land Register (*Tingbogen*) a public registration fee of 0.6% of the agreed purchase price of the real property is payable. Again, if a business transfer includes the transfer of real property, it is advisable to separately indicate the agreed purchase price of the real property in order to document the basis of calculation of the registration fee.

3. Other Tax Issues

Apart from the usual income tax considerations on the side of both seller and purchaser, there are no other tax issues in connection with an asset transfer.

J. Bankruptcy Law

1. Challenge of Asset Transfer in Case of Insolvency

If the seller, subsequent to the asset transfer, becomes subject to insolvency proceedings, in principle, the receiver or alternatively one or more creditors may claim that the transaction is invalid if the purchase price was clearly not equal to fair value. If the purchaser is truly independent of seller, such invalidity claims are rarely made, unless the cash part of the purchase price (if any) was not paid effectively but by set-off against purchaser's claim against seller for earlier trade.

If the seller is close to insolvency proceedings, a purchaser should insist on preparing and agreeing to exhaustive or exemplary schedules or lists of either included or excluded assets, as the creditors of seller may contest the transfer of title to various individual assets to purchaser unless the assets have been reasonably identified and specified as part of the purchase. Vis-à-vis the creditors of seller, general or generic descriptions do not suffice, if each asset may reasonably be specified or identified in detail.

2. Acquisition of Assets that are Subject to Insolvency Proceedings

There are no specific rules with regard to an acquisition of assets from a seller who is subject to insolvency proceedings at the time of the transfer except that the receiver (i.e. the insolvency administration) is negotiating on behalf of the insolvent seller (and not the board/management) and in some cases, a committee of creditors must approve the transfer. It must be noted that relevant contracts with suppliers, customers or the like may already be terminated for breach due to the insolvency of seller.

K. Timing and Costs

1. Timeframe of Asset Transfer

As there are no notarization, registration or similar requirements, a sale/acquisition of a business by way of an asset deal may, after completion of due diligence and contract negotiations, be completed or closed in a few days, except if real property is concerned, as registration in the Land Register may take two to six weeks. However, with a deposit of the purchase price or a portion thereof in escrow until registration in the Land Register (*Tingbogen*) has occurred, most of the completion or closing may be dealt with in days rather than weeks.

2. Costs of Asset Transfer

There is no stamp duty on documents regarding transfers of tangible assets, IP Rights, receivables, a business or real property, etc. However, if a transfer of real property is concerned, a public registration fee of 0.6% of the value/purchase price of the real property is payable for the registration of the separate deed of transfer in the Land Register (*Tingbogen*). There are no notarization requirements under Danish law, and, consequently, there are no costs for notarization.

L. Miscellaneous

1. Choice of Foreign Law

Danish laws on conflict of laws or international private law allow the choice of foreign laws to govern a contract for the sale of assets and real property in Denmark, provided that at least one of the parties is a non-resident. The parties to an agreement on sale of real property may not agree to opt-out of the Danish rules regarding registration of title in, e.g., the Land Register (*Tingbogen*). Danish statutory rules for the protection of employees still must be observed vis-à-vis the employees, even if the parties choose the laws of a foreign jurisdiction.

2. (International) Arbitration, Choice of Venue

The parties to a business/asset sale and purchase agreement may agree on arbitration in Denmark or abroad as exclusive forum for dispute settlement, and may also agree on venue for ordinary courts outside of Denmark. Such arbitration/venue agreement should be in writing.

3. Other Distinctions, Characteristics

In most cases, licenses or permits granted by virtue of environmental acts and legalization (e.g., to operate certain polluting industries) automatically transfer from seller to purchaser without the need for renewed filings or applications or without the risk of the environmental agencies introducing more burdensome conditions, unless the business or production facilities are relocated due to the change of ownership of the business. However, purchaser must continue to comply and/or fulfill the emission thresholds and conditions, etc., in the license as such obligations also automatically transfer to purchaser.

The public license (required in order to permit emissions of CO2 in such quantities as is stipulated in the awarded CO2 quotas) to operate a fixed fuel-driven power plant (for production of electricity or heating or for industry process purposes) and plants for production of ferrous metals, tiles/bricks, glass, paper, etc., over certain capacity thresholds does not automatically transfer to a purchaser of the production business and plants. The approval by the Ministry of Transport and Energy is required. Upon such approval, the purchaser (i.e. the new operator) also assumes full liability for all obligations accrued during the time when the seller (i.e. the previous operator) was the responsible operator with respect to the CO2 system, e.g., for fees payable if the emission of CO2 in the relevant preceding periods have been higher than the quotas awarded (or acquired).

M. Literature

Jan Schans Christensen, Grænseoverskridende virksomhedsoverdragelser – tilrettelæggelse, forhandling, aftaleudarbejdelse og opfølgning, 1st Edition, 1998

Eigil Lego Andersen, Kontrakter om virksomhedskøb, 1st Edition, 1991

England & Wales

By *Andrew Gillen* and *Fay Anthony*

A. General Aspects

1. Asset Deal vs. Share Deal: Essential Considerations

There are various factors to consider when determining whether to structure a transaction as a share transfer or as an asset transfer.

In broad terms, asset transfers are considered to be more complex and are typically less commonly used than share transfers as a medium for the sale of a business. In circumstances where the commercial agreement between a purchaser and seller relates to a limited proportion of a targets company's assets, it may be more appropriate for the transaction to be structured as an asset sale. However, where the commercial agreement relates to a transfer of the assets and liabilities comprising an entire business or a division of a business, an asset sale will generally be a more complex structure for both the purchaser and the seller:

- in an asset transfer, the purchaser and seller will need to carefully identify and stipulate in the transfer documentation all of those assets and liabilities which are to transferred: save for the provisions relating to the transfer of employees in a going concern business (see G and H below) and those relating to contaminated land (see G below), there are no provisions at law for the automatic transfer of business assets and liabilities in the context of an asset transfer;
- third party consent may be required for the transfer of certain assets (e.g., contracts with third parties), given that, by way of contrast to a share transfer, the counterparty to the contract or the owner of the relevant asset will not be the same party following completion of the agreement and commercial contracts will often prohibit assignment without consent. By contrast, on a share transfer, such consents are rarely required (although a termination right may be triggered on a share transfer, by "change of control" clauses in financing and other major contracts);
- if the business being transferred requires certain permits or approvals (such as regulatory authorization), then the purchaser will need to ensure that it has sought and obtained the necessary permits and approvals in advance of completion, since these may be required from that time to ensure continuity of operations.

However, from a purchaser's perspective there are certainly advantages to proceeding by way of an asset transfer, since it will not involve the wholesale assumption of potentially undisclosed liabilities, which is a feature of a share transfer. Conversely, a seller may have little appetite for retaining a shell entity with residual liabilities in circumstances where the key assets of the company have been sold.

There are, however, ways of minimizing the impact of the factors referred to above when drafting either the asset sale documentation or the share sale documentation (e.g., (i) "sweeper" provisions in an asset transfer, to ensure that all assets are caught, and/or (ii) carefully drafted warranties and disclosure process in a share sale to ensure that the assumption of a company's liabilities is carried out on a more informed basis).

In the majority of cases, one of the most decisive factors in determining whether to proceed by means of a share or asset transfer will be the respective tax benefits and disadvantages from the purchaser and seller's perspective. The key tax considerations include the following:

- Where the transaction is a share sale, the taxable disposal will be made directly by the selling shareholder(s). Where the transaction is an asset sale, the taxable disposal will be by the asset-holding entity and a further taxable event may occur when the proceeds of sale are returned to shareholders.
- The tax liability may depend on the base cost in the shares/assets. The base costs will depend on the particular facts and circumstances but it is possible for different amounts of tax to arise on the sale of the assets or shares.
- Certain assets have special tax regimes, including intangible assets, assets on which capital allowances (the UK's form of tax depreciation) are claimed and loan relationships derivative contracts, which may mean that an asset sale is treated differently to a share sale. The intangibles regime, in particular, can be advantageous to an incoming third party purchaser where intangible assets make up a material part of the asset base.
- An exemption exists (the "substantial shareholding exemption") for sales of substantial shareholdings (broadly, at least 10%) in trading companies or the holding companies of trading groups. There are a number of conditions (including a minimum holding period). Where applicable, this could make a share sale exempt from tax whereas an asset sale has no equivalent exemption.
- Transfer taxes on an asset transfer including value added tax ("**VAT**") (where applicable – see below) currently at 15% but expected to revert to 17.5%, stamp duty land tax at up to 4% in the case of land and stamp duty at 0.5% in the case of stock and marketable securities. For share sales, only the 0.5% rate of transfer tax applies, albeit on the full amount of the consideration. Thus, transfer taxes may be higher for a share or asset transfer depending on the facts and circumstances, and in particular depending on the assets concerned.
- Degrouping charges may apply on the sale of a company, broadly where that company has acquired assets from another member of the relevant tax group within a specified period. These changes can arise under various of the UK's tax regimes including those for chargeable gains tax, stamp duty land tax, derivative contracts and loan relationships.

- As mentioned above, on a share sale all of the relevant company's assets and liabilities will remain with the company. This includes the company's tax liabilities. For this reason, it is sometimes preferable for the purchaser to acquire specific assets from a company rather than acquire the entire company. If the parties decide to opt for a share deal, it is more usual than not for some form of tax indemnity to be given by the seller to the purchaser. Equally (and subject to detailed anti-avoidance rules), it may be preferable to acquire a company rather than assets if the company has valuable carried forward losses, as these losses would not generally transfer on an asset sale.

Overall, therefore, it is not uncommon for the seller to want a share sale (in particular, where the substantial shareholding exemption applies) and for the purchaser to favor an asset purchase (particularly where the intangible asset regime is of significant value). The outcome will depend on commercial negotiations.

On an asset deal, one of the key tax considerations is whether the transfer will constitute a supply of goods or services on which VAT is payable. In general, VAT will be payable at a rate of 15% but expected shortly to revert to 17.5% on the acquisition of assets unless the acquisition constitutes a "transfer of a going concern" for the purposes of the relevant legislation (or the assets transferred are exempt or zero-rated or the seller and the purchaser are in the same VAT group). Transfers of a going concern are described further under I, 1 below. Broadly, if the effect of the transaction is to put the transferee in possession of a going concern, the activities of which he can carry on (and intends to carry on) without interruption then it may be that the transfer is not treated as a supply of goods or services and no VAT is payable.

2. Distinction between Sale and Transfer in Rem

English law does not recognize the distinction referred to as a point of legal principle with respect to all categories of asset. This said, the agreement for sale will not be sufficient in itself to effect the transfer of title to certain categories of asset and certain additional formalities will need to be complied with to effect the transfer of such assets (e.g., land, shares, intellectual property rights and effective assignment of debtors).

Typically, an asset transfer agreement will be entered into, pursuant to which the parties will agree to comply with any additional formalities required to effect the transfer of title to relevant categories of asset on completion of the agreement: these are normally expressed to be completion deliverables to the sale contract. Title to the remaining assets will be transferred by the operative provisions of the sale agreement itself.

Dependent upon the structure that was required to be achieved, it would, in broad terms, be possible to enter into a master agreement that contained certain preconditions to completion and which would stipulate that the various asset transfers would occur pursuant to the terms of separate ancillary transfer agreements upon the satisfaction of the condition or conditions set out in the master agreement.

Exchange of contracts takes place at the point that a binding contract is entered into for the sale of certain assets. Completion of the sale takes place when the conditions to completion (if any) are satisfied in accordance with the terms of the sale agreement, and the completion obligations set out in the sale agreement are complied with (which would include an obligation on the purchaser and/or seller as the case may be to enter into any necessary documentation to comply with any requisite formalities).

3. Regional Differences

There are no regional differences within England and Wales as regards the legal requirements in connection with the transfer of assets. England and Wales is a single jurisdiction. However, Scottish companies and certain assets located within Scotland will be subject to Scottish law, which is different in some respects to the law of England and Wales (but is outside of the scope of this chapter). This will be of particular relevance in relation to transfers of property.

4. Acquisition by Foreigners

As far as employees are concerned, if the business (or a distinct part of it) is being transferred to a foreign purchaser based outside the UK, the Transfer of Undertakings (Protection of Employment) Regulations 2006 ("**TUPE**") (the UK's regulations implementing the Acquired Rights Directive ("**ARD**")) could nevertheless apply. The TUPE (ARD) regime applies whenever UK-based employees transfer along with a business.

There may, however, be some practical distinctions when a business is sold to a foreign purchaser based outside the UK. In particular, the fact that a purchaser is based outside the UK may have a bearing on whether employees would be prepared to relocate. For example, this may mean that employees who would otherwise transfer to a foreign purchaser by operation of TUPE: (i) are redeployed by the seller within its own organization (and are, therefore, not transferred with the business at all); (ii) formally opt out of the TUPE transfer (see H, 1 below, under the heading "opting out", for more details) in advance of the business sale (in which case they are regarded as leaving the employment of the seller, but are not regarded as having been dismissed by the seller); (iii) are made redundant by the purchaser (in which case the purchaser may wish to seek a contribution from the seller to redundancy and other severance payments, as part of the commercial terms of the transfer). Other issues may also arise, for example relating to immigration, continuation of benefits (as the employees will have been participating in UK-based schemes) and the currency in which salary is paid.

5. Public Registers, Records and Databases

There is no central public repository of information relating to all of the assets held by an English or Welsh company, but there are public databases of certain assets and company information.

Dependent upon the assets being transferred, the following registers will be of relevance:

Companies House

Where the purchaser and/or seller is a company incorporated and registered in England and Wales, copies of the constitutional documentation and information relating to the officers of the company and the holders of the issued shares of these companies can be obtained from Companies House. This information can be accessed by application or online via their website. Of more immediate relevance to an asset transfer, details of the current charges and mortgages over of a company's assets may also be obtained from this register. It is also worthwhile checking at Companies Court with respect to whether any winding-up petitions have been submitted in relation to a particular company.

Land Registry

Ownership of interests in land is recorded at the Land Registry and also, in respect of land which has not yet been registered and in respect of the possible bankruptcy of the purchaser and any guarantor, at the Land Charges Department.

There are also numerous searches which can be carried out at the Land Registry or on other dedicated data-bases to discover whether a property is affected by any encumbrances. The common searches are as follows:

- a search at the local Land Registry;
- enquiries of the local authority (including building regulations, planning consents, commons registration, highways authority);
- drainage and water enquiries;
- specific enquiries of the seller;
- obtaining official copies of any entries at the Land Registry;
- an index map search at the Land Registry;
- a coal mining and subsidence search;
- a desktop search of environmental data;
- where dealing with residential property, a disadvantaged area search; and
- any other searches applicable to the locality or type of property e.g., waterways search if the property borders a canal, railways searches if the property is near railways lines or tunnels, or tin mining if the property is in a relevant location.

There are also the following searches which are sometimes advisable in connection with an acquisition of real property:

- companies searches at Companies House (as referred to above);
- searches of the winding-up petitions at the Companies Court (as referred to above); and
- searches with the various gas, telephone and electricity companies.

UK Intellectual Property Office

Information relating to registered intellectual property (copyright, designs, patents and trademarks) may be obtained from the UK Intellectual Property Office. This is available on application or via their website.

6. Purchase Price Requirements

There are no specific provisions under English law, which stipulate the choice of currency for a sale contract or which prescribe how consideration should be apportioned between assets that are being transferred, but tax considerations will usually be relevant to the apportionment of the consideration.

In most circumstances, on an asset transfer it will be necessary to apportion the aggregate consideration between the assets given that: (i) the transfer of certain assets may be subject to stamp taxes and it would, therefore, be necessary to identify the specific amount of consideration paid in respect of these assets in order to determine the amount of stamp taxes to be paid; and (ii) the allocation of the consideration will affect the purchaser's base cost and the seller's disposal amount (and consequently any gain or loss that each may make in respect of an asset) for the purposes of determining its tax liability. It is possible that the parties' interests may not be entirely aligned for the purposes of this allocation exercise. However, it is possible that the values attributed to the assets may be subject to HMRC ("Her Majesty's Revenue & Customs") review and, accordingly, both parties should ensure that reasonable, sustainable values are attributed to the assets in order to minimize the scope for the values (and the tax liability fixed in relation to them) to be questioned.

Also, on the assumption that both of the purchaser and the seller are companies incorporated in England, then the directors will need to comply with their statutory duties towards the company, which include, amongst others, the overriding duty to promote the success of the company. Therefore, the directors of each company will need to give careful thought to: (i) the choice of currency to ensure that it does not expose the company concerned to any foreign exchange risks; and (ii) the aggregate amount and the apportionment of the consideration, to ensure that it reflects a sustainable arms' length value for the various assets.

B. Tangible/Movable Assets

1. Characteristics as to:

a) Language of Documentation. The transfer of tangible assets will be governed by the main asset transfer agreement.

The asset transfer agreement may be drafted in a language other than English, if the parties choose. This will apply even where the contract is governed by English law. In theory, it would be possible to execute the documentation bilingually although it would be advisable to stipulate which version should prevail in the event an inconsistency between the versions is identified. In practice, however, most sale documentation relating to a UK-based business will be drafted in English.

b) Form of Documentation. The sale contract will usually be capable of execution by a corporate seller or purchaser under hand by one of its directors, or another appropriately authorized individual. Where there is no consideration for the sale, where the agreement contains a guarantee or in certain other circumstances where statute requires a deed, the contract will require execution as a deed.

To the extent that separate documentation needs to be executed to comply with any relevant formalities governing the transfer of title to certain assets, this will need to be completed in the prescribed form: please refer to Sections C and E below in respect of real property and intellectual property respectively.

A document governed by English law need not be executed in England. However, if the companies executing the documentation are incorporated and tax resident in England and Wales, then thought should be given as to whether executing documentation overseas may be problematic, in particular if this is done on a regular basis or in respect of particularly significant agreements.

A sale contract may be executed in counterparts. The typical approach would be to include a provision to the effect that the agreement may be executed in counterparts and that all of the counterparts shall constitute one and the same instrument.

c) Specification of Assets. It is in both parties' best interests to identify clearly which assets are being transferred pursuant to the terms of the sale agreement (and which, if any, are to be retained). This will minimize the scope for future dispute with the other party or parties to the sale contract, as well as possible disputes with third parties. Accordingly, where possible, best practice would be to produce detailed schedules of the various assets being transferred, which provide a clear record of what is being transferred under the agreement. However, inevitably there will be certain categories of tangible assets which it will be extremely difficult to identify in this specific manner, and, on that basis, there is some scope for the use of generic language to ensure that all relevant assets within a given category are caught (if this is what has been agreed from a commercial perspective). The determining factor in each case will be whether the drafting in the contract is sufficiently precise to identify unambiguously which assets are being transferred. If the purchaser is only acquiring certain assets (or liabilities) of the business, the schedules of those assets (or liabilities) will be particularly important in determining what it has and has not acquired.

2. Administrative, Corporate and Other Approvals

Administrative/Regulatory Approvals

If the transfer of tangible assets is a part of a business or wider asset transfer, then the requirement for U.K. and/or EC merger control filings and consents will need to be considered. In addition, and dependent upon the relevant business sector concerned, further regulatory approvals may be required. Specific advice should be sought on a case by case basis, but, by way of overview, the following non-exhaustive list of regulatory approvals may need to be considered, dependent upon the assets to be transferred: (i) telecommunications, broadcasting and media; (ii) water, electricity and gas supply; (iii) rail and air transport; (iv) defense; (v) postal; (vi) financial services; (vii) insurance; (viii) pensions; and (ix) banking.

Corporate Approvals

It is best practice to ensure that any transfer documentation has been approved and authorized for signature at a validly convened meeting of the board of the directors of both purchaser and seller and to ensure that this approval process has been appropriately minuted. However, certain executive directors may have delegated authority to enter into certain types of contract on behalf of the relevant company, and so it is possible that a specific board authorization may not be required.

A third party who is dealing with a company in good faith is entitled to rely upon a contract executed by this company. However, where the directors have acted beyond the powers conferred on them by the company's constitution, the company may then be unable to rely on the contract. In these circumstances, further steps may need to be taken by the company to ratify the contract.

There is no general requirement at law that stipulates that a company's shareholders must approve an asset transfer. There are specific circumstances where shareholder approval will be needed, for example where: (i) the constitutional documents or the shareholders' agreement relating to the purchasing or selling company require shareholder approval; (ii) the transaction falls within the parameters of certain statutory provisions, which prescribe that a specified level of shareholder approval is required (e.g., substantial property transactions involving directors); (iii) if shares are being issued as all or part of the consideration, shareholder approval may be required for the directors to be granted authority to issue the shares; and/or (iv) the securities in either the purchaser or the seller are listed, in which case shareholder approval may be required under the rules of the relevant market, provided the transaction is of a certain size – for companies listed on the Official List of the UK Listing Authority, shareholder approval will generally be required if any of the "class tests" by which the size of the transaction is measured exceed 25% and for an AIM company if such tests exceed 100% or result in a fundamental change in the AIM company's business.

Security Holders

If the purchaser has actual or constructive notice that the relevant assets are encumbered, then the terms of the relevant security should be considered to determine whether or not the security holder's consent is required to the transfer.

As a general principle, if a purchaser acquires an encumbered asset and has notice (whether actual or constructive) of the encumbrance, then he will acquire the asset subject to the encumbrance. However, the terms of the security in question should be considered. The transfer of an asset that is subject to a fixed charge is likely to be in breach of the terms of that charge and the transfer of an asset that is subject to a floating charge is likely to have the effect of crystallizing the floating charge.

Standard practice is to ensure that any assets that are subject to fixed charges are released from the charge prior to or at the point of sale and that a certificate of non-crystallization is obtained in relation to any floating charges. A standard form asset transfer agreement will typically include a warranty to be given by the seller that the assets transferred under the agreement are being transferred with full title guarantee and free from all encumbrances, (which would include fixed and floating charges, pledges, liens and mortgages): it would not be market practice in the UK to deviate from this and to sell assets subject to existing encumbrances.

3. Filing Requirements

Subject to the comments at B, 2 above in relation to regulatory consents and submissions, no special filings are required other than any filings that may be required to comply with the provisions of the Data Protection Act 1998 (“**DPA**”).

Where the asset transfer includes a transfer of personal data (such as names and contact details in a database) from the seller to the purchaser, both the seller and purchaser must comply with the DPA in respect of that transfer. This should include obtaining the data subjects’ consent to the transfer (which in practice is often obtained after the event), although official best practice guidelines indicate that consent is not required where the purchaser continues to use the data in exactly the same way and for exactly the same purposes as the seller used the data. The purchaser should also ensure that it has officially notified the Information Commissioner’s Office, the body responsible for administering the DPA, that it is a data controller as defined in the DPA.

4. Automatic Transfer of Encumbrances

The assets will only be transferred free of the encumbrances, if the purchaser acquires the assets free of the non-registrable encumbrances (for example equitable charges and mortgages), if the purchaser acquires the assets free of actual or constructive knowledge of the prior ranking encumbrance and if it is a bona fide purchaser for value.

Where the asset is subject to a registrable charge and the security interest has been duly registered in accordance with the relevant formalities, then, save where a purchaser could argue that it could not reasonably be deemed to have constructive knowledge of the pre-existing security interest, it will acquire the asset subject to the encumbrance. It is unlikely that a purchaser would be able to maintain successfully that it did not have constructive knowledge of a charge or other security interest that was correctly registered on a publicly-maintained register.

As referred to at B, 2 above, the sale of an encumbered asset is likely to be in breach of the terms of any fixed charges that a seller has given over its assets and, furthermore, is likely to crystallize any floating charges that the seller has granted in respect of any assets to be transferred.

C. Real Property

1. Characteristics as to:

a) Language of Documentation. There is no specific land law rule as to the language of documents, but in practice if a deed or document is to be registered at the Land Registry then it should be in English or Welsh and must be executed in accordance with practice guide 8:

http://www.landreg.gov.uk/docs/html/practice—guides/lrpg008.htm

b) Form of Documentation. Save for a few exceptions, a contract for the sale of land needs to be in written form in order to comply with Section 2 of the Law of Property (Miscellaneous Provisions) Act 1989. The transfer deed then needs to be by deed, and should be in form TR1 in order to register it at the Land Registry.

Documents can be executed outside the jurisdiction. Documents can be signed in counterpart but the Land Registry might require sight of all parts before registration is completed.

c) Specification of Assets. The transfer document should always contain a detailed description of the property and should refer to the title number if the land is registered. It should also contain a plan which will accord with the Land Registry's requirements whether or not the land is registered.

2. Administrative, Corporate and Other Approvals

Administrative/Regulatory Approvals

Subject to the comments referred to at B, 2 above, no special governmental or administrative approvals will be required.

Corporate Approvals

Please refer to the response at B, 2 above: the same principle applies.

Security Holders

As referred to above, a financial charge will usually be released when the transfer is completed, or else the purchaser will take the property subject to the charge. If the property owner is granting a new lease then (if the terms of the mortgage so require) the mortgagee's consent must be obtained or else the owner will be in breach of the mortgage and the principle sum becomes payable immediately.

3. Filing Requirements

A transfer of real estate must be registered at the Land Registry, otherwise the transfer will be void (Section 6 Land Registration Act 2002). The Land Registry will not complete the registration unless the purchaser can produce evidence that it has paid Stamp Duty Land Tax on the purchase.

4. Automatic Transfer of Encumbrances

As referred to above, financial charges will usually be released on completion of the transfer, when the seller will redeem the mortgage.

Broadly speaking, any other third party right will automatically transfer to the purchaser unless it is expressly released by the party who benefits from it. The answer depends slightly on whether the land in question is registered at the Land Registry or not, because if the third party rights are not registered then the purchaser will only be subject to them if he has notice of them.

A release of such rights should be by deed and should clearly identify the land which is the subject of the rights but there are no other formalities required. It should then be lodged at the Land Registry.

5. Automatic Transfer of Lease Agreements

A lease will almost always automatically transfer to the purchaser. The only situation where this might not be the case is where:

- the lease is not in writing;
- it is not registered at the Land Registry;
- it is not disclosed by the seller to the purchaser; and
- the tenant was not in occupation at the time of the purchase,

when the purchaser might be able to argue that he did not have notice of the existence of the lease and should, therefore, not be fixed with it.

None of parties (seller, purchaser or tenant) can terminate the lease purely by reason of the sale of the freehold.

D. Contracts

1. Characteristics as to:

a) Language of Documentation. Please refer to the response at B, 1, a above: the same principle applies.

b) Form of Documentation. Please refer to the response at B, 1, b above: the same principle applies.

c) Specification of Contracts. Please refer to the response at B, 1, c above: the same principle applies.

2. Administrative, Corporate and Other Approvals

Administrative/Regulatory Approvals

Please refer to the response at B, 2 above: the same principle applies.

Corporate Approvals

Please refer to the response at B, 2 above: the same principle applies.

Counterparty of the Contract

As a general principle of English contract law, it is possible for a party to a contract to assign the benefit (but not the burden) of a contract to a third party without the consent of the counterparty to the contract. The third party to whom the benefit of the contract has been assigned may then assert the contractual rights assigned to it directly against the counterparty. Conversely, whilst it is possible to assign contractual obligations and liabilities as between a party to a contract and a third party, the contractual relationship will remain between the original parties to the contract. The original counterparty to the contract will, therefore, still be able to assert its contractual rights against the original party (i.e. the assignor). In these circumstances, the assigning party will need to rely on the terms of the assignment to the third party to protect itself with respect to the performance of these contractual obligations, since it will have continuing obligations under the terms of the original contract. In particular, the seller should ensure that it obtains an indemnity from the purchaser in respect of any failure to perform the contract post completion.

The only way in which the seller can fully dispose of its contractual liabilities is by novating them to a third party with the counterparty's consent by way of a deed of novation between the seller, purchaser and the original contract counterparty.

If, however, a contract contains specific provisions stipulating either that consent to assignment is required or where some other form of waiver or approval is required, then if the contract in question is material, the purchaser should secure any requisite consents prior to entry into the asset sale agreement.

Sometimes for reasons of confidentiality, time constraints or other reasons, the parties agree that these consents will not be sought prior to entry into the sale agreement. In order to protect both parties in this situation, the asset sale agreement would typically include provisions such as the following: (i) a procurement obligation on the purchaser and/or seller to secure any necessary consents to assignments or novations as soon as possible; (ii) a provision that until such consent is given or such novation or assignment is entered into, the seller will continue its corporate existence and hold the contracts in question on trust for the purchaser (although this is a purchaser-friendly provision, the effectiveness of which may be susceptible to legal challenge); and (iii) a provision that if consent is not obtained prior to a specified long-stop date, then the parties will try to put in place alternative arrangements in relation to a contract.

These provisions should not be relied upon in relation to a specific material contract or in relation to a number of contracts which, when taken together, would be material in the context of the assets being sold.

3. Automatic Transfer of Contracts (Other than Lease and Employment Agreement)

There are none other than contracts relating to employment arrangements where TUPE applies, as referred to under H below.

4. Filing Requirements

Save for any contracts which must be filed with public authorities or databases as a result of any regulatory or other approval process (as referred to at B, 2 above) and any notifications that need to be made in compliance with the provisions of the DPA (as referred to at B, 3 above), there is no specific requirement to make submissions in relation to the transfer of contracts.

5. Treatment of Existing Contractual Claims and Obligations

As described above, contractual obligations will not automatically transfer – only the benefit, not the burden of a contract may be transferred by assignment without consent. As noted above, indemnification should be sought by the seller for the performance of the contract by the purchaser post completion and often by the purchaser for the performance by the seller prior to completion.

6. Warranty Claims Resulting from Events prior to Transfer

Typically liability in respect of warranty claims relating to the period prior to the transfer date will be for the seller's account. However, this is a matter for commercial negotiation and would be addressed in the terms of the sale and purchaser agreement and, if applicable, the deed of novation. Sometimes, the sale and purchase agreement will seek to transfer all liability in respect of the period pre-completion to the purchaser – this must, however, be expressly set out in the sale and purchase agreement and will not take effect automatically.

Please also refer to the response to G, 4, c below.

E. IP Rights

1. Characteristics of Intellectual Property Rights (e.g., Trade Marks, Patents, Utility Models, Domain Names) ("*IP Rights*") as to:

a) Language of Documentation. The sale and transfer documents regarding IP Rights may be drafted in any language. However, it is advisable, although not mandatory, for the documents to provide that one particular language will be definitive and will prevail over the other versions, in the event of any inconsistency and that the documents are translated into another language for purely informational purposes. In order to comply with any special filing requirements for registered IP Rights (see the response to E, 3 below), if any documentary evidence is submitted in a language other than English, the UK Intellectual Property Office may require certified translations.

b) Form of Documentation. The transfer of IP Rights must be in writing and signed by (or on behalf of) the assignor to be effective. In the case of unregistered trade marks, their transfer can only be effected by also simultaneously assigning, in writing, the goodwill that resides in them. The transfer documents may be executed outside the UK (although please note the comments at B, 1, b above in this regard). Signing in counterparts is permissible (unless the transfer document specifies that it must be jointly signed).

c) Specification of IP Rights. The IP Rights to be transferred must be specified in the transfer agreement to such an extent that the purchaser and any third party will be able to clearly distinguish the assets from any other retained assets. In order to achieve this if the assets comprising an entire business are being acquired, the approach usually taken is to have a general "cover all" assignment (e.g., covering all IP Rights owned by the seller and which relate exclusively to the business) with a specific identification of registered and material unregistered IP Rights. The specific identification is usually achieved by the use of lists and/or tables (usually set out in a schedule to the transfer document) clearly stating which IP Rights are included in the transfer. Using schedules to clearly identify the IP Rights to be transferred is therefore recommended but is not mandatory. However in order to enable a formal transfer of registered IP Rights (see E, 2 below) it will be necessary to ensure that the registrar is able to identify clearly that the documentation covers a particular right.

2. Administrative, Corporate and Other Approvals

Administrative/Regulatory Approvals

Subject to the comments at B, 2 above, the transfer of IP Rights does not require special governmental or administrative approvals.

Corporate Approvals

The specific approval of corporate bodies in the seller's and/or purchaser's group is generally not required for the transfer of IP Rights unless otherwise provided in the seller's and/or purchaser's articles of association, any shareholder or partnership agreements, or other agreements relating to the seller or purchaser. Generally, please refer to the response at B, 2 above: the same point of principle applies.

Security Holders

If the IP rights are encumbered, the security documentation is likely to prohibit or require the approval of the security holder before a transfer of IP Rights occurs. The consequences of an attempt to transfer IP Rights in breach of such an approval will depend on the nature of the security over the IP Rights, whether the proposed transferee is a bona fide purchaser for value without notice of the security holder's claim and whether the IP Rights in question are registered or unregistered.

If the security holder has a legal mortgage over the IP Rights, the legal title to the IP Rights will be vested in it and the person granting the mortgage will not be able to transfer the IP Rights to a third party. If the security holder has an equitable charge over the IP Rights, a purchaser for value of the IP Rights without notice of the security holder's claim could acquire the IP Rights free of the security holder's claim. A security granted over the IP Rights of a company registered in England and Wales, Scotland or Northern Ireland should be registered at the relevant Companies House under the Companies Act. However, case law suggests that a court may not conclude that registration of that security at Companies House will always constitute notice to a purchaser of the IP Rights for value. If the IP Right in question is registered and the security interest can be registered at the relevant registry (e.g., the UK Intellectual Property Office), the registration of that security will mean the security holder's claim "trumps" that of any purported transferee

3. Filing Requirements

There is no legal obligation to notify public authorities of the transfer of IP Rights but where the IP Rights in question are registered, a proper filing puts third parties on notice of the change of ownership. It also has a number of other advantages. For example, in relation to patents, an assignee who fails to register an assignment within six months of its effective date may be prevented from recovering the costs of a successful infringement claim. It is therefore imperative that a filing should be made in respect of the transfer as soon as possible after completion. The transfer of unregistered IP Rights (namely, unregistered trade marks, unregistered design rights and copyright) does not require any special filings or registrations.

4. Applicable International (Multilateral) Agreements or Treaties

In relation to IP Rights in general, the UK participates in the TRIPS Agreement, in the WIPO Convention and in the Paris Convention for the Protection of Intellectual Property.

Regarding trade marks, the UK signed the Madrid Protocol, the Nice Agreement and the Singapore Treaty, and is subject to the Council Regulation on the Community Trade Mark of the European Community.

Regarding copyright, the UK is signatory to the Berne Convention, the Universal Copyright Convention, the Rome Convention, the WIPO Copyright Treaty, the WIPO Performances and Phonograms Treaty and the Phonograms Convention.

Regarding patents, the UK is a signatory to the Patent Co-operation Treaty, the Patent Law Treaty, the Strasbourg Agreement and the Budapest Treaty and participates in the European Patent Convention.

Regarding designs, the UK participates in the Locarno Agreement and is subject to the Council Regulation on the Community Design Right.

F. Receivables

1. Characteristics as to:

a) Language of Documentation. Please refer to the response to B, 1, a above: the same principle applies.

b) Form of Documentation. Please refer to the answer provided to question B, 1, b above: the same principle applies to receivables.

c) Specification of Receivables. Please refer to the response to B, 1, c above: the same principle applies.

2. Administrative, Corporate and Other Approvals

Administrative/Regulatory Approvals

Please refer to the response to B, 1, a above: the same principle applies.

Corporate Approvals

Please refer to the response to B, 1, b above: the same principle applies.

Approval of Debtors

Subject to any specific provisions in any documentation governing individual book debts or receivables, which the purchaser should consider as part of its diligence process, there is nothing at law which would require a debtor's consent to the proposed assignment. However, for the assignment to be effective a notice of the assignment must be served on the debtors in the form prescribed by Section 136 Law of Property Act 1925.

3. Filing Requirements

Regarding filings with public authorities or registrations into registers or (online) databases, please refer to the responses to B, 2 and B, 3 above: the same principle applies. Regarding the requirement to notify the debtors, please refer to F, 2 above.

G. Liabilities

1. Characteristics as to:

a) Language of Documentation. Please refer to the response to B, 1, a above: the same principle applies.

b) Form of Documentation. Please refer to the response to B, 1, b above: the same principle applies.

c) Specification of Liabilities. Please refer to the response to B, 1, c above: the same principle applies.

2. Administrative, Corporate and Other Approvals

Administrative/Regulatory Approvals

Please refer to the response to B, 2 above: the same principle applies.

Corporate Approvals

Please refer to the response to B, 2 above: the same principle applies.

Approval of Creditors

Please refer to the response at D, 2 above with respect to the assignment and novation of contractual liabilities. For the most part creditors are likely to stipulate in their standard (or specific) terms and conditions whether or not their consent is required for assignment and/or whether novation is required and so the specific terms of any material contracts should be considered. In certain circumstances, failure to obtain the required consent may result in a termination of the arrangements in question, which could result in an acceleration of payment obligations.

3. Filing Requirements

Subject to the comments in relation to merger and other regulatory approvals referred to at B, 2 above and in relation to the DPA at B, 3 above, there are no requirements for any special filings to be made with public authorities or registrations with registers or (online) databases.

There is no obligation at law to notify trade creditors of the assignment of the contract. However, please refer to the comments at F, 2 above in relation to the situation where consent is required from the creditor to the assignment.

4. Purchaser's Liability for:

a) Tax Obligations. Unlike share acquisitions, tax liabilities and tax assets do not in general pass with the asset concerned. It is, however, common to exclude such liabilities from those assumed by the purchaser.

b) Environmental Contamination. Liability for environmental contamination arises primarily under Part IIA of the Environmental Protection Act 1990 – the Contaminated Land Regime (the "**Regime**") where the enforcing authority can require those responsible for contaminating land to ensure that the land is cleaned up, even if the contamination was lawful when it took place. There is no limit (other than evidential) to how far back in time the Regime can reach. The main objective of the Regime is to ensure that the polluter pays. The Regime distinguishes between a Class A Appropriate Person (the polluter or knowing permitter) and a Class B Appropriate Person (the owner or occupier). Only if the original polluter cannot be found after "reasonable enquiry" will liability fall on the current innocent owner or occupier of the land.

Responsibility for environmental contamination is a potentially significant risk in transactions involving UK property assets. The risks include: (i) contamination arising from activities by the seller; and (ii) any liabilities that the seller may have for contamination arising from previous activities or occupants at a property. The system is risk-based and it is only where there is a "significant risk of significant harm" that liability for the clean-up of contaminated land is triggered. The nature and extent of any such contamination is usually assessed by following a phased program of investigations, in the first instance this would involve commissioning a desk-top study. This does not involve any site work but provides an initial assessment of risk by examining historic land uses at a site to determine whether or not potentially contaminative sources existed and assessing the local environmental sensitivity. More detailed investigations might be appropriate were it known or reasonably anticipated that a property was formerly in industrial use, or was in an area where neighboring operators could have polluted the site.

c) Products Sold or Services Rendered by the Seller to Third Parties. On an asset transfer, the purchaser assumes no liabilities which relate to the business during the period prior to the acquisition (other than those which it specifically agrees to acquire in the transfer documentation); such liabilities remain with the seller (or other relevant person).

5. Automatic Transfer of Other Liabilities

TUPE (see A, 4 above) provides that, except where an employee objects to the transfer and opts out (see H, 1 below, under the heading "opting out", for more details), there is an automatic transfer to the purchaser of the employment contract of any employee working wholly or mainly in the transferring business immediately before the transfer. All of the seller's rights, powers, duties and liabilities under or in connection with that employment contract will transfer to the purchaser, although there are some exceptions in relation to occupational pension schemes (as detailed in the pensions section at H below). In addition, any pre-transfer act or omission of the seller in relation to the employment contract will, following the transfer, be deemed to be an act or omission of the purchaser. These principles also apply to any employee who is dismissed prior to the transfer for a reason connected with it.

6. Contractual Protection as to 4 and 5 above

Environmental

In transactions involving freehold properties, liability for environmental contamination may be addressed in a number of ways including a reduction in price, the use of indemnities, or bespoke environmental insurance policies. These should be clearly documented in the sale and purchase agreement or in a separate a stand alone 'agreement on liabilities'.

For leasehold properties many older leases will not have any specific provisions relating to contamination. Where the tenant under a lease is the party that caused or knowingly permitted the relevant substances giving rise to the contamination to be present, they will be the party that should be identified as being responsible for the clean up. In those circumstances, it should not in fact matter what the provisions of the lease are. However, if there is a clear agreement on liabilities in a lease, this will generally determine who is liable for historic environmental contamination. If there is no such agreement, then this responsibility will be shared between the owner and tenant on the basis of various tests set out in relevant statutory guidance. The key point is that liability should rest with those who own the capital value in the lease. This is a question that would require valuation input.

Employees

It is customary to include indemnities and other provisions in the business/sale transfer agreement dealing with employee-related liabilities (see further H, 3 below). The nature and extent of the indemnities and other provisions will usually depend on the relative negotiating/bargaining positions of the parties. Typical provisions would include: (i) an indemnity from the seller to the purchaser for any liability which transfers under TUPE (see A, 4 above) for the pre-transfer acts or omissions of the seller (often referred to as a "line in the sand" indemnity); and (ii) indemnities from the seller in relation to specific employee-related liabilities identified by due diligence (e.g., employment tribunal claims).

Commercial Contracts

Regarding the response to G, 4, c above, it is customary for the seller to indemnify the purchaser from and against all actions, proceedings, damages, costs, claims and demands arising in respect of any liabilities arising before the acquisition.

Tax

In the case of an asset acquisition where the assets include shares, the purchaser will often require some form of tax indemnity to cover tax liabilities of the target company arising in the period before completion of the acquisition; and the share purchase agreement will also commonly include tax warranties aiming to obtain disclosure of material potential tax liabilities. Generally, such provisions will not be required otherwise in the case of an asset acquisition as the liabilities will not generally transfer. Limited warranties may be required, in particular in respect of VAT, stamp taxes and employee incentives.

H. Employees

1. Transfer of Employees

If there is a transfer of a business (or part of a business), TUPE (see A, 4 above) is likely to apply. If there is a transfer of specific assets (but not the entire business or a part of the business) TUPE is unlikely to apply.

Effect of a TUPE Transfer

If TUPE applies, the employment contracts of all employees wholly or mainly working in the transferring business at the point that the business transfers automatically transfer from the seller to the purchaser. (See G, 5 above in relation to the employment-related liabilities which transfer.) There is deemed to be no dismissal and statutory continuity of service is unbroken. Employees transfer on their existing terms and conditions of employment and this means that the purchaser (with some limited exceptions, in the case of occupational pension arrangements) is obliged to continue to provide the same (or, in limited cases, substantially equivalent) benefits post-transfer (please refer to the pensions Section below). In addition, any rights or benefits enshrined in a collective agreement, and, in most cases, trade union recognition, will transfer to the purchaser. Any attempt to change terms and conditions of employment will be void if the sole or main reason for the change is the TUPE transfer.

Opting Out

Employees have a right voluntarily to object to, and opt out of, the transfer for any reason. Any requirements in the employment contract for prior notice from the employees are waived in these circumstances. The opt out has the effect of ending their employment with the seller, although they are not regarded as being dismissed by the seller, and therefore have no right to dismissal payments, in these circumstances. However, where substantial changes to terms and conditions of employment are proposed (or made) post-transfer to the material detriment of an employee, the employee may regard himself as dismissed. This could potentially trigger claims for constructive unfair dismissal in an employment tribunal.

Information/Consultation

The seller is obliged to inform (and, in some cases, to consult) representatives of employees affected by the transfer (including trade unions if they are recognized) about the consequences and implications of the transfer in good time before the transfer takes place. There are potential financial sanctions of 13 weeks' pay per affected employee for the failure to inform/consult. The seller is also required to inform the purchaser in writing of key information relating to the employees (known as employee liability information) in advance of the transfer. This includes details of employees' terms and conditions of employment, and information about grievance/disciplinary procedures or court cases applicable to the employees in the past two years. An employment tribunal can make a financial award against the seller (on an application by the purchaser) for the failure to provide this information (subject to a minimum award of GBP 500 per employee). The amount of the award is based on the loss referable to the failure to provide the information, as well as any provisions on this issue in the business transfer agreement.

Dismissals and Severance Payments

Any dismissals made in connection with the TUPE transfer, or where the sole or principal reason for the dismissal is the transfer, are automatically unfair. Whether something is "in connection with" the transfer is broadly construed, and there is case law which indicates that dismissals over a year after the transfer can still be "connected" to the transfer. The exception to this rule is that dismissals may be effected (and will not be automatically unfair, but could still be unfair under normal principles) if there is an economic, technical or organizational reason for the dismissals entailing changes in headcount (broadly, where there is a genuine redundancy reason).

In the case of a genuine redundancy dismissal, an employee with more than two years' continuous service (i.e. two years' prior service with the seller) will, as a minimum, be eligible to receive a statutory redundancy payment (calculated according to a formula based on salary, age and length of service, and currently capped at a maximum of GBP 10,500).

Pensions

Vested past service pension rights are preserved in the seller's pension scheme and may be transferred. The effect of the transaction on employees' rights to future pension provision depends upon the type of pension arrangement in place immediately before the transfer, as follows:

- rights to contributions to a personal pension (including group personal pensions arranged by the employer) transfer automatically by law (see the discussion in relation to TUPE provisions above). The purchaser must therefore pay contributions at the same rates as the seller did;
- rights to contributions to a defined contribution occupational (i.e. privately administered) pension scheme, or to accrual under a defined benefit occupational pension scheme, generally do not transfer. There is a possible exception, however, in respect of pensions payable on compulsory (and perhaps also voluntary) early retirement pensions. There is, in any event, a minimum level of pension provision that must be made by the purchaser in respect of employees who were members of an occupational pension scheme immediately before the transfer. This requirement can be satisfied by providing matched contributions of 6% of basic salary;
- rights to lump sum life assurance cover generally transfer automatically by law (see the discussion in relation to the TUPE provisions above).

2. Approval of Works Council, Trade Union or Other Institutions

There is no general UK legal requirement for formal approval to the business transfer by any of the above bodies. However, trade union/collective agreement/works council agreements particular to the seller may make special provisions for the seller to notify or seek the agreement of the trade union or works council in advance of the business transfer.

There is also a requirement to inform, and in some cases, to consult, with trade union and other representatives of affected employees in advance of the transfer (see H, 1 above, under the heading "Information/Consultation").

3. Contractual Protection as to Labor Issues

It is customary to include indemnities and other provisions relating to employees in the business/sale transfer agreement. The nature and extent of the indemnities and other provisions will depend on the relative negotiating/bargaining positions of the parties.

Provisions typically seen in the business/sale transfer agreement are as follows: (i) a list of the transferring employees so that the purchaser is clear which employees will transfer to it; (ii) provisions determining what happens to employees not on the list of transferring employees who nevertheless transfer to the purchaser by operation of TUPE; (iii) an indemnity from the seller to the purchaser in relation to any pre-transfer acts or omissions (liability for which transfer to the purchaser under TUPE); and (iv) a requirement on the seller to disclose in full the terms and conditions of employment and other key employee information to the purchaser, and to indemnify the purchaser to the extent that any loss results from the failure to provide complete or accurate information.

I. Tax Implications

1. Value Added Tax

The following applies where UK VAT is potentially applicable. The place of supply for VAT purposes should be considered at an early stage, in order to determine whether the transfer is within the scope of UK VAT.

When acting for a seller, it is essential that the sale agreement provides that the consideration does not include any VAT which may be chargeable, since the price will otherwise be deemed to be VAT inclusive.

Generally, the consideration payable under the sale agreement will attract VAT (at a current rate of 15% but expected to revert to 17.5% from January 1, 2010) unless:

- the purchaser and seller are VAT grouped; or
- the assets in question are exempt or zero rated for VAT purposes; or
- the transaction qualifies as a transfer of a going concern (“**TOGC**”).

If the transaction is a TOGC, it will be treated as neither a supply of goods nor a supply of services for VAT purposes. TOGC treatment is mandatory in cases to which it applies (i.e. the parties cannot opt out of TOGC treatment if it does not suit them).

In determining whether a transaction is a TOGC, the principal consideration is whether the effect of the transaction is to put the transferee in possession of a going concern, the activities of which he can, and does in practice, carry on without interruption. Cases where there might be problems include where the purchaser intends to change the type of business, or where the purchaser will be closing down for a while for refurbishment. Relevant considerations will include whether goodwill, customer lists, staff, premises, contracts, plant and machinery, stock and the business name are transferred, and whether the seller enters into restrictive covenants, but none of these will be conclusive one way or the other. A business does not need to be profitable to be transferred as a going concern.

Even if the sale can be classified as a transfer of a business as a going concern, it will only qualify to be treated as neither a supply of goods nor a supply of services if certain further conditions are satisfied relating principally to the use of the assets and the VAT registration position of the parties. In particular, if the business to be transferred includes any land, there will be additional requirements to be fulfilled to benefit in full from the TOGC provisions.

The VAT position as regards supplies made by and to the business will need to be considered, particularly where the business sale includes a transfer of trade (or book) debts owed to the seller or where the purchaser is assuming trade creditors.

2. Real Property Transfer Tax

If there is a transfer of any interest in UK land, the transfer may attract stamp duty land tax (“**SDLT**”). This applies to freeholds, leaseholds, and also to other land-related rights or powers such as rights of way or the benefit of a restrictive covenant. Additionally, it would not be unusual for the seller to agree to grant the purchaser certain land-related rights, such as a sub-lease or right of way, in connection with the sale of the business. These may also attract SDLT.

The rate of SDLT for non-residential property is nil if the consideration is less than GBP 150,000, 1% if the consideration is between GBP 150,000 and GBP 250,000, 3% if the consideration is between GBP 250,000 and GBP 500,000, and 4% if the consideration is over GBP 500,000. If any relevant threshold is exceeded the higher rate is payable on the whole amount of the consideration, not just the surplus. If any lease is to be granted as part of the transfer of the business, SDLT may also be due on any rental element. If VAT is payable on a land transaction, SDLT is payable on the VAT component as well.

3. Other Tax Issues

Certain tax implications are discussed in the response at A, 1 above.

If the assets being acquired include UK shares and/or marketable securities, stamp duty or stamp duty reserve tax will be chargeable on 0.5% of the consideration apportioned to the relevant share transfer.

If the business includes assets on which the seller has been claiming capital allowances (the UK’s form of tax depreciation), a sale to a third party purchaser may trigger balancing charges to the extent that the sale proceeds exceed the written down value of the assets. If the written down value of the assets is greater than the sale proceeds, there may be balancing allowances. In certain circumstances if the seller and the purchaser are in the same group the transfer is ignored for capital allowances purposes, so that the purchaser obtains the same allowances and suffers the same charges as the seller would have done had it continued to own the business.

There are further corporation tax consequences of a business sale and acquisition. One is that, if the seller ceases to trade, it will forfeit any carried forward losses of that trade. Cessation of trade also terminates an accounting period for the seller, unless it is continuing to carry on a different trade. This may accelerate the payment of any corporation tax for that period. If the purchaser and the seller are in the same group, the purchaser may be able to benefit from trading losses.

Generally, the employer's liability to national insurance contributions (social security) and income tax in respect of the employees of the business should be apportioned on a time basis, so that it is borne by the seller for periods up to and including completion, and by the purchaser thereafter.

The original employer may retain its obligation to account for income tax in respect of share options which are granted before but exercised after completion. However, the obligation to account for national insurance contributions thereon will become the responsibility of the purchaser as the new employer. This can be the case even if the options were granted as part of the seller's incentive scheme and/or the shares to be issued when the options are exercised will be in a company in the seller's group.

J. Bankruptcy Law

1. Challenge of Asset Transfer in Case of Insolvency

If a corporate seller or purchaser becomes subject to an administration or liquidation process following the asset transfer, there are a number of potential grounds upon which the administrator or liquidator may be able to set aside the asset transfer.

If the asset transfer was, from the perspective of the company in administration or liquidation, a transaction at an undervalue (i.e. the value of what the insolvent company received was less than the value of what it gave to the other party) and the administration or liquidation process commenced within two years of the asset transfer and at the time of the asset transfer the insolvent company was unable to pay its debts (within the meaning given in Section 123 of the Insolvency Act 1986) then the court may make an order setting aside the transaction. However, the court will not make this order if satisfied that the company entered into the asset transfer in good faith, for the purpose of carrying on its business, and at the time there were reasonable grounds for believing that the transaction would benefit the company.

Similarly, if the asset transfer constitutes a preference, then a court may make such order as it deems fit to restore the position to what it would have been if the insolvent company had not given the preference. A preference occurs where the transaction was designed to put a creditor into a position which, in the event of insolvent liquidation, will be better than the position in which it would have otherwise been. For a preference to take place, the administration or liquidation must commence within six months of the transaction or two years where the transaction was to a connected party. In the context of an asset sale, a preference may, for example, be an issue where part or all of the purchase price is set-off against amounts owed by the seller to the purchaser. The court may not however make an order setting aside the transaction if it can be demonstrated that there was no desire on the part of the insolvent company to prefer the creditor.

In addition to transactions at an undervalue and preferences, certain office holders also have the ability to investigate transactions conducted prior to the commencement of a formal insolvency process where such transactions were conducted to the detriment of the company's creditors (e.g., extortionate credit transactions and transactions defrauding creditors).

2. Acquisition of Assets which are Subject to Insolvency Proceedings

Insolvency practitioners appointed in respect of a company are able to sell the company's assets. The terms of such sales are, in the ordinary course, conducted on an "as seen" basis and without the benefit of representations or warranties on the part of the seller (acting by the relevant insolvency practitioner).

In a winding up by the court, any disposition of the company's property made after the commencement of the winding up is, unless the court otherwise orders, void. When an order is made for the winding up of a company, the commencement of the winding up is deemed to be the date on which the winding up petition was presented (or in certain circumstances earlier). Consequently, the insolvency legislation can operate with retrospective effect to avoid an asset transfer that takes place after the date on which a winding up petition was presented but before the company enters a formal winding up. A transaction poses no serious risk to creditors or which is likely to improve the position of its creditors may result in the court exercising its discretion to validate the transaction.

K. Timing and Costs

1. Timeframe of Asset Transfer

The main driver of the timetable in an asset or business transfer is likely to be whether any third party consents or approvals are required. There are various other timing constraints need to be considered both prior to and after completion of an asset transfer. These are discussed below:

- environmental desk top studies can be turned around in 1–2 days whereas a detailed site investigation and risk assessment can take several weeks or more;
- a standard set of conveyancing searches usually takes about two weeks;
- for a straightforward sale, registration at the Land Registry is usually processed in 18–21 working days;
- pre-exchange searches into registered IP Rights and subsequent registration of IP Rights will also require several weeks;
- where shares have been acquired, stamping of the stock transfer forms with HMRC can take several weeks. In the case of other assets, registration for VAT and/or a rul-

ing on whether the transfer constitutes a "transfer of a going concern" can also take a number of weeks.

2. Costs of Asset Transfer

It is difficult to estimate costs with any degree of precision. However, the following may provide some indication of relevant areas where non-advisory costs may be incurred. As a general point, documents executed by companies incorporated in England and Wales and which are governed by English law will not require notarization.

- environmental desk top studies cost in the order of GBP 250; phase I studies including a site visit can cost in the order of GBP 1,500, whereas a detailed site investigation and risk assessment can cost anything between GBP 5,000–GBP 20,000 or more depending on area of site and complexity. For some transactions there will need to be a transfer of authorizations, licenses, permits etc for which there will be fees, the level of which needs to be confirmed with the relevant Regulator in each case;
- property search fees vary according to the searches undertaken and the data providers concerned, but usually cost between GBP 600 and GBP 1000;
- Land Registry fees range between GBP 40 (for the registration of a property with a value of under GBP 50,000) to GBP 700 (for a property which is worth over GBP 1 million);
- broadly, stamp taxes apply to transfers of interests in UK land (as referred to below), shares and marketable securities and certain transfers of partnership interests. On a transfer of shares or securities in a UK company, or shares or securities which are registered in a register held in the UK, stamp duty or stamp duty reserve tax will be payable at a rate of 0.5% of the consideration;
- as regards stamp duty land tax, the rates of duty are calculated as a percentage of the consideration for the transfer of an interest in land or as a percentage of the rent amount in the case of grants of leases. The current applicable percentages vary between 1% to 4% for transfers of an interest in land and up to 1% of the net present value of the rent for grants of lease interests;
- no costs are incurred when notifying the UK Intellectual Property Office of a transfer of IP Rights (other than a nominal charge for the assignment of registered trade marks). Registration costs are incurred on the initial registration, and subsequent renewal, of an IP Right (up to several hundred pounds depending on the individual IP Right);
- mergers that qualify for reference to the Competition Commission are subject to a fee. The level of the fee may vary from GBP 15,000 to GBP 45,000, according to the value of the UK turnover of the acquired business. Some small and medium-sized companies are exempt from payment of merger control fees.

L. Miscellaneous

1. Choice of Foreign Law

As a point of principle two English companies may elect to make an agreement for the transfer of assets subject to foreign law, although it would be unusual. However, thought would also need to be given to the related question of which courts would have jurisdiction in relation to any disputes arising out of the sale contract. The standard approach would be to choose the governing law under which one of the parties to the contract has been incorporated, and for the courts of that country to have jurisdiction.

As a related point, the parties should be alive to the risk that it may be difficult to enforce judgments in one jurisdiction against a company incorporated in another if the governing local laws relating to the recognition and enforceability of judgments are not favorable.

2. (International) Arbitration, Choice of Venue

It is possible for the parties to provide that disputes arising under the sale agreement should be referred to arbitration. They may prescribe who the relevant body should be, and this can be an international arbitral body, if desired. There are no restrictions with respect to choice of venue. However, to reduce costs, it would be typical to select a body situated in the jurisdiction in which either the seller or purchaser is incorporated.

3. Other Distinctions, Characteristics

The key issues of relevance have all been addressed above.

Estonia

By *Paul Künnap* and *Toomas Prangli*

A. General Aspects

Under Estonian law, there are two types of transactions that could be regarded as asset deals: transfer of a business as a going concern (transfer of enterprise) and piece-by-piece asset transfer. It should be noted that if a piece-by-piece asset transfer as a whole is deemed to constitute a transfer of a business as a going concern, the creditors may treat the transaction as a transfer of an enterprise regardless of how the parties structured the transaction.

The Estonian law operates with the term "enterprise" which is an active economic unit consisting of assets, rights and obligations related to and serving the purpose of the economic unit whether specifically assigned to the unit or not. Exact delineations can be difficult, sometimes a specific business line of a company might be regarded as an enterprise. The delineation difficulties are somewhat mitigated by the fact that the regulation of enterprises applies also to organizationally whole units even if from the business perspective they only form a part of the enterprise. Thus there is considerable flexibility in determining what constitutes the enterprise.

Court practice has confirmed that in order to rely on the creditor protection provisions of the transfer of enterprise regulation, the creditor does not have to produce a transfer of enterprise agreement as evidence and need only prove that the economic activity has in fact continued as an on-going concern.

Due to the risk of a transaction being deemed a transfer of an enterprise and due to the beneficial VAT treatment of transfer of an enterprise, few piece-by-piece asset transactions are concluded.

1. Asset Deal vs. Share Deal: Essential Considerations

The main reason for favoring an asset deal over a share deal is that an asset deal allows more control over what aspects of the business are transferred to the purchaser and the purchaser has thus less historical "baggage" to worry about. Since transactions often involve some separation of businesses, an asset deal can be a natural way of completing the reorganization at the same time as the completion of the transaction.

Asset deals are, however, not always possible due to regulatory issues. For example, usually various licenses and registrations are specific to the legal entity and are not transferable along with the assets. Also, sometimes asset deals are not possible due to requirements of third-party consents. For example, it is not possible to transfer certain databases containing personal data without the consent of the subjects of the database.

If the assets consist of considerable amounts of real property or other similar registered property, the transaction costs can favor a share deal over an asset deal. Also, in such cases the structure of an asset deal would be more complex than a share deal.

Estonia treats the transfer of an enterprise as VAT exempt turnover and there is no annual corporate income tax, so in most cases the differences in taxation between asset deals and share deals are minimal. A notable exception is if the shareholders of the target company are natural persons whose capital gains in the case of share deal would be immediately taxable – an asset deal in this situation can defer the tax consequences for the shareholders.

In practice, despite the advantages of asset deals, share deals are more common than asset deals. Sometimes the sellers are not even willing to consider an asset deal as they do not wish to retain the legal entity nor want to deal with its liquidation after the transaction.

2. Distinction between Sale and Transfer in Rem

Estonian law does distinguish between the sale and transfer in rem and it is possible to structure the transaction in separate documents for the sale and the transfer of ownership. In fact, in real property transactions a separate expressis verbis transfer in rem agreement is required (although it can be included in the sale agreement document).

3. Regional Differences

There are no regional differences as regards legal requirements in connection with the transfer of assets.

4. Acquisition by Foreigners

Under a general rule, equal business conditions should be ensured to domestic and foreign investors. The investor has the right to manage, use and dispose of the object of investment in compliance with the Estonian laws. Thus, generally, there should be no distinctions with regard to the acquisition of assets by foreign persons. However, the laws may contain some restrictions concerning certain types of assets.

Transactions with forest and agricultural land plots exceeding 10 ha (hectare) in area as well as real property on some islands and border areas are restricted and sometimes require special consents from the authorities.

5. Public Registers, Records and Databases

In Estonia, there is no central institution that retains all relevant information in connection with an asset transfer. The following publicly available databases allow access to the data, depending on the amount of information, either free of charge or for a certain fee. Public access may be restricted to specific information included in the registration files of companies or real property.

Corporate details about the seller and the purchaser can be obtained from the public Commercial Register (kept regionally by certain courts) which shows the basic details as to (i) legal form, (ii) powers of representation, (iii) registered share capital, and (iv) certain corporate events such as mergers or capital increases. Further, corporate information including financial statements, articles of association and history of changes can be obtained in the corporate information. All this is available via internet to everyone:

www.rik.ee/e-ariregister/teabesusteem.

Information on commercial pledges can be obtained from the Commercial Pledge Register (kept with the Commercial Register, the same website as for the Commercial Register), also available to everyone.

Information as to the real property, including ownership and encumbrances, can be obtained from the Public Title Book (kept regionally by certain courts, www.rik.ee/e-kinnistusraamat). The information is available to everyone.

Information on motor-vehicles, trailers and recreational crafts is kept by the Vehicle Register (kept by Motor Vehicle Registration Centre, www.ark.ee). The information is available to the owners of motor-vehicles, trailers and recreational crafts.

Information on vessels (at least 12 m of length) and vessels under construction is included in the Ship Title Book (kept regionally by certain courts). In order to access the information, the person must have an Estonian personal identity card which enables identification via internet. The information is available to everyone.

Information as to the number and type of an aircraft is indicated in the Aircraft Register (kept by the Civil Aviation Administration). This information is available to everyone.

Finally, information as to the intellectual property rights such as trademarks, inventions (patents and utility models), industrial designs and geographical indications is maintained by the respective registers kept by the Patent Office (www.epa.ee). This information is available to everyone.

Information on domain names ending with ".ee" can be obtained from www.eenet.ee. This information is available to everyone.

6. Purchase Price Requirements

The parties are free in determining the purchase price, which can be stated in any currency and can also be paid by any third party (e.g., parent company).

The laws do not explicitly require indicating the price for each particular asset, however, in some cases, this may be required due to different tax implications or for determining notary fees (in case of real property) and state duties.

B. Tangible/Movable Assets

1. Characteristics as to:

a) Language of Documentation. Generally, there are no language requirements for the documentation. However, in case of vessels and certain other assets where a notarized transfer agreement is required, the language is restricted to what the notary accepts. Notaries rarely accept any language other than Estonian.

Any documents that must be submitted to authorities must be submitted with an Estonian translation.

Agreements can be concluded bilingually.

b) Form of Documentation. As a general rule, the transfer of tangible assets does not require any special form; agreements may be executed in oral form as well. However, obviously, a form leaving documentary evidence of the parties' intention is recommendable if the agreement ever needs to be enforced.

Estonian law distinguishes between written form and forms that can be reproduced in writing. The former means the agreement is signed by own hand by both parties, the latter can mean any other form including fax or e-mail exchange or parties signing on separate documents. There are no restrictions on executing written form or other agreements abroad.

It is permissible to sign the documents in counterparts.

In certain cases, the laws may require executing the agreement in a certain form; for example, in case of transfer of vessels (considered to be immovables). The notary can verify a transaction only in his/her jurisdiction (limited by counties) and with all parties present. Although the notary cannot travel abroad to verify the transaction, and the transaction cannot validly be verified by a foreign notary, the notary can accept powers of attorney verified by a foreign notary. If, by law, the agreement requires a notarized form, then any pre-agreements for such transaction shall also require notarized form.

c) Specification of Assets. To avoid disputes, the description of assets should be such as to be clear to the parties. Language like "all assets related to the business," or "all inventories located in ", etc. are often used and may be sufficient depending on the circumstances.

It is often most practicable to attach a list of assets to the transaction, whereas the list does not have to specify every individual asset but can identify groups of assets like "all inventories located at X warehouse."

2. Administrative, Corporate and Other Approvals

The transfer of tangible assets generally does not require special governmental or administrative approvals. However, exceptions may apply to specific categories of assets. Generally, failure to comply with such requirements may lead to the invalidity of the transfer; however, this should be analyzed on a case-by-case basis.

The competence of corporate bodies of a company is established in the articles of association of the company and the Commercial Code. Although the management board is usually the sole body authorized to represent the company, it often needs the consent of the supervisory board or shareholders' meeting to transfer an enterprise. Non-compliance with corporate governance rules does not render the transfer invalid. The validity may be objected to by third parties concerned (e.g., shareholders of the company) only in cases where a counterparty was acting in bad faith.

Under a general rule, in case of a transfer of encumbered (pledged) assets, approval of the security holder is not required. However, agreements establishing such encumbrance often require consent of the security holder for disposal of the asset. In such a case, transfer of the assets without the required consent does not render the transfer invalid. Commercial pledges encumbering an enterprise remain in force even after the transfer of the enterprise.

3. Filing Requirements

No filings or entries in public registers or databases are required, unless assets are registered with a certain register (e.g., vehicles, trademarks).

4. Automatic Transfer of Encumbrances

Generally, encumbrances on assets transfer to the new owner together with such assets. In case the encumbrances on assets have to be registered, only the registered encumbrances should be transferred to the new owner.

In case of assets under retention of title, the title transfers to the purchaser if the assets were in the possession of the seller and if the purchaser acquired the assets in good faith not knowing about the retention of title. If the purchaser knew or should have known about the retention of title, the title is not transferred to the purchaser and instead of transferring the assets per se, the contract containing the right to obtain the assets under retention of title should be transferred.

C. Real Property

1. Characteristics as to:

a) Language of Documentation. Since agreements for transferring real property must be verified by the notary, the language of the agreement is restricted to what the notary accepts. Notaries usually still do not accept any language other than Estonian, but the practice is gradually changing and English language agreements are getting more common.

In any case, the agreement must be translated to Estonian before it can be submitted to the Public Title Book.

b) Form of Documentation. Real property transfer (sale-purchase) agreements must be concluded in writing and notarized. Failure to comply with the notarization requirement renders the agreement invalid. The notary can verify a transaction only in his/her jurisdiction (limited by counties) and with all parties present. Although the notary cannot travel abroad to verify the transaction, and the transaction cannot validly be verified by a foreign notary, the notary can accept powers of attorney verified by a foreign notary. If the agreement requires a notarized form by law, then pre-agreements for such transaction shall also require notarized form.

Real property sale-purchase agreements must be registered with the Public Title Book. Only upon entry in the respective Public Title Book is the title deemed transferred.

c) Specification of Assets. The real property sale-purchase agreement must identify the specific real estate in question (by reference to the Public Title Book registration code) and cannot contain a general reference to all real property or group of real properties.

2. Administrative, Corporate and Other Approvals

Transactions with forest and agricultural land plots exceeding ten hectares in area as well as real estate on some islands and border areas are restricted and sometimes require special consents from the authorities. Failure to secure such consent renders the transaction invalid.

Transfer of real property containing or near certain culturally valuable sites or nature protection areas may incur the pre-emption right of the state or municipality. In such a case, the state or municipality can enter into the transaction instead of the purchaser on the same terms as originally agreed with the purchaser.

Competence of corporate bodies of a company is established in the articles of association of the company and the Commercial Code. In case of public limited companies, consent of the supervisory board, as a rule, is required for transactions involving real property. For further details, please refer to B, 2 above.

Generally, in case of a transfer of encumbered (mortgaged) real property, approval of a security holder is not required. However, agreements establishing such encumbrance often require consent or notification of the security holder for the disposal of the asset. In such a case, transfer of the assets without required consent does not render the transfer invalid.

3. Filing Requirements

Title to real property must be registered with the Public Title Book. All third persons have the right to rely on the information in the Public Title Book and the title is not deemed passed before a respective entry is made in the Public Title Book.

4. Automatic Transfer of Encumbrances

Real property's encumbrances transfer to the new owner together with the real property, provided the encumbrances have been entered into the Public Title Book.

A waiver of encumbrances in the Public Title Book requires their removal from the Public Title Book, which requires a notarized application by the person in whose favor the encumbrance was created.

5. Automatic Transfer of Lease Agreements

In case of a transfer of title to the real property, all lease agreements executed by the former owner of the real property and registered in the Public Title Book are automatically assigned to the new owner of the real property. If the lease agreement is not registered (which is most often the case), the new owner has a right to terminate the lease agreement by giving three months notice. However, the right of extraordinary termination applies in case of residential or commercial premises only if the new owner has a pressing need to use the premises for its own purposes.

D. Contracts

1. Characteristics as to:

a) Language of Documentation. The laws do not establish special language requirements for the transfer of a contract, and, therefore, general rules described in B, 1, a would apply.

b) Form of Documentation. There is no general form requirement regarding the transfer of contracts. Specific form may be required depending on the type and form of the agreement transferred. For example, transfer of notarized agreements may require a notarized agreement.

Unless notarization is required, the sale and transfer documents may be executed abroad. Signing in counterparts is permissible.

c) Specification of Contracts. The contracts have to be specified sufficiently. Schedules or lists of contracts are not required, however, might be recommendable depending on the details of the transaction.

Please note that upon transfer of an enterprise (but not in a genuine piece-by-piece asset transfer), all obligations attributable to the enterprise are deemed transferred automatically; thus, it is theoretically possible that if there is no agreement regarding the transfer of rights under the agreement, the rights will not transfer, but the obligations transfer automatically.

2. Administrative, Corporate and Other Approvals

A transfer of contracts does not require special governmental or administrative approvals.

As regards corporate approvals, the laws do not establish special requirements for transfer of contracts, therefore, general rules described in B, 2 above would apply.

A transfer of obligation generally requires the consent of the creditor under law, and often this is reinforced by contractual obligation. In case of transfer of enterprise, the transfer of an obligation does not require the consent of the creditor unless otherwise specified by law (for example, in the case of lease agreements, the landlord must consent to the transfer) and the creditors must only be informed of the transfer.

3. Automatic Transfer of Contracts (Other than Lease and Employment Agreements)

Estonian law provides for the automatic transfer of asset-related insurance agreements. Insurance providers may, however, terminate such agreements with one-month notice.

4. Filing Requirements

The transfer of contracts does not require special filings with public authorities or registrations in registers or (online) databases.

5. Treatment of Existing Contractual Claims and Obligations

If and to the extent the counterparty consents to the transfer of contract, the respective claims and/or obligations from such contract do automatically transfer to the purchaser. Also, in case of a transfer of an enterprise, all obligations attributable to the enterprise transfer automatically. Therefore, it is advisable to include special provisions (e.g., indemnifications) into the contract transfer agreement.

6. Warranty Claims Resulting from Events prior to Transfer

Provided that the asset transfer constitutes transfer of enterprise and the warranty claims are attributable to the enterprise, the liability for the warranties transfers automatically to the purchaser (although the seller of the enterprise remains jointly and severally liable with the purchaser for five years). It is customary to address this issue by including respective indemnification clauses in an asset (contracts) transfer agreement.

If the asset transfer does not constitute a transfer of an enterprise, the liability for warranty claims does not transfer to the purchaser unless otherwise agreed and with the third party consenting to such transfer of liability.

E. IP Rights

1. Characteristics of Intellectual Property Rights (e.g., Trademarks, Patents, Utility Models, Domain Names) ("*IP Rights*") as to:

a) Language of Documentation. The laws do not establish special language requirements for the transfer of IP Rights, and, therefore, general rules described in B, 1, a would apply.

Please note that in case of registered IP Rights, certain documents are required to be in Estonian for filing purposes, e.g., in order to register the transfer of rights with the Patent Office (which registers trademarks, patents, designs and topographies of semiconductor products).

b) Form of Documentation. Form requirements for documentation differ depending on the object of the transfer. The laws do not foresee special form requirements for the transfer of copyright, trademarks, designs and domain names. Agreements on transfer of patents and topographies of semiconductor products have to be executed in a form that can be reproduced in writing. Nonetheless, since registration of transfer is required, some written documentation will be needed with respect to the transfer of all kinds of objects of IP Rights.

The documents can be executed outside Estonia. Signing in counterparts is permissible.

c) Specification of IP Rights. IP Rights to be transferred should be described in a manner making it possible to identify which IP Rights were transferred. Depending on the circumstances, in general, all IP Rights related to the business clause might be sufficient. However, in most cases identification of separate IP Rights or groups of IP Rights is advisable. A transfer of registered IP Rights generally requires that the IP Rights are identified individually in the transfer documents or separate documents are concluded for registering the changes.

A separate schedule or list of IP Rights is not required, however, is often advisable.

2. Administrative, Corporate and Other Approvals

The transfer of IP Rights does not require special governmental or administrative approvals.

As regards corporate approvals, the laws do not establish special requirements for the transfer of contracts, therefore, the general rules described in B, 2 above would apply.

If the IP Rights are encumbered, approval of the security holder is not required. In case of a pledge, if the right of ownership of the collateral is transferred, the right to the pledge remains due when the object of the pledge was transferred to the pledgee or when the pledge bond was registered in the respective IP register.

3. Filing Requirements

If and to the extent the IP Rights to be transferred are registered, the change of ownership requires registration with the relevant registers. In case of trademarks, patents, design and topographies of semiconductor products, the transfer of these objects becomes effective only upon and from the date of registration of the transfer with the respective register. Rights to the domain names are transferred when the technical transfer procedures with the domain name register are completed.

4. Applicable International (Multilateral) Agreements or Treaties

Estonia participates in the following treaties and agreements:

(i) WIPO Conventions:

- Patent Cooperation Treaty, Washington 1970
- Berne Convention for the Protection of Literary and Artistic Works
- Nice Agreement Concerning the International Classification of Goods and Services for the Purposes of the Registration of Marks
- Protocol Relating to the Madrid Agreement Concerning the International Registration of Marks
- Budapest Treaty on the International Recognition of the Deposit of Microorganisms for the Purposes of Patent Procedure
- Trademark Law Treaty
- World Intellectual Property Organization Performances and Phonograms Treaty
- World Intellectual Property Organization Copyright Treaty
- The Geneva Act (1999) of the Hague Agreement Concerning the International Registration of Industrial Designs

(ii) Conventions of the United Nations:

- International Convention for the Protection of Performers, Producers of Phonograms and Broadcasting Organizations
- Convention for the Protection of Producers of Phonograms Against Unauthorized Duplication of their Phonograms

(iii) Other:

- Convention on the Grant of European Patents (European Patent Convention)
- Trade-Related Aspects of Intellectual Property Rights (TRIPS)
- Treaties and agreements in which European Community participates are also relevant to Estonia.

F. Receivables

1. Characteristics as to:

a) Language of Documentation. The laws do not establish special language requirements for the transfer of receivables, and, therefore, the general rules described in B, 1, a would apply.

b) Form of Documentation. There are no form requirements for the transfer of receivables. The sale and transfer documents may be executed outside Estonia. Signing in counterparts is permissible.

c) Specification of Receivables. Following the general rule described in B, 1, c, receivables have to be specified sufficiently. Schedules or lists of receivables are not required, however, might be advisable depending on the details of the transaction.

2. Administrative, Corporate and Other Approvals

The transfer of receivables does not require special governmental or administrative approvals.

As regards corporate approvals, the laws do not establish special requirements for the transfer of contracts, therefore, general rules described in B, 2 above would apply.

The transfer of receivables does not require the prior consent of the debtor. It is possible to limit the right to transfer or assign rights from the agreement to third persons by agreement.

3. Filing Requirements

Transfer of receivables does not require filings with public authorities or registrations in public registers or databases.

The notification of the transfer to the debtors is not required but advisable. As long as the debtors are not aware of the transfer, payments on the receivables can still be made to the former owner of the receivables.

G. Liabilities

1. Characteristics as to:

a) Language of Documentation. The laws do not establish special language requirements for transfer of liabilities, and, therefore, the general rules described in B, 1, a would apply.

Bilingual documents are permitted.

b) Form of Documentation. There are no form requirements for the transfer of obligations. The sale and transfer documents may be executed outside Estonia. Signing in counterparts is permissible.

c) Specification of Liabilities. Following the general rule described in B, 1, c, liabilities have to be sufficiently specified. Schedules or lists of liabilities are not required, however, might be advisable depending on the details of the transaction.

2. Administrative, Corporate and Other Approvals

The transfer of liabilities does not require special governmental or administrative approvals.

As regards corporate approvals, the laws do not establish special requirements for the transfer of contracts, therefore, the general rules described in B, 2 above would apply.

The transfer of liabilities requires the prior consent of the creditor. If the consent of the creditor for the transfer of liabilities is not obtained, the transfer of liabilities is null and void.

An important exception to the requirement of creditor's consent is the transfer of liabilities in case of a transfer of an enterprise. However, in such a case the original debtor remains jointly and severally liable with the new debtor for five years for any liabilities incurred prior to the transfer.

3. Filing Requirements

No filings with public authorities or registrations in public registers or databases are required to transfer liabilities.

Due to the fact that the transfer of liabilities is subject to the creditors' consent, a separate notification to the creditors is not necessary.

4. Purchaser's Liability for:

a) Tax Obligations. In case of a transfer of an enterprise, the obligations attributable to the enterprise, which would include tax obligations related to particular assets (e.g., land tax) would transfer to the purchaser of the assets, but the original debtor remains jointly and severally liable to the tax authorities for five years after the transfer.

In a genuine piece-by-piece transfer of assets, the tax obligations of the seller do not transfer to the purchaser.

b) Environmental Contamination. The polluter is liable for the environmental contamination. In case of transfer of the enterprise and provided the pollution occurred in the course of business of the enterprise, the obligations of the polluter would transfer to the purchaser of the assets but the original polluter remains jointly and severally liable for five years after the transfer.

If the polluter cannot be determined or does not remediate the pollution, the owner of the assets is deemed liable for the pollution. Thus, it is also the case in a piece-by-piece asset transfer that the purchaser may end up being liable for the seller's actions.

c) Products Sold or Services Rendered by the Seller to Third Parties. In case of a sale of an enterprise, all obligations of the enterprise with regard to products sold or services already rendered transfer to the purchaser, but the seller will remain jointly and severally liable to the customers for five years.

5. Automatic Transfer of Other Liabilities

In case of the acquisition of an enterprise, the purchaser will assume all the obligations attributable to the acquired assets (business).

In case of genuine piece-by-piece asset transfer, the obligations of the seller transfer to the purchaser only in specified cases (e.g., certain lease of premises agreements as described above).

6. Contractual Protection as to 4 and 5 above

It is customary and advisable to include special provisions (e.g., indemnifications) as to the issues mentioned under 4 and 5 into the asset transfer agreement.

H. Employees

1. Transfer of Employees

In case of a transfer of an enterprise, the employees transfer automatically to the purchaser. The transfer does not change any of the employment terms nor does it grant any additional rights to terminate the agreements. Often the transfer is used as a convenient junction to review and amend the employment agreements, but the employees are under no obligation to accept any amendments.

If the transfer of assets also involves a transfer of employees, it is likely that such a transaction would be considered a transfer of an enterprise. If, however, the assets are transferred piece-by-piece and the business does not continue to be an on-going concern, then the employees do not transfer automatically and transferring the employees would require separate agreements with each employee.

2. Approval of Works Council, Trade Union or Other Institutions

The transfer of an enterprise does not require any approval from works councils or other institutions. If employees are to be transferred with the enterprise, the employees must be notified of this at least 30 days in advance and given a chance to express their views and proposals. The employer is obliged to review the proposals but is not bound by them in any way. Nevertheless, the employer must justify refusal to take into account the proposals from the employees.

3. Contractual Protection as to Labor Issues

It is customary to include indemnifications regarding employees in the asset transfer agreements. In particular, the purchaser is often interested in some guarantees that the seller has disclosed all employees eligible for automatic transfer.

I. Tax Implications

1. Value Added Tax

The transfer of an enterprise is deemed as tax-exempt for VAT purposes.

Sale of assets piece-by-piece by a seller registered as taxable person to an Estonian purchaser will likely include a transfer of assets that incurs VAT. The current VAT rate is 20%.

2. Real Property Transfer Tax

Transfer of real property incurs notary fees and state duties. The notary fee and state duty is calculated based on the value of the transaction. Regardless of the amount of transaction, the state fee never exceeds EUR 2,556. The notary's fees usually vary between 0.1% to 5% of the transaction value. For example, in case of a transaction with a value of EUR 500,000, the notary's fee is approx 0.3% of the transaction value.
There is no land transfer tax in Estonia.

3. Other Tax Issues

An asset transfer itself does not generally incur any tax implications for Estonian entities, as the capital gain of corporations is generally not taxed in Estonia. Please note that in case changes are made to the operations of business, tax implications may occur. This is subject to case-by-case analyses.

J. Bankruptcy Law

1. Challenge of Asset Transfer in Case of Insolvency

In case of insolvency proceedings, there is a risk of a challenge of the asset transfer: as of the effective date of the court decision to initiate insolvency proceedings of the seller or purchaser. Transactions can be declared invalid if concluded up to one year before initiating the insolvency proceedings and if the other party knew or should have known the transaction to be damaging to the creditors' interests. If the debtor intentionally damaged the interests of the creditors, the transactions can be declared invalid for three years or five years, if the other party is associated with the debtor.

2. Acquisition of Assets that are Subject to Insolvency Proceedings

The assets of an insolvent company should generally be sold on auction. Other methods of sale are possible only upon the creditors' general meeting or committee approval.

K. Timing and Costs

1. Timeframe of Asset Transfer

If the transfer of assets involves transfer of employees, 30 days must be allowed for notifying the employees. Otherwise, the timeframe is determined by the practical aspects of the transactions; for example, on whether and when stock inventories can be conducted, etc.

2. Costs of Asset Transfer

Since generally the transfer of assets does not require notarization or registration there are no additional costs. However, real estate and vessel transfers incur notary's fees and state duties both depending on the value of the transaction. Transfer of vehicles, trademarks, patents and some other IP Rights incur state duties.

L. Miscellaneous

1. Choice of Foreign Law

The asset transfer agreement might be governed by foreign law. However, Estonian mandatory legal rules would apply in any case.

2. (International) Arbitration, Choice of Venue

The parties to the asset transfer deal may use international arbitration.

3. Other Distinctions, Choice of Venue

The relevant legislation regulating asset transfer is heavily influenced by German and Dutch civil codes; thus, the legislation is not particularly unusual.

M. Literature

Sorainen, Handbook of the Baltic Business Law, 4th Edition, 2004

France

By *Bénédicte Bremond*

A. General Aspects

1. Asset Deal vs. Share Deal: Essential Considerations

In France, there are various considerations that have to be taken into account when deciding whether a transaction should be structured as a share deal or as an asset deal.

One significant reason for structuring a transaction as a share deal is simplicity (and, consequently, speed and cost effectiveness). Under French Law, a transfer of shares can be completed through the mere execution by the seller of a share transfer order (*ordre de mouvement*) and the payment of the purchase price by the purchaser, whereas the transfer of a business (*fonds de commerce*) is regulated by specific and more complex regulations. French law does not specify which assets have to be transferred to subject the transfer to the these regulations, however, French case law has made clear that a business is composed of customers and all assets necessary for the development of the clientele (*clientèle*).

For example, the French Commercial Code provides for certain mandatory representations and statements to be included in the business transfer agreement (mainly the name of the former seller of the business and the acquisition price, the description of all liens or preferential rights affecting the business, the turnovers and profits realized by the seller over the past three years, the conditions of the lease, if any, and the name and address of the lessor). In the absence of such provisions in the business transfer agreement or inaccuracy/incompleteness of such representations or statements, the purchaser may request the rescission of the sale on the ground that its consent was vitiated.

The French Commercial Code further provides for certain publication formalities (see A, 5 below), triggering a 10-day period for creditors of the seller to oppose payment of the purchase price by the purchaser. As a consequence, the parties might want to consider placing all or part of the price in escrow until the end of such opposition period (see A, 6 below).

In the case of a purchase of shares, the purchaser takes all assets and liabilities of the purchased entity regardless of whether such purchaser is aware of such assets and liabilities; in case of a business transfer, the parties must specifically and individually determine which assets and liabilities will be transferred and which will not. Unless otherwise agreed, only the assets composing the business transferred (mainly the clientele, the trade name or trademark, the commercial lease and the goods and equipment relating to the business) will be transferred. On the one hand, this allows the purchaser to select which particular assets and liabilities he wants to buy. On the other hand, the listing of all assets and liabilities contemplated to be transferred then has to be accurate, specific and complete on the date of the transfer of the business, which can be challenging. In particular, except for certain contracts, the transfer of which is regulated by law, the contracts related to the business will not be automatically transferred to the purchaser and the contractor's prior consent will have to be obtained (see D below); whereas, in a share purchase, except where contracts include change of control provisions, the contracts of the target company will be indirectly transferred to the purchaser, with no third-party consent required.

Tax aspects are also worth taking into account. While, the transfer of a business triggers the payment by the purchaser of a progressive registration duty from 3% to 5% based on the transfer price or the market value of the tangible and intangible assets transferred (whichever is higher) with a franchise for transactions below EUR 23,000, the rate of the registration duty applicable to stock generally amounts to 3% of the agreed price of the shares, with a cap at EUR 5,000. However, depending on the corporate form of the target company, if shares (*parts sociales*) are transferred instead of stock (*actions*), the registration duty of 3% of the purchase price will not be capped. In addition, capital gains realized by the seller on the sale of a business are normally taxable at the ordinary rate of corporate income (i.e. currently an effective rate of 34.43%) whereas capital gains on the sale of shares may benefit, under certain conditions, from a 95% capital gains tax exemption.

Another issue worth bearing in mind when structuring a transaction is financial assistance and up-stream guarantee-related issues. French law prohibits the grant by a company of financial assistance (whether by granting a loan, a guarantee or security) for the purchase or subscription of its own shares. Breach of this prohibition makes the transaction void and is a criminal offence. The granting of a guarantee and of security interests by a French company to secure the indebtedness of its parent company or of an affiliate can therefore be a delicate matter. These issues are more easily handled in the context of an asset deal where the purchaser is usually able to grant security over the acquired assets to the benefit of its lenders, if need be.

2. Distinction between Sale and Transfer in Rem

Under French law, a sale of assets will be deemed complete upon signing of an agreement between the seller and the purchaser in which they agree on the assets to be transferred and on the price to be paid. Nothing prevents the parties from providing that the completion of the transfer will occur at a date that differs from the date of signing of such an agreement. But it has to be explicitly stated in the agreement. If the seller and the purchaser wish to defer the completion of the sale, e.g., satisfaction of certain conditions, such conditions must be clearly provided for in the transfer agreement as conditions precedent to the completion of the transaction.

In the event of an international sale of assets, it is possible to provide for the main terms of the sale in a master agreement with the condition precedent that a local agreement be executed for the effective transfer of the assets located in France. The drafting of such local agreement for the transfer of French businesses is even preferable since the requirements (for certain mandatory representations and statements to be provided and for certain registration formalities to be completed) will be more easily addressed at the level of a local agreement than in a master agreement.

Regarding registration formalities, the signing of a local agreement will enable the parties to avoid the disclosure of their entire agreement as well as having to translate it into French if it has been drafted in another language. One should, however, note that when registration with the French tax administration is required in order to pay the applicable transfer duties, it is recommended to avoid any reference to the master agreement in the French local agreement because such a reference could cause the French tax administration to request that the parties register the entire master agreement (translated into French) together with the local agreement.

3. Regional Differences

Under French law, there are no regional differences as regards the legal requirements in connection with the transfer of assets.

4. Acquisition by Foreigners

With regard to the acquisition of assets by foreigners or foreign entities, in France, the acquisition by foreigners of assets comprising the business of a French entity, whether directly or indirectly, is subject to an administrative declaration to the French Minister for the Economy, which must be filed after the acquisition. Failure to comply with this declaration is subject to a fine of EUR 750.

Furthermore, for specific areas of the economy deemed essential for public interests (such as businesses that participate in the exercise of public authority, which could jeopardize public order, public safety or national defense interests or activities linked to arms, munitions, explosive substances), foreign investments are subject to the prior authorization of the Minister for the Economy. Therefore, if a foreign person or entity acquires all or part of a line of business of a company whose activities fall within the scope of any of these protected areas, the completion of such acquisition will be subject to the prior authorization of the Minister for the Economy.

The duty of the French Ministry of Economy is to safeguard the protection of national interests by insuring that any investment described above does not adversely affect public policy (*ordre public*), public safety or national security. If the French Ministry of Economy believes that these national interests could be adversely affected, particular conditions may be imposed for the realization of the foreign investment or the French Ministry of Economy may refuse its authorization if it believes that conditions alone will not be sufficient to safeguard the national interests in question or that there is a strong probability that the foreign investor is likely to commit one of the crimes prohibited by these regulations (money laundering, acts of terrorism or financing terrorism, corruption and influence peddling, etc.).

The French Ministry of Economy may then render its decision in a number of ways: (i) there may be no response within the two-month timeframe imposed by law and the authorization will be deemed tacitly granted, (ii) it may issue an authorization (with or without conditions) in the form of correspondence to the foreign investor, which authorization may or may not be subject to official publication, or (iii) it may confirm its refusal to authorize in the same manner as the foregoing. The decision of the French Ministry of Economy is subject to full review and foreign investors may contest the conditions imposed for the authorization or the refusal to authorize before the administrative law courts.

Regarding the risks and sanctions for violation of the above-mentioned obligations, the French regulations provide that any undertaking, agreement or contractual clause that, directly or indirectly, results in a foreign investment in an activity mentioned above is null and void if such investment has not been granted prior authorization as required. The French Ministry of Economy may then issue an injunction prohibiting the foreign investor from proceeding with the transaction, or to amend the transaction or to restore the status quo at its own cost if it has been ascertained that such investment is being or has been carried out. In addition, if such an injunction has not been complied with, the French Ministry of Economy may, without prejudice to the re-establishment of the former situation, impose a financial sanction, the maximum amount of which is twice the amount of the amount of the unlawful investment.

5. Public Registers, Records and Databases

In France, information is filed with several registries depending mainly upon the type of assets concerned.

In the event of a business transfer, the following formalities will have to be completed:

(i) the registration of the purchase agreement with the tax authorities,

(ii) the registration of the transfer with the public Commerce and Companies Registry (*Registre du Commerce et des Sociétés*),

(iii) the publication of a notice of the transfer in a legal newspaper and in the official gazette of civil and commercial notices, the *Bulletin Officiel des Annonces Civiles et Commerciales* ("BODACC"),

(iv) the filing of various declarations with the social and labor authorities.

Corporate details about the seller and the purchaser can further be obtained from the public Commerce and Companies Registry, which may provide (mainly on a so-called *K-bis* Extract) basic details on the company (legal form, registered office, registered share capital, legal representatives, financial statements, certain corporate events such as capital increases, mergers, business transfers, pledges granted by the company on certain of its assets, insolvency proceedings against the company). The French Commerce and Companies Registry has a website where this information is available (www.infogreffe.fr). These sources are available to the public.

Information relating to real property including ownership, transfers and mortgages can be obtained from the Mortgage Registry (*Bureau de Conservation des Hypothèques*) and plans of real property from the Land Registry (*Cadastre*). Anyone can request information from these two registries.

Finally, information relating to the transfer of registered intellectual property rights (such as trademarks, patents, designs) is available at the French Trademark and Patent Registry (*Institut National de la Propriété Intellectuelle* or INPI).

6. Purchase Price Requirements

The parties are free to determine the purchase price to be paid in connection with an asset deal, which can be stated in euros or in any other currency. However, since the transfer duties relating to the business transfer are calculated as a percentage of the purchase price and are paid in euros, the price equivalent in euros will have to be determined for the calculation of such transfer duties. It is recommended that the exchange rate for determining such price equivalent in euros be established in the business transfer agreement.

The purchase price will have to be allocated to groups of assets. Under French law, a business transfer agreement must give a break-down of the purchase price regarding the portion of such price attributable to each of the following categories of assets transferred: (i) the fixed intangible assets, (ii) the equipment and (iii) the goods (inventory). This is required to enable the seller to exercise its preferential right in the event of a deferred payment of the price. In such case, the seller benefits from a priority against other creditors on the payment of each of these separate prices.

Allocation of the price to each category of assets may further be required to ensure the application of the relevant tax regime to the transfer of each such category of assets. As an example, if no distinction is made between the price of the real property transferred and the price of the other assets, transfer duties relating to the conveyance of the real property may be calculated on the whole price. More generally, the parties will also want to provide such allocation of the purchase price to each category of assets transferred for accounting purposes in order to justify the value granted to each such category of assets in their respective accounts.

In addition, it must be noted that the French tax authorities can modify the purchase price of a business transfer if they consider it lower than the market value of the business or assets transferred. Such modification would lead to a tax reassessment with respect to corporate income tax at the level of the seller and also with respect to registration duty at the level of the purchaser, the seller being jointly and severally liable for such payment.

Furthermore, under French law, the creditors of the business transferred (including the French tax authorities) have a direct right to the purchase price. Creditors may oppose the payment of the purchase price to the seller during a certain period of time (i.e. ten days) from the publication of the notice of the business transfer in the BODACC (see A, 5 above). It is common practice for the purchase price to be escrowed until the end of the opposition period or until all the creditors have been paid, the rationale being that if the purchaser has paid the purchase price to the seller before the end of the opposition period available to the creditors, the purchaser remains liable to the creditors up to the purchase price amount and therefore is exposed to paying the purchase price twice. The creditors opposing the payment of the price or those which had pledges registered on the transferred assets also have the right to acquire the business under certain circumstances with a higher bid than the initial purchaser.

B. Tangible/Movable Assets

1. Characteristics as to:

a) Language of Documentation. The documentation relating to the transfer of tangible assets may be drafted in any language. Bilingual documents are permitted, in which case it is recommended to specify which of the two versions will prevail in the event of dispute or discrepancy between them.

However, if tangible assets are transferred as part of a business transfer, the business transfer agreement will have to be registered in the French language with the tax authorities. The parties can therefore either execute the agreement in both languages or, if the agreement is only executed in a foreign language, the parties will have to procure an official translation in French prepared by a translator approved by French Courts, which translation is acceptable for registration purposes.

b) Form of Documentation. As a general rule, French law does not require a special form of documentation for the transfer of tangible assets, but it is customary to execute a written document to ensure that the parties have agreed on the assets transferred and on the price thereof.

If the tangible assets are transferred as part of a business transfer, a written agreement will have to be executed (i) for the registration formalities relating to the business transfer (see A, 5 above), (ii) to enable the seller to benefit from its preferential right (see A, 6 above), and (iii) to include the mandatory representations and statements requested by French law (see A, 1 above).

The documents relating to the transfer may be executed outside France but, as previously mentioned, registration in France may be required.

Signing in counterparts is not allowed under French law and all parties to an agreement subject to French law must execute the same original document. Instruments under private signature that contain obligations binding upon all parties are valid only insofar as they have been made in as many originals as there are parties having a distinct interest. One original suffices for all the persons who have the same interest. Each original copy must indicate the number of originals that have been executed. Original copies may further be needed for the purpose of completion of the necessary filings with French public authorities. As an example, with respect to a business transfer agreement, one additional original copy will be required for the filing with the French tax authorities.

c) Specification of Assets. If the transfer of tangible assets occurs as part of a business transfer, the goods and equipment relating to such business will automatically be transferred with the business, even if they are not specifically identified, and unless otherwise specified by the parties. Therefore a description in general (e.g., "all tangible assets related to the business or to a certain unit of an entity") or a generic description (e.g., "all inventories located in") of such assets in the transfer agreement would be sufficient. To avoid any dispute among the parties as well as for accounting and tax purposes, it is, however, common practice in France to attach to the business transfer agreement an exhaustive list of all tangible assets transferred as part of the business as well as an inventory of the goods transferred.

For any other assets transferred with the business or for assets transferred on a stand alone basis, they will be transferred only if specifically referred to in the transfer agreement, the simple listing of categories of assets will not be sufficient.

2. Administrative, Corporate and Other Approvals

Special Governmental or Administrative Approvals

As a general rule, the transfer of tangible assets does not require special governmental or administrative approvals. However, exceptions may apply with regard to special categories of assets (such as drugs or war-related materials) or certain categories of businesses (such as drinking establishments, pharmacies, travel agencies). Certain types of sales are also specifically regulated, such as mail order sales or discount or liquidation sales.

If the tangible assets are transferred as part of a business transfer, one must confirm whether the transaction falls within the scope of any anti-trust regulations (whether national or European) requiring prior authorization from the anti-trust authorities.

In case of a transfer of a business that is located in special areas that have been identified by the city (*commune*) as areas where the diversity of businesses shall be protected, then the city may have a preemptive right over the transferred business. In order that the city may have an opportunity to exercise this right, the proposed transfer shall be notified to the city, which must respond within two months. Failure to provide notice will invalidate the transfer.

Approval of Corporate Bodies Regarding the Seller and/or the Purchaser

If the seller is a corporate entity, the transfer of tangible assets will usually be validly decided by any legal representative of the seller (or by any employee having been granted such powers), subject only to such transfer complying with the seller's corporate interest.

However, in the event of a business transfer, if the business transferred constitutes the sole activity or the most significant part of the activities of the seller, the sale of such business may deprive the selling company of its corporate purpose and therefore the prior authorization of its shareholders will be requested prior to completion of such sale.

Depending upon the corporate form of the selling or purchasing company, specific authorizations may also be required. For example, if the seller/purchaser is a *société anonyme*, a prior approval from the board of directors will have to be obtained, if the asset transfer agreement is entered into, either directly or through an intermediary, between the seller/purchaser and its general manager, one of its assistant general managers, one of its directors or one of its shareholders holding a fraction of the voting rights greater than 10%. Same rule would apply if any manager or director of the seller/purchaser is the owner, a general partner, a manager, a director or in any way involved in the management of the purchaser/seller of the assets.

The seller's and/or purchaser's by-laws may further provide that a specific prior approval from the board of directors or from the shareholders is required. Please, however, note that such limitations to the power of representation of the legal representatives will only have effect vis-à-vis the shareholders of the company concerned and will not be enforceable against third parties, unless it can be proven that the third party, given the circumstances, could not have been ignorant of that fact, and the mere publication of the by-laws does not suffice to constitute such proof.

Regarding business transfers, if the seller or the purchaser has a works council (employees' representatives), the transaction must be submitted to such works councils for the purpose of receiving their opinion prior to the signing of any binding agreement (see H, 2 below). While the parties are not bound by the works council's opinion, this requirement may delay the whole process.

Approval of Security Holders in Case the Assets are Encumbered

Under French law, the rules governing security interests may differ depending upon the type of assets secured. Specific rules govern the pledge of a business (*nantissement de fonds de commerce*), the pledge on tools and equipments (*nantissement du materiel et de l'outillage*) or the pledge on inventory (*gage de stocks*). Where no specific regime exists, the general rules governing the pledge will apply.

The prior approval of the security holder in the event of a transfer of the secured assets is not always required by provision of law but the pledge agreement will usually contain a provision preventing the debtor from transferring the secured assets without having obtained the prior approval of the security holder. Furthermore, if there are no legal provisions requiring its prior approval, the security holder is usually granted a preferential right, a so called droit de suite, which authorizes him to enforce the pledge notwithstanding the transfer to the purchaser (see B, 4 below). As a result, the purchaser will always want to ensure that the obligations secured by the pledge have been satisfied prior to the transfer of the secured assets in order to avoid any further claim of the security holder.

The main legal provisions applicable under the various regimes to the transfer of secured assets are further summarized below:

(i) In the event of a transfer of a business subject to a business pledge (*nantissement de fonds de commerce*): the prior consent of the pledgor is not required, but the pledgor acting as a creditor may oppose the payment of the purchase price of the business to the seller (see A, 6 above) and the pledgor will further benefit from a *droit de suite,* which authorizes him to enforce the pledge notwithstanding the transfer (see B, 4 below).

(ii) In case of a transfer of tools or equipment subject to a pledge (*nantissement du materiel* et *de l'outillage*), French law requires the seller to obtain the prior consent of the pledgor or an authorization from the president of the commercial court deciding under summary proceedings (*statuant en référé*). If such consent or authorization is not obtained, the pledgor will be granted a *droit de suite* under the conditions described below in D, 4, provided that the tools and equipment transferred have been duly marked as pledged under the conditions provided for by French law.

(iii) In case of a pledge on inventory (*gage de stocks*), the debtor has the obligation to maintain the inventory in quality and quantity equal to that existing at the date of creation of the pledge. Subject to satisfaction of this requirement, the debtor can sell the inventory and the pledge will continue on the goods that will constitute the new inventory. If the value of the inventory is reduced by more than 20%, the pledgor can require the debtor to restore the inventory or repay part of its debt.

(iv) Finally, if the tangible assets are secured under the common rules of the pledge, the debtor will be prohibited from selling the pledged assets without the prior consent of the pledgor. In case of non-compliance of the debtor with such prohibition, the secured creditor may exercise its rights against the purchaser of the secured assets in order to preserve the pledge.

3. Filing Requirements

As a general rule, the transfer of tangible assets does not require special filings or registrations. However, exceptions may apply with respect to special categories of assets (e.g., vehicles, ships, boats, aircrafts) whose transfer of ownership has to be mentioned in the relevant registries.

If the tangible assets are transferred as part of a business transfer, the registration formalities described in A, 5 above will apply.

4. Automatic Transfer of Encumbrances

If the assets transferred are subject to encumbrances, such encumbrances will transfer to the purchaser. As previously mentioned (see B, 2 above), in case of a transfer of pledged assets or of a pledged business, the security holder may be granted a preferential right (*droit de suite*). As a result, the security holder may require the sale of the assets/business at public auction notwithstanding the fact that the assets/business have been transferred to a third party purchaser.

Purchasers generally want to avoid such situation by serving notice of the transfer to the pledgor and offering to satisfy immediately all obligations secured by the pledge (up to the amount of the purchase price). The pledgor may accept such offer and release the pledge, or require that the assets/business be sold at a public auction (if he believes that the assets/business can be sold at a higher price than that offered by the purchaser), the proceeds of such sale being used to satisfy the debts owed to the pledgor. To protect purchasers from abuse of this provision, where a pledgor requests the sale of the assets/business at public auction, he must offer to purchase the assets/business from the purchaser for 110% of the purchase price agreed upon between the purchaser and the seller.

C. Real Property

1. Characteristics as to:

a) Language of Documentation. Agreements relating to the transfer of real property will always be drafted in French since they must be recorded with the Mortgage Registry (*Bureau des Hypothèques*) and take the form of a notarized act for which the use of the French language is mandatory.

b) Form of Documentation. Agreements relating to the transfer of real property must take the form of a formal deed of sale in the authentic form duly prepared by a French public notary. As a result, the transfer documents relating to real property will have to be executed in France. Such agreements must also be recorded in the Mortgage Registry in order to be binding against third parties.

Such formal requirements will apply even if the real property is transferred simultaneously with a business. The transfer of the real property cannot be included in the transfer of the business but shall be completed through the execution of a separate agreement.

Since the completion of all of the formalities relating to the transfer is time-consuming, the parties often execute a unilateral or bilateral option agreement that immediately creates obligations between them but that does not transfer title to the real property. One should note, however, that in order to be valid a unilateral purchase option must be filed with the tax authorities (and the corresponding registration tax paid) no later than ten days after its execution.

c) Specification of Assets. The real property transferred must be clearly identified, with reference to its section in the Land Registry. The seller has the obligation to deliver to the purchaser the exact real property as described in the sale agreement, as well as all intangible real property rights relating thereto and, unless otherwise provided, all personal property relating thereto that is deemed to constitute real property by its purpose or because it relates to real property.

The history of the real property title must also be set forth in the transfer deed. As a general rule, no document may be recorded in the Mortgage Registry if the title to the real property concerned has not already been the subject of a recording in such registry. Thus, a title search must be performed in connection with each conveyance of a real property interest.

Furthermore, it is a statutory obligation for the seller to provide the purchaser with certain specific information regarding the environmental condition of the property (e.g., asbestos report, termites' survey).

2. Administrative, Corporate and Other Approvals

Special Governmental or Administrative Approvals

As a general rule, the transfer of real property does not require special governmental or administrative approval. However, pursuant to French law relating to the protection of the environment, the operation of certain installations and equipment that may represent a danger to the environment or health ("classified installations") is subject to a prior authorization or notification to the environmental authorities depending on the size and nature of such installations or equipment.

Furthermore, in order to prevent speculation in real estate and to permit the application of zoning laws to certain areas, a preemptive right is granted to local governmental authorities to purchase real property that the owner intends to sell. In such cases, notice of the sale of such real property must be given to the local governmental authorities prior to the completion of the sale.

The Approval of Corporate Bodies Regarding the Seller and/or the Purchaser

If the seller or the purchaser is a corporate entity, the transfer of the real property can be made by any of its legal representatives subject to compliance of this transfer with its corporate interest. Depending upon the corporate form of the selling or purchasing company specific authorizations may be required. As an example, if the seller is a *société anonyme* with a management board and supervisory board, prior authorization of the supervisory board is required for the transfer of real property. Similar rules as those described for the transfer of tangible assets in B, 2 above may further apply.

Approval of Security Holders in Case the Real Property is Encumbered

If the real property is encumbered, no prior authorization from the security holder is required in the event of a transfer of the real property, except if otherwise provided for in the mortgage agreement. But, as indicated below (see C, 4 below), the mortgage will not be affected by the transfer and the security holder will benefit from a *droit de suite* on the real property. Therefore, purchasers will always seek the prior approval of the security holders or request that the seller obtain the release of the mortgage prior to the transfer.

3. Filing Requirements

In order to be enforceable against third parties, all conveyances of real property must be recorded with the Mortgage Registry of the locality in which the real property is situated. In the event that a seller conveys the same interest in real property to two purchasers, the purchaser who is the first to record his acquisition will prevail.

The transfer deed will also have to be registered with the tax authorities.

4. Automatic Transfer of Encumbrances

A duly recorded interest of a creditor of the owner of real property that is secured by such real property, e.g., a mortgage, will continue as an encumbrance on the real property notwithstanding a transfer of such property by the owner thereof. This continuity of recording is known as the *droit de suite*. Such an encumbrance will only be cleared upon the deletion of its recording from the Mortgage Registry. Where the obligation underlying a recorded encumbrance is satisfied, the recording thereof in the Mortgage Registry is deleted from such registry either by operation of law or upon the petition of the purchaser of the real property.

If the purchaser requests the waiver of a recorded encumbrance, he must have a notice of the sale of the real property served upon all security holders and expressly offer to satisfy immediately all of the obligations secured by the recorded encumbrance, provided, however, that the purchaser is not obligated to pay more in satisfaction of such obligations than the purchase price for the real property. The security holders may either accept the offer of the purchaser or petition the court for an order that the real property be sold at public auction (if he believes that the offered price is understated), the proceeds of such sale being used to satisfy the debts owing to them. Where a security holder requests the sale of the real property at public auction, he must offer to purchase the real property from the purchaser for 110% of the purchase price that was agreed upon between the purchaser and the seller.

5. Automatic Transfer of Lease Agreements

In the event that all or part of the real property transferred is subject to lease agreements, the French Civil Code provides that the lease agreements will automatically transfer to the purchaser of the real property, provided that such lease agreements have been entered into in the authentic form or that the signing date of such lease agreements is undisputable.

There is no specific requirement to notify the tenant of the transfer of the real property; the registration formalities with the Mortgage Registry required to enforce the conveyance of the real property to third parties is deemed sufficient to enforce the transfer towards the tenant.

Except if otherwise provided in the lease agreement, notwithstanding the sale of the real property and the transfer of the lease agreement, the seller will remain liable for the reimbursement at the end of the lease of the deposit initially paid by the tenant to the seller. To avoid this situation, it is customary that the lessor and the tenant agree in the lease agreement that the deposit will be transferred by the lessor to the purchaser of the real property and therefore that the tenant will claim the repayment of the deposit from the purchaser at the end of the lease.

There is no extraordinary right for the purchaser or the tenant to terminate the lease agreements following the transfer of the real property. The lease agreement continues under the same terms and conditions notwithstanding the sale of the real property.

The French Civil Code, however, authorizes the lessor to provide in the initial lease agreement that he can terminate the lease in the event of a transfer of the real property, provided that the tenant is indemnified. Regarding commercial leases, such right to terminate the lease cannot be enforced prior to the end of the minimum initial period of nine years during which the lessor cannot terminate the lease and, thereafter, only if six-months notice is given.

If the real property is used for residential purposes, the lessor/seller may refuse to renew the lease upon expiration thereof in order to sell the real property, in which case the tenant is granted a preemptive right to purchase the leased premises. The seller must notify the tenant of the price and other terms and conditions of the sale and the tenant must, within two months, indicate if it wishes to exercise its preemptive right.

Similar preemptive rights are provided for by French law in other specific instances, such as the sale of a residential building containing more than 10 apartments (*vente en bloc*) or the sale of residential premises subsequent to the first subdivision of all or part of the building in which the rented premises are located.

D. Contracts

1. Characteristics as to:

a) Language of Documentation. The documentation relating to the transfer of contracts may be drafted in any language. Bilingual documents are permitted.

b) Form of Documentation. The assignment of a contract is permissible under French law except, however, (i) if the obligations to be transferred may only be adequately performed by the assignor, in which case the contract creating such obligations is said to have been entered into *intuitu personae* and may not be transferred, or (ii) if the parties to such contract have expressly stated that such transfer is prohibited.

Except where the contract provides otherwise or for certain contracts that are automatically transferred with the business by provision of law (see below D, 3), no contract can be assigned without the contractor's consent.

The parties to a contract are free to determine the conditions for the consent to be granted. It may be granted in advance by inclusion of a provision in the contract itself, even if the parties are not aware of the identity of the transferee. Unless otherwise provided for in the contract, such consent may be deemed obtained, even in the absence of written notification thereof, through the mere performance of the contract by the parties concerned with the new contractor.

A transfer of all or part of the contractual rights and obligations to third parties may also result from other mechanisms known under French law as *novation* or delegation and are further described below in I.

c) Specification of Contracts. Except for certain contracts that automatically transfer with the business (see D, 3 below), a contract will be transferred only if specifically referred to in the transfer agreement, a description in general (e.g., "all contracts related to the business") or a generic description (e.g., "all customer contracts") will not be sufficient. Given that the transfer of a contract is governed by the provisions thereof, the seller and the purchaser will also have to carefully review the provisions of each contract transferred to ensure that its transfer is authorized and to identify under which conditions the approval of the counterparties must be obtained. It is thus customary to attach to business transfer agreements an exhaustive list of all contracts transferred as well as a copy of such contracts.

The business transfer agreement will also usually provide for an undertaking on the part of the seller to obtain any prior consent required from all counterparties thereto in compliance with the terms and conditions of the contracts transferred. It is advisable to determine in the business transfer agreement the consequences of a failure to obtain the approval of a counterparty to the transfer of a contract. For contracts that are material to the conduct of the business transferred, the obtaining of the prior consent of the counterparties, if required, will usually be set as a condition precedent to the completion of the business transfer.

2. Administrative, Corporate and Other Approvals

Under French law, except for special categories of contracts (e.g., military contracts, contracts entered into with administrative authorities), the transfer of contracts will not require special governmental or administrative approvals.

If the contracts are transferred as part of a business transfer, one must check if the authorizations referred to in B, 2 above will apply.

Regarding the approval of corporate bodies of the seller or the purchaser, the transfer of contracts will generally be validly decided by any legal representative of the seller and of the purchaser subject to compliance of this transfer with their corporate interest. The same rules as those described for the transfer of tangible assets in B, 2 above may apply.

As previously mentioned in D, 1 above, approval of the transfer by the counterparties to the contract is required under the conditions set forth in the contract, except if such parties have already authorized such transfer in advance. The transfer of the contract would not be enforceable vis-à-vis the counterparties to the contract transferred if such transfer has not been performed or authorized in compliance with its provisions.

3. Automatic Transfer of Contracts (Other than Lease and Employment Agreements)

Certain contracts are automatically transferred with the business to which they relate. This rule applies in particular to employment agreements (see H below), insurance contracts relating to the business and to editorial contracts (if the business transferred is an editorial business).

For other contracts, the parties thereto can agree in advance that such contract will be automatically transferred to the purchaser in the event of an asset deal and may include a provision to that effect in the contract itself.

A specific regime applies to lease agreements in the event of a business transfer. The commercial lease relating to the premises in which the business is conducted will be transferred automatically with the business, except if otherwise specifically agreed between the seller and the purchaser.

The commercial lease will be transferred to the purchaser notwithstanding any provision to the contrary contained in the lease agreement. The French Commercial Code declares null and void any provisions of the lease agreement pursuant to which the lessor would prohibit the tenant from transferring the lease to the purchaser of its business. However, provisions that restrict the right to transfer the lease to the purchaser of the business that fall short of an absolute prohibition to transfer the lease are valid. As an example, a clause providing for the prior authorization of the lessor for the transfer of the lease or granting the lessor a preemption right on the transfer of the business would be enforced. Therefore, it will be necessary to verify whether certain conditions and formalities relating to the transfer of the lease are contractually required under the lease agreement.

To be binding upon the lessor, the transfer of the lease will further have to be duly notified to it under the conditions set forth in the French Civil Code for the transfer of receivables (notification of the transfer by a French bailiff (*huissier*) or through a writ of summons or formal acceptance by the lessor to the transfer in a notarized deed (*acte authentique*) witnessed by a French public notary).

4. Filing Requirements

Except for contracts regarding categories of assets or services that require special filings (such as, for example, a license agreement on intellectual property rights), there is no general rule requiring the filing of the transfer agreement with public authorities or registrations with registers or (online) databases.

If the contracts are transferred as part of a business transfer, the registration formalities described in B, 5 above will apply.

5. Treatment of Existing Contractual Claims and Obligations

In the absence of any legal provisions relating to the transfer of contracts, it is customary to include, in the business transfer agreement, special provisions to determine the allocation of any outstanding claims or obligations under the transferred contract between the seller or the purchaser. It may thus be provided that the purchaser will be responsible for the performance of all obligations outstanding under the transferred contract only as from the date of the transfer, and therefore that the seller will indemnify the purchaser against any claim resulting from the performance of the contract prior to its transfer.

In relation to the other parties to the contract, the seller will be fully discharged from all obligations resulting from the transferred contract only if the other parties thereto have expressly agreed to such discharge. Otherwise, the seller will remain liable towards the other parties for the due performance by the purchaser of its obligations under the transferred contract, provided, however, that if the seller is held liable, he may make a claim against the purchaser under the conditions set forth in the business transfer agreement.

6. Warranty Claims Resulting from Events prior to Transfer

Except for specific items mentioned in G, 4 and 5 below, a business transfer does not trigger the automatic transfer of the liabilities of the business but only those that are specifically listed in the business transfer agreement. Therefore, in an asset deal, the parties will determine on a case by case basis which liabilities (if any) will transfer to the purchaser. This greatly reduces the level of risk assumed by the purchaser and, consequently, the need for contractual protection through indemnification provisions.

E. IP Rights

1. Characteristics of Intellectual Property Rights (e.g., Trademarks, Patents, Utility Models, Domain Names) ("*IP Rights*") as to:

a) Language of Documentation. The documents relating to the assignment of IP Rights may be drafted in English or any other language.

With respect to registered IP Rights (e.g., trademarks, patents, designs), a French language translation needs to be provided together with the foreign language agreement for registration purposes with the French Trademark and Patent Office (*Institut National de la Propriété Intellectuelle*, or *INPI*). No official translation is required. Furthermore, since it is possible to just register extracts of the assignment agreement with the INPI (mostly for confidentiality purposes), the translation to be provided with the INPI will be limited to those extracts.

The documents can be executed bilingually. In this case, it is possible to register the bilingual agreement with the INPI.

b) Form of Documentation. The assignment of trademarks and patents must be in writing. Failure to comply will nullify the assignment. There is no such express requirement concerning designs, copyright or domain name assignments, although it is highly advisable to conclude such assignment agreements in writing.

The documents relating to the assignment of IP Rights may be executed outside France.

If the agreement is subject to French law, signing in counterparts will not be allowed. If the agreement is subject to foreign law, the question whether the parties may sign on separate documents or must sign on the same document may arise if registration is required with the INPI. Although the INPI may sometimes accept for registration an agreement signed in counterparts in cases where foreign parties are involved, there are no written rules and it is advisable to the parties to sign the agreement on the same document in order to avoid any registration problems with the INPI.

c) Specification of IP Rights. As a general rule, except if otherwise provided in the assignment agreement, the IP Rights owned by the seller and relating to the business will automatically be transferred with such business. It is nevertheless common practice in France to provide a complete list of the IP Rights that will be assigned to the buyer in the assignment agreement in order to avoid any dispute among the parties, as well as for accounting and tax purposes.

2. Administrative, Corporate and Other Approvals

The assignment of IP Rights does not require any special governmental or administrative approval.

Regarding the approval of corporate bodies of the seller or the purchaser, the transfer of IP Rights will generally be validly decided by any legal representative of the seller and the purchaser subject to compliance of this transfer with their corporate interest. The same rules as those described for the transfer of tangible assets in B, 2 above may apply.

Regarding the approval of security holders where IP Rights are encumbered, in most cases the applicable rules will be those governing common pledge under French law, and the debtor will be prohibited from selling the pledged IP Rights without the prior consent of the pledgor. Should the debtor not comply, the secured creditor may exercise its rights against the purchaser of the secured IP Rights in order to preserve the pledge.

3. Filing Requirements

As far as registered IP Rights are concerned (i.e., patents, trademarks and designs), it is necessary to register their assignment with the INPI in order for them to be enforceable against third parties. This formality, however, does not affect the validity of the assignment.

4. Applicable International (Multilateral) Agreements or Treaties

France is party to all major international IP Treaties, such as:

(i) Paris Convention for the Protection of Industrial Property 1883

(ii) Madrid Agreement concerning the International Registration of Marks 1891

(iii) The Hague Convention on the International Registration of Designs 1925

(iv) Patent Co-operation Treaty 1970

(v) Berne Convention for the Protection of Literary and Artistic Works 1971 (Berne Convention)

(vi) European Patent Convention 1973

(vii) WTO Agreement on Trade-Related Aspects of Intellectual Rights 1994 (TRIPS)

As a member state of the European Union, France is also subject to EC directives and regulations relating to IP Rights (e.g., EC Regulation No. 40/94 on the Community Trade Mark and EC Regulation No. 6/2002 on Community Designs).

F. Receivables

1. Characteristics as to:

a) Language of Documentation. The documentation relating to the assignment of receivables can be drafted in English or bilingually. However, as further explained below in F, 1, b, a notice of the assignment will have to be given to the debtor of the receivables and such notice will have to be drafted in French.

b) Form of Documentation. Pursuant to the French Civil Code, delivery takes place between the assignor and the assignee of the receivable by handing over the instrument of title. To avoid any future claim, it is, however, customary that the parties execute a written document that specifies that the transfer qualifies as a transfer of receivables under French law (*cession de créance*) and sets forth the conditions of such transfer. This document can be executed outside France. Signing in counterparts is not allowed if the transfer agreement is subject to French law (see B, 1, b above).

The French Civil Code further provides that an assignment of receivables will only be enforceable against the debtor and third parties if the following conditions are met: (i) the debtor has been notified of the transfer by a French bailiff (*huissier*) or through a writ of summons or (ii) the debtor has formally accepted the transfer in a notarized deed (*acte authentique*) witnessed by a French public notary. In both cases, the notice of the assignment to the debtor or the notarized deed will have to be executed in France and drafted in French. These rules apply as soon as the debtor of the receivables is located in France and even if the assignment of receivables occurs as part of a business transfer.

It should be noted that specific rules are provided for by French law to facilitate the assignment of professional receivables to the benefit of credit establishments.

c) Specification of Receivables. There are no specific legal requirements regarding the description of the receivables in the transfer agreement. They must be sufficiently clearly identified to avoid any further dispute among the parties as to the scope of the transfer.

2. Administrative, Corporate and Other Approvals

The transfer of receivables does not require special governmental or administrative approvals, nor specific approval of corporate bodies regarding the seller and/or the purchaser. Regarding the approval of corporate bodies, the same rules as those described in B, 2 above may apply.

As indicated in F, 1, b above, notice of the transfer must be served upon the debtor of the receivable. As a result, if the debtor has paid the assignor before the debtor has been given notice by the assignor or the assignee, he is lawfully discharged.

3. Filing Requirements

Except for the notification to the debtor, no other notifications or special filings with public authorities or registrations are required for the transfer of receivables.

G. Liabilities

1. Characteristics as to:

a) Language of Documentation. The assignment of liabilities is prohibited as such under French law. Liabilities can therefore only be transferred as part of the transfer of a contract containing rights and obligations. However, French law provides for specific mechanisms known as novation or delegation, which enable the substitution of a new debtor for the original one. The documentation relating thereto can be drafted in French, in English or bilingually.

b) Form of Documentation. Under French law, the transfer of liabilities may result from a novation or a delegation, both of which are regulated by the French Civil Code.

A novation may result from three different situations: (i) where a debtor contracts towards his creditor a new debt which is substituted for the old one, which is extinguished, (ii) where a new debtor is substituted for the old one who is discharged by the creditor, and (iii) where, by the effect of a new undertaking, a new creditor is substituted for the old one, towards whom the debtor is discharged. The novation described in (ii) will result in a transfer of liabilities. The novation may not be presumed; the wish to bring it about must clearly result from the agreement of all parties concerned. There is no legal requirement regarding the form of this agreement.

Delegation is defined as a situation where a party transfers an obligation to perform a duty to a third party. If the creditor of the transferred obligation accepts the delegation and agrees to discharge the original debtor, a novation occurs and the transaction is known as *delegation parfaite.* If the creditor does not agree to the delegation, the transaction is known as *delegation imparfaite* and the original debtor is not discharged vis-à-vis said party until the obligation to perform has been fully satisfied. There is no legal requirement regarding the form of the delegation agreement nor regarding the form of the agreement of the creditor thereon, if any.

In both cases there is no requirement that the documentation be executed in France.

c) Specification of Liabilities. The liabilities must be clearly identified to enforce a novation or a delegation and therefore to be transferred to the new debtor.

2. Administrative, Corporate and Other Approvals

The transfer of liabilities does not require special governmental or administrative approvals, or specific approval of corporate bodies regarding the seller and/or the purchaser.

The approval of the creditor is required to fully enforce the substitution of the new debtor for the original debtor and to discharge the latter of its obligations under the liabilities transferred. If such approval is not granted, the original debtor will remain liable to the new debtor for the fulfillment of the transferred obligations.

3. Filing Requirements

The transfer of liabilities does not require special filings with public authorities or registrations into registers or (online) databases. Notification to the creditors and obtainment of their approval is required to discharge the original debtor.

4. Purchaser's Liability for:

a) Tax Obligations. According to French tax law, the purchaser may be liable for the payment of taxes related to the purchased assets.

When a business is sold, the seller is liable for corporate income tax with respect to the profits derived from the operation of the business up until the acquisition date. The purchaser is normally jointly liable for the payment of this corporate income tax and certain ancillary taxes to the tax authorities up to the amount of the purchase price for a period of three months as from the date the sale was registered with the tax authorities.

The seller and the purchaser are also jointly liable to the tax authorities for the payment of registration duties payable in connection with the sale of the business or of certain assets, even if the sale agreement provides that those duties must be paid and/or borne solely by the purchaser or the seller.

Finally, if the purchase of assets is subject to VAT, the seller is normally liable for the payment of VAT. Nonetheless, the purchaser is also responsible for the payment of VAT in some circumstances (e.g., intra-Community acquisition of goods and fraud). This being said, the transfer of a whole business normally benefits from a VAT exemption.

b) Environmental Contamination. According to French law, the purchaser of a business operated on a classified installation will be substituted as new operator of the site vis-à-vis the French public authorities and therefore can be held directly liable for environmental contamination of the acquired assets even in periods prior to the acquisition. Environmental representations and warranties are usually included in the business transfer agreement to provide that the seller will indemnify the purchaser for any detriment resulting from environmental claims relating to contamination prior to the date of transfer.

c) Products Sold or Services Rendered by the Seller to Third Parties. Except as otherwise provided for by law or specifically agreed upon by the seller and the purchaser, the transfer of assets does not result in the automatic transfer of any related liability. Thus, in the event of a transfer of a business, except if otherwise agreed among the parties, the purchaser will not be held liable for claims resulting from products sold or services rendered by the seller to third parties prior to the business transfer.

5. Automatic Transfer of Other Liabilities

If a commercial lease is transferred with the business, except if otherwise specifically agreed with the lessor, French case law has held the purchaser liable towards the lessor for any deterioration of the premises even if it results from the operation of the business by the seller.

6. Contractual Protection as to 4 and 5 above

It is customary to include special provisions (e.g., indemnification) as to the issues mentioned (tax, environmental, other liabilities) in the asset sale and/or transfer agreement.

H. Employees

1. Transfer of Employees

Under French labor law, in case of an asset transfer, all existing employment agreements attached to the sold business are automatically transferred to the purchaser by virtue of Article L.1224-1 of the French Labor Code, provided that (i) the business transferred constitutes an "autonomous economic entity", i.e. an organized unit of personnel and tangible or intangible assets that enables the continued running of an economic activity with its own objective, and that (ii) the transferred entity maintains its identity despite the transfer. This rule does not apply if the transaction only involves select assets that do not form an "autonomous economic entity."

All employment agreements in force at the date of the transfer, including for those employees who perform their trial period, notice period or whose employment agreement is temporarily suspended for whatever reason, will automatically be transferred.

Under French labor law, the seller, the purchaser and the employees do not have a right to object to such transfer.

As a consequence of the transfer, the purchaser becomes the new employer and is bound by the terms and conditions of the transferred employment agreements. The purchaser may not modify or amend the employment agreements at the time of the transfer. The employee's waiver of part of his/her rights would not be enforceable. However, the purchaser may amend the transferred employment agreements once the transfer has been finalized, provided that the employee agrees to such amendments.

As a general rule, termination of an employment agreement by the seller or the purchaser merely due to the transfer of business is void. However, termination for other reasons, if any, would be possible, although the Court would carefully verify the alleged grounds of termination to ensure that it was not pretense for bypassing the rules as regards the automatic transfer, and the Courts would be suspicious of any termination notified just before or after the transfer.

As to the collective bargaining agreements or company agreements, and pursuant to Article L.2261-14 of the French Labor Code, these will automatically terminate in the event of an asset transfer triggering the automatic transfer of the employees. Such agreements will, however, remain applicable for a maximum time period of 15 months during which new agreements should be entered into as substitution agreements. If at the end of such 15-month period no such agreement is concluded, the seller's agreements will no longer be applicable but the transferred employees will continue to benefit from individual acquired rights. Should the purchaser be subject to collective agreements, the transferred employees will benefit from the more favorable provisions of either ones until a new agreement is entered into or until the end of the 15-month period, and will then only benefit from the purchaser's collective agreements.

As far as customary terms and conditions (*usages*) are concerned, they transfer to the purchaser, who may nevertheless alter them subject to compliance with a specific procedure. The same principle applies to the employer's unilateral undertakings (*engagements unilatéraux*).

Thus, the consequences as regards non-mandatory pension schemes and benefits, etc. will vary depending on the way such schemes have been implemented.

Specific rules apply to profit sharing (mandatory or voluntary schemes). If the purchaser has a mandatory and/or a voluntary scheme, the transferred employees will automatically benefit from it/them. If such a scheme is not in place, the seller's schemes will be transferred unless it is legally or financially impossible; in any case, the employees will not lose the rights acquired with respect thereto prior to the transfer.

Finally, the purchaser must inform the transferred employees that it is now their employer, and must inform them of their rights and benefits.

2. Approval of Works Council, Trade Union or Other Institutions

According to Article L.2323-6 and L.2323-19 of the French labor code, the purchaser and the seller have to inform and consult their respective works council, if any, prior to the contemplated transfer. The role of the works council is limited to expression of its opinion on the transaction (sale or acquisition of the business) and its consequences on employees. It has no veto right. If the seller or purchaser fails to properly inform and consult its works council, it may (i) face a claim by the works council asking for the suspension or postponement of the transaction, and (ii) be held criminally liable for infringement of the works council's rights (*délit d'entrave*).

In the event of a partial transfer of business, the transfer of "protected employees," e. g., in particular employee delegates, members of the works council, trade union representatives, is subject to the Labor Inspector's prior authorization, to be requested at least 15 days prior to the contemplated date of transfer.

3. Contractual Protection as to Labor Issues

As regards the asset sale and/or transfer agreement, it is customary to include special provisions, e.g., guarantees and indemnifications, as to employees, such as general guarantees regarding the legal compliance of employment agreements, collective agreements or other transferred collective status. The agreement should further (i) provide for the split between the purchaser and the seller of the employees related to costs as from the date of the transfer, and (ii) list the transferred employees together with certain elements such as remuneration, bonus, accrued rights as regards paid holidays, training, any specific severance provision, etc.

I. Tax Implications

1. Value Added Tax

A transfer of a whole business normally benefits from a VAT exemption. In addition, although it would normally be subject to VAT at the appropriate rate depending upon the asset concerned (normal rate of 19.6%), a transfer of one or several assets may benefit from a VAT exemption if such transfer also gives rise to the transfer of a clientele. In such case, only transfer taxes are due. As an exception, the parties may elect to subject the transfer of inventories to VAT, in which case transfer taxes are not due on the related portion of the sale price.

2. Real Property Transfer Tax

Transfers of real estate properties are normally subject to land transfer tax at the rate of 5.09% (to which must be added notary fees generally at a rate of around 1%). In the case of a combined sale of movable and immovable assets, the land transfer tax applies to the sole portion of the sale price of the immovable assets, provided the respective value of the movable and immovable assets are clearly identified in the sale agreement. A recording fee (*salaire du conservateur des hypothèques*) will also have to be paid upon the recording of the transfer with the Mortgage Registry, which is equal to 0.1% of the fair market value of the real property conveyed and is paid by the purchaser.

3. Other Tax Issues

Certain taxes (business tax, real estate tax on built and un-built properties, for example) are due in respect of the ownership of the asset or business on January 1st of the year concerned. In the case of a sale of such asset or business, the person liable for such taxes remains the one who is the owner on January 1st of the year during which the sale takes place. Although this has no particular effect vis-à-vis the French tax authorities, it is customary that the parties agree in the sale agreement that the burden of such tax will be borne on a pro rata basis by the purchaser and the seller.

J. Bankruptcy Law

1. Challenge of Asset Transfer in Case of Insolvency

In the event seller or purchaser, following the asset transfer, becomes bankrupt or subject to insolvency proceedings, the receivers or the public prosecutor may be entitled to challenge the asset transfer, provided that it has occurred after the seller or purchaser become unable to pay its debts as they fall due out of its available assets. In order for this challenge to be exercised, the sale would either have to have (i) been on terms significantly unfavorable to the company against which the insolvency proceedings will be opened, (ii) provided for means of payment that are unusual in normal business practice, or (iii) been entered into with the knowledge that the contracting party was in suspension of payments.

2. Acquisition of Assets that are Subject to Insolvency Proceedings

Under French law, either isolated assets or a group of assets that may be operated as a business may be acquired out of insolvency proceedings. In both cases, the insolvency court decision authorizing the sale is insufficient to effect the transfer and proper documentation, as required by the nature of the assets transferred (e.g., real estate, business), must be executed. The content of this documentation and the formalities to which the sale is subject are, with certain exceptions, those that would apply to such a sale outside of an insolvency context. No warranties will be given by the insolvent seller, and it is the purchaser's responsibility to perform his due diligence to evaluate the condition of the assets.

In both cases, interested parties will submit bids to acquire the assets. Isolated assets will be sold to the highest bidder. Groups of assets that may be operated as a business will be sold to the bidder that is in the best position, in the eyes of the insolvency court, to preserve the activity of the business and the jobs of the related employees. As opposed to the general regime of transfers of businesses outside of insolvency described above, all contracts necessary for the operation of the business are transferred to the purchaser, provided that he has requested such transfer; the consent of the co-contracting party is not required.

K. Timing and Costs

1. Timeframe of Asset Transfer

Before the final documentation relating to an asset deal is executed, the parties generally undertake certain preliminary steps that may take several weeks. Such steps mainly cover the carrying out of due diligence, the definition of the scope of the transfer (identification of the assets and liabilities to be transferred, any prior consent required for the transfer of contracts, and any other prior authorization, if any, from public authorities), the drafting and negotiating of the documentation, and the consulting with the employees representatives.

If the business transfer triggers any prior authorization (such as resulting from the application of the antitrust regulations or the foreign investment regulations), such authorization will have to be obtained prior to the completion of the business transfer.

If the business transferred is located in an area where the city has been granted a preemptive right (see B, 2 above), the proposed transfer must be notified to the city prior to completion and the city is granted a two-month period to respond.

The business transfer agreement will also have to be registered by the purchaser with the French tax administration (and the registration fees will have to be paid) within 15 days of its date. Publication of the transfer with a legal newspaper must occur within the same 15-day period and, within 15 days of this first publication, a second announcement of the transfer will have to be made by the Office of the Clerk of the Commercial Court in the official gazette of civil and commercial notices, the "BODACC." The creditors of the business have 10 days from the date of this second publication to object to the payment of the purchase price to the seller. During the period prior to the expiration of the aforementioned objection period (and for any subsequent period necessary to address the objections, if any), it is common practice for the purchase price to be escrowed for the benefit of creditors.

Negotiations between the purchaser and the union delegates, if any, may also take place to discuss amendments to the collective bargaining agreement, it being mentioned that the former collective bargaining agreement will continue to apply by virtue of law during a 15-month period (see H, 1 above).

2. Costs of Asset Transfer

An asset deal will mainly trigger the following costs:

(i) a progressive registration duty based on the transfer price or the market value of the business transferred (whichever is higher) with a franchise for transactions below EUR 23,000 the portion of the price/value between EUR 23,000 and EUR 200,000 being subject to a 3% duty and the portion of the price/value exceeding EUR 200,000 being subject to a 5% duty;

(ii) if real property is transferred simultaneously, a land transfer tax at the rate of 5.09% (to which must be added notary fees, generally at a rate of approx. 1%) and a recording fee amounting to 0.1% of the fair market value of the real property.

L. Miscellaneous

1. Choice of Foreign Law

The transfer agreement may be subject to foreign law (other than local law) designated by the parties.

However, certain aspects of the transfer agreement will necessarily be subject to French imperative regulations (*lois de police*) if the business is located in France. As such, the law of the jurisdiction where the business is located (*lex rei sitae*) will govern, inter alia, the formalities that need to be accomplished in the course of the transfer of the business (such as the drafting of a written agreement containing mandatory representations or statements or the registration formalities relating to the transfer).

2. (International) Arbitration, Choice of Venue

The parties to a transfer agreement may submit their dispute to (international) arbitration, provided that there is an arbitration clause in their agreement and that they are acting "by reason of a professional activity" (Section 1443 of the French Code of Civil Procedure and Section 2061 of the French Civil Code).

Similarly, the parties to a transfer agreement will have the ability to include a jurisdiction clause (*clause attributive de competence*) in their transfer agreement, provided that such clause has been provided for in "an explicit manner" and the agreement has been entered into between "merchants" (Section 48 of the French Civil Procedure Code).

3. Other Distinctions, Characteristics

Our jurisdiction does not provide for any other distinctions or unusual characteristics noteworthy in connection with a customary asset deal.

M. Literature

Lamy Droit Commercial – Fonds de commerce (Lamy Commercial Law – Business Concern), 2008

Frédéric Masquelier, Transmission et cession d'entreprise (Transfer and Sale of a Business), 2008

Barthélemy Mercadal, Memento Droit Commercial – Fonds de commerce – Cession (Commercial Law – Business Concern – Sale), 2008

Germany

By *Gero Pfeiffer*, *Sven Timmerbeil* and *Frederik Johannesdotter*

A. General Aspects

1. Asset Deal vs. Share Deal: Essential Considerations

There are various considerations that have to be taken into account when deciding whether a transaction to be carried out in Germany should be structured as a share deal or as an asset deal.

Probably the most important aspect is how the transaction will be taxed. The purchaser of a business is interested in deducting the acquisition costs as operating expenses. Thus, it is preferable to structure the transaction as a purchase and acquisition of assets so that the purchaser is able to increase the depreciation basis, i.e. the net book value of the depreciable assets, by the difference between the purchase price paid and the book value of the assets ("step-up"). On the other hand, the seller can obtain significant tax benefits if the transaction is structured as a sale and transfer of shares. If the seller is a corporate entity, which, in Germany, is a stock corporation (*AG*), limited liability company (*GmbH*) or limited partnership on shares (*KGaA*), 95% of capital gains from the disposal of the shares are tax exempt unless such shares have been received in connection with a tax-free contribution in kind. The remaining 5% of the capital gains are deemed to be operating expenses and are non-deductible.

Usually, the accomplishment of the transfer of a business by way of a transfer of its assets is more complex since you have to identify the assets belonging to such business and have to make sure that all such assets are validly transferred. On the other hand, however, in case of a purchase and acquisition of assets, the purchaser may choose the assets and liabilities that he intends to purchase and acquire, while in a purchase and acquisition of shares the purchaser has to take all assets and liabilities owned by the respective entity no matter whether he is aware of such assets and liabilities. Thus, a share deal bears the risk of assuming undisclosed liabilities.

Another aspect that might be relevant in determining the structure of the transaction is the requirement that governmental or administrative permits have to be obtained. Under German law, some businesses require permits that are either tied to the business itself or to its owner. While permits associated with the business usually are transferred together with the assets of the business, the permits associated with the owner do not transfer. Thus, the purchaser would potentially have to apply for new permits. In contrast, in a share deal this issue does not arise since the owner of the business, i.e. the entity owning the assets forming the business, does not actually change.

Finally, an asset deal may serve as a way of avoiding the German Public Acquisition Takeover Act, which is only applicable to the acquisition of shares traded on regulated markets.

As a general rule, in Germany, the acquisition of a business by way of purchasing and acquiring the shares of the entity operating the respective business is more common than an asset acquisition since it is less complex.

2. Distinction between Sale and Transfer in Rem

German law distinguishes between the sale of assets (i.e. obligation to transfer) and the transfer in rem as the fulfillment of the transfer obligation (principle of separation). A valid transfer in rem can be effected even if the sale and purchase agreement is invalid. In this case, however, the seller is basically entitled to claim a re-transfer of the assets.

If assets are to be sold and transferred in multiple jurisdictions, it might be recommendable to cover the sale in a single master purchase agreement while the assets can be transferred in the respective jurisdictions via local transfer agreements. The benefit of such an approach is that local transfer requirements can be fulfilled by the local transfer agreement without affecting the master purchase agreement. This also avoids the disclosure of the entire asset transfer (including the master purchase agreement) in the event the transfer has to be filed with any authorities.

3. Regional Differences

Since the essential rules applicable to the sale and transfer of assets are part of German federal law, there are no regional differences regarding the legal requirements applicable to an asset transfer within Germany.

4. Acquisition by Foreigners

As a general rule, there are no restrictions or special requirements impacting foreigners or foreign entities who wish to acquire assets located in Germany. By way of exception, the Department of Trade and Industry must be informed of a transaction if foreigners or foreign entities intend to acquire a German industrial business that manufactures vehicles, material or services that are of relevance to the military. Under certain circumstances the Department has the right to prohibit the acquisition. In particular, the Department has the right to prohibit the acquisition by foreign investors regardless of the industry sector to protect the free and democratic order of the Federal Republic of Germany.

Finally, there are some trade embargos pursuant to the resolutions of the United Nations for the states of Somalia, Rwanda, Sierra Leone, Iraq, Congo, Liberia, Zimbabwe, Myanmar, Cote d'Ivoire, Sudan, Uzbekistan, Lebanon, North Korea, Iran and all individuals related to the Taliban or Al-Qaeda.

5. Public Registers, Records and Databases

In Germany, there is no central institution that maintains all relevant information in connection with an asset transfer.

Corporate details about the seller and the buyer can be obtained from the public Commercial Registers (*Handelsregister*) which show basic details as to (i) legal form, (ii) powers of representation, (iii) registered share capital, and (iv) certain corporate events, such as capital increases or mergers. Additional corporate information including financial statements can be obtained from the Commercial Register files and the Electronic Business Register (www.unternehmensregister.de). These sources are available to everyone.

Information as to real property, including ownership and encumbrances, can be obtained from the Land Register (*Grundbuch*) and the Land Registry Office (*Katasteramt*). In contrast to the Commercial Register, access to the Land Register requires the declaration of a qualified interest by the interested party.

Finally, information regarding intellectual property rights such as trademarks and patents and the ownership of internet domains is publicly available on the websites of the German Patent and Trademark Office (www.dpma.de) and, respectively, the Central Registry for the Top Level Domain ".de" (www.denic.de). No such information is available regarding copyrights, since a general copyright register does not exist in Germany.

6. Purchase Price Requirements

The parties of an asset deal are free in determining the purchase price, which can be stated in every currency and paid by any third party (e. g., parent company). In the event of separation of sale and transfer (see A, 2 above) the transfer agreement does not need to state a purchase price, whereas the sale and purchase agreement must provide for a purchase price. However, in case the parties are required to disclose the transfer to the tax authorities (e.g., in case real property is involved) and they want to avoid submitting the sale and purchase agreement (e.g., the whole master agreement), it may be advisable to also provide for the purchase price in the relevant transfer agreement. Alternatively, in a notarized master purchase agreement, a notary can provide an excerpt of the relevant passages. Furthermore, for tax and accounting purposes, an allocation of the purchase price to individual assets or groups of assets may be recommendable as well.

B. Tangible/Movable Assets

1. Characteristics as to:

a) Language of Documentation. The sale and transfer documents regarding tangible assets may be drafted in any language. Bilingual documents are permitted. Since there is no need to file such documents with public authorities, a German translation is not required.

b) Form of Documentation. The transfer of tangible assets does not require a special form; oral agreements are valid. For evidentiary purposes, the written form is nonetheless recommendable. If the sold assets constitute the entire estate of the seller, notarization of the sale and purchase agreement (i.e. the transfer obligation) might be required under certain circumstances. This applies particularly if the seller sells "any and all present assets" without drawing a distinction between individual assets. Since the underlying provision of the German Civil Code is designed to protect the seller against rash actions without due consideration, the sale is not considered a sale of the entire estate if it is evident from the sale and purchase agreement that the seller's primary intention is not to sell "anything and everything" but a sum of individual assets, even if such sum economically constitutes seller's entire estate.

The sale and transfer documents may be executed outside Germany. Signing in counterparts is permissible.

The transfer in rem of movable assets basically requires that seller and purchaser are in agreement regarding the transfer and that the purchaser takes possession of the assets. The taking of possession may be substituted by transfer to the purchaser of the claim for surrender against a third party (in case a third party is in possession of the assets) or the creation of a legal relationship between seller and purchaser according to which the purchaser obtains indirect possession (in case the seller is to remain in possession of the assets).

c) Specification of Assets. As a general rule, the assets to be transferred must be specified in the transfer agreement to such an extent that any third party will be able to distinguish the assets from any other non-transferred assets (principle of identification). In order to comply with such principle the use of asset lists (or schedules) is recommendable but not mandatory. A specification by category or location is sufficient provided that identification is possible without recourse to any legal valuation or discretion. The transfer of "all assets" located at a certain place (e.g., a certain warehouse) meets those requirements.

If and to the extent the asset specification is insufficient, the assets are not transferred, but remain with the seller. In this case the purchaser is still entitled to claim a valid transfer in rem, since the principle of identification does not affect seller's transfer obligation contained in the sale and purchase agreement (see A, 2 above regarding the legal distinction between sale and transfer in rem). In particular, the sale and purchase agreement does not have to specify the assets in order to be valid.

2. Administrative, Corporate and Other Approvals

The transfer of tangible assets generally does not require special governmental or administrative approvals. However, exceptions might apply with regard to special categories of assets (e.g., certain weapons, dangerous substances). Non-compliance renders the transfer invalid.

The approval of any corporate bodies is basically not required unless otherwise provided for in seller's and/or purchaser's articles of association, partnership agreement or any other corporate document. If the seller is a stock corporation or a limited liability company the approval of its shareholders' meeting might be required if the sold assets form a substantial part of seller's business even if such approval is not expressly provided for in the corporate documents. Non compliance with any corporate approval requirement does not affect the validity of the transfer. However, it could subject management to personal liability under certain circumstances.

If the assets are encumbered or used as collateral the following applies: If, despite of the encumbrance or the use as collateral, the seller is the owner of the sold assets (e.g., in case the assets are pledged), no such approval is required. If, due to the encumbrance or the use as collateral, a third party becomes the owner of the assets (e.g., retention of title, security assignment), the transfer is basically invalid unless the purchaser acquired the assets in good faith (bona fide principle).

3. Filing Requirements

Regarding the transfer of tangible assets, no filings with public authorities or registrations in public registers or databases are required.

4. Automatic Transfer of Encumbrances

As a general rule, encumbrances regarding tangible assets automatically transfer to the purchaser. In particular, pledged assets remain pledged, and assets that are subject to retention of title clauses in favor of suppliers remain in the ownership of such suppliers. However, this does not apply where the purchaser acquires the assets in good faith (bona fide principle).

C. Real Property

1. Characteristics as to:

a) Language of Documentation. The sale and transfer documents regarding real property may be drafted in every language, provided that the notary in charge is in command of such language. Bilingual documents are permitted. Due to the fact that the transfer deed must be filed with the Land Register, a bilingual version or a certified German translation is necessary. The same applies with regard to the tax authorities, who must also be provided with a document showing the purchase price (see A, 6 above regarding the inclusion of the purchase price into the transfer agreement).

b) Form of Documentation. With respect to real property, notarization of both the sale and purchase agreement (obligation to transfer; see A, 2 above regarding the legal distinction between sale and transfer in rem) and the transfer agreement is basically required. However, if the sale and purchase agreement (e.g., master agreement) is not notarized, this defect may be cured upon a duly notarized transfer agreement and registration in the Land Register. The notarization requirement is very comprehensive and extends to any documents and agreements legally and economically connected with the sale and purchase and/or transfer agreement, such as side letters, agreements regarding collaterals, as well as any schedules.

The sale and purchase agreement may be executed outside Germany, provided that the local form requirements concerning real property are complied with, and provided that execution abroad does not aim at an avoidance of the German form requirements. The transfer in rem, however, necessarily requires notarization (if not executed before court).

Signing in counterparts is permissible, provided that both the seller and the purchaser appear before a notary.

c) Specification of Assets. The principle of identification (see B, 1, c above) also applies to the transfer of real property. The property thus has to be specified sufficiently. In order to comply with such requirements it might be recommendable to refer to the relevant sections in the Land Register containing a detailed description of the property.

2. Administrative, Corporate and Other Approvals

The transfer of real property basically does not require special governmental or administrative approvals. If the property is subject to certain measures of city planning the approval of the municipality may be required. As a general rule, the transfer of agricultural property requires the approval of the relevant agricultural agency.

The approval of any corporate bodies is basically not required unless otherwise provided in seller's and/or purchaser's articles of association or partnership agreement (such provisions are customary in case of real property). For further details, please refer to B, 2 above.

In the event the real property is encumbered with mortgages, land charges or usufruct rights, the transfer is not subject to the approval of the security holders, who continue to be secured following the transfer due to the fact that the encumbrances automatically transfer to the purchaser (see C, 4 below).

3. Filing Requirements

The transfer of any real property needs to be registered in the Land Register and is not valid before such registration. The relevant filings have to be made by the notary in charge. In addition, the notary is obliged to provide the tax authorities with copies of the executed and notarized transfer documents.

If the approval of the municipality or the agricultural agency is required (see C, 2 above), the relevant authorities must be notified of the transfer.

4. Automatic Transfer of Encumbrances

In case the real property is subject to encumbrances (e.g., mortgages, usufruct rights) registered in the Land Register, such encumbrances remain valid following the transfer of the real property. As a consequence, the purchaser acquires encumbered real property, which usually leads to a reduction of the purchase price.

A waiver of encumbrances regarding real property does not require notarization or any other special form. However, the waiver must be registered in the Land Register and is not valid before such registration.

5. Automatic Transfer of Lease Agreements

Any lease agreements that the real property is subject to automatically transfer to the purchaser, who assumes all rights and obligations under such lease agreements vis-à-vis the tenant. Neither the purchaser nor the tenant has an extra-ordinary termination right due to the transfer.

D. Contracts

1. Characteristics as to:

a) Language of Documentation. The sale and transfer documents regarding contracts may be drafted in every language. Bilingual documents are permitted. Since there is no need to file these documents with public authorities, a German translation is not required.

b) Form of Documentation. The transfer of contracts does not require a special form unless the conclusion of the contract to be transferred requires a specific form. For evidentiary purposes, the written form is nonetheless recommendable. If the contracts constitute the entire estate of the seller, notarization of the sale and purchase agreement (i.e. the transfer obligation) might be required under certain circumstances (see B, 1, b above).

The sale and transfer documents may be executed outside Germany. Signing in counterparts is permissible.

c) Specification of Contracts. The principle of identification (see B, 1, c above) also applies to the transfer of contracts. The contracts thus have to be specified sufficiently. In order to comply with such requirements it is recommendable to list the contracts to be transferred in schedules to the asset transfer agreement, specifying subject, parties and date of the relevant agreements.

2. Administrative, Corporate and Other Approvals

The transfer of contracts does not require special governmental or administrative approvals.

The approval of any corporate bodies is basically not required unless otherwise provided in seller's and/or purchaser's articles of association or partnership agreement. For further details, please refer to B, 2 above.

Under German law, the transfer of contracts requires the consent of the other party to the contract to be transferred. For certain types of contracts (e.g., employment agreements, lease agreements, certain types of insurance agreements) exceptions apply (see D, 3 and H, 1 below as well as C, 5 above). Non-compliance may render the transfer invalid.

3. Automatic Transfer of Contracts (Other than Lease and Employment Agreements)

Besides lease and employment agreements (see H, 1 below and C, 5 above), German law provides for the automatic transfer of certain types of asset-related insurance agreements, such as certain property insurances. The ratio of such rule is the avoidance of insurance gaps in case the insured assets are transferred. However, the parties to the insurance agreement have special termination rights following the completion of the transfer.

4. Filing Requirements

Regarding the transfer of contracts, no filings with public authorities or registrations into public registers or databases are required.

5. Treatment of Existing Contractual Claims and Obligations

If and to the extent the other party to a contract consents to the transfer of such contract, the respective claims and/or obligations arising from such contract do automatically transfer to the purchaser. This also applies to unfulfilled or partially fulfilled contracts unless otherwise provided for in the transfer agreement. The issue of unfulfilled of partially fulfilled contracts is usually addressed in the purchase price adjustment mechanism (e.g., working capital adjustment). An alternative treatment of such issue would be to include a respective indemnification clause into the asset sale and/or transfer agreement.

6. Warranty Claims Resulting from Events prior to Transfer

As a general rule, the transfer of a contract also includes the transfer of any claims and any obligations related to such contract, since the required consent of the other contractual party usually also covers such claims and obligations. This also applies to warranty claims resulting from events prior to the transfer of such contract if not otherwise provided for in the asset sale and/or transfer agreement. The potential exposure is customarily covered by representations and warranties and/or indemnifications.

E. IP Rights

1. Characteristics of Intellectual Property Rights (e. g., Trademarks, Patents, Utility Models, Domain Names) ("*IP Rights*") as to:

a) Language of Documentation. The sale and transfer documents regarding IP Rights may be drafted in every language. In case of registered IP Rights (e. g., trademarks, patents, design patents, domain names) a German translation is recommendable for filing purposes; bilingual documents are permitted. However, if the seller and the purchaser jointly apply for the transcription of registered IP Rights there is basically no need to file such documents and, therefore, a German translation is not required.

Please note that, according to German law, the transfer of copyrights is not possible; only a license can be granted.

b) Form of Documentation. The transfer of IP Rights does not require a special form; oral agreements are valid. For evidentiary purposes, the written form is nonetheless recommendable. In case the IP Rights constitute the entire estate of the seller, notarization of the sale and purchase agreement (i.e. the transfer obligation) might be required under certain circumstances (see B, 1, b above).

The sale and transfer documents may be executed outside Germany. Signing in counterparts is permissible.

Please note that, in case of sale of a business or a business unit, trademarks and design patents (*Geschmacksmuster*) related to such business or business unit automatically transfer to the purchaser if not otherwise agreed.

c) Specification of IP Rights. The principle of identification (see B, 1, c above) also applies to the transfer of IP Rights. The IP Rights thus have to be specified sufficiently. In order to comply with such requirements the use of lists (or schedules) is recommendable but not mandatory. See E, 1, b above as regards cases of transfer by operation of law.

2. Administrative, Corporate and Other Approvals

The transfer of IP Rights does not require special governmental or administrative approvals.

The approval of any corporate bodies is basically not required unless otherwise provided in seller's and/or purchaser's articles of association or partnership agreement. For further details, please refer to B, 2 above.

If the IP Rights are encumbered or used as collateral the following applies: If the seller is the owner of the IP Rights (e. g., in case the IP Rights are pledged), no such approval is required. If a third party is owner of the assets (e. g., in case of security assignment), the transfer is invalid.

3. Filing Requirements

If and to the extent the IP Rights to be transferred are registered in public registers (e.g., trademarks, patents, design patents, domain names), the change of ownership requires the filing with the relevant public registers. However, such registration is merely of a declaratory nature and does not affect the validity of the transfer.

4. Applicable International (Multilateral) Agreements or Treaties

Germany participates in the TRIPS Agreement and in the Paris Convention for the Protection of Industrial Property. In addition, Germany signed the Madrid Agreement and the Madrid Protocol regarding trademarks. Finally, Germany is subject to the Council Regulation on the Community Trademark of the European Community.

F. Receivables

1. Characteristics as to:

a) Language of Documentation. The sale and transfer documents regarding receivables may be drafted in any language. Bilingual documents are permitted. Since there is no need to file such documents with public authorities, a German translation is not required.

b) Form of Documentation. The transfer of receivables does not require a special form; oral agreements are valid. For evidentiary purposes, the written form is nonetheless recommendable. If the sold receivables constitute the entire estate of the seller, notarization of the sale and purchase agreement (i.e. the transfer obligation) might be required under certain circumstances (see B, 1, b above).

The sale and transfer documents may be executed outside Germany. Signing in counterparts is permissible.

c) Specification of Receivables. The principle of identification (see B, 1, c above) also applies to the transfer of receivables. The receivables must therefore be specified sufficiently. In order to comply with this requirement, it is recommendable to list the receivables to be transferred in schedules to the asset transfer agreement, specifying the underlying legal relationships and the outstanding amount of the relevant receivables.

2. Administrative, Corporate and Other Approvals

The transfer of receivables does not require special governmental or administrative approvals.

The approval of any corporate bodies is basically not required unless otherwise provided in seller's and/or purchaser's articles of association or partnership agreement. For further details, please refer to B, 2 above.

The validity of the transfer is not subject to the approval of the debtors provided that the underlying agreement does not state otherwise.

3. Filing Requirements

Regarding the transfer of receivables, no filings with public authorities or registration in public registers or databases are required. The notification of the transfer to the debtors is not required but recommendable. As long as the debtors are not aware of the transfer, payments on the receivables can still be made to the former owner of the receivables.

G. Liabilities

1. Characteristics as to:

a) Language of Documentation. The sale and transfer documents regarding liabilities may be drafted in every language. Bilingual documents are permitted. Since there is no need to file such documents with public authorities, a German translation is not required.

b) Form of Documentation. The transfer of liabilities does not require a special form; oral agreements are valid. For evidentiary purposes, the written form is nonetheless recommendable.

The sale and transfer documents may be executed outside Germany. Signing in counterparts is permissible.

c) Specification of Liabilities. The principle of identification (see B, 1, c above) also applies to the transfer of liabilities. The liabilities must therefore be specified sufficiently. In order to comply with this requirement, it is recommendable to list the liabilities to be transferred in schedules to the asset transfer agreement, specifying the underlying legal relationships and the outstanding amount of the relevant liabilities.

2. Administrative, Corporate and Other Approvals

The transfer of liabilities does not require special governmental or administrative approvals.

The approval of any corporate bodies is basically not required unless otherwise provided in seller's and/or purchaser's articles of association or partnership agreement. For further details, please refer to B, 2 above.

Under German law, the transfer of liabilities requires the consent of the creditors. Non-compliance renders the transfer invalid.

3. Filing Requirements

Regarding the transfer of liabilities, no filings with public authorities or registration in public registers or databases are required. Due to the fact that the transfer is subject to the creditors' consent, a separate notification to the creditors is not necessary.

4. Purchaser's Liability for:

a) Tax Obligations. Where the entire business or a separately conducted business division is acquired by way of an asset deal, the purchaser is liable for any tax obligations arising from the conduct of business as well as for any withholding tax amounts, provided that such taxes or withholding amounts (i) have accrued from the beginning of the calendar year prior to the calendar year in which the business is acquired, and (ii) are assessed or declared within one year after notifying the tax authorities of the acquisition. The purchaser's aggregate liability is limited to the value of the acquired assets.

Taxes arising from the conduct of business within the meaning of the aforementioned paragraph are trade/commercial tax (*Gewerbesteuer*) and VAT (*Umsatzsteuer*) as well as any consumption taxes (*Verbrauchssteuern*) connected with the business. In contrast, corporate income tax (*Körperschaftssteuer*) or wage tax (*Einkommensteuer*) personally owed by the proprietor of the sold business are not subject to the purchaser's liability, as such taxes do not refer to the conduct of business but to the entity or person carrying on the business.

Withholding tax amounts within the meaning of the first paragraph are amounts that have to be paid on a third party's account, such as wage tax owed by employees, which the employer is obliged to pay to the tax authorities.

b) Environmental Contamination. In Germany, the issue of environmental contamination becomes relevant only in connection with real property. If real property located in Germany forms part of the asset deal, considerable liability might arise for the purchaser in its capacity as new owner of the real property, where it is liable for any environmental contamination irrespective of the time of its origin.

According to the German Soil Protection Act, the owner is basically obliged to remove any contamination at its own expense. Apart from the owner, any person who caused the contamination as well as the person in possession of the real property is also responsible for the removal. However, in most cases, the public authorities in charge will address the current owner, as such owner can be easily identified from public records.

Furthermore, any former owner may be obliged to remove contamination if the former owner transferred the real property after March 1, 1999 and, at the time of transfer, had actual or potential knowledge of the contamination, unless the former owner itself had once acquired the real property in good faith.

c) Products Sold or Services Rendered by the Seller to Third Parties. In an asset deal, there are no specific liability risks for the purchaser as regards products sold or services rendered by the seller to third parties, provided that the products were sold or the services were rendered prior to the asset acquisition. This is due to the fact that German law strictly distinguishes between a business as an economic unit and the owner or proprietor of such business. Since the relevant product and warranty liability provisions under German law exclusively refer to the legal person or entity acting as seller, producer, importer or supplier of goods or services, though not to the business where such goods or services were produced/rendered, an asset deal generally could not lead to the purchaser's liability for such goods or services even if the entire business is acquired by the purchaser.

This does not apply, of course, in the event the purchaser assumes such product or warranty liability under the sale and transfer agreement.

5. Automatic Transfer of Other Liabilities

Where the purchaser acquires the entire business and continues to use the previous business name following the acquisition, the purchaser vis-à-vis third parties automatically assumes all liabilities and obligations of the seller arising from the conduct of business. Such automatic transfer to the purchaser may be excluded vis-à-vis third parties only through registration of the exclusion in the Commercial Register, or by separate notification to the relevant third parties by the seller or the purchaser.

6. Contractual Protection as to 4 and 5 above

Regarding the issues mentioned under 4 and 5 above, it is customary to include special provisions (e.g., indemnifications) in the asset sale and/or transfer agreement.

Particularly with regard to potential liability caused by environmental contamination, the purchaser may require indemnification rules in the asset sale and/or transfer agreement. The aggregate amount of such indemnification, however, is often capped by the purchase price. An alternative would be a step-by-step reduction of the cap in the course of time (a so-called sliding scale).

As to tax liabilities, the asset sale and/or transfer agreement often provides for a reference date that is relevant for the allocation of liabilities between seller and purchaser.

H. Employees

1. Transfer of Employees

According to mandatory German law, all existing employment agreements pertaining to the sold business automatically transfer to the purchaser by operation of law. This does not apply if the transaction only involves selected assets that do not form a distinct business unit. As a general rule, service agreements with board members or managing directors are not subject to such transfer.

As a consequence of the transfer, the purchaser becomes part of the employment agreement and is bound to its terms and conditions as well as to any arrangements stipulated between the seller and the affected employee (including collective bargaining agreements and shop agreements). The seller, jointly with the purchaser, remains liable vis-à-vis the employees as regards obligations arising from the employment relationships that were incurred prior to, and become due within one year following, the transfer.

Prior to a transfer of a business, the seller or the purchaser has to inform the affected employees in written form on, inter alia, the transfer date, the reason for the transfer, as well as the legal, economic and social impact of the sale on the employees. The employees then may object to the transfer within one month after having received such notification. If an employee objects to the transfer, he/she remains the employee of the seller, although his/her employment agreement may be terminated by the seller under certain circumstances (e.g., if the affected employee's position no longer exists due to the transfer of business).

As a general rule, the termination by the seller or the purchaser of an employment agreement solely due to the transfer of business is void. However, termination for other reasons, if any, is permissible.

2. Approval of Works Council, Trade Union or Other Institutions

In general, the transfer of a business by way of transferring the individual assets does not trigger codetermination rights of the works council, if any. Exceptions may apply if only parts of the business are transferred, i.e. the business is split, or if the transfer is accompanied by substantial redundancies or reorganization measures. In such cases, a social plan and an equalization of interest agreement have to be negotiated with the works council prior to the transfer of the business.

3. Contractual Protection as to Labor Issues

The asset sale and/or transfer agreement usually includes special provisions dealing with employees. In particular, most agreements include a guarantee by the seller that there is only a certain number of employees which are, therefore, transferred to the purchaser. Due to the fact that the purchaser becomes party to the employment agreement and any other employment related arrangements (see H, 1 above), most asset sale and/or transfer agreements also include guarantees as to the terms and conditions of such employment agreements and arrangements.

The breach of such guarantees triggers claims for damages for the purchaser's benefit. According to German law, it is not clear if and to what extent the assumption of an employee who is able and willing to work for the new employer constitutes a damage. Therefore, from a purchaser's perspective, the asset sale and/or transfer agreement should also include an indemnification procedure in the event more employees than provided for in the agreement are assumed by the purchaser due to a breach of the respective seller's guarantee.

I. Tax Implications

1. Value Added Tax

The regular VAT (*Umsatzsteuer*) rate in Germany is 19%; for some products and services of public interest there is a reduced rate of 7%. However, the transfer of assets is exempt from VAT if it constitutes a transfer of an entire business or of all assets of an independently operated business unit. The basis for calculating VAT is the total value of the assets, i.e. the purchase price.

Since it might not be absolutely clear whether the foregoing exception applies, it is recommendable to include in the asset transfer agreement a provision clarifying which party bears the VAT if the tax authorities deem the transaction to be subject to VAT. If in such case the purchaser undertakes to reimburse the seller for the payment of the VAT, the seller should be obliged under the asset transfer agreement to issue an invoice to the purchaser on the basis of which it can enforce his input VAT. Alternatively, purchaser transfers such input refund claim to seller who can meet its VAT liability by such input refund claim.

2. Real Property Transfer Tax

The transfer of real estate in Germany triggers a real property transfer tax in the amount of at least 3.5% of the purchase price. The real property transfer tax is due upon the conclusion of the purchase agreement, not when the transfer of the real property is completed and registered in the Land Register.

3. Other Tax Issues

Since the German tax system is very complex, the asset deal might trigger further tax issues. Details depend on the individual circumstances. At any rate, it is highly recommendable to seek tax advice at each stage of the transaction.

J. Bankruptcy Law

1. Challenge of Asset Transfer in Case of Insolvency

In the event seller or purchaser, following the asset transfer, becomes bankrupt or subject to insolvency proceedings, German law generally provides for the opportunity to challenge the transfer under certain circumstances. How such challenge may be effected and who will be entitled to challenge the asset transfer depends on whether or not formal insolvency proceedings within the meaning of the German Insolvency Code have already been initiated at the time of challenge.

Following the initiation of insolvency proceedings, only the insolvency receiver is entitled to challenge a preceding asset transfer. The challenge is subject to the German Insolvency Code and requires that the transfer disadvantages the insolvency creditors. Furthermore, the receiver's challenge will only be successful if at least one of the requirements described in Sections 130 to 136 of the German Insolvency Code is met at the time of the asset transfer. Sections 130 to 136 German Insolvency Code, inter alia, comprise the following cases: (i) the asset transfer took place within three months prior to the application for insolvency proceedings and the other party knew about the insolvency; (ii) the asset transfer took place within ten years prior to the application for insolvency proceedings and the insolvent debtor intentionally caused the insolvency creditors to sustain damages due to the transfer; or (iii) the asset transfer was carried out gratuitously within four years prior to the application for insolvency proceedings. In the event of a successful challenge, the affected assets must be re-transferred to the insolvency estate.

Prior to the formal initiation of insolvency proceedings, any disadvantaged creditor is entitled to challenge the asset transfer effected by its debtor according to the provisions of the German Act on Creditors' Avoidance (*Anfechtungsgesetz*), provided that (i) the creditor has an enforceable title against the debtor, (ii) the creditor's claim is due, (iii) legal enforcement measures did not or would not lead to a full settlement of the creditor's claims, and (iv) at least one of the requirements described in Sections 3 to 6 of the aforementioned act – which are more or less similar to the abovementioned requirements under the German Insolvency Code – are met at the time of the asset transfer. In the event of a successful challenge, the creditor may claim the re-transfer of the assets to the extent necessary to settle his claims.

2. Acquisition of Assets that are Subject to Insolvency Proceedings

German law basically does not provide for specific rules with regard to the acquisition of assets that are subject to insolvency proceedings. However, following the initiation of insolvency proceedings, only the receiver is entitled to dispose of the insolvency estate. Disposals made by the bankrupt entity, thus, are essentially void if not made by the receiver or with the receiver's approval.

If the sale and purchase agreement was concluded prior to the initiation of insolvency proceedings regarding the sold assets and the seller and/or purchaser, at the time of initiation, have not completed performance under the agreement, the receiver basically is entitled to opt for performance or non-performance of the sale agreement. If the receiver elects performance, the agreement has to be performed as if no insolvency proceedings were initiated; if the receiver elects non-performance, the other party, regarding the claim for performance, becomes an insolvency creditor.

K. Timing and Costs

1. Timeframe of Asset Transfer

The timeframe for the sale/acquisition of a business through an asset deal depends on the individual circumstances, such as registration, authorization or notarization requirements, as well as the scope and the kind of assets sold. In simple cases the transfer can take place within one day; in more complex cases the whole transaction may require up to three months.

2. Costs of Asset Transfer

The costs involved for notarizations, if any, and registrations as well as administration fees are all dependent on the value of the acquired assets and will have to be determined in each case.

L. Miscellaneous

1. Choice of Foreign Law

Regarding the question of whether or not the sale and/or transfer agreement can be made subject to foreign law (other than local law), the principle of separation (see A, 2 above) has to be considered. While the parties are free to choose any foreign law for the sale agreement, the transfer in rem is mandatory subject to the law applicable to the jurisdiction where the respective assets are located.

2. (International) Arbitration, Choice of Venue

Under German law, arbitration (including international arbitration) is permissible and popular, in particular to avoid public litigation. The parties of an asset deal thus may arrange for arbitration clauses in the sale and purchase and/or transfer agreement. To be enforceable in Germany, the arbitral award requires a declaration of enforcement by a German court. With respect to international arbitration awards, the jurisdiction for such declarations is assigned to the Higher Regional Courts (*Oberlandesgerichte*), which are bound to the New York Convention on the Recognition and Enforcement of Foreign Arbitration Awards of June 10, 1958. In Germany, arbitration proceedings are generally more time consuming and more expensive than court proceedings.

As a general rule, the parties of an asset deal may agree on the venue in the sale and purchase and/or transfer agreement. Some restrictions may arise from the German Procedural Code or the European Convention on Jurisdiction and Enforcement of Judicial Judgments in Civil and Commercial Matters of September 27, 1968. Details depend on whether or not the parties reside in Germany.

3. Other Distinctions, Characteristics

Please note that German law provides for many further distinctions and characteristics that could become relevant in connection with an asset deal, always subject to the individual circumstances, such as line of business, structure of the deal or associating legal measures. From the authors' experience regarding asset deals in Germany, it is particularly important to keep in mind that if the seller is an individual person rather than a legal entity and if he/she is married, the consent of his/her spouse is required regarding the transfer of the assets, provided that the assets to be transferred constitute the entire or almost the entire estate of the seller. Without such consent the transfer of the assets is not valid.

M. Literature

Hans-Joachim Holzapfel and *Reinhard Pöllath*, Unternehmenskauf in Recht und Praxis (Legal and Practical Aspects of Business Acquisition), 13th Edition, 2008

Daniel Beisel and *Hans-Hermann Klumpp*, Der Unternehmenskauf (Acquisition of a Business), 6th Edition, 2009

Hungary

By *Péter Berethalmi*

A. General Aspects

1. Asset Deal vs. Share Deal: Essential Considerations

In Hungary, a share transfer is more commonly used than an asset transfer as a form of a transaction.

An asset transfer may be preferable when tax issues are identified during a due diligence investigation and the purchaser does not wish to address such issues after the acquisition. Alternatively, parties may also opt for the asset transfer when the number or nature of the assets to be transferred make it unreasonable to transfer the shares of an entire company.

An asset transfer, however, may involve higher transaction costs, as additional transfer taxes may arise as compared to a share deal (please note that as of January 1, 2010, new transfer tax rules will be introduced regarding share deals). Also, approval from third parties is required in many instances in order to continue certain contracts or otherwise. Also, the parties may face license and/or permit issues as certain licenses and/or permits may require special procedures in order to be transferred or may not be transferred at all.

With respect to merger clearance, there is no difference as to whether a transaction is accomplished via an asset transfer or share transfer, as it is always the business unit acquired that is relevant and not the form of the acquisition.

2. Distinction between Sale and Transfer in Rem

Hungarian law does not distinguish between sale and 'transfer in rem'. Nevertheless, the Hungarian legal system also acknowledges title transfer by way of mere endorsement of bearer securities or notes in certain cases, but such arrangement would not necessarily equal a 'transfer in rem.'

In general, in Hungary, for the acquisition of ownership, in addition to the contract for transfer and other legal titles, the item must be handed over. The handover shall be accomplished by the actual transfer of possession of the asset or in any other way to substantiate beyond doubt that control of the asset has been conveyed from the seller to the purchaser.

There are special cases, however, where there are further formalities that need to be followed in order to complete a title transfer.

3. Regional Differences

In Hungary, there are no regional differences as regards the legal requirements in connection with the transfer of assets.

4. Acquisition by Foreigners

In Hungary, in general, there is no distinction with regard to the acquisition of assets by foreign entities, however, in some cases there are restrictions or approval requirements. For example, purchasing real property by foreigners may be excluded or may be subject to authorization.

5. Public Registers, Records and Databases

In Hungary, there is no central institution that maintains all relevant information concerning asset transfers.

The Register of Companies includes relevant company information (e.g., legal form, powers of representation, registered capital, capital increases, etc.). In addition to this, the register includes the financial statements of the companies, if they have been filed. These sources are available to everyone. The applicable laws determine the obligations related to registration as well as the consequences thereto. Also, strict procedural rules are specified by such laws.

The Land Registration Office issues land certificates (*tulajdoni lap*) regarding real property in Hungary, including size, qualification, ownership and charges. The land certificates, which include public information, can be obtained and inspected by everybody, however, the documents in which the registration is based can be inspected only with the approval of the interested parties. The applicable laws determine the obligations related to registration as well as the consequences thereto. Also, strict procedural rules are specified by such laws. Most of the registered information may be relied upon by any third party, however, there is certain information that is available only for information purposes.

The Land Registration Office issues land usage certificates (*földhasználati lap*), as it has a public registration regarding usage rights (*használat*) and usufruct leases (*haszonbérlet*) in Hungary. Again, there are detailed procedural rules regarding registration and to what extent the public can rely on the registered information.

Liens concerning movable assets and floating charges must be recorded in the register maintained by the Hungarian Association of Notaries Public (lien register), which can be inspected by everybody. Again, there are detailed procedural rules established regarding the registered information.

Finally, patents, plant variety protections, utility model protections, trademarks, industrial designs and other IP rights are registered by the Hungarian Patent Office, which is public. However, regarding the copyrights, no such information is available as copyright registration is not required in Hungary.

6. Purchase Price Requirements

There are no restrictions as to currency. There is no minimum price regulated, but price should be fixed with respect to each asset. There are various tax and accounting laws to be taken into account (e.g., fair price at arm's length, etc).

B. Tangible/Movable Assets

1. Characteristics as to:

a) Language of Documentation. The transfer documents regarding tangible assets can generally be prepared in any language. However, depending on the specific tangible asset, the document may need to be submitted to various authorities (e.g., real property transfer) in which case an official translation is required. If for technical reasons the official translation would be incapable of registration (due to improper expression etc.), the Hungarian version should be prepared as the controlling version.

b) Form of Documentation. The transfer of tangible assets generally does not require special form and therefore may be concluded either in written or oral form, except, however, in certain cases (e.g., transfer of real property) where the special form and special signature (e.g., countersigning by attorney-at-law) is required. The documents can be executed outside Hungary, except where in certain cases (e.g., transfer of real property) a special verification procedure would be required for the signing abroad (e.g., apostille). Signing in counterparts is not specifically restricted but it is advisable to check this issue in light of the specific transaction since some authorities may not accept signing in counterparts.

c) Specification of Assets. A general description of the assets to be transferred is not sufficient. In order to ensure that anyone can identify the assets to be transferred without any doubt, the transfer requires that each asset be described. In certain cases there are specific requirements (e.g., in case of real property transfer, please see below).

2. Administrative, Corporate and Other Approvals

(i) The transfer of tangible assets generally does not require special governmental or administrative approvals, however, in some cases, authority approval is needed (i.e. in the case of the transfer of firearms, nuclear weapons, etc.). If such consent is required for the validity of the agreement, the agreement shall not come into existence until this approval has been given. In the absence of consent or approval, the agreement is invalid. For special rules regarding real property please see below.

(ii) The approval of corporate bodies regarding the seller and/or the purchaser is not required by the law, however, the articles of association or the deed of foundation of the company could stipulate these approvals. If such approval is not granted or is missing, then the so concluded agreement would not automatically become invalid. Instead, the internal limitations, in the event that the document is signed by a duly authorized representative, are ineffective vis-à-vis third parties.

(iii) In case the assets are encumbered, the approval of the security holder is not required as a general rule.

3. Filing Requirements

Regarding the transfer of tangible assets, there is generally no requirement that a filing be made with public authorities or that registrations be made in public registers or databases; however, in certain cases such filings and registrations are required (e.g., real property, motor vehicle, etc.) and the transfer may not be completed without registration.

4. Automatic Transfer of Encumbrances

If the assets are subject to encumbrances, such encumbrances are fixed on the asset and not linked with the owner of the asset, as a general rule. Therefore, such encumbrances would continue to encumber the assets even after the purchaser acquires title to them.

The seller shall be entitled to retain title of ownership only upon the execution of the agreement, in writing, until the purchase price is paid in full. During the operative period of title retention, the purchaser shall not alienate and/or encumber the asset.

C. Real Property

1. Characteristics as to:

a) Language of Documentation. The sale and purchase agreement concerning real property could be prepared in any language, however, as per Hungarian laws, the sale and purchase agreement regarding real property shall be countersigned by a Hungarian attorney at law or a notary public and the transfer document shall be filed with the Hungarian Land Registry Office and Hungarian Tax Authority, therefore, the bilingual version of the documents or official translation thereof is necessary.

b) Form of Documentation. The transfer of a real property and any transaction for the creation, modification or termination of ownership, beneficial ownership, right of use, appurtenant easement, purchase right or mortgage (independent lien) may be registered on the basis of a notarial document or a private document countersigned by a Hungarian attorney-at-law. In addition, there are several formal requirements specified by law as to contents of the transfer document.

The documents can be executed outside Hungary, however, the formal requirements of an execution in a foreign country (notarization, apostille, legalization) should be considered.

Signing in counterparts is permissible if all other formal requirements are fulfilled with respect to each version.

c) Specification of Assets. A general description of the real property is not sufficient, the precise description of real property is necessary for the registration and therefore for the title transfer. The description shall include the city where the property is located and the topographical lot number of the property (*helyrajzi szám*). In practice, parties include other information as well, such as size and number of rooms.

2. Administrative, Corporate and Other Approvals

(i) Arable land: Under Hungarian law, the transfer of the ownership rights of arable land is subject to restrictions and prohibitions. Hungarian private individuals or legal entities may purchase real property freely; however, in the case of arable land, a Hungarian private individual may acquire ownership rights up to the limit of 300 hectares in terms of size or 6000 Gold Crowns (*Aranykorona*) in terms of quality rating. In addition, Hungarian legal entities or organizations that are not legal entities may not acquire ownership rights of arable land. The provisions pertaining to resident private individuals shall apply to the EU national wishing to settle in Hungary to independently engage in agricultural production, and who has been legitimately residing in Hungary for at least three consecutive years and is pursuing agricultural activities. EU nationals are required to provide proof of eligibility for acquiring title of ownership in the form of official certificates. They are also required to provide guarantees for future commitments fixed in a private document of full probative force or in a public document.

Non-arable land: Non-resident legal entities or private individuals may acquire title of ownership to real property not qualifying as arable land by authorization from the administrative authority of competence. EU nationals and legal persons and entities without legal personality established in any Member State of the European Union, in a Member State that is a party to the Agreement on the European Economic Area, or in other similar States, may acquire title of ownership of non-agricultural land under the same conditions applicable to resident persons (without special permission) with the exception of properties serving as a secondary place of residence, which may be acquired subject to permission by the administrative authority until December 31, 2011. From this time on, the restrictions will be deleted. EU nationals shall be entitled to acquire only one property under the title of principal place of residence during this transitional period.

Any agreements on the transfer of real property breaching the restrictions detailed above (for example, an agreement on the transfer of arable land to a non-resident legal entity) are null and void. In case of transfer of non-arable land to a non-resident legal entity or private, the agreement qualifies as non-existing without the approval of the administrative authority.

(ii) The approval of corporate bodies regarding the seller and/or the purchaser is not required by the laws, however, the articles of association or the deed of foundation of the company could stipulate these approvals. If such approval is not granted or missing, then the concluded agreement would not automatically become invalid. The internal limitations, in case the document is signed by duly authorized representative, are ineffective vis-à-vis third parties.

(iii) In case the real property is encumbered, the approval of the security holder is not needed for the transfer.

3. Filing Requirements

In case of transfer of real property, an application must be filed with the Land Registration Office within 30 days as of the date of the document (or statement) that is the basis of registration or, if an authority approval is needed for registration, within 30 days as of the authority approval. The document that is the basis of registration and other documents must be also filed along with the application. The Land Registration Office notifies the Tax Authority regarding the application and the Tax Authority deals with transfer tax issues accordingly. If the application and the filed documents are capable of being registered, the Land Registration Office registers the transfer.

In fact, registration by the Land Registration Office shall create the ownership right for the purchaser based on the transfer document. Without registration, the purchaser does not acquire proper title effective vis-à-vis all third parties. Nevertheless, it is possible to acquire title outside the scope of land registration, but such title is ineffective vis-à-vis bona fide third parties that rely on the land registration.

4. Automatic Transfer of Encumbrances

In case the real property is subject to encumbrances, the transfer of the title to the property would not effect the existence and registration of such encumbrances.

The waiver of encumbrances shall be made in such special form as the creation of such encumbrance requires. In certain cases formalities are not that strict; for example, banks may issue their waiver of mortgages by the mere execution of their duly authorized representatives.

5. Automatic Transfer of Lease Agreements

If the real property is subject to a lease agreement, such lease agreement is automatically transferred to the purchaser. There is no automatic right for the purchaser or the tenant to terminate the lease agreement upon acquisition.

A lease agreement concluded for an indefinite period of time may be terminated by either party by a notice specified in the agreement or the law. A lease agreement concluded for a definite period of time cannot be terminated by the purchaser unless the tenant has misled the purchaser regarding the existence of the lease or material lease conditions.

D. Contracts

1. Characteristics as to:

a) Language of Documentation. According to Hungarian legal rules, transfer of contracts is not possible, and 'novation' does not exist in Hungary. However, parties may transfer contracts de facto by way of simultaneous assignment of claims and assumption of debts, which requires the consent of third parties. The document regarding the de facto transfer of contracts can be prepared in any language. Bilingual documents are permissible.

There are some exceptions to the general rule. For example, employment contracts are automatically transferred to the new owner in an asset transfer and certain contract portfolio transfers may be possible pursuant to specific laws. In these cases, no consent is required from third parties but specific laws require a licensing procedure to effect the closing of the transfer (e.g., Insurance Act, Act on Investment Firms, Banking Act, etc).

b) Form of Documentation. As a general rule, the documentation does not have to adhere to a special form, therefore, the agreement may be concluded either in written or oral form, however, the written form is strongly recommended for evidentiary purposes. There are some cases (e.g., specified by the Labor Code, Insurance Act, Act on Investment Firms, Banking Act, etc). when special formalities must be complied with in order to complete the transfer.

Documents can be executed outside of Hungary, in which case the authentication of the signature may be required. Signing in counterparts is permissible as general rule.

c) Specification of Contracts. The general description of contracts would not be sufficient unless each contract could be identified without any doubt based on such general description. The list of contracts (claims and debts) may be attached to the agreement, but this is not compulsory.

2. Administrative, Corporate and Other Approvals

(i) As a general rule, the transfer of contracts (assignment of claims and assumption of debts) does not require special governmental or administrative approvals.

However, there may be certain cases when an authority approval is required for the validity of the agreement, in which case the agreement shall not come into existence until this approval has been given (e.g., in the case of transfer of portfolio as regulated in the Banking Act, Act on Investment Firms, Insurance Act, etc.). In the absence of approval, the agreement is invalid.

(ii) The approval of corporate bodies regarding the seller and/or the purchaser is not required by law, however, the articles of association or the deed of foundation of the company could stipulate these approvals. If such approval is not granted or is missing, then the so concluded agreement would not automatically become invalid. The internal limitations, in case the document is signed by duly authorized representative, are ineffective vis-à-vis third parties.

(iii) Under Hungarian law, claims that are bound to the person of the claimant and claims whose assignment is not permitted by legal regulation shall not be assigned. The debtor must be notified of the assignment, otherwise the debtor is entitled to perform services to the seller of the receivable notification.

In the case of assumption of debts, the approval of the claimant is required. If the claimant does not give such consent, the purchaser shall make arrangements to enable the seller as obligor to perform at maturity, however, the agreement between the seller and the purchaser is valid. If the claimant approves the assumption of debts, the person assuming the debt shall subrogate the seller.

For certain types of contracts (e.g., employment agreements, lease agreements, etc.) exceptions apply. Failure to comply will invalidate the transfer.

3. Automatic Transfer of Contracts (Other than Lease and Employment Agreements)

Security contracts creating encumbrances transfer automatically as they have in rem effect.

4. Filing Requirements

As a general rule, the transfer of contracts (assignment of claims and assumption of debts) does not require filings with public authorities or registration in registers or (online) databases, except in the special cases mentioned above relating to transfer of portfolio as defined in the Banking Act, Insurance Act, Act on Investment Firms, etc.

5. Treatment of Existing Contractual Claims and Obligations

In the case of assignment of claims, the assignee shall be entitled to enforce the objections and offset the counterclaims against the assignee that arise with regard to the assignee on the legal grounds prevailing at the time of notifications. The assignor shall, as a suretyship, be liable for the obligor's services to the assignee, up to the value of the consideration received in return for the assignment unless (i) he has assigned the claim to the assignee expressly as an indefinite claim, or (ii) he has otherwise excluded his liability.

In the case of assumption of debts, if the claimant approves the assumption of debts, the person assuming the debt shall subrogate the seller as obligor. Such person shall be entitled to all rights to which the seller was entitled in respect of the claimant, however the purchaser shall not be entitled to offset the seller's existing claims against the claimant. The suretyship and liens securing a claim shall cease to exist upon the assumption of debt in the absence of statements of approval from the surety and the obligor of the lien. Please see also D, 2 above.

6. Warranty Claims Resulting from Events prior to Transfer

As a general rule, in the case of assumption of debt the purchaser assuming the debt shall subrogate the seller. Therefore, the purchaser liable for warranty claims resulting from events prior to the transfer of the assets affected. In case of consumer contract, the purchaser as the obligor of the consumer contract shall be entitled to demand compensation from the previous obligor, i.e. from the seller. Special provisions concerning indemnifications are recommended, but not mandatory.

E. IP Rights

1. Characteristics of Intellectual Property Rights (e.g., Trademarks, Patents, Utility Models, Domain Names) ("*IP Rights*") as to:

a) Language of Documentation. The sale and purchase documents regarding intellectual property rights may be concluded in any language. With respect to registered IP Rights (trademarks, patents, domain names, etc.) the documents to be submitted in some cases shall be in Hungarian also, therefore, the preparation of bilingual documents is strongly recommended. In addition to this, a Hungarian representative (patent attorney or attorney at law) shall be appointed in the case of a non-Hungarian applicant appearing before the authorities, except if the registered seat or the address of the applicant is in the territory of the European Economic Area.

Please note that according to the Hungarian law, in the case of copyrights, the author cannot assign or waive its moral rights, and economic rights can be assigned and transferred in the cases and under the conditions specified in law.

b) Form of Documentation. In some cases, the sale and transfer documents concerning IP Rights require written form (e.g., assignment of economic rights, transfer of collective trademarks, licensing agreements, etc.). In addition to this, the transfer documents generally shall be filed with the relevant authorities in order to register the purchaser as the new owner of the IP Rights, therefore, the documents shall be in written form. The documents can be executed outside Hungary, and signing in counterparts is permissible.

Please note that in case of a sale of a business or a business unit, the legal successor of a legal entity also obtains the trademark unless the parties specify to the contrary, or the circumstances clearly dictate otherwise.

c) Specification of IP Rights. The principle of identification shall be applied to the transfer of IP Rights; therefore, the IP Rights to be transferred shall be specified identifiably. To that end, the appending of a list of IP Rights to the documents is recommended.

2. Administrative, Corporate and Other Approvals

The transfer of IP Rights does not require special governmental or administrative approvals. The law does not require the approval of corporate bodies regarding the seller and/or the purchaser.

In case the IP Rights are encumbered, the approval of security holder is not needed for the transfer. For further details, please see B, 2 above.

3. Filing Requirements

Except for copyright, the IP Rights require special filings with public authorities or registrations in registers or databases. If the IP Rights are transferred, the change of the ownership rights shall be registered, as well. However, such registration is merely of a declaratory nature and does not affect the validity of the transfer.

In opposition to any third parties who have obtained rights in good faith in exchange for consideration, any rights pertaining to trademark protection may only be referred to if they have been recorded in the Trademark Register.

4. Applicable International (Multilateral) Agreements or Treaties

Hungary participates in the following agreements and conventions:

- TRIPS Agreement,
- Paris Convention for the Protection of Industrial Property,
- Universal Copyright Convention,
- Bern Convention,
- WIPO Copyright Treaty,
- WIPO Performances and Phonogram Treaty, and
- Patent Cooperation Treaty.

In addition to this, Hungary signed the Trademark Law Treaty, Madrid Agreement and the Madrid Protocol regarding trademarks and the Nice Agreement.

F. Receivables

1. Characteristics as to:

a) Language of Documentation. The transfer documentation can be prepared in any language, including English. The documents can be executed bilingually.

b) Form of Documentation. The transfer of receivables is basically an assignment of debts (*engedményezés*) in Hungary. The assignment may be made with a contract in any form, and the written form is not mandatory. However, to avoid any disputes, the written form is recommended.

Upon assignment, the debtor must be notified regarding the assignment, otherwise the debtor may continue to perform with respect to the seller until such notice.

The transfer documents can be executed outside Hungary and signing in counterparts is permissible.

c) Specification of Receivables. The description of the receivables must be detailed, and a general description is not sufficient. There are no requirements that schedules or lists of receivables be attached to the agreement, however, this is recommended.

2. Administrative, Corporate and Other Approvals

(i) As a general rule, the transfer of receivables does not require special governmental or administrative approvals. If the consent of an official or third party is required for the validity of the agreement, the agreement shall not come into existence until this approval has been given. In the absence of approval, the agreement is invalid.

(ii) The approval of corporate bodies regarding the seller and/or the purchaser is not required by the law, however, the articles of association or deed of foundation of the company could stipulate these approvals. If such approval is not granted or missing, then the so concluded agreement would not automatically become invalid. Instead, the internal limitations, in case the document is signed by a duly authorized representative, are ineffective vis-à-vis third parties.

(iii) The assignment of a debt does not require the consent of the debtor.

3. Filing Requirements

The transfer of receivables does not require special filings with public authorities or registration in registers or (online) databases. Upon assignment the debtor must be notified regarding the assignment, otherwise the debtor may continue to perform with respect to the seller of the receivable until such notice.

G. Liabilities

1. Characteristics as to:

a) Language of Documentation. The transfer documentation can be prepared in any language, including English. The documents can be executed bilingually.

b) Form of Documentation. The transfer of liabilities is a transfer of debts (*tartozás átvállalása*) in Hungary. The transfer may be made with a contract in any form, and the written form is not obligatory. However, to avoid any disputes, the written form is recommended.

The transfer is effective with respect to the creditor only once the creditor has approved the transfer.

The transfer documents can be executed outside Hungary and signing in counterparts is permissible.

c) Specification of Liabilities. The description of the receivables must be detailed, and a general description is not sufficient. There are no requirements for attaching schedules or lists of receivables to the agreement, however, this is recommended.

2. Administrative, Corporate and Other Approvals

(i) As a general rule, the transfer of liabilities generally does not require special governmental or administrative approvals. If the consent of official approval or third party is required for the validity of the agreement, the agreement shall not come into existence until this approval has been given. In the absence of approval, the agreement is invalid.

(ii) The approval of corporate bodies regarding the seller and/or the purchaser is not required by the laws, however, the articles of association or deed of foundation of the company could stipulate these approvals. If such approval is not granted or missing, then the so concluded agreement would not automatically become invalid. Instead, the internal limitations, in case the document is signed by a duly authorized representative, are ineffective vis-à-vis third parties.

(iii) Approval from the creditor is necessary. The transfer is effective with respect to the creditor only once the creditor approved the transfer.

3. Filing Requirements

(i) As a general rule, the transfer of liabilities does not require special filings with public authorities or registrations into registers or (online) databases. However, there are certain liabilities that require an authority filing and approval (e.g., transfer of an environmental liability).

(ii) No notification is required to the creditor, but the creditor should approve the transfer; please see above.

4. Purchaser's Liability for:

a) Tax Obligations. The purchaser is not liable for tax obligations unless tax liabilities are attached to the asset (e.g., tax on real property etc.).

b) Environmental Contamination. Liability for environmental damage or for any risk to the environment shall be joint and several – pending proof to the contrary – upon the person who is registered as the owner or possessor (user) of the property after environmental damage or threat to the environment has occurred on which the activity resulting in damage to the environment or posing imminent threat to the environment was carried out. The owner shall be exempt from joint and several liability if it is able to identify the actual user of the real property and to provide proof beyond reasonable doubt that liability does not lie with the owner. These provisions shall apply to the owners and the possessors (users) of non-stationary (mobile) contaminating sources.

Damage caused to other parties by virtue of activities or negligence entailing the utilization of the environment shall qualify as damage caused by an activity endangering the environment. If the person or the entity performing an unlawful activity changes, the rules of the liability of the legal successor shall be applied to the person or entity performing the activity, unless the parties have agreed otherwise in an agreement.

c) Products Sold or Services Rendered by the Seller to Third Parties. As a general rule, in case of assumption of debt, the purchaser assuming the debt shall subrogate the obligor (seller). Therefore, the purchaser liable for warranty claims resulting from events prior to the transfer of the assets affected. In case of a consumer contract, the purchaser, as the obligor of the consumer contract, shall be entitled to demand compensation from the previous obligor, i.e. from the seller.

5. Automatic Transfer of Other Liabilities

No liabilities of the seller automatically transfer to the purchaser except as described under G, 4 above.

6. Contractual Protection as to 4 and 5 above

It is customary to include special provisions such as indemnifications clauses regarding those issues.

H. Employees

1. Transfer of Employees

The employees of the seller automatically transfer to the purchaser due to the asset transfer. (Pursuant to the Hungarian Labor Code, an asset transfer occurs when an independent unit (such as a strategic business unit, plant, division, workplace or any section of these) or the material and non-material assets of the employer are transferred by an agreement to an organization or person, if such transfer takes place within the framework of a sale and purchase agreement).

In connection with legal succession, the rights and obligations of the predecessor (seller) concerning the employment relations existing at the time of succession shall be transferred to the successor (purchaser) at the time of succession. This means that the terms of employment (such job profile, remuneration, benefits, hours, location, etc.), not including the work order, as prescribed in the collective agreement applicable to the predecessor at the time of succession, if any, shall be honored by the successor employer, in respect to the employees affected by the succession (In case of an existing collective agreement, there are special rules regarding its cancellation).

The asset transfer does not require the modification of the employment agreements of the employees concerned by the transfer, but it does not exclude the modification of the existing employment contracts nor the termination thereof, both with the mutual consent of those employee that are transferred to the purchaser.

Judicial practice and commentary establish that the mere fact of asset transfer shall not give rise to grounds to serve ordinary notice to employees transferred to the purchaser; however, should the operation of the affected activity require fewer employees as a result of the asset transfer, the purchaser may serve ordinary notice to those employees whose work is not required any more. (If an employment relationship is terminated by ordinary notice, the employee shall be entitled to a notice period and severance payment, the amount of which depends on the length of his/her employment with the employer.)

The predecessor (seller) and the successor (purchaser) employer shall be subject to joint and several liability for liabilities incurred prior to legal succession if such claims are enforced within one year of the legal succession.

If an employee is terminated by the legal successor employer within one year of the date of legal succession (i) by ordinary dismissal for reasons in connection with the employer's operations or (ii) by termination of the employment relationship concluded for a definite period of time, the legal predecessor employer shall, as a surety, be liable for the employee's compensation due upon termination of the employment. The surety liability shall apply if (i) the predecessor employer, (ii) the company controlled by the predecessor employer, (iii) the majority owner of the predecessor employer, or (iv) the company in which the majority owner is an organization referred to above (iii) holds more than fifty percent of the votes in the supreme body of the successor employer.

2. Approval of Works Council, Trade Union or Other Institutions

Employers (both seller and purchaser) shall consult the trade union or workers' council, if any, prior to adopting a decision in connection with the plans for actions affecting a large group of employees, in particular those related to proposals for the employer's reorganization, transformation, the conversion, privatization and modernization of a strategic business unit into an independent organization.

During the consultations, the predecessor and the successor employer shall, within 15 days prior to the date of successions, inform the local trade union branch, or, if there is no trade union, the workers' council, or, if there is no workers' council, the committee formed from the representatives of non-union employees, concerning (i) the schedule or proposed date of legal succession, (ii) the reasons, (iii) the legal, economic, and social consequences affecting the employees, and shall initiate talks aiming to reach an agreement concerning other proposed actions that affect the employees.

If an employer violates the rights of the workers' council or the trade union detailed above, the workers' council or the trade union affected may seek remedy in court.

3. Contractual Protection as to Labor Issues

Depending on the circumstances of the given transaction it may be customary to include special provisions as the employees in the asset sale and/or transfer agreement.

I. Tax Implications

1. Value Added Tax

On June 1, 2009, the general rate of 20% applies, with some minor exceptions. As from July 1, 2009 the general rate shall increase to 25%.

2. Real Property Transfer Tax

In Hungary, the purchaser of real property shall pay a so-called duty on the transfer of real property to the tax authority. In case of an onerous transfer, the rate of the duty is 10% of the market value of the respective piece of real property, that is, in most cases 10% of the purchase price established in the sale and purchase agreement. The rate of the duty is different in apartment purchases, since it is 2% of the market value up to 4 million HUF and 6% of the part above 4 million. Companies dealing in the sale and purchase of real property as their primary business, shall pay 2% duty (please note that as of January 1, 2010 new rules will be introduced).

The duty on transfer is already due upon the conclusion of the sale and purchase agreement and not only after the transfer of the piece of real property is completed and registered in the land register.

Gifts of real property or gifts of movable property (non onerous transactions) shall be subject to duty payment on gifts. The rate and base of the duty depends on the subject of the gift and its market value as well as the status of the parties to the transaction.

3. Other Tax Issues

There are no other noteworthy tax issues.

J. Bankruptcy Law

1. Challenge of Asset Transfer in Case of Insolvency

According to the Hungarian law, all assets held by the "economic operator" under bankruptcy or liquidation proceeding at the time of the opening of proceedings, as well as all assets acquired during the proceeding, shall be the subject of the bankruptcy or liquidation proceedings. The assets of an economic operator shall comprise all assets it owns or controls. Assets or subsidiary companies shall also be considered assets of the economic operator.

Any creditor or the liquidator (receiver) may bring action during the liquidation proceeding for the court to establish that the former executives of the economic operator failed to properly represent the preferential rights of creditors in the span of the three years prior to the opening of liquidation proceedings in the wake of any situation carrying potential danger of insolvency (including the clearing up of environmental damages), in consequence of which the company's assets diminished to the extent specified.

In addition to this, the creditor, and the receiver, on behalf of the debtor, may file for legal action before the court within 90 days from the time of gaining knowledge or within one year from the date of publication of the notice of liquidation to contest concerning (i) contracts concluded by the debtor within five years preceding the date of when the court received the petition for opening liquidation proceedings or thereafter, or his other commitments, if intended to conceal the debtor's assets or to defraud any one creditor or the creditors, and the other party had or should have had knowledge of such intent, (ii) contracts concluded by the debtor within two years preceding the date of when the court received the petition for opening liquidation proceedings or thereafter, or its other commitments, if intended to transfer the debtor's assets, or if the stipulated consideration constitutes unreasonable and extensive benefits to a third party, (iii) contracts concluded by the debtor within 90 days preceding the date on which the court received the petition for opening liquidation proceedings or thereafter, or its other commitments, if intended to give preference and privileges to any one creditor, such as the amendment of an existing contract to the benefit of a creditor, or to provide financial collateral to a creditor that does not have any.

In respect of the liquidation of a company under control by a qualified majority or a single member company, the controlling party or the sole member (shareholder) shall be responsible without limitation for those of the company's liabilities that are not covered by the debtor's assets during the liquidation proceedings, if the court has established the unlimited and full responsibility of such member (shareholder) for the company's liabilities pursuant to a claim filed by the creditor during the liquidation proceedings or within a 90-day forfeit deadline following the final conclusion of liquidation proceedings, on account of such member (shareholder) having had a history of making unfavorable business decisions from the standpoint of the debtor company.

Where the court of registry has launched dissolution proceedings against a debtor before the opening of liquidation proceedings, and the debtor has accumulated debts in excess of 50% of its equity capital at the time of the opening of liquidation proceedings, upon the request lodged by the liquidator or a creditor the court shall establish that a former member (shareholder) with majority control, who transferred his share within three years before the opening date of the liquidation procedure, is subject to unlimited liability for the debtor's outstanding liabilities, unless it is able to prove that the debtor was solvent at the time of said transfer, and that the loss of assets took place after that time, or that it acted in good faith in transferring its shares even though the debtor was insolvent.

2. Acquisition of Assets that are Subject to Insolvency Proceedings

The receiver shall collect the claims of the debtor when due, enforce its claims and sell its assets. If consented by the creditors, the receiver may invest the debtor's property in private limited-liability companies, public limited liability companies or cooperatives as non-pecuniary assets (contribution) if it promises to obtain a better price this way.

The receiver shall dispose of the debtor's assets through public sales at the highest price that can be obtained on the market. The receiver shall effect the sale by way of tender or auction, and may forego the application of these procedures only upon the prior consent of the select committee, or if the estimated proceeds are insufficient to cover the costs of sale or in the difference between the prospective proceeds and the estimated cost is less than HUF 100,000 (approx. USD 500). In this case, the receiver may apply other public forms of sale for the purpose of achieving a more favorable result.

The party acquiring ownership or any other rights of value may not apply a setoff at the public sale with the debtor. If the liquidator fails to comply with the obligation to observe one's right of first refusal concerning the debtor's assets, the person holding such right shall be entitled to bring the case to court.

K. Timing and Costs

1. Timeframe of Asset Transfer

The timeframes applicable to the sale/acquisition of a business by way of an asset deal depend on the asset deal in question (movable assets or real property, liens/mortgages, IP Rights, etc.). However, the timeframe of the deal could be two or three months.

2. Costs of Asset Transfer

The notarization costs, the registration costs and the stamp duties depend on the given situation (e.g., the costs of the notarization generally depend on the value of the project).

L. Miscellaneous

1. Choice of Foreign Law

As per the Hungarian legal rules, the sale and/or transfer agreement could be subject to foreign law other than Hungarian law, if the parties selected the applicable law and if the asset transfer contains non-Hungarian part. In the absence of selection, the law relating to the agreement shall be the law of the state in which the seller has its central office at the date of the conclusion sale and purchase agreement.

2. (International) Arbitration, Choice of Venue

In case of asset transfer, arbitration and international arbitration is permissible without any restriction.

3. Other Distinctions, Characteristics

There are no other noteworthy distinctions or characteristics as to the transfer of assets under Hungarian law.

M. Literature

András Kisfaludi, Az adásvételi szerződés (The sale and purchase agreement), 2nd Edition, 2007

György Gellért (Editor), A Polgári Törvénykönyv Magyarázata 1–2. (Commentary on the Civil Code of Hungary 1–2.), 1st Edition, 2007

Gábor Hidas, *Gyula Horváth*, *András Urbán* and *Gábor Kőszegi*, Az ingatlanjog nagy kézikönyve (Grand manual to real property law), 1st Edition, 2007

Tamás Sárközy (Editor), Csődjog (Bankruptcy law), 2nd Edition, 2007

László Leszkoven, Az engedményezés új szabályai a kötelmi javaslat szövegtervezetében (New provisions regarding assignment in the draft text of the proposal for contract law), *Kötelmi jogi kodifikációs tanulmányok (Contract law codification studies)*, 2005, 311–323

László Leszkoven, A fiduciárius engedményezés jogi természetéről (On the legal nature of fiduciary assignment), *Gazdaság és jog (Economics and law)* 3/2002, 13–17

India

By *Shourya Mandal* and *Orijit Chatterjee*

A. General Aspects

1. Asset Deal vs. Share Deal: Essential Considerations

The following are the essential considerations for a seller and a purchaser in structuring a transaction by way of an asset deal as opposed to a share deal:

(i) Stamp duty and VAT payable on an asset deal would be much higher than in the case of a transfer of shares.

(ii) In an asset deal, consideration must be given to whether there are expenses involved in obtaining permits and/or licenses that cannot be transferred from the seller to the purchaser. In such cases it is advisable to opt for a share deal.

(iii) The contracts (including leases for real property) existing in the name of the company have to be considered since they would be required to be assigned to the purchaser in case of an asset deal. The assignment of contracts may require approval of third parties and may also involve payment of stamp duty based on the value of the assignment.

(iv) In a share deal, all liabilities (including hidden liabilities) of the companies would be assumed by the purchaser. In an asset deal, it is possible to exclude certain liabilities. Some statutory liabilities, such as income tax liabilities or any potential liability for statutory violations, can be avoided in an asset deal.

2. Distinction between Sale and Transfer in Rem

Under Indian law it is possible to enter into an obligation to transfer through execution of a sale and purchase agreement between the purchaser and seller and thereafter fulfill the obligation to transfer the assets by a separate transfer deed/conveyance in respect of the individual assets.

In multi-jurisdictional transactions, it is common to have a master agreement and a separate business transfer agreement for the Indian assets.

3. Regional Differences

The general law for transfer of assets is similar across India except that different states have different rates regarding stamp duty and registration fees under the Indian Stamp Act and Registration Act, respectively.

There are also some states in India where ceilings are applicable with regard to ownership of land. In case the transfer of assets that leads to ownership of land exceeding the limits, prior permission of the prescribed authorities would be required to acquire the excess land.

4. Acquisition by Foreigners

There are certain regulations under the Foreign Exchange Management Act, 1999 that are required to be complied with by foreigners for acquiring assets in India. These relate to acquisition of real property (rights, title and interest) in India, delivery of assets and payment of consideration value for the assets. There are no restrictions on the purchase of moveable assets (e.g., goods other than stock, shares and money) for use in India. However, a non-resident entity (such as a foreign company) cannot undertake any business in India.

Foreign nationals are generally not permitted to acquire any real property in India. However, a branch office of a foreign company is permitted to acquire real property for the purpose of setting up an office in India that is necessary for or incidental to carrying out such activities, provided that all applicable laws, rules, regulations or directions in force are duly complied with.

It is common practice for a foreign company to purchase a business or real property in India in the name of an Indian subsidiary. In such case the consideration for purchasing such real property would have to be paid in Indian rupee through the Indian subsidiary and not directly by the foreign company to the seller. There are some restrictions on foreigners holding shares in Indian companies. However, it is possible for a foreigner to hold up to 100% of a company engaged in most type of manufacturing activities.

5. Public Registers, Records and Databases

With respect to real property, public records are maintained with the District Registrar/Additional District Sub Registrar having jurisdiction over the place where the property is situated.

For the purpose of ascertaining any disputes related to the real property, a search may also be conducted in the records of the Court (District and High Courts) having jurisdiction where the real property is situated.

Searches may also be conducted with the Registrar of Companies with regard to charges created on its assets by a company. In most cases, the information is available online.

6. Purchase Price Requirements

There are no special rules regarding the purchase price in an asset deal. However, if real property is transferred, most states require that stamp duty be payable on the market value of such property irrespective of the value assigned to the property by the parties. For restrictions in case of the purchase of real property by a foreign company through its Indian subsidiary please refer to A, 4 above.

B. Tangible/Movable Assets

1. Characteristics as to:

a) Language of Documentation. The language of documentation is usually English. However, the documentation may also be in the local language of the place where the assets are located. Use of local language is not mandatory. Documents are generally not executed bilingually.

b) Form of Documentation. Under Indian law, a contract for sale of goods (tangible assets) is a sale and purchase agreement whereby the seller transfers or agrees to transfer the property in goods to the purchaser at a consideration. Such transfer of tangible assets may be made either orally or in writing or partly orally and partly in writing.

There is no prescribed form for such transfer, and the documents may be executed outside India. The parties must sign on the same documents. No signing in counterparts is permitted.

The transfer of title may take place by virtue of the sale and purchase agreement or by delivery of possession subsequent to the execution of a sale and purchase agreement. Stamp duty is payable in some states if the transfer of title takes place by the contract. Therefore, it is common practice to transfer title to movable assets by delivery. The parties would sign a receipt showing the consideration paid and goods delivered.

c) Specification of Assets. No specific form is prescribed under Indian law for the transfer of tangible assets. However, in the usual course of practice, the sale and purchase agreement may provide for a generic description of the assets to be transferred that could be described in more detail in a schedule annexed to the sale and purchase agreement.

2. Administrative, Corporate and Other Approvals

The transfer of tangible assets generally does not require any governmental or statutory approvals. No corporate approvals are necessary for such transfers unless such approvals are specifically required to be obtained under the provisions of the articles of association of a party that is a company or the constitutional documents of any other corporate entity. In a case where the tangibles assets are the only assets of the business and the business is being transferred, it may be necessary to obtain prior approval of the shareholders in case the seller is a public limited company (whether listed or unlisted). In case approvals for such transfers are not obtained, if required, such transfers may be invalid and can be declared void in case the same is challenged in a court of law.

No consent or approval is required from the security holders under Indian law if the assets are encumbered. However, the encumbrance would remain and the title in favor of the purchaser would be subject to the existing encumbrance.

3. Filing Requirements

In case of transfer of tangible assets, no filing/reporting is required to be made in any public register or database.

4. Automatic Transfer of Encumbrances

Encumbrances related to the tangible assets would automatically transfer to the purchaser together with such assets. Please also refer B, 2 above.

C. Real Property

1. Characteristics as to:

a) Language of Documentation. The language of documentation is usually English. However, the documentation may also be in the local language of the place where the property is located. Use of local language is not mandatory. Documents are generally not executed bilingually.

b) Form of Documentation. Transfer of real property in India is primarily governed by the Transfer of Property Act, 1882 ("**TOPA**"). Under the TOPA, the transfer of real property can be made only by an instrument in writing and must be registered under the Indian Registration Act, 1908.

It is possible to execute the sale and purchase agreement outside India. However, in such event persons in India would have to be authorized to submit the sale and purchase agreement for registration in India with the Registrar of Assurances or the District Registrar or District Sub-Registrar having jurisdiction over the place in which the property to be transferred is located. However, it is common for the parties outside India to authorize someone in India to execute the sale and purchase agreement and submit it for registration in India.

It is not possible for the parties to sign the sale and purchase agreement in counterparts. The sale and purchase agreement must be submitted for registration in India.

c) Specification of Assets. The real property must be described in detail in the sale and purchase agreement along with reference to land registration details. It is also common to attach a map to the sale and purchase agreement for the purpose of identifying the land.

2. Administrative, Corporate and Other Approvals

The selling company requires the approval of its Board of Directors prior to such transfer. It is not mandatory to obtain shareholder's approval to such transfer unless the company is a public limited company (listed or unlisted) or when otherwise stated in the articles of association of the selling company.

The purchasing company would also require the approval of its Board of Directors prior to such purchase. Shareholder approval does not have to be obtained to purchase real property unless otherwise stated in the articles of association of the purchaser.

In some states, there is a ceiling on the amount of land that can be held by any person if such person wishes to hold land beyond the limit as prescribed. The owner may require specific approval to hold such land prior to its acquisition.

Approval of a security holder does not have to be obtained prior to the transfer if the property is encumbered. The purchaser would obtain the title to the property subject to existing encumbrances.

In case of leasehold property, transfer of such assets would be subject to the provisions of the lease.

3. Filing Requirements

Any transfer of real property must occur by way of execution of an instrument in writing, i.e. the sale and purchase agreement, which is required to be registered under the Indian Registration Act, 1908. After registration, the name of the purchaser would have to be recorded in the land records and the records of the relevant municipal authorities or local body.

4. Automatic Transfer of Encumbrances

It is possible to transfer real property that is encumbered. In such case, the real property is transferred to the purchaser along with all encumbrances. There is no prescribed form under Indian law with respect to waiver of encumbrance. In the case of transfer of encumbered assets by a company, under the Indian Companies Act, 1956 the company is required to notify the Registrar of Companies of the payment or satisfaction in full of such encumbrance within thirty days from the date of such payment or satisfaction in the prescribed form.

In case the real property is subject to lease agreements, such leases would automatically transfer to the purchaser of such real property. There is no extraordinary right for the purchaser or the tenant to terminate the lease following the acquisition. The seller does not have any right to terminate the lease agreements following the transfer. The purchaser may terminate such lease agreement after the transfer under the conditions prescribed by the TOPA and the terms of the lease.

D. Contracts

1. Characteristics as to:

a) Language of Documentation. The language of the documentation is usually English. However, the documentation may also be in the local language. Use of local language is not mandatory and the documents may be executed either in English or in the local language.

b) Form of Documentation. Under Indian law, there is no prescribed form for such transfer. It is possible to execute the documents outside India, but not possible for the parties to sign the transfer documents in counter-parts.

c) Specification of Contracts. The contracts proposed to be transferred must be clearly specified in the sale and purchase agreement. Usually a generic description is given in the sale and purchase agreement and a broad description of the contracts is annexed to the agreement. After the execution of the sale and purchase agreement, each contract must be assigned by the seller in favor of the purchaser by a separate deed of assignment. Separate assignment deeds for each contract to be transferred are essential in addition to the sale and purchase agreement. Through the assignment deed the said third party consents to such transfer of the contract in favor of the purchaser.

2. Administrative, Corporate and Other Approvals

No special governmental approval is required for transfer of contracts.

If the purchaser and/or the seller are companies, approval of the respective Board of Directors is required. Approval of third parties may also be necessary if the same is a condition mentioned in the contract being transferred. If the contract is silent, the seller may transfer the contract to the purchaser without obtaining approval.

In case there is a prohibition on the assignment of a contract and the contract is transferred in violation of such clause, the transfer is not valid and cannot be enforced.

3. Automatic Transfer of Contracts (Other than Lease and Employment Agreements)

Except for employment contracts, no contracts are automatically transferred to the purchaser in the acquisition of assets.

4. Filing Requirements

No filing with public authorities or registration is required for the transfer of contracts.

5. Treatment of Existing Contractual Claims and Obligations

The liability of the purchaser will depend on the terms of the sale and purchase agreement between the purchaser and the seller and the terms of the contract. Special indemnity clauses may be included in the sale and purchase agreement with regard to such obligations and liabilities.

6. Warranty Claims Resulting from Events prior to Transfer

The purchaser may be liable for warranty claims resulting from events prior to the transfer date. It is usual to have indemnities between the purchaser and seller in the sale and purchase agreement.

E. IP Rights

1. Characteristics of Intellectual Property Rights (e. g., Trademarks, Patents, Utility Models, Domain Names) ("*IP Rights*"), as to:

a) Language of Documentation. The language of the documentation is usually English. Agreements for transfer of IP Rights are generally not made in the local language.

b) Form of Documentation. Under Indian law there is no prescribed form for effecting such a transfer. There is no specific law that requires joint signing of the sale and purchase agreement. Thus, execution in counterparts is permitted. However, it is common for parties to sign the same document.

The sale and purchase agreement should be duly stamped.

c) Specification of IP Rights. As mentioned above, since no specific form is prescribed under Indian law for transferring IP Rights, in the usual course of practice the sale and purchase agreement may provide for a generic description of the rights to be transferred that could be described in more detail in the schedule to the sale and purchase agreement.

There is no specific requirement under Indian law for attaching schedules or lists of IP Rights to the sale and purchase agreement.

However, after the execution of the sale and purchase agreement, the title to the IP Rights are transferred by a separate document. In such document, the IP Rights have to be described in detail. Separate documents are usually executed for different classes of IP Rights, such as trademarks, copyrights, patents, etc. Separate transfer documents can also be executed in the English language.

2. Administrative, Corporate and Other Approvals

No special governmental or administrative approvals are required for transfer of IP Rights.

The selling company must be appropriately authorized by a resolution passed in a meeting of the Board of Directors to transfer the IP Rights and the purchasing company must always be authorized by a resolution passed in a meeting of its Board of Directors to purchase such IP Rights from the seller.

No approval of the security holders is required if IP Rights are encumbered.

3. Filing Requirements

The following filings are required after transfer of IP Rights:

Patents: A certified copy of the agreement (not the sale and purchase agreement) affecting the title of the patent is required to be submitted to the Controller of Patents. The purchaser is required to apply for registration of its name. Registration of the document of transfer is compulsory for recording and establishing the title of the purchaser and transactions that are based on unregistered transfer documents are not valid.

Copyrights

No filing and/or registration is required for transfer of copyrights.

Designs

The purchaser is required to file an application in the prescribed format with the Controller of Designs to enter its name as subsequent proprietor of the design. The original deed of transfer should be filed with such application.

Trademarks

If the purchaser becomes entitled by assignment or transmission to a registered trademark, it is required to apply in the prescribed manner to the Registrar of Trade Marks to register its right, title and interest in the trademark. The Registrar shall, upon receipt of the application and proof of title of the trademark, register the applicant as the proprietor of the trademark with respect to the goods or service on which the assignment or transmission has effect and shall cause particulars of the assignment or transmission to be entered in register of trademarks.

These filings and registrations are essential to prove and establish the title of the purchaser as owner of such IP Rights, i.e. ownership of patents, designs and trademarks requires registration in order to be effective.

4. Applicable International (Multilateral) Agreements or Treaties

India is a party to the Trade Related Aspects of Intellectual Property Rights (TRIPS) Agreement and is a member of World Intellectual Property Organization (WIPO), Paris Convention for the Protection of Industrial Property (relating to patents, trademarks, designs, etc.) of 1883 and the Berne Convention for the Protection of Literary and Artistic Works (relating to copyright) of 1886. Apart from these, India is also a member of the Patent Cooperation Treaty (PCT), which facilitates obtaining of patents in several countries through the filing of a single application.

F. Receivables

1. Characteristics as to:

a) Language of Documentation. The language of documentation is usually English. However, the documentation may also be provided in the local language. Such use of local language is not mandatory and the documents may be executed either in English or in the local language.

b) Form of Documentation. It is possible to execute the documents outside India. It is not possible for the parties to sign the sale and purchase agreement in counterparts. It is, however, common for parties outside India to authorize someone in India to sign the transfer documents.

The transfer document should be duly stamped.

c) Specification of Receivables. As mentioned above, since no specific form is prescribed under Indian law for transferring the assets, the sale and purchase agreement may provide for a generic description of the assets to be transferred, which could be more fully described in the schedule appended to the document.

However, the document that transfers title to the receivable must sufficiently specify the receivable.

2. Administrative, Corporate and Other Approvals

No special governmental or administrative approval is required for transfer of receivables.

The transfer of receivables requires prior approval of the Board of Directors of the seller.

The approval of the debtor will be necessary in the event it is required under the contract between the debtor and the seller. Thus, if the contract is silent, the debtor's consent is not required. In the event the approvals mentioned above are not granted, the transfer cannot be effected.

3. Filing Requirements

The transfer of receivables does not require any special filings with public authorities or registration.

The seller should notify the debtor of such transfer. Until the time the debtor is notified, any payment by the debtor to the seller is a valid payment.

G. Liabilities

1. Characteristics as to:

a) Language of Documentation. The language requirements correspond with those applicable to the case of a transfer of contracts. Please refer to D, 1, a above in this respect.

b) Form of Documentation. The form requirements correspond with those applicable to the a transfer of contracts. Please refer to D, 1, b above in this respect.

c) Specification of Liabilities. The specification requirements correspond with those applicable to the transfer of contracts. Please refer to D, 1, c above in this respect.

2. Administrative, Corporate and Other Approvals

The required approvals correspond with those applicable to the transfer of contracts. Please refer to D, 2 above in this respect.

3. Filing Requirements

The filing requirements correspond with those applicable to the transfer of contracts. Please refer to D, 3 above in this respect.

4. Purchaser's Liability for:

a) Tax Obligations. Various types of tax obligations are discussed below:

Excise duty is payable upon the manufacture of goods. Such liability generally remains with the business, and the purchaser may become liable for such obligation even for the period prior to the acquisition;

With regard to the sales tax and VAT, liability will generally remain with the seller for the period prior to the acquisition;

With regard to the customs duty and other similar duties, the seller has the primary liability for the period prior to the acquisition. However, in the event that any customs duty is payable or due with respect to assets being transferred, the Tax Authority may enforce its claim against these specific assets, even after the acquisition.

b) Environmental Contamination. There is no general rule regarding environmental contamination related to the acquired assets for the periods prior to the acquisition. However, it is generally agreed between the seller and the purchaser that the purchaser shall be indemnified for all environmental liabilities that may exist pertaining to the period prior to the acquisition. In case there is no such indemnity, the purchaser would be liable for all such environmental claims arising with respect to the property.

c) Products Sold or Services Rendered by the Seller to Third Parties. Generally, any liability relating to products sold by the seller to third parties prior to the acquisition will remain with the seller.

5. Automatic Transfer of Other Liabilities

By operation of law, the purchaser may become liable for all statutory and other liabilities in relation to employees, even for the period prior to the acquisition.

6. Contractual Protection as to 4 and 5 above

Indemnity clauses are generally inserted in the agreement as a special provision to indemnify the purchaser in case of liabilities arising on account of issues mentioned in I, 4 and I 5 above.

H. Employees

1. Transfer of Employees

When the ownership of a business or part of business is transferred by an agreement from the employer (seller) to a new employer (purchaser) and the seller's employees are to be transferred, some of the employees may decide to terminate their services while the rest decide to continue their employment.

The transfer of employees to the purchaser is subject to compliance with provisions under Section 25FF of the Industrial Disputes Act, 1947. Under the Act, where the seller's employees decide to terminate their employment, every employee who has been in continuous service for more than one year in such business immediately before such transfer shall be entitled to notice and compensation in accordance with other provisions in the Act as if the employee had been retrenched.

Where the employees continue with their employment, the provisions under the Act shall not apply to those employees, if

(i) the service of the employee has not been interrupted by such transfer;

(ii) the terms and conditions of service applicable to the employee after such transfer are not in any way less favorable to the employee than those applicable to him immediately before the transfer; and

(iii) under the terms of such transfer or otherwise, the purchaser is legally liable to pay to the workman in the event of his retrenchment compensation on the basis that his service has been continuous and has not been interrupted by the transfer.

If the business is transferred, the purchaser will agree to engage the employees of the business and fulfill the conditions mentioned above, which are recorded in the sale and purchase agreement. The employees will thereafter transfer to the purchaser automatically.

2. Approval of Works Council, Trade Union and Other Institutions

No prior approval is required from any works council, labor agency, trade union or other institution if the transfer is made in accordance with the law.

3. Contractual Protection as to Labor Issues

It is customary to have a provision in the sale and purchase agreement pursuant to which the seller indemnifies the purchaser in relation to any claim arising in respect of the employees prior to the date of the asset transfer.

I. Tax Implications

1. Value Added Tax

Every state in India has its own VAT laws. Generally, VAT is payable in an asset deal on transfer of machinery, inventory, raw material and other tangible assets.

VAT is charged at various rates (ranging from 4% to 12.5%) in various states depending on the nature and character of the goods on which such charge is levied. Generally, VAT is 12.5%.

2. Real Property Transfer Tax

Under Indian law, any transfer of real property requires the payment of stamp duties and registration fees under the Indian Stamp Act and Registration Act, respectively.

The rate of stamp duty and registration fees depends on where the property is located, as different rates of duties and fees are prescribed for every state and would also depend on whether the transfer is by way of lease, license or sale.

The rate of stamp duty may vary from 2% to 16% of the market value of the property.

Registration fees in some states are charged on the basis of the value of the property and can be high as 2% of the market value.

3. Other Tax Issues

With regard to transfer of receivables and assignment of contracts, the stamp duty may be payable on the same rate as applicable to the sale of the real property. In case of transfer of receivables, the debtor usually agrees to make payment in favor of the purchaser directly in order to avoid payment of the stamp duty. In this case, no specific assignment of the receivable is made.

With respect to the assignment of a contract, stamp duty is also payable at the same rate for transfer of real property. However, the value assigned to such transfer can be reduced, thereby reducing the stamp duty payable.

J. Bankruptcy Law

1. Challenge of Asset Transfer in Case of Insolvency

In the event the seller is wound up following the asset transfer, the liquidator may challenge the transfer, provided that the transfer was made within a period of one year before the presentation of the petition for winding up. In such case, the purchaser is required to show that the asset transfer was made in the ordinary course of business or in favor of a purchaser, in good faith and for valuable consideration. If the purchaser is able to establish the aforesaid, then the purchaser may be protected from the acts of the liquidator.

2. Acquisition of Assets that are Subject to Insolvency Proceedings

In India, certain companies experiencing financial difficulty are referred to the Board for Industrial and Financial Reconstruction (**"BIFR"**) under the Sick Industrial Companies (Special Provisions) Act, 1985. If a company is referred to BIFR, the assets of the company can be sold, subject to the orders that may be passed by the BIFR.

K. Timing and Costs

1. Timeframe of Asset Transfer

The sale of a business in India by way of an asset deal takes approximately six months.

2. Costs of Asset Transfer

The relevant costs would depend on the value of the assets proposed to be transferred and the State in which the assets are located. The stamp and registration fees can be quite substantial, as discussed in Section I above.

L. Miscellaneous

1. Choice of Foreign Law

The sale and purchase agreement may be governed by foreign law and obligations under it may be enforced in a foreign court. However, the transfer of assets and liabilities by virtue of the parties to such agreement would have to be in accordance and in conformity with Indian laws applicable in this regard. Therefore as mentioned earlier, it is not unusual to have a separate sale and purchase agreement for Indian assets, and for this agreement to be governed by Indian law.

2. (International) Arbitration, Choice of Venue

It is possible to provide for international arbitration.

There is no restriction on the choice of venue. However, if both seller and purchaser are Indian entities, it is usual for the arbitration to take place in India.

3. Other Distinctions, Characteristics

There are no other distinctions or noteworthy characteristics with regard to the transfer of assets in India.

Italy

By *Carlo Pianese* and *Elia Ferdinando Clarizia*

A. General Aspects

1. Asset Deal vs. Share Deal: Essential Considerations

The decision as to whether to structure a transaction as an asset deal or share deal depends on a variety of considerations.

Primarily, both the seller and the purchaser will look at the tax implications.

In an asset deal, the price paid will correspond to the fiscal price (the value of the assets as recognized by the tax authority) of the assets for the purchaser and, as a consequence thereof, the purchaser will benefit from (i) a higher annual deduction of depreciation charges of the purchased assets (as it will be able to increase the depreciation basis), and (ii) lower taxation as capital gain when the purchaser, in turn, sells the relevant assets. On the other hand, in a share deal, the fiscal value of the underlying assets (the assets owned by the relevant company purchased) keeps the fiscal value at the level prior to the relevant transfer, therefore the purchaser may not benefit from the mentioned step-up of the fiscal value of the assets.

Furthermore, in an asset deal the purchaser can limit its liability by applying for a tax certificate from the relevant tax authority (in which case the liability is limited to the tax required under the certificate). In this way the purchaser can be certain of the amount of the tax liability attached to the relevant business, obviating the need for due diligence with respect to tax liability.

On the other hand, share deals are more convenient from an indirect tax (e.g. VAT and registration tax) liability perspective and, subject to certain requirements, also in terms of direct tax liability (e.g. corporate taxes).

As far as indirect taxes are concerned, a transfer of business triggers a registration tax amounting to 3% (unless the business includes land and buildings, in which case indirect taxes are due up to 18%) on the net value of the assets being transferred, including goodwill. On the contrary, share deals do not trigger any indirect taxes (save for minor registration tax amounting to EUR 168).

With reference to direct taxes, in case of assets deals, the seller is subject to a 27.5% corporate tax on the fiscal capital gain (the seller is, however, entitled to deduct such tax costs with fiscal losses of the current and previous fiscal years). If the going concern being disposed of has been owned by the seller for at least three years, taxation of capital gains can be deferred pro-rata over a maximum of five-year period.

Also, in the case of share deals, the seller is subject to a 27.5% corporate tax on the fiscal capital gain (being such tax costs deductible with fiscal losses of the current and previous fiscal years); however, provided that certain requirements are met, the seller may benefit from the participation exemption (i.e. the exemption from taxation granted to shareholders on dividends and capital gains in order to avoid double taxation) and will therefore be subject to 27.5% of corporate tax only on 5% of the capital gain.

Besides tax considerations, further considerations are based on the different legal consequences of the two alternatives. In the case of a direct transfer of the business, the transferee only assumes liabilities that are recorded in the mandatory accounting books of the going concern and, with reference to such liabilities, becomes jointly and severally liable with the transferor. In a share deal, however, the transfer involves the acquisition of an existing company, with all its assets and past and current liabilities (recorded, contingent or otherwise).

Additionally, in an asset deal the purchaser may benefit from the protection granted by the Italian Civil Code should the assets have latent defects. On the contrary, in a share deal the Civil Code protection is limited to the direct subject matter of the sale (the shares) and does not extend to the indirect subject matter of the transfer (the underlying assets owned by the target company), as the seller transfers the shares of the relevant company (the status of shareholder, with the relevant rights and obligations). It follows that in order to obtain satisfactory legal protection in a share deal, the purchaser will seek to include detailed and extensive representations and warranties in the relevant transfer agreement.

2. Distinction between Sale and Transfer in Rem

Under Italian law, upon execution of a sale and purchase agreement the transfer of the business is completed, i.e. the purchaser acquires full title to and ownership of the relevant asset.

However, it is common practice for the parties to first execute a preliminary sale and purchase agreement where they agree to execute the transfer deed at a later stage. The preliminary sale and purchase agreement is binding, i.e. the parties commit themselves to close the transfer by signing the transfer deed within a certain timeframe and/or subject to the occurrence of certain conditions precedent (e.g., clearance by the antitrust authority).

Should a party fail to comply with the preliminary sale and purchase agreement (i.e. one party fails to sign the transfer deed on the agreed date), the other party may benefit from different contractual remedies under the Civil Code as specific performance (i.e. obtaining a judgment completing the transfer) and recovery of damages. It is common practice for the purchaser to make a down payment at signing of the preliminary sale and purchase agreement which will be counted towards the payment price on closing, or, alternatively, if the transfer is not closed due to the purchaser's breach, the seller is entitled to retain such down payment. If it is the seller who fails to close, the purchaser is entitled to ask the seller for double the amount of the down payment.

Generally, representations and warranties, indemnification provisions, and other relevant clauses are provided for in the preliminary sale and purchase agreement, whereas the transfer deed simply provides for the transfer provisions, as well as the identification of the subject matter of the transfer and the price thereof.

If assets are to be transferred in different jurisdictions, it is possible for the parties to execute a master sale and purchase agreement governed by the law of their choice, and providing, as far as the transfer of the assets located in Italy is concerned, for an obligation of the parties to execute a specific transfer deed related to those assets.

It is advisable that the transfer deed relating to the assets located in Italy does not mention the master sale and purchase agreement nor the total price thereof, otherwise there is a risk that the tax authority (i) calculates the registration tax on the global price, instead of just the price allocated to the assets located in the Italian jurisdiction; and/or (ii) challenges the portion of the price allocated to the Italian business.

3. Regional Differences

In Italy, the only material regional difference with respect to the legal requirements in connection with the transfer of assets relates to the transfer of real estate in Trentino-Alto Adige. Therefore, if the business includes real property located in that region, it is necessary to bear in mind that the transfer of the relevant asset will not be completed upon execution of the transfer deed of the business by the parties, but the transfer shall also be registered at the local Land Registry. Such registration is not only necessary as a form of publicity and to render the transfer enforceable against third parties but also to perfect the transfer inter partes, i.e. to close the transfer of the real property vis-à-vis the seller and the purchaser, granting the latter full title to the relevant asset.

4. Acquisition by Foreigners

On a general basis, in Italy there are no distinctions with regard to the acquisition of assets by foreigners or foreign entities.

5. Public Registers, Records and Databases

There is no central register in Italy that retains all relevant information regarding an asset transfer. Information relating to companies may be found at the local companies registry where it is possible to find corporate details such as the articles of association and by-laws, financial statements, list of shareholders, powers of attorneys granted to directors, number of employees of the company, as well as information relating to certain corporate events (amendments of by-laws, capital increases, institution and relocation of secondary branches, etc.).

Information concerning real property may be found at the local Land Registry, including details on the owner of the relevant land, encumbrances, easements, etc. As far as leaseholds are concerned, they only have to be registered if the relevant lease agreement has an initial term exceeding nine years.

Finally, information relating to patents and trademarks can be found at the Italian Patent and Trademark Office (*Ufficio Italiano Brevetti e Marchi*).

6. Purchase Price Requirements

The parties may freely agree on the currency to be used for the payment of the purchase price. The transfer deed relating to a business must be executed before a notary public (by way of public deed or private deed with notarized signature) and registered at the local tax office (*Agenzia delle Entrate*), subject to the payment of a registration tax. As the registration tax is a percentage of the purchase price, if a currency other than the euro is the agreed-upon currency, the tax office will calculate the purchase price in euros and determine the registration tax due accordingly.

The parties are free to agree on any price for the transfer of the business. The transfer deed must provide for the actual purchase price. If a transfer deed sets forth a price that is objectively too low, the tax office may object to it, as it could allege that the transfer deed provides for a lower price than the one actually paid in order to reduce the registration tax on the transfer. In this case, it is the parties' burden to prove that the price set forth in the transfer deed reflects the genuine economic agreement of the parties.

The parties may allocate part of the price to the different assets composing the business. This is actually advisable, as certain assets of a going concern, when transferred, are subject to a specific rate of registration tax. As an example, registration tax on goodwill is 3%; registration tax for the transfer of immovables varies from 3% to 15% (depending on the type of immovable), and is 7% in the majority of cases.

The registration tax applies on the net value of the assets being transferred (the liabilities related to the going concern are allocated to the different assets/rights proportionally to their respective values) at different rates depending on the nature of each asset.

Additionally, it is advisable to allocate a portion of the price to the different assets composing the business for depreciation purposes, considering that different depreciation rules govern different categories of assets.

As mentioned in Section A, 2 above, it would be advisable for the parties not to refer to the master sale and purchase agreement in the local transfer deed in order to avoid the tax office making the parties pay the registration tax on the global price rather than on the price allocated to just the business located in Italy.

B. Tangible/Movable Assets

1. Characteristics as to:

a) Language of Documentation. Under Italian law the transfer of a business must be executed before a notary public (by way of public deed or private deed with notarized signature) and subsequently registered at the local tax office (*Agenzia delle Entrate*) subject to the payment of a registration tax, and at the Companies Registry. This is mandatory, even in cases where the business does not include any real property.

In order for a transfer deed to be registered at the tax office, it must be in the Italian language. It is possible to have the transfer deed drafted and executed bilingually, provided, of course that one of the two languages is Italian.

However, if the tangible assets to be transferred do not constitute a business (i.e. a pool of assets suitable for carrying out an entrepreneurial activity and potentially capable of generating revenues), then the relevant transfer agreement may be executed as private agreement (*scrittura privata*) in any language selected by the parties, as the relevant transfer agreement is not subject to registration tax (provided that the transfer is completed by way of exchange of correspondence) but is generally subject to VAT.

b) Form of Documentation. With reference to the form of documentation, a distinction shall be made between a transfer of tangible assets within a transfer of a business (where such tangible assets are part of the going concern) and a transfer of tangible assets alone (that do not form a business).

In the former case, the formalities set forth above with reference to the transfer of a business shall apply.

In the latter case, no formalities must be adhered to, as the relevant transfer agreement may be verbal or written, and, in the latter case, the relevant transfer agreement may be executed outside Italy, as well as in counterparts (by way of exchange of correspondence of proposal and acceptance).

c) Specification of Assets. In order for the transfer to be valid, the subject matter shall be determined or determinable. It follows that the sale and purchase agreement shall identify the relevant assets. This may be done by a generic description, to the extent that such description renders those assets distinguishable (for instance, referring to the stock in a warehouse as of a certain date). For this purpose it is common practice to provide schedules to the sale and purchase agreement. There are no specific requirements as to the drafting of such schedules, provided that the descriptions of the assets set forth therein comply with the above-mentioned rule of making the subject matter of the transfer determined or determinable.

2. Administrative, Corporate and Other Approvals

Generally, no special governmental or administrative approvals are required for the transfer of tangible assets.

Sale or purchase of assets is a decision to be resolved by the administrative body of the company, this being either a joint stock company or a limited liability company, although in the latter type of corporation, there might be cases where such decision shall be resolved at the shareholders' level. Sometimes the board of directors delegates certain powers (including decisions relating to the sale or purchase of assets) to one or more directors, and, in these cases, no resolution by the board of directors is needed to approve a transfer.

In order to verify the authority of the signatories to act on behalf of the purchaser or of the seller, it is sufficient to check an updated abstract from the companies registry, where all the relevant powers of the board of directors and single directors are reported. If the decision to sell or purchase pertains to the board of directors, the other party of the contract may require the signatories to produce evidence that such decision has been taken (for example, a copy of the relevant resolution of the board of directors could be delivered to the other party).

Directors are the legal representatives of the company and may enter into contracts in the name of and on behalf of the company. Limitations on the powers of the directors set forth in the by-laws or in resolutions appointing the relevant director(s) are not effective vis-à-vis third parties, unless it can be established that such third parties acted with the intention of harming the company.

If the assets are pledged, the owner may sell such assets without the consent of the pledgee. However, the purchaser cannot take possession of the relevant assets. In fact, under Italian law, perfection of the pledge requires dispossession, i.e. the pledgor must deliver the pledged asset to the pledgee or to a third party designated by both the pledgor and the pledgee. In this case the pledgor retains title of ownership but without possession.

It follows that if the pledged asset is then sold to a third party by the pledgor, the third party purchaser will acquire title of ownership to the asset but no possession as long as the asset remains pledged.

3. Filing Requirements

Generally, transfer of tangible assets does not require special filings with public authorities or registrations in public registers or databases. However, there are certain categories of tangible assets (automobiles, vessels and aircraft) that have a special register, and any agreement relating to transfer of title on those categories of assets must be duly registered therein. Registration is not required to complete the transfer inter partes but in order to render the transfer enforceable against third parties.

4. Automatic Transfer of Encumbrances

If an asset is transferred by the pledgor to a third party purchaser, the pledge is enforceable vis-à-vis such third party. The latter will acquire the title of ownership to the asset (subject to pledge) but not the possession – which will remain with the pledgee. The dispossession of the pledged asset constitutes a form of publicity. In fact, as there is no registry for movables, the only way to publicize an encumbrance on a tangible asset is the dispossession from its owner. This way an envisaged third party purchaser, learning that the asset is not possessed by the seller, will become aware that such asset may be subject to an encumbrance.

C. Real Property

1. Characteristics as to:

a) Language of Documentation. As mentioned above, under Italian law the transfer of a business must be executed before a notary public (by way of public deed or private deed with notarized signature) and subsequently registered at the local tax office (*Agenzia delle Entrate*), subject to the payment of a registration tax. This is mandatory, even in cases where the going concern is not composed of any real property.

In order for a transfer deed to be registered at the tax office, it must be in Italian. It is possible having the transfer deed drafted and executed bilingually, provided that one of the two languages is Italian.

If the relevant property is transferred itself (and not as part of a business), the transfer deed must still be notarized and registered at the tax office. Therefore, as the transfer deed is subject to registration, it must be in Italian (or bilingual).

b) Form of Documentation. A distinction is to be made with reference to the preliminary sale and purchase agreement and the transfer deed.

If the preliminary sale and purchase agreement (or the master sale and purchase agreement, in case of a multi-jurisdiction transaction) is governed by a law other than Italian law, then the relevant rules as to the formality of execution will apply.

If the preliminary sale and purchase agreement is governed by Italian law, then the parties may execute the document either in or outside Italy by both parties signing the same document or by way of exchange of correspondence (i.e. parties signing counterparts, where one party sends out the proposal containing the preliminary sale and purchase agreement and the other party returns an acceptance thereof).

Execution by way of correspondence is advisable, as by this means the parties do not have to pay registration tax on the preliminary sale and purchase agreement (even where a down payment is paid at signing).

The execution of a transfer deed must adhere to certain formalities. As mentioned, the deed must be executed before a notary public (by way of public deed or private deed with notarized signature) and registered at the local tax office, subject to the payment of a registration tax, the cadastral tax and the mortgage tax, where applicable. Additionally, the transfer deed must be registered with the relevant local Land Registry.

c) Specification of Assets. The transfer deed must specifically identify each real property that is intended to be transferred by referring to the identification data set forth in the cadastral registry.

2. Administrative, Corporate and Other Approvals

Transfer of real properties does not require special governmental or administrative approvals.

Sale or purchase of assets is a decision to be resolved by the administrative body of the company, this being either a joint stock company or a limited liability company. In the latter type of corporation, there might be cases where such decision shall be resolved at the shareholders' level. As stated in B, 2 above, sometimes the board of directors delegates certain powers (including decisions relating to sale or purchase of assets) to one or more directors, and, in these cases, no resolution by the board of directors is needed.

In order to verify the authority of the signatories on behalf of the purchaser or of the seller, it is sufficient to check an updated abstract from the Companies Registry, where all the relevant powers of the board of directors and single directors are reported. If the decision to sell or purchase pertains to the board of directors, the other party to the contract may require the signatories to produce evidence that such decision has been taken. A copy of the relevant resolution of the board of directors is delivered to the other party.

If the real property is encumbered with a mortgage, the owner may still transfer the asset. In this case the mortgage is enforceable against the third party purchaser, provided that it has been duly registered with the Land Registry before registration of the relevant transfer.

3. Filing Requirements

Upon completion of the transfer of a real property, the transfer shall be registered with the Land Registry identifying the purchaser as the new owner. The transfer is perfected with the execution of the transfer deed, and upon such execution, the transfer is valid and enforceable vis-à-vis the seller and the purchaser. The registration in the Land Registry is necessary in order to render the relevant transfer enforceable against third parties (e.g., against a mortgagee acquiring a mortgage on the real property following registration of the relevant transfer).

4. Automatic Transfer of Encumbrances

In case the real property is subject to encumbrances (e.g., mortgages, usufruct rights), such encumbrances automatically transfer to the purchaser. Release of an encumbrance shall have the form of a public deed or a private deed with notarized signature and shall be registered at the Land Registry.

5. Automatic Transfer of Lease Agreements

In the event that the real property is the subject matter of the transfer and such real property is subject to a lease agreement, such lease agreement is automatically transferred to the purchaser upon completion of the transfer. The transfer does not allow either party of the lease agreement to terminate upon or following completion of the transfer.

D. Contracts

1. Characteristics as to:

a) Language of Documentation. The assignment of a contract to a third party does not require specific formalities, unless it is otherwise provided in the contract to be assigned.

The assignment agreement may be drafted in English or in any other language. It is also possible to draft the relevant documents bilingually.

b) Form of Documentation. As mentioned, there are no specific formalities that are applicable to complete an assignment of a contract, unless the relevant contract provides otherwise. It is possible for the assignment agreement to be executed outside Italy, as well as to be executed by way of exchange of correspondence, (i.e. by signing in counterparts as proposal and acceptance thereof).

An assignment is valid to the extent that the assigned party accepts the assignment thereof. Such acceptance may be made in advance (for instance, it could already be provided for in the contract to be assigned), or at the time of completion of the assignment. In the former case, the assignment becomes effective upon notification of the assignment to the assigned party of the contract.

The approval of the other parties to the contract is necessary, unless the assignment of contracts is made within the context of a transfer of business. When a business is transferred, all the contracts pertaining to the business are transferred to the purchaser by operation of law.

It follows that the purchaser of a business will replace the seller as the party to the pending agreements that are related to the business being transferred, provided that such agreements are not of a "personal" nature. However, the other parties to the assigned agreements could terminate the relevant assigned agreement for good cause within three months from the date such parties have acquired knowledge of the occurred sale of the business.

The provision mentioned above applies to all contracts that may be considered to pertain to the business and give rise to a potential liability for the purchaser vis-à-vis the third party from possible breaches of the assigned agreements made by the seller before completion of the sale. In light of the above, the purchaser should seek protection against such liabilities by asking the seller for specific representations and warranties on the relevant agreements and the performance thereof.

c) Specification of Contracts. The contracts to be assigned shall be duly identified in the assignment agreement, indicating the parties, the date of execution and other elements that could be necessary for the identification thereof. The identification may be made in a schedule of the assignment agreement. When a business is transferred, all the contracts pertaining to the business are transferred to the purchaser by operation of law, therefore, in such case, there is no need to identify the relevant contracts.

2. Administrative, Corporate and Other Approvals

The assignment of a contract does not require special governmental or administrative approvals, unless the relevant public authority is a party to the contract to be assigned or such authority has a qualified interest therein.

If the assignor or the assignee is a company, then the relevant by-laws should be checked, together with an abstract from the Companies Registry, to verify whether the relevant decisions can be resolved by the board of directors or whether the relevant powers have been granted to a director or an executive officer of the company.

3. Automatic Transfer of Contracts (Other than Lease and Employment Agreements)

See D, 1, b above.

4. Filing Requirements

The transfer of contracts does not require special filings with public authorities or registrations unless the contracts are transferred as part of a business.

5. Treatment of Existing Contractual Claims and Obligations

If a contract is not completely fulfilled at the time of completion of the transfer of the business, the relevant contractual position is automatically assigned to the purchaser of the business, to the extent that the relevant sale contract pertains to such business.

It is common practice in a business sale, for the sale and purchase agreement to provide specific representations and warranties as to the validity of contracts pertaining to the business, the due past performance by all the contractual parties, as well as the lack of pending or threatened disputes relating to such contracts.

6. Warranty Claims Resulting from Events prior to Transfer

The purchaser is liable for warranty claims resulting from events prior to the transfer of the assets affected, as the purchaser replaces the seller in the relevant contractual position. In this respect, as mentioned, it is common practice for the sale and purchase agreement to provide specific representations and warranties relating to, inter alia, the lack of pending or threatened disputes relating to such contracts.

E. IP Rights

1. Characteristics of Intellectual Property Rights (e. g., Trademarks, Patents, Utility Models, Domain Names) ("*IP Rights*") as to:

a) Language of Documentation. The transfer documents regarding intellectual property rights may be drafted either in Italian or in a foreign language, as well as bilingually.

b) Form of Documentation. No formalities are required for the valid transfer of trademarks or patents between the parties; however, as the relevant transfer shall be registered with the Italian Patent and Trademark Office, the written form is necessary in order to effect valid registration. Upon registration, the transfer becomes effective and enforceable vis-à-vis third parties.

c) Specification of IP Rights. A specific description (mentioning the elements of their registration with the Italian Patent and Trademark Office) of the IP Rights that constitute the subject matter of the transfer is necessary in order to define them precisely and effect registration with the Italian Patent and Trademark Office.

2. Administrative, Corporate and Other Approvals

The transfer of IP Rights does not require special governmental or administrative approvals. With respect to the approval of corporate bodies regarding the seller and/or the purchaser, and the approval of security holders in case IP Rights are encumbered, please refer to the discussion above relating to the transfer of real property.

3. Filing Requirements

See E, 1, b above.

4. Applicable International (Multilateral) Agreements or Treaties

Italy is a party to the major international IP conventions, including the Paris Convention for the Protection of Industrial Property of March 20, 1883, as subsequently amended.

F. Receivables

1. Characteristics as to:

a) Language of Documentation. The transfer of receivables may be drafted in English, as well as bilingually.

b) Form of Documentation. Save for certain exceptions (for instance, receivables vis-à-vis the public administration), the documentation for transfer of receivables does not require a specific form. The documents may be executed outside Italy, and it is possible for the parties to execute the documents by way of exchange of correspondence and signing in counterparts.

c) Specification of Receivables. The documentation shall describe the receivables to be transferred by providing for the identifying elements of the relevant credits (i.e. parties, amount of credit, title upon which the credit arises). There is no specific requirement for attaching schedules or lists of receivables to the transfer agreement, even though in practice the receivables are identified in schedules of the transfer agreement for convenience purposes.

2. Administrative, Corporate and Other Approvals

The assignment of a contract does not require special governmental or administrative approvals unless the relevant public authority is a party to the contract to be assigned or such authority has a qualified interest therein.

If the assignor or the assignee is a company, then the relevant by-laws should be reviewed, together with an abstract from the Companies Registry, to verify whether the relevant decisions can be resolved by the board of directors or the relevant powers have been granted to a director or an executive officer of the company.

The approval of the debtor is not required unless the original title from which the receivables arise provided for a non-assignability of the receivables.

3. Filing Requirements

The transfer of receivables does not require special filings with public authorities or registration in registers or databases.

The transfer shall, however, be notified to the relevant debtors. The transfer becomes effective vis-à-vis the debtors upon notification of the transfer or, alternatively, upon acceptance of the transfer by the relevant debtors.

The transfer is enforceable against third parties following notification to the debtors or, alternatively, when the debtors have accepted the transfer by means of a deed executed on a certain date (e.g., a notarized deed).

When the transfer of receivables is made within the context of a transfer of business, the transfer of the receivables pertaining to the business is effective towards the debtors from the time of the registration of the sale of business with the Companies Registry even in the absence of the notification or the debtor's consent. However, a debtor would be released from its obligations in the event it paid, in good faith, its debt to the seller of the business. For this reason, although not required by provisions of law, a communication to the transferred debtors is usually effected.

G. Liabilities

1. Characteristics as to:

a) Language of Documentation. Liabilities are transferred together with the relevant business to which they pertain, therefore the formalities described above with reference to the transfer of a going concern will apply. The transfer of a business must be executed in Italian before a notary public (by way of public deed or private deed with notarized signature) and subsequently registered at the local tax office (*Agenzia delle Entrate*), subject to the payment of a registration tax, and in the Companies Registry.

With reference to the form of documentation, the formalities set forth above with reference to the transfer of a business shall apply. The transfer of a business must be executed before a notary public (by way of public deed or private deed with notarized signature). It follows that the documents may be executed outside Italy, to the extent that the transfer deed is notarized in the place where it is executed. Depending on the jurisdiction where the document has been executed, the document is sometimes apostilled in order for it to be recognized in Italy. In any case, the parties must sign the same document and may not sign in counterparts.

b) Specification of Liabilities. A description of the liabilities is not required. As already mentioned in A, 1 above, when the business is transferred, the transferee only assumes those liabilities that are recorded in the mandatory accounting books of the going concern and, with reference to such liabilities, becomes jointly and severally liable with the transferor.

2. Administrative, Corporate and Other Approvals

The transfer of liabilities, being part of the transfer of the business, does not require the approval of creditors.

With respect to the approval of corporate bodies regarding the seller and/or the purchaser, please refer to B, 2 above.

3. Filing Requirements

The transfer of liabilities does not require any special filing except for the filings mentioned above and required for the transfer of the business (registration at the local tax office (*Agenzia delle Entrate*), subject to the payment of a registration tax, and in the Companies Registry).

4. Purchaser's Liability for:

a) Tax Obligations. In general terms, the transferee becomes jointly liable with the transferor for tax liabilities pertaining to the business before the transfer is completed. In this case the purchaser's liability is subordinated (i.e. the tax authority will go after the purchaser only after having unsuccessfully tried to collect the taxes and fines from the seller of the business). The tax liabilities of the purchaser cannot exceed the value of the purchased going concern.

The transferee can limit its liability by applying for a tax certificate from the relevant tax authority (in which case the liability is limited to the tax required under the certificate). For instance, if the relevant tax certificate states that there are no tax liabilities with reference to the relevant business, the transferee is free from any tax liability relating to the business in the period preceding the completion of transfer of the going concern.

b) Environmental Contamination. The general rule under Italian law is that the person responsible for the clean-up of contaminated land is the person responsible for the contamination itself. The purchaser of the relevant business is not jointly liable. However, practically speaking, should the seller (if it is the party responsible for the contamination) fail to pay for the clean-up, the purchaser shall bear the relevant clean-up works costs.

c) Products Sold or Services Rendered by the Seller to Third Parties. Matters relating to the liability arising from defective products sold or services rendered by the seller to third parties prior to the acquisition shall be evaluated in connection with succession of existing contracts.

In fact, as general rule, upon completion of a business transfer, all the relevant pending contracts pertaining to the business are automatically transferred to the purchaser by operation of law. Such automatic transfer operates at any stage of an existing agreement, i.e. until such an agreement produces effects. Therefore, in case liability arises from the performance of an agreement by the seller, such liability passes to the purchaser of the business upon completion of the relevant transfer. It is therefore advisable for the purchaser to obtain adequate protection in the sale and purchase agreement providing specific representations and warranties relating to the duly and timely performance of contracts by the seller, as well as the absence of any pending or threatened dispute connected to contracts pertaining to the business.

5. Automatic Transfer of Other Liabilities

As general rule, the transferee of a commercial business is liable for debts pertaining to the transferred business and arising before the transfer, provided that these debts are recorded in the mandatory accounting books of the transferor. According to case law, the purchaser's mere knowledge of the existence of a debt (which has not been recorded in the accounting books of the seller) is not by itself insufficient to create the joint liability for that debt. The seller of the business is not released from the above debts unless the relevant creditors have granted their consent to such release. Any different contractual arrangement between the seller and the purchaser is lawful and enforceable as between the parties but cannot be enforced toward any third parties.

6. Contractual Protection as to 4 and 5 above

Regarding the question as to whether it is customary to include special provisions (e.g., indemnifications) regarding the issues mentioned under G, 4 and 5 above into the asset sale and/or transfer agreement, please see G, 4, c above for details.

H. Employees

1. Transfer of Employees

Whenever a transfer of business takes place, the employment relationships of the personnel employed in the transferred business continue with the transferee by operation of law, and the employees who are transferred maintain all the rights deriving from the employment agreements in force at the time of the transfer.

The transferor and the transferee are jointly liable for the employees' credits accrued and existing as at the date of the transfer. However, subject to certain procedures, the employees can discharge the transferor from the obligations deriving from the employment relationships.

The transferee is required to apply the economic and legal treatment set forth by the national, territorial and company collective agreements in force at the time of the transfer until their expiration, unless they are replaced by other collective agreements applicable to the transferee at the same level (i.e. national, territorial, company).

The transfer of a business is not by itself a cause for termination of the employment relationships. However, the employees whose employment conditions are substantially affected as a result of the transfer may resign for cause during the three months following the transfer date. Resignation for cause permits the employees to be entitled to the statutory termination payments (i.e. mandatory severance payment, indemnity in lieu of unused holidays, etc.), as well as to payment in lieu of the notice period they would have been entitled to in case of dismissal.

2. Approval of Works Council, Trade Union or Other Institutions

In the event of a sale of a going concern employing more than 15 employees, the seller and the purchaser must provide at least 25 days before completion of the transfer a joint advance notice in writing to their respective internal unions' representatives. In the absence of internal unions' representatives, the notice must be given to the trade associations belonging to the major national workers' unions. The notice shall contain: a) the date the execution of the final sale agreement is scheduled; b) the reasons of the proposed sale; c) the legal, economic and social consequences for the employees; and d) the proposed measures, if any, affecting the employees.

Upon written request of the internal union representatives or the trade associations, to be conveyed within seven days from the receipt of the abovementioned notice, the seller and the purchaser shall commence, within seven days as of the receipt of such request, joint consultation with the unions. The consultation shall be deemed terminated within ten days from the start of the consultation even if no agreement is reached, since there is no obligation of the purchaser and seller to come to an agreement with the unions. The breach by the seller or the purchaser of the consultation requirements constitutes anti-union conduct. As consequence thereof, trade unions may seek a court order mandating that the employer remove the effects of such conduct. An employer who does not observe the consultation requirements and fails to comply with the court order is subject to imprisonment up to three months or a fine.

3. Contractual Protection as to Labor Issues

It is market practice to include specific representations and warranties relating to the employees in the business sale and purchase agreement. Such representations and warranties relate to the past treatment of employees, compliance with labor legislation and absence of any liability. Contrary to representations and warranties relating to other areas of the business, the representations and warranties regarding employees generally have a duration equal to the statutory limitations of the rights of the employees. No specific indemnities are usually inserted in the relevant sale and purchase agreement, unless specific potential liabilities are discovered by the purchaser during the due diligence exercise or are disclosed by the seller.

I. Tax Implications

1. Value Added Tax

The transfer of a business is not subject to VAT but to a registration tax. This applies only if the pool of assets that constitutes the subject matter of the transfer is qualified as a "business", i.e. a pool of assets suitable for carrying out an entrepreneurial activity and potentially capable of generating revenues.

To the contrary, if the relevant pool of assets does not constitute a "business", then the VAT shall be applicable to the price allocable to each single asset, with the general VAT rate equal to 20%. Specific rules are provided for some assets – i.e. transfer of receivables are generally subject to registration tax of 0.5%.

In order to establish whether the sale and purchase is a simple sale of a pool of assets or a transfer of a going concern, the intention expressed by the parties is largely irrelevant; the Italian Registration Tax Code allows the tax authority to apply registration tax on a substantive basis, irrespective of the qualification provided for by the parties to a specific agreement, in application of the "substance over form" principle.

2. Real Property Transfer Tax

If the business that constitutes the subject matter of the transfer includes land or other immovable property, then the price allocated to the land or other immovable property is subject to two further indirect taxes (in addition to registration tax) i.e. (i) cadastral tax (*imposta catastale*) equal to 1%, and (ii) where applicable, mortgage tax (*imposta ipote-*

caria) amounting generally to 2–3% of the relevant price. Unlike registration tax on real property (which is calculated based on the price of the same, net of relevant liabilities), cadastral tax and mortgage tax are calculated based on the price of the land without deducting liabilities.

3. Other Tax Issues

There are no other tax issues in connection with an asset transfer.

J. Bankruptcy Law

1. In Challenge of Asset Transfer in Case of Insolvency

In general terms, in the event that the seller or the purchaser, following the asset transfer, becomes bankrupt or subject to insolvency or similar proceedings, the receiver may challenge the asset transfer under certain claw-back provisions. In particular, the transfer may be subject to claw-back (upon an ad-hoc legal claim to be filed by the receiver) if (i) the insolvency is declared within twelve months from completion of the relevant transfer of business, and (ii) the price (received or paid, depending whether the insolvent company is the seller or the purchaser) is disproportionate as compared to the relevant business.

2. Acquisition of Assets that are Subject to Insolvency Proceedings

Within the context of bankruptcy proceedings, the receiver may decide to sell the assets of the insolvent company (whether or not they constitute a business) to third parties in order to distribute the proceeds to the insolvent company's creditor.

Different formalities apply depending on whether the assets to be sold are solely movables or also include immovables.

Generally, the assets of the insolvent company are sold by way of a public auction, even though the bankruptcy court or administrator may opt for a private auction (inviting selected bidders) or by way of private negotiations with a single proposed purchaser, bypassing any auction procedure.

If the assets sold constitute a business, the rules above relating to the sale of a going concern apply, with the exception that the sale of a business within a bankruptcy proceeding does not include the liabilities of the insolvent company pertaining to the relevant business. The going concern will be sold free from liabilities, as such liabilities will be satisfied with the proceeds of the sale of the business, together with the proceeds of the sale of other assets of the distressed company, if any.

K. Timing and Costs

1. Timeframe of Asset Transfer

Completing a transfer of a business is relatively a straightforward proceeding. Unless specific conditions precedent must be satisfied under the relevant sale and purchase agreement (e. g., antitrust clearance), no preliminary actions are required before executing the transfer deed, except for the trade unions' consultation in the event that the business to be transferred includes employees. In such event, the consultations proceedings with the trade unions shall start at least twenty five days before the completion of the business transfer is scheduled.

2. Costs of Asset Transfer

As far as the relevant costs of the transfer are concerned, besides the registration tax and other indirect taxes described above, parties have to pay the notarial fees, which are generally not a material cost in mid-sized and large transactions, as they usually amount to a few thousand euros at most.

L. Miscellaneous

1. Choice of Foreign Law

The sale and transfer agreement can be made subject to foreign law. However, the choice of foreign law will not limit the rights of third parties to whom Italian law grants special protection. For instance, as far as the employees of the business are concerned, they will be protected by the mandatory rules under Italian law described above. These apply because the employees are not party to the business sale and purchase agreement between the seller and the purchaser. However, even where the employees were party to such agreement, Article 7, first paragraph, of the Rome Convention on the applicable law on contractual obligations (1980) would apply. Such provision ("the mandatory rules of other countries") would probably require the court adjudicating the dispute arising in connection with the relevant business sale and purchase agreement to apply mandatory Italian laws, as such agreement relating to a business located in Italy would obviously have a close connection to the Italian jurisdiction.

Moreover, even where the business sale was governed by foreign law, Italian law would still govern the consequences of a business transfer with respect to third parties. For instance, as seen above, contracts pertaining to the business will be automatically transferred to the purchaser upon completion of the sale. Parties to such contracts would still be subject to such rule by operation of Italian law, notwithstanding the business sale being governed by a foreign law. While the rights and obligations of the seller and the purchaser arising from the business sale could be governed by a foreign law chosen by the parties, all the consequences of a transfer of a business located in Italy affecting third parties would still be governed by Italian law.

In practice, parties tend to chose Italian law for the transfer of a business located in Italy. This is even in case where the master agreement is governed by foreign law. This is not inconsistent, as all the major provisions arising from the master agreement (representations, warranties, indemnities, covenants, conditions precedent) are governed by the foreign law chosen by the parties, while the sole consequences directly arising from the Italian transfer are governed by local law.

2. (International) Arbitration, Choice of Venue

The parties may freely decide on a domestic or international arbitration.

3. Other Distinctions, Characteristics

There are no other distinctions or unusual characteristics noteworthy in connection with a customary asset deal.

M. Literature

Alessanro Cotto, Luca Fornero and *Gianluca Odetto*, Cessione, conferimento, affitto e donazione d'azienda, Ipsoa (Transfer, Contribution, Lease and Donation of a Business), 2nd Edition, 2008

Ugo Draetta and *Carlo Monesi*, I contratti di acquisizione di società ed aziende (Companies and Business Acquisition Contracts), 1st Edition, 2007

Japan

By *Kengo Nishigaki* and *Rodell Molina*

A. General Aspects

1. Asset Deal vs. Share Deal: Essential Considerations

A share transfer is easier and simpler in Japan than a share deal because the parties do not have to identify each asset to be transferred. Only the number and type of shares must be identified. Further, the purchaser may continue to enjoy the benefit of limitation of liabilities, and the loss will be, at least theoretically, limited to the share purchase price. However, under a share deal, the purchaser may not be able to select assets or liabilities to be transferred unlike in an asset transfer deal. Thus, if the parties intend to transfer part of the businesses or if the parties do not intend to transfer some hidden liabilities, such as product liabilities, the asset transfer structure is preferable.

Further, the tax implications are one of the most important issues to be considered in selecting the scheme. Under the share transfer scheme, the gain on the sale of the shares is recognized as a capital gain subject to corporate tax and all carry-over losses are transferred to the purchaser. On the other hand, such transfer of losses is not recognized under the asset transfer structure. In addition, consumption tax, real estate acquisition tax, and registration tax will be imposed on an asset transfer as described in I below. Thus, the parties should consider the tax structure carefully in order to minimize tax exposure.

2. Distinction between Sale and Transfer in Rem

The Japanese law distinguishes between sale and transfer in rem, meaning that a sale is an agreement that does not necessarily result in the transfer of assets. This is based on the Civil Code's basic principles inherited from German law where rights in personam are clearly distinguished from rights in rem. However, according to established and fixed court precedents and doctrines, unless otherwise provided in the agreement, the transfer occurs at the same time that the agreement becomes effective. Therefore, it is critical to provide for the timing of transfer in an asset sale agreement.

Under this legal structure, it is possible to provide for the sale and the transfer/conveyance in separate documents. However, parties usually prefer to include them in one document. This practice was influenced by M&A practices in the US where the execution (signing) of an asset sale agreement is separated from its implementation, even though the execution and the implementation are usually included in the same document.

3. Regional Differences

There are no regional differences in Japan as regards the legal requirements in connection with the transfer of assets. This is because Japan has a unitary rather than a federal system of government in which not relatively little autonomy is granted to local governments. Local governments (prefectural and municipal governments) may enact ordinances only to the extent that the scope of such ordinances is related to municipal governance (Article 92 of the Japanese Constitution). Therefore, local governments may not enact laws on asset transfers that are beyond their municipal governance.

4. Acquisition by Foreigners

If the target assets include an asset that falls within the scope of the following regulations, a notification to and/or approval from the government will be required.

The following transactions between residents and non-residents fall within the scope of "capital transactions," where the Foreign Exchange Law of Japan requires post-transaction notifications within twenty days of the acquisition to the Finance Ministry through the Bank of Japan:

(i) a resident sells loans exceeding 100 million yen (approximately USD 1,049,318 as of December 1, 2008) in value to a non-resident;

(ii) a resident sells securities as a portfolio investment exceeding 100 million yen in value to a non-resident; or

(iii) a non-resident buys real estate or any rights to it from a resident (except as a purchase of a residence or purchase of an office for its business).

The following transactions by foreign investors fall within the scope of a "direct investment," where the Foreign Exchange Law of Japan requires notification of the Finance Ministry through the Bank of Japan within 15 days of the investment in general:

(i) a foreign investor purchases shares in non-listed companies; or

(ii) a foreign investor purchases shares in listed companies, resulting in the ownership of 10% or more of all the issued and outstanding shares.

If such transactions are related to restricted industries such as the manufacturing of airplanes, arms or gunpowder, industries regarding nuclear energy or space development, manufacturing of narcotics, police security services, agriculture, oil or leather, etc., the foreign investor must submit an application to the Finance Ministry and a minister in charge of such business area three months prior to the purchase, instead of the 15-day prior notification mentioned above. The screening period is usually 30 days, but this may be extended to up to five months. If a transaction is not related to restricted industries, the filing of a post-transaction notice within 15 days from the transaction is sufficient for these purposes.

5. Public Registers, Records and Databases

There is no similar registration system for asset transfers per se. However, basic company information such as the official company name, date of incorporation, directors, representative directors, statutory auditors, and the transactional history may be viewed in a company's corporate registration (with the Legal Affairs Bureau, "**LAB**"). Therefore, before a purchaser enters into an asset purchase agreement, it usually reviews the most recent copy of the company's commercial registration, which is available at the LAB that has jurisdiction over the company.

Information on ownership of shares in the target company is not public. However, under the Japan Corporations Law, any corporation that issues shares (*Kabushiki Kaisha*; "**KK**"), whether publicly listed or not, must keep a share register to identify who the shareholders of the company are.

Information on ownership of some types of assets such as real property, automobiles, ships and intellectual property (patents and trademarks) are available at the local LAB or other governmental agencies.

Under the Antimonopoly Law of Japan, an acquirer of assets must file an Assets Purchase Report to the Japan Fair Trade Commission (the "**JFTC**") if the following requirements are met (this filing is not required if the parties are in the relationship of parent-subsidiary or share the same parent company):

The acquirer is a domestic or foreign company that has more than ten billion yen in gross assets (this gross includes those of the company's domestic parent company and subsidiaries); and

(i) if the seller is a domestic corporation, and the sale is to transfer all of the assets of the seller, the gross assets amount will exceed one billion yen; or

(ii) if the seller is a domestic corporation, and the sale is intended to transfer part of the seller's assets, the annual sales in connection with the portion of sale will exceed one billion yen; or

(iii) if the seller is a foreign corporation, the annual domestic sales in connection with the target assets will exceed one billion yen.

If this filing is required, the parties may not transfer the assets for 30 days from the filing. However, the JFTC may shorten this 30-day waiting period if the acquirer shows that the asset transfer does not create any anti-trust issues.

The JFTC may review the transfer (to determine whether it would cause a substantial restraint in a relevant market) by requiring the parties to file detailed report. The investigation period shall occur within the later of 120 days after the filing or 90 days after the JFTC receives additional information (if applicable).

6. Purchase Price Requirements

Under the general principles of freedom of contract, there are no such distinctions or special rules regarding the purchase price. Thus, the parties may freely agree on the amount, currency, and allocation to groups of assets or individual assets. However, if the allocation or valuation of an asset is "outrageous," a gift tax could be imposed under the Corporation Tax Law.

B. Tangible/Movable Assets

1. Characteristics as to:

a) Language of Documentation. There is no rule on the language of documentation. It is common to see asset purchase agreements written in English or in both English and Japanese, especially when one of the parties is an international company.

However, under Japan Court Rules, all court proceedings must be conducted in Japanese; thus, if an agreement that was written and executed in a foreign language is litigated, a Japanese translation must be procured by the party wanting to enforce the agreement.

b) Form of Documentation. Even though Japan has a notarization system where contents and signatures of an agreement may be notarized, it is rarely used for an asset purchase agreement. Thus, such an agreement is usually executed through signing or affixing a certified corporate seal by the company's representative. Further, there is no requirement that an agreement must be signed in Japan, and each party may sign a separate document (signing in counterparts).

c) Specification of Assets. In Japan, there is no requirement that each asset be specified. Therefore, even an agreement that states that "all assets and liabilities of Company A shall be transferred for the consideration of X yen" is valid.

However, unless the parties have no time to do so, they usually make some effort to specify the scope of assets in order to avoid future disputes.

Attaching schedules or lists of assets is preferable, but not mandatory.

2. Administrative, Corporate and Other Approvals

No governmental or administrative approvals are required for the transfer of tangible assets except as the law prohibits or highly restricts their transfer (e.g., drug, narcotic, guns, and counterfeit), the transaction itself is prohibited or restricted by regulatory laws or antitrust laws.

If the seller is a KK, it must obtain a special resolution of the shareholders adopted at a general shareholders meeting at which there is a quorum (the attendance of shareholders who have a majority of all the outstanding voting shares). The approval of two thirds of attending shareholders is required if all of the following conditions are present (Article 467 of the Company Law):

(i) the target assets constitute a business. According to a case decided by the Supreme Court on September 11, 1986, the target assets are "assets organized for a certain business and organically working as a whole.". This means that a mere aggregate of individual assets (such as personal computers in a warehouse X) do not constitute a business;

(ii) the target assets are "material." This is interpreted to be more than ten percent of all the business of the seller judging from major factors such as sales, profits and the number of employees; and

(iii) the target assets consist of more than 20% of all the gross assets of the seller.

For the purchaser, if it is a KK and the following conditions are present, it must obtain the approval of a special resolution as described above:

(i) the target assets constitute a business as described above;

(ii) the target assets constitute all or substantially all of the assets of the seller; and

(iii) the consideration to be paid is more than 20% of the total net asset of the purchaser.

In addition, regardless of the fulfillment of such requirements, if the transaction is reasonably considered "material" and the seller or purchaser corporation has a board of directors, it must obtain the approval of the board of directors (Article 362 of the Company Law).

Such special resolutions at shareholders meetings are not required with respect to the seller or purchaser as long as the seller or purchaser holds 90% or more of all the outstanding voting shares in the other party (Article 468 of the Company Law)

No approval of security holders is required for the transfer of title as long as the purchaser accepts the encumbrance as it is. If the security holder and the seller have agreed that the transfer of title on the encumbered asset requires the consent of the security holder, although non-compliance with this requirement will technically constitute a breach of contract, it will not result in the invalidity of the transfer itself.

3. Filing Requirements

No filings for the transfer of tangible assets are required except for special products such as weapons, drugs, airplanes, ships and automobiles.

4. Automatic Transfer of Encumbrances

Encumbrances such as mortgages and pledges will be automatically transferred to the purchaser of the title. One exception is a lien over tangible assets, which is established by operation of law (e.g., a lien on the employer's assets is automatically granted to employees to secure up to six months salary.) This lien is extinguished if the assets subject to the lien are transferred.

C. Real Property

1. Characteristics as to:

a) Language of Documentation. There is no requirement that an asset purchase agreement be executed in English or in both Japanese and English. However, in order to register the transaction with the Legal Affairs Bureau so that the purchaser will be able to exercise its rights against third parties, the parties have to prepare and submit an application for real estate registration in accordance with the Real Estate Registration Law. The application, which may be submitted in hard copy or electronic form, contains information that must be written in Japanese or bilingually, that is, both in Japanese and English. The agreement of sale itself does not have to be attached to the application for registration.

b) Form of Documentation. As noted above, an asset purchase agreement itself does not have to be submitted to the Legal Affairs Bureau for registration. Therefore, the formality of the agreement itself is not regulated at all. However, as stated in B, 1, a above, an application for the registration of real property must be prepared and submitted by the seller in accordance with the Real Estate Registration Law. In general, such applications must be prepared and submitted by both parties, who must execute the same application sheet by affixing their seals on the same document.

c) Specification of Assets. As long as the parties are able to identify which real property is going to be transferred, it is not necessary to describe the real property in detail. In most cases, the parties identify and specify the real property to be transferred by describing the following items:

For land: the address, location number, type of land (e.g., land for housing,), and area (square meters); and

For building: the location, structure (e.g., two-story steel-frame concrete structure), floor area (in square meters) and house number.

2. Administrative, Corporate and Other Approvals

Real property in Japan is generally transferable without any governmental or administrative approvals; however, if the property is designated as farm land, the transfer needs to be approved by a competent Agriculture Committee, and if the purchaser intends to use the farm land for other purposes, the approval of the governor of the prefecture in which the real property is located is required.

If the seller is a KK and the real property to be transferred is one of the important assets of the seller, taking into account the value and function of the property and the size of the company, it must obtain the approval of (i) the board of directors (if the KK has a board of directors) or (ii) the majority of the shareholders in a shareholders meeting (if the KK does not have a board of directors). Further, if the transfer is part of the transfer of its business, a special resolution of a general shareholders meeting will be required if the conditions mentioned above are present.

No approval of security holders is required for the transfer of title as long as the purchaser accepts the encumbrance "as is". The most typical security on real property are mortgages, which appear on most real estate titles in Japan. Thus, before purchasing real estate, purchasers have to confirm the existence of a mortgage by examining the real estate registration, which is available at the LAB having jurisdiction over the property.

3. Filing Requirements

Japan has a Real Estate Registration System in which a seller and a purchaser must submit an application for registration of the transaction to a local Legal Affairs Bureau so that the purchaser may exercise its right to the property with respect to any third parties. The Real Estate Registration System is based on "race statute," which means that whoever records first "wins" (Article 177 of the Civil Code). For example, if the seller that has sold the property to the first purchaser (the **"First Purchaser"**) then sells the same real estate to another purchaser (the **"Second Purchaser"**) and it has completed the registration before the registration by the First Purchaser, the Second Purchaser will be the party that has the title (unless the Second Purchaser had a malicious intent to harm the First Purchaser; simple acknowledgement by the Second Purchaser that the real estate has been sold to the First Purchaser does not disqualify the Second Purchaser's priority based on its registration). Under this registration system, a potential purchaser may confirm that the target real estate has not yet been sold to a third party based solely on the Real Estate Registration. Therefore, it is critical for parties to a real estate transaction to complete a Real Estate Registration as soon as possible.

Records of Real Estate Registration are available for inspection by any person at the competent Local LAB.

4. Automatic Transfer of Encumbrances

If the real property is subject to encumbrances (typically, mortgages), such encumbrances automatically transfer to the purchaser. There is no mandatory form for the waiver of encumbrances, and even an oral statement of waiver is valid. However, as to encumbrances that have been registered with the Real Estate Registration, the purchaser must ask the beneficiary of the encumbrances to submit an application to the competent LAB in order to eliminate the encumbrance records on the Registration. Otherwise, to eliminate the mortgage record at the LAB the purchaser will have to seek declaratory judgment.

5. Automatic Transfer of Lease Agreements

If the lessee already occupies the premise, it may insist its lease right against any third party, including the current owner and any new owner. Therefore, if the real property is transferred, the purchaser will have to respect the lease right and may not terminate it unilaterally. From the lessee's perspective, the lessee may not terminate the lease by claiming that the property has been transferred without its consent, because such transfer will not adversely affect the lease.

D. Contracts

1. Regarding the transfer of contracts, are there any characteristics as to:

a) Language of Documentation. There is no regulation regarding the language of documentation. Thus, documentation may be drafted in English, another language or bilingually.

b) Form of Documentation. There are no rules regarding documentation. The documents can be executed outside Japan, and may be signed on the same or separate documents (signing in counterparts).

c) Specification of Contracts. Either a general description or a generic description is sufficient; however, parties usually specify at least the material contracts by attaching a list of contracts to the asset transfer agreement.

2. Administrative, Corporate and Other Approvals

No governmental approvals are required. If the contract is "material" to the seller or purchaser, it must obtain a resolution of the board of directors and the shareholders meeting with a simple majority. If the asset transaction as a whole meets the conditions stated in B, 2 above, a special resolution of the shareholders in a shareholders meeting is required.

Contracts usually consist of rights and obligations. The transfer of "rights" generally does not require the approval of the other parties to the contract (one of the exceptions is a lease agreement where the transfer of the right to use the property must be approved prior the transfer). However, the transfer of "obligations" does require the approval of the other parties. If such approval is not obtained, the other parties may terminate the contract itself and/or claim that the transfer is void.

3. Automatic Transfer of Contracts (Other than Lease and Employment Agreements)

As a general rule, contracts are not transferred automatically to the purchaser in the event of an asset deal. The parties must agree on the transfer of contracts.

4. Filing Requirements

There are no filing or registration requirements with respect to the transfer of contracts.

5. Treatment of Existing Contractual Claims and Obligations

If the purchaser announces that it has assumed the business, including the contracts from the seller, the other party to the contract may require the purchaser to perform the unfulfilled obligations thereunder. It is customary to include indemnifications or limitations on such assumptions of obligations in the asset sale/transfer agreement so that the purchaser's obligations will be controllable and manageable.

6. Warranty Claims Resulting from Events prior to Transfer

If the purchaser announces that it has assumed the business, including the contracts from the seller, it will be liable for warranty claims resulting from events prior to the transfer of the assets affected. It is customary to include special provisions (typically, indemnification) in the asset sale/transfer agreement.

E. IP Rights

1. Characteristics of Intellectual Property Rights (e.g., Trademarks, Patents, Utility Models, Domain Names) ("*IP Rights*") as to:

a) Language of Documentation. There is no regulation regarding the language of documentation. Thus, the documentation may be drafted in English, any another language or bilingually.

b) Form of Documentation. There are no rules regarding the form of documentation. The documents can be executed outside Japan, and may be signed on the same or separate documents (signing in counterparts).

c) Specification of IP Rights. A general description is sufficient; however, parties usually specify the IP Rights to be transferred by attaching a list to the asset transfer agreement.

2. Administrative, Corporate and Other Approvals

No governmental approvals are required.

If the sale of IP Rights is a material activity for the seller or the purchaser, it must obtain an approval of (i) the board of directors (if the KK has a board of directors) or (ii) the shareholders in a shareholders meeting with a simple majority (if the KK does not have a board of directors). If the asset transfer including the sale of the IP Rights constitutes the transfer of the business as discussed in B, 2 above, a special resolution of the shareholders meeting will be required.

The approval of security holders is not required, as long as the purchaser accepts the encumbrances on its IP Rights.

3. Filing Requirements

There are registration systems and databases at the Japan Patent Office and the Agency of Cultural Affairs where IP Rights such as patents, trademarks and copyrights are registered. While the registration of the transfer of patents and trademarks is required to effectuate the transfer, transfer registration is not a requirement for the transfer of copyrights. For the first acquirer to exercise its right against third parties, registration is necessary only where the same registered copyright is sold to two or more persons.

4. Applicable International (Multilateral) Agreements or Treaties

Japan became a signatory to the Paris Convention in 1899, the Nice Agreement in 1990, the TRIPS in 1996, the Trademark Law Treaty in 1997, and the Madrid Protocol in 2000.

F. Receivables

1. Characteristics as to:

a) Language of Documentation. There is no regulation regarding the language of documentation. Such documents may be drafted in English, Japanese or other languages, or even bilingually.

b) Form of Documentation. There are no rules regarding documentation. Thus, the documents can be executed outside Japan, and may be signed on the same document or on a separate document (signing in counterparts).

c) Specification of Receivables. A general description is sufficient. Schedules/lists of receivables do not have to be attached to the transfer agreement.

2. Administrative, Corporate and Other Approvals

There is no requirement for governmental approvals, however, no one except for lawyers licensed in Japan and servicers who have acquired an approval by the Minister of Justice may engage in the business of collecting receivables purchased or entrusted from a third party.

If the sale is a material activity for the seller or purchaser, it must obtain an approval of the board of directors (if the KK has a board of directors) or the shareholders in a shareholders meeting (if the KK does not have a board of directors) with a simple majority. If the asset transfer transaction itself constitutes the transfer of business referred to in B, 2 above, a special resolution of the shareholders meeting will be required.

In general, approval of debtors is not required unless there is an agreement between the seller and the debtors that the transfer is subject to the consent of the debtors. However, unless the purchaser knows the existence of such agreement or its failure to know of it constitutes gross negligence, the transfer itself will be valid (Article 466, paragraph 2 of the Civil Code).

3. Filing Requirements

Under Article 467, paragraph 1 of the Civil Code, in order to transfer receivables in a debtor-creditor legal relationship, the original creditor (i.e., the seller) must give notice of the transfer to the debtor or have the debtor send the seller or purchaser acknowledgement of the transfer. Otherwise, the debtor may refuse the purchaser's request to pay the receivables.

Further, under Article 467, paragraph 2 the Civil Code, in the event that the seller would double-sell the receivables to third parties, the purchaser may secure its receivables against any third parties by having the seller give the debtor notice with "date certification" (including a notice letter by way of content-certified mail or notarization). The priority between the purchaser and any other third parties will be determined by which notice has been served first (not by the dates certified by such "date certifications"). However, this method of securing receivables against any other third parties is used only for bankruptcy-related transactions where the near-insolvent seller may double-sell its receivables to third parties. In ordinary transactions, the parties tend to avoid this, as debtors who would receive notice may misinterpret the notice as a sign of insolvency.

This notice with "date certification" may be replaced with a commercial registration under the Law of Special Treatment on Assertion of Movables and Receivables Transfer (No. 104, June 12, 1998) where the seller may register the transfer of receivables at the Legal Affairs Bureau having jurisdiction. Under this system, the seller does not have to give notice to the debtors, and the purchasers may do so when they would like to exercise their claims against the debtors. The priority with respect to any other third parties will be determined by the date of such commercial registration (not the date of notice). However, this registration is designed mainly for finance schemes in which creditors such as banks would want to secure their claims by establishing collaterals on borrower's receivables without giving notice to borrower's debtors (as such notice might make debtors mistake the borrower as insolvent). Thus, this system is rarely used in a typical M&A transaction between corporate entities.

G. Liabilities

1. Characteristics as to:

a) Language of Documentation. There are no rules regarding the language of documentation. Therefore, the documents may be drafted in Japanese, English or other languages, or bilingually.

b) Form of Documentation. There are no rules regarding the form of documentation, location for the execution, and how to sign them.

c) Specification of Liabilities. A generic description is sufficient to transfer liabilities as long as the seller obtains consents of the creditors. The purchaser is interested in limiting and defining the scope of liabilities to be transferred and tries to minimize the risk of acceptance of hidden or incidental liabilities. Thus, the purchaser usually asks the seller to identify the quantity and nature of liabilities by attaching a list of liabilities, and to indemnity the purchaser from any hidden/incidental liabilities.

2. Administrative, Corporate and Other Approvals

Generally, neither governmental nor administrative approval for the transfer of liabilities is required. However, in some highly regulated areas such as banking, securities, agriculture, and public utility, certain governmental approvals are required for asset transfer.

If the seller is a KK and the sale of liabilities is a material transaction, it must obtain the approval of the board of directors (if the KK has a board of directors)or the shareholders in a shareholders meeting (if the KK does not have a board of directors) with a simple majority vote. Further, if the assets transferred fall within the scope of B, 2 above above, a special resolution at the shareholders meeting is required.

The transfer of liabilities requires the consent of individual creditors. However, in practice, as it is difficult to obtain all the written consents of the creditors, parties to the asset transfer usually obtain only consents of important creditors, such as banks, major customers and suppliers. Other creditors are sent notification letters to inform them of the asset transfer. If such minor creditors do not object for a certain period of time, the parties will deem the non-objection as de-facto consent, even though such de-facto consents are not so clear from a legal perspective.

If the transfer is made without consents of creditors, the transfer of liabilities without consent will be invalid as far as the legal relationship between the debtor and creditor is concerned; thus, the creditors may claim and exercise their rights against the original debtor (i.e., the seller) before they accept the performance of obligation by the new debtor (i.e., the purchaser).

3. Filing Requirements

Neither filing/registration nor notification to the creditors is required regarding the transfer of liabilities in general.

An exception is found in Article 17 of the Commercial Code that provides that (i) a merchant purchaser who has purchased a business and continued to use the seller's trade name shall be responsible for all the debts accrued in connection with the business before the sale, but (ii) if the purchaser registers with the competent LAB immediately after the sale, providing that it will not assume such liabilities, it will not be responsible for such liabilities.

4. Purchaser's Liability for:

a) Tax Obligations. In general, no tax liabilities will be transferred to the purchaser unless the seller has tax liabilities that have already become due, and the purchaser is a family-owned company of the seller or has obtained assets from the seller for free or at an unreasonably low price.

b) Environmental Contamination. Under Article 7, paragraph 1 of the Soil Pollution Act, a governor of a prefecture may require an owner, occupier or administrator of a land that is designated by the governor to clean up the contamination. Thus, even if the previous owners contaminated the land, the current owner must clean the land at its own cost.

c) Products Sold or Services Rendered by the Seller to Third Parties. If the asset purchase agreement does not explicitly exclude such product/service liabilities to third parties, it is highly likely that such liabilities will be transferred to the purchaser. Therefore, it is imperative that the purchaser exclude or limit the assumption of liabilities.

5. Automatic Transfer of Other Liabilities

There is no automatic transfer of other liabilities; provided, however, that a merchant purchaser who has purchased a business and continued to use the seller's trade name shall be responsible for all the debts accrued in connection with the business before the sale (see G, 3 above).

6. Contractual Protection as to 4 and 5 above

Most asset purchase agreements between companies include special provisions of indemnifications regarding tax, environment and product liability exposures.

H. Employees

1. Transfer of Employees

No employees will automatically be transferred due to the asset transfer. Thus, parties that wish to transfer the relevant employees must explicitly agree to the transfer in the asset purchase agreement. In most cases, a list of employees to be transferred is attached to the agreement. Further, to transfer employees, consents from such individual employees are required.

2. Approval of Works Council, Trade Union and Other Institutions

No approval of the works council, trade union or similar institution is required unless the employer has agreed with a labor union in writing that the transfer of employees must not be done without the union's consent.

3. Contractual Protection as to Labor Issues

It is customary to include indemnifications in which the seller shall indemnify the purchaser from any labor-related liabilities (such as unpaid salaries, including overtime or pension fund liabilities).

I. Tax Implications

1. Value Added Tax

Consumption tax (similar to VAT) will be imposed at a 5% rate on the transfer of taxable assets such as inventories and fixed assets (both tangible and intangible) except real estate and goodwill.

2. Real Property Transfer Tax

Real property acquisition tax is imposed on the purchaser, which is assessed on acquisitions on land and buildings at the rate of 3% of the property value that the government announces annually (not the transaction price). Further, to register the transaction at a local LAB, 2% of the value announced by the government must be paid.

3. Other Tax Issues

An asset transfer is a cash transaction that is a taxable transaction for Japanese tax purposes. Gains from the sale of assets are taxable to the seller under the Corporation Tax Law. Correspondingly, any built-in gain in the transferred assets (in other words, booked value of the asset is less than the market value, which is usually the transfer price) will be recognized and taxed to the seller. If there is no built-in gain in the assets to be transferred, generally no undesirable tax consequences should arise.

Net loss carryovers and reserves, such as a retirement allowance reserve, held by the seller cannot be transferred to the purchaser.

If the purchaser pays less than the fair market value for the assets, it will incur a taxable gain. If a corporation transfers an asset for less than fair market value, the difference between the fair market value of the asset and the consideration may be deemed a donation from the transferor to the transferee. As a deduction for the donation is denied to the extent that it exceeds the statutory limitation covering all corporate donations and contributions, a purchaser will be deemed to have sold the assets at the fair value and recognized the amount of "donation" as gain. Accordingly, a purchase below fair market value creates a risk of double taxation.

J. Bankruptcy Law

1. Challenge of Asset Transfer in Case of Insolvency

The receiver or creditors may deny the asset transfer if it has unreasonably harmed the creditors' position. Typically, if the consideration for the assets is unreasonably low, the transfer will harm creditors of the seller. Even if the consideration itself is fair, the transaction will liquidate the assets to cash, which the debtor may conceal easily. Thus, if the purchaser knew the debtor's intent to hide the value of the assets, the transaction is deemed unfair regardless of the valuation of the assets. In addition, if the transfer is made to fulfill part of the creditors' rights to the seller as payment substitutes when the seller is insolvent or close to be insolvent, the transfer will be deemed to harm the equality of creditors.

Under such circumstances, the creditors (or after bankruptcy, the receiver) may deny the validity of the asset transfer and require the purchaser to return the assets.

2. Acquisition of Assets that are Subject to Insolvency Proceedings

If the seller is involved in formal bankruptcy proceedings (including reorganization proceedings), the receiver or debtor in possession must obtain an approval for the asset transfer from the court. In addition, under reorganization procedures, the receiver or debtor in possession must go through hearing procedures with the creditors and employees.

K. Timing and Costs

1. Timeframe of Asset Transfer

Excluding the period for negotiations for the letter of intent and the definitive agreement, the parties tend to agree on a one-month timeframe between the signing of the definitive agreement and the closing in order to complete the transition of assets and obtain some business licenses. However, if the business is highly restricted by regulatory laws (such as banking or securities business) or a special resolution of the shareholders meeting is required to be obtained for a party that is listed on a stock exchange, it is not uncommon that the parties will agree to a three- to six-month period between the signing and closing.

2. Costs of Asset Transfer

In Japan, the relevant costs for an asset transfer agreement are minimal as far as the target assets do not include real estate, the transfer of which would require payment of a registration fee as stated in I above. Notarization is not a requirement to effectuate the asset transfer agreement. The only regular cost associated with an asset transfer is a stamp duty for the asset agreement, which is progressive and assessed on the amount of the purchase price stated in the agreement. The maximum amount of stamp duties for an asset transfer agreement that creates a payment obligation of more than five billion yen (approximately USD 52,465,897 as of December 1, 2008) is 600,000 yen (approximately USD 6,295.90 as of December 1, 2008).

L. Miscellaneous

1. Choice of Foreign Law

Under Article 7 of the Law of Application of Laws (No. 78, 2006), it is permissible to agree that foreign law is the governing law of the sale and/or transfer agreement; however, Article 13 of the Law provides that actions in rem must be subject to the law of the location of the assets, and that in particular, an acquisition of the rights to assets in rem must be governed by the law of the location where the assets existed at the time when the cause of action (i.e., the sale) was completed.

2. (International) Arbitration, Choice of Venue

Arbitration is one of the dispute resolution alternatives available in Japan, since it is one of the signatories of New York Convention, in which the enforceability of arbitration judgment is secured among the signatory nations. There is no restriction on the choice of venues as long as the arbitration venue is held within the territory of a signatory nation.

In practice, Japan is not usually designated as a venue, and dispute resolutions in courts are preferred. Even Japan's largest arbitration organization, the Japan Commercial Arbitration Association, handles fewer than 20 cases annually.

3. Other Distinctions, Characteristics

There are no distinctions other than those outlined above.

M. Literature

Kenjiro Egashira, Laws of Stock Corporations, 2nd Edition, 2008

Takashi Uchida, Civil Law II, 2nd Edition, 2007

Katsuro Kanzaki, Kantaro Toyoizumi, Toshikazu Nakanishi and *Akinori Uesugi*, Asset Sales and Purchase Handbook, 2nd Edition, 1999

Latvia

By *Agris Repšs*, *Eva Berlaus-Gulbe*, *Lauma Bērziņa* and *Ūve Zosārs*

A. General Aspects

1. Asset Deal vs. Share Deal: Essential Considerations

Asset deals are typically favored over share deals because asset deals allow the purchaser to choose more freely what aspects of the business are acquired and what are not. In a share deal, in order to attain the same result, the transaction would require two steps – separation of the business to be acquired and then completing the purchase transaction. An asset deal reaches the same result in a single step.

However, in practice the transactions for a purchase of assets are more difficult to carry out, as one must carefully consider transferability of each and every asset in question. For example, sometimes asset deals are not possible due to regulatory issues. Usually various licenses and registrations are specific to the legal entity and are not transferable along with the assets. Also, sometimes asset deals are not possible due to requirements of third party consents. For example, it is not possible to transfer certain databases containing personal data without the consent of the subjects of the database. Further, due to the undeveloped legal framework, there are many unclear legal issues related to asset transfers that may complicate the transaction. For instance, although it is generally possible to re-register a mortgage registered in the Land Register in favor of the seller of the business in the name of the purchaser of the business without the consent of the debtor, only some of the Land Register judges recognize that the prohibition notes registered along with the mortgages (for example, a prohibition against selling the mortgaged property without the creditor's consent) can also be transferred in the same way.

If the assets consist of considerable amounts of real property or other similar registered property, the transaction costs can favor a share deal over an asset deal. Also, in such cases the structure of an asset deal would be more complex than a share deal. In practice, despite the advantages of asset deals, share deals are more common than asset deals.

A share deal raises no complex tax issues with the exception of a foreign shareholder selling shares in a company that is considered a real estate company because more than 50% of its assets are directly or indirectly comprised of real property located in Latvia. If the purchaser of the shares is a Latvian entity, a 2% Latvian withholding tax will be payable on the sale price of the shares. In these circumstances, the sale is considered to be the equivalent of the sale of real property located in Latvia, which is also subject to a

2% withholding tax. There is no Latvian tax applicable if the purchaser of the shares is not a Latvian resident.

Latvia's Corporate Income Tax ("**CIT**") and Value Added Tax ("**VAT**") laws provide that in the context of a defined reorganization, methods whereby assets are transferred in accordance with these methods, the transfers will be tax neutral for both CIT and VAT purposes.

Asset sales and transfer transactions outside the defined reorganization transactions can be subject to CIT and VAT liabilities.

If carry-forward tax losses exist, structuring a transaction by way of a share deal also allows for the existing carry-forward tax losses to be continued to be utilized after closing of the transaction. However, if a change in the control of the company occurs because of the share deal, existing carry-forward tax losses can only continue to be utilized if the company continues to operate for 5 years following the year control changed, the same principle business it operated during the 2 years prior to the year control changed.

2. Distinction between Sale and Transfer in Rem

Latvian law does not make a clear distinction between the sale of assets (i.e. obligation to transfer), on the one hand, and the transfer in rem (fulfillment of the obligation to transfer) on the other hand. The general rule of Latvian Civil Law is that the title to the asset under transfer passes to the purchaser upon payment of the purchase price, unless the agreement establishes otherwise. The parties are not obligated to conclude a separate transfer-acceptance deed. It should be noted that special regulations apply to the transfers of immovable property.

The parties are free to structure their transaction as they deem appropriate. As is often the case in cross-border acquisitions, the transfer of assets is covered by a single master purchase agreement while the assets can be transferred in the respective jurisdictions on the basis of local transfer agreements. The benefit of such an approach is that local transfer requirements can be fulfilled by the local transfer agreement without affecting the master purchase agreement, which would serve as a framework of the whole transaction.

3. Regional Differences

There are no regional differences as regards legal requirements in connection with the transfer of assets.

4. Acquisition by Foreigners

Under a general rule, equal business conditions should be guaranteed to domestic and foreign investors. The investor has the right to manage, use and dispose of the object of investment in compliance with the Latvian laws. Thus, generally, from the point of view of contract law, there are no distinctions with regard to the acquisition of assets by foreign persons. However, the laws may contain some restrictions concerning certain types of assets.

The restrictions regarding real estate acquisition in Latvia refer to land plot purchases. After the accession to the EU as of May 1, 2004, land plot acquisition in Latvia has become more liberalized for EU citizens and legal entities. Foreigners from non-EU states should consider that there are many restrictions to acquire land plots in Latvia.

The Latvian law does not impose any particular restrictions or obstacles on foreigners buying commercial property.

There are no restrictions imposed on the acquisition of real property by companies registered in the Register of Enterprises of the Republic of Latvia in the following cases:

If more than ½ of the company's share capital is owned by Latvian citizens, the state or a municipality; or

If more than ½ of the capital is owned by foreign natural persons or undertakings, and Latvia and the relevant foreign country have concluded agreements on mutual promotion and protection of investments (Latvia has signed such agreements with most European countries, Canada and the USA); or

If the company is a public limited liability company, the shares of which are listed on the Riga Stock Exchange.

If after the land acquisition, the shareholders' structure of an undertaking is changed so that it no longer corresponds to the requirements of the law, permission from the municipality must be obtained to retain the particular land in ownership. If the local municipality does not issue the permission, the land must be transferred to another person within two years.

Should the potential foreign purchasers fail to fulfill the criteria listed above, they must apply for permission from the local municipality that has the discretion to accept or reject such application. Permission is necessary, regardless of the size of the land plot to be purchased.

However, permission is required only for acquisition of land. Therefore, apartments or buildings may be acquired without further restrictions and limitations, unless the land beneath such apartments or buildings is included in the deal. In most cases an apartment ownership also comprises a certain ideal part of the land plot, the land plot being in the co-ownership of all apartment owners in the building.

Certain restrictions are applicable to foreigners if the land is located in the state border territories and preservation zones.

As of May 1, 2011 (expiry of transitional period), EU citizens and legal entities domiciled in EU Member States will be permitted to acquire land on the same conditions as citizens of Latvia. During the transitional period, EU citizens may only acquire agricultural land or forestry if they live in Latvia permanently and have owned agricultural land there within the last three years.

There are no restrictions on EU citizens and legal entities acquiring land plots in the cities of Latvia.

5. Public Registers, Records and Databases

In Latvia, there is no central institution that records all relevant information in connection with an asset transfer. The following publicly available databases allow access to the data, depending on the amount of information, either free of charge or for a fee.

Corporate details about the seller and the purchaser can be obtained from the public database of the Latvian Enterprise Register, which shows the basic details as to (i) legal form, (ii) powers of representation, (iii) registered share capital, (iv) shareholders of private limited liability companies (SIA), (v) certain corporate events such as mergers, capital increases, liquidations and insolvency procedures, (vi) commercial pledges, (vii) registration prohibitions imposed by the State Revenue Service, and (viii) financial statements submitted by the company to the Enterprise Register. All this is available via internet to any registered user (most of the information for a certain fee) (www.lursoft.lv).

Information as to real property, including ownership and encumbrances, can be obtained from the electronic database of the Land Book (www.zemesgramata.lv). The information is available to everyone.

Information on motor vehicles is recorded in the State Motor Vehicle and Drivers Register (maintained by the Road Traffic Safety Directorate, www.csdd.lv). All information on vehicles, with the exception of the data on natural persons owning the vehicle, are available via increased tariff phone or sms-numbers indicated on www.csdd.lv. The information is available to everyone. The same information is available via internet to any registered user (by fee) at www.lursoft.lv. This website also provides information on tractor machinery kept by the State Agency for Technical Surveillance in the Tractor register.

Information on vessels (except for vessels shorter than 12m in length that are not yachts or vessels used for business activities) and vessels under construction is included in the Ship Register maintained by Maritime Administration of Latvia. Information is available to everyone (for a fee) who submits an application to the Maritime Administration of Latvia.

Information on aircraft registered in Latvia is recorded in the Aircraft Register (maintained by the Civil Aviation Agency). The electronic version, which is updated once every month or two, can be found at the webpage of the Civil Aviation Agency (www.caa.lv). This information is available to everyone.

Information on domain names (.lv) can be obtained from www.nic.lv. This information is available to everyone.

6. Purchase Price Requirements

The parties are free in determining the purchase price, which can be stated in any currency and can also be paid by any third party (e.g., parent company).

The laws do not explicitly require indicating the price for each particular asset, however, in some cases, it might be required due to different tax implications or for determining notary's fees (in case of real property) and state duties.

If the parties are related parties for Latvian CIT purposes, the purchase price must comply with transfer pricing rules which set market or arms'-length prices.

B. Tangible/Movable Assets

1. Characteristics as to:

a) Language of Documentation. Generally, there are no language requirements for the transaction documentation. However, in case of vessels and certain other assets where a notarized transfer agreement is required, the language is restricted to what the notary accepts. Notaries rarely accept any language other than Latvian.

Any documents that must be submitted to authorities must be submitted with a Latvian translation.

Agreements can be concluded bilingually.

b) Form of Documentation. As a general rule, the transfer of tangible assets does not require any special form. Agreements may be made orally as well. However, a written memorialization of the parties' intention is needed in order for an agreement to be enforced in court. It is not possible for a court to enforce a claim based on an oral contract of sale.

There are no restrictions for executing written form or other agreements abroad.

It is permissible to sign the documents in counterparts; joint signing is not mandatory.

c) Specification of Assets. To avoid disputes, the description of assets should be such as to be clear to the parties. Language like "all assets related to the business", "all inventories located in ", etc. are often used and can be sufficient, depending on the circumstances.

It is often most practicable to attach a list of assets to the transaction, whereby the list does not have to specify every individual asset but can identify groups of assets.

2. Administrative, Corporate and Other Approvals

<u>Special Governmental or Administrative Approvals</u>

The transfer of tangible assets generally does not require special governmental or administrative approvals. However, exceptions may apply to specific categories of assets.

Generally, non-compliance with such requirements may lead to an invalidation of the transfer; however, this is analyzed on a case-by-case basis. In addition, the transfer may also require the consent of the antitrust authorities if the asset transaction qualifies as a merger subject to merger control.

Approval of Corporate Bodies Regarding the Seller and/or the Purchaser

In general, pursuant to the Latvian Commercial Law, the decision to sell certain assets or a business would be up to the management board. However, the articles of association of a company often prescribe that for concluding certain transactions, which may include, for example, any business transfers, the management board needs to obtain prior written consent by the supervisory board. Generally, such a limitation is only internally enforceable; i.e. if the management board concludes a business sale agreement without receiving consent of the supervisory board, the transaction would be binding on the company; however, the company would have a claim against the management board. Nevertheless, the validity of the transaction could be questioned if it is established that the purchaser was aware of the limitations provided in the articles of association of the selling company.

In addition, the Latvian Commercial Law provides for a possibility of extending competencies of the general meeting of shareholders of a private limited liability company (SIA). Thus, practically speaking, for some companies the decision regarding selling/acquiring a business or assets of certain value can be in the competence of the general meeting of shareholders.

Approval of Security Holders

The transfer of encumbered tangible assets, except for real property, requires the approval of the security holder. For more information on real property encumbrances, please refer to B,4 below.

3. Filing Requirements

No filings or entries into public registers or databases are required, unless assets are registered in a certain register (e.g., vehicles, vessels, immovable property).

4. Automatic Transfer of Encumbrances

Tangible assets owned by a company, except for real property and certain limited categories of movable assets (cash, financial instruments, and claims arising out of cheques and promissory notes (bills of exchange)), can be encumbered with a commercial pledge. As a general principle, such assets may not be alienated by the pledgor without the consent of the pledgee. If, however, such an asset is sold without the consent of the pledgee, then:

(i) provided that the purchaser knew that the asset was pledged and the consent of the pledgee had not been obtained, the pledge will continue to bind the purchaser;

(ii) provided that the asset sold was an asset subject to public registration (e.g. a vehicle), shares, certain types of bonds, or if the asset sold is evidently not the type of asset usually sold or produced by the seller, or if assets usually sold or produced by the seller are sold in unusually large quantities, the purchaser will be under obligation to check whether the asset is pledged, and provided that the asset was pledged and the consent of the pledgee had not been obtained, the pledge will continue to bind the purchaser;

(iii) in all other cases the purchaser will be deemed to be acting in good faith and the pledge will cease to cover the sold asset.

C. Real Property

1. Characteristics as to:

a) Language of Documentation. Private companies can execute documentation in a foreign language. However, the documents that have to be submitted to the state institutions, local governments, or to the judicial institutions of the Republic of Latvia should be drafted in Latvian or, alternatively, in a foreign language with a notarized translation into the Latvian language attached thereto.

Title to real property is transferable subject to registration with the Land Register. The Land Register is an institution belonging to the judicial system of the Republic of Latvia. Thus, the Land Register must have at least a translation of the purchase agreement in Latvian and one copy of the original agreement, with the exception of an application to the Land Register for registration of a title. The registration application shall be executed in Latvian and in the presence of a notary public in Latvia.

Documents may also be executed bilingually. In practice, the Land Register sometimes refuses to register title to an object if the prevailing language is not Latvian.

b) Form of Documentation. Transactions involving real property must be in writing to be binding. There are no requirements for notarization of the transaction documents, except for an application to the Land Register for a registration of a title. The registration application has to be signed by the seller and the purchaser in the presence of a notary public in Latvia.

Transaction documents can be executed outside Latvia with the exception of an application to the Land Register for registration of a title. This application shall be signed in the presence of the notary public in Latvia. It should be noted that although transaction documents may be executed outside Latvia, Latvian laws govern the real property transaction documents. The parties do not have the freedom to choose the applicable law should the transaction involve rights in rem to the real property in Latvia.

Joint signing is a common practice. Signing in counterparts is rarely used but not forbidden if executed in the form of an offer and acceptance.

c) Specification of Assets. The transfer requires a precise and detailed description of the real property. Most often, this description is limited to the address, reference to a cadastral number or compartment number in the Land Register, size of the land plot, the number of buildings on the land plot, number of floors, etc. Additionally, a plan of the real property might be attached to the agreement to establish proper understanding on the subject matter of the transaction between the parties.

In the event the subject matter of the transaction is parts of a real property or the real property is divided up into sections, the layout of the respective part of the real property must be enclosed to the agreement and submitted to the Land Book.

2. Administrative, Corporate and Other Approvals

Governmental or Administrative Approvals

The transfer of real property does not require special governmental or administrative approvals; however, it might be subject to pre-emption rights, certain restrictions and competition restraints.

(i) Pre-emption Rights

The local governments have pre-emption rights with respect to the acquisition of real property located in their territory, should the real property be sold, but not alienated in any other manner. Only after the local government has decided not to exercise its pre-emption rights may the purchase agreement be registered with the Land Register and the ownership transferred to the purchaser.

The state has pre-emption rights on the sale of cultural monuments of state importance and land plots in protected areas. Furthermore, there are pre-emption rights of legal entities upon the sale of the land in ports and special economic zones.

Should the building and the land plot have different owners, the owner of the building situated on the land plot to be sold has pre-emption rights with respect to the land plot and vice versa. Also, co-owners of real estate have pre-emption rights with respect to the ideal part (legal share) of the real property being sold.

Pre-emption rights may also be agreed upon between the parties, e.g., to a lease agreement and are in force based on their agreement.

Generally, pre-emption rights are exercised within two months after the purchase agreement is submitted to the persons entitled to such rights. The local government shall decide on using pre-emption rights within 20 days after the purchase agreement is submitted to it.

In case the person entitled to the pre-emption rights has not been notified of the transfer of real property, such person may claim the buy-out of the real property from the seller and the purchaser on the terms and conditions agreed upon between the seller and the purchaser.

(ii) Restrictions

As a result of the accession of Latvia to the EU, certain restrictions on acquisition of agricultural land plots are set up for EU citizens and legal entities. Restrictions are limited to the transitional period. The transitional period ends on May 1, 2011. There are no restrictions on EU citizens and legal entities acquiring land in the cities of Latvia.

There are many restrictions on acquiring land plots in Latvia for non-EU citizens.

Latvian law does not impose on foreigners any particular restrictions on the purchase commercial property.

(iii) Competition Restraints

The transfer of real property (most often properties in portfolio) can also be subject to prior approval by the Latvian Competition Council where:

Market participants are engaged or plan to be engaged in the economic activities in the territory of Latvia or their activities affect or may affect the competition within the territory of Latvia; and

The combined turnover of the market participants from the territory of Latvia during the previous financial year was at least LVL 25 million, except if the turnover of one of the market participants during the previous financial year on aggregate is LVL 1.5 million or less.

Please note that the sale of assets may also be subject to merger notification if the assets are deemed to be an enterprise (business unit) and the turnover in question can be attributed to such business unit.

The turnover comprises products sold and services provided by market participants to customers in the territory of Latvia during the last financial year.

The notification shall be made before the asset transfer is completed, i.e. after the signing of the agreement, since the agreement will have to be submitted to the Latvian Competition Council before the agreement enters into force.

Approval of Corporate Bodies

The Latvian law does not require the approval of corporate bodies for the transfer of real property. By-laws or shareholders' agreements, however, may establish certain restrictions.

Approval of Security Holders

In terms of the law, the transfer of encumbered real property does not require the approval of the security holder. The obligation to request the approval of the security holder may be established in the agreement between the owner and the security holder and be registered with the Land Register as a prohibition note. Typically, the prohibition note contains the prohibition on alienating, donating, dividing and encumbering the real property with rights in rem without a written consent of the security holder.

Encumbrances follow the real property and are binding upon the purchaser even if the real property is sold without the approval of the security holder.

3. Filing Requirements

The transfer of real property requires filings with the Land Book. After the title transfer, the new owner shall apply to the local government for real estate tax purposes.

Certain types of property are when purchased entitled to have a VAT deduction, the claim must be registered with the Latvian State Revenue Service.

4. Automatic Transfer of Encumbrances

In case the real property is subject to encumbrances, such encumbrances automatically follow the real property and are binding upon the purchaser. A waiver of encumbrances shall be executed in writing in the presence of a notary public in Latvia.

5. Automatic Transfer of Lease Agreements

According to the law, lease agreements automatically transfer to the purchaser in the event that they are registered with the Land Register. The new owner is bound by the lease agreement concluded by the former owner (seller). The purchaser may terminate the lease agreement pursuant to the terms and conditions of the inherited lease agreement and the rules of law. There are no extraordinary rights for the purchaser or the tenant to terminate the lease agreement because of the transfer.

If the lease agreement is not registered with the Land Register, the new owner is entitled to terminate the agreement, and the seller shall compensate for all loss the early termination has caused to the lessee. The new owner, on the other hand, shall grant the lessee sufficient time to vacate the real property.

D. Contracts

1. Characteristics as to:

a) Language of Documentation. The laws do not establish special language requirements for transfer of contract, and therefore general rules described in B, 1, a would apply.

b) Form of Documentation. There is no general form requirement. Specific form may be required depending on the type and form of the agreement transferred. For example, a transfer of notarized agreements may require a notarized agreement.

Unless notarization is required, the sale and transfer documents may be executed abroad. Signing in counterparts is permissible.

c) Specification of Contracts. The contracts have to be specified sufficiently. Schedules or lists of contracts are not required, but, might be advisable depending on the details of the transaction.

Please note that upon transfer of an enterprise (but not in a genuine piece-by-piece asset transfer) all rights and obligations attributable to the enterprise are deemed transferred automatically.

2. Administrative, Corporate and Other Approvals

Transfer of contracts does not require special governmental or administrative approvals.

As regards corporate approvals, the laws do not establish special requirements for transfer of contracts, therefore, general rules described in B, 2 above would apply.

Transfer of obligation generally requires the consent of the creditor, and often this is reinforced by contractual obligation.

3. Automatic Transfer of Contracts (Other than Lease and Employment Agreements)

Latvian law provides for the automatic transfer of asset-related insurance agreements. In case of the transfer of an enterprise (undertaking), employment contracts will be transferred automatically. Employees, however, may object to being transferred. In such a case they would remain with the previous employer, who most likely would have the grounds to terminate the employment depending on particular circumstances.

4. Filing Requirements

The transfer of contracts as such does not require special filings with public authorities or registrations in registers or (online) databases.

5. Treatment of Existing Contractual Claims and Obligations

If and to the extent the counterparty consents to the transfer of a contract, the respective claims and/or obligations from such contract do automatically transfer to the purchaser. Also, in case of transfer of a business enterprise, all rights and obligations attributable to the enterprise transfer automatically. Therefore, it is recommendable to include special provisions (e.g., indemnifications) into the transfer agreement.

6. Warranty Claims Resulting from Events prior to Transfer

Provided that the asset transfer constitutes the transfer of an enterprise and the warranty claims are attributable to the enterprise, the liability for the warranties transfers automatically to the purchaser (although the seller of the enterprise remains jointly and severally liable with the purchaser for five years). It is customary to address this issue by including respective indemnification clauses in an asset (contracts) transfer agreement.

If the asset transfer does not constitute a transfer of an enterprise, the liability for warranty claims does not transfer to the purchaser unless otherwise agreed and with the third party consenting to such transfer of liability.

E. IP Rights

1. Characteristics of Intellectual Property Rights (e. g., Trademarks, Patents, Utility Models, Domain Names) ("*IP Rights*") as to:

a) Language of Documentation. The laws do not establish special language requirements for the transfer of IP Rights, and, therefore, general rules described in B, 1, a would apply.

Please note that in the case of registered IP Rights, certain documents in the Latvian language are required for filing purposes, e. g., in order to register a transfer of rights with the Patent Office (which registers trademarks, patents, designs and topographies of semiconductor products).

b) Form of Documentation. Form requirements for documentation differ depending on the object of the transfer. The laws do not foresee special form requirements for a transfer of copyright, trademarks, designs and domain names. Agreements regarding the transfer of patents and topographies of semiconductor products have to be executed in a form that can be reproduced in writing. Nonetheless, since registration of the transfer is required, some written document will be needed with respect to the transfer of all kinds of objects of IP Rights.

The documents can be executed outside Latvia. Signing in counterparts is permissible.

c) Specification of IP Rights. IP Rights to be transferred should be described in a manner making it possible to identify which IP Rights were transferred. Depending on the circumstances, a general description of all IP Rights related to the business might be sufficient. However, in most cases identification of separate IP Rights or groups of IP Rights is advisable. The transfer of registered IP Rights generally requires that the IP Rights are identified individually in the transfer documents or separate documents are concluded for registering the changes.

A separate schedule or list of IP Rights is not required, but is often recommended.

2. Administrative, Corporate and Other Approvals

The transfer of IP Rights does not require special governmental or administrative approvals.

As regards corporate approvals, the laws do not establish special requirements for transfer of contracts, therefore, the general rules described in B, 2 above would apply.

If the IP Rights are encumbered, approval of the security holder is not required for the transfer. In case of pledges, if the right of ownership of the collateral is transferred, the right to the pledge remains due when the object of the pledge was transferred to the pledgee or when the pledge bond was registered in the respective IP register.

3. Filing Requirements

If and to the extent the IP Rights to be transferred are registered, the change of ownership requires registration with the relevant registers. In case of trademarks, patents, design and topographies of semiconductor products, the transfer of these objects becomes effective only upon and from the date of registration of the transfer with the respective register. Rights to the domain names are transferred when the technical transfer procedures with the domain name register are completed.

4. Applicable International (Multilateral) Agreements or Treaties

Latvia participates in the following treaties and agreements:

(i) WIPO Conventions:

- Patent Cooperation Treaty, Washington 1970
- Berne Convention for the Protection of Literary and Artistic Works
- Nice Agreement Concerning the International Classification of Goods and Services for the Purposes of the Registration of Marks
- Protocol Relating to the Madrid Agreement Concerning the International Registration of Marks
- Budapest Treaty on the International Recognition of the Deposit of Microorganisms for the Purposes of Patent Procedure
- Trademark Law Treaty
- World Intellectual Property Organization Performances and Phonograms Treaty
- World Intellectual Property Organization Copyright Treaty
- The Geneva Act (1999) of the Hague Agreement Concerning the International Registration of Industrial Designs

(ii) Conventions of the United Nations:

- International Convention for the Protection of Performers, Producers of Phonograms and Broadcasting Organizations
- Convention for the Protection of Producers of Phonograms Against Unauthorized Duplication of their Phonograms

(iii) Other:

- Convention on the Grant of European Patents (European Patent Convention)
- Trade-Related Aspects of Intellectual Property Rights (TRIPS)

- Treaties and agreements in which European Community participates are also relevant to Latvia

F. Receivables

1. Characteristics as to:

a) Language of Documentation. The laws do not establish special language requirements for transfer of receivables, and, therefore, the general rules described in B, 1, a above would apply.

b) Form of Documentation. There are no form requirements for the transfer of receivables. The sale and transfer documents may be executed outside Latvia. Signing in counterparts is permissible.

c) Specification of Receivables. Following the general rule described in B, 1, c, receivables have to be specified sufficiently. Schedules or lists of receivables are not required, however might be recommendable depending on the details of the transaction.

2. Administrative, Corporate and Other Approvals

The transfer of receivables does not require special governmental or administrative approvals.

As regards corporate approvals, the laws do not establish special requirements for the transfer of contracts, therefore, the general rules described in B, 2 above would apply.

The transfer of receivables does not require the prior consent of the debtor. It is possible to limit the right to transfer or assign rights from the agreement to third persons by agreement.

3. Filing Requirements

Transfer of receivables does not require filings with public authorities or registrations in public registers or databases.

The notification of the transfer to the debtors is not required but advisable. As long as the debtors are not aware of the transfer, payments on the receivables can still be made to the former owner of the receivables.

G. Liabilities

1. Characteristics as to:

a) Language of Documentation. The laws do not establish special language requirements for the transfer of liabilities, and, therefore, general rules described in B, 1, a would apply.

Bilingual documents are permitted.

b) Form of Documentation. There are no form requirements for the transfer of obligations. The sale and transfer documents may be executed outside Latvia. Signing in counterparts is permissible.

c) Specification of Liabilities. Following the general rule described in B, 1, c, liabilities have to be specified sufficiently. Schedules or lists of liabilities are not required, however, might be recommendable depending on the details of the transaction.

2. Administrative, Corporate and Other Approvals

The transfer of liabilities does not require special governmental or administrative approvals.

As regards corporate approvals, the laws do not establish special requirements for transfer of contracts, therefore, the general rules described in B, 2 above would apply.

The transfer of liabilities requires the prior consent of the creditor. If the consent of the creditor for the transfer of liabilities is not obtained, the transfer of liabilities is null and void.

An important exception to the requirement of creditor's consent is the transfer of liabilities in the case of a transfer of an enterprise. However, in such a case the original debtor remains jointly and severally liable with the new debtor for five years for any liabilities incurred prior to the transfer.

3. Filing Requirements

No filings with public authorities or registrations in public registers or databases are required to transfer liabilities.

Due to the fact that the transfer of liabilities is subject to the creditors' consent, a separate notification to the creditors is not necessary.

4. Purchaser's Liability for:

a) Tax Obligations. With regard to real property, the obligation to pay Real Estate Tax arises beginning one month after the new owner is registered as owner of the property.

With respect to assets that are transferred as part of a recognized reorganization, the question concerning tax liabilities is more complicated, as there are no clear guidelines from the law. We consider that in case of a transfer of an enterprise, the state tax authorities may consider the purchaser of the assets (business) liable for the periods prior to the transfer of assets (business). Each specific case will need to be examined and it is advisable to regulate any liability issues in asset (enterprise) purchase agreements by indemnifications or warranties.

b) Environmental Contamination. The general principle under Latvian law is that the polluter is liable for environmental contamination. In a transfer of an enterprise and provided that the polluting occurred in the course of the business of the enterprise, the obligations of the polluter would transfer to the purchaser of the assets, but the "original" polluter remains jointly and severally liable for five years after the transfer.

If the polluter cannot be determined or does not remediate the pollution, the owner of the assets is deemed liable for the pollution. Thus, also in the case of a piece-by-piece asset transfer, the purchaser may end up being liable for the seller's actions.

c) Products Sold or Services Rendered by the Seller to Third Parties. In case of a sale of an enterprise, all obligations of the enterprise with regard to products sold or services already rendered transfer to the purchaser, but the seller will remain jointly and severally liable to customers for five years.

5. Automatic Transfer of Other Liabilities

In the case of the acquisition of an enterprise, the purchaser will assume all the obligations attributable to the acquired assets (business).

In case of a genuine piece-by-piece asset transfer, the obligations of the seller transfer to the purchaser only in specified cases (for example certain lease of premises agreements as described above).

6. Contractual Protection as to 4 and 5 above

It is customary and advisable to include special provisions (e.g., indemnifications) as to the issues mentioned under G, 4 and 5 above into the asset transfer agreement.

H. Employees

1. Transfer of Employees

In case the asset transfer falls within the scope of a "transfer of undertaking" within the meaning of the Latvian Labor Law and Council Directive 2001/23/EC of March 12, 2001 on the approximation of the laws of the Member States relating to the safeguarding of employees' rights in the event of transfers of undertakings, businesses or parts of undertakings or businesses, the employees transfer automatically to the purchaser. The seller or the purchaser who, due to the transfer, is planning on performing organizational, technological or sociological activities with respect to the employees has an obligation to commence consulting with representatives of its employees no later than three weeks prior to that, in order to reach an agreement on such activities. Both, the seller and the purchaser of the enterprise must notify the employees in question at least one month in advance. The transfer does not change any of the employment terms nor grant any additional rights to terminate the agreements. Unless agreed otherwise between the employee and the new employer, the employment with the purchaser of the enterprise continues in the same manner as with the seller. For example, any unused vacation days and any employee benefits, if agreed in the employment contracts or otherwise, are also transferred to the purchaser. The employees are not entitled to any severance payments due to the transfer of an enterprise. However, the employees may refuse to be transferred to the purchaser, and in such case their employment continues with the seller. The refusal of the transfer to the purchaser may not serve as a ground for termination of the employment contract by the seller and the employee can be dismissed only on general grounds of dismissal provided by the Labor Law.

If the transfer of assets involves also transfer of employees, it is likely that such a transaction would be considered a transfer of undertaking within the meaning of Labor Law and the Directive 2001/23/EC. If, however, the assets are actually transferred piece-by-piece and the business does not continue on as a going concern, then it might be the case that the employees do not transfer automatically and transferring the employees would require separate agreements with each employee.

2. Approval of Works Council, Trade Union or Other Institutions

The asset transfer as such does not require any approval from works councils or other institutions. For information and consultative obligations if the asset transfer falls within the scope of "transfer of undertaking," please see J, 1 above.

3. Contractual Protection as to Labor Issues

It is customary to include guarantees and indemnifications regarding employees in the asset transfer agreement. In particular, the purchaser is often interested in guarantees stating that the seller has disclosed all employees eligible for automatic transfer and that all information regarding the employment legal relationship (most important, regarding all duties of the employer in relation to the employees) is completely disclosed.

I. Tax Implications

1. Value Added Tax

The general rate of Latvian VAT applicable to the sale of assets is 21%. However, where an entity subject to VAT as a result of a reorganization is divided or assets are transferred into a new entity, which within 30 days of its registration in the Latvian Commerce Register is registered with the Latvian State Revenue Service (**"SRS"**) as an entity subject to VAT, VAT will not be payable on the assets transferred. In these situations what must be transferred out to the new entity is a distinct and complete operational line of business. Stripping out selected assets to the new entity will not receive the favorable treatment.

Alternatively, where an entity subject to VAT is joined to another entity or two or more entities subject to VAT are merged and the resulting entity takes over all the rights and liabilities of the previous entities that were taken over or merged, VAT will not be payable on the assets transferred.

Asset transfers outside these situations will therefore generally be subject to Latvian VAT. However, there are many exceptions in the law regarding VAT, thus every single case should be analyzed on a separate basis.

Latvian law also has a requirement that "unused" immovable property acquired by the taxable person, as well as constructed, reconstructed, renovated or restored immovable property, should be registered with the SRS. When registering the property, the total amount of input VAT thus paid, is advised to the SRS taking into account the amount of taxable and non-taxable sales transactions for which the property will be used for. The allowable amount of input VAT claimed in the year of registration is then adjusted over the next ten years if the original percentage of taxable use changes.

If the property is sold within ten years of its registration, the taxable person should refund the State a certain amount of input VAT. It will be calculated by multiplying one-tenth of the deducted input VAT with the number of years that are left in the ten years. This refundable amount of input VAT has to be included in the cost-price of the immovable property.

2. Real Property Transfer Tax

When registering the acquisition of real property, a corporation must pay a transfer duty of 2% of the higher of the contract or cadastral value of the land, but no more than LVL 30,000.

The law also applies a transfer tax and treats a share sale as an asset sale regarding a transfer of shares in a 'real property company'. This will occur if shares held by a foreign entity are sold in a company that, in the year of the share sale or the prior year, directly or indirectly held assets that were real property located in Latvia and that comprised more than 50% of the assets held by the company. If these shares are sold to a Latvian purchaser they will be treated as the sale of real property and will be subject to a 2% withholding tax on the total sale price, which should be withheld by the purchaser and paid to the Latvian State. If a foreign entity sells shares in such a company to a non-resident of Latvia, the withholding tax does not apply and the sale is not subject to Latvian taxes.

3. Other Tax Issues

There are various aspects of the tax laws that should be taken into account when executing asset deals. We consider that the most important are those related to VAT and corporate profit taxation. As regards corporate profit taxation, which in Latvia is a flat rate of 15%, income received from the sale of assets by a Latvian company will be recognized as taxable. On the other hand, the purchaser of the assets (if it is a Latvian company) might be able to consider the acquisition costs as allowable deductions.

As a general rule any merger should be tax-neutral, i.e. should not create any adverse tax consequences for the parties involved. Where assets are transferred as part of a reorganization, the calculation of taxable income does not take into account the results of the revaluation of assets and liabilities transferred to the transferring, merging or dividing companies. In calculating the depreciation of fixed assets transferred as part of a reorganization, any revaluation shall not be taken into account (except the exceptional cases) in relation to the residual value of fixed assets, which the acquiring company has received in relation to the transfer, merger or division.

If a purchaser and seller of a business are "related parties" for Latvian corporate taxation purposes, the transfer values will have to accord with transfer pricing rules.

J. Bankruptcy Law

1. Challenge of Asset Transfer in Case of Insolvency

In the event the seller or the purchaser, following the asset transfer, becomes subject to insolvency proceedings, the receiver is entitled to claim the transfer to be declared void. The challenge of the transfer is subject to the following criteria:

The asset transfer is concluded after the insolvency occurred or in a one-month period before the insolvency and has caused loss to the legal entity in insolvency. In such cases, the other party is prevented from arguing that it was not aware of the fact that the transaction caused loss to the insolvent entity and the creditors; or

The asset transfer is concluded in the five years prior to the insolvency, it has caused loss to the legal entity under insolvency, and the other party to the transaction was aware or should have been aware of such loss.

2. Acquisition of Assets that are Subject to Insolvency Proceedings

The acquisition of assets subject to insolvency proceedings is organized pursuant to the procedure prescribed by the Insolvency Law. According to this law, the assets subject to the insolvency proceedings can be sold in public auctions or in any other manner, subject to the approval of the creditors' meeting.

The assets shall be appraised before they are placed up for auction. Auctions shall be announced in advance in the official gazette of the Republic of Latvia – *Latvijas Vestnesis*.

K. Timing and Costs

1. Timeframe of Asset Transfer

If the transfer of assets involves transfer of employees, then 30 days must be allowed for notifying the employees. Otherwise, the timeframe is determined by the practical aspects of the transactions, e.g., whether any third party consents must be received, whether any registrations in public registers are required, whether and when stock inventories can be conducted, etc.

2. Costs of Asset Transfer

As the transfer of assets typically does not require notarization or registration, there are no additional administrative costs. However, real estate and vessel transfers incur notary fees and state fees. Transfer of vehicles, trademarks, patents and some other IP Rights also incur state duties.

L. Miscellaneous

1. Choice of Foreign Law

The asset transfer agreement might be governed by foreign law. However, Latvian mandatory legal rules would apply in certain cases. For example, in case of immovable property, vessels and other assets, local law with respect to form, notarization, registration would apply.

2. (International) Arbitration, Choice of Venue

The parties to the asset transfer deal are free to agree upon international arbitration. There are no restrictions as to the venue of the arbitration.

3. Other Distinctions, Characteristics

The relevant legislation regulating asset transfer is heavily influenced by German law, thus the legislation is not particularly unusual.

M. Literature

Sorainen, Handbook of the Baltic Business Law, 4th Edition, 2004

Lithuania

By *Mantas Petkevičius* and *Laimonas Skibarka*

A. General Aspects

Under Lithuanian law, there are two types of transactions that could be regarded as asset deals: transfer of a business as a going concern (transfer of enterprise) and a piece-by-piece asset transfer.

A piece-by-piece asset transfer refers to one or a series of separate ordinary asset transactions under which particular assets (and liabilities) are transferred. Depending on the structure of the transaction, the parties may conclude one transfer agreement or several connected asset transfer agreements.

Transfer of a business as a going concern (transfer of enterprise) refers to the specific type of transactions regulated by a specific chapter of the Lithuanian Civil Code. Pursuant to the Civil Code, the acquisition of a business in the form of a transfer of an enterprise (transfer of business as a going concern) is a transaction whereby a seller undertakes to transfer into the ownership of a purchaser, as a complex of assets, the whole enterprise or a substantial part thereof.

It should be noted that effective legislation does not provide for clear guidelines as to whether an acquisition of all assets of a company or of a substantial part thereof could be performed in the a form of a piece-by-piece acquisition, or whether the procedure of a transfer of enterprise established in the Civil Code should always be followed in such case. This is open to varying interpretations, as a result.

Regulation of the sale of an enterprise is a relatively new and fragmentary concept in Lithuania and there is no reliable judicial practice. Due to this and the fact that the established procedure is rather burdensome, parties generally tend to perform piece-by-piece acquisitions even in cases where the transferred assets should be considered a substantial part of the company's business. It appears that the prevailing opinion among practitioners is that the transfer of an enterprise is not a mandatory transaction structure but rather a possible alternative to a piece-by-piece asset transfer.

This chapter focuses on piece-by-piece acquisitions unless specific reference to a transfer of enterprise (transfer of business as a going concern) is made. For more comments on the transfer of an enterprise please also see the last section of this chapter.

1. Asset Deal vs. Share Deal: Essential Considerations

There are various considerations that have to be taken into account when deciding whether the transaction should be structured as a share transfer or as an asset transfer. Some of the more significant among these are tax considerations, relative complexity of the deal structures, including procedural requirements, ability to transfer governmental licenses/permits and to "cherry-pick" the assets to be transferred.

Proceeds received from the sale of assets (in both piece-by-piece transfers and transfers of enterprises) of a Lithuanian company normally will be recognized as taxable income of that Lithuanian company and will be subject to Corporate Profit Tax. On the other hand, the purchaser of the assets might be able to consider the acquisition costs as allowable deductions. In addition, a transfer of assets will normally be subject to VAT. It is noteworthy that Lithuania does not recognize transfer of business as a VAT-exempt transaction. Therefore, the transfer of business will be subject to general VAT rules applicable to transfers of assets and, in order to determine whether the VAT is applicable, each category of assets under transfer should be analyzed separately. Tax laws do not contain clear directions regarding VAT application on certain categories of assets under transfer, e. g., on remuneration for the assignment of business claims or rights and benefits of the insurance contracts. Therefore, such uncertainty leads to increased taxation risks.

The sale of shares in a Lithuanian company would be exempt from taxation in Lithuania if the seller is not a Lithuanian tax resident. Certain tax exemptions are applicable if the seller of shares is a Lithuanian tax resident. In particular, the transaction will be exempt from Lithuanian Corporate Profit Tax where shares are held by the Lithuanian company, provided that the company has held more than 25% of shares for more than two years prior to the transaction. Further, transfer of shares is generally not subject to VAT in Lithuania.

Asset deals are usually more complex than share purchase deals. In principle, in a share transfer, the procedural requirements mainly relate to the exercise of the preemption rights of the company's shareholders (these usually apply in private companies, but not in public companies) and respective registration of the change of the shareholders. A share purchase agreement should be executed in writing, but notarization of the agreement is not required.

In a transfer of assets, general requirements of the Civil Code applicable to the form of particular agreements should be followed (e. g., with respect to the transfer of real estate, the agreement must be notarized). As to the procedure, the general requirements of the Civil Code are applicable as well, e. g., a party is generally entitled to transfer its obligations under a contract concluded with a third party only upon a prior written consent of that third party (i.e. as a general rule, a written consent of the counterparty to transfer a particular agreement would have to be received).

As regards the transfer of an enterprise, the agreement on the transfer of the enterprise should be verified and certified by a notary. In addition, extensive formal requirements, especially related to the protection of the creditors' rights (notification of the creditors, appointment of a third party (a bank, other credit institution or an insurance company) to settle with creditors, appointment of an independent auditor to evaluate the assets of the company), are applicable. Furthermore, as already mentioned above, the concept of a transfer of an enterprise is relatively new and fragmentary in Lithuania and there is no reliable court practice. All this makes the procedure rather complicated and burdensome as well as somewhat uncertain. Nevertheless one should not consider that transfer of an enterprise (transfer of business as a going concern) is not possible or does happen at all in practice. Further, while this is outside the scope of this questionnaire, worth to note that business as a going concern might also be transferred in the form of in-kind contribution to the share capital of a third party.

Another aspect that might be relevant in determining the structure of the transaction are governmental licenses/permits. As a general rule, change of shareholders of the company does not affect the licenses/permits held by that company. While in a transfer of assets (including the transfer of an enterprise) the licenses/permits can be transferred only in specific cases where this is provided for in the legislation or a license/permit itself (which is normally not the case), i.e. under general rule the licenses cannot be transferred.

On the other hand, in an asset transfer (particularly piece-by-piece), the purchaser may select or "cherry-pick" the assets to be transferred and acquire them separately from the other company's (seller's) liabilities (this would not be the case in case of a transfer of an enterprise, though it may also allow at least limited cherry-picking). Therefore, asset transfers may enable the purchaser to acquire the assets of a target company without the history and past or contingent liabilities related thereto.

In Lithuania the acquisition of a business by way of acquiring the shares of the entity operating that business is more common and generally more convenient than an asset acquisition.

2. Distinction between Sale and Transfer in Rem

Lithuanian law does not make clear the distinction between the sale of assets (i.e. obligation to transfer) on the one hand and the transfer in rem (fulfillment of the obligation to transfer) on the other hand. Pursuant to the Lithuanian Civil Code, as a general rule, the title to the asset under transfer passes to the purchaser from the moment of delivery of the asset to the purchaser, unless the agreement establishes otherwise. The parties are not obligated to conclude a separate transfer-acceptance deed. Note, however, that special regulations apply to the real property transfers (see C, 1, b below).

Nevertheless, in multinational acquisitions, it may be practical to cover the transfer of assets with a single master purchase agreement while the assets can be transferred in the respective jurisdictions on the basis of local transfer agreements. The benefit of such an approach, which is rather often used in practice, is that local transfer requirements can be fulfilled by the local transfer agreement without affecting the master purchase agreement, which can serve as a framework for the whole transaction.

3. Regional Differences

Taking into account that uniform rules apply to the transfer of assets throughout Lithuania, there are no regional differences. However, some practical differences may arise when dealing with local institutions in the course of the transaction (e. g., different municipalities may have slightly different practices as to required documentation for the issuance of new licenses that would be required for the purchaser after the completion of an asset deal).

4. Acquisition by Foreigners

Under a general rule, equal business conditions should be ensured to domestic and foreign investors. The investor has the right to manage, use and dispose of the object of investment in compliance with the Lithuanian laws. Thus, generally, there should be no distinction with regard to the acquisition of assets by foreign persons. However, the laws may provide for some specific regulation or restrictions concerning certain types of assets. Sale or acquisition of assets by a foreign entity may also produce different tax consequences (e.g., where a foreign entity sells a real property located in Lithuania, its income from such sale would be subject to withholding tax in Lithuania).

5. Public Registers, Records and Databases

The list below states the main public registers and databases that contain information that might be relevant in an asset transfer:

- the Commercial Register (Register of Legal Entities) contains information on the main data of the Lithuanian companies, including code, registered address, share capital, identity of members of the supervisory and management bodies, legal status (entries are made when bankruptcy proceedings are commenced, the company undergoes liquidation, reorganization or transformation) etc.; respective records are made in the Register of Legal Entities in case of an asset transfer. Franchise agreements are also registered with the Register of Legal Entities;
- the Real Estate Register contains information related to real property (including real property transfer, lease and other agreements related to real property, encumbrances, etc.); transfer of enterprise agreements should also be registered with the Real Estate Register;
- the Mortgage Register contains information on pledges and mortgages of the real property and other assets and rights;
- the Seizure Register contains information on seized (arrested) property;
- the database of the State Personal Data Inspectorate contains information related to processing of the personal data (e.g., companies entitled to process personal data are indicated with the register);
- the database of the State Patent Bureau contains information related to IP Rights (e.g., ownership to IP property, license agreements etc.);

- the Contract Register contains information on registered financial lease agreements, sale-purchase agreements with redemption rights etc.;
- the Register of Tax Payers contains information on tax payers, including their tax registration and VAT numbers.

Some other specialized online databases of the state institutions responsible for supervision of the licensed activities contain information on licenses granted to the companies.

The parties are free in determining the purchase price, which may be stated in every currency and be paid by any third party (e.g., parent company) on behalf of the purchaser. Pursuant to the effective legislation, in Lithuania payments in cash may be made in Litas and Euros only whereas payments made by means other than cash may also be made in any other foreign currency agreed by the parties.

The laws do not explicitly require indicating the price for each particular asset, however, in some cases, this might be required due to different tax implications. For example, some assets might be subject to VAT and some not, or the sale of different assets may trigger different capital gains. In such a case, in order to avoid negative tax implications or uncertainties, the parties should state the price for individual assets or groups of assets.

B. Tangible/Movable Assets

1. Characteristics as to:

a) Language of Documentation. Pursuant to the Lithuanian Law on State Language, all transactions between Lithuanian companies must be executed in the Lithuanian language. Translations into one or more other languages may be attached to the agreements. Further, the Law on State Language establishes that transactions with foreign persons must be executed in Lithuanian and another language acceptable to both parties (i.e. bilingual documents are allowed in such case and it is permissible to have a foreign language version prevail). Violations of the Law on State Language may result in minor administrative liability of the company's management; however, generally it does not affect the validity of the agreement.

It is not unusual for Lithuanian companies to disregard the said requirements of the Law on State Language and conclude agreements with foreign companies in foreign language only. We are not aware of any substantial penalties incurred by the companies for failure to comply with the requirements of the Law on State Language.

If the transaction documents would have to be submitted to state authorities (e.g., if transaction involves assets, rights or obligations that are subject to registration (e.g., vehicles, IP Rights, franchise contracts etc.) or state authorities (e.g., state tax authorities) require to present the documents in other cases, a Lithuanian translation would be required in any case.

b) Form of Documentation. As a general rule, transfer of tangible assets does not require any special form; agreements may be executed in oral form as well. However, written form is always recommendable for the sake of provability and certainty.

In certain cases, the laws may require executing the agreement in a certain form, e.g., preliminary agreements must be concluded in written form whereas pledge bonds must be notarized. Failure to comply with the established form requirements may cause invalidity of the agreement (in case of failure to comply with the notarization requirement) or restriction to use witnesses in order to prove execution of the agreement (where there is a failure to comply with the written form requirement).

Transaction documents may be executed outside Lithuania. Signing in counterparts is permissible.

c) Specification of Assets. Generally, the assets to be transferred should be specified in the transfer agreement in a manner such that any third party could identify the transferred assets from other non-transferred assets. The assets under transfer may be characterized both by individual characteristics or by their kind (generic description). The assets to be transferred are deemed to have been agreed on by the parties in case the contract allows determining the name and quantity of the assets to be transferred. In order to comply with such criteria, the use of asset lists (or schedules) is recommendable, but generally not mandatory. However, a list (inventory) of assets transferred through a transfer of enterprise transaction has to be attached as a schedule to the enterprise transfer agreement.

The laws do not provide for clear guidelines as to whether the reference to a particular location or business is sufficient. Such a reference may not be sufficient if it is not possible to identify name and quantity of the transferred assets from their definition in the agreement. Therefore, the use of asset lists (or schedules) is recommended for practical reasons.

2. Administrative, Corporate and Other Approvals

The transfer of tangible assets generally does not require special governmental or administrative approvals. However, exceptions may apply to specific categories of assets, such as, poisonous or dangerous substances. Generally, non-compliance with such requirements may invalidate the transfer; however, this is analyzed on a case-by-case basis.

Competence of corporate bodies of a company is established in the articles of association of the company and the Lithuanian Law on Companies. Under a general rule, the managing director of the company represents the company in relations with third parties as well as in court and arbitration proceedings. In the company's relations with third parties, the managing director acts at his own discretion on behalf of the company and is entitled to enter into transactions autonomously. In case a board is formed in the company (formation of a board is not mandatory), certain management decisions are allocated to the competence of the board. In particular, pursuant to the Law on Companies, the board must make decisions on sale or acquisition (as well as other decisions on disposal or encumbrance) of the long-term assets of the company, the value of which exceeds 1/20 of the company's share capital. However, the articles of association of the company may establish broader competence of the management board. Where a certain decision is allocated to the competence of the management board, the managing director may enter into a respective transaction only if the management board adopts a respective resolution or grants consent. It is noteworthy that the articles of association of the company may establish a joint representation rule, under which the company can be represented by a managing director jointly with other member(s) of the management bodies or procura holders.

Failure to comply with corporate governance rules does not render the transfer invalid and contracts concluded by the managing bodies of a company by exceeding their competence will nevertheless be binding for the company. However, this will not be the case if it is established that counterparties were aware or, due to certain circumstances may not have been unaware, of the fact that an unauthorized contract was concluded by the managing body of the company, i.e. where a counterparty was acting in bad faith. It is noteworthy that such a rule does not apply to the violation of the joint representation rule, i.e. the contracts concluded in violation of the joint representation rule will not bind the company provided that the joint representation rule is duly established in the articles of association and registered with the Register of Legal Entities.

Generally, a transfer of encumbered (pledged) assets does not require the approval of security holders. However, the standard pledge bond (deed) form (which must be used) contains a field that specifically requests whether the consent of the security holder is required for disposal of the asset. It is a standard practice in Lithuania to include provisions requiring such approvals into the pledge bonds.

If the encumbrances on assets have to be registered with the public register, only the registered encumbrances shall be transferred to the new owner together with the assets. In such case the security holder is entitled to satisfy its claim from pledged assets irrespective of the ownership towards the assets.

It must be noted that the Lithuanian legislation does not explicitly specify consequences of non-compliance with the requirement to obtain security holder's consent for transfer of assets where such consent is required. While it is not clear whether a failure to obtain consent may lead to invalidity of the transaction, we consider that it may trigger the right of the security holder to demand early execution of the secured obligation, and accordingly the satisfaction of the claim from the pledged asset that was transferred.

3. Filing Requirements

Under a general rule, no filings or entries in public registers or databases are required, unless assets are registered with a certain register (e.g., vehicles).

4. Automatic Transfer of Encumbrances

Generally, encumbrances on assets transfer to the new owner together with such assets. In case the encumbrances on assets are subject to mandatory registration, only duly registered encumbrances would normally transfer to the new owner.

C. Real Property

1. Characteristics as to:

a) Language of Documentation. The laws do not establish special language requirements for transfer of real property, and, therefore, general rules described in B, 1, a above would apply. Taking into account that the real property transactions are subject to verification of the notary public, usually they must be executed either in Lithuanian or, if agreements are bilingual, the Lithuanian language should be the prevailing language of the agreement.

b) Form of Documentation. Real property transfer (sale-purchase) agreements must be concluded in writing and be notarized. Failure to comply with the notarization requirement renders the agreement invalid. Real property sale-purchase agreements must be registered with the Real Estate Register. Only registered agreement might be invoked against third persons. Title to the real property passes to the purchaser from the moment of delivery of the real property to the purchaser, which is evidenced by conclusion of the transfer-acceptance deed. A real property transfer agreement may provide that it functions as a transfer-acceptance deed as well. The law does not require notarization of a transfer-acceptance deed if it is executed as a separate document.

Due to the fact that a real property sale-purchase agreement must be notarized, it may not be executed outside Lithuania. In addition, while it is not expressly provided for in the law, common practice dictates that Lithuanian notaries should not accept signing in counterparts.

c) Specification of Assets. The real estate sale-purchase agreement must contain a precise and detailed description of the property. The seller should also represent that there are no violations or restrictions of public law affecting the real property that may affect ownership rights. Further, layout of the real property (land plot or building) must be attached to the agreement and the exact location of the real property must be indicated in such a layout.

In practice, descriptions of real property are quite detailed. General references would not be sufficient.

2. Administrative, Corporate and Other Approvals

The transfer of real property generally does not require special governmental or administrative approvals. However, each particular transaction should be analyzed on a case-by-case basis, e.g., in case the property has historical or cultural value or falls in the influence zone of such territory (e.g., Vilnius old town). Prior inspection of the property by the municipality may be required.

As regards corporate approvals, the laws do not establish special requirements for transfer of real property. General rules described in B, 2 above would apply to the transfer of real property.

Under a general rule, in a transfer of encumbered (mortgaged) real property, approval of a security holder is not required. However, the standard mortgage bond form (which must be used) contains a field that specifically requests whether the consent of the security holder is required for disposal of the real property. It is a standard practice in Lithuania to include provisions requiring such approvals into the mortgage bonds. The notary should certify the real property transfer agreement and must check whether respective consents of security holders are duly obtained. If consent of the security holder is required for the transfer of the real property, the notary should not notarize the real property transfer agreement until such consent is obtained.

3. Filing Requirements

Title to real property must be registered with the Real Estate Register. The purchaser may not invoke a real property sale-purchase agreement against third parties in case it is not registered with the Real Estate Register.

4. Automatic Transfer of Encumbrances

Real property's encumbrances transfer to the new owner together with the real property. In case the encumbrances on real property are subject to mandatory registration, as a general rule only duly registered encumbrances would transfer to the new owner.

5. Automatic Transfer of Lease Agreements

In case of a transfer of title to the real property, all lease agreements executed by the former owner of the real property and registered with the Real Estate Register are automatically assigned to the new owner of the real property. It is noteworthy that only the registered lease agreements may be invoked by the tenants against the new owner of the property, i.e. lease agreements that are not registered with the Real Estate Register will not bind the new owner. On the other hand, tenants have a statutory right to terminate the lease agreement in case of a change of owner of the leased property.

D. Contracts

1. Characteristics as to:

a) Language of Documentation. The laws do not establish special language requirements for a transfer of contracts, and, therefore, the general rules described in B, 1, A above would apply.

b) Form of Documentation. Since Lithuanian laws do not provide for any specific rules regarding transfer of contracts, general rules would apply (see B, 1, b above). However, depending on the particular situation, certain form requirements may exist, e.g., the transferred contract may establish that any transfer thereof might be effectuated in writing only.

The sale and transfer documents may be executed outside Lithuania. Signing in counterparts is permissible.

c) Specification of Contracts. Following the general rule described in B, 1, c above, the contracts have to be specified sufficiently. Schedules or lists of contracts are not required but might be recommendable depending on the details of the transaction.

2. Administrative, Corporate and Other Approvals

Under a general rule, the transfer of contracts does not require special governmental or administrative approvals. However, special governmental or administrative approvals might be required depending on the circumstances of the transaction.

As regards corporate approvals, the laws do not establish special requirements for the transfer of contracts, therefore, the general rules described in B, 2 above would apply.

Under Lithuanian law, the transfer of contracts requires the prior consent of the counterparty, unless it is otherwise provided for in the contracts to be transferred. Non-compliance may invalidate the transfer. For certain types of contracts (e.g., certain types of insurance contracts) exceptions may apply.

3. Automatic Transfer of Contracts (Other than Lease and Employment Agreements)

Lithuanian law provides for the automatic transfer of asset-related insurance agreements, except where otherwise provided for in the insurance agreement (in practice, insurance agreements tend to limit automatic transfer or establish additional requirements).

Further, utilities contracts related to the transferred real estate do not transfer to the purchaser automatically. In practice, the transfer often takes place by virtue of actions; for example, the transfer might occur as the purchaser starts using the real property and pays for utility services, and the utility service provider starts issuing the invoices to the purchaser without signing a new contract.

4. Filing Requirements

Under a general rule, the transfer of contracts does not require special filings with public authorities or registrations with registers or (online) databases. However, filings with public authorities might be required in a particular transaction, e.g., special filings would be required in a transfer of the registered contracts. The list below states the most common types of contracts subject to registration with public authorities:

- real property transfer, lease and other agreements related to the real property are registered with the Real Estate Register;
- pledge/mortgage bonds are registered with the Mortgage Register;
- contracts related to the use of personal data are registered with the State Personal Data Inspectorate;
- franchise agreements are subject to registration with the Register of Legal Entities;
- contracts regarding certain IP Rights are registered with the State Patent Bureau;
- financial lease agreements, sale purchase agreements with redemption rights etc. are subject to registration with the Contract Register; etc.

5. Treatment of Existing Contractual Claims and Obligations

If and to the extent the counterparty consents to the transfer of a contract, the respective claims and/or obligations from such contract do automatically transfer to the purchaser. Therefore, it is customary to include special indemnifications in the contract transfer agreement in case it is agreed that the seller should take such a risk.

6. Warranty Claims Resulting from Events prior to Transfer

If and to the extent the counterparty consents to the transfer of a contract, the purchaser will be liable for respective warranty claims under the transferred contracts even where claims result from events prior to the transfer. It is customary to address this issue by including respective indemnification clauses in the asset (contracts) transfer agreement.

In a sale of the company as a business (to be effected by the agreement on transfer of enterprise), the purchaser will be similarly liable for respective warranty claims related to the transferred assets even if the claims results from events prior to the transfer of the assets (business). It is customary to address this issue by including respective indemnification clauses in business (contracts) transfer agreement also.

E. IP Rights

1. Characteristics of Intellectual Property Rights (e. g., Trademarks, Patents, Utility Models, Domain Names) ("*IP Rights*") as to:

a) Language of Documentation. The laws do not establish special language requirements for the transfer of IP Rights, and, therefore, the general rules described in B, 1, a above would apply.

Please note that in case of registered IP Rights, certain documents in Lithuanian are required for filing purposes, e.g., in order to register transfer of rights with the State Patent Bureau (which registers trademarks, patents, designs and topographies of semiconductor products); these documents must be submitted in Lithuanian.

b) Form of Documentation. Form requirements for documentation differ depending on the object of the transfer. The laws do not foresee special form requirements for transfer of trademarks, designs and domain names, therefore the general rules described in B, 1, b above would apply. Agreements regarding the transfer of copyright, patents and topographies of semiconductor products have to be executed in writing. Nonetheless, since registration of transfer is required, some written documents will be required with respect to transfer of all kinds of objects of IP Rights. In most cases, the following alternative documents may be submitted: the transfer agreement, a notarized extract from the transfer agreement, or a standard form of the State Patent Bureau on transfer of rights signed by the parties to the transaction.

The documents can be executed outside Lithuania. Signing in counterparts is permissible.

c) Specification of IP Rights. As described in B, 1, c above, the contracts have to be specified sufficiently enough. Identification of separate IP Rights is advisable for practical purposes, since the transfer would have to be registered with respect to individual objects of IP Rights. Moreover, in case of copyright, it is presumed that only those proprietary rights that are explicitly identified are transferred. For these reasons it is advisable to always include descriptions of each IP Right.

A separate schedule or list of IP Rights is not required but is advisable.

2. Administrative, Corporate and Other Approvals

Generally, the transfer of IP Rights does not require special governmental or administrative approvals. There may be specific exceptional cases where certain IP Rights are subject to a permit of state authorities that is issued personally to a specific entity; such cases would include transfer of trademarks containing a state symbol, flag or country name. The purchaser of such IP Rights would have to obtain a new permit.

As regards corporate approvals, the laws do not establish special requirements for the transfer of contracts, therefore, the general rules described in B, 2 above would apply.

If the IP Rights are encumbered, approval of the security holder is not required. In case of pledges, if the right to ownership of the collateral is transferred, the pledge remains due when the object of the pledge was transferred to the pledgee (beneficiary) or when the pledge bond was registered in the Register of Mortgages.

3. Filing Requirements

If and to the extent the IP Rights to be transferred are registered, the change of ownership requires registration with the relevant registers. In case of trademarks, patents, design and topographies of semiconductor products, the transfer of these objects becomes effective only upon and from the date of registration of the transfer with the State Patent Bureau. Rights to the domain names are transferred when the technical transfer procedures with the .lt domain name register are completed.

4. Applicable International (Multilateral) Agreements or Treaties

Lithuania participates in the following treaties and agreements:

WIPO Conventions:

- Patent Cooperation Treaty, Washington 1970
- Berne Convention for the Protection of Literary and Artistic Works
- Nice Agreement Concerning the International Classification of Goods and Services for the Purposes of the Registration of Marks
- Protocol Relating to the Madrid Agreement Concerning the International Registration of Marks
- Budapest Treaty on the International Recognition of the Deposit of Microorganisms for the Purposes of Patent Procedure
- Trademark Law Treaty
- World Intellectual Property Organization Performances and Phonograms Treaty
- World Intellectual Property Organization Copyright Treaty
- The Geneva Act (1999) of the Hague Agreement Concerning the International Registration of Industrial Designs

Conventions of the United Nations:

- International Convention for the Protection of Performers, Producers of Phonograms and Broadcasting Organizations
- Convention for the Protection of Producers of Phonograms Against Unauthorized Duplication of their Phonograms

Other:

- Convention on the Grant of European Patents (European Patent Convention)
- Trade-Related Aspects of Intellectual Property Rights (TRIPS)
- Treaties and agreements in which European Community participates are also relevant to Lithuania.

F. Receivables

1. Characteristics as to:

a) Language of Documentation. The laws do not establish special language requirements for the transfer of receivables, and, therefore, the general rules described in D, 1, a above would apply.

b) Form of Documentation. Since Lithuanian laws do not provide for any specific rules regarding transfer of receivables, the general rules would apply (see B 1, b above).

The sale and transfer documents may be executed outside Lithuania. Signing in counterparts is permissible.

c) Specification of Receivables. Following the general rule described in B, 1, c above, receivables have to be specified sufficiently. Schedules or lists of receivables are not required, however, might be recommendable depending on the details of the transaction.

2. Administrative, Corporate and Other Approvals

Under a general rule, the transfer of receivables does not require special governmental or administrative approvals. However, they might be required depending on the circumstances of the transaction.

As regards corporate approvals, the laws do not establish special requirements for the transfer of receivables, therefore, the general rules described in B, 2 above would apply.

Under Lithuanian law, the transfer of receivables does not require the prior consent of the debtor unless the creditor's person is of essential importance to the debtor. The assessment of whether the person of the creditor is of essential importance to the debtor should be made in each particular case individually.

3. Filing Requirements

Under a general rule, the transfer of receivables does not require filings with public authorities or registration in public registers or databases.

G. Liabilities

1. Characteristics as to:

a) Language of Documentation. The laws do not establish special language requirements for a transfer of liabilities, and, therefore, the general rules described in D, 1, a above would apply.

b) Form of Documentation. Since Lithuanian laws do not provide for any specific rules regarding the transfer of liabilities, the general rules would apply (see B 1, b above).

The sale and transfer documents may be executed outside Lithuania. Signing in counterparts is permissible.

c) Specification of Liabilities. Following the general rule described in D, 1, c above, liabilities have to be specified sufficiently. Schedules or lists of liabilities are not required, however, might be recommendable depending on the circumstances of the transaction.

2. Administrative, Corporate and Other Approvals

The transfer of liabilities basically does not require special governmental or administrative approvals. However, they might be required depending on the circumstances of the transaction.

As regards corporate approvals, the laws do not establish special requirements for the transfer of contracts, therefore, the general rules described in B, 2 above would apply.

Under Lithuanian law, as a general rule, the transfer of liabilities requires the prior consent of the creditor. When the consent of the creditor for the transfer of liabilities is not obtained, the transfer of liabilities is normally null and void.

3. Filing Requirements

Under a general rule, the transfer of liabilities does not require any filings with public authorities or registration in public registers or databases.

4. Purchaser's Liability for:

a) Tax Obligations. Under a general rule, all tax liabilities for the purchaser arise after the acquisition of the assets. For instance, the purchaser should not be liable for payment of the immovable property tax for periods prior to the acquisition of the immovable property, since under Lithuanian law the immovable property tax should be calculated as of the month when the title to the immovable property is acquired, the immovable property starts to be used for economic activities or is assumed by the company. Therefore, the seller of the assets should be liable for the tax obligations related to the periods prior to the transfer of the asset.

However, in a transfer of the enterprise, the question concerning tax liabilities is more complicated as there are no clear guidelines provided for in the Lithuanian law. We consider that in case of a transfer of an enterprise, state tax authorities may consider the purchaser of the assets (business) liable for the periods prior to the transfer of assets (business). It is recommendable to regulate liability issues in an asset (enterprise) purchase agreement through indemnifications.

b) Environmental Contamination. Pursuant to the general principle established in Lithuanian environmental regulations, the polluter should be liable for the environmental contamination. However, we consider that there is a risk that the state authorities may try to claim compensation or fines from the current owner of the asset, in particular in case the current owner was aware of the problem when it acquired the asset.

c) Products Sold or Services Rendered by the Seller to Third Parties. In case of a piece-by-piece acquisition of assets, the purchaser should acquire the asset free from liability towards third parties. However, in a transfer of contracts, the purchaser will be liable under the transferred contracts even in cases where claims result from events prior to the transfer.

In a sale of an enterprise the general rule is that the purchaser, due to the acquisition of enterprise, must also assume all rights and obligations related thereto. Therefore, the purchaser will assume all liabilities related to products sold or services rendered by the seller to third parties prior to the acquisition of the enterprise.

5. Automatic Transfer of Other Liabilities

As a general rule, acquisition of assets in piece-by-piece transactions should not result in the purchaser's liability towards third parties. However, each case should be analyzed separately.

In the acquisition of an enterprise, under the general rule, the purchaser will assume all the rights and obligations related to the acquired assets (business).

6. Contractual Protection as to 4 and 5 above

It is customary and recommendable to include special provisions (e. g., indemnifications) in the asset transfer agreement.

H. Employees

1. Transfer of Employees

The Acquired Rights Directive (Council Directive 2001/23/EC of March 12, 2001 on the approximation of the laws of the Member States relating to the safeguarding of employees' rights in the event of transfers of undertakings, businesses or parts of undertakings or businesses which codifies Council Directive 77/187/EC as amended by Council Directive 98/50/EC) has not been properly transposed into the Lithuanian law. Pursuant to Lithuanian labor laws there is no automatic transfer of employees in either a transfer of particular assets or a transfer of business (transfer of enterprise). The Lithuanian Labor Code only establishes that the transfer of a business may not be considered a legal ground for the termination of employment. However, pursuant to our understanding, the major aim of this clause is to establish an obligation for the seller not to dismiss the employees rather than for the purchaser to take over the employees.

In practice, the seller and the purchaser may (and often do) agree that the employees will be transferred to the seller upon transfer of assets/business. In such case the employers (seller and purchaser) should conclude an agreement on transfer of employees. The agreement on transfer of employees should discuss terms and conditions of the transfer of employees. Further, in practice, the employees are usually transferred by terminating their employment contracts with the seller and concluding new employment contracts with the purchaser. It is noteworthy that such transfer is possible only where the employee in question consents to his/her transfer.

There are no clear guidelines under Lithuanian law on whether the purchaser assumes the liability related to the employment relations related to the events occurred prior to the transfer of employees. According to our understanding, such a risk exists. Therefore, it is recommendable to regulate liability issues in the employees transfer agreement.

The employee transfer agreement should also discuss other terms and conditions of transfer of employees, e.g., parties may agree that the employees' length of service (and related rights) with the seller should be included in the calculation of the length of service with the purchaser.

It is noteworthy that the seller and the purchaser are prohibited from terminating employment of the employees due to a transfer of business; nonetheless, such prohibition may not prevent termination of employment on other grounds, e. g., due to structural changes of the seller.

The seller and the purchaser have an obligation to inform and consult with their employees on the issues related to the future activities of the seller of the purchaser, respectively, and possible changes in their employment structure. The order and conditions for providing the information and carrying the consultations should be established by laws, collective agreements and agreements between the employers and representatives of the employees.

Our understanding on the transfer of employees is based on current Lithuanian legislation and the fact that there is no court practice related to the rights of employees in a transfer of business; however, there is a risk that the court may interpret Lithuanian laws in the light of the Directive and decide that an automatic transfer of employees should occur.

2. Approval of Works Council, Trade Union or Other Institutions

As a general rule, an asset transfer does not require the approval of works councils or other institutions. Lithuanian laws establish certain consultation or notification requirements related to asset transfers that may affect the employees, including where the asset transfer leads to substantial redundancies that may be carried out because of the asset transfer.

3. Contractual Protection as to Labor Issues

It is customary and recommendable to regulate the seller's and purchaser's liability issues through the employee transfer agreement and, if necessary, to include respective indemnifications.

I. Tax Implications

1. Value Added Tax

In general, for VAT purposes the transfer of assets is treated as a supply of goods. Thus, if a transferor is a VAT payer, the assets are in the territory of Lithuania, and the transferee obtains the right to dispose of the assets as the owner, then the Lithuanian VAT of 19% (in July 2009, the Lithuanian Parliament decided to increase VAT rate to

21% as of September 1, 2009) shall be applied. The Law on VAT contains many exceptions as to the particular type of assets and, therefore, every single case should be analyzed separately.

Lithuania does not recognize a business transfer as a VAT-exempt transaction. Therefore, the transfer of business will be subject to general VAT rules applicable to an asset transfer. Consequently, in order to determine whether VAT is applicable, each category of assets under transfer should be analyzed separately. It is noteworthy that tax laws do not contain clear directions regarding VAT application on certain categories of assets, e. g., on remuneration for the assignment of business claims or rights and benefits of the insurance contracts. Such uncertainty leads to increased taxation risks.

2. Real Property Transfer Tax

There are no transfer taxes, including real property or land transfer tax, in Lithuania.

3. Other Tax Issues

There are various aspects of the tax laws that should be taken into account when executing asset deals. The most important are those related to VAT (see I, 1 above) and corporate profit taxation. As regards corporate profit taxation, income received from the sale of assets (both piece-by-piece and transfer of enterprise) of a Lithuanian company will be recognized as taxable income of that Lithuanian company and will be subject to Corporate Profit Tax. On the other hand, the purchaser of the assets (if it is the Lithuanian company) might be able to consider the acquisition costs as allowable deductions.

J. Bankruptcy Law

1. Challenge of Asset Transfer in Case of Insolvency

In bankruptcy proceedings, as of the effective date of the court decision to initiate bankruptcy proceedings involving the company, the company's bankruptcy administrator should examine the contracts the company entered into within (at least) the last 36 months prior to the effective date of the above-referenced court decision. In some cases (when the court declares fraudulent bankruptcy) the company's bankruptcy administrator shall examine the contracts the company entered into within (at least) 5 years prior to the effective date of the above-referenced court decision. The company's bankruptcy administrator is entitled to bring actions to court for invalidation of the contracts that are contrary to the objectives of the company's activities and/or which could have led to the inability of the company to settle with creditors. Therefore, there may be a risk of a challenge to the asset transfer in case of bankruptcy proceedings.

2. Acquisition of Assets that are Subject to Insolvency Proceedings

The assets of the company in bankruptcy and the receivables thereof are appraised and sold in the following manner: immovable assets are sold by auction, and the procedure of sale of other assets (except for the pledged assets) is determined by the creditors of the company in bankruptcy. Unsold assets may be transferred to the creditors of the company in bankruptcy. Securities held by the company in bankruptcy are sold in accordance with the procedure determined by laws regulating the trading in securities, except for private companies' shares, which are sold in the manner established by the creditors' meeting. Pledged assets are sold by auction upon notifying the pledge or the mortgage creditor thereof. In practice, assets (business) of companies in bankruptcy are often sold as complex.

K. Timing and Costs

1. Timeframe of Asset Transfer

Timing of the transaction depends on the particularities of the transaction in question. Taking into account that usually no advance consents of the governmental authorities are required (please see L, 3 below regarding competition clearance), timing largely depends on the parties (length of negotiations). In case certain matters should be registered with state registers due to the transaction, usually the registration procedure takes up to five business days. However, timing of a particular transaction should be assessed on case-by-case basis.

2. Costs of Asset Transfer

Transaction-related costs depend on the peculiarities of the transaction in question. For example, where real property is transferred, state duties for the registration of the change of the ownership rights to the real estate would not be substantial and vary depending on the market value of the real estate and whether the owner is a natural or legal person. The registration duties would be calculated separately for each real estate object. For instance, if the average market value of the building or premises exceeds LTL 3,000,000 (approx. EUR 868,860), the registration duties for a legal person will amount to LTL 1,715 (approx. EUR 497) plus 0.05% of the amount exceeding LTL 3,000,000 (approx. EUR 868,860), however, not more than LTL 5,000 (approx. EUR 1,448). The notary fee amounts to 0.5% (0.45% in case of natural persons) of the value of the transaction, however, should not exceed LTL 20,000 (approx EUR 5,792) in case one real property object is transferred or LTL 50,000 (approx EUR 14,481) in case multiple real property objects are transferred by one asset transfer agreement.

L. Miscellaneous

1. Choice of Foreign Law

The asset transfer agreement might be governed by foreign law. However, Lithuanian mandatory legal rules may apply irrespective of choosing foreign law.

2. (International) Arbitration, Choice of Venue

The parties may agree on international arbitration. It might be noted that in larger transactions it is common to choose international arbitration (Stockholm, London).

3. Other Distinctions, Characteristics

Competition Issues

According to Lithuanian legislation, transfer of assets (both in piece-by-piece acquisitions and transfers of enterprise) may qualify as a concentration under the Lithuanian competition laws and be subject to the notification and relevant permission by the Lithuanian Competition Council. The transfer of assets may require permission of the Lithuanian Competition Council if the transferred assets constitute 25% or more of the seller's assets and generate annual turnover of more than LTL 5 million (approx. EUR 1.45 million). In such case, concentration clearance would be required provided that: (i) combined aggregate income of the undertakings (income of the purchaser plus income generated by the assets under transfer) concerned exceeded LTL 30 million (approx. EUR 8.69 million) in the fiscal year preceding the transfer of assets, and (ii) the aggregate income of each of the undertakings concerned exceeded LTL 5 million (approx. EUR 1.45 million) in the fiscal year preceding the transfer of assets. Competition clearance is required only if both criteria (LTL 5 million and LTL 30 million) are met. Pursuant to the Lithuanian competition laws, the Competition Council must issue permission within one month with a possibility to extend the term for additional three months. In practice, where the contemplated transaction does not create serious competition concerns, permission is usually issued within one month.

Transfer of Enterprise

Contrary to the customary piece-by-piece asset deals, the Lithuanian laws (the Civil Code) provide for the possibility to structure the deal as the transfer of enterprise (transfer of enterprise). According to the Civil Code, the acquisition of business in the form of a transfer of an enterprise is a transaction whereby a seller undertakes to transfer into the ownership of a purchaser, as a complex of assets, an enterprise or a substantial part thereof, except for the non-transferable rights and obligations.

It must be noted that the laws do not clearly define what type of rights or obligations cannot be transferred in a transfer of enterprise, except for licenses and permits. The Civil Code explicitly establishes that licenses and permits can be transferred only in cases where this is provided for in the legislation or in a license or permit itself. The Code further specifies that the transfer of obligations to the purchaser that he cannot perform due to the lack of a specific license should not release the seller from liability to creditors for non-performance of such obligations. In such cases the seller and purchaser would be jointly liable to creditors for non-performance of such obligations.

In a transfer of enterprise, IP Rights, including the business name of the company, trademarks, etc. are transferred together with the assets, unless explicitly agreed otherwise.

The Civil Code establishes certain mandatory requirements for the transfer of enterprise, which could generally be summarized as follows:

- Prior to signing of the agreement on transfer of enterprise, the following documents should be drawn up, agreed upon and signed by the parties and attached to the agreement:
  - assets inventory act (this is an inventory of assets, not a law);
  - balance sheet;
  - independent auditor's opinion on the composition of the assets and the value thereof;
  - the list of liabilities (obligations) of the company, specifying the amount of the liabilities, time limits for the performance and kinds of security of obligations, creditors and their addresses.
- Notification of the creditors about the intended transfer of enterprise. The Civil Code establishes rather strict requirements related to protection of the creditors' interests. The purchaser has to notify all the creditors of the company of the transfer of enterprise at least 20 days prior to the execution of the sale-purchase agreement. In the event of a failure by the purchaser to fulfill the above duty, the seller's creditors are entitled to submit their claims directly to the purchaser. Advance notification of the creditors is required unless the enterprise purchase price is paid in cash and the amount thereof is sufficient and allocated to settle with all the creditors of the company.
- Appointment of a third party (a bank, other credit institution or an insurance company) to perform settlements with creditors. According to the Civil Code, under a general rule in the course of transfer of enterprise the companies should settle with the creditors of the transferred enterprise. Settlement with the creditors should be performed via a third party and cannot be performed directly by the companies involved. In accordance with the established procedure, the purchaser should transfer a part of the enterprise purchase price to such third party (as specified in the agreement) who is obliged to settle with the creditors of the company. The seller and the purchaser of an enterprise are jointly and severally liable for the actions of a third party who was appointed to settle with the creditors (the liability of the purchaser is limited to the value of the purchased assets).

Obviously, in most cases the obligation to settle with the creditors of the transferred enterprise would constitute a deal breaker. The parties may avoid this obligation only where the purchaser grants to the creditors a security to ensure due satisfaction of all the creditors' claims that is acceptable to all the creditors. The Code does not specify what type of security should be granted to the creditors in this case. According to our understanding, e.g., a parent company or bank guarantee might be sufficient provided that it is acceptable to all creditors.

In addition, the Civil Code does not explicitly establish that a transfer of enterprise should be regarded as the universal transfer of the assets and liabilities of the business in question. We would support an interpretation that it should be the case and, therefore, the transfer of assets and liabilities should not be subject to consents of the creditors of the company. However, due to the fragmentary regulation and lack of authoritative court practice, the opposite interpretation cannot be precluded. Therefore, there is a risk that the counterparties under transferred contracts may dispute the transfer on the grounds that their prior consent was not obtained.

In addition, particular agreements may establish restrictions on the transfer of agreements by way of the sale of an enterprise without the prior consent of the other party (e. g., it is rather customary to include such restrictions in agreements with banks and other credit institutions).

Further, please note that an agreement on the transfer of enterprise must be notarized (the failure to comply with the requirements of the form of the agreement renders the contract null and void) and registered with the Real Estate Register and respective records have to be made with the Register of Legal Entities. Taking into account that both notaries and registers are not familiar with this type of transaction, in practice it might be difficult to prove that the structure and conditions of a particular transaction correspond to the requirements of the laws.

To conclude, regulation of the sale of an enterprise is relatively new and fragmentary in Lithuania and there is no reliable judicial practice. Due to the fact that the established procedure is rather burdensome and somewhat uncertain, in practice parties usually perform assets transfers as piece-by-piece acquisitions rather than a transfer of enterprise.

M. Literature

Sorainen, Handbook of the Baltic Business Law, 4th Edition, 2004

Malaysia

By *Ang Siak Keng*, *Chew See Khee*, *Tan Lay Choo*, *Gooi Kathleen* and *Teoh Pei Pei*

A. General Aspects

1. Asset Deal vs. Share Deal: Essential Considerations

There are various aspects to be considered by a seller and a purchaser in deciding whether to structure a transaction by way of an asset deal in contrast to a share deal. The most important aspect would be the liabilities that are to be assumed by the purchaser. For example, in a share deal, the company has its own existence independent of its shareholders, and accordingly the change of ownership does not generally affect its assets and liabilities. The purchaser has to accept all assets and assume all liabilities that come with the share deal. However, in an asset deal, the purchaser may choose the assets it wishes to acquire, and, most importantly, which liabilities it will assume.

Another aspect that may be significant in determining the structure of the transaction would be the time frame of the transaction. A share deal involves a shorter process than an asset deal because the liabilities and assets in an asset deal would have to be separately identified and transferred, and this involves greater administrative complexity as well as several legal transfer documents to consummate the transaction.

The seller and the purchaser would also take into consideration the cost involved in structuring the transaction as a share or asset deal. Though both structures require payment of stamp duties based on the value of the transaction, different stamp duties are payable on asset deals and share deals; for a transaction of substantial value, a transaction structured as an asset deal will incur a higher stamp duty.

Another consideration that might be of relevance are the approvals or consents to be obtained from the relevant government authorities. In an asset deal, certain licenses of the seller, approvals or consents granted to seller cannot be transferred to the purchaser pursuant to the terms attached to the approvals or consents. Thus, the purchaser has to apply for new licenses, approvals or consents and this will consume time. In contrast, where an acquisition occurs by way of acquiring the shares in the company, the issue of approvals or consents does not arise, as there is no change in the owner of the business even though in certain types of licenses there may be restrictions or conditions imposed on a change in shareholders.

2. Distinction between Sale and Transfer in Rem

The Malaysian jurisdiction distinguishes between the sale (obligation to transfer) and the transfer in rem of assets. It is possible to provide for the sale and the transfer/conveyance in separate documents where, for example, when real property is involved, there is a master sale and purchase agreement and another separate transfer in rem document for the transfer of the real property. Where an asset deal involves shares of another company, there may be a share purchase agreement and a separately prescribed form for the actual transfer of the shares.

3. Regional Differences

Generally, the same law applies throughout Malaysia. However, different state laws apply to Peninsular Malaysia (or West Malaysia) and East Malaysia (which covers the states of Sabah and Sarawak). The information provided in this report applies to Peninsular Malaysia and West Malaysia only.

4. Acquisition by Foreigners

There are distinctions with regard to the acquisition of assets by foreigners or foreign entities as compared to locals and local entities.

Foreigners or foreign entities acquiring assets in Malaysia from local and other foreign entities are subject to the guidelines issued by the Foreign Investment Committee ("**FIC**") of the Economic Planning Unit of the Prime Minister's Department, and depending on the types of assets to be acquired and the percentage of interest to be acquired (in respect of shares in a company), prior approval/consent is required.

In granting their consents, FIC may impose certain conditions.

Certain categories of real properties will require foreign entities to obtain the prior approval of the state authorities in which the real properties are situated prior to any acquisition.

Foreigners or foreign entities acquiring assets from sellers who are specifically licensed (for example, who have a manufacturing license) may require the sellers to obtain the consent from the relevant authorities who issued the licenses.

5. Public Registers, Records and Databases

In Malaysia, there are certain central or local institutions where searches can be conducted to determine the ownership, encumbrances, and financial standing of seller and/or purchaser.

For example, title searches can be conducted at the relevant Land Offices, Road Transport Department, Port of Registry and Intellectual Property Corporation of Malaysia to determine the ownership and other interests of lands, vessels, and intellectual property respectively.

A company or a business search can be conducted at the Companies Commission of Malaysia to obtain corporate information regarding a company and business, such as the identity of its directors, shareholdings, existing charges created and financial information. A winding-up search and a bankruptcy search can be conducted at the Insolvency Department of Malaysia to determine whether a seller is bankrupt or has been wound up.

Additionally, a Professional Body Search with the Malaysian Bar Council, the Construction Industry Development Board Search and Business Partnership Search can also be conducted to determine the good standing of an entity.

6. Purchase Price Requirements

In Malaysia, there are no distinctions or special rules with regard to payment and satisfaction of the purchase price in connection with an asset deal or share deal and neither is there a minimum price for such deal(s).

The Central Bank of Malaysia has rules with regards to the payment of foreign currencies (i.e. currency other than Ringgit) to or from Malaysian entities.

The purchase price does not have to be allocated to each group of assets or individual asset. However for accounting and taxation purposes, it is advisable to allocate the purchase price. Where the transfers or conveyances of assets requires the payment of stamp duties, an allocation of the purchase price to each class of asset is necessary for purposes of determining the stamp duty payable.

B. Tangible/Movable Assets

1. Characteristics as to:

a) Language of Documentation. Regarding the transfer of tangible assets, the agreement can be drafted in English and can be executed bilingually.

b) Form of Documentation. Verbal agreements are valid in Malaysia. Most of the tangible assets (save for real property) are not required to be registered with any public authorities and are normally evidenced by way of physical possession. As such, transfer by way of written form or notarization is not required. However, it is advisable to transfer by written form to avoid future dispute/uncertainty and as good form of written evidence.

For the transfer of some tangible assets (real property excluded), written agreements are required as the assets have to be registered with particular governmental departments. These include motor vehicles, vessels and shares in a company and there are usually prescribed forms to effect the transfers.

The agreement and forms can be executed outside the Malaysian jurisdiction with the condition that the execution of certain transfer forms is to be witnessed by a notary public or other prescribed qualified persons.

Signing the agreement in counterparts is permissible but usually not permissible for the execution of prescribed forms.

c) Specification of Assets. Although it is not mandatory to describe the assets in details in a sale agreement, it is normal to attach schedules or lists of assets to the transfer agreement for certainty and ease of identification. At the very least, a generic description is recommended to identity the subject matters of a sale, so long as the process of identification does not involve specific legal requirements or expert opinions.

For those assets that are to be transferred via the prescribed transfer forms, specific descriptions and identifications are necessary.

2. Administrative, Corporate and Other Approvals

Special Governmental or Administrative Approvals

The transfer of tangible assets generally does not require special governmental approvals and administrative approvals, except for certain types of tangible assets (for example, dangerous drugs, weapons, rubber, and machinery with a certificate of fitness). Certain machinery requires a certificate of fitness to be issued by the governmental body prior to it being used. These include steam boilers, unfired pressured vessels, pipelines and gas cylinders.

In the event the transferee intends to export the assets, the approval of the custom authorities is required. Any transfer of assets by a seller situated in the Free Trade Zone needs the prior approval of the Free Trade Zone authorities.

The Approval of the Corporate Bodies

For any sale and purchase of assets, board of directors' resolutions and shareholders' resolutions have to be passed in accordance with the Memorandum and Articles of Association and the Companies Act, 1965 for any disposals or acquisitions of assets by both the seller and purchaser, if they are companies incorporated in Malaysia.

The Companies Act of 1965 in Malaysia prohibits the directors of a company from carrying into effect any arrangement of transaction for the acquisition or disposal of an undertaking or property of a substantial value unless such arrangement or transaction has been approved by the company in a general meeting.

For a company where all or any of its shares are listed for quotation on the official list of a stock exchange, the term substantial value shall mean the same value prescribed by the provisions in the listing requirement of the stock exchange for which compliance is also required by the company concerned.

The Approval of Security Holders

Generally, for assets owned by the seller, approval by the security holders for the sales is not required if the purchasers are buying the assets subject to the encumbrances and interests of the security holders.

For assets under hire purchase or where titles have not passed, the approval of the security holders is required, otherwise the transfer will be invalid.

If a purchaser is buying the assets free of encumbrances, it is normal for the purchaser to obtain information on the amount required to redeem the assets.

3. Filing Requirements

The transfer of tangible assets normally does not require special filings with public authorities except for certain tangible asset as follows:

- Motor vehicles – to be filed with the Road Transport Department.
- Ship vessels – to be filed with the relevant port of registry.
- Shares – to be filed with the Companies Commission of Malaysia.

4. Automatic Transfer of Encumbrances

Generally, encumbrances on assets are automatically transferred to the purchaser.

In Malaysia, a company must lodge the registration of charge with the Company Commission of Malaysia within thirty days after the creation of the charge. Therefore, the purchaser shall be deemed to have knowledge of the charge prior to the purchase of the assets by conducting a company search on the company.

C. Real Property

1. Characteristics as to:

a) Language of Documentation. Regarding the transfer of real property, the agreement can be drafted in English and may be executed bilingually.

The transfer form for real property under the National Land Code shall only be drafted in the local language.

b) Form of Documentation. It is a mandatory requirement under the relevant statute that the transfer in rem of real property shall be effected using instruments in the prescribed forms. Further, no instrument effecting any such dealing shall operate to transfer the title or create or affect any interest until it has been duly registered in accordance with the relevant statute.

The agreement and transfer form can be executed outside the Malaysian jurisdiction. In the event the transfer form is executed by a natural person in West Malaysia, it shall be attested to by a magistrate, the State Director, the Registrar, a Land Administrator, an advocate and solicitor or a notary public. In the event the instrument is executed outside Malaysia in India, Pakistan, Singapore, Sri Lanka, Brunei and any other Commonwealth country, attestation by a notary public having an official seal is necessary. For the State of Taiwan, the attestation by the President, Deputy President and the

Economic Director of the Malaysian Friendship and Trade Council is acceptable. In places other than those mentioned above, the attestation by a diplomatic officer in Malaysia or any person or class or description of persons approved on behalf of the Minister on the recommendation of the National Land Council is required.

Signing the agreement in counterparts is permissible but not the execution of the transfer form.

c) Specification of Assets. For the transfer of real property, the description of the property shall be made in accordance with the details in the title of the property.

2. Administrative, Corporate and Other Approvals

Special Governmental or Administrative Approvals

Generally, the transfer of real property in Malaysia does not require special governmental or administrative approvals. Special governmental or administrative approvals are only required in the following circumstances:

(i) if there is a restriction on the interest in the title of the real property that requires the transferor to apply for state consent prior to the transfer of the real property, the transferor shall apply for the necessary state consent to transfer the real property to the transferee;

(ii) in the event the land is a Malay Reserved Land or a native land, the transferor shall apply for the necessary local state consent to transfer the real property;

(iii) the approval of Estate Land Board is required for the transfer, conveyance and disposal of estate land; and

(iv) if the land is transferred to a foreign company/individual, the necessary consent of the local state authority is required, except where the real property is categorized as industry land wherein consent from the FIC is required.

The Approval of the Corporate Bodies

For any sale and purchase of assets, board of directors' resolutions and shareholders' resolutions have to be passed in accordance with the Memorandum and Articles of Association for both the transferor and the transferee in the event the transferor and the transferee are corporate bodies incorporated in Malaysia.

The Companies Act 1965 in Malaysia prohibits the directors of a company from carrying into effect any arrangement of transaction for the acquisition or disposal of an undertaking or property of a substantial value, unless such arrangement or transaction has been approved by the company in a general meeting.

For a company where all or any of its shares are listed for quotation on the official list of a stock exchange, the term substantial value shall mean the same value prescribed by the provisions in the listing requirement of the stock exchange for which compliance is also required by the company concerned.

The Approval of Security Holders

Generally, for assets owned by the seller, approval of the security holders for the sales is not required so long as the purchasers are buying the assets subject to the encumbrances and interests of the security holders.

For assets under hire purchase where title has not passed, the approval of the security holders is required, otherwise the transfer will be invalid.

If a purchaser is buying the assets free of encumbrances, it is normal for the purchaser to obtain information on the amount required to redeem the assets.

3. Filing Requirements

The transfer of the real property shall be registered at the respective Land Registry or Land Office depending on the nature of the document of title. Prior to the registration, the transfer form shall be submitted to the Stamp Office for adjudication purposes to determine the amount of stamp duty payable by the transferee in respect of the transfer of the real property.

4. Automatic Transfer of Encumbrances

The transfer of the property will be subject to all encumbrances and such encumbrances will automatically be transferred to the purchaser.

The waiver or discharge of encumbrances can only be accomplished with the consent of the parties having interests in such encumbrances and requires the execution of a prescribed form under the relevant statue.

5. Automatic Transfer of Lease Agreements

State law in Malaysia allows a lease (which is a tenancy exceeding three years) to be registered on the title to the real property. Once registered, the lease would automatically be transferred to the purchaser. The rights of the lessee (tenant) and purchaser are contained in the lease agreement executed between the seller and the lessee and there is no extraordinary right to termination outside the agreement.

D. Contracts

1. Characteristics as to:

a) Language of Documentation. The agreement setting out the terms and conditions of the transfer of contracts can be drafted in English and executed bilingually.

b) Form of Documentation. Verbal contracts are valid in Malaysia. As such, transfer of contracts by way of written form or notarization are not required. However, it is advisable to transfer by written form to avoid uncertainty and for evidentiary purposes.

The agreement can be executed outside Malaysia and signing in counterparts is permissible.

c) Specification of Contracts. Although it is not mandatory to describe the contracts in detail in a purchase agreement, it is normal to attach schedules or lists of assets to the transfer agreement for certainty and ease of identification. At the very least, a generic description is recommended to identify the subject matters of a sale so long as the process of identification does not involve specific legal requirements or expert opinions.

2. Administrative, Corporate and Other Approvals

Special Governmental or Administrative Approvals

The transfer of contracts generally does not require special governmental approvals and administrative approvals, except where there are express provisions to the contrary in the contract or the particular circumstances for those types of contracts (for example, contracts involving dangerous drugs, weapons, rubber, machinery with a certificate of fitness) require them.

The Approval of the Corporate Bodies

For any sale and purchase of assets, board of directors' resolutions and shareholders' resolutions have to be passed in accordance with the Memorandum and Articles of Association for both the transferor and the transferee in the event the transferor and the transferee are corporate bodies incorporated in Malaysia.

The Companies Act 1965 in Malaysia prohibits the directors of a company from carrying into effect any arrangement of transaction for the acquisition or disposal of an undertaking or property of a substantial value unless such arrangement or transaction has been approved by the company in a general meeting.

For a company where all or any of its shares are listed for quotation on an official stock exchange, the term substantial value shall mean the same value prescribed by the provisions in the listing requirement of the stock exchange.

Approval of the Other Parties to the Contract

The written consent of the other parties should be obtained in the form of a novation agreement (except for rights under a contract related to real property that has been registered with the relevant land registry) where all the rights, obligations and liabilities of the contract are passed to the purchaser.

If the approval of the other party cannot be obtained, the other way to transfer the contract is by way of legal assignment where the rights under the contract are assigned absolutely to the purchaser. If the contracts are assigned absolutely to the purchaser, a written notice (as opposed to consent) of such assignment to the other party of the contract shall suffice. The limitation of such assignment is that the obligations and liabilities in the contract cannot be assigned.

3. Automatic Transfer of Contracts (Other than Lease and Employment Agreements)

In Malaysia, besides registered leases of real properties and insurance contracts relating to certain assets, there are no automatic transfers of other kinds of contracts to the purchaser in an asset deal. For employment agreements, the existing employees will not be transferred to the purchaser unless and until they have accepted the offers made to them by the purchaser.

4. Filing Requirements

The transfer of contracts does not require special filings with public authorities.

5. Treatment of Existing Contractual Claims and Obligations

In the event sold contracts are not completely fulfilled and if the sold contracts are novated to the purchaser, which is the preferred form for transfers of contracts, the respective claims and/or obligations arising from such contracts would automatically be transferred to the purchaser. Conversely, an assignment would only entail the rights arising from the contracts being transferred to the assignee and as such the obligations/claims are not transferred to the assignee. In any case, it is always prudent to include a special indemnification clause in such transfer agreements to protect the interests of the purchaser and seller.

6. Warranty Claims Resulting from Events prior to Transfer

The transfer of a contract by novation would also include the transfer of any rights to claims, warranties and obligations related to such contract, and as such the purchaser would be liable for any warranty claims resulting from events prior to the transfer of the assets affected. Accordingly, it is usual to include special indemnification provisions in the asset sale/or the transfer agreement.

E. IP Rights

1. Characteristics of Intellectual Property Rights (e. g., Trademarks, Patents, Utility Models, Domain Names) ("*IP Rights*") as to:

a) Language of Documentation. There are no restrictions as to the language of documentation for the transfer of IP Rights. The documents may be drafted in English and may also be executed bilingually.

b) Form of Documentation. Generally, there are different sets of rules and regulations pertaining to the form of documentation required for the assignment of each class of intellectual properties:

(i) For trademarks, these are transferable/assignable subject to the approval of the Registrar of Trademarks where written application shall be made to the Registrar of Trademarks in the prescribed form and fees.

(ii) For industrial designs, these are transferable/assignable and the assignment must be in writing. The person for whose benefit the assignment is made shall apply to the Registrar of Industrial Designs for the transfer/assignment to be recorded in the Register; without such recording the assignment shall not have any effect as against third parties.

(iii) For copyrights, these are assignable as movable property and the assignment must be in writing.

(iv) For patents and patents application, these are transferable/assignable and the transfer/assignment must be in writing. The person for whose benefit the assignment is made shall apply to the Registrar of Patents for the transfer/assignment to be recorded in the Register where without such recording the transfer/assignment shall not have any effect as against third parties.

(v) For layout design, these are completely or partially transferable/assignable and the transfer/assignment must be in writing, with notice to the third party of the transfer/assignment.

The documents can be executed outside the jurisdiction, and proper notarization of the documents needs to be effected; execution in counterparts is permissible.

c) Specification of IP Rights. Each of the transfer or the assignment of the IP Rights should be described individually in detail, in particular those IP Rights that have been registered and granted individual references or identifications. Even though there is no requirement for attaching schedules or lists of IP Rights to the transfer agreement, it is advisable to attach a schedule or a list of the IP Rights to the transfer agreement. This is particularly so in cases where the business relies heavily on IP Rights.

2. Administrative, Corporate and Other Approvals

Special Governmental or Administrative Approvals

The assignment of certain IP Rights, such as Trademarks, requires the approval of the Registrar of Trademarks. However, IP Rights are generally assignable without the consent from the relevant authority, save for the application to the respective Registrars to record (as opposed to approval) the assignment for it to have legal effect as against third parties.

The Approval of the Corporate Bodies

For any sale and purchase of assets, board of directors' resolutions and shareholders' resolutions must be passed in accordance with the Memorandum and Articles of Association for both the transferor and the transferee in the event the transferor and the transferee are corporate bodies incorporated in Malaysia.

The Companies Act 1965 in Malaysia prohibits the directors of a company from carrying into effect any arrangement of transaction for the acquisition or disposal of undertaking or property of a substantial value, unless such arrangement or transaction has been approved by the company in a general meeting.

For a company where all or any of its shares are listed for quotation on an official stock exchange, the term substantial value shall mean the same value prescribed by the provisions in the listing requirement of the stock exchange.

The Approval of Security Holders in Case the IP Rights are Encumbered

Generally, for IP Rights owned by the seller, approval from the security holders for the sale of such rights is not required so long as the purchasers are buying the assets subject to the encumbrances and interests of the security holders.

For assets under hire purchase or where titles has not passed, the approval of the security holders are required, otherwise the transfer will be invalid.

If a purchaser is buying the assets free of encumbrances, it is normal for the purchaser to obtain information on the sum required to redeem the assets.

3. Filing Requirements

For the transfer of IP Rights, the Transferee shall apply to the Registrar in the prescribed forms with payment of the prescribed fees to have such transfer or assignment recorded in the Register.

Except for trademarks, filings or registrations are merely declaratory in nature but the transfer or assignment of the IP Rights will only have legal effect against third parties in the event such IP Rights have been duly recorded by the Registrar into his Register.

4. Applicable International (Multilateral) Agreements or Treaties

Malaysia is a signatory to the TRIPS agreement and the Paris Convention for the Protection of Industrial Property of March 20, 1883 (revised in Stockholm on July 14, 1967).

F. Receivables

1. Characteristics as to:

a) Language of Documentation. The agreement setting out the terms and conditions of the transfer of receivables can be drafted in English and executed bilingually.

b) Form of Documentation. For the transfer of receivables, written form or notarization is not required. However, it is advisable to transfer by written form to avoid uncertainty and as good form of written evidence for future use.

The agreement can be executed outside the Malaysian jurisdiction and signing in counterparts is permissible.

c) Specification of Receivables. Although it is not mandatory to describe the receivables in detail in a purchase agreement, it is normal to attach schedules or lists of receivables to the transfer agreement for certainty and easy identification. At the very least, a generic description is recommended to identify the subject matters of sale so long as the process of identification does not involve specific legal requirements or expert opinions.

2. Administrative, Corporate and Other Approvals

Special Governmental or Administrative Approvals

The transfer of receivables generally does not require special governmental or administrative approvals.

The Approval of the Corporate Bodies

For any sale and purchase of asset, board of directors' resolutions and shareholders' resolutions have to be passed in accordance with the Memorandum and Articles of Association for both the transferor and the transferee in the event the transferor and the transferee are corporate bodies incorporated in Malaysia.

The Companies Act 1965 in Malaysia prohibits the directors of a company from carrying into effect any arrangement of transaction for the acquisition or disposal of an undertaking or property of a substantial value unless such arrangement or transaction has been approved by the company in a general meeting.

For a company where all or any of its shares are listed for quotation on the official list of a stock exchange, the term substantial value shall mean the same value prescribed by the provisions in the listing requirement of the stock exchange.

Approval of the Other Parties to the Contract

The transfer of receivables is by way of legal assignment where the rights under the contract are assigned absolutely to the purchaser and a written notice of such assignment to the other party of the contract is sufficient.

3. Filing Requirements

The transfer of receivables does not require special filings with public authorities or registrations into registers or (online) databases, but would require written notification to the debtors concerned.

G. Liabilities

1. Characteristics as to:

a) Language of Documentation. The agreement setting out the terms and conditions of the transfer of liabilities can be drafted in English and executed bilingually.

b) Form of Documentation. No special form of documentation is required to transfer liabilities. The documents can be executed outside the jurisdiction and parties are allowed to sign in counterparts. However, it is advisable to transfer the liabilities in written form to avoid uncertainty and as a good form of evidence for future use.

c) Specification of Liabilities. Liabilities are not required to be described in detail in a transfer agreement. However, it is recommended that a schedule or lists of liabilities be attached to the transfer agreement for certainty and easy identification. At the very least, a generic description is recommended for the identification of separate classes of liabilities. This will at least ensure that those liabilities intended to be transferred can easily be identified under that particular generic description without requiring separate description of each of the liabilities.

2. Administrative, Corporate and Other Approvals

Special Government or Administrative Approvals

The transfer of liabilities does not require special governmental or administrative approval and the approval of corporate bodies regarding the seller and/or the purchaser.

The Approval of the Corporate Bodies

For any sale and purchase of asset, board of directors' resolutions and shareholders' resolutions must be passed in accordance with the Memorandum and Articles of Association for both the transferor and the transferee in the event the transferor and the transferee are corporate bodies incorporated in Malaysia.

The Companies Act 1965 in Malaysia prohibits the directors of a company from carrying into effect any arrangement of transaction for the acquisition or disposal of an undertaking or property of a substantial value, unless such arrangement or transaction has been approved by the company in a general meeting.

For a company where all or any of its shares are listed for quotation on the official list of a stock exchange, the term substantial value shall mean the same value prescribed by the provisions in the listing requirement of the stock exchange.

Approval from Creditors

For the transfer of liabilities, consents from the creditors are needed because consents in the form of a novation are the only method whereby the seller (original obligor) can effectively be replaced by the purchaser. If there are no consents from the creditors, the transfers are not valid. The creditors may then proceed against the sellers as they are still the contracting parties.

3. Filing Requirements

The transfer of liabilities does not require any special filings with public authorities or registrations into registers or (online) databases. Further notifications to the creditors are not sufficient and instead consents in the form of executed novation agreements are required.

4. Purchaser's Liability for:

a) Tax Obligations. In an asset purchase and transfer, the purchaser does not have any tax obligations with respect to the assets for periods prior to the acquisition; the tax obligation lies with the seller.

b) Environmental Contamination. The purchaser may be liable for environmental contamination caused by the acquired assets for periods prior to the acquisition. The legislation permits enforcing action against the new owner of contaminated land.

If, pursuant to a transfer agreement, the purchaser has to make an application under the applicable environmental legislation for a license due to the fact that the activities to be carried out are prescribed activities, then, in calculating the prescribed fee, the following factors shall be taken into consideration: (i) the quantity of the wastes discharged; (ii) the pollutant or class of pollutants discharged; (iii) the existing level of pollution by the previous occupier i.e. the seller. If it is ascertained upon investigation by the relevant authority that the pollutants or class of pollutants discharged, emitted or deposited is different in nature or greater in quantity from that declared by the seller, the fees may be recoverable in respect of that pollutant or class of pollutant or extra quantity of discharge, emission or deposit. It shall be deemed that the seller discharged, emitted or deposited that pollutant or class of pollutants or that quantity of wastes for a period of six months preceding the inspection in the calculation of the fees payable or, if the application was made less than six months prior to the inspection, for the period beginning from the application up to the inspection. However, the additional fees shall not be payable by the purchaser if the additional sum is less than ten percent of the fees paid by the seller during the corresponding period.

c) Products Sold or Services Rendered by the Seller to Third Parties. The purchaser does not assume liability for the products sold or services rendered prior to the acquisition unless the purchaser has specifically agreed to do so.

5. Automatic Transfer of Other Liabilities

The other liabilities of the seller do not automatically transfer to the purchaser due to the acquisition of assets.

6. Contractual Protection as to 4 and 5 above

It is recommended that an indemnification clause be included to protect the interest of the purchaser in an asset sale and/or transfer agreement.

H. Employees

1. Transfer of Employees

The employees of the seller are not automatically transferred to the purchaser in an asset transfer.

If the purchaser intends to take over the employees, notice has to be given by the seller to the employees to terminate the employment contract. In this event, termination benefits shall be paid to the employees. The employees shall not be entitled to any termination benefits if within seven days of the change of ownership, offers are made by the purchaser to the employees to continue to employ the employees under the terms and conditions of employment not less favorable than those under which the employees were employed before the change occurs and the employees unreasonably refuse the offer. In the event the purchaser does not offer to continue to employ the employees as mentioned above, the contract of service shall be deemed to have been terminated and the seller shall be liable for payment of all termination benefits.

In any event, if an employee is employed for less than twelve months on the date of termination or after receiving due notice of termination, the employee leaves the services without employer's prior consent or without paying the employer the indemnity due under the employment agreement, then he is not entitled to any termination/lay-off benefits.

2. Approval of Works Council, Trade Union or Other Institutions

Generally, the asset transfer does not require the approval of any works council, labor agency, trade unions or other institution unless the asset transfer would result in a major redundancy or retrenchment scheme and the employees are members of any trade unions. In this sense, where a collective agreement has been executed between the employer and the trade union there is usually a clause in which such major redundancy or retrenchment must be negotiated with the trade union for the protection of the employees who are members of such trade union. The absence of such approvals of any work council, labor agency and trade unions will not invalidate the asset transfer.

3. Contractual Protection as to Labor Issues

It is normal for asset transfer contracts to include indemnification clauses as to employees, e.g., the seller will indemnify the purchaser in respect of any liabilities that may be incurred arising out of or in connection with the employment or termination of employment of each and every employee prior to or on the completion date of the asset transfer and any claim by an employee or trade union arising out of the seller's failure to comply with any laws or regulations.

I. Tax Implications

1. Value Added Tax

There is no VAT in Malaysia.

2. Real Property Transfer Tax

Under the Malaysian Real Property Gains Tax Act 1976 (the "**Act**"), a tax will be imposed on gains derived from the disposal of real property. Disposal under the Act shall mean sell, convey, transfer, assign, settle or alienate whether by agreement or by force of law while real property means any land situated in Malaysia and includes any interest, option or other right in or over such land. The rate of tax ranges from 30% to 5% depending on the category of disposal, i.e. whether the disposal is within two (30%) to six years (5%) after acquisition of the real property. However, via an Exemption Order, currently all gains are exempted from the Real Property Gains Tax.

3. Other Tax Issues

Other tax issues are import/export duties/taxes on tangible assets. When a purchaser acquires assets subject to import/export duties/taxes or from a seller situated in tax privileged area, the purchaser has to ensure that it obtains similar or necessary exemptions to complete the purchase of the tangible assets.

J. Bankruptcy Law

1. Challenge of Asset Transfer in Case of Insolvency

With respect to a company, any transfer of property made by a company that, had it been made or done by an individual, would be void or voidable under bankruptcy of the individual, shall be void and voidable if the company is liquidated in the like manner.

Due to bankruptcy legislation in Malaysia, transfers made within two years prior to the commencement of bankruptcy are absolutely void unless the transfers are made in favor of purchasers in good faith and for valuable consideration. Any transfers are also void if made within five years prior to the commencement of bankruptcy unless the persons remained able to pay their debts after the transfer and had disposed of their interest in the property.

2. Acquisition of Assets that are Subject to Insolvency Proceedings

As soon as there is a commencement of a winding up by the court, any disposition of property, things in action, transfer of shares in the company shall be void unless the court orders otherwise.

When a winding up order has been made, the liquidator takes into custody all the property and things in action to which the company is or appears to be entitled and the liquidator has the power to sell and transfer to any person or company the immovable and movable property and things in action of the company by way of public auction, public tender or private contract.

K. Timing and Costs

1. Timeframe of Asset Transfer

The timeframe applicable to the sale/acquisition of a business by way of an asset deal will depend on whether regulatory consents are required. If no consents from the local authorities are required, completion is approximately three months from the date of the agreement. If consents are required from the local authorities, completion is approximately six months from the date of the agreement.

2. Costs of Asset Transfer

Regarding the relevant costs (other than advisors' fees), please see the following overview:

<u>Notarization</u>

Approximately RM 100 –150 per notarization

<u>Stamp Duty on Conveyance of Real Properties:</u>

Consideration	Stamp Duty Payable
For the first RM 100,000.00	1% of the consideration
For the next RM 400,000.00	2% of the consideration
Amount in excess of RM 500,000.00	3% of the consideration

<u>Registration Fees for Conveyance of Real Properties:</u>

Note: The followings are only applicable to the state of Penang and an example on the tabulation of the registration fees based on the value of the land/property. Different land offices charge different registration fees for the relevant category of value of Land/Property.

Value of Land/Property	Registration Fee Payable
Value up to RM 25,000.00	RM 50.00
RM 25,000.00 to RM 50,000.00	RM 75.00
RM 50,000.00 to RM 100,000.00	RM 125.00
RM 100,000.00 to RM 200,000.00	RM 250.00
RM 200,000.00 to RM 300,000.00	RM 375.00
RM 300,000.00 to RM 400,000.00	RM 500.00
RM 400,000.00 to RM 500,000.00	RM 625.00
RM 500,000.00 to RM 600,000.00	RM 750.00
RM 600,000.00 to RM 700,000.00	RM 875.00

Value of Land/Property	Registration Fee Payable
RM 700,000.00 to RM 800,000.00	RM 1,000.00
RM 800,000.00 to RM 900,000.00	RM 1,125.00
RM 900,000.00 to RM 1,000,000.00	RM 1,250.00
Value above RM 1,000,000.00	RM 1,250.00 for the first RM 1 million plus 0.5% of the valuation above RM 1 million calculated to the nearest Ringgit

Consent Fees for Application for Permission to Transfer and Charge in Compliance with Restriction in Interest Endorsed on the Document of Title

Each and every state where the real property is located has its own fees for the application.

Consent Fees for Application for Permission to Transfer Properties to Foreigners and Foreign Entities

Matters	Individuals	Company
Residential Buildings	RM 1,000.00	RM 2,000.00 per lot
Commercial Buildings	RM 2,000.00	RM 4,000.00 per lot
Agriculture	RM 2,000.00	RM 4,000.00 per lot

Stamp Duty Payable on Transfer of Shares

RM 3.00 for every RM 1,000.00 or fractional part of RM 1,000.00.

Stamp Duty on Agreements

RM 10.00 for each copy

L. Miscellaneous

1. Choice of Foreign Law

The sale and/or transfer agreement may be made subject to foreign law other than the laws of Malaysia.

2. (International) Arbitration, Choice of Venue

International arbitration is permissible with no restriction on the choice of venue.

3. Other Distinctions, Characteristics

The Malaysian jurisdiction does not provide for any other distinctions or unusual characteristics noteworthy in connection with a customary asset deal.

Mexico

By *Eugenio Bernal* and *Lizette Neme Bechara*

A. General Aspects

1. Asset Deal vs. Share Deal: Essential Considerations

In Mexico, the main consideration in structuring an acquisition as an asset deal in contrast to a share deal is first and foremost the risk of contingencies not disclosed in the target's financials, coupled with the credit risk associated with any indemnity provisions to be included in the purchase agreement; i.e. when a purchaser perceives a heightened risk that there will be material contingencies that are not or not fully disclosed in the target's financial statements, and the credit risk it would assume by accepting indemnities from the seller is not optimum, the purchaser is more likely to seek to structure the transaction as an asset deal, as opposed to a share deal.

A second concern (that is more readily measurable than the first) is tax considerations. In a share deal, for instance, the shareholders of the target company are the sellers. As such, they would have a taxable income on the positive difference between the purchase price and the tax base (tax cost) of the shares per selling shareholder. Conversely, in an asset deal, the seller is the target company, which would therefore have a taxable gain to the extent the purchase price exceeds the tax base of each asset sold.

Other considerations include mainly:

(i) the need for corporate consents: a purchase of assets may require a resolution by a qualified majority at a shareholders' meeting of the seller, and its creditors may oppose the sale arguing fraudulent conveyance or "fire sale" of assets, whereas a share deal will require the consent of the seller of the stock but may trigger change of control provisions in material agreements and may be subject to provisions of shareholders' agreements (such as rights of first refusal, puts, calls, tag-alongs, drag-alongs, etc.);

(ii) labor issues: in an asset deal, employees may have to be transferred to purchaser under an "employer substitution" regime (see H below), where the employee's consent is not required, whereas in an share deal there is usually no action required regarding employees; and

(iii) regulatory concerns: in Mexico, some governmental authorizations are not transferable and therefore, in regulated industries, a sale of assets may not be the optimum alternative, whereas in a share deal no specific authorization will be required unless the situation is specifically contemplated in the authorizations held by the target.

2. Distinction between Sale and Transfer in Rem

In general terms, Mexican law considers a sale as perfected and fully binding the moment the seller and the purchaser have agreed on (i) the asset to be sold and (ii) the price to be paid for the asset, even when the asset has not yet been delivered or the price has not yet been paid. Therefore, usually the obligation to transfer and the actual transfer are evidenced by the same document. It is possible, however, to separate the two by means of a promissory agreement, where the parties agree simply to execute the sale agreement at a point in the future. This is done frequently, for a number of specific reasons, when the parties wish to subject the sale transaction to conditions precedent. The promissory agreement must be in writing, contain the essential elements of the agreement object of the promise (in this case, the sale agreement) and be subject to a certain deadline, and may be otherwise made as simple or complex as needed. When using a promissory agreement, one must be careful, among other things, to avoid the risk that an escrow or similar payment might be reinterpreted as an installment of the price for tax purposes.

3. Regional Differences

Depending mainly on the object of the sale, the transaction may be subject to federal or state law. Real estate transactions, in general, are subject to state civil law, while stock purchases are subject to federal commercial law. For purposes hereof, we refer to Mexican federal law and/or the state laws applicable in the Federal District, as the case may be. It is fair to say, nonetheless, that, to a considerable extent, the civil laws of many states in Mexico are tailored after those of the Federal District.

4. Acquisition by Foreigners

Although the general rule is that foreign investment is permitted in Mexico, Mexican law does provide for specific limits to the participation of foreign investment in certain activities or companies. Except for real estate, however, Mexican law does not generally limit the acquisition of specific assets by foreigners.

The Mexican Constitution provides that foreigners may acquire real estate within the Mexican territory, provided they agree to be considered as Mexican nationals and not to request the protection of their respective governments with regard to such property, under penalty of forfeiting such property in favor of Mexico. The Constitution further provides that foreigners may not acquire direct domain of real estate within the restricted zone, which is a strip of land 100 kilometers wide along the borders and 50 kilometers wide along the sea coast (the **"Restricted Zone"**). Beyond that, Mexican law provides for certain requirements and procedures for a foreigner to acquire real estate in Mexico. Such requirements and procedures are different for properties within the Restricted Zone (which is more highly regulated) and for properties outside of it.

There are also differentiated requirements in the case of properties located in the Restricted Zone depending on whether the properties are intended for residential purposes or not.

In general, foreign entities and individuals may invest in real estate in Mexico in the following manner:

(i) Outside the Restricted Zone:

- directly,
- through a Mexican entity, or
- through a Mexican trust.

(ii) Within the Restricted Zone:

- for non-residential purposes, through a Mexican entity, with certain special provisions to be included in by-laws, or
- for residential purposes, through a Mexican trust, approved by the Ministry of Foreign Affairs.

5. Public Registers, Records and Databases

There is no central institution that collects relevant information in connection with asset transfers in Mexico.

Information regarding real estate property, including title and liens, can be obtained from the local Public Registry of Property, depending on the location of each property. This information is publicly available. Information on real estate property subject to special agrarian regulation (*ejidos*) is available at the National Agrarian Registry.

Other than the above, there are some specialized public registries for certain specific types of assets, including, among others, aircraft (the Mexican Aeronautical Registry), sea vessels (the National Maritime Public Registry), railway equipment (the Mexican Railway Registry), assets related to public telecommunications concessions, permits and other related acts (the Telecommunications Registry), mines (the Public Registry of Mining and Mining Cartography), intellectual property (the Mexican Institute of Intellectual Property) and copyrights (*derechos de autor*, the Public Registry of Copyrights).

General information about corporate sellers and purchasers can be obtained from the local Public Registry of Commerce (depending on the corporate domicile of each entity). The information available in such registry usually includes (i) the legal type of the entity, (ii) any general powers of attorney, (iii) the entity's fixed capital stock, and (iv) certain corporate events, such as any amendments to its by-laws and any mergers or spin-offs. Special situations such as judicial declarations of insolvency are also recorded in this registry. When a seller or purchaser is a public entity, further corporate information, including financial statements, may be obtained from the Mexican Stock Exchange.

6. Purchase Price Requirements

Generally, the parties are free to agree upon the purchase price. The price agreed may or may not coincide with the market value at the time and place that the purchase takes place. The purchaser must pay the price pursuant to the terms and conditions agreed to in the purchase agreement. In the absence of such terms and conditions, the price must be paid in cash and at the time and place of delivery of the purchased asset. Regardless of any other currency agreed upon for payment of the price, the purchaser will always be entitled to pay the price in Mexican pesos.

B. Tangible/Movable Assets

1. Characteristics as to:

a) Language of Documentation. The transfer documents regarding personal property may be drafted in any language. Bilingual documents are permitted. Furthermore, as long as there is no need to file such documents with authorities, a Spanish translation will not be required for documents drafted in a different language. Conversely, where such documents are to be filed with any authority (including any public registry), an official Spanish translation will generally be required. Official Spanish translations will also be required in the case of a dispute submitted to Mexican courts.

b) Form of Documentation. The transfer of personal property in Mexico does not generally require a special form; verbal agreements are valid but are the rare exception. Documenting the agreement in written form is nonetheless always advisable, especially for evidentiary purposes. The transfer documents may generally be executed outside Mexico. Signing in counterparts is permissible.

c) Specification of Assets. As a general rule, the assets to be transferred must be specified in the transfer agreement, provided that general or generic descriptions are not necessarily invalid. Depending on the nature and situation of the assets, however, it is advisable for the agreement to include a description as precise as possible.

Also as a general rule, purchases of assets that are customarily tasted, weighed or measured become effective only after they have been tasted, weighed or measured.

Furthermore, when the assets are determined and perfectly known, the transfer may be agreed upon samples.

In the two foregoing cases, the transfer shall be deemed perfected upon the parties reaching agreement as to the price.

2. Administrative, Corporate and Other Approvals

(i) The transfer of personal property in Mexico per se generally does not require special governmental or administrative approvals. Depending on the specific nature and object of the contract, however, certain filings could be required, for instance, in connection with assets related to the rendering of a public service by a private party under a concession granted by the corresponding authorities.

(ii) Except in connection with public companies (which are subject to specific requirements set out in Mexican securities laws), the approval of any corporate bodies is usually not required in connection with transfers of assets, unless otherwise provided for in seller's and/or purchaser's by-laws. Depending, among other things, on either party's knowledge (or deemed knowledge) of any such requirement in the by-laws, non-compliance therewith might affect the validity of the transfer.

(iii) In case the assets being transferred are subject to a security interest, no approval from the holder thereof is generally required, but the purchaser may not demand delivery of the assets sold except upon payment of the secured obligation, together with all accessories thereto.

3. Filing Requirements

Generally, the transfer of personal property does not require any such filing. Exceptionally, the transfer of certain specific types of assets, including, without limitation, aircraft, sea vessels, railway equipment, assets related to public telecommunications concessions and permits, mines and intellectual property, among others, does require special filings (see A, 5 above).

4. Automatic Transfer of Encumbrances

Security interests in personal property transfer automatically to the purchaser.

C. Real Property

1. Characteristics as to:

a) Language of Documentation. Transfer agreements regarding real estate property could, in theory, be drafted in any language, but because they must be formalized before a notary public and filed with the corresponding Public Registry of Property, they must be either drafted in Spanish or translated by an official translator (see A, 5 above). Bilingual documents are permitted.

b) Form of Documentation. Transfers of real estate property must be made in writing. In the event the value of the property does not exceed a certain threshold (currently 365 times the daily minimum wage for the Federal District (which is MXN 52.59 for 2008), a private document signed by the parties and two witnesses is sufficient, with the signatures being ratified before a notary public, competent judge or the Public Registry of Property. When the value exceeds such amount, the transfer must necessarily be made before a notary public, in a public deed.

Because most transfers of real estate property must be notarized and recorded with the Public Registry of Property pursuant to the above, the corresponding transfer agreement must be executed in Mexico and execution in counterparts is not possible.

c) Specification of Assets. A general description of a real estate property is typically not sufficient. The transferred property must be described in detail, usually specifying metes, bounds and surface, and the agreement should reference the property's file with the Public Registry of Property.

2. Administrative, Corporate and Other Approvals

In general, the transfer of real estate property does not require special governmental or administrative approvals. In the event the real estate property is subject to special agrarian regulation (*ejidos*), the approval of the communal owners' meeting may be required. The transfer shall be invalid if such approval is not requested and granted. Similarly, the purchase of real property by foreigners or foreign entities is subject to certain restrictions, as described in C.4 above.

Except in connection with public companies (which are subject to specific requirements set out in Mexican securities laws), the approval of any corporate bodies is usually not required in connection with transfers of real estate property, unless otherwise provided for in seller's and/or purchaser's by-laws. Depending, among other things, on either party's knowledge (or deemed knowledge) of any such requirement in the by-laws, non-compliance therewith might affect the validity of the transfer.

In case the property being transferred is subject to a mortgage, no approval from the holder thereof is generally required, but the mortgage will survive the transfer and continue to encumber the property to the detriment of its new owner.

3. Filing Requirements

Transfers of real estate property must generally be registered before the Public Registry of Property of the location of such property in order for them to become effective before third parties.

4. Automatic Transfer of Encumbrances

As a general rule, encumbrances regarding real property automatically transfer to the purchaser. The waiver of encumbrances generally requires the same formalities as their granting (usually notarization and registration).

5. Automatic Transfer of Lease Agreements

Lease agreements to which the real property is subject automatically transfer to the purchaser, who assumes all rights and obligations under such lease agreements vis-à-vis the tenant. Neither the purchaser nor the tenant nor the seller has any extraordinary termination rights by reason of the transfer.

D. Contracts

1. Characteristics as to:

a) Language of Documentation. Transfer documents regarding contracts may be drafted in any language. Notwithstanding, in the event the transfer or assignment agreement must be formalized before a notary public or filed before governmental authorities, it must either be drafted in Spanish or accompanied by an official Spanish translation. Bilingual documents are permitted.

b) Form of Documentation. As a general rule, the transfer of bilateral contracts must be formalized in a private agreement, executed by the parties to the transfer and two witnesses. In addition, the transfer of bilateral contracts requires the consent of the other party to the contract being transferred (see D, 2 below).

Other than the above, the transfer of contracts does not require a special form, unless the original execution of the contract to be transferred required a specific form. In general, unless notarization is required, the transfer documents may be executed outside Mexico and execution in counterparts is permissible.

c) Specification of Contracts. Similar to transfers of personal property, as a general rule, the contracts to be transferred must be specified in the transfer agreement, provided that general or generic descriptions are not necessarily invalid. Depending on the nature and situation of the contracts, however, it is advisable for the transfer agreement to include as precise a description as possible.

2. Administrative, Corporate and Other Approvals

As with personal property, the transfer of contracts in Mexico generally does not require special governmental or administrative approvals.

Similarly, except in connection with public companies (which are subject to specific requirements set out in Mexican securities laws), the approval of any corporate bodies is usually not required in connection with transfers of contracts, unless otherwise provided for in seller's and/or purchaser's by-laws. Depending, among other things, on either party's knowledge (or deemed knowledge) of any such requirement in the by-laws, non-compliance therewith might affect the validity of the transfer.

Under Mexican law, the transfer of contracts generally requires the consent of the other party to the contract being transferred. For certain types of contracts (e. g., lease agreements, employment agreements), however, exceptions apply (see H, 1 below and C, 5 above, respectively, and F, 3 below). Non-compliance usually leads to invalidity of the transfer.

3. Automatic Transfer of Contracts (Other than Lease and Employment Agreements)

In general, insurance agreements covering damages also transfer automatically in case the insured assets are transferred, provided that the insurance company is entitled to terminate the agreement within the 15 days following the date it became aware of the transfer. In addition to this (and to lease and employment agreements), there could be other exceptional contracts that could, under certain specific circumstances and depending on arrangements between the parties thereto, transfer automatically to the purchaser.

4. Filing Requirements

No filings with public authorities or registrations in public registers or databases are required by reason of the transfer of contracts per se.

5. Treatment of Existing Contractual Claims and Obligations

If and to the extent a party to a contract consents to the transfer of such contract by the seller, and absent specific provisions to the contrary, the respective claims and/or obligations arising from such contract do automatically transfer to the purchaser. If there is a perceived likelihood or considerable risk that potential contingencies will arise from a breach of the transferred contract, this is often addressed by means of either a tailored indemnity clause (sometimes coupled with an escrow-like device) or a purchase price adjustment mechanism.

6. Warranty Claims Resulting from Events prior to Transfer

As a general rule, and absent specific provisions to the contrary, upon transfer of a contract the purchaser will also be liable for warranty claims, even if resulting from events prior to the transfer. The potential resulting exposure is customarily covered by representations and warranties and/or indemnification provisions. More elaborate alternatives (such as those referred to in D, 6 above, i.e. escrow equivalents or price adjustment mechanisms) may also be used for specific potential contingencies where there is greater concern.

E. IP Rights

1. Characteristics of Intellectual Property Rights (e. g., trademarks, patents, utility models, domain names) ("*IP Rights*"), as to:

a) Language of Documentation. The transfer documents regarding IP Rights may be drafted in any language, except that in the case of IP Rights registered with the Mexican Institute of Intellectual Property and of copyrights (*derechos de autor*) registered with the Public Registry of Copyrights, an official Spanish translation must be attached for filing purposes. Bilingual documents are permitted. Official Spanish translations will also be required in the case of a dispute submitted to Mexican courts.

It is important to note that, according to Mexican law, the non-economic rights over copyrights (*derechos de autor*) are not transferable, and may only be licensed to a third party.

b) Form of Documentation. The transfer of IP Rights does not require a special form; verbal agreements are valid, but – again – are the rare exception. Documenting the agreement in written form is generally advisable, especially for evidentiary purposes.

The transfer documents may generally be executed outside Mexico, and signing in counterparts is permissible.

c) Specification of IP Rights. As a general rule, the IP Rights to be transferred must be specified in the transfer agreement, provided that general or generic descriptions are not necessarily invalid. Depending on the specifics of the IP Rights, however, it is advisable for the agreement to include as precise a description as possible.

2. Administrative, Corporate and Other Approvals

As a general rule, the transfer of IP Rights in Mexico per se does not require special governmental or administrative approvals.

Except in connection with public companies (which are subject to specific requirements set out in Mexican securities laws), the approval of any corporate body is usually not required in connection with transfers of IP Rights, unless otherwise provided for in seller's and/or purchaser's by-laws. Depending, among other things, on either party's knowledge (or deemed knowledge) of any such requirement in the by-laws, non-compliance therewith might affect the validity of the transfer.

In case the IP Rights being transferred are subject to a security interest, no approval from the holder of the IP Rights is generally required, but the purchaser may not demand delivery of the titles evidencing ownership of the IP Rights sold except upon payment of the secured obligation, together with all accessories thereto.

3. Filing Requirements

As the IP Rights are subject to recordation with the Mexican Institute of Intellectual Property, any change of ownership requires filing of the transfer with such registry. Such registration, however, is merely of a declaratory nature and does not affect the validity of the transfer, provided that it will only become effective against third parties upon registration.

4. Applicable International (Multilateral) Agreements or Treaties

Mexico participates in the Agreement on Trade-Related Aspects of Intellectual Property Rights, as in Annex 1C of the Marrakesh Agreement Establishing the World Trade Organization, and in the Paris Convention for the Protection of Industrial Property. In addition, Mexico signed, among others, the Strasbourg Arrangement regarding the International Classification of Patents dated March 24, 1971 and amended on September 28, 1979, as well as the Patents Cooperation Agreement dated June 19, 1970 and its Rules of February 3, 1984 and September 29, 1992.

F. Receivables

1. Characteristics as to:

a) Language of Documentation. The transfer documents regarding receivables may be drafted in any language. Bilingual documents are permitted. Furthermore, as long as there is no need to file such documents with any authority, a Spanish translation will not be required for documents drafted in a different language. Conversely, where such documents are to be filed with any authority (including any public registry), an official Spanish translation will generally be required. Official Spanish translations will also be required in the case of a dispute submitted to Mexican courts.

b) Form of Documentation. As a general rule, the transfer of receivables that are not documented in a security must be formalized in a private agreement, executed by the parties to the transfer and two witnesses. Conversely, transfer of receivables documented in a security must be done in accordance with the rules applicable thereto, usually consisting of endorsement (where the assignor signs the back of the security as evidence of the transfer), delivery of the endorsed security to the assignee and/or an entry regarding the transfer in the registry of the issuer of the security.

In order for a transfer of receivables to be enforceable against the debtor thereof, the assignee must give notice of the transfer to such debtor, whether judicially or extrajudicially (in the latter case, before two witnesses or via a notary public).

Furthermore, the transfer of receivables not documented in a security will only be effective against third parties as of the date (i) it is recorded with the corresponding Public Registry of Property, regarding receivables that are recordable therewith, (ii) it is notarized, if so documented, (iii) it is recorded with a public registry in the case of private documents, (iv) of death of any of the signatories of the document, or (v) it is delivered to a public servant by reason of his or her office.

Except when notarization is required, the transfer documents may be executed outside Mexico, and execution in counterparts is permissible, unless it must be formalized before a notary public.

c) Specification of Liabilities. Similar to transfers of contracts, as a general rule, the receivables to be transferred must be specified in the transfer agreement, provided that general or generic descriptions are not necessarily invalid. Depending on the nature and situation of the receivables, however, it is advisable for the transfer agreement to include as precise a description as possible.

2. Administrative, Corporate and Other Approvals

As with contracts, the transfer of receivables in Mexico generally does not require special governmental or administrative approvals.

Similarly, except in connection with public companies (which are subject to specific requirements set out in Mexican securities laws), the approval of any corporate body is usually not required in connection with transfers of receivables, unless otherwise provided for in seller's and/or purchaser's by-laws. Depending, among other things, on either party's knowledge (or deemed knowledge) of any such requirement in the by-laws, non-compliance therewith might affect the validity of the transfer.

Under Mexican law, the validity of the transfer is not subject to the approval of the debtors, provided that the underlying agreement does not state otherwise.

It is important to note that the above rules do not apply to bank and mortgage loans, which are subject to much more specific rules in Mexico.

3. Filing Requirements

No filings with public authorities or registrations into public registers or databases are required by reason of the transfer of receivables per se. Again, it is important to note that this does not apply to bank and mortgage loans, which are subject to much more specific rules in Mexico.

As mentioned above, in order for a transfer of receivables to be enforceable against the debtor thereof, the assignee must give notice of the transfer to such debtor, whether judicially or extra-judicially (in the latter case, before two witnesses or via a notary public). Furthermore, the transfer of receivables not documented in a security will only be effective against third parties as of the date (a) it is recorded with the corresponding Public Registry of Property, regarding receivables that are recordable therewith, (b) it is notarized, if so documented, (c) it is recorded with a public registry in the case of private documents, (d) of death of any of the signatories of the document, or (e) it is delivered to a public servant by reason of his or her office.

G. Liabilities

1. Characteristics as to:

a) Language of Documentation. The transfer documents regarding liabilities may be drafted in any language. Bilingual documents are permitted. Furthermore, as long as there is no need to file such documents with any authority, a Spanish translation will not be required for documents drafted in a different language. Conversely, where such documents are to be filed with any authority (including any public registry), an official Spanish translation will generally be required. Official Spanish translations will also be required in the case of a dispute submitted to Mexican courts.

b) Form of Documentation. The transfer of liabilities per se in Mexico does not require a special form; verbal agreements are valid but the rare exception. Documenting the agreement in written form is always advisable, especially for evidentiary purposes. In general, unless notarization is required, the transfer documents may be executed outside Mexico and execution in counterparts is permissible.

c) Specification of Liabilities. Similar to transfers of contracts and receivables, as a general rule, the liabilities to be transferred must be specified in the transfer agreement, provided that general or generic descriptions are not necessarily invalid. Depending on the nature and situation of the liabilities, however, it is advisable for the transfer agreement to include as precise a description as possible.

2. Administrative, Corporate and Other Approvals

The transfer of liabilities in Mexico per se generally does not require special governmental or administrative approvals (but see G, 4, b below). Depending on the specific nature and object of the liabilities, however, certain filings could be required.

Except in connection with public companies (which are subject to specific requirements set out in Mexican securities laws), the approval of any corporate bodies is usually not required in connection with transfers of liabilities, unless otherwise provided for in the transferor's and/or the transferee's by-laws. Depending, among other things, on either party's knowledge (or deemed knowledge) of any such requirement in the by-laws, non-compliance therewith might affect the validity of the transfer.

Under Mexican law, the transfer of liabilities does require the consent of the creditors, whether express or tacit. Non-compliance will invalidate the transfer.

3. Filing Requirements

No filings with public authorities or registrations in public registers or databases are required by reason of the transfer of liabilities per se.

As indicated above, the transfer of liabilities is subject to the creditors' consent. No other notification to the creditors is necessary.

4. Purchaser's Liability for:

a) Tax Obligations. Purchasers of an ongoing business are jointly liable for the seller's unpaid taxes up to the amount of the fair market value of the ongoing business. The purchase of an ongoing business is deemed to have occurred if the assets, employees, goodwill, rights and liabilities in connection with a business are acquired and such business continues as an ongoing concern after the acquisition.

b) Environmental Contamination. Under Mexican law, an owner (including upon purchase) or a possessor is jointly liable for any required remediation of environmental contamination related to the acquired (or possessed) assets for periods prior to the acquisition, together with the person(s) actually responsible for such contamination. The law grants a purchaser the right to make a claim against the person who actually caused the contamination for reimbursement of the costs incurred in remediating such contamination. In addition to the above, it is customary in Mexico for asset purchase agreements to include indemnity provisions in favor of the purchaser (and against the seller) in connection with any such environmental liability. The transfer of assets contaminated with hazardous waste in Mexico may require the approval of the environmental authorities.

c) Products Sold or Services Rendered by the Seller to Third Parties. In Mexico, there is no general liability for the purchaser regarding products sold or services rendered by the seller to third parties prior to the acquisition.

5. Automatic Transfer of Other Liabilities

Other liabilities of the seller that automatically transfer to the purchaser due to the acquisition of the assets include so-called "propter rem" liabilities, which are liabilities that naturally follow a given asset. A common example is maintenance quotas when acquiring a real estate property subject to condominium regime.

6. Contractual Protection as to 4 and 5 above

Special provisions as to liabilities regarding tax and environmental (and labor) issues arising prior to the perfection of the transfer agreement are customary in Mexico, usually in the form of indemnities or escrow-equivalent devices.

H. Employees

1. Transfer of Employees

Pursuant to Mexican Labor Law, unless the employees are duly terminated and paid all benefits and indemnities due under law, the transfer of a business, structured through an asset sale, is considered an "employer substitution."

Upon the occurrence of an employer substitution, labor relationships continue unaffected. The substitute employer is bound to honor all the accrued rights of the employees (such as seniority premiums, continuity, and preference right in the employment), and will (i) generally assume all liabilities related to the labor relationships with the employees, and (ii) be jointly liable with the substituted employer for labor contingencies arising before the employer substitution and for a period of six months after the substitution occurs. Such six-month period shall be counted as from the date in which the notice of such substitution is given to the union or to the employees. Until such notice is given, the joint obligation will survive indefinitely. Once the notice has been properly given and the six-month period has elapsed, the substitute employer shall remain the sole obligor for any labor contingencies related to the employees.

These obligations cannot be waived.

2. Approval of Works Council, Trade Union or Other Institutions

In Mexico, no approval of any works council, labor agency, trade union or other institution is required for an asset transfer.

3. Contractual Protection as to Labor Issues

Special provisions as to liabilities regarding labor issues arising prior to the perfection of the transfer agreement are customary in Mexico, usually in the form of indemnities or escrow-equivalent devices.

I. Tax Implications

1. Value Added Tax

The current regular VAT rate in Mexico is 15%. In general, asset transfers in Mexico incur VAT. The basis for calculating VAT is the price or the agreed consideration, which may include any other amount collected from or chargeable to the purchaser either for other taxes, governmental fees, interests (ordinary or delinquent), liquidated damages or any other applicable concept. Asset transfers trigger VAT at the moment of payment.

There are certain cases where the 15% rate is reduced or in which the payment of VAT is exempted, including the following:

10% rate in border zones: VAT is 10% when the taxable acts or activities are carried out by residents of geographic regions close to the borders, and as long as the physical delivery of the property or the rendering of the services is done within any such region. This reduced rate, however, does not apply to transfers of real estate property.

There is no VAT on the transfer of, among other things, equity quotas, receivables and negotiable instruments.

2. Real Property Transfer Tax

VAT

The transfer of real estate property destined for commercial or industrial purposes in Mexico triggers VAT at the rate of 15%. The transfer of empty lots (with no construction) and residential homes (*casa-habitación*) is exempt from VAT.

Income Tax

Individuals and entities are obligated to pay income tax in the following cases: (i) Mexican residents, with respect to all revenue, regardless of the location of the source of wealth from which they arise; (ii) non-residents with a permanent establishment within Mexico, with respect to revenue attributable to such permanent establishment; (iii) non-residents without a permanent establishment within the country, with respect to revenue arising from sources of wealth located within Mexico, or if having a permanent establishment, when such revenue is not attributable thereto.

The Income Tax rate is currently 28%.

The transfer of real estate owned by non-residents and located in Mexico is taxed in Mexico. For such purposes, the tax must be calculated and paid under one of the following alternatives: (i) by applying a 25% rate to the gross consideration perceived ("full sale price"), with no deductions allowed; or (ii) by applying a 28% rate to the net income obtained ("actual gain") from the transfer, with certain deductions being allowed, such as improvements made to the property. In order to pay the tax under this second alternative, certain requirements must be met, such as the execution of the transaction before a notary public.

The seller is exempt from the payment of Income Tax when the residential home (*casa-habitación*) is being transferred, in the event the transfer price does not exceed the current equivalent of approximately MXN 6,000,000, and the transfer is formalized before a notary public. This limit is not applicable when the seller had been living in such residential home during the five immediately previous years

Flat Rate Business Tax (Impuesto Empresarial a Tasa Única)

Individuals and entities transferring real estate property, including empty lots and construction sites, whether Mexican residents or non-residents with a permanent establishment in Mexico, must pay flat tax over the income obtained from the sale by applying a 17.5% rate to the amount resulting from decreasing authorized deductions from the total income received for such transfers. This tax may be accredited against the amount to be paid for Income Tax, and the excess must be paid.

Local Tax on Acquisition of Real Estate (*Impuesto sobre la Adquisición de Inmuebles*)

In the Federal District, there is an additional local tax for the acquisition of real estate, which is calculated pursuant to the following progressive scale, as applied to the highest of: (i) the commercial price, (ii) the appraisal value, or (iii) the cadastral value of the property:

Range	**Inferior Limit**	**Superior Limit**	**Fixed Rate**	**Factor to be Applied to the Excess of the Inferior Limit**
A	0.11	73,531.32	138.62	0.00000
B	73,531.33	117,650.05	138.63	0.03163
C	117,650.06	176,474.91	1,534.10	0.03261
D	176,474.92	352,949.92	3,452.38	0.03261
E	352,949.93	882,374.80	9,207.23	0.03696
F	882,374.81	1,764,749.61	28,774.78	0.04565
G	1,764,749.62	And over	69,055.19	0.04565

(amounts in Mexican Pesos; one Mexican Peso, as of June 1, 2009, corresponds to approximately USD 0.075)

The formula to calculate the tax is as follows: Acquisition value minus the inferior limit per the factor plus the fixed rate, this is ((acquisition value – inferior limit) * factor) + fixed rate.

Registration Rights

Finally, registration duties must be paid to the Public Registry of Property in order to register the transfer. For 2008, the standard duties amount to a fixed amount of MXN 10,019.00.

J. Bankruptcy Law

1. Challenge of Asset Transfer in Case of Insolvency

In the event seller or purchaser, following the asset transfer, becomes bankrupt or subject to insolvency or similar proceedings, there are risks that the asset transfer will be challenged, depending whether the transfers are consummated or non-consummated.

Consummated Transfers

Regarding consummated transfers, transfers for consideration shall be deemed ineffective in the event they were executed during the two hundred and seventy calendar days prior to the date of the bankruptcy resolution (retroactive term), with the purpose of defrauding the creditors and when the purchaser knew about such fraud. On the other hand, all gratuitous transfers shall always be deemed ineffective if executed during such retroactive term.

The 'bad faith' purchaser will be responsible for damages and lost profits related to the transfer of assets or the loss of the assets before third purchaser parties of good faith.

Non-Consummated Transfers

Regarding non-consummated transfers, their legitimate owners may request that the bankruptcy judge rule to separate the assets that were not transferred by a definitive legal and irrevocable act from the bankruptcy estate, in which case the legitimate owner shall comply with all pending obligations regarding the transfer.

The bankruptcy or insolvency proceeding shall not affect the validity of the transfers of strictly personal, non-economic or similar assets, whose management is maintained by the party subject to insolvency and such assets are non-transferable, not subject to seizure or to negative prescription.

The preparatory or definite acts, pending execution, must be executed by the party subject to insolvency, unless the conciliator opposes such completion in the interest of the bankruptcy estate.

If the seller of a real estate property is declared bankrupt or insolvent, the purchaser may claim the delivery of the asset prior to payment of the purchase price, in the event that the sale is perfect pursuant to legal provisions. If the purchaser is the party subject to bankruptcy or insolvency proceedings, the delivery cannot be claimed unless the price is paid or the payment secured.

2. Acquisition of Assets that are Subject to Insolvency Proceedings

Specific rules apply with regard to the acquisition of assets that are subject to insolvency proceedings or similar proceedings in connection with bankruptcy at the time of transfer, as follows:

(i) In case the seller maintains the management of the company, transfers of the company's assets, other than those executed in the normal course of business, must be approved by the conciliator, with the prior opinion of the inspectors.

(ii) In case the conciliator already manages the company, the conciliator shall have all the rights and obligations of the management of the company.

Following the bankruptcy resolution (whereupon the role of the conciliator ends and a receiver is appointed), the receiver shall proceed to the sale of all the assets that comprise the bankruptcy estate, trying to obtain the best price for their sale. This sale shall be carried out through a public auction, which shall take place within a period not less than ten and not more than ninety calendar days from the date in which the invitation for the bidders to the auction is published.

The receiver may request that the judge authorize the transfer any kind of assets or group of assets from the bankruptcy estate through any way other than a public auction when the receiver considers that a higher value may be obtained.

Once a period of six months has elapsed from the beginning of the bankruptcy proceeding without the transfer of all the assets being made, any interested person may file an offer to the bankruptcy judge to purchase the assets.

K. Timing and Costs

1. Timeframe of Asset Transfer

Both the timing and cost of an asset deal in Mexico may vary substantially, depending mostly on (i) whether the assets involved comprise real estate property or not, and (ii) whether the industry involved is specifically regulated or not.

In the first case, the presence of real estate property as part of the assets to be transferred implies the drafting, execution and registration of notarized public deeds, which may take anywhere between two weeks to a month, depending mostly on the number, size, legal situation and geographical location of the properties. In this last respect, if the properties are located in different States, the corresponding public deeds must be registered in each such State. Notarial and registration fees and costs (the latter of which vary from State to State) will often be a factor to be considered.

In the second case, the procedure and costs involved in obtaining the corresponding authorizations are also frequently a factor to consider, which may vary depending on the nature of the assets and the process required by the regulating entity.

Subject to the above considerations, and absent any complications or protracted negotiation, an asset deal in Mexico not comprising real estate will usually take between two to five months, whereas one involving real estate will usually take between three to eight months.

2. Costs of Asset Transfer

Notarization costs are calculated pursuant to the value of the transaction. Notaries may not charge more than a fixed amount of MXN 4,302.00 in case the value of the transaction does not exceed MXN 118,303.01. In case the transaction's value is higher, to the mentioned fixed amount an additional factor must be added, which must be calculated pursuant to the following chart:

Transaction Value		Cumulative Additional Factor over the excess of the inferior limit
More than	Up to	
118,303.01	236,608.00	1.125%
236,608.01	473,214.00	0.975%
473,214.01	946,428.00	0.825%
946,428.01	1,892,857.00	0.675%
1,892,857.01	3,785,714.00	0.525%
3,785,714.01	7,571,428.00	0.375%
7,571,428.01	15,142,855.00	0.225%
15,142,855.01	onwards	0.075%

(amounts in Mexican Pesos; one Mexican Peso, as of June 1, 2009, corresponds to approximately USD 0.075)

Additionally, a registration fee can add up to MXN 10,643.00.

L. Miscellaneous

1. Choice of Foreign Law

Sale and/or transfer agreements executed in Mexico may be subject to foreign law, except if real estate property is being transferred, in which case the agreement will be subject to Mexican law, regardless of what the transfer agreement may provide.

2. (International) Arbitration, Choice of Venue

International arbitration is possible. There are no restrictions in Mexico as to the choice of venue.

3. Other Distinctions, Characteristics

Asset deals in Mexico rarely include any other distinctions or unusual noteworthy characteristics other than as described above.

M. Literature

Rafael Rojina Villegas, Derecho Civil Mexicano: Contratos, 8th Edition, 2001

Manuel Borja Soriano, Teoría General de las Obligaciones, 18th Edition, 2001

Francisco Lozano Noriega, Cuarto Curso de Derecho Civil: contratos, 3rd Edition, 1982

Netherlands

By *Kim F. Tan*

A. General Aspects

1. Asset Deal vs. Share Deal: Essential Considerations

The decision to transfer a business by way of an asset transfer in contrast to a transfer of shares may be subject to various considerations.

One advantage of a transfer of assets is that the assets and liabilities to be transferred can be exactly distinguished from any assets or liabilities that should remain with the seller. In particular, when assets are purchased, the purchaser will not automatically assume any corresponding (undisclosed) liabilities unless such liabilities are expressly distinguished and assumed. Obviously, a proper due diligence may be supportive when determining which assets and liabilities are to be transferred from seller to purchaser.

From a practical point of view, however, the transfer of assets may prove to be more cumbersome than a transfer of shares, as each asset will need to be identified and transferred separately in accordance with the applicable legal transfer formalities.

Furthermore, certain transfers will require the co-operation of third parties. For instance, existing contracts with business relations of the acquired business will need to be transferred, which may result in time consuming re-negotiations or even termination of existing business relations.

Also, licenses, permits and other governmental approvals may be terminated upon a transfer of a business or may remain with the seller. Consequently, the purchaser may need to apply for new permits or at least secure the amendment or renewal of existing permits.

Finally, from a tax perspective, a transfer of assets is more complex than a transfer of shares. A transfer of assets may trigger transfer and/or income taxes. In addition, the purchaser will not be able to carry forward any tax losses that pertain to the business being acquired. On the other hand, the purchaser will generally be entitled to write off the acquisition costs for tax purposes. The tax implications should therefore be thoroughly considered in deciding between a transfer of assets versus a transfer of shares.

In the Netherlands, due to the complexity of asset transfers, share transactions are generally preferred.

2. Distinction between Sale and Transfer in Rem

Dutch law distinguishes between the creation of an obligation to transfer assets on the one hand and the actual transfer of legal ownership of such assets on the other. The former is usually laid down in a sale agreement between the seller and purchaser, which sets out the (commercial) terms and conditions that apply to the sale between the seller and purchaser. The latter (i.e. the fulfillment of the obligation to transfer) is effected in accordance with the specific transfer requirements that are applicable to the relevant assets to be transferred.

In some cases, the obligation to transfer assets and the actual transfer of assets may be combined in one and the same agreement, but it may be advantageous to provide for the sale and transfer in separate documents. In particular, when various types of assets (subject to different transfer requirements) are to be transferred or when assets are located in multiple jurisdictions, a "master purchase agreement" accompanied by local transfer agreements may be the most practical approach. From a timing perspective, the master purchase agreement could provide for a limited time frame during which the local transfer requirements will need to be completed.

3. Regional Differences

There are no regional differences as regards the legal requirements in connection with the transfer of assets in the Netherlands.

4. Acquisition by Foreigners

The acquisition of assets by foreigners and/or foreign entities is normally not subject to any Dutch governmental consent or foreign exchange regulations. The applicability of the EC Merger Control Regulation and Dutch Competition Act should always be taken into account.

5. Public Registers, Records and Databases

Prior to acquiring a business and depending on the assets and liabilities constituting such business, relevant information may be obtained from various public registers.

The most commonly consulted register is the Trade Register (*Handelsregister*) of the Chamber of Commerce (*Kamer van Koophandel*) that provides basic corporate information on the seller and/or purchaser such as (i) legal form, (ii) directors and officers and their powers of representation, (iii) registered share capital, (iv) sole ownership, (v) trade names, (vi) articles of association and (vii) financial statements.

The information with the Dutch Land Registry (*Kadaster*) is also publicly available and includes information on ownership of real property and possible encumbrances.

Information on certain intellectual property rights such as trademarks that are valid in the Benelux (i.e. Belgium, Netherlands and Luxembourg) can be obtained from the Benelux Office for Intellectual Property.

6. Purchase Price Requirements

From a legal perspective, there are no restrictions as to the purchase price to be paid in connection with an acquisition of assets in the Netherlands. The amount, currency and method of payment (e.g., by a third party on behalf of the purchaser) of the purchase price may be freely agreed upon between the parties involved. In order for a sale to be valid, an identifiable purchase price will need to be stipulated in the sale agreement. In general, any ancillary transfer agreements (i.e. documents effecting the actual transfer of legal ownership) do not necessarily have to refer to a purchase price.

For tax and accounting purposes it may be recommended that the sale agreement includes a price allocation between the assets to be transferred.

B. Tangible/Movable Assets

1. Characteristics as to:

a) Language of Documentation. The documentation governing the sale and transfer of tangible assets may be drawn up in any language or in multiple languages. For the latter it is recommended to stipulate which language will prevail in the event of any discrepancies.

b) Form of Documentation. In general, there are no format requirements as to documenting a sale and transfer of tangible assets, although the written form is certainly recommendable. A transaction between a sole shareholder and a Dutch company represented by such sole shareholder must be in writing. All documents may be signed outside the Netherlands and, if necessary, in counterparts.

c) Specification of Assets. In order for an asset transfer to be valid, the assets transferred should be sufficiently identifiable, i.e. it should be evident which assets are being transferred to the purchaser and which assets will remain with the seller. When identifying the assets, the level of detail required will depend on the facts and circumstances. In practice, asset lists are often used to identify the transferring assets, although in some cases a more generic asset description (e.g., "all assets located in a certain warehouse") is acceptable as well.

2. Administrative, Corporate and Other Approvals

Safe for certain specific assets (e.g., weapons, certain chemicals), the transfer of tangible assets does not require any governmental or administrative approvals.

In general, no corporate approvals are required for the transfer of assets unless the articles of association of the seller and/or purchaser provide that the approval of a corporate body is required. Such a corporate approval requirement has an internal effect only, which means that the absence of approval cannot be invoked against third parties and does not have an impact on the validity of the transfer. Notwithstanding the foregoing, if a Dutch company is selling and transferring its entire or a substantial part of its business, by virtue of Dutch law, the prior approval of its shareholders meeting will be required.

In the event the assets transferred are encumbered, approval of the security holder will not be required for a valid transfer of assets. Nevertheless, contractual arrangements may require notification to or approval by the security holder.

3. Filing Requirements

The transfer of tangible assets does not require any specific filings with public authorities or registrations in public registers or databases.

4. Automatic Transfer of Encumbrances

Upon a transfer of assets, any encumbrances (e. g., pledges) remain in existence unless the acquirer acted in good faith and did not know or could not have known about the encumbrance on the assets transferred.

C. Real Property

1. Characteristics as to:

a) Language of Documentation. The documents governing the sale and transfer of Dutch real property may be drawn up in any language or even in multiple languages. However, as the transfer of legal ownership of real property requires the execution of a transfer deed by a Dutch notary and registration thereof with the Dutch Land Registry (*Kadaster*), such transfer deed must be drawn up in Dutch. If necessary, a translation of the transfer deed will be provided by the notary.

b) Form of Documentation. A sale and purchase agreement regarding Dutch real property may be drawn up as a private deed and does not necessarily need to be executed before a notary. The subsequent transfer of legal ownership of the real property requires (i) execution of a transfer deed by a Dutch notary and (ii) registration of such transfer deed with the Dutch Land Registry.

The sale and purchase agreement may be signed outside the Netherlands and in counterparts if necessary. However, the required transfer deed must be executed by and before a Dutch notary. In case the parties are not able to appear before the notary, the transfer deed may be executed on the basis of powers of attorney.

c) Specification of Assets. As the real property being transferred must be sufficiently identified, the necessary notarial transfer deed will make reference to the relevant sections in the Dutch Land Register.

2. Administrative, Corporate and Other Approvals

The transfer of real property may be subject to prior governmental or administrative approvals. The Dutch notary involved in the transfer of the real property (see C, 1 above) will perform the relevant searches to identify any approval requirements.

As for the requirement of corporate approvals, reference is made to B, 2 above.

Strictly, the transfer of real property that is subject to encumbrances (e. g., mortgages, usufructs etc.) does not require the approval of the relevant security holder. Nevertheless, contractual arrangements may require notification to or approval by the security holder.

3. Filing Requirements

In order for a transfer of real property to be valid, such transfer must be registered with the public registers, including the Dutch Land Registry. The transfer deed will also be submitted to the Dutch Tax Authorities.

4. Automatic Transfer of Encumbrances

Upon a transfer of real property, any encumbrances (e. g., mortgages) remain in existence. The notary involved in the transfer of the property will perform a search with the public registers to identify any existing encumbrances.

The waiver or termination of existing encumbrances requires the cooperation of the beneficiary and registration with the Dutch Land Registry.

5. Automatic Transfer of Lease Agreements

By virtue of Dutch law, the acquirer of leased property will automatically acquire all rights and assume all obligations of the lease agreement to which a property is subject. The acquirer will only be bound to the provisions of the lease agreement that directly relate to the use of the property and consideration to be paid. There are no specific rights for the purchaser or tenant to terminate the lease agreement following the acquisition.

D. Contracts

1. Characteristics as to:

a) Language of Documentation. The documentation governing the transfer of contracts may be drawn up in any language and can even be drawn up in multiple languages. For the latter, the language that will prevail in case of any discrepancies should be stipulated.

b) Form of Documentation. Dutch law requires the transfer of contracts to be memorialized in a deed (in writing). All documents may be signed outside the Netherlands and, if necessary, in counterparts.

c) Specification of Contracts. Similar to the transfer of tangible assets, the transfer of contracts requires that such contracts are sufficiently identifiable, i.e. it should be evident which contracts are being transferred to the purchaser and which contracts will remain with the seller. Please see B, 1, c above for further information.

2. Administrative, Corporate and Other Approvals

In general, the transfer of contracts does not require any governmental or administrative approvals.

As for the requirement of corporate approvals, reference is made to B, 2 above.

For a contract to be transferred, Dutch law requires the cooperation of the other contract party. Under certain circumstances (e.g., lease agreements and employment agreements) exceptions may be applicable. Absence of the aforementioned cooperation results in an invalid transfer of the contract.

3. Automatic Transfer of Contracts (Other than Lease and Employment Agreements)

Rights deriving from contracts that by nature only benefit the holder of a certain asset may transfer by operation of law to the acquirer (purchaser) of such asset. For example, under certain circumstances, the rights pursuant to non-competition arrangements with prior employees of a certain business may transfer to the new owner of the business.

4. Filing Requirements

The transfer of contracts does not require any specific filings with public authorities or registrations in public registers or databases.

5. Treatment of Existing Contractual Claims and Obligations

Provided that a contract has been validly transferred, any claims and/or obligations arising from the contract will have automatically transferred to the purchaser unless specifically agreed otherwise upon the transfer of the contract. In case claims or obligations are existing or expected, this may result in an adjustment to the purchase price or require an indemnification from the seller.

6. Warranty Claims Resulting from Events prior to Transfer

Unless agreed otherwise upon the transfer of a contract, all claims and obligations related to such contract will transfer to the purchaser. Consequently any warranty claims from events prior to the transfer will be for the account of the purchaser. The agreement governing the sale and transfer of the contract may provide for certain warranties and/or indemnifications in that regard.

E. IP Rights

1. Characteristics of Intellectual Property Rights (e. g., Trademarks, Patents, Utility Models, Domain Names) ("*IP Rights*") as to:

a) Language of Documentation. The documentation governing the sale and transfer of intellectual property rights may be drawn up in any language and can even be drawn up in multiple languages. For the latter it is recommended that it be stipulated which language will prevail in case of any discrepancies. As the relevant transfer instrument may need to be registered (e.g., with the Benelux Office for Intellectual Property), the documents should be drawn up in the Dutch or English language.

b) Form of Documentation. The sale and transfer of intellectual property rights should be memorialized in writing (i.e. in a private or notarial deed). Otherwise there are no specific format requirements. All documents may be signed outside the Netherlands and, if necessary, in counterparts.

c) Specification of IP Rights. Similar to the transfer of tangible assets, the transfer of intellectual property rights requires that such rights are sufficiently identifiable, i.e. it should be evident which rights are being transferred to the purchaser and which rights will remain with the seller (e.g., by making reference to certain registration numbers). Please see B, 1, c above for further information.

2. Administrative, Corporate and Other Approvals

In general, the transfer of intellectual property does not require any governmental or administrative approvals.

As for the requirement of corporate approvals, reference is made to B, 2 above.

The transfer of intellectual property subject to encumbrances does not require the approval of the relevant security holder. Nevertheless, contractual arrangements may require notification to or approval by the security holder.

3. Filing Requirements

Depending on the type of IP Rights being transferred, registration may be required (e.g., the transfer of trademarks is registered with the Benelux Office for Intellectual Property). Registration is not a constitutive requirement for the transfer to be effective. However, until registration has been completed, the transfer has no effect as against third parties.

4. Applicable International (Multilateral) Agreements or Treaties

The Netherlands is party to various international agreements and treaties in relation to IP Rights such as the Treaty of Paris for the Protection of Industrial Property, the European Patent Convention, the Patent Cooperation Treaty and the Strasbourg Convention. The Netherlands is also a party to the Agreement on Trade-Related Aspects of Intellectual Property Rights (TRIPS Agreement).

F. Receivables

1. Characteristics as to:

a) Language of Documentation. The documentation governing the transfer of receivables may be drawn up in any language and can even be drawn up in multiple languages. For the latter, it should be stipulated which language will prevail in case of any discrepancies.

b) Form of Documentation. Dutch law requires the transfer of receivables to be laid down in a deed (i.e. written form). All documents may be signed outside the Netherlands and, if necessary, in counterparts.

c) Specification of Receivables. Similar to the transfer of tangible assets, the transfer of receivables requires that such receivables are sufficiently identifiable, i.e. it should be evident which receivables are being transferred to the purchaser and which receivables will remain with the seller. Reference is made to B, 1, c above for further information.

2. Administrative, Corporate and Other Approvals

The transfer of receivables does not require any governmental or administrative approvals.

As for the requirement of corporate approvals, reference is made to B, 2 above.

The transfer of receivables will only be valid after the debtor has been notified of such transfer by either the seller or purchaser. The validity of the transfer is, however, not subject to the approval of the debtor.

3. Filing Requirements

The transfer of receivables does not require any specific filings with public authorities or registrations in public registers or databases. Until the debtor has been notified of the transfer, such transfer will not be valid and payments in discharge of the receivable can still be made to the seller.

G. Liabilities

1. Characteristics as to:

a) Language of Documentation. The documentation governing the transfer of receivables may be drawn up in any language and can even be drawn up in multiple languages. For the latter it is recommended to stipulate which language will prevail in case of any discrepancies.

b) Form of Documentation. In general there are no format requirements as to documenting a transfer of liabilities although written form is certainly recommendable. A transaction between a sole shareholder and a Dutch company represented by such sole shareholder must be laid down in written form. All documents may be signed outside the Netherlands and, if necessary, in counterparts.

c) Specification of Liabilities. Similar to the transfer of tangible assets, the transfer of liabilities requires that such liabilities are sufficiently identifiable, i.e. it should be evident which liabilities are being transferred to the purchaser and which liabilities will remain with the seller. Reference is made to B, 1, c above for further information.

2. Administrative, Corporate and Other Approvals

The transfer of liabilities does not require any governmental or administrative approvals.

As for the requirement of corporate approvals, reference is made to B, 2 above.

The transfer of liabilities will only be valid upon the consent of the creditor after having been notified of such transfer by either the seller or purchaser.

3. Filing Requirements

The transfer of liabilities does not require any specific filings with public authorities or registrations in public registers or databases. Until the creditor has been notified of the transfer and has granted its consent, such transfer will not be valid.

4. Purchaser's Liability for:

a) Tax Obligations. Upon a transfer of assets, any tax obligations generally remain with the seller. However, there may be some exceptions. For instance, in case the transfer of assets can be qualified as a transfer of a whole enterprise, liability for certain social security contributions may pass to the new owner.

b) Environmental Contamination. In principle, the owner of certain assets is liable for any environmental contamination unless it can be proven that the prior owner is responsible for such contamination. For this reason, it is highly recommended that an environmental investigation be performed in the context of a proper due diligence.

c) Products Sold or Services Rendered by the Seller to Third Parties. In principle, the original manufacturer is liable for any products sold or services rendered prior to the acquisition. However, on a contractual basis, purchasers often also assume liabilities related to the business are being transferred. Therefore, it is recommended to clearly indicate the liabilities being assumed and exclude any unknown liabilities.

5. Automatic Transfer of Other Liabilities

In general, no other liabilities of the seller transfer automatically to the purchaser following the acquisition of assets. However, reference is made to G, 4 above and H, 1 below.

6. Contractual Protection as to 4 and 5 above

It is customary to include specific provisions in the relevant asset transfer agreement as to liabilities that transfer to a purchaser by operation of law. The provisions could include an indemnification by the seller or a limitation thereto. In certain cases this may also be reflected in a purchase price adjustment mechanism.

H. Employees

1. Transfer of Employees

By operation of Dutch law, all rights and obligations deriving from employment agreements that pertain to the transferred business will automatically transfer from the seller to the purchaser in case the transferred assets constitute a distinct business or undertaking (an economic unit). If the transferred assets do not constitute such economic unit, all rights and obligations arising from the employment agreements will remain with the seller.

In principle, obligations arising from existing pension schemes will also transfer to the purchaser. However, if the purchaser has established its own pension scheme, it may, under certain strict conditions, opt to provide the transferring employees with its own pension scheme as of the transfer date.

After the transfer, the transferred employees will in principle remain employed based on the terms and conditions of employment that were in place with the seller. A subsequent harmonization of terms and conditions of employment cannot be related to the transfer itself and must be based on economic, technical or organizational reasons.

For one year after the transfer of an undertaking, the seller, jointly with the purchaser, can be held fully liable for any and all obligations arising from the transferred employment agreements that came into existence prior to the transfer.

An employee may object to the transfer of his/her employment to the purchaser. However, this will result in the automatic termination of the existing employment agreement. The employee also has the option to request the competent court for dissolution of the employment agreement, in case he/she can substantiate that the transfer is disadvantageous to him/her. In such case, the court may award a severance payment.

The employer (whether it is the seller or the purchaser) is not allowed to dismiss an employee based on a transfer of undertaking. The dismissal must be based on economic, technical or organizational reasons. Any termination by the seller based on the transfer alone may be declared void.

2. Approval of Works Council, Trade Union or Other Institutions

Under the Dutch Works Council Act, businesses with fifty or more employees are obliged to establish a works council. The proposed transfer of a business must be presented to the respective works councils of the seller and the purchaser in order to obtain their advice on the proposed transaction. A written request for advice must be presented to the works council in good time and must allow the works council to still have an impact on the contemplated decision. The request for advice must stipulate the reasons for the proposed transaction and describe the expected consequences for the employees.

After the works council has given its advice, the entrepreneur must inform the works council of its final decision. If the advice of the works council is not followed, the implementation of the decision must be suspended for a one-month period during which the works council may appeal to the decision with the Companies' Chamber of the Amsterdam Court of Appeals.

Companies that employ between ten and fifty employees may establish personnel representation. The company is obliged to request the advice of personnel representation on any decision that may lead to a loss of jobs or major changes in the type of work done, employment conditions or the working conditions if at least 25% of the employees working within the company is involved.

In case a company employs between ten and fifty employees and has not established personnel representation, the employees are entitled to give their advice in an all-staff meeting regarding an intended decision that may result in a loss of jobs or in major changes in the type of work done, employment conditions or the working conditions if at least 25% of the employees working within the company is involved.

In the two situations described above, it is likely that the transfer of a business and its consequences would be subject to the prior advice from the personnel representation or the all-staff meeting. One important aspect of these proceedings is that negative advice from either body does not preclude the company from executing the asset transfer.

If no works council or employee representation is in existence, the seller will need to inform the transferring employees in good time of the proposed date of the asset transfer, reasons for the transfer, legal, social and economic implications for the employees and any measures (such as relocations or changes to reporting lines) that are contemplated in relation to the employees.

3. Contractual Protection as to Labor Issues

It is customary to include special provisions regarding the employees in an asset sale and/or transfer agreement. The guarantees and indemnifications to be included are dependent on the issues that were discovered during any due diligence review. In any case, the asset transfer agreement may include a provision pursuant to which the seller will discharge all its obligations regarding the transferred employees for its own account up to the date of the asset transfer and will indemnify the purchaser against all liabilities arising from the seller's failure to discharge such obligations.

I. Tax Implications

1. Value Added Tax

The current VAT rate in the Netherlands amounts to 19%. The transfer of assets is generally taxable at a rate of 19% if the assets are located in the Netherlands at the time of transfer. However, it is in some cases possible to claim relief from VAT (by way of a credit). This is the case if a transfer can be regarded as a "transfer of going concern", meaning that the assets transferred constitute a business as a whole or a part of a business that can operate independently. The purchaser must intend to operate the business or the part of the business transferred and not simply to immediately liquidate the activity concerned and sell the stock, if any. Unjust application of VAT relief could incur VAT liability of 19% of the transfer value. This liability will, from a formal tax law perspective, be for the account of the seller. To mitigate the VAT liability for the seller, the tax/VAT provisions in the asset transfer agreement must provide for a provision stipulating which party will bear the costs in case the transfer of assets results in a chargeable transaction for VAT purposes and how these cost can be reduced as much as possible. Often, parties opt for obtaining a binding ruling from the local tax authorities.

2. Real Property Transfer Tax

The transfer of real property is in principle subject to Dutch Real Estate Transfer Tax at a rate of 6%. This may include the transfer of economic ownership of real property and the transfer of shares in a real estate entity (i.e. an entity of which 70% of the assets relates to commercial real estate in the Netherlands). The Real Estate Transfer Tax is calculated on the higher of the purchase price or the market value. Although transfer tax is due and payable by the purchaser, the parties may agree on who will effectively bear the costs. Under certain conditions, exemptions may apply. For instance, this is the case for transfers within the scope of internal reorganizations or for certain transfers that are subject to VAT; whether an exemption may apply must be reviewed on a case-by-case basis.

3. Other Tax Issues

In general, asset transfers are relatively complicated from a tax perspective and require prior planning, as income and/or transfer taxes may be triggered. Moreover, the right to carry forward tax losses may not be transferred to the purchaser.

J. Bankruptcy Law

1. Challenge of Asset Transfer in Case of Insolvency

In the event seller or purchaser, following a transfer of assets for consideration, becomes bankrupt and provided that the other party knew or should have known that the transaction would prejudice certain creditors, such prejudiced creditors may have the transaction declared void. A trustee in bankruptcy may even declare the transaction void without court intervention.

2. Acquisition of Assets that are Subject to Insolvency Proceedings

A trustee in bankruptcy may decide not to transfer assets even though an asset purchase agreement has been entered into. Any agreements that have been executed prior to bankruptcy may be declared void. After commencement of bankruptcy proceedings, the authority to enter into agreements and dispose of assets of the company is vested in the trustee only. The trustee will need to verify whether the assets are subject to a right of retention by third parties. In addition, the trustee may need to obtain approval from a supervisory judge.

K. Timing and Costs

1. Timeframe of Asset Transfer

The timing of the sale/acquisition of a business by way of an asset deal very much depends on the type of assets to be transferred and the availability of the relevant information for the legal and tax advisors involved. Assuming that all information is readily available and that no specific issues arise, a transfer of assets may be completed in a relatively short timeframe. When time is of the essence, parties may wish to agree to transfer the beneficial ownership of the assets immediately, whereas the local transfer requirements for the transfer of legal ownership will be complied with within an agreed period of time (e.g., 30 days) after the transaction date.

2. Costs of Asset Transfer

In addition to potential advisors' fees, asset transfers may trigger certain notarization and registration costs. Notarization costs will be incurred upon the transfer of real property and registered shares in Dutch companies. Registration costs with the Dutch local authorities (e.g., Land Registry) are generally minimal.

L. Miscellaneous

1. Choice of Foreign Law

A sale and transfer agreement regarding a business located in the Netherlands may be governed by foreign (i.e. non-Dutch) law. The sale and transfer agreement will create an obligation to transfer the legal title to assets and liabilities. For the latter (i.e. the transfer in rem) local Dutch transfer formalities must be complied with.

2. (International) Arbitration, Choice of Venue

The parties to an asset transfer may agree to choose to settle their disputes by arbitration rather than in court. Reference can be made to an existing arbitration institute such as the Netherlands Arbitration Institute, which has its own arbitration rules that may be adopted by the parties. The Netherlands is a party to the New York convention on the recognition and enforcement of foreign arbitral awards so that arbitral decisions from other member states can be easily enforced in the Netherlands.

3. Other Distinctions, Characteristics

It is recommended that proper legal advice be engaged when entering into an asset deal, regardless of the circumstances.

Russia

By *Alexander Kalinov* and *Nadezhda Drobilko*

A. General Aspects

1. Asset Deal vs. Share Deal: Essential Considerations

There are a number of considerations to take into account when structuring a transaction as a share or asset deal:

Tax

The sale of shares in a joint-stock company (**"JSC"**) or interest in a limited liability company (**"LLC"**) is not subject to VAT. With certain exceptions, the sale of assets is subject to VAT.

Timing

Generally, a share deal takes less time to accomplish.

State Registration and Regulatory Approvals

By contrast with an asset deal, a share deal allows the avoidance of state registration of the transfer of qualified assets, such as objects of real estate.

Liabilities

The downside of a share deal is that the acquiring company acquires the target company with all rights, obligations and liabilities, while asset deals allow a "pick and choose" approach.

Antitrust Requirements

Under certain circumstances, both share and asset deals may be subject to antitrust approval.

Licenses and Permits

As a general rule, licenses and permits are not transferable. Therefore, if necessary, in an asset deal the acquiring company will need to obtain licenses and permits in its own name.

Corporate Matters

An asset deal may be subject to corporate approval by the seller and/or purchaser. A share deal may be subject to preemptive rights of other stakeholders of the target company.

Integrity of Business

To insure the integrity of the acquired business, in an asset deal it may be necessary to effectuate auxiliary transactions, such as transferring rights to intellectual property, transferring key employees to a new company, etc., which could be time-consuming and expensive process.

It should be noted that Russian law distinguishes a special type of asset deal – the sale of an enterprise, as a special type of real estate object. Under this type of asset deal, the acquiring company purchases assets as well as liabilities related to the assets, trademarks, etc. This type of asset deal is cumbersome, requires notification of creditors and is subject to state registration. Therefore, it is rarely used in Russia.

2. Distinction between Sale and Transfer in Rem

Russian law distinguishes between the obligation to transfer and the fulfillment of the obligation to transfer (transfer in rem) in the following sense. A sale and purchase contract is deemed executed when the parties have reached an agreement with respect to all material terms. Under Russian law, a sale and purchase contract is a consensual contract, meaning that as soon as the contract is signed, the seller is obligated to transfer the assets and the purchaser is obligated to pay for such assets; however, the sale and purchase contract does not imply that signing of the contract means the actual transfer of the assets (real contract).

In all other material aspects, transfer in rem is inseparable from the underlying obligation to transfer. Therefore, if the underlying obligation is deemed null and void after the transfer in rem takes place, the applicable remedy is restitution in integrum. If the underlying transaction is voided prior to the transfer in rem, the effectuating of such transfer will have no contractual ground.

Since there is usually an interval of time between undertaking an obligation to transfer and fulfillment of such obligation, it is customary in Russia to evidence the actual transfer of assets by an act of transfer and acceptance signed by both parties to the transaction.

3. Regional Differences

There are no regional differences as regards the legal requirements applicable to an asset transfer in Russia because the sale and transfer of assets, being part of Russian civil law, are within the jurisdiction of federal authorities and, therefore, are governed by Russian federal laws and regulations and not by regional laws and regulations.

4. Acquisition by Foreigners

As a general rule, the same legal regime applicable to asset transfers applies to both foreign and Russian individuals and legal entities, unless otherwise expressly provided for by Russian federal law. Certain restrictions are set forth by federal law with regard to the acquisition of real estate by foreigners. For instance, foreign individuals and legal entities are prohibited from owning agricultural lands and land plots adjacent to the state border. Also, with respect to the acquisition of nuclear materials, foreign legal entities should receive approval from the Russian Federation ("**RF**") Government.

Also, Russian authorities recently implemented certain measures towards restricting foreign investment in strategic industries (such as encryption services, distribution and maintenance of cryptographic means, development, production, repair and sale of arms and military goods, space industry and aeronautical engineering). Such investments generally require preliminary approval by the state authorities.

5. Public Registers, Records and Databases

There are several state registers in Russia containing publicly available information that may be required in connection with asset transfers. They are the following:

(i) The Unified State Register of Legal Entities ("**EGRUL**"). This register is maintained by the tax authorities and contains basic information with regard to legal entities and individual entrepreneurs, such as legal form, state registration number, taxpayer identification number, registered share capital, description of certain corporate events (capital increases/decreases, reorganizations and liquidations) and information on the status of individuals who are registered as individual entrepreneurs. This information may be obtained from EGRUL upon written request filed with the tax authorities, and limited data is made available on the Internet.

(ii) The Unified State Register of Rights to Real Estate and Transactions Therewith. This register contains information with regard to real estate, its owners and encumbrances thereon. Information on the state registration of titles to real estate is public.

(iii) Intellectual Property Registers. There is no single unified register that contains all relevant information on intellectual property rights.

Intellectual property and respective intellectual property rights are registered in the following registers depending on the category of the particular item of intellectual property: (i) State Register of Inventions; (ii) State Register of Utility Models; (iii) State Register of Industrial Designs; (iv) State Register of Trademarks and Service Marks; (v) State Register of Appellations of Places of Origin of Goods; and (vi) State Register of Protected Selection Achievements. In addition, state registers of topologies of integral microcircuits, software and databases are maintained in Russia. However, the registration of intellectual property with these registers is optional.

The official website of the Federal Service for Intellectual Property, Patents and Trademarks ("**Rospatent**") (www.fips.ru) provides on-line access to the registers listed in points (i) through (v) above and to the list of trademarks in Russia. Information from the State Register of Protected Selection Achievements is available on the website of the RF State Commission for Trial and Protection of Selection Achievements (www.gossort.com).

As a general rule, the transfer of intellectual property or granting of rights to use intellectual property under license agreements, agreements on the transfer of exclusive rights or franchising agreements are subject to state registration, which is recorded in the foregoing state registers. If an agreement that is subject to mandatory registration is not registered, it should be deemed invalid.

With respect to a general copyright register, we note that such register does not exist in Russia.

(iv) Registers of Means of Transportation. Russian law requires the registration of qualified means of transportation and their transfer, such as aircrafts, spacecrafts and vessels. The ownership rights to vessels, as well as their encumbrances, are registered in the appropriate state register (there are currently five different vessel registers, in particular, the State Shipping Register, the Vessel Book, the Bareboat Charter Register, the Register of Vessels under Construction and the Russian International Register of Vessels). The information in the State Shipping Register is public. Civil aircraft are subject to state registration in the State Civil Aircraft Register. After September 14, 2009, when the RF Law on State Registration of Aircraft and Transactions Therewith enters into force, information from this register will become public. Spacecraft should also be subject to state registration; however, the registration procedure has not yet been implemented.

6. Purchase Price Requirements

The parties are free to determine the purchase price, which can be stated in the agreement in any currency. However, with few exceptions, settlements among Russian legal entities and/or individuals shall be effectuated in the Russian ruble (RUB).

For taxation purposes, the price set forth by the parties in a contract is deemed to be within market pricing range. However, Russian tax authorities are authorized to make transfer pricing adjustments if the price under a controlled transaction deviates from the market price by more than 20%. Controlled transactions include transactions between related parties, foreign trade contracts, exchange transactions and transactions that deviate by more than 20% from transactions with similar assets of the same seller (or purchaser, as the case may be).

For tax and accounting purposes, it is advisable to specify in the contract both the total purchase price and the individual purchase prices of each particular asset (category of assets).

B. Tangible/Movable Assets

1. Characteristics as to:

a) Language of Documentation. Sale and purchase agreements and other documents regarding tangible assets can be drafted in any language. However, Russian law requires that the records (including corporate, accounting and taxation records) of a Russian company be maintained in Russian. If an agreement between Russian and foreign companies should be submitted to Russian state authorities, such agreement should be executed in Russian or bilingually or be accompanied with a certified Russian translation. Agreements between Russian companies are generally executed in Russian.

b) Form of Documentation. As a general rule, agreements between legal entities and between a legal entity and individual with respect to the transfer of tangible assets should be executed in writing. However, oral agreements are permitted if they are performed at the time of their execution, e.g., purchase of agricultural produce from individuals. Consumer transactions are not required to be in writing, but they should be evidenced by a receipt. Failure to comply with the written form does not invalidate the transaction, unless otherwise stated in the law or agreed by the parties, but prohibits the parties from calling witnesses in the event of a dispute involving the transaction. Russian law establishes that failure to comply with the requirement of a written form of the agreement in a foreign trade transaction or in a sale and purchase of works of art or antiques makes such transactions void. The law or the parties to the agreement themselves may set forth additional requirements for the form of the agreement, such as its notarization, affixing a seal, etc. The sale and transfer documents may be executed outside Russia. Signing in counterparts is permissible.

c) Specification of Assets. Under Russian law, a contract for the sale and purchase of assets should provide for a description of the assets that would be sufficient to properly identify the assets subject to the transfer (e.g., type of asset, quantity, model/ registration number (if any), technical documentation, etc.). Therefore, each asset (or group of homogeneous assets) should be described in the contract or listed in an annex to the contract. Similarly, the act of transfer and acceptance of the assets under a contract shall provide for a description of assets being transferred.

If the assets are not described in the contract in sufficient detail, the agreement may be deemed to have not been concluded, in which case neither the seller nor purchaser is entitled to claim performance thereunder. If the description of assets in the act of transfer and acceptance is not sufficient to identify such assets, no assets would be deemed to have been transferred under such act.

2. Administrative, Corporate and Other Approvals

(i) The law may require that the transfer of tangible assets be approved by relevant state authorities. For instance, according to Russian antitrust legislation, the transfer of assets may be subject to preliminary approval by antitrust authorities depending on a number of factors, e. g., value of acquired assets, aggregate value of the assets of the seller, purchaser and their groups, total proceeds of the seller and the purchaser for the year preceding the transaction, etc. Failure to obtain antitrust approval when required may result in invalidation of a transaction by the courts in the event that such transaction adversely affected or may adversely affect market competition. Also, administrative fines may be imposed on a legal entity for such failure. Another example of a transaction that requires special governmental approval would be the acquisition of nuclear materials by foreign legal entities, which must be approved by the RF Government. The right to explore and develop oil and gas fields, gold-mines and other mineral deposits in inland sea waters and on the continental shelf of the RF is granted by resolution of the RF Government.

(ii) The approval of a competent corporate body is required for major and interested party transactions and in other cases specified by the company's charter. Failure to obtain such approval may result in the invalidation of the transaction in court.

(iii) As a general rule, the pledgor has the right to dispose of the encumbered asset only with the consent of the pledgee unless it is otherwise stipulated by law or by the pledge agreement.

The transfer of a jointly-owned asset requires the consent of the other owners. The transfer of a share in a jointly-owned asset belonging to two or more persons is subject to the preemptive right of other co-owners of such asset to acquire the offered share in the asset.

3. Filing Requirements

The law may require that an agreement for the transfer of tangible assets be registered with relevant state authorities. For instance, transactions with qualified museum collections require state registration. Also, in certain cases, the antitrust authorities must be notified about qualified transactions.

4. Automatic Transfer of Encumbrances

As a general rule, upon the sale of tangible assets, the purchaser automatically substitutes for the pledgor in its role unless otherwise agreed by the purchaser and the pledgee.

C. Real Property

1. Characteristics as to:

a) Language of Documentation. Due to the fact that the documents substantiating real property sale and purchase transactions must be filed with the state authorities, a Russian or bilingual version or a certified Russian translation of the documentation is necessary.

b) Form of Documentation. An agreement for the sale and purchase of real property should be in writing as a single document signed by both parties. Signing in counterparts is not permitted. If the agreement does not comply with these requirements with respect to form, it is deemed null and void. The transfer of real property should be evidenced by an act of transfer and acceptance signed by both parties. The sale and purchase agreement may be executed outside Russia, provided that the mandatory rules of Russian law governing real property are complied with.

The transfer of rights to real property is subject to state registration. In addition to the state registration of the transfer of rights, the law requires the state registration of certain transactions with real property. For example, in the event of an acquisition of residential premises or an enterprise as a property complex or the shared participation in the construction of multi-apartment buildings, the underlying agreements are subject to state registration. If the transaction (and not only the transfer of rights) is subject to state registration, the agreement is deemed concluded upon the state registration thereof and the purchaser acquires the title to real property only upon the state registration of such transfer rather than upon the execution of the agreement.

c) Specification of Assets. According to Russian law, an agreement on the sale and purchase of real property should name the property and specify its location, cadastral number and other material details (such as the size of the land plot or location of premises in a building). A general description would not be sufficient for proper transfer of the title. Similarly, the act of transfer and acceptance of real property under the agreement shall provide for a description of the property being transferred.

2. Administrative, Corporate and Other Approvals

The transfer of real property may require approval by state authorities, such as the antitrust authorities, in cases specified by law as discussed in Section B, 2 above. In certain cases, the failure to obtain such approval may result in the invalidation of the transaction by a court and the imposition of an administrative fine.

The approval of a competent corporate body is required for major and interested party transactions and in other cases specified by the company's charter. Failure to obtain such approval may result in the invalidation of a transaction by the courts.

In the event real property is encumbered by a mortgage, the transfer is subject to the approval of the mortgagee. Failure to comply with this requirement may result in the invalidation of a transaction by the courts or in earlier foreclosure of the mortgaged property by the mortgagee.

In the event real property is leased or encumbered with an easement, the title transfer does not affect the lease or easement, accordingly, both of which are deemed automatically assigned to the purchaser.

3. Filing Requirements

Under Russian law, the transfer of title to real property shall be registered with the Unified State Register of Rights to Real Estate and Transactions Therewith maintained by the Federal Service on State Registration, Cadastre and Cartography. Title to real property is deemed to be transferred only upon such state registration.

In addition to land plots, subsoil, buildings, unfinished constructions and any other objects which may not be moved without prejudice to their designated purpose, under Russian law, vessels, aircrafts and spacecrafts are also deemed real property and are subject to registration in various registers referred to above (see Section A, 5, (iv) above).

4. Automatic Transfer of Encumbrances

For the purposes of state registration, Russian law interprets as a restriction of rights to real property (encumbrance over real property) (i) easements, (ii) mortgages, (iii) lease rights, and (iv) other rights of third parties (such as special protection zones, including electric lines zones, water bodies, protection zones, etc.). Real property is deemed encumbered with an easement or mortgage as of the moment of state registration of such encumbrance. As a general rule, encumbrances on real property that were registered in the state register are not affected by, and remain in effect after, the transfer of real property.

We also note that by virtue of law, unless otherwise is stated in the purchase agreement, real property is deemed mortgaged to the seller until the purchaser discharges its payment obligations under the purchase agreement in full.

Russian law does not recognize the legal concept of a waiver of encumbrance.

5. Automatic Transfer of Lease Agreements

Agreements on the lease of real property survive the transfer of such property to the purchaser and the latter replaces the seller as a landlord in the lease agreement. Russian law does not provide for special termination rights of the purchaser or the tenant in the event of the transfer of the leased property. However, the lease agreement may provide for the change of ownership as a ground for termination of the lease agreement. Also, if the real property lease agreement is entered into for an unspecified period of time, any party to the agreement may terminate the lease agreement by giving three-month's written notice to the other party, unless the agreement provides for a different termination notice term.

D. Contracts

1. Characteristics as to:

a) Language of Documentation. Under Russian law, a "transfer of contract" takes the legal form of a substitution of one party to the contract by another through the assignment of rights of such party as an obligee (creditor) to the assignee and/or transfer of the debt (obligations) of such party to the assignee. In other words, a transfer of contracts constitutes an assignment of rights and obligations under such contracts to a third party. For consistency purposes, the transfer of rights and obligations under a contract is hereinafter referred to as the "assignment agreement."

The assignment agreement can be executed in any language. However, it is customary that an assignment agreement that is between Russian companies and individuals be drafted in Russian. Also, Russian law requires that the records of a Russian company be maintained in Russian and, therefore, if a party to the assignment agreement is a Russian company, it may be necessary to have the assignment agreement translated into Russian. The assignment agreement could be executed bilingually. Finally, if the assignment agreement is to be filed with a Russian state authority, it should be in Russian, bilingual or accompanied with a certified Russian translation.

b) Form of Documentation. The assignment agreement should be executed in the same form as the contract that is subject to the assignment, i.e., as a general rule, it should be in writing and may also be subject to notarization and/or registration requirements if the original contract is subject to such requirements (for more details, please refer to B, 1, b above). The parties to the original contract may also establish additional requirements for its form (such as execution as a single document), which should be complied with upon execution of the assignment agreement. As a matter of practice, in addition to the assignment agreement, it may sometimes be reasonable to make a supplemental agreement to the contract that is subject to the assignment agreement to reflect the change in the contracting parties to such contract.

The assignment agreement may be executed outside of Russia. Signing in counterparts is permitted unless the law specifically requires the execution of such agreement as a single document signed by all parties.

c) Specification of Contracts. The assignment agreement must specify in each contract the rights and obligations that are subject to the assignment in a sufficiently detailed manner in order to identify the contract. It is customary to provide the following information in the assignment agreement with respect to the assigned contract: parties to the contract, date of execution, title of the contract, its number and the subject matter. If all rights and obligations under the contract are subject to assignment under the assignment agreement, it is sufficient to indicate in such agreement that "all" rights and obligations are subject to transfer without listing them. The assignor should transfer to the assignee the documents evidencing the rights being transferred, including, inter alia, the original contract, and also make available to the assignee the information necessary for the latter to exercise its rights under the assigned contract. Also, the parties to the assignment agreement may agree on a different scope of rights being transferred or different terms and conditions of their exercising, which should be also set forth in the assignment agreement.

Under Russian law, a party to the contract may assign only its rights or obligations or both (in part or in whole) under the contract. The assignment agreement should specify exactly the scope of the rights and/or obligations being transferred.

There is no specific requirement for attaching schedules or lists of contracts to the assignment agreement.

2. Administrative, Corporate and Other Approvals

Rules with respect to statutory and corporate approvals applicable to commercial contracts generally apply to assignment agreements. Please refer to B, 2 above for more details.

Russian legislation provides for different rules with regard to the transfer of rights and transfer of obligations under a contract. Obligations under the contract could be assigned only upon consent of the other party to the contract. Failure to obtain such consent would result in the invalidity of the transfer of obligations.

Rights under the contract could be transferred to a third party without the consent of the other party (the debtor), unless otherwise expressly provided for by law or set forth in the contract. However, notification of the debtor about the assignment of rights under the contract is highly advisable because the failure to notify the debtor may result in adverse consequences for the new creditor. For instance, fulfillment of obligations by the debtor to the initial creditor will be deemed as due performance of obligations by the debtor.

3. Automatic Transfer of Contracts (Other than Lease and Employment Agreements)

Under Russian law, pledge, mortgage and lease rights are automatically transferred to the purchaser, together with the assets that are subject to the pledge, mortgage or lease, respectively. In addition, Russian law provides for the automatic transfer of asset-related insurance agreements (property insurance) together with the transfer of rights to the insured assets. In this case the insurer should be notified immediately of the transfer in writing.

According to Russian law, in the event of the sale and purchase of an enterprise (as a property complex) all obligations under each contract recorded as part of the enterprise are deemed to be transferred to the purchaser, provided the respective creditor was notified of the sale of the enterprise and unless the creditor required termination or acceleration of performance under the respective contract.

Also, the rights under a contract are deemed to be transferred to the surety-grantor or pledgor by operation of law, in the event the surety-grantor or pledgor (as the case may be) performed the secured obligation under such contract for the debtor.

4. Filing Requirements

Assignment agreements are subject to the same registration requirements as the contracts, the rights and obligations under which are subject to the transfer. Therefore, if the contract itself is subject to filing or registration with authorities or registrars, the assignment agreement shall be subject to the applicable filing or registration as well.

5. Treatment of Existing Contractual Claims and Obligations

Unless otherwise provided for by law or agreement, all rights and obligations under the contract are transferred to the "purchaser" of the contract pursuant to the assignment agreement. If a third party entirely replaces the original party to an unfulfilled contract, such third party assumes all rights and obligations of the original party and may present claims arising out of the contract on grounds that existed prior to the transfer, unless otherwise provided for by law or agreement. With respect to the obligations transfer, the new debtor may use arguments based on the relationship that existed between the creditor and original debtor against claims of the creditor. Similarly, with respect to the rights transfer, the debtor may use arguments which he may have had previously against the original creditor against claims of the new creditor. The original creditor may not be held liable to the new creditor for the debtor's failure to fulfill obligations under the assigned contract, unless the original creditor acts as surety under the debtor's obligations. However, the original creditor is liable to the creditor in the event the assigned contract is invalid.

6. Warranty Claims Resulting from Events prior to Transfer

Under Russian law, the "transfer of the contract" means the assignment of all rights and assignment of all obligations under the contract and, as a result, substitution of a party to the contract by a third party. As a general rule, the transfer of contractual obligations under the contract of the original debtor to the third party could only be made with the consent of the creditor. Therefore, if the creditor consented to the transfer of the obligations of the original debtor to the third party and such third party assumed such obligations, then such third party will be responsible before the original creditor under the transferred obligations.

The concept of indemnity is not expressly recognized under Russian law in assignment agreements. Usually, parties to an agreement use contractual liability and other contractual instruments to reach the same ends for which the concept of indemnity is used.

E. IP Rights

1. Characteristics of Intellectual Property Rights (e.g., Trademarks, Patents, Utility Models, Domain Names) ("*IP Rights*") as to:

a) Language of Documentation. Documents regarding the transfer of IP Rights could be drafted in any language. However, it is customary that such documents executed between Russian companies and individuals be drafted in Russian. Also, Russian law requires that the records of a Russian company be maintained in Russian and, therefore, if a party to IP Rights transfer documents is a Russian company, it may be necessary to have the documents translated into Russian. The documents could be executed bilingually. Finally, if the documents are to be filed with a Russian state authority, they should be in Russian, bilingual or accompanied by a certified Russian translation.

b) Form of Documentation. Agreements regarding the transfer of IP Rights should be executed in writing. Certain intellectual property is protected in the RF only if registered. The transfer of registered intellectual property or granting of rights to use registered intellectual property (under license agreements, agreements on the transfer of exclusive rights to intellectual property, franchise agreements, etc.) should be registered with the Rospatent (see A, 5, (iii) above). Agreements for the transfer of intellectual property not subject to mandatory registration do not require any special registration. If the agreement for the transfer of IP Rights is not registered with the appropriate authorities when so required by law, it is deemed void. Notarization of sale and transfer agreements regarding IP Rights is not required.

In a sale of an enterprise (as a property complex), IP Rights of the seller related to the enterprise are transferred to the purchaser together with other property constituting the enterprise, unless otherwise provided for in the sale and purchase agreement. Such IP Rights transfer may be subject to two state registrations: (i) as part of the enterprise, a sale and purchase transaction; and (ii) as a separate transaction with IP Rights (in the event of registered IP).

The Russian law governing agreements on the transfer of IP Rights may be executed outside of Russia. Joint signing of one and the same document is not required by law; however, it is customary in Russia that the parties sign a single document.

c) Specification of IP Rights. Under Russian law, the subject matter of the agreement should be properly described, which implies that IP and IP Rights subject to transfer should be described in the agreement in all material aspects, including references to documents confirming the IP Rights (certificates, patents, etc.).

There is no requirement provided for by Russian law regarding the attachment of schedules and lists to the agreements.

2. Administrative, Corporate and Other Approvals

The transfer of IP Rights is subject to governmental or administrative approvals or approval by a corporate body if such approvals are specifically required by law or the charter documents of the company. Please refer to B, 2 above for more details.

If IP Rights are encumbered with a pledge, the pledgor may alienate such IP Rights only upon consent of the pledgee, unless otherwise provided for by law or contract. In the event of failure to obtain the consent of the pledgee, the pledgee is entitled to demand acceleration of the performance of the secured obligation. We note that the pledge of IP Rights is a new legal construction in Russian law and, therefore, its application in practice has not been widely tested.

3. Filing Requirements

If IP Rights are subject to state registration with relevant state authorities, the transfer of such IP Rights also requires state registration. In this case, the transfer of IP Rights is registered by way of registration of the underlying transfer agreement, and the IP

Rights are deemed transferred at the moment of such registration. Failure to register the agreement renders the respective transaction void.

4. Applicable International (Multilateral) Agreements or Treaties

The Russian Federation is a party to the following international treaties and conventions regarding the protection of IP Rights:

- Convention Establishing the World Intellectual Property Organization, Stockholm, July 14, 1967;
- Paris Convention for the Protection of Industrial Property, March 20, 1883;
- Patent Cooperation Treaty, Washington, June 19, 1970;
- Eurasia Patent Convention, 1994;
- Madrid Agreement Concerning the International Registration of Marks, April 14, 1891;
- Trademark Law Treaty, Geneva, October 27, 1994;
- International Convention for the Protection of Performers, Producers of Phonograms and Broadcasting Organizations, Rome, October 26, 1961;
- Convention for the Protection of Producers of Phonograms Against Unauthorized Duplication of Their Phonograms, October 29, 1971; and
- Berne Convention for the Protection of Literary and Artistic Works, September 9, 1886.

F. Receivables

1. Characteristics as to:

a) Language of Documentation. Under Russian law, receivables could be transferred from one party to another through the assignment of rights (claims) to receive such receivables under the contract. The assignment agreement could be executed in any language. However, it is customary that an assignment agreement between Russian companies be drafted in Russian. Also, Russian law requires that the records of a Russian company be maintained in Russian; therefore, it could be necessary to have the document in question translated into Russian. Finally, it may be necessary to translate the agreement into Russian if it must be submitted to the state authorities. The documents could be executed bilingually.

b) Form of Documentation. The assignment agreement effectuating the transfer of receivables, i.e., assignment of a right (claim), should be executed in the same form as the contract under which the rights are assigned, i.e., it should be in writing and may be subject to notarization and/or registration requirements if the contract under which the rights are assigned was notarized and/or registered, respectively.

The assignment agreement may be executed outside of Russia. Signing in counterparts is generally permitted, unless the law requires execution of such agreement as a single document signed by all parties (for example, in the event of assignment under a real property purchase agreement).

c) Specification of Receivables. Receivables may be transferred to a third party through an assignment of rights under particular contracts and, therefore, it may be difficult to document the transfer of all receivables owed to the transferor by different debtors under a single assignment agreement. The assignment agreement should provide for the description of assigned rights, which would allow proper identification of them, e. g., specify the agreement under which the receivables are assigned, rights that are subject to transfer, amount of receivables, etc.

Russian law does not provide for a special requirement for attaching schedules and lists of receivables to the transfer agreement.

2. Administrative, Corporate and Other Approvals

The transfer of receivables is subject to governmental or administrative approvals or approval by corporate bodies if such approvals are specifically required by law or by the charter documents of the company. Please refer to B, 2 above for more details.

Consent of the debtor is not required for the transfer of the receivables, although the latter should be notified of such transfer, unless otherwise set forth by law or agreement. For instance, the law provides that if the identity of the creditor is material for the debtor (e. g., under a joint-venture agreement), the rights may not be assigned to a third party without consent of the debtor, and failure to comply with the consent requirement renders the assignment void. Failure to notify the debtor of the assignment of receivables may result in adverse consequences for the creditor. For instance, the fulfillment of obligations to the initial creditor will be deemed as due performance of obligations by the debtor.

3. Filing Requirements

The law may require that the agreement for the transfer of receivables be registered with the relevant state authorities. For example, antitrust authorities must be notified of qualified transactions; and assignment occurring through transactions concerning real property should be registered.

Notification of the debtor is also necessary; otherwise, performance to the initial creditor will be deemed due performance.

G. Liabilities

1. Characteristics as to:

a) Language of Documentation. Under Russian law, the liabilities under the contract could be transferred to a third party through the assignment of debt (obligations) of the party to such contract. The assignment agreement could be executed in any language. However, it is customary that such document executed between Russian companies be drafted in Russian. Also, Russian law requires that the records of a Russian company be maintained in Russian; therefore, it could be necessary to have the document in question translated into Russian. Finally, it may be necessary to translate the assignment agreement into Russian if it must be submitted to the state authorities. The documents could be executed bilingually.

b) Form of Documentation. The assignment agreement should be executed in the same form as the initial contract under which the obligations are subject to assignment, i.e., it should be in writing and may be subject to notarization and/or registration requirements if the original contract was notarized and/or registered. For more detail, please refer to B, 1, b above.

The assignment agreement and other related documents may be executed outside of Russia. Signing in counterparts is generally permitted, unless execution of a single document is required by law (e. g., assignment under a real property sale and purchase agreement).

c) Specification of Liabilities. The assignment agreement should provide for a description of the assigned obligations, which would allow proper identification of the assigned obligations, e. g., specify the agreement under which the liabilities are assigned, obligations that are subject to transfer, outstanding amounts of liabilities, etc. Russian law does not provide for a special requirement for attaching schedules and lists of receivables to the transfer agreement.

2. Administrative, Corporate and Other Approvals

The transfer of liabilities is subject to governmental or administrative approvals or approval by corporate bodies if such approvals are specifically required by law or by foundation documents of the company. Please refer to B, 2 above for more detail.

The debtor may not transfer its obligations (debt) to a third party without the consent of the creditor. Failure to comply with the consent requirement renders the assignment void.

3. Filing Requirements

The law may require that an agreement regarding the transfer of liabilities be registered and/or filed with the relevant state authorities. For example, antitrust authorities must be notified about qualified transactions; and assignment through transactions concerning real property should be registered.

The transfer of liabilities is subject to the creditor's consent and, therefore, separate notification of the creditor is not required.

4. Purchaser's Liability for:

a) Tax Obligations. Under Russian tax law, taxes due from a person should be paid personally, i.e. at such person's expense and on its own behalf. Subsequently, tax liabilities related to the periods preceding the asset acquisition could not generally be transferred to the purchaser.

b) Environmental Contamination. As a general rule, a party in breach of environmental laws will be liable for the breach, with certain exceptions. For example, the customer under a construction project may be held liable for the environmental contamination at its construction site, irrespective of whether caused by the customer or its contractors. The purchaser would generally be held liable for a breach of environmental requirements if it is established that the breach is caused by the actions (or omissions) of the purchaser.

Damage caused to the environment should be recovered in full by the breaching party. Russian law provides for property, disciplinary, administrative and criminal liability for violation of environmental laws. Both legal entities and individuals may be subject to administrative liability, while disciplinary liability and criminal liability may be imposed on individuals only. In terms of administrative liability, the statute of limitations for holding an entity or individual liable for a breach of environmental laws is one (1) year from the date when the breach was committed or revealed.

c) Products Sold or Services Rendered by the Seller to Third Parties. With certain exceptions, under Russian law, a person, such as the purchaser, is not liable for the action or failure to act for another person, such as the seller. However, the agreement on assignment of the entire initial contract (or all of the obligations of the seller) may provide for the transfer of obligations of the seller to the purchaser under claims of third parties arising out of products sold and services rendered by the seller under such initial contract prior to the assignment of the contract.

5. Automatic Transfer of Other Liabilities

As a general rule, the seller's liabilities are not automatically transferred to the purchaser in an asset deal. The purchaser and seller may reach an agreement that the purchaser becomes fully liable under the obligations of the seller in relation of the transferred assets. Liabilities in tort are not generally transferred to the purchaser.

6. Contractual Protection as to 4 and 5 above

The concept of indemnity is not expressly recognized under Russian law. However, the agreement may provide for contractual liability, such as recovery of damages or punitive damages.

H. Employees

1. Transfer of Employees

Under Russian law, employees of the seller are not automatically transferred to the purchaser as a result of the asset transfer. Employees may be transferred from the seller to the purchaser upon their consent (or upon their request, as the case may be) through termination of employment with the seller and execution of a labor agreement with the purchaser. The two companies may also enter into an agreement on the transfer of employees, in which the terms of such transfer would be addressed.

There are a few exceptions to the foregoing rule. For instance, upon the sale of an enterprise (as a property complex) during bankruptcy proceedings, all existing labor agreements as of the sale date remain effective, and the purchaser of the enterprise assumes the rights and obligations of the employer.

2. Approval of Works Council, Trade Union or Other Institutions

The asset transfer itself does not require the approval of any works council, labor agency, trade union or other institution, unless it results in the reduction of personnel, which reduction requires notification of the trade union (if any) by the employer.

3. Contractual Protection as to Labor Issues

It is not customary to include special provisions (e. g., guarantees, indemnifications) regarding employees in the asset sale and/or transfer agreement; however, this inclusion is not prohibited.

I. Tax Implications

1. Value Added Tax

Under Russian law, the sale of assets is generally subject to VAT if the assets are located in, or imported to, Russia and would not be transported abroad. Certain transactions are exempt from VAT, such as the sale of land plots and portions thereof, residential premises, uncut diamonds and qualified drugs, the export of assets, contributions to charter capitals of business entities, the sale of securities and transfer of IP rights. Small businesses (having less than two million rubles in proceeds for three consecutive months) are entitled to apply for exemption from payment of VAT. Generally, VAT is payable by the seller; however, if, for example, the seller is a foreign entity that is not subject to mandatory registration as a taxpayer with Russian authorities, VAT is payable by the purchaser as tax agent of the seller.

Current VAT rate is 18%. VAT at the rate equal to 0% and 10% as well as VAT deductions could be applied to transactions specified in law.

2. Real Property Transfer Tax

Russian law does not provide for a land transfer tax.

3. Other Tax Issues

Russian law additionally provides for the following taxes related to an asset transfer:

(i) Profit Tax. Generally, profit gained by taxpayers is taxable by tax on profit. Taxpayers are Russian legal entities and foreign legal entities operating through a permanent establishment in Russia and/or gaining profit from sources located in Russia. The current tax rate is 24%. Lower tax rates may apply in cases specified in Russian law and/or international treaties of the Russian Federation on the avoidance of double taxation.

(ii) Property Tax. Generally, movable and immovable property deemed to be fixed assets (except for land plots, bodies of water and other natural objects) of Russian legal entities and foreign legal entities having a permanent establishment in Russia are subject to property tax. However, if a foreign legal entity does not have a permanent establishment in Russia, only immovable property owned by such entity will be taxed. Taxpayers are exempted from the payment of property tax on certain assets, such as spacecraft and vessels registered in the Russian International Vessel Register; and entities registered in free economic zones of the Russian Federation are exempt from the payment of property tax on their assets during five years from the acquisition of each particular asset. Tax rates are set forth by territorial subdivisions of the Russian Federation; however, the tax rate may not exceed 2.2% per annum. Russian law also sets forth provisions addressing double taxation issues with respect to those assets of Russian entities that are located, and are subject to taxation, in foreign jurisdictions.

(iii) Land Tax. Land plots are subject to land tax (except for those that may not be privately owned). Tax rates are established by local municipal authorities; however, the tax rate may not exceed 0.3% or 1.5% per annum, depending on the category of land.

J. Bankruptcy Law

1. Challenge of Asset Transfer in Case of Insolvency

Under Russian law, certain qualified asset transfer transactions could be challenged if the purchaser or seller is subject to bankruptcy proceedings. We also note that, in contrast to the usual course of business, in a bankruptcy, the circle of persons entitled to challenge the transactions is wider and the list of grounds for challenge is more extensive. For instance, in the course of bankruptcy proceedings the appointed receiver (*vneshniy upravlyayuschiy*) is entitled to challenge on behalf of the insolvent company any transaction on the grounds set forth under federal law. On its own behalf, the appointed receiver may challenge interested party transactions, and such transactions could be invalidated if their fulfillment has resulted or may result in damages to the insolvent company or its creditors. Further, the appointed receiver may challenge any transaction entered into within the six-month period prior to filing for bankruptcy if such transaction resulted in the creation of preferences of one creditor before others in satisfying their claims. Also, a company's distribution of assets to its shareholders or interest holders that took place within the six-month period prior to the filing for the bankruptcy could be challenged by creditors or the appointed receiver, etc.

Within three months from the date of establishment of external management over the insolvent company, the appointed receiver may refuse to perform under certain agreements of such insolvent company. Therefore, if the asset transfer has not been finalized before the foregoing date, the insolvent company may refuse to pay for the assets or transfer them, as the case may be.

2. Acquisition of Assets that are Subject to Insolvency Proceedings

The regulation of assets acquisition during insolvency proceedings varies depending on the type of proceeding to which the insolvent company is subjected at the time of the acquisition (supervision, external management, financial rehabilitation or bankruptcy proceedings).

Russian bankruptcy regulations set forth several measures that could be implemented by the appointed receiver to restore the solvency of the company. Such measures include the sale of some of the assets of the insolvent company. Such sale and transfer of the assets of the insolvent company is subject to special regulations. The sale of assets is prohibited if such sale would result the company being unable to conduct its business. As a general rule, assets may only be sold at public auctions. The assets should be appraised by an independent appraiser and the minimum bid price shall be determined by the meeting of creditors (creditors committee) based on such appraisal.

Also, special rules apply to the sale of assets of a company that was declared bankrupt by the court. The asset sale and purchase agreement shall contain a clause to the effect that the payment for the sold assets be made not later than one month from the date of the sale and purchase agreement or within seven days from the date of the transfer of the title to such assets. As a general rule, such assets may only be sold at public auctions. The minimum bid price shall be determined by an independent appraiser.

K. Timing and Costs

1. Timeframe of Asset Transfer

The timing of the asset transfer transaction mostly depends on whether it is subject to corporate approvals, state registration and/or antitrust clearance. If the transaction requires approval by a shareholders' or interest holders' meeting, e. g., as a major or interested party transaction, such approval may take 45 days or more for limited liability companies and 40 days or more for joint stock companies. If the transaction is subject to the board of directors' approval only, such approval could be obtained in a shorter period of time.

In the best case scenario, the registration of rights to immovable property will be made by the relevant authorities within one month from the date of submission of all necessary documents. In practice, such registration may take longer due to various reasons.

The registration of agreements with respect to the transfer of the rights to IP takes, in the best case scenario, two months from the date of submission of the relevant application and all required documents to the registration authorities.

An application for antitrust approval, if necessary for an asset transfer transaction, should be reviewed by the antitrust authorities within 30 days from the date of submission of the application with all necessary documents. However, the antitrust authority may extend its review period up to 90 days.

2. Costs of Asset Transfer

(i) Notarization Fees

Notarization fees are controlled by the state and their amounts are set forth by law. There are two schedules of notarization fees. One schedule applies to notarization actions that are mandatory under Russian law and another schedule applies to notarization actions that are not mandatory. Fees for the mandatory notarization vary depending on the type of document to be certified, specific notary action to be performed by the notary public, monetary value of the agreement, etc. Although the fees for mandatory notarizations may vary, the range of these fees for notary actions that may be applicable to transactional matters is the following: the minimum fee is RUB 100 (e.g., for the certification of a translated document) and the maximum is RUB 30,000 (e.g., for the certification of an agreement for the pledge of sea vessels).

A different schedule of fees applies to the notarization of documents and performance of other actions by a notary public in instances where such notarization and actions are not mandatory, for instance in a situation where parties agreed to notarize an agreement that is not subject to mandatory notarization. The fee varies depending on the nature of the agreement; for example, it is twice as expensive to certify an agreement for the alienation of real estate than an agreement for the alienation of movable property. Fees are also tied to the value of the contract and consist of a fixed part specified in rubles and variable part set forth as a percentage of the contract value of the agreement. The variable part utilizes a regressive scale, i.e., the percentage of the rate declines with an increase in the contract value of the agreement. The maximum fee rate is set forth for a transaction with real estate valued at more than RUB ten million and constitutes RUB 77,500 plus 0.5% of the value of the contract exceeding RUB ten million.

(ii) State Duties for Registration

If the agreement or transfer of the title or transfer of rights is subject to state registration, such registration is subject to the payment of state duty in the amount set forth by the law. As a general rule, state duties applicable to legal entities are higher than state duties applicable to individuals. Most typical registration fees are the following:

- registration of the transfer of rights to an enterprise – 0.1% of the enterprise's value, but not more than RUB 30,000;
- registration of an agreement on the sale and purchase of immovable property, registration of an agreement on the assignment of rights and obligations under the agreement which was subject to state registration – RUB 500 for individuals and RUB 7,500 for legal entities;
- registration of a mortgage – RUB 500 for individuals and RUB 2,000 for legal entities.

State duties for the registration of license agreements with respect to the transfer of IP Rights depend on the object of such IP and vary from RUB 600 to 8,000.

(iii) Fee for Antitrust Approval

The fee for the review of an application for obtaining antitrust approval of a transaction is RUB 10,000.

L. Miscellaneous

1. Choice of Foreign Law

As a general rule, Russian law applies to agreements entered into by residents of the Russian Federation. In certain cases foreign law may apply to an agreement of the parties (for example, if a party to the agreement is a foreign entity, or the asset subject to sale is located abroad, or performance under the agreement should take place abroad).

2. (International) Arbitration, Choice of Venue

Under Russian law, disputes involving a foreign party could be submitted to international commercial arbitration upon agreement of the parties, except for cases specifically provided for by Russian law (e.g., bankruptcy matters). Russian law provides that the following disputes could be submitted to international commercial arbitration:

- disputes arising from contractual and other civil law relations related to foreign trade activities and other international business relations, if the commercial enterprise of at least one of the parties is located abroad; and
- disputes between companies with foreign investments, disputes between international associations and organizations organized in the Russian Federation, as well as disputes among their participants/shareholders, disputes between companies

with foreign investments and Russian entities and disputes between international associations and organizations organized in the Russian Federation and Russian entities.

A case could be submitted to international arbitration if the parties entered into an arbitration agreement or included an arbitration clause in their contract. Russia is a party to the 1958 New York Convention on Recognition and Enforcement of Foreign Arbitral Awards and, therefore, Russian state courts are entitled to rule on the enforcement of arbitration awards in Russia.

If the dispute could be submitted to international arbitration, the parties to such dispute may select a venue for arbitration of their choice (e. g., LCIA, ICA at ICC or SCC Arbitration Institute).

3. Other Distinctions, Characteristics

Our jurisdiction does not provide for any other distinctions or unusual characteristics noteworthy in connection with a customary asset deal.

M. Literature

M. I. Braghinsky and *V. V. Vitryansky*, Contract Law. Book 1: General Provisions, Statut, Moscow, 2008

M. I. Braghinsky and *V. V. Vitryansky*, Contract Law. Book 2: Agreements on Disposal of Property, Statut, Moscow, 2008

O. Yu. Skvortsov, Transactions with Real Property in Commercial Turnover, 1st Edition, 2006

Singapore

By *Colin Ong Pang Huan*

A. General Aspects

Singapore was a British crown colony until 1959. The general law applicable is the English common law, and therefore, the common law of Singapore has it roots in English jurisprudence. The Application of the English Law Act, Chapter 7A of Singapore (the "**Application of the English Law Act**"), provides that the common law of England, to the extent it was part of the law of Singapore before November 12, 1993, will continue to be part of the law of Singapore, subject to any modifications as circumstances may require. Section 4 of the Application of the English Law Act, read with the First Schedule, specifies the English enactments that apply or continue to apply in Singapore, subject to Singapore statutes.

Access to Singapore statutes is available without charge at the Singapore Government Statutes Online website at http://statutes.agc.gov.sg.

1. Asset Deal vs. Share Deal: Essential Considerations

The main consideration for any deal would necessarily be an economic one – would any given structure be more cost efficient, assuming equal risks are involved (legal or otherwise)?

The requirement to pay taxes is one key consideration. There would be a number of key tax considerations:

- Goods and Services Tax (or "**GST**") is not payable in a share deal, but may be triggered in an asset deal. However, an exemption from GST is available in the event that certain conditions are fulfilled in an asset deal. (See I, 1 below)
- Stamp Duty: sale of certain assets, such as real property and shares, would attract stamp duty. (See I, 2 below)
- Income Tax: profits derived from the sale of shares are usually treated as being capital in nature (unless the seller is in the business of trading shares), and do not attract income tax. Profits derived from a sale of assets that constitutes part of trading stock would constitute income, and would attract income tax at the prevailing rates.

Another consideration is the scope of the assets (and liabilities) to be purchased. An asset acquisition allows for the transfer of the assets only, as opposed to the transfer of liabilities (which would occur in a share deal). Furthermore, the purchaser would be entitled to "cherry-pick" by purchasing only the assets he requires in an asset deal.

Assuming the commercial decision is to purchase all the assets and liabilities of the seller, it would be more convenient to do a share deal, given that there would be no need to transfer or novate contracts (including those of employees – see H, 1 below), and to transfer licenses, with the exception of contracts and licenses that terminate upon a change of control of the seller. This is due to the doctrine regarding the separate legal personality of companies under Singapore law.

The takeover rules set out in the Singapore Code on Takeovers and Mergers would also be triggered in a share deal involving a public company in Singapore, although this may not necessarily be an impediment if the purchaser's intention is to acquire the entire share capital in the target company. However, if the intention is to acquire the assets of a public company, it may be more convenient to do an asset deal (which typically requires either the consent of the board of directors or of a majority of shareholders) rather than to make a tender offer to acquire the shares belonging to all of the other shareholders.

2. Distinction between Sale and Transfer in Rem

Singapore law generally does not distinguish between the sale and the transfer in rem of an asset as a point of legal principle in respect of all categories of assets. However, the sale agreement would not in itself be sufficient to effect the transfer of title to certain categories of assets, and certain additional steps or formalities will need to be taken or fulfilled in order to effect the transfer of such assets. Examples of categories of assets where a sale agreement itself does not effect transfer of the property, and where a separate instrument of transfer will need to be executed in order to transfer the title of the asset include real (or immovable) property and shares in a company. Such transfers would require the execution of separate transfer instruments.

In the case of immovable property, legal interest is only obtained by the purchaser at the time of the transfer, and not at the time of signing the contract for sale. For instance, in the case of land falling under the jurisdiction of the Land Titles Act, Chapter 157 of Singapore ("**LTA**"), the purchaser will only obtain indefeasible title to the land when the interest is registered. However, where the contractual documents for the sale of land have been signed by all parties, the contract in most cases will be specifically enforceable, given that real property is unique and monetary damages are not considered as being an adequate remedy for a breach of the contract to transfer real property. This is unlike most other contracts, where the usual remedy for breach of contract is damages.

A binding contract is in existence at the point of entry between the parties, assuming the presence of all the elements for the formation of a contract, and the absence of any vitiating factors. A sale agreement would typically state that the completion of the obligations of the contract would occur upon the satisfaction of the conditions to completion (if any) in accordance with the terms of the agreement. Asset sale agreements entered into between the seller and the purchaser typically provide, as conditions precedent to completion, that any additional steps or formalities required to effect the transfer of title to relevant categories of assets (for instance, the execution of the transfer instruments, or the delivery of the asset itself, where relevant) must be fulfilled by the seller prior to completion of the obligations under the agreement. Title to the remaining assets (which do not require any additional formalities) will be transferred by the operative provisions of the sale agreement itself.

3. Regional Differences

Singapore only has one set of laws, which is uniformly applied across the entire jurisdiction. There are no "federal" or "state" laws for which a distinction must be made.

4. Acquisition by Foreigners

With the exception of residential property, which foreigners are prohibited from purchasing (see C, 2 below for a more detailed discussion), there are generally no restrictions or special approval requirements to be fulfilled in order for foreigners to acquire assets in Singapore.

5. Public Registers, Records and Databases

There is no central registry or depositary of information in Singapore where a person can obtain all relevant information in connection with an asset transfer for assets generally. Certain types of assets have public ownership records, which are accessible to the public upon the payment of a prescribed fee. These include shares in Singapore incorporated companies, intellectual property rights registered in Singapore, Singapore real estate and Singapore registered motor vehicles. Ownership information on assets owned by a corporation whose shares are listed on the Singapore Exchange Securities Trading Limited ("**SGX-ST**") may also be disclosed in its published annual report, which will be made available online on the SGX-ST website.

Assuming that the seller and purchaser are Singapore incorporated companies, information relating to such entities (including the paid-up share capital, identities of shareholders and officers, copies of constitutive documents (namely, the memorandum and articles of association), and the legal form of such entity – e. g., whether the entity is limited by shares or otherwise) can be obtained from records maintained by the Accounting & Corporate Regulatory Authority of Singapore ("**ACRA**") upon payment of a fee. A business profile search, which would reveal certain summary information of a Singapore incorporated company, can be conducted online. Copies of documents filed by the corporate purchaser or seller can also be extracted from ACRA upon payment of a prescribed fee. In addition, ACRA also maintains a record of registered charges over the assets of a Singapore incorporated company, which is similarly accessible to the public upon payment of a prescribed fee.

Information relating to registered intellectual property rights (such as registered trademarks, patents and registered designs) can be obtained from the public records maintained in the appropriate registries. However, there are no equivalent searches that will reveal information on non-registered intellectual property rights, such as copyright.

Ownership information on real property falling within the ambit of the LTA can be obtained from the public records maintained by the Singapore Land Authority (a statutory board under the Singapore Ministry of Law) upon payment of a prescribed fee. Similar information can be obtained in respect of real property not falling within the Torrens system (i.e. non-LTA land) if the owners and secured lenders have registered their respective interest in such real property. Although registration of interests in respect of land falling outside of the LTA is not compulsory, registration secures priority in the event of conflicting or competing interests, and an unregistered deed is not admissible in court as evidence of title to land. (See C, 3 below.)

Ownership information on Singapore registered motor vehicles can be obtained from the Registrar of Vehicles, Singapore, upon payment of a prescribed fee (See Rule 13 of the Road Traffic (Motor Vehicles, Registration and Licensing) Rules).

Information relating to litigation commenced by or against a party in Singapore can also be obtained from the records maintained by the Singapore courts, upon the payment of a prescribed fee. Similarly, information on bankruptcy or winding up/liquidation actions commenced against a person in Singapore can also be extracted from these records.

6. Purchase Price Requirements

The seller and purchaser in Singapore are generally free to agree on the purchase price to be paid in connection with an asset deal and the currency in which it is denominated. However, for the purpose of computing stamp duties payable in Singapore (such as in the event of a transfer of real property or of shares), the higher of the actual purchase price or the market value of the asset will be used for such computation. (See I, 2 below.)

A prior sale made at a value below fair-market by a bankrupt entity can be challenged by the liquidator of the bankrupt seller within the prescribed period. (See J, 1 below.)

B. Tangible/Movable Assets

1. Characteristics as to:

a) Language of Documentation. Generally, a contract for the transfer of assets can be in writing or oral, although it is generally not advisable for such a contract to be made in oral form. In addition, an agreement in writing for a transfer of assets can be drafted in a language other than English. The term "writing" has been defined in the Interpretation Act, Chapter 1 of Singapore, to include "printing, lithography, typewriting, photography and other modes of representing or reproducing words or figures in visible form." There is also recent local case law suggesting that contracts concluded through an exchange of electronic mail will satisfy the requirements of writing and signature.

A written contract may, in the absence of a specific requirement to the contrary, be drafted in a language other than English. One notable exception to the above proposition involves the grant or transfer of a lease in land exceeding seven years, which requires a deed made in the English language (see C, 1, a below).

For oral contracts, parties should also note the requirements of Section 6(e) of the Civil Law Act, Chapter 43 of Singapore (the **"Civil Law Act"**), which states that an agreement that is not performed within the space of one year from the date it was made is not enforceable unless it was first memorialized in writing and signed by the party required to perform the agreement.

Documents can, generally, be executed bilingually, although a question may arise as to whether an agreement was actually in existence given the difference in the language of offer and acceptance. However, this must necessarily be examined in the context of the totality of the factual evidence present.

A contract can be translated into different language versions, but it is common (and prudent) to state that the version of the contract drafted in a certain language would take precedence over all the other versions in the event of any conflict in the meaning/ interpretation of the various versions. Alternatively, it can be clearly specified that only one version of the contract would have legal effect, while the others are provided for reference only.

b) Form of Documentation. Unless specifically required under law for a particular class of assets (e. g., interest in real property exceeding seven years in duration, for which a prescribed form of transfer would need to be executed – see C, 1, a below), there are no specific forms of documentation generally required for the transfer of assets. The existence of a written agreement would, however, aid parties seeking to prove the existence and terms of the agreement in question.

Documents can be executed outside of Singapore, and, if agreed to between the parties, may be executed in counterparts.

c) Specification of Assets. Generally, a description relating to the sale of assets should be adequately detailed so that there is no ambiguity as to the identity of the assets transferred. While there is no legal requirement, a detailed description of the assets to be transferred (either in the main body of the agreement or as a separate schedule, asset list or annex attached to or referred to in the agreement) would be helpful for identification purposes. A specification of assets by category or location may be sufficient if the assets can be clearly identified without ambiguity and without reference to any discretion of the parties. Accordingly, an agreement to transfer "all assets" (without exception) located in a specific location or building would satisfy the above.

2. Administrative, Corporate and Other Approvals

Generally, the transfer of tangible assets does not require special governmental or administrative approvals. Some exceptions to this rule exist, e.g., the transfer of assets of certain companies (such as telecommunication companies – see Section 34 of the Telecommunications Act, Chapter 323 of Singapore) are subject to the approval of the relevant regulatory authorities. Any transfer made in breach of law would generally be void ab initio, or voidable at the direction of the relevant authorities.

Depending on the terms of their respective constitutive documents (namely, the memorandum or articles of association), certain acquisitions or disposals may be subject to the approval of the seller's and/or purchaser's shareholders. Furthermore, a disposal of all or substantially all of the assets of a Singapore incorporated company is subject to the approval of such company's shareholders in a general meeting (see Section 160 of the Companies Act, Chapter 50 of Singapore), although such disposal would be valid and enforceable by a purchaser providing good value, and without any actual notice of this contravention. A corporation whose shares are listed on the SGX-ST also may not engage in transactions involving the acquisition or disposal of assets beyond a certain threshold (relative to the value of its total assets, its net profits or market capitalization) without the approval of its shareholders in a general meeting.

The prior approval of security holders is typically required for the transfer of assets that are subject to encumbrances, although this would largely depend upon the terms of the relevant security documents. The seller may, under certain circumstances, be permitted to transfer the assets subject to the prior interest of the security holder. Transfers made in breach of such obligations may lead to a trigger of the security holder's right to enforce the security. Note also that non-disposal covenants commonly found in loan documents may prohibit the disposal of certain assets. A breach of such covenants usually would not invalidate the transfer but may lead to the occurrence of events of default under the relevant agreements.

Transfers between parties where a director of the transferor holds a substantial stake in the transferee, or which involve listed entities, are subject to special rules.

3. Filing Requirements

A transfer of tangible assets does not typically require special filings with public authorities or registrations in public registers or databases, with the exception of certain classes of assets, including interests in real estate (see C, 3 below), Singapore registered ships and Singapore registered motor vehicles.

4. Automatic Transfer of Encumbrances

Encumbrances are generally attached to the asset and would automatically transfer to the purchaser. The exception to this rule would apply in the case of transfers made to purchasers who qualify as "Equity's darlings," or bona fide purchasers who had acquired the assets for good value without having any prior notice of the encumbrances. However, as a matter of practice, it is not uncommon to find that the instruments creating the encumbrances, such as mortgage documents, would contain provisions requiring the consent of the security holder (e.g., a mortgagee) for the transfer of the encumbered asset.

C. Real Property

1. Characteristics as to:

a) Language of Documentation. Section 53(1) of the Conveyancing and Law of Property Act, Chapter 61 of Singapore, provides that any conveyance of any estate or interest in land other than a lease for a period not exceeding seven years at a rack rent shall be void at law unless it is conveyed by a deed in the English language. Conveyances relating to a lease of land not exceeding seven years may be made by way of an oral grant (subject to the requirements of Section 6(d) of the Civil Law Act being satisfied – see C, 1, b below), or a written agreement.

Grants of leases for periods not exceeding seven years may be drafted in a language other than English. Although not prohibited, the use of bilingual agreements is discouraged unless it is clear that one language version of the agreement would take precedence over the other in the event of any conflict between the two different versions. (See B, 1, a above.)

In the case of land under the LTA (which accounts for the majority of land in Singapore), Section 51(1) of the LTA states that approved forms shall be used for all instruments intended to affect registered land, although the Registrar of Land Titles has the discretion to register any instrument that deviates from the approved form. The approved forms are drafted in the English language.

b) Form of Documentation. Section 6(d) of the Civil Law Act states that all contracts for the sale or disposition of immovable property, or any interest therein, shall be unenforceable in the absence of a written memorandum or note (duly signed by the party enforced against) evidencing such contract. It is therefore a requirement that the contract for the transfer of property must be evidenced in writing. (See also B, 1, a above on what satisfies the requirement of writing.)

Save as discussed in C, 1, a above, there are no other formal requirements for the contract, although the instrument for transfer will have to be stamped and registered for title of the property to pass in the case of registered land.

There is no legal requirement for documents to be executed in Singapore. If agreed to between the parties, the document may also be executed in counterparts, although as a matter of practice, sale documents relating to real property are usually executed by the parties on the same document. It may also be noteworthy that, although not a strict legal requirement, sale documents relating to Singapore real property executed outside Singapore are typically notarized for evidentiary purposes.

c) Specification of Assets. Given that certainty is of paramount importance in transactions involving land, it is unlikely that a general description of the property would suffice. Generally, the cornerstones of a contract for the sale of land are the parties, the property and the price. These elements must be stated with sufficient clarity for the contract to be enforceable. A failure to do so may render the contract unenforceable for want of certainty. Therefore, precise descriptions of the property are typically required in transactions involving the transfer of real property in Singapore.

In the case of land under the LTA, the prescribed form for transfer requires a brief description of the land in question. Particulars required include the property address and lot number, which can be obtained by making the necessary title searches with the Singapore Land Authority. (See A, 5 above.)

2. Administrative, Corporate and Other Approvals

The transfer of real property typically does not require any special governmental or administrative approvals, or (save as discussed in B, 2 above) the approval of corporate bodies regarding the seller and/or the purchaser. However, two points should be noted, namely: (i) transfers of residential properties in Singapore (other than flats in any building or development permitted to be used for residential purposes, units in developments designated as condominiums, or units in developments under the executive condominium scheme established under the Executive Condominium Housing Scheme Act, Chapter 99A of Singapore) to foreign persons (including foreign companies and companies having shareholders that are foreign persons) are prohibited and will be null and void under the Residential Property Act, Chapter 274 of Singapore, unless prior approval from the Land Dealings (Approval) Unit of the Singapore Land Authority is first obtained, and (ii) the transfer of leasehold properties leased from the Singapore government and government statutory boards will usually require prior consent of the Singapore government or the relevant statutory boards, such as the Jurong Town Corporation (or **"JTC"**), the Singapore government's corporate vehicle, which leases state-owned land, and the Housing and Development Board (**"HDB"**), Singapore's public housing authority.

The transfer of properties leased from the JTC will usually require its prior consent. Under Section 38 of the Jurong Town Corporation Act, Chapter 150 of Singapore, no flat, house or building that has been sold by the JTC shall be sold, leased, mortgaged, transferred or charged without the written consent of the JTC. The Registrar of Deeds (for common law land) and the Registrar of Titles (for LTA land) shall not register the assurance, lease, mortgage, transfer or charge if it is in contravention of Section 38, and to the extent that any registrations are made, these may be declared void by the JTC through the lodgment of an instrument. Any sales, leases, mortgages or other disposals of flats, houses or buildings originally sold by the HDB without its prior written consent may be similarly declared by the HDB as void (see Section 50 of the Housing and Development Act, Chapter 129 of Singapore).

The transfers of leases of state land are also typically subject to approval of the Singapore government.

Security documents also typically provide that real property provided as collateral cannot be transferred without the prior approval of the security holders. Security holders would typically also have a caveat lodged against the real property that is subject to encumbrance, so there is only a very small possibility of the transfer being made without the knowledge (and consent) of the security holder. As a matter of practice, a security holder would typically require the repayment of the loan and discharge of the encumbrance prior to any such transfer.

3. Filing Requirements

In the case of registered land, an instrument purporting to pass title to land is not effective until such instrument has been registered with the Singapore Land Authority (Section 45 of the LTA).

For land not falling under the LTA, interest in land passes when the deed of transfer is signed, sealed and delivered. However, it is advisable to register the deed (i) to secure priority where there are conflicting or competing interests, and (ii) for use as evidence, given that Section 4 of the Registration of Deeds Act, Chapter 269 of Singapore provides that a registrable deed that is not registered is not admissible in any court of law as evidence of title to land.

4. Automatic Transfer of Encumbrances

In the case of land falling under the LTA, a purchaser of registered land shall hold that land free from all encumbrances, liens, estates and interests except as such may be registered or notified in the land register, subject to, inter alia, a tenancy that does not exceed seven years (Section 46 of the LTA). Accordingly, a purchaser of real property will take interest subject to any encumbrances registered or notified in the land register, or to tenancies/leases of tenor not exceeding seven years.

Waiver of encumbrances for land under the LTA must follow some formal requirements. For example, an instrument for the surrender of a lease has to be registered, as in the case of an instrument for the discharge of a mortgage or a charge.

Similarly, for land not under the LTA, the purchaser of the land shall take the land subject to all prior registered encumbrances. Easements and other covenants that run with the land will also bind all purchasers of such land, other than purchasers who qualify as "Equity's darlings." (See B, 4 above.)

5. Automatic Transfer of Agreements

In the case of land falling under the LTA, prior registered leases, as well as leases not exceeding seven years, will not be affected by any subsequent sale of the land. These leases automatically transfer to the purchaser.

There is no extraordinary right for the purchaser or landlord to terminate the leases beyond what is provided for within the lease agreement entered into between the previous landlord (the seller) and the tenant.

D. Contracts

1. Characteristics as to:

a) Language of Documentation. Rights arising under a contract are choses in action, which is a category of personal rights or property that can only be claimed or enforced by action, rather than by taking physical possession.

The transfer of legal choses in action is statutorily allowed by virtue of Section 4(8) of the Civil Law Act, subject to the requirements that (i) the assignment must be absolute (i.e. not a conditional assignment, an assignment by way of charge, or an assignment of part only of a debt), (ii) the assignment must be in writing, and (iii) written notice must be provided to the debtor. Accordingly, the agreements relating to the transfer of contracts can be in writing made in English or any other language. (See B, 1, a above for the definition of "writing.") The documents can be executed bilingually, although please refer to the discussion in B, 1, a above in relation to the issue concerning the existence of such bilingual agreements.

If, however, the three requirements for a statutory assignment (discussed above) are not fulfilled, the transfer of a contract will be void as a statutory assignment, but may nevertheless constitute a valid equitable assignment. The creation of a valid equitable assignment of a chose in action only requires a clear intention to create the chose in action. No particular form is required to constitute a valid equitable assignment of a chose in action, although a notice to the debtor (which is not strictly required under law) will prevent the debtor from paying the assignor, and will afford the assignee priority over other assignees who had not given such notice.

The main disadvantage in the case of an equitable assignment of a chose in action is that the assignee will not be entitled to sue the debtor to recover in its own name (at common law a chose in action cannot be assigned). This has the consequence of requiring the assignee to join the assignor either as co-plaintiff or co-defendant in the action at hand.

Further, under Singapore contract law, only rights under a contract (as opposed to liabilities) may be transferred unilaterally. (See G below.) In order to transfer liabilities, the consent of the other party to the contract must be obtained. It is therefore common for parties to enter into novation agreements to transfer both rights and liabilities to a third party. (See G below.)

b) Form of Documentation. Unless specifically required under law for a particular class of assets (e. g., interest in real property exceeding seven years in duration), there are no specific forms of documentation required for a statutory assignment of contracts, although this will need to be in written form. (See D, 1, a above.) An equitable assignment can, however, be oral, although the existence of a written agreement would aid parties seeking to prove the existence of, and the terms of the agreement in question. Documents can be executed outside of Singapore, and if agreed among the parties, may be executed in counterparts.

c) Specification of Contracts. As discussed in B, 1, c above, a description relating to the actual contracts to be transferred should be adequately detailed so that there is no ambiguity as to the contracts that are actually transferred. Although there is no legal requirement, a listing of the contracts to be transferred (either in an attached schedule or a list) would be helpful for identification purposes. Note that only rights (and not liabilities) can be unilaterally transferred under Singapore law. (See D, 1, a above.)

2. Administrative, Corporate and Other Approvals

The transfer of contracts typically does not require governmental or administrative approvals, and unless specifically required under the seller's or the purchaser's respective memoranda or articles of association, or where the contract purports to transfer all or substantially all of the seller's assets (see B, 2 above), does not require the consent of the seller's or purchaser's shareholders (in the case of corporate sellers or purchasers). Under Singapore law, a seller is also permitted to transfer his rights under a contract without consent of the other contracting party (unless otherwise provided for in the contract), although a written notice must be given to the other contracting party. Liabilities under a contract cannot be transferred without the consent of the other parties. (See D, 1, a above.)

In the event that any requisite approvals are not obtained, the transfers may be invalidated, and the seller may also be in breach of its obligations under the relevant contracts. Note that certain contractual rights are incapable of assignment, such as rights under contracts involving personal skill or confidence.

3. Automatic Transfer of Contracts (Other than Lease and Employment Agreements)

With the exception of lease agreements and employment agreements (see C, 5 above and H, 1 below), rights and obligations under contracts do not typically transfer automatically to a purchaser of assets, unless this has been originally contemplated by and agreed to among the parties to such contract(s). For instance, some standard form contracts (e.g., manufacturing contracts) may provide that the rights and obligations thereunder may be automatically transferred in the event that the assets and business of a seller is transferred to another party. In such cases, the transfers will take effect in accordance with the terms agreed to between the original contracting parties.

4. Filing Requirements

No public filings or registrations are typically required in connection with the transfer of contracts.

5. Treatment of Existing Contractual Claims and Obligations

Following a statutory assignment of rights under a contract by a seller to a purchaser, the purchaser will be entitled to enforce all rights under the contract so assigned. As discussed above (see D, 1, a above), liabilities under a contract cannot be unilaterally transferred without the consent of the other contracting party, unless this has been provided for expressly under the terms of the contract itself. Typically, a tripartite novation agreement is entered into between the purchaser, the seller and the other contracting party, whereby the other contracting party agrees to the substitution of the seller with the purchaser. The parties have freedom to structure the terms of the deal, and the parties could agree that the seller assumes all liability under the contract prior to the substitution of the purchaser, or that the purchaser assumes all liability from the date of the original contract. Similarly, the seller and purchaser may agree that the seller will provide an indemnity in respect of its unfulfilled obligations under the contract, or for the inclusion of a price adjustment mechanism in the sale contract, or the purchaser and seller could collectively agree on a sale price that would take into account the seller's unfulfilled obligations under the contract.

Note that a novation agreement is a new contract between the parties allowing for the substitution of the seller with the purchaser under the original contract, rather than a transfer of liabilities from the seller to the purchaser. (See G, 1 below.)

6. Warranty Claims Resulting from Events prior to Transfer

For the discussion on the liability of the purchaser for warranty claims resulting from events prior to the transfer of the assets affected, see D, 5 above and G, 4, c below.

E. IP Rights

1. Characteristics of Intellectual Property Rights (e. g., Trademarks, Patents, Utility Models, Domain Names) ("*IP Rights*") as to:

a) Language of Documentation. The sale and transfer documents relating to IP Rights in Singapore (such as patents, trademarks, registered designs and copyright) may be drafted in English or any other language. The relevant statutes provide that the assignment must be in writing and signed by the assignor in order to be valid. If these requirements are not complied with, the assignment of patents will be void, and the assignment of registered trademarks, registered designs and copyright will not be effective. (See B, 1, a above for the definition of "writing.")

The documents can be executed bilingually, although please refer to the discussion in B, 1, a above in relation to the issue concerning the existence of the agreement.

b) Form of Documentation. There are no special forms of documentation required for the transfer of IP Rights, although the relevant legislation specifically provides that the assignments of patents are void unless made in writing and signed by the parties to the assignment (Section 41(6) of the Patents Act, Chapter 221 of Singapore (the "**Patents Act**")), and that the assignment of trademarks, registered designs and copyright shall not be effective unless it is in writing and signed by or on behalf of the assignor (see Section 38(3) of the Trade Marks Act, Chapter 332 of Singapore (the "**Trade Marks Act**"), Section 32(6) of the Registered Designs Act, Chapter 266 of Singapore (the "**Registered Designs Act**"), and Section 194(3) of the Copyright Act, Chapter 63 of Singapore). Such agreements can be executed outside of Singapore, and if agreed to between the parties, may be executed in counterparts.

c) Specification of IP Rights. As discussed in B, 1, c above, a description relating to the IP Rights to be transferred should be adequately detailed so that there is no ambiguity as to the rights transferred. Depending on the terms of the licenses for use of certain IP Rights, these licenses may or may not be transferred. Although there is no legal requirement, a listing of the specific IP Rights to be transferred (either in an attached schedule or a list) would be helpful for identification purposes.

2. Administrative, Corporate and Other Approvals

The transfer of IP Rights typically does not require governmental or administrative approvals, and unless specifically required under the seller's or the purchaser's respective memoranda or articles of association, or where the contract purports to transfer all or substantially all of the seller's assets (e. g., in situations where the seller's assets are predominantly IP Rights, in which case see B, 2 above), do not require the consent of the seller's or purchaser's shareholders (in cases where the seller or purchaser are corporate entities). Depending on the terms of its licenses to use IP Rights licensed by third party licensors, such licensors' prior consent may be required for the transfer of such IP Rights. In the event that the requisite approvals are not obtained, the transfers may be invalidated, and the seller may also breach its obligations under the license.

Where the IP Rights are encumbered or used as collateral, the approval of the security holders may be required, depending on the terms of the relevant security documents. (See B, 2 above.)

3. Filing Requirements

A distinction must be made between the IP Rights requiring registration, such as patents, registered trademarks and registered designs, and those that do not, such as copyright, for which there is no registration mechanism. In respect of IP Rights not requiring registration, no filings with public authorities or registrations into registers or databases are required. In respect of registered trademarks and registered designs, assignments that are not registered in the respective registers maintained by the authorities will be ineffective against any persons acquiring a conflicting interest in such IP Rights in ignorance of the transferee's interest in the IP Right (see Section 39(3) of the Trade Marks Act and Section 34(3) of the Registered Designs Act). In respect of patents, a subsequent registered assignment of a patent affords the assignee thereof priority against the assignee of an earlier unregistered assignment of the same patent (Section 43(1) of the Patents Act).

4. Applicable International (Multilateral) Agreements or Treaties

Singapore has ratified the Agreement on Trade Related Aspects of Intellectual Property Rights ("**TRIPS**"), and has implemented a TRIPS-compliant IP Rights legislative and administrative regime. In addition, Singapore is also a signatory to the following international conventions on IP Rights:

- Paris Convention for the Protection of Industrial Property;
- Berne Convention for the Protection of Literary and Artistic Works;
- Brussels Convention Relating to the Distribution of Programme-Carrying Signals Transmitted by Satellite;

- Protocol Relating to the Madrid Agreement Concerning the International Registration of Marks;
- Nice Agreement Concerning the National Classification of Goods and Services for the Purposes of the Registration of Marks;
- Patent Cooperation Treaty;
- Budapest Treaty on the International Recognition of the Deposit of Microorganisms for the Purposes of Patent Procedure;
- Convention Establishing the World Intellectual Property Organization;
- WIPO Copyright Treaty;
- WIPO Performances and Phonograms Treaty;
- International Convention for the Protection of New Varieties of Plants;
- Convention on Biological Diversity;
- The Geneva Act (1999) of the Hague Agreement concerning the International Registration of Industrial Designs; and
- Singapore Treaty on the Law of Trademarks.

Sources:

http://www.ipos.gov.sg;

http://www.wipo.int/treaties/en/index.jsp;

http://www.wto.org/english/tratop_e/trips_e/trips_e.htm; and

http://www.cbd.int/

F. Receivables

1. Characteristics as to:

a) Language of Documentation. As is the case for rights arising under a contract, receivables are also choses in action. See D, 1, a above on the discussion relating to the law on the transfer of legal choses in action.

The agreements relating to the transfer of receivables can be in writing in English or any other language. (See B, 1, a above for the definition of "writing".) The documents can be executed bilingually, although please refer to the discussion in B, 1, a above in relation to the issue concerning the existence of a bilingual agreement.

If a transfer of receivables does not satisfy the requirements for a statutory assignment, it will be void as a statutory assignment, but may nevertheless constitute a valid equitable assignment. (See discussions in D, 1, a above.)

Note that a partial transfer of receivables is not an absolute assignment, and consequently cannot be effected by means of a statutory assignment. Accordingly, a partial transfer of receivables can only be effected by way of an equitable assignment. (See D, 1, a above.)

b) Form of Documentation. There are no specific forms of documentation required for a statutory assignment of receivables, although it must be in writing. (See D, 1, a above.) An equitable assignment can, however, be oral, although the existence of a written agreement would aid parties seeking to prove the existence and terms of the agreement in question. Documents can be executed outside of Singapore, and if agreed to between the parties, may also be executed in counterparts.

c) Specification of Receivables. As discussed in B, 1, c above, a description relating to the actual receivables to be transferred should be adequately detailed so that there is no ambiguity as to which receivables are transferred. Although not legally required, a listing of the receivables to be transferred (either in an attached schedule or a list) would be helpful for identification purposes.

2. Administrative, Corporate and Other Approvals

The transfer of receivables typically does not require governmental or administrative approvals, and unless specifically required under the seller's or the purchaser's respective memoranda or articles of association (which is not typical), or where the receivables transferred comprises all or substantially all of the seller's assets (in which case, see B, 2 above), do not require the consent of the seller's or purchaser's shareholders (in cases where the seller or purchaser are corporate entities). Generally, no consent of debtors is required unless such consent is required under the terms of the agreement with the debtor, although a debtor would need to be notified in writing (see D, 1, a above). In the event that the requisite approvals are not obtained, the transfers may be invalidated, and the seller may also be in breach of its obligations under the contracts.

3. Filing Requirements

The transfer of receivables does not typically require any special filings with public authorities or registration in public registers or databases. Under Section 4(8) of the Civil Law Act, an absolute assignment by writing of a debt or other legal chose in action of which an express notice in writing has been given to the debtor will be deemed effective under the law. (See D, 1, a above.)

G. Liabilities

1. Characteristics as to:

a) Language of Documentation. As discussed in D, 1, a above, liabilities cannot be transferred unilaterally under Singapore law. Novation (in essence, a contract to extinguish the original obligor's (i.e. the seller's) existing obligation to the transferee (i.e. the creditor), and the concurrent assignment of the same obligation to the transferee (i.e. the purchaser)) is the only method through which the original obligor can be replaced by another party (i.e. the purchaser). (See D, 5 above for details.) An agreement to novate the obligations of one party can be drafted in English or any other language. The documents can be executed bilingually, although please refer to the discussion in B, 1, a above in relation to the issue concerning the existence of a bilingual agreement.

b) Form of Documentation. There is no specific form of documentation generally required for novation agreements, and oral agreements are valid. The existence of a written agreement would, however, aid parties seeking to prove the existence of, and the terms of the agreement in question. Documents can be executed outside of Singapore, and if agreed to between the parties, may be executed in counterparts.

c) Specification of Liabilities. As in the case of a transfer of assets discussed in B, 1, c above, a description relating to the actual liabilities to be novated should be adequately detailed so that there is no ambiguity as to the liabilities actually novated. Although there is no legal requirement, a listing of the liabilities to be novated (either in an attached schedule or a list) would be helpful for identification purposes.

2. Administrative, Corporate and Other Approvals

The novation of liabilities, in itself, does not require any special filings with public authorities or registration in public registers or databases, or (in the case of an obligor that is a corporate entity), and unless specifically provided for in the seller's and/or purchaser's constitutive documents (which is not typical), the approval of the seller's and/or purchaser's shareholders. However, given that only a novation is effective to "transfer" the original obligor's liabilities to another party, the consent of the creditor would necessarily be required. (See G, 1, a above.)

In the absence of a novation (i.e., the absence of consent by the creditor to a transfer of the original obligor's liabilities), a creditor would retain its rights to sue the original obligor to enforce its rights under the liabilities, although the assignment may be binding between the original obligor (i.e. the seller) and the new obligor (i.e. the purchaser).

3. Filing Requirements

The transfer of liabilities does not require any special filings with public authorities or registration in public registers or databases. Given that the consent of the creditor is required (in order to effect a novation), mere notification to the creditor would not suffice. (See G, 1 and G, 2 above.)

4. Purchaser's Liability for:

a) Tax Obligations. As tax on real property is an in rem and not in personam liability, such tax is payable by the owner of the property at the time when the tax becomes payable. A purchaser of property will therefore assume liability in respect of all outstanding property taxes in arrears on such property. Thus, it is commonly provided for in the sale and purchase agreement that the seller will be responsible for all property taxes payable for the period up to and including the day fixed for completion of the sale of real property. It is also not uncommon for legal counsel to perform checks to ascertain whether there are any outstanding property taxes prior to the close of a property sale transaction.

In contrast, other tax obligations (such as personal income taxes and corporate taxes) are personal in nature. Goods and Services Tax (or GST), which is a value-added tax on a supply of goods or services, is the liability of the person making the supply and becomes due at the time of supply (see Section 8(3) of the Goods and Services Tax Act, Chapter 117A of Singapore (the "**GST Act**")). See I, 1 below. Liability for such taxes is therefore personal to the seller, and does not transfer to the purchaser unless the contract for sale otherwise provides.

Dutiable goods, such as motor vehicles, tobacco and alcoholic beverages, are subject to taxes on importation into Singapore for local consumption. Purchasers of such goods while they are still duty-exempt or unpaid (for instance, while still located in a bonded warehouse) would normally assume the liability to pay these taxes upon the removal of the goods from the bonded warehouse (see Section 27 of the Customs Act, Chapter 70 of Singapore, and Regulation 10 of the Customs Regulations).

b) Environmental Contamination. The Director-General of Environmental Protection has been granted wide-ranging powers under the Environmental Protection and Management Act, Chapter 94A of Singapore (the "**EPMA**") to require the removal or cleaning up of pollutants, and the rectification of damage caused through pollution. The liability for such acts attaches to the persons to whom a notice or order has been served by the Director-General, typically the persons carrying out the polluting activity, or the owner or occupier of the property on which such activity had taken place. The Director-General may also choose to carry out the rectification works, and claim all costs and expenses from the person served with the notice.

Section 63 of the EPMA provides that a seller of property in respect of which costs and expenses have been incurred by the Singapore National Environment Agency in connection with the execution of any work the costs of which are recoverable from the owner thereof, shall continue to be liable for the payment of such costs and expenses in respect of the property, in addition to the performance of all other obligations imposed by the EPMA.

In the case of land leased from the JTC, the JTC will, under certain circumstances, require as a condition to the assignment of the lease, an Environmental Baseline Study ("**EBS**") to be conducted on the land in question to establish the level of potential contaminants in the soil and groundwater beneath the site and to determine the extent of contamination of the site. The EBS is required where the seller's usage or the purchaser's proposed industry or activity falls within a list of activities, including storage or processing facilities for petrochemicals and hydrocarbons, chemical plants, chemical warehouses and terminals, shipyards, power stations and waste treatment facilities. The JTC will typically require the seller to rectify any damage caused through pollution before permitting the assignment of the lease, although it may in certain cases permit the purchaser to assume responsibility for such rectification.

c) Products Sold or Services Rendered by the Seller to Third Parties. Product liability can exist either under contract law (for instance, in the contract for sale between a supplier and the customer) or tort law (for instance, the tort of negligence). However, in either case liability attaches to a legal entity rather than to the product itself. Accordingly, a seller of products or services would be liable to a third party purchaser in respect of defective products sold or services rendered by such seller prior to the acquisition by the purchaser, although this liability could be assumed by the purchaser under the sale contract. It is common for contracts for the sale of assets to expressly provide that the seller shall indemnify the purchaser in respect of all liabilities that the latter may incur due to any products or services previously sold by the seller.

5. Automatic Transfer of Other Liabilities

Other than the liabilities of the seller in respect of certain employees (including unpaid salaries) (see H, 1 below) that transfer by operation of law, the liabilities of the seller do not automatically transfer to the purchaser due to the acquisition of assets. Please also refer to the discussions above relating to whether existing encumbrances on the assets will be automatically transferred to the purchaser. See B, 4; C, 4; C, 5; D, 5 and D, 6 above.

6. Contractual Protection as to 4 and 5 above

Whether (and what) special provisions (such as guarantees or indemnifications) are included with respect to the issues discussed above in asset sale and/or transfer agreements is largely dependent on the commercial arrangements behind the sale. The parties could decide that the aggregate consideration for the asset would include all or some of the liabilities arising from these issues that occur prior to the transfer date, but to the extent this is not the business arrangement, the seller would customarily provide either guarantees or indemnities to the purchaser in respect of such liabilities, or the parties could agree to an adjustment in the sale price. The indemnity to be provided could take the form of an absolute indemnity for all liabilities, or an indemnity in respect of any amount of liabilities incurred above a certain agreed threshold amount.

H. Employees

1. Transfer of Employees

Section 18A of the Employment Act, Chapter 91 of Singapore (the **"Employment Act"**), provides for the automatic transfer of employment for employees of the seller to the purchaser, in the event of a transfer of a business as a going concern. The terms and conditions of such employee's employment contracts are preserved, including any benefits attributable to seniority and length of service. Generally, any prior acts or omissions of the seller in respect of the employee (including salary accrued but unpaid) shall, following such transfer of employment, be treated as the acts or omissions of the purchaser. This similarly applies in respect of acts and omissions of the employee so transferred, vis-à-vis the purchaser. Accordingly, it is commonly provided in asset sale agreements that the seller shall indemnify the purchaser in respect of an agreed portion (or all) of the purchaser's liability towards the employees transferred, in respect of acts/omissions prior to the transfer date.

The Employment Act, however, only provides for the automatic transfer of a limited class of employees, typically blue-collar workers or workers involved in manual or menial labor, and certain classes of persons employed in confidential positions (such as secretaries and human resource clerks), with a specific exclusion of seamen, domestic workers and persons employed in managerial or executive positions. In respect of the employees whose employment contracts will not be transferred by operation of law (under the Employment Act), their employment contracts must be novated across to the purchaser, or the "transfer" must be consented to by the employee in question.

2. Approval of Works Council, Trade Union or Other Institutions

There is no requirement under Singapore law to obtain the approval of any works council, labor agency or trade union, unless specifically provided for in the collective agreement entered into with the relevant trade union(s). However, the Employment Act requires the seller of the business to notify the affected employees and the trade unions of such affected employees as soon as it is reasonable before the transfer of employment, in order to enable consultations to take place between the seller, the affected employees and the relevant trade unions. Information required to be furnished by the seller include the fact that the transfer will be taking place, the reason for the transfer and the approximate date of transfer, the implications of the transfer and the measures that the seller and purchaser will take in relation to the affected employees. Any disputes or disagreements arising from an automatic transfer of employment under law may be referred to the Commissioner for Labor for adjudication.

3. Contractual Protection as to Labor Issues

Whether provisions for guarantees or indemnifications are included in asset sale and/or transfer agreements is largely dependent on the commercial arrangements behind the sale. The parties could decide that the aggregate consideration for the asset would include all liabilities attributable to the employees that occur prior to the transfer date, but to the extent this is not the case, the seller would customarily provide either guarantees or indemnities to the purchaser in respect of liabilities relating to the employees, or the parties could agree to an adjustment in the sale price. The indemnity to be provided could take the form of an absolute indemnity, or an indemnity in respect of any amount of liabilities incurred above a certain agreed threshold amount.

I. Tax Implications

1. Value Added Tax

Value Added Tax in Singapore is known as Goods and Services Tax, or GST, and is a broad-based consumption tax that is levied on the import of goods, as well as a majority of the supply of goods and services in Singapore (other than for exempt supplies of goods). Such a supply of goods and services is known as a "taxable supply." GST is charged on a supply of goods or services made in Singapore by a "taxable person" (namely, a person who is listed in the First Schedule of the GST Act), who would be required to be registered under the GST Act.

The GST Act states that, subject to certain exceptions, the transfer or disposal of goods forming part of the business assets by a person will be treated as a supply of such goods by such person for the purposes of the GST Act (see Paragraph 5 of the Second Schedule of the GST Act).

An exemption for GST is available under the GST Act for the transfer of a business as a going concern, where all of the following conditions are satisfied:

- the supply of assets is made in relation to a transfer of the business or part thereof to the transferee;
- the assets to be transferred are intended for use by the transferee in carrying on the same kind of business as the transferor;
- in the case where only part of the business is transferred, that portion that is transferred must be capable of being operated independently;
- the business or part thereof must be a going concern at the time of the transfer;
- the transferee must be a GST registered person at the time of the transfer; and
- both the transferor and transferee must maintain sufficient records on the transferred assets.

The current rate of GST (effective as of July 1, 2007) is 7.0%.

2. Real Property Transfer Tax

The grant, assignment or surrender of an interest in or a right over land is treated as a supply of goods for the purposes of the GST Act (see Paragraph 4 of the Second Schedule of the GST Act). Note that the sale and lease of residential properties are exempt supplies under the GST Act, and do not attract GST. An exemption for GST is available in respect of the transfer of real property pursuant to the transfer of a business as a going concern. (See I, 1 above.)

Stamp duties are also chargeable upon the transfer of real property (whether residential or non-residential). This is calculated based on the higher of the actual purchase price or the market value of the property. The rate of stamp duty in respect of real property transfer is set out below:

(i) SGD 1.00 payable on every SGD 100 or part thereof of the first SGD 180,000;

(ii) SGD 2.00 payable on every SGD 100 or part thereof of the next SGD 180,000; and

(iii) SGD 3.00 payable on every SGD 100 or part thereof of the remainder.

3. Other Tax Issues

In addition to property tax and GST (which are discussed in G, 4, a above), stamp duty and income tax would be relevant considerations. (See discussions in A, 1 and I, 2 above.)

For the purposes of sales between related parties, the tax authorities may determine that the sale price for purposes of computation of income tax could differ from the actual price paid, based on general anti-avoidance provisions or relevant provisions of an applicable double taxation treaty.

J. Bankruptcy Law

1. Challenge of Asset Transfer in Case of Insolvency

In the event the seller or the purchaser, following an asset transfer, becomes bankrupt or subject to insolvency or similar proceedings, the asset transfer may be challenged. There are two main grounds for such a challenge, namely that (i) the transfer was, at the time it was entered into, made at an undervalue, or that (ii) the transfer resulted in an unfair preference being made by the bankrupt or insolvent party to its creditor, or to a surety or guarantor of its debts. A transaction is made at an undervalue if the value of the asset, in money or money's worth, is significantly less than the value of the consideration paid for it, in money or money's worth, or *vice versa*, and an unfair preference occurs when an individual does (or allows to be done) anything that has the effect of putting its creditor into a position that, in the event of such individual's bankruptcy, will be better than the position he would have been in if that dealing had not been done (see Sections 98 and 99 of the Bankruptcy Act, Chapter 20 of Singapore (the "**Bankruptcy Act**")). For the purpose of identifying undervalue transactions, the trustee in bankruptcy has the ability to look towards all transactions within a period of five years immediately prior to the day on which a bankruptcy application (pursuant to which an individual is adjudged bankrupt) is made on such individual, and in the case of unfair preferences which are not transactions made at an undervalue, the trustee in bankruptcy has the ability to look at transactions occurring within a period of two years (in the case of unfair preferences involving an associate of the bankrupt individual) or six months (in all other cases) prior to such date (see Section 100(1) of the Bankruptcy Act).

2. Acquisition of Assets that are Subject to Insolvency Proceedings

Under the Bankruptcy Act, the trustee in bankruptcy is authorized to take possession of a bankrupt party's property (see Section 107 of the Bankruptcy Act), and to dispose of all or part of such property (see Section 111(a) of the Bankruptcy Act), including the goodwill of the bankrupt's business and the book debts due or accruing due to him, by way of tender, public auction or private contract.

K. Timing and Costs

1. Timeframe of Asset Transfer

The amount of time required to complete a sale/acquisition of a business by way of an asset deal would necessarily depend on a number of factors, including the size of the transaction (in monetary terms), the personalities of the purchaser and the seller, the nature of the asset (and whether the transfer involves any regulatory approvals or transfers of licences/permits), and whether there are time pressures involved for closing the deal. Rather than suggest a ballpark timeframe for the entire transaction, the following gives a breakdown per segment of the process, which may or may not be relevant for the transaction in question:

- Where shareholders' approvals are required (see B, 2 above), appropriate time must be set aside to convene a shareholders' meeting. The notice period for Singapore incorporated companies (subject to the terms of each company's constitutive documents) is typically either 14 or 21 days, although this duration can be reduced with the consent of shareholders. In situations involving publicly listed companies, additional time would need to be factored in to allow for the preparation of the circular to be delivered to shareholders in order to convene the meeting.
- Where the consideration for the sale is entirely or partially paid for using equity (i.e. shares) of the purchaser, the purchaser would require its shareholders' approval. Where the purchaser is a company listed and trading on the SGX-ST, the SGX-ST would also need to approve the listing of the new consideration shares. The SGX-ST approval process typically takes three to four weeks, from the time of submission of the application.
- Where due diligence is required, an appropriate duration should be factored in for this. The actual duration would depend on a number of factors, including the number and nature of the assets, the availability of information and the extent and depth of the due diligence required. This could be completed within a few days, or take up to a few months.
- Where the transaction requires governmental or third party approvals, or the assignment of governmental permits and/or third party licenses, an appropriate duration should be factored in for this. This would depend on a number of factors, including the complexity of the matter and the nature of the business/assets transferred (for instance, a sale involving sensitive assets (such as assets with a potential military application, telecommunication assets or banking business/assets) may require governmental approval). Third party approvals would tend to be easier (and faster) to obtain, as compared with governmental approvals, which could take up to a few months (or longer).

- Where the transaction includes the transfer of real property, or the assignment of IP Rights requiring registration (see E, 3 above), time should also be set aside for the registration of such transfers:
  - Registration of assignments of the aforesaid IP Rights would take place following submission of the relevant forms to the authorities. An online submission form for the registration of the assignment for trademarks is available.
  - In respect of the registration of assignment of real property, registration under the Registration of Deeds Act (in respect of common law land) would be completed within a few days of filing the application form, and instruments filed in respect of assignments relating to LTA land will be provisionally accepted at the time of lodgment. Electronic lodgment of instruments relating to LTA land is available.

Note that the above can be structured as pre-conditions to execution of the sale/acquisition documents, or as conditions precedent to closing.

2. Costs of Asset Transfer

In addition to advisors' fees, the main costs would be taxes and registration fees:

Taxes:

- *Goods and Services Tax*: GST is currently 7.0% (see I, 1 above);
- *Stamp Duties*: See I, 2 above; and
- *Income Tax:* Income of resident individuals is taxed at a progressive rate. A maximum tax rate of 20% applies for resident individuals in respect of the year of assessment 2007 onwards. Income of companies is taxed at a fixed rate of 18% in respect of the years of assessment 2008 and 2009, and will be reduced to 17% in respect of the year of assessment 2010 onwards.

Registration Fees for:

- lodgment of instruments of transfer under the Land Title Rules – SGD 68.30 per instrument.
- lodgment of instruments under Registration of Deeds Rules – SGD 28.00 per instrument.
- assignment of patents – SGD 70.00 per patent.
- assignment of trademarks – SGD 80.00 or SGD 88.00 per trademark (being the rates for online filing and manual filing, respectively).
- assignment of registered designs – SGD 80.00 per registered design.

Due diligence is also typically conducted on the assets to be acquired and/or on the sellers either prior to the execution of the sale agreements or the completion of the sale. The cost of the searches vary: for example, a business profile search (with ACRA) to obtain certain basic information relating to a Singapore-incorporated company would cost SGD 5.00, and a title search (with the Singapore Land Authority) on real property in Singapore would cost SGD 15.75. In relation to searches made on the records maintained by the Singapore courts, a composite litigation search (on the records maintained by the Supreme Court and the Subordinate Courts of Singapore, either as plaintiff or defendant) would cost SGD 37.00, and a winding-up search (on a corporate seller) and a bankruptcy search (on an individual seller) would cost SGD 13.00 and SGD 6.00, respectively, in respect of each year of data.

L. Miscellaneous

1. Choice of Foreign Law

The sale and/or transfer agreement can be made subject to foreign law; Singapore courts will give effect to a choice of law provision in the sale and/or transfer agreement unless the choice is not bona fide or legal, or is contrary to public policy. Singapore courts do not require any connection between the parties or the transaction and the country which law is chosen, and have taken a very narrow approach to the limitations to party autonomy in choice of law. In effect, the only qualification to the parties' choice of law is the principle that if the sole purpose of the choice of law was to evade the operation of the law of a country that would otherwise have applied to the contract in the absence of an express choice of law, then the choice of law would not be regarded as bona fide.

Parties should note that contracts for the sale and/or transfer of real property in Singapore typically provide that Singapore law will govern, given that the transfer of title of real property in Singapore would need to be governed by Singapore law.

2. (International) Arbitration, Choice of Venue

International arbitration is permissible under Singapore law. Singapore has adopted (with the exception of Chapter VIII thereof) the UNCITRAL Model Law on International Commercial Arbitration adopted by the United Nations Commission on International Trade Law on June 21, 1985 (the "**Model Law**"). Under the International Arbitration Act, Chapter 143A of Singapore, arbitration is international if:

- at least one of the parties to an arbitration agreement, at the time of the conclusion of the agreement, has its place of business in any State other than Singapore; or
- one of the following places is situated outside the State in which the parties have their places of business:
  - the place of arbitration if determined in, or pursuant to, the arbitration agreement;
  - any place where a substantial part of the obligations of the commercial relationship is to be performed or the place with which the subject-matter of the dispute is most closely connected; or

- the parties have expressly agreed that the subject-matter of the arbitration agreement relates to more than one country.

Article 5 of the Model Law provides that the parties to an arbitration agreement are free to agree on the place of the arbitration, and that failing such agreement, the arbitration tribunal may determine the venue, after having regard to the circumstances of the case, including the convenience of the location to the parties.

3. Other Distinctions, Characteristics

There are no any other distinctions or unusual characteristics noteworthy in connection with a customary asset deal.

M. Literature

There are no local legal publications dealing specifically with this topic. For a general overview of the commercial laws of Singapore, please visit *www.singaporelaw.sg*.

South Africa

By *Madelein Burger-van der Walt*, *Brian Dennehy*, *Bernadette Heever* and *Claire Gaul*

A. General Aspects

1. Asset Deal vs. Share Deal: Essential Considerations

General

It should be considered that, in a sale of business, the purchaser can select which assets and concomitant liabilities it is willing to assume, whereas in respect of a sale of shares, the purchaser is obligated to invest in all assets and liabilities of the company. However, the risks in the case of a sale of shares may be negated by the inclusion of extensive warranties and indemnities by the seller. Depending on the nature of the assets and possible exposures that cannot be covered by warranties, the purchaser may prefer to structure the transaction as a sale of business to ensure that it knows exactly which liabilities it will be assuming.

Section 34 of the South African Insolvency Act, 1936

Section 34(1) of the South African Insolvency Act, 1936 (**"the Insolvency Act"**) provides that, in the case of a sale of business, if a trader sells its business without having advertised the sale in the Government Gazette and two issues of Afrikaans and English newspapers circulating in the district in which that business is operated within a period not less than 30 days and not more than 60 days before the date of such transfer, the said transfer shall be void as against his creditors for a period of six months after such transfer, and shall be void against the trustee of his estate, if his estate is sequestrated at any time within this period.

From the seller's perspective, this should be avoided at all costs, as all debts immediately become claimable by the seller's creditors. The publication also adds to additional timing and implementation considerations.

In the case of a sale of shares, no notice in terms of Section 34 of the Insolvency Act is required.

Section 228 of the South African Companies Act, 1973

In the case of a sale of business, Section 228 of the South African Companies Act, 1973 (**"the Companies Act"**) provides that the directors of a company shall not have the power, save by a special resolution of its members (i.e. a resolution passed by shareholders holding 75% of the votes at a meeting at which shareholders holding at least 25% of the votes are present), to dispose of the whole or the greater part of the undertaking of the company or the whole or the greater part of the assets of the company.

The requirement adds to the timetable for a sale of business, allowing for the notice for the passing of the special resolutions (21 days), and, thereafter, registration with the Registrar of Companies.

The above is not required in the case of a sale of shares (except if the shares are the whole or the greater part of the undertaking of the seller or the whole or the greater part of the assets of the seller).

Contracts

In a sale of a business, as far as contracts are concerned, unless they permit the seller to assign them without the consent of the other parties (which would be highly unusual), the seller would not be legally entitled to delegate its obligations under those contracts, although it could cede its rights (assuming there is nothing in the agreements to prohibit cessions, which could well be the case). If there are any such contracts that have obligations attached to them that are large in value or lengthy in duration, consideration should be given to making it a suspensive condition of the agreement that the other parties to the agreements consent to their assignment to the purchaser.

In a sale of shares, there will be no change as regards the legal entity that entered into the contracts for the business, and accordingly no consents are required. However, if the contract prohibits a change of control of the contracting party, such consent may have to be obtained if the shares in the contracting party are sold such that a change of control takes place.

Labor Law

In the case of a sale of business, in terms of Section 197 of the South African Labor Relations Act, 1995, all contracts of employees are automatically assumed by the purchaser.

Effective Date

The selection of the effective date is far more significant in a sale of a business than in a sale of shares. If possible, it should coincide with the date upon which the purchaser physically takes over the assets and liabilities, otherwise any problems which may arise will be the responsibility of the party for whom profits/losses accrue during the interim period. If the sale is subject to suspensive conditions, the agreement must stipulate for whose benefit profit and losses will accrue during the interim period and who will be liable for income tax.

Regulatory Approvals Required

The parties should consider various regulatory approvals that may be applicable to the proposed structure of the sale, such as compliance with the Securities Regulation Code on Takeovers and Mergers (**"the Code"**), JSE Listings Requirements, approval by the competition authorities, exchange control approval from the South African Reserve Bank and industry or sector specific approvals and permits. Additionally, certain licenses and permits are not transferable and as such, in a sale of business, the purchaser would have to reapply for such permit or license, although parties generally provide that the sale is conditional upon the purchaser acquiring such license or permit. A license or permit may also prohibit a change of shareholding as regards the person to whom the license or permit has been issued, in which case the sale should be conditional upon a waiver of this requirement being obtained.

Tax Considerations

In an asset deal, various levels of taxes may become payable by the seller, including:

(i) income tax at 28% (if the seller is a corporate entity) on any recoupments realized (generally speaking, a recoupment represents the difference between the original cost of an asset and its tax value);

(ii) capital gains tax at 14% (if the seller is a corporate entity) (“**CGT**”) on the difference between the selling price for each asset and the CGT base cost thereof;

(iii) value-added tax (“**VAT**”) at 14% of the purchase consideration for the assets, unless (generally speaking) the assets comprise a business that is being disposed of as a going concern, in which case VAT would be payable at the rate of 0%;

(iv) secondary tax on companies (“**STC**”) at 10% on the net distribution (if any) of the sale proceeds to the company’s shareholders. STC will be abolished during 2010 and replaced with a dividends withholding tax system, also applying a flat rate of 10%, subject to reduction (maximum 5%) in accordance with any applicable double tax agreement (i.e. in the case of non-resident shareholders);

(v) transfer duty at a flat rate of 8% for corporate entities (in the case of natural persons a sliding scale applies) to the extent that the assets purchased comprise immovable (real) property if the transaction is not subject to VAT (for example, if the seller is not a registered VAT vendor). Any transfer duty paid by the purchaser in this regard can be claimed as a deemed input deduction for VAT purposes, assuming that the purchaser is or becomes a registered VAT vendor;

(vi) any unutilized assessed losses in the seller cannot be transferred to the buyer; and

(vii) in the case of a sale of business, book debts that are not recoverable are generally not allowed as a deduction for income tax purposes. Usually, therefore, the sale of book debts is subject to a resolutive condition that they are duly collected, failing which they ceded back to the seller as an adjustment to the purchase price.

By contrast, in a share deal, the following taxes may become payable by the sellers:

(i) income tax, to the extent that the sellers dispose of their shares on revenue account (28% for corporate shareholders, 40% for trusts, maximum marginal rate of 40% for individuals);

(ii) CGT, to the extent that the sellers dispose of their shares in a capital account (14% for corporate shareholders, 20% for trusts, maximum marginal rate of 10% for individuals);

(iii) generally speaking, shares (listed or unlisted) held for at least three years are deemed to be held on capital account;

(iv) the purchaser will ultimately incur securities transfer tax on the acquisition of the shares in the target company, which is payable at 0.25% of the greater of the purchase consideration or market value of such shares acquired (if different); and

(v) interest incurred on debt funding raised to acquire local shares is generally not deductible for income tax purposes.

2. Distinction between Sale and Transfer in Rem

In order to perfect the sale there must be a valid obligation to sell accompanied by the actual (or constructive) transfer in rem. The obligation to transfer and the transfer in rem must be provided for in the same contract, as these are essential for the classification of a contract of sale as such and therefore it is not possible to conclude agreements dealing separately with the obligation to transfer and the transfer in rem unless the main agreement cross references and incorporates by reference the separate local agreements.

3. Regional Differences

There are no regional differences. The laws of the Republic of South Africa, including the legal requirements for the transfer of assets, are equally applicable throughout all nine provinces.

4. Acquisition by Foreigners

Non-residents may invest freely in South Africa and hold shares in South African entities, provided that suitable documentary evidence is viewed by the Exchange Control Department of the South African Reserve Bank in order to ensure that such transactions are concluded at arm's length, at fair market related prices and are financed in an approved manner. Restrictions in this regard relate inter alia to the terms of loans being made to South African entities and the basis for disinvesting from South Africa. Shares held by foreign entities are stamped "non-resident" by authorized dealers (the major banks acting as agent for the South African Reserve Bank in this regard).

In terms of the Companies Act, an external company (a company incorporated outside of South Africa) must, if it is to establish a place of business in South Africa, register with the Registrar of Companies within 21 days after establishing itself. The external company must register a certified copy of its memorandum with the Registrar, and if the memorandum is not in one of the official languages of South Africa, a certified translation must be registered. The Companies Act sets out further requirements, such as information regarding the directors and the like. An external company may not own immovable (real) property in South Africa unless it is so registered.

5. Public Registers, Records and Databases

In relation to intellectual property, specifically patents, designs and trade marks, information in respect thereof is available at the Companies and Intellectual Properties Registration Office.

Immovable (real) property information is available at the different Deeds Registry Offices in South Africa (**"Deeds Office"**) and on a database known as "WinDeed." Mortgage Bonds registered against immovable (real) property are noted in the Deeds Office and on WinDeed.

Information as to a party's creditworthiness may be obtained from Credit Agencies.

As regards shareholding, each company is obliged in terms of the Companies Act, to keep a register of all shareholders at its registered address. In the case of entities listed on the JSE Limited, the information and register can be obtained from the relevant Transfer Secretary.

6. Purchase Price Requirements

Our tax authorities will not question the overall purchase price payable between unconnected persons dealing at arm's length, as such price will represent a willing buyer/willing seller market value. However, the allocation of such purchase price between the respective asset categories is closely scrutinized, as there would invariably exist the potential for tax arbitrage if a disproportionate amount was allocated to assets subject to CGT (for example, goodwill), versus assets subject to income tax and CGT (for example, fixed assets that have previously qualified for capital allowances/deductions in the seller's hands).

Consequently, the allocation of purchase price between the various assets disposed of must be made at market value. In practice, this allocation is made by asset group.

In transactions between connected persons, the overall purchase consideration is always deemed to be at market value.

Furthermore, if one of the parties to the transaction is a foreign entity, the requirements of the Exchange Control Department of the South African Reserve Bank will have to stipulate that the purchase price amounts to at least the fair market value of a disinvestment and that no more than fair market value is being paid if the acquisition is being made by a South African entity.

B. Tangible/Movable Assets

1. Characteristics as to:

a) Language of Documentation. Section 6 of the Constitution of the Republic of South Africa Act, 1996, sets out the eleven official languages of the country and promotes the equal treatment of all official languages. To date, our experience has shown that the documentation accompanying the disposal of an asset is usually drafted in English and Afrikaans. There is no reason, however, to prevent any legal document from being drafted in any one of the eleven official languages. The documentation may be executed bilingually.

b) Form of Documentation. It is not a requirement of South African law that the asset purchase agreement be reduced to writing and signed by the parties, save for under certain circumstances, such as the sale of immovable (real) property and credit agreements. A valid sale may be concluded in terms of a verbal agreement. It is, however, common practice to reduce such agreements into a written contract for evidentiary purposes, as the written agreement becomes the sole memorial of the parties' respective rights and obligations.

It is possible for documents to be executed outside of South Africa and for documents to be signed in counterparts. Rule 63 of the High Court Rules of South Africa sets out the procedure to follow regarding the authentication of documents that are executed outside of South Africa, for use in South Africa.

Section 63 states that any deed, contract, or power of attorney shall be deemed to be sufficiently authenticated if such document bears the signature and seal of office of:

(i) the head of a South African Diplomatic or consular mission;

(ii) a consul-general, vice-consul or consular agent of the United Kingdom;

(iii) any government authority of such foreign place charged with the authentication of documents under the law of that foreign country;

(iv) any person duly authorized to do so, as evidenced by a certificate by an person cited above;

(v) a notary public in the United Kingdom, Zimbabwe, Lesotho, Botswana or Swaziland; or

(vi) a commissioner of oaths in the South African Defence Force in the case of a document executed by any person in active service.

If the country in which such document has been executed is a member state to The Convention Abolishing the Requirement of Legislation for Foreign Public Documents (to which South Africa is also a member state), then the only requirement regarding the authentication of documents is that a certificate described as an Apostille, issued by a competent authority of the State from which the document emanates, be attached. In South Africa, any magistrate, registrar, assistant registrar of the High Court, any person designated by the Director General of Justice and any person designated by the Director General of Foreign Affairs may provide an Apostille.

c) Specification of Assets. A generic description will suffice. Of course, for the sake of certainty, a description of each asset or class and/or aggregate of assets is preferable. In terms of the specificity principle, a transfer is accomplished by the transfer of each separate asset or aggregate of assets, thus it is advisable to attach a schedule of assets to the transfer agreement, though not mandatory.

2. Administrative, Corporate and Other Approvals

Administrative Approvals

There may be certain sector and industry-specific approvals in relation to the transfer of the tangible assets, for example in the banking or insurance industries, and non-compliance with such regulatory approval renders the sale invalid. The transfer of mineral and petroleum rights (for example, exploration rights or production rights) would require ministerial consent. The relevant provisions distinguish between whether non-compliance will render the transfer invalid or not.

The parties should have to consider various regulatory approvals that may be applicable to the proposed structure of the sale such as such as the compliance with the Code, JSE Listings Requirements, approval by the competition authorities (non-compliance will render the transfer invalid and expose the parties to penalties), exchange control approval from the South African Reserve Bank (non-compliance will lead to the transfer being void from the start) and industry or sector specific approvals and permits (each provision separately provides for the consequences of non-compliance).

Corporate Approvals

As mentioned above, in terms of Section 228 of the Companies Act, the directors of a company shall not have the power, save by a special resolution of its members (i.e. a resolution passed by shareholders holding 75% of the votes at a meeting at which shareholders holding at least 25% of the votes are present), to dispose of the whole or the greater part of the undertaking of the company or the whole or the greater part of the assets of the company. The transaction can be ratified, but if it is not, it is invalid.

A sale of shares and a sale of assets will require a resolution passed by the directors of the relevant selling company. Furthermore, the constitutional documents or shareholders' agreement in respect of a company may also require additional consents, e. g., that of shareholders or a certain minimum of shareholders.

Other Approvals

In case the assets are encumbered, the approval of the relevant security holders would be required to effect the valid transfer of the encumbered asset, unless the contrary is provided for in the relevant security document. A transfer without the consent of the security holder will not necessarily make the transfer invalid, but may lead to the security being enforced.

3. Filing Requirements

In the case of a change of control and subject to certain monetary thresholds having been met, a sale of assets or sale of shares may be notifiable in terms of the South Africa Competition Act, 1998.

If one of the parties is foreign, a transfer may require the notification (and approval) of the Exchange Control Department of the South African Reserve Bank.

The special resolution referred to in B, 2 (Corporate Approvals) above must be lodged with the Registrar of Companies within one month from passing such special resolution. Any special resolution of which a copy is not lodged with the Registrar and registered within six months from the date of the passing of that resolution will, unless the Court otherwise directs, lapse and be void.

The transfer of intellectual property in respect of patents, designs and trade marks applied for or registered, must be lodged with the Patent, Designs or Trade Marks Offices at the Companies and Intellectual Properties Registration Office.

The transfer of immovable (real) property must be registered with the relevant Deeds Office.

The transfer of motor vehicles has to be registered with the local authorities.

4. Automatic Transfer of Encumbrances

The assets will be sold subject to any existing encumbrances, and depending on what type of encumbrance the asset is subject to, the prior consent of the relevant security holder will be required before such asset may be validly transferred. For example, the consent of a mortgage bond holder will be necessary before the mortgage bond may be cancelled in the Deeds Office and the property transferred.

C. Real Property

1. Characteristics as to:

a) Language of Documentation. Documents registered at the Deeds Office must be executed in either English or Afrikaans. Furthermore, all title deed conditions contained in a deed of transfer must be carried through in exactly the same language as they appear and cannot be translated.

b) Form of Documentation. Documents must be in writing and executed by a notary. Please also refer to the commentary in Section D 1, b below.

c) Specification of Assets. Regulation 28(1) of the Deeds Registries Act 47 of 1937 prescribes that the following detail be disclosed in any deed in which land is described:

- the name of the registration division, administrative district and province in which the land is situated, or in the case of land situated in a township, the registration division concerned, administrative district, the name of such township and the province; and

- the registered number of such land.

The manner in which farm land is described differs slightly, in that it contains:

- the name of the farm;
- the number of the farm;
- the registration division;
- the province in which the farm is situated; and
- the number of the plot.

2. Administrative, Corporate and Other Approvals

Administrative Approvals

In any property transaction, a clearance certificate issued by the local municipality must be produced before transfer can be effected. This clearance certificate confirms that all fees and taxes due to the local municipality have been settled in full by the seller.

Similarly, the South African Receiver of Revenue (**"Receiver of Revenue"**) must confirm in writing that all property taxes due and payable have been paid and that the property may be transferred.

In some instances, it would be necessary to obtain the consent of the Master of the High Court of South Africa, where the transfer of the property occurs from the deceased estate of an individual to a third party.

Corporate Approvals

Where property is transferred or acquired by a corporate entity, such entity is meant to consent to the disposal or acquisition of such asset in terms of a resolution passed by its directors. Similarly, a trust may only acquire or dispose of property if the trustees have been provided with the power to do so in terms of the trust deed.

Other Approvals

In instances where the property is encumbered, a transfer is only possible once the bondholder has consented to the cancellation of the bond over the property. The bondholder consents to cancellation based on the understanding that upon transfer of the property, it will receive all monies due to it, in terms of its bond, from the proceeds of the purchase price. The transfer of property and cancellation of a bond occur simultaneously.

Given the manner in which the South African land registration process works, it is impossible for transfer to be effected if the necessary consents have not been obtained.

3. Filing Requirements

In a change of control and subject to certain monetary thresholds having been met, a sale of real property may be notifiable in terms of the South Africa Competition Act, 1998.

All property transfers are processed through the Deeds Offices and therefore all transfer of property and registration of endorsements against property is documented by the Deeds Office. It is therefore very easy to establish the ownership of any piece of land situated anywhere in South Africa, because of the practice that requires all property transfers be registered by the Deeds Office. Properties in South Africa are recorded in different registers at the Deeds Office, depending on the nature of the property. Township property is filed in the township register while farm property is filed in the farm register. The Registrar of Deeds is obliged to ensure that these registers are continuously maintained.

4. Automatic Transfer of Encumbrances

As mentioned in C, 2 (Other Approvals) above, all encumbrances on a property would have to be cancelled before such property may be transferred. The bondholder must provide his written consent to the cancellation for the Deeds Office to give effect to such cancellation. Section 57 of the Deeds Registries Act does, however, allow for the substitution of debtors under a mortgage bond in certain circumstances.

Should a servitude be registered against or in favor of a specific piece of land, such servitude will be enforceable in favor of the land, regardless of the ownership of the land, and is transferred to the purchaser.

If however a servitude is registered in favor of an individual, so that the right vests in the individual and not in favor of the land, then such a right (with the exception of some special classes of rights such as usufructs) lapses upon transfer by virtue of the fact that it is personal in nature. The lapsing of such right may occur in one of the following manners:

(i) be means of a notarial deed whereby the individual transfers his rights to the existing owner of the property;

(ii) by means of a deed of transfer where the individual together with the existing owner transfers full ownership of the property to the purchaser;

(iii) by means of a notarial cancellation of the servitude, and

(iv) by means of an underhand waiver of the individual's rights in favor of the existing owner.

5. Automatic Transfer of Lease Agreements

A lease agreement would automatically transfer to the purchaser not only if it is a condition of the sale agreement, or, if the lease is registered against the property as a long term lease (i.e. a lease for a period of greater than ten years) but also due to the common law principle of *huur gaat voor koop*, which loosely translates to "hire goes before sale." The common law principle states that, not withstanding the sale of immoveable property, if such property is subject to a lease agreement, the rights of the lessee will survive the transfer.

It is always possible, however, to terminate a lease agreement by agreement between the parties and in accordance with the conditions of the lease agreement. The transfer of property and cession of lease agreements would generally occur simultaneously, and therefore it would not be possible for a seller to terminate a lease agreement after transfer has taken place.

D. Contracts

1. Characteristics as to:

a) Language of Documentation. Please refer to B, 1, a above.

b) Form of Documentation. Generally, contracts are not required to be in writing. There are, however, certain statutory exceptions that require the contract to be reduced to writing and require that certain formalities be followed. Various contracts that must be reduced to writing include: the sale, exchange or donation of land; credit agreements; bills of exchange and cheques; and contracts of suretyship. Mineral lease agreements must be in writing and registered in the Deeds Office to be enforceable against third parties. In addition, long term leases, notarial cession agreements, notarial bonds (both general and specific) and servitude agreements must be written and attested to by a notary and registered in the Deeds Office.

Please also refer to our comments in B, 1, b above.

c) Specification of Contracts. Please refer to our comments in B, 1, c above.

2. Administrative, Corporate and Other Approvals

Administrative Approvals

Generally, transfer of contracts to do not require governmental or administrative approvals. Depending on the industry and relevant legislations, approvals may, however, be required.

There may be certain sector and industry specific approvals in relation to the transfer of contracts.

The parties should consider various regulatory approvals that may be applicable to the transfer of contracts, e.g., approval by the competition authorities (non-compliance will render the transfer invalid and expose the parties to penalties), exchange control approval from the South African Reserve Bank (non-compliance will lead to the transfer being void from the start) and industry or sector specific approvals and permits (each provision provides itself what the consequences of non-compliance would be).

Corporate Approvals

As mentioned above, in terms of Section 228 of the Companies Act, the directors of a company shall not have the power, save by a special resolution of its members (i.e. a resolution passed by shareholders holding 75% of the votes at a meeting at which shareholders holding at least 25% of the votes are present), to dispose of the whole or the greater part of the undertaking of the company or the whole or the greater part of the assets of the company. This will also apply if the relevant contract being transferred is the main major asset of the company. The transaction can be ratified, but if not it is invalid.

The transfer of contracts will generally require a resolution passed by the board of directors of the relevant contract parties. The constitutional documents or shareholders' agreement in respect of a company may also require additional consents, e. g., that of shareholders, or may delegate the authority authorizing different people to authorize the transfer of a contract. If the transfer was not approved at all by the directors of the company, the transfer will be invalid, unless an officer of the company, authorized in terms of the company's memorandum and articles of association, entered into the transferring agreement, in which case the person will be deemed to have had the necessary authority in terms of South African company law. If the transfer was subject to internal approvals of the relevant company, third parties may assume that the necessary approvals have been obtained.

Other Approvals

The approval of other parties to the contract may be required, depending on the wording of the contract. The contract may have a provision that, save with the consent of the other party, the contract may not be assigned nor may its rights or obligations be ceded or delegated. If such consent is required, the transfer will, unless the contract provides differently, be valid, but the party will be in breach of the contract, which may entitle the other contract party to cancel the transferred contract (or sue for damages or claim specific performance).

3. Automatic Transfer of Contracts (Other than Lease and Employment Agreements)

The consent of the insurer is required if an insurance contract is to be assigned and there is to be a substitution of the insured, such as in the case of the sale and transfer of an insured's property.

Generally, a sale of an asset agreement provides that the rights and obligations of any contracts sold will be ceded and assigned to the purchaser.

4. Filing Requirements

Please refer to D, 2 above.

5. Treatment of Existing Contractual Claims and Obligations

Once the contracts have been ceded and assigned to the purchaser, the rights and obligations will automatically transfer to the purchaser. Depending on which party one is acting for, it may be advisable to provide for indemnities in the asset sale agreement, indemnifying the purchaser from any onerous obligations that it may incur with respect to the sold contracts.

6. Warranty Claims Resulting from Events prior to Transfer

Once the rights and obligations have been ceded and assigned to the purchaser, the purchaser will be liable for any warranty claims. It is customary to include warranties and indemnities to protect the purchaser against any contingent liabilities. Generally, a thorough due diligence investigation will be undertaken to determine any contingent liabilities, which will enable the purchaser to include the price of the risk of such warranty claims in the purchase consideration.

E. IP Rights

1. Characteristics of Intellectual Property Rights (e. g., Trademarks, Patents, Utility Models, Domain Names) ("*IP Rights*") as to:

a) Language of Documentation. All documents must be filed in one of the official languages of the Republic. The documents can be drafted in English and can be executed bilingually.

b) Form of Documentation. The deed of assignment and power of attorney do not require notarization. The documentation can be executed outside South Africa and can be signed in counterparts.

c) Specification of IP Rights. The IP Rights should be described in full. The trademarks, designs and patents must be identified with the trademark, patent and design numbers. There is no requirement for schedules or lists to be attached provided the IP Rights are identified clearly in the deed of assignment.

2. Administrative, Corporate and Other Approvals

If IP Rights are being transferred from a South African entity to a foreign entity, exchange control approval must be obtained from the South African Reserve Bank in terms of the Currency and Exchange Act 9 of 1933. Approval is never granted in respect of sales to connected persons.

It is not necessary to obtain the approval of corporate bodies regarding the seller and/or purchaser.

If IP Rights are encumbered it is necessary to obtain the security holders' consent.

If the above approvals and/or consents are not granted and/or obtained, the assignment is invalid against third parties.

3. Filing Requirements

The assignment must be recorded at the Trademarks, Designs and/or Patent Offices in order to be effective against third parties.

4. Applicable International (Multilateral) Agreements or Treaties

South Africa is party to the Agreement on Trade-Related Aspects of Intellectual Property Rights (**"TRIPS"**), the Paris Convention and the Berne Convention.

F. Receivables

1. Characteristics as to:

a) Language of Documentation. Please refer to the comments in B, 1, a above.

b) Form of Documentation. Please refer to the comments in B, 1, b above.

c) Specification of Receivables. Please refer to the comments in B, 1, c above.

2. Administrative, Corporate and Other Approvals

Generally, the transfer of receivables does not require governmental or administrative approvals. Depending on the industry and relevant legislations, approvals may, however, be required.

As mentioned above, in terms of Section 228 of the Companies Act, the directors of a company shall not have the power, save by a special resolution of its members (i.e. a resolution passed by shareholders holding 75% of the votes at a meeting at which shareholders holding at least 25% of the votes are present), to dispose of the whole or the greater part of the undertaking of the company or the whole or the greater part of the assets of the company. This will also apply if the receivables being transferred are the main major asset of the company. The transaction can be ratified, but if not, it is invalid.

The transfer of receivables will generally require a resolution passed by the board of directors of the relevant contract parties. The constitutional documents or shareholders' agreement in respect of a company may also require additional consents, e. g., that of the shareholders, or may delegate the authority, authorizing different people to authorize the transfer of a contract. If the transfer was not approved by the directors of the company, it will be invalid, unless an officer of the company, authorized in terms of the company's memorandum and articles of association, entered into the transferring agreement, in which case the person will be deemed to have had the necessary authority under South African company law. If the transfer was subject to internal approvals of the relevant company, third parties may assume that the necessary approvals have been obtained.

Generally, the approval of debtors is not required.

3. Filing Requirements

There are no public registers for receivables and no special filings are required. The notification of debtors may be required, depending on the wording of the agreement.

G. Liabilities

1. Characteristics as to:

a) Language of Documentation. Please refer to the comments in B, 1, a above.

b) Form of Documentation. Please see the comments in B, 1 b above.

c) Specification of Liabilities. Please refer to the comments in B, 1, c above.

2. Administrative, Corporate and Other Approvals

Generally, the transfer of liabilities does not require governmental or administrative approvals. Depending on the industry and relevant legislation, approvals may, however, be required.

The transfer of liabilities will generally require a resolution passed by the boards of directors of the relevant contract parties. The constitutional documents or shareholders' agreement in respect of a company may also require additional consents, e. g. that of shareholders or may delegate the authority authorizing different people to authorize the transfer of liabilities. If the transfer was not approved at all by the directors of the company, the transfer will be invalid, unless an officer of the company, authorized in terms of the company's memorandum and articles of association, entered into the transferring agreement, in which case the person will be deemed to have had the necessary authority in terms of South African company law. If the transfer was subject to internal approvals of the relevant company, third parties may assume that the necessary approvals have been obtained.

Generally, the approval of creditors is required. A transfer without the approval will generally remain valid, although the transferring party may have breached the agreement with the creditor and the creditor will have its normal remedies in law for breach.

3. Filing Requirements

There are no filing requirements. Notification of the creditors may be required depending on the wording of the agreement.

4. Purchaser's Liability for:

a) Tax Obligations. All tax obligations for periods prior to the acquisition remain for the seller's account.

b) Environmental Contamination. The purchaser's liability in this respect will primarily arise from Section 28 of the National Environmental Management Act, 1998 (**"NEMA"**). NEMA imposes a duty of care on every person who causes, has caused or may cause significant pollution or degradation of the environment to take reasonable measures to prevent the pollution or degradation of the environment from occurring, continuing or reoccurring. Insofar as such harm to the environment is authorized by law or cannot reasonably be avoided, NEMA requires that the pollution or degradation must be minimized and rectified (see Section 28(1) of NEMA).

The persons on whom the duty of care rests include, inter alia, an owner of land or premises, a person in control of land or premises or a person who has a right to use the land or premises on which or in which

- any activity or process is or was performed or undertaken; or
- any other situation exists,

which causes, has caused or is likely to cause significant pollution or degradation of the environment (Section 28(2) of NEMA).

The "reasonable measures" referred to above may include measures to:

- investigate, assess and evaluate the impact on the environment;
- remedy the effects of the pollution or degradation;
- inform and educate employees about the environmental risks of their work and the manner in which their tasks must be performed in order to avoid causing significant pollution or degradation of the environment;
- eliminate any source of the pollution or degradation;
- contain or prevent the movement of pollutants or the cause of the degradation; or
- cease, modify or control any act, activity or process causing the pollution or degradation (see Section 28(3) of NEMA).

The state may direct any person who fails to take these reasonable measures, to commence, continue and complete the reasonable measures. Should a person fail to comply with a directive, the State may itself take the reasonable measures to remedy the situation and recover all the costs of remediation from specified persons, which include, inter alia, the person who failed to take the reasonable measures, the owner of the land, the person in control of the land and/or the person who has or had a right to use the land. Liability may be apportioned according to the degree to which each person was responsible for the harm to the environment.

In *Bareki v Gencor* 2006 (1) SA 432 (T) at pages 439–441, the Transvaal Provincial Division of the High Court of South Africa held that the provisions of Section 28 of NEMA are not retroactive and, accordingly, the obligation to take the reasonable measures does not apply where the acts of pollution and degradation complained of were caused or began prior to January 29, 1999 (the date NEMA went into effect).

The Court further held that the effect of Section 28 of NEMA is that an owner or possessor of land on whose land an activity or process causing pollution has been performed without his knowledge and consent, prima facie, incurs an obligation to take reasonable corrective measures. In this case there is prima facie absolute liability, which precludes not merely the element of fault, but also the element of unlawful conduct. Sections 28(1) and (2) of NEMA therefore create at least a strict liability and in some cases they may even create an absolute liability. As an example of absolute liability, the Court noted that in terms of the latter part of Section 28(1) of NEMA, even where significant pollution or degradation of the environment is authorized by law or cannot be reasonably avoided or stopped, the person who causes, has caused or may cause such pollution or degradation must take reasonable measures to minimize and rectify such pollution or degradation of the environment. Conduct that is not unlawful because it is authorized by law nevertheless gives rise to a duty to take reasonable measures, meaning that the liability is absolute.

The Court observed that there is no monetary limit to such liability, and so the liability is potentially extensive.

In a nutshell, the purchaser in the transaction will be liable to take reasonable measures to remedy existing pollution caused between January 29, 1999 and the date of the acquisition.

c) Products Sold or Services Rendered by the Seller to Third Parties. The purchaser will be liable for any defects in the products sold or services rendered at the date that the parties agree that the risk and benefit in the asset passes to the purchaser. Manufacturers of products are strictly liable for latent defects in the products sold, and may be liable for consequential loss suffered by the purchaser of such products. The manufacturer may, however, protect itself by contracting around such loss. It should be noted, however, that comprehensive statutory consumer protection legislation has been passed, in the form of the Consumer Protection Act 68 of 2008, which is to come into effect during the first quarter of 2010, and will limit the general ability of manufacturers and suppliers to contract out of liability.

5. Automatic Transfer of Other Liabilities

Except as concerns employees (see H, 1 below), there is no automatic transfer of other liabilities.

6. Contractual Protection as to 4 and 5 above

Generally warranties and indemnities are provided to cover such liabilities.

H. Employees

1. Transfer of Employees

Employees automatically transfer to the employ of a purchaser of a business, or part thereof, as a going concern. With regard to a sale of assets, to the extent that the transaction is, in substance, a transfer of a business as a going concern, all affected employees will be transferred from the seller, referred to as the 'old employer,' to the purchaser, referred to as the 'new employer'. This is not applicable in other circumstances, such as a sale of shares. The transfer of employees must occur on the same or similar terms and conditions of employment. The 'old employer' is required to calculate accrued leave, notional severance pay, and any other payments that may become due to the affected employees as at the date of transfer, and the parties must agree which will assume liability for these payments should they become payable. The amounts must be disclosed to the affected employees. The 'new employer' and the 'old employer' are jointly and severally liable for a period of twelve months after the transfer in the event that an employee becomes entitled to receive any of the payments referred to above as a consequence of such employee being dismissed for operational requirements (referred to as retrenchments). Employees' years of service remain uninterrupted notwithstanding the transfer. This has consequences for the payment of severance amounts that may become payable to the employee in the event of a dismissal for operational requirements, since the law dictates that an employee is entitled to severance pay in an amount equivalent to one week's remuneration for every completed year of service. Employees may not be dismissed – either by the 'old employer' or the 'new employer' - for any reason related to a transfer of a business, as this is expressly prohibited under South African labor legislation, and constitutes what is known as an 'automatically unfair dismissal.' In such circumstances, dismissed employees may be awarded compensation in an amount equivalent to 24 months' remuneration.

The transfer of pension funds is dependant upon the type and rules of the pension fund and it is generally accepted that employees may be transferred to a new pension fund where circumstances warrant this (for example, when the pension fund is a closed fund and the new employer may not, therefore, participate in the fund) subject to compliance with pension legislation. The transfer of benefits is not expressly regulated by labor legislation and the onus is on the employer to ensure that employees' benefits are not detrimentally affected by the transfer. This is dealt with on a case-by-case basis.

Since the new employer effectively steps into the shoes of the old employer, everything done in relation to the transferring employee prior to the transfer (for example, a dismissal) is considered to have been done by the new employer. The new employer and the old employer are jointly and severally liable in respect of any claim concerning any terms and condition of employment that arose prior to the transfer.

Since the transfer of employment occurs by operation of law employees may not refuse to transfer into the employ of the new employer. Labor legislation does, however, allow for the conclusion of an agreement between the old employer, one or more of the affected employees, and the new employer to vary the consequences of the automatic transfer; i.e. it is possible for the parties to agree that the employee(s) will not transfer into the employ of the purchaser of the business as a going concern.

2. Approval of Works Council, Trade Union or Other Institutions

Works Councils are not applicable within the South African context. The consent of the employees and the trade union (to the extent that a trade union is present within the workplace) is not required prior to the transfer of the employees nor is there any consultation obligation imposed upon either the 'old employer' or the 'new employer'. Notwithstanding the absence of a statutory duty to consult, it accords with sound human resource policy to disclose the pertinent aspects of the transfer either to the employees directly or the employees' representative (such as a trade union).

3. Contractual Protection as to Labor Issues

It is essential that the 'old employer' and the 'new employer' negotiate indemnities and warranties, usually contained in an annexure to the sale agreement, in order to regulate the liabilities referred to above.

I. Tax Implications

1. Value Added Tax

VAT is levied at a flat rate of 14% when a registered vendor disposes of assets (excluding financial instruments). This rate is reduced to 0% in certain circumstances – for example, when the assets are disposed of as part of a going concern between VAT vendors.

2. Real Property Transfer Tax

The disposal of real property is subject to transfer duty at a flat rate of 8% (other than in the case of natural persons, in which case a sliding scale applies), but only if such disposal is not subject to VAT in the seller's hands.

Any transfer duty paid by the purchaser in this regard can be claimed as a deemed input deduction for VAT purposes, assuming of course that the purchaser is or becomes a registered VAT vendor.

3. Other Tax Issues

Although there is no group tax relief in South Africa, the South African Income Tax Act provides for, in specific circumstances, relief from income tax, CGT, VAT, STT, and (in certain circumstances) STC to facilitate corporate reorganizations. The transactions contemplated include asset-for-share transactions, amalgamation transactions intra-group transactions, unbundling transactions, and liquidation distributions

J. Bankruptcy Law

1. Challenge of Asset Transfer in Case of Insolvency

If a company is being wound up and is unable to pay all of its debts, every disposition by the company of its property that, if made by an individual, could, for any reason be set aside in the event of his insolvency, may, if made by a company, be set aside, and the laws relating to insolvency will be applied to any disposition *mutatis mutandis*.

The Insolvency Act provides that any disposition (which is defined broadly and includes, inter alia, a sale lease, mortgage, payment, and pledge, etc.) may be declared voidable and set aside in the following circumstances:

(i) a disposition not for value: a disposition by a company of its assets not for value may be declared void if the disposition was made within two years of the winding-up and the person in whose favor the disposition was made cannot prove that immediately after the disposition the assets of the company exceeded its liabilities. If the disposition was made more than two years before the winding-up, it is voidable only if the liquidator can prove that immediately after the disposition the liabilities of the company exceeded its assets. If the value of the property disposed of exceeds the amount whereby the liabilities exceed the assets, the disposition may be set aside only to the extent of such excess;

(ii) voidable preference: every disposition made by a debtor not more than six months before the winding up of the company, which has the effect of favoring one creditor above another may be set aside if, immediately after the disposition, the liabilities of the company exceeded the value of its assets, unless the person in whose favor the disposition was made can prove that the disposition was made in the ordinary course of business and was not intended to favor one creditor over another;

(iii) undue preference to creditors: if a debtor makes a disposition of property at a time when its liabilities exceed its assets with the intention of preferring one creditor over another, such disposition may be set aside;

(iv) collusive dealing: after the sequestration of a debtor's estate, the court may set aside any transaction entered into by the debtor before the sequestration, whereby such debtor, in collusion with another person, disposed of property belonging to it in a manner that had the effect of prejudicing its creditors or of preferring one of its creditors above another; and

(vi) voidable sale of business as a trading company: if a trading company transfers in terms of a contract its business or the goodwill of the business or any property (except for stock in trade in the ordinary course of business or for securing payment of a debt) and such trader has not published a notice of such intended transfer in the Government Gazette and daily newspapers in the district in which the business is operated within a period of not less than 30 days and not more than 60 days before the date of transfer, and such company is wound up within six months after transferring the property, such transfer may be declared void as against its creditors and liquidator for a period of six months after such transfer.

The Insolvency Act does not deprive creditors of various common law remedies, and where disposition are made in fraud of creditor (i.e. with the intention of favoring one creditor over another), such disposition may be rescinded.

In return for any disposition liable to be set aside under the Insolvency Act, any person who has parted with any property or security that he held or who has lost any right to as against another person is not obliged to restore any property or other benefit received under such disposition, provided that such person has acted in good faith, unless the liquidator has indemnified him for parting with such property or security or for losing such right. Where a person has acquired property from a person other than a company that is subsequently wound up in good faith and for value, then the rights of such person are not affected by the provisions of the Insolvency Act relating to voidable dispositions.

2. Acquisition of Assets that are Subject to Insolvency Proceedings

In terms of the Companies Act, after the liquidator has been granted the necessary authority by the creditors and members or the Master of the High Court, the liquidator has the power to sell any asset (movable or immovable) or the business of the company by way of public auction or private contract. Where, however, the liquidator sells an asset or whole or part of the business of a company in return for shares in the buyer, the liquidator may only do so if it has the specific consent of the shareholders in the form of a special resolution and/or the consent of three-fourths of the creditors at a meeting of creditors.

A company may be placed under judicial management in circumstances where through mismanagement or otherwise it is unable to pay its debts, but there is a reasonable probability that if it is under such management, it will be able to pay its debts and meet its obligations. In such circumstances, the judicial manager is empowered to sell the assets of the company only if they are sold in the ordinary course of business of the company (i.e. trading stock).

K. Timing and Costs

1. Timeframe of Asset Transfer

In a sale of business, Section 228 of the Companies Act provides that the directors of a company shall not have the power, save by a special resolution of its members (i.e. a resolution passed by shareholders holding 75% of the votes at a meeting at which shareholders holding at least 25% of the votes are present), to dispose of the whole or the greater part of the undertaking of the company or the whole or the greater part of the assets of the company.

The requirement adds to the timetable for a sale of business, allowing for the notice for the passing of the special resolutions (21 days) and thereafter registration with the Registrar of Companies.

Furthermore, should the disposal of the assets be in terms of Section 228 of the Companies Act (a disposal of the whole or greater part of the assets of the company) and the disposing entity is a company listed on the JSE or otherwise falls within the scope of the Code, such disposal will be governed by the Code. The Code provides for strict time periods. Once announcement is made of the intent to dispose, the posting of the offer document must occur within 30 days. The board of the seller must advise its shareholders of its views of the offer within 14 days after posting the offer acceptance periods, and the offer must be open for acceptance for 21 days after the posting of the offer. The offer must be declared unconditional within 60 days of the posting of the offer, or the offer will lapse. Once the offer has been declared unconditional, the offer must remain open for a further 14 days, and the consideration payable by the purchaser must posted to within seven days to the shareholders of the target company within seven days of the later of the offer becoming unconditional or the offer being accepted.

The constitutional documents of the relevant parties may require additional consents and provide for time periods in that regard (e. g., board approvals, shareholder approvals, etc).

The registration of the transfer of immovable (real) property in the Deeds Office or the registration of intellectual property at the Companies and Intellectual Properties Registration Office generally takes between six to 12 weeks.

The timing regarding competition approval depends on the size of the merger:

(i) an intermediate merger is one in which consolidated annual turnover of the seller in, into or from South Africa is South African Rand (“**ZAR**”) 80 million or more, or an asset value in South Africa of ZAR 80 million or more, and the combined annual turnover or assets (whichever is greater) in, into or from South Africa of the purchaser and the seller is ZAR 560 million or more, but less than ZAR 6.6 billion. A large merger is where the seller has a consolidated turnover in, into or from South Africa of ZAR 190 million or more, or an asset value of in South Africa of ZAR 190 million or more, and the combined annual turnover or assets in, into or from South Africa of the purchaser and the seller is ZAR 6.6 billion or more. Small mergers do not have to be notified, unless required by the Competition Commission (“**Commission**”), and may be implemented without competition approval.

(ii) in the case of an intermediate merger the Commission has 20 business days to consider the merger, which may be extended for a further 40 business days in which to approve the merger. The time periods are longer in the case of a large merger, where the Commission has an initial 40 business days in which to consider the merger, which may be extended by up to 15 business days at a time on application to the Competition Tribunal (“**Tribunal**”). After considering the application, the Commission is obliged to refer the matter to the Tribunal with its recommendation in relation to the matter. Once the Commission has referred the matter to the Tribunal for consideration, the Tribunal must set a date for hearing the matter within 10 business days. The date for hearing the matter may be extended by 10 business days by the Tribunal or for a further period as agreed between the parties. The Tribunal must issue a certificate reflecting its decision in the matter within ten business days after the completion of the hearing.

2. Costs of Asset Transfer

The statutory merger filing fee for an intermediate merger is ZAR 100,000 (approx. USD 12 515) and ZAR 350,000 (approx. USD 43 800) for a large merger.

The purchaser will indirectly incur securities transfer tax on the acquisition of the shares in the target company, which is payable at 0.25% of the greater of the purchase consideration or market value of such shares acquired (if different).

The fees charged in terms of the notarization and registration of documents in the Deeds Registry are governed by a tariff schedule, and the fees vary depending on the type of document to be notarized or the size of the bond to be registered. Notaries may also charge a fee for their preparation of the relevant documents.

Please refer to the comments in A, 1 above regarding transfer duties, VAT and other taxes.

L. Miscellaneous

1. Choice of Foreign Law

The parties are free to elect which law will govern their contractual relationship, and in terms of case law, it has been held that the proper law of the contract is that the law of the country which the parties have agreed or intended will govern the contract.

2. (International) Arbitration, Choice of Venue

The Arbitration Act, 1965 covers both international and domestic arbitration in South Africa. Parties to a sale of assets can agree to insert an arbitration clause and may agree on which rules of procedure will be followed, such as the Arbitration Foundation of South Africa's rules or the rules of the International Chamber of Commerce (**"the ICC"**). The parties are free to adopt the procedure of their choice, and the parties are free to choose the venue of the arbitration.

South Africa is not yet a party to the 1965 Washington Convention on the Settlement of Investment Disputes between States and Nationals of Other States (**"the ICSID Convention"**), though many of the contracts that the South African government and its agencies have concluded with foreign bodies and investors provide for compulsory international arbitration under the ICSID Convention Rules, the ICC Rules or the United Nations Commission on International Trade Arbitration Rules. South Africa has also ratified many Bilateral Investment Treaties with foreign countries and these BITs usually provide for compulsory international arbitration. In addition, South Africa is a party to the 1958 New York Convention on the Recognition and Enforcement of Foreign Arbitral Awards.

3. Other Distinctions, Characteristics

If the seller is a natural person, as opposed to a legal entity, and if such seller's marital regime is one subject to community of property, the consent of the other spouse is required before any assets comprising the joint estate may be sold and transferred. If the asset sought to be transferred is immovable (real) property and forms part of the joint estate, the written consent of both spouses, together with the attestation of two competent witnesses, is required before such immovable (real) property may be sold, except where such disposal of the immovable (real) property is made in the ordinary course of that spouse's profession, business or trade. If no consent is given in such circumstances, the agreement is voidable, however, the other spouse may ratify the agreement.

M. Literature

T. M. Mohan, Purchase and Sale of Movable Property, Butterworths Forms and Precedents, January 2004

D. R. Clarke, Sale of Business, Butterworths Forms and Precedents, November 1996

IBFD Tax Travel Companions, M&A Tax Fundamentals 2008

Lynette Olivier, Tax implications of the sale of a business, *South African Law Journal*, 2007, Volume 124(3), page 600–617

Spain

By *Juan Manuel De Remedios*, *Paco Iso*, *Xavier Pujol* and *Manuel Deó*

A. General Aspects

1. Asset Deal vs. Share Deal: Essential Considerations

In an asset deal, the purchaser chooses or "cherry picks" each and every asset and liability to be acquired since only those assets and liabilities expressly agreed upon in the corresponding agreement by the parties are transferred (with the exception of certain liabilities towards employees and Spanish social security, as well as certain taxes). On the other hand, in a share deal, by means of the acquisition of the shares, all assets and liabilities of the target company are acquired by the purchaser, including any liabilities that the purchaser might not be aware of or certain assets that the purchaser might not desire. Therefore, if the seller is only interested in certain assets held by the purchaser, an asset deal may be the best way to structure the transaction.

Since the purchaser does not acquire hidden or undisclosed liabilities in the target company, very often the purchaser will be expecting the seller to provide fewer representations and warranties (normally with a higher limitation of liability) in an asset deal than in a share deal. On the other hand, since the purchaser in a share deal acquires all assets and liabilities of the target company, the purchaser will often expect more representations and warranties from the seller.

Another important consideration is that the transfer procedure in a share deal is technically more simple than in an asset deal. While in a share deal, the transfer of the shares is enough to effectively transfer the assets and liabilities, in an asset deal the transfer agreement and the transfer formalities are normally more complex, since each and every asset and liability must be effectively transferred. Therefore, each such asset and liability must be specifically and individually identified in the transfer agreement and a price must be allocated to each asset or, in the event of assets of the same kind, to each group of assets.

This implies that in an asset deal more third-party consents or clearances are usually involved in order to complete the transfer (e. g., clients or governmental authorities). However, as in many other jurisdictions, third-party consents are also included as a condition precedent to the completion of many share deals.

More in depth, the purchaser may prefer an asset deal to a share deal when the company selling the asset is the company that was responsible for the building or manufacture of the asset (e. g., real property or machinery), in particular when the asset is in the course of building or manufacture at the time of sale. The reason for this is that a transfer of shares in such cases would entail the transfer of the builder's or manufacturer's responsibility, the scope of which the purchaser cannot assess at the time of the acquisition. The risk attached to the transfer of the builder's or manufacturer's liability is increased if the company whose shares are being sold is a partnership (*sociedad colectiva*) rather than a limited liability company.

Furthermore, among certain type of purchasers (e. g., private equity firms) an asset deal might be preferable due to the advantages it offers in terms of avoiding the financial assistance prohibition set out in Spanish regulations for the purchase of shares of Spanish limited liability companies (*sociedad anónima* and *sociedad de responsabilidad limitada*), to the extent that the shares or assets of the target company are given as collateral in order to finance or repay the acquisition of the target company's shares. Having said that, market practice has shown that there has been an evolution in the application of the financial assistance regime and that private equity firms have not abused the asset deal structure.

The sale of certain assets may be subject to pre-emption rights in favor of third parties. The sale of leased premises, for instance, is subject to a pre-emption right in favor of the tenant in the event there is a sale of the building being leased to it. On the other hand, a transfer of the shares of a company is normally not subject to third-party pre-emption rights, unless the articles of association of the target company (or a shareholder agreement, if any) contain clauses providing for restrictions on the transfer of shares (e. g., pre-emption rights and tag along and drag along rights).

Broadly speaking, asset deals could be subject to more taxes than a share deal. An asset deal is normally subject to value added tax (*Impuesto sobre el Valor Añadido*), transfer tax (*Transmisiones Patrimoniales Onerosas*), stamp duty (*Actos Jurídicos Documentados*) and, in the event of real property, and taxes on the increase in value of urban land (*Impuesto sobre el Incremento de Valor de los terrenos de Naturaleza Urbana*). On the other hand, share deals are in principle only subject to transfer taxes (*Transmisiones Patrimoniales Onerosas*).

2. Distinction between Sale and Transfer in Rem

As many other continental European jurisdictions, Spanish law distinguishes between the sale (obligation to transfer) and the transfer in rem (fulfillment of the obligation to transfer) of assets. As a general rule, the transfer of an asset under Spanish law is a twofold transaction which requires

- a valid agreement or title; and
- the effective and actual transfer of the asset to the purchaser, which may or may not take place simultaneously. Although the parties concerned may agree that the assets will be transferred at a later stage, the entering into of a private purchase agreement will give the purchaser a legal right to acquire the assets under the terms and conditions set out therein.

Any private purchase agreement by means of which the parties outline the terms and conditions of the transfer is deemed a valid agreement. The parties also agree on both the specific assets and liabilities to be transferred and the representations and warranties to be given by the seller, plus the relevant indemnification procedures in case of misrepresentation.

Having said that, the actual transfer is completed only upon the delivery of the asset, which takes place when such asset is under the power and possession of the purchaser. In the event the transfer is entered into by means of a public deed, the granting of such deed will be the equivalent to the delivery of the transferred asset, and will be deemed to have taken place automatically.

Depending on the specific assets to be transferred, the public deed may be replaced by other transfer systems (e. g., in the event of a moveable tangible asset, the delivery of the keys to the place where the asset is stored).

In this respect, it is possible under Spanish law to enter into a master agreement, which can be subject to foreign law, regarding the sale and purchase of certain assets and then execute one or more separate local agreements, which can also be subject to foreign law, regarding the transfer of an individual asset or group of assets. However, note that, unless other specific transfer systems are available for the asset, the relevant local agreement is then usually formalized into a public deed in order for the actual transfer to be deemed completed. Such public deed must be drafted in Spanish since it is granted before a Spanish notary public.

3. Regional Differences

Spain is a regional state, where the legislative power is shared between the State and the regions (*Comunidades Autonomas*) with varying degree of autonomy. While state law regulates most of the civil law, there are regional differences with regards to the legal requirements for the transfer of assets. For instance, the taxation scheme, or liability regime, may vary significantly from one region to the other. As such, the remainder of this text will focus exclusively on state law.

4. Acquisition by Foreigners

Current Spanish regulations include some particularities, authorizations and restrictions for the acquisition of assets by foreign investors. Among the most relevant are the following:

- Energy sector: According to a recent ruling from the Spanish Energy Commission (*Comisión Nacional de la Energía*), the acquisition of energy assets (*activos energéticos*) by a non-EU purchaser will require prior administrative authorization by such commission. Prior to July 2008, this authorization requirement applied to any acquisition of energy assets made by any Spanish or foreign purchasers. However, the European Court of Justice ruled that this administrative requirement was contrary to the EC Treaty and, since then, such requirement is only applicable to non-EU purchasers.
- Foreign investments in Spain over EUR 3,005,060.52 must be declared to the Investments Register of the Spanish Ministry of Industry, Tourism and Commerce

(*Registro de Inversiones Exteriores del Ministerio de Industria, Turismo y Comercio* within thirty (30) days from the date the investment has been carried out) for administrative, statistical and economic purposes only, with certain exceptions.

- Investments made from territories or countries considered to be "tax havens," which generally have to be notified beforehand.
- Foreign investments in activities directly related to national security or defense, and real estate investments for diplomatic missions by states that are not members of the European Union, which require prior approval from the Spanish Council of Ministers (*Consejo de Ministros*). In addition, the Spanish Council of Ministers may decide to suspend general deregulation measures in the event that the relevant investments affect the exercise of public power, public order, security or public health. In this case, it would be necessary to request administrative authorization prior to the investment.
- There are also special conditions that affect foreign investment in Spain in matters of air transport, radio, minerals, mineral raw materials of strategic interest and mining rights, manufacturing of weapons, television, gambling and telecommunications.

For instance, foreign shareholders in companies carrying out gambling activities cannot exceed a given percentage. In any case, the shareholding by a foreign entity or individual of any percentage in such companies requires prior administrative authorization. In addition, in order to acquire a shareholding exceeding 15% in the share capital of a bank or credit institution, authorization is required from the Bank of Spain (*Banco de España*).

5. Public Registers, Records and Databases

The Spanish real property registry (*Registro de la Propiedad*) contains plenty of information regarding transactions and agreements relating to real property, and other in rem rights, with information provided by the parties. Registration is not a legal requirement for the valid transfer of property, but is what parties do in order to protect the purchaser vis-à-vis third-party claims and ownership disputes. The registry includes information relating to sales and purchases, the creation of mortgages, easements, and any pending disputes over the real estate assets. Preliminary agreements such as letters of intent or private sale agreements cannot be registered.

In addition, the Spanish moveable assets registry (*Registro de Bienes Muebles*) has similar information regarding moveable assets, also voluntarily provided by interested parties. Information typically found in such registry might be:

- information regarding vessels and airplanes and any agreements or encumbrances concerning them;
- information on hire sale and purchase agreements of moveable, tangible non-consumable and identifiable assets;
- information regarding loan facility agreements for the financing of the purchase of the foregoing assets;

- information on leasing, lease-back or renting agreements over movable assets;
- information regarding mortgage or chattel mortgage over movable assets; and
- information on general conditions of contract. The registry includes information relating to sales and purchases, the creation of mortgages, easements, and any pending disputes over the moveable assets.

The following Spanish registries available online include information that may be relevant in connection with an asset transfer:

- the Spanish Commercial Registry (*Registro Mercantil*), which includes, among other things, the directors of the company, the powers of attorney, the annual accounts of each Spanish company with information on assets and liabilities; and
- the Spanish Intellectual Property Registry (*Registro de Propiedad Intelectual*) and the Spanish Patents and Trademarks Office (*Oficina Española de Patentes y Marcas*), which provides up-to-date information regarding intellectual or industrial property rights enforceable in Spain (mainly the name of the holders, opposition proceedings, expiration date and scope and class of the relevant rights).

6. Purchase Price Requirements

The main consideration with respect to the purchase price to be paid in an asset deal is that a price must be allocated to each asset or, in the event of assets of the same kind, to each group of assets.

B. Tangible/Movable Assets

1. Characteristics as to:

a) Language of Documentation. Under Spanish law it is possible to enter into a private agreement drafted bilingually or even drafted in a foreign language. However, in the event the actual transfer of the relevant asset is carried out by means of a public deed granted before a Spanish notary, then such deed must be drafted in Spanish as it is witnessed by the Spanish notary public and, in some cases is filed in a Spanish registry (e.g., *Registro de Bienes Muebles*) in order to protect the purchaser vis-à-vis third-party claims and conflicts relating to ownership. In this respect, the relevant public deed of transfer, although drafted in Spanish, may attach the private agreement that is drafted in a foreign language. The Spanish notary public will state in the relevant public deed, among other information, the parties involved, the agreed price, the date of completion and a full description of the asset or assets transferred, but the Spanish notary public will not witness the contents of the private agreement drafted in a language he does not understand.

b) Form of Documentation. The private transfer agreement can be entered into in written or oral form and can be executed in Spain or outside Spain, both in counterparts or in a single document. However, note again that the actual transfer of the asset to the purchaser, which may or may not take place simultaneously with the entering into of the private agreement, can take place by means of different systems.

In the event the actual transfer needs to be carried out by means of a public deed (i.e. transfer of real property or a data protection base), the granting of the public deed will be deemed the delivery of the transferred asset, and, therefore, the actual transfer will be completed. As previously noted, the public deed of transfer must be drafted in Spanish and executed by all parties, either personally or duly represented before a Spanish Notary Public, who will certify the capacity and authorization of each party in order to complete the transfer. In the event any of the parties is unable to attend the meeting at the Spanish Notary Public's office, the relevant party must grant a power of attorney in favor of an individual who can attend such meeting in his name and on his behalf.

Notwithstanding the above, the transfer of tangible movable assets can also be carried out by

- the delivery of the keys to the place where the asset is located, stored or kept; and
- the agreement of both parties when the possession of the asset cannot be delivered to the purchaser in the moment of the entering into of the transfer agreement or when the purchaser already holds the relevant asset before the entering into of such transfer agreement.

c) Specification of Assets. In an asset deal, each and every asset and liability must be individually identified and a price must be allocated to each asset, setting out the type of asset and the model and, if possible, the identification number. In this respect, the validity of the agreement could be challenged by any third-party with a legitimate interest in the transfer agreement (e.g., debtor) on the basis of the uncertainty of the object of the agreement.

However, it is possible to make groups of assets as long as each group is made up of assets of identical or very similar characteristics (e.g., screws, hammers, etc.). In this respect, it is customary in Spain to group assets according to the groups of assets set out in the Spanish Generally Accepted Accounting Principles (*Plan General de Contabilidad*). However, note that even if assets of the same kind are grouped, the transfer agreement must specify the number of assets actually transferred (e.g., 100 screws) and, as stated above, with the model or identification number of the relevant asset (e.g., screw type A model E-131).

Finally, in the event that the assets and liabilities transferred (i) could be considered to be a single business unit ("*rama de actividad*") and (ii) are listed as required elements of the business unit, then the description of the assets and liabilities can be more generic.

2. Administrative, Corporate and Other Approvals

The transfer of tangible assets does not require special governmental or administrative approvals, except for special conditions that affect assets related to the air transport, radio, minerals, utilities, mineral raw materials of strategic interest and mining rights, television, gambling and telecommunications.

In the event the seller or the purchaser is a company, the validity of the transfer may be subject to the approval of the Board of Directors or the General Shareholders Meeting of the company if this is contemplated in their by-laws (e. g., machinery over certain market value), or if the entering into of the relevant sale and purchase agreement exceeds the powers of the director or the person who may be entitled to enter into the agreement. In that case, the absence of approval may invalidate or void the transfer.

The authorization would generally be issued before the transfer takes place. However, in its absence, the transfer could be ratified *a posteriori* by the corresponding corporate body. In addition, note that even if not stated in the relevant by-laws of the seller or purchaser, it is customary in Spain to approve such transfer or purchase, as the case may be, by the relevant corporate bodies of the companies.

Although the validity of the transfer of the tangible asset is not impaired by the lack of approval of the transfer by any security holders, the legal effects will vary depending on whether or not the security holders give such approval. In the event the transfer is carried out without the prior approval of the security holders, the seller will not be released from the obligations towards the security holders. However, in the event the security holders give their consent to such transfer, such obligations would be transferred automatically with the asset and the seller would be released from such obligations.

3. Filing Requirements

There are no special filings required except with respect to some assets, such as data protection information and intellectual property rights.

Registration of the transfer of tangible assets (out of the ones described) with the Spanish moveable assets registry (*Registro de Bienes Muebles*) is not a legal requirement for the transfer of property, but is nevertheless the common market practice and is recommended in order to protect the purchaser vis-à-vis third-party claims and conflicts relating to ownership.

4. Automatic Transfer of Encumbrances

The encumbrances will be transferred along with the assets. To duly complete such transfer, the security holders must provide their prior consent to release the seller from any obligation linked to such asset towards the security.

C. Real Property

1. Characteristics as to:

a) Language of Documentation. The transfer of real property under Spanish law is a two-fold transaction that requires (i) a valid agreement (title); and (ii) the effective and actual transfer of the possession of the real property to the purchaser, which may or may not take place simultaneously.

A private transfer agreement can be drafted in any foreign language or even bilingually. Having said that, note that the transfer of the real property is normally completed by means of public deed that must be drafted in Spanish.

b) Form of Documentation. The form required for the transfer of the property is a written agreement, and it will normally be a public deed. In more detail, a public deed of transfer of real property is deemed as the delivery and actual transfer of ownership of such real property and therefore replaces the need to evidence the possession of the purchaser. In this sense, public deeds granted in Spain before Spanish notary publics must be drafted in Spanish and shall include all signatures (therefore, signing in counterparts is not an option). However, the relevant public deed of transfer – although drafted in Spanish – may attach the private agreement drafted in a foreign language (which could be signed in counterparts).

In addition, the only documents that can be filed with the Spanish real property registry (*Registro de la Propiedad*) are public documents (e. g., public deeds) and such filing is highly recommended in order to protect the purchaser vis-à-vis third-party claims and conflicts relating to ownership.

c) Specification of Assets. The transfer of the real property requires a detailed description of the assets to be transferred. In this respect, it is customary in Spain to identify the real property with its real estate registry details which could be obtained from the real estate registry (*Registro de la Propiedad*).

2. Administrative, Corporate and Other Approvals

As a general rule, the transfer of real property that has all licenses does not require additional government or administrative approvals. Having said that, the valid transfer of some real estate assets will require special authorizations (i.e. investments in real property made from territories or countries considered to be tax havens which must be notified beforehand).

If the seller or purchaser is a company, the validity of the transfer may be subject to the approval of the Board of Directors or the General Shareholders Meeting of the company if contemplated in their by-laws (e.g., real property over certain market value), or if the entering into of the relevant transfer agreement exceeds the powers of the director or the person who may be entitled to enter into the agreement. In that case, the absence of approval may invalidate or void the transfer.

The authorization would generally be issued before the transfer takes place. However, an a priori vitiated transfer could be ratified a posteriori by the corresponding corporate body. In addition, note that even if not stated in the relevant by-laws of the seller or purchaser, it is customary in Spain to approve such transfer or purchase, as the case may be, by the relevant corporate bodies of the companies.

If the transfer is carried out without the prior approval of the security holders, the seller will not be released from the obligations towards the security holders. However, if the security holders provide their consent to such transfer, such obligations would be transferred automatically with the asset and the seller would be released from such obligations.

3. Filing Requirements

The public deed of transfer of real property can be registered in the Spanish real estate property registry (*Registro de la Propiedad*). This filing is voluntary, but it is nevertheless common market practice and is recommended to protect the purchaser from any third-party claims and disputes relating to ownership.

With the sole registration of the public deed in the Spanish real property registry (*Registro de la Propiedad*) the purchaser may:

- be considered the sole and true owner of the real property unless a court says otherwise in a final judgment;
- be protected from any claims made by the creditors of the seller on the real property;
- be protected from unregistered encumbrances over the real property;
- obtain legal and judicial protection against any challenges vis-à-vis the purchaser's free possession and ownership;
- deny the registration with the real estate registry of any right over the real property without his prior consent;
- grant a mortgage over the property; and
- be registered for tax purposes as new owner in the cadastre.

Furthermore, subsequent sales of a registered real property that are not registered in the Spanish real property registry (*Registro de la Propiedad*) have no effects vis-à-vis third parties.

Finally, there is also a cadastral registry (*Registro del Catastro*). The information recorded in such registry is publicly available, except for any personal information recorded therein. The cadastral registry (*Registro del Catastro*) is an administrative registry where rural and urban property is filed voluntarily. It contains information on the physical, legal and economic characteristics of the property, including the location, reference, surface, use, designation, type of cultivation, construction, a plan and the cadastral value.

4. Automatic Transfer of Encumbrances

The encumbrances will be transferred together with the asset if the real property transferred is subject to an encumbrance and such burden is duly registered in the Spanish real property registry (*Registro de la Propiedad*).

The transfer of any rights over real property assets must be granted in a public deed. In addition, the granting of a mortgage over real property is conditioned on its notarization in a public deed and on the due registration of such public deed in the Spanish real property registry (*Registro de la Propiedad*). A non-registered mortgage is an ordinary loan and, therefore, does not constitute a preferential charge on the real property.

5. Automatic Transfer of Lease Agreements

The transfer is subject to a pre-emption right in favor of the tenant in case the real property has a lease agreement, and the landlord intends to sell it to a third party.

There are some exceptions in the event that

- the real property is sold by the landlord jointly with other real property premises that are part of the same building, or
- the entire real property is sold jointly by different sellers to the same acquirer.
- However, a tenant can carve-out this right
- in commercial leases and
- in residential leases where the lease has been granted for a period of more than five years.

In case such pre-emption right is not exercised by the tenant, the lease agreement would then be transferred to the purchaser, which would therefore be subrogated to the position of the seller (as landlord) during the first five years of the lease agreement.

In the event such lease agreement has a longer term, the purchaser will be subrogated to the sellers' position as a landlord during all its term, unless

- the purchaser ignored in good faith the existence of the lease agreement; and
- such agreement is not duly registered in the Spanish real property registry (*Registro de la Propiedad*). In such case, the purchaser acting in good faith would only have to observe the lease agreement until its fifth year. After such date, the lease agreement could be terminated early by the purchaser and the seller would have to indemnify the tenant in an amount equal to one monthly installment per each year beyond the first five-year term that remains.

In addition, if the parties to the lease agreement agree that the sale of the real property terminates the lease agreement, the purchaser would only have to observe the lease until its fifth year.

Other than any general termination cause set forth in the lease agreement (e. g., breach of material obligations, unauthorized subleases or assignments, etc.) neither the purchaser, the seller nor the tenant have any extraordinary right to early terminate the lease agreement following the transfer of the real property.

D. Contracts

1. Characteristics as to:

a) Language of Documentation. A private agreement transferring contracts can be drafted in Spanish or in any foreign language agreed on by the parties (except if the contract purpose of the transfer requires that the assignment should be done in Spanish).

If the agreement needs to be formalized in a public deed, then such public deed must be drafted in Spanish and executed by all parties, either personally or duly represented, before a Spanish Notary Public. However, the relevant public deed can attach the private contract drafted in a foreign language.

b) Form of Documentation. Contracts can be assigned in most cases with no mandatory formal requirements except if otherwise provided in the contract. Without prejudice of the above, the law foresees that the contract of any rights arising from acts that have been carried out through the granting of a public deed should be executed in the same form. In this case, all parties will need to execute the Spanish public deed instead of signing a separate document.

The possibility of executing the documents in another jurisdiction will depend on whether the transfer is granted or not by means of a public deed. If no public deed is granted, the parties are free to decide where to enter into the contract in written or oral form, in Spain or outside Spain, both in counterparts or in a single document.

c) Specification of Contracts. In order to provide legal certainty regarding the object of the transfer it is necessary to include a complete description of the contracts with reasonable detail, including references to the contractual parties, execution date, location and subject or purpose of the agreement. Having said that, the contract could be categorized and listed under such criteria.

2. Administrative, Corporate and Other Approvals

As a general rule, the assignment of a contract does not require special governmental or administrative approval, except for special conditions that may affect contracts in matters related to air transport, radio, minerals, mineral raw materials of strategic interest and mining rights, television, gambling and telecommunications. The legal consequences in case such approvals vary on a case-by-case basis.

In the event the seller or the purchaser is a company, the validity of the assignment may be subject to the approval of the board of directors or the general shareholders meeting of the company if this is contemplated in their by-laws (e. g., contracts over certain market value), or if the entering into of the relevant transfer agreement exceeds the powers of the director or the person who may be entitled to enter into the contract. In that case, the absence of approval may invalidate or void the transfer.

The authorization would generally be issued before the transfer takes place. However, an a priori vitiated transfer could be ratified a posteriori by the corresponding corporate body. In addition, note that even if not stated in the relevant by-laws of the assignor or assignee, it is customary in Spain for such assignment to be subject to approval by the relevant corporate bodies of the companies.

The validity of the assignment of the contract is conditioned on its approval by all the parties to the original contract and the assignee.

The consent to such assignment by the other parties to the original contract can either occur prior to, concurrent with or after the assignment of the contract. In the event the consent is given by the other parties prior to the assignment of the contract, then such assignment of the contract will not be effective until such other parties are notified of the entering into of the assignment.

3. Automatic Transfer of Contracts (Other than Lease and Employment Agreements)

The transfer of an asset includes any third party ancillary right to it, such as an encumbrance, and any contract that was entered into regarding the granting of such rights. These rights are held by a third party and are considered a burden encumbering the asset, and as a result the seller cannot unilaterally terminate them.

In the event a transfer contract regarding real property subject to a lease contract is entered into and the lessee does not exercise its pre-emption right over such real property, the lease contract will be automatically transferred and assigned to the purchaser, being subrogated in all the rights and obligations of the seller under such lease contract.

In the event of the transfer of an insured asset, the purchaser is automatically subrogated to the rights and obligations of the seller upon entering into the transfer contract, except otherwise agreed in the general conditions in respect of nominative insurance policies for non-mandatory damages (*pólizas nominativas para daños no obligatorios*).

4. Filing Requirements

As a general rule, the transfer of contracts does not require special filings with public authorities, registers or online databases. However, there are certain exceptions.

For instance, contracts transferring rights over movable assets like vessels or aircraft must be registered with the Spanish movable property registry (*Registro de Bienes Muebles*) in order to be enforceable vis-à-vis third parties. Furthermore, the transfer of registered trademarks will only be effective vis-à-vis third parties in the event the change of ownership has been previously registered with the Office of the Spanish Registry of Patents and Trademarks (*Registro de la Oficina de Patentes y Marcas*).

Furthermore, in the event the contract subject to transfer entails the assignments of in rem rights over real property, although not mandatory, it is strongly recommended that such transfer be filed in the Spanish real property registry (*Registro de la Propiedad*) in order to receive stronger protection and, if necessary, enforce such rights vis-à-vis third parties.

5. Treatment of Existing Contractual Claims and Obligations

In the event sold contracts are not completely fulfilled, the respective claims and/or obligations do automatically transfer to the purchaser.

The assignment to the purchaser of the obligations under the contract requires the other party or parties to the contract to expressly agree to such assignment. Provided such consents are obtained and the assignment has been entered into for valuable consideration (*título oneroso*), the assignor

- will be held liable for the existence and legitimacy of the contract unless it has been assigned as doubtful (*dudoso*); and
- will not be held liable for the solvency of the debtor, unless expressly agreed or if such insolvency was public and well-known. However, in the event the assignment was entered into for lucrative title (*título gratuito*), the assignor will not be held liable for the existence and legitimacy of such contract. In addition, note that a bad faith (*mala fe*) assignor will be always held liable for any damages caused to (or expenses incurred by) the assignee.

In addition and unless otherwise expressly agreed, the assignor will not be responsible for the complete and correct fulfillment of the obligations under the assigned contract. Therefore, all claims regarding the fulfillment of the obligations will automatically be transferred to the assignee, except for any damages arising from acts carried out before such assignment, for which the assignor will be held liable.

Finally, it is customary under Spanish law to include special provisions (e.g., indemnifications) in the asset sale and/or transfer contract in order to provide for a specific remedy in the event of breach.

6. Warranty Claims Resulting from Events prior to Transfer

The purchaser will only be liable for warranty claims from third parties resulting from events prior to the transfer of the asset if,

- it is expressly agreed upon by the purchaser and the seller in the relevant agreement; or,
- the purchaser was aware, or should have been aware, of such events on the date of the contract and therefore such events are deemed to have been tacitly accepted by the purchaser when the transfer was executed.

Finally, it is customary under Spanish law to include special provisions (e. g., indemnification provisions) in the asset sale and/or transfer contract in order to provide for a specific remedy in the event of breach.

E. IP Rights

1. Characteristics of Intellectual Property Rights (e. g., Trademarks, Patents, Utility Models, Domain Names) ("*IP Rights*") as to:

a) Language of Documentation. A private agreement transferring IP Rights can be drafted in Spanish or in any foreign language agreed upon by the parties (except if the contract purpose of the transfer requires that the assignment should be done in Spanish).

b) Form of Documentation. The transfer agreements of IP Rights must be drafted in written form. In addition, the parties are free to decide where to enter into the contract in Spain or outside Spain, both in counterparts or in a single document.

c) Specification of IP Rights. In order to provide legal certainty regarding the object of the transfer it is necessary to include a complete description of the IP Rights with reasonable detail, including references to the class, type, effectiveness and registry details

Therefore, and although there is no legal requirement for attaching schedules or lists of IP Rights to the transfer agreement, in order to obtain such certainty on the object of the contract it is customary to cross-reference an attached schedule or list of IP Rights.

2. Administrative, Corporate and Other Approvals

No special governmental or administrative approvals are needed regarding the transfer of IP Rights. However, the execution of the transfer agreement must be authorized by the corporate bodies of the relevant entities in accordance to Spanish corporate law and by-laws.

The transfer of an IP Right is not deemed valid until any security holder (if any) has given its consent to such transfer.

3. Filing Requirements

The transfer of patents, trademarks and other "industrial" IP Rights must be duly registered with the relevant public registries in order to be effective vis-à-vis third parties whereas the transfer of copyrights must not be filed or registered with any public registry in order to be effective.

4. Applicable International (Multilateral) Agreements or Treaties

Among other treaties, Spain is party to

- Annex 1C of the Marrakesh Agreement Establishing the World Trade Organization (WTO) signed in Marrakesh (Morocco) dated April 15, 1994 (The Uruguay Round) (TRIPS Agreement (Trade-Related Aspects of Intellectual Property Rights));
- Paris Convention for the Protection of Industrial Property dated March 20, 1883;

- Berne Convention for the Protection of Literary and Artistic Works dated September 9, 1886;
- Regulation of January 15, 1996 of the implementation of the agreement of Madrid related to the International Registry of Trademarks and Protocols approved in Geneva dated January 18, 1996; and
- the International Rome Convention for the Protection of Performers, Producers of Phonograms and Broadcasting Organizations at Rome dated October 26, 1961.

F. Receivables

1. Characteristics as to:

a) Language of Documentation. As a general rule, the assignment agreement by means of which a receivable is transferred can be drafted in Spanish or in any foreign language agreed upon by the parties. In addition, such documents can be drafted, for example, in English or bilingually.

However, the assignment of any receivables arising from transactions that have been formalized in a public deed should be executed in a public instrument.

Such public instrument, in order to be valid and enforceable under Spanish law, must be drafted in Spanish and executed by all parties, either personally or duly represented, before a Spanish Notary Public. In such case, the private document of transfer could be drafted in Spanish or in any foreign language agreed by the parties and then attached into a Spanish public instrument.

b) Form of Documentation. As a general rule, it is not compulsory, although highly recommended, that both the seller and the purchaser enter into a transfer agreement in written form in order to evidence the terms and conditions of the transfer agreement. Agreements that amount to more than EUR 9 must be entered into in writing.

Although receivables can be assigned in most cases with no mandatory formal requirements, as stated above, the law contemplates whether the assignment of any rights arising from transactions that have been formalized in a public deed should be executed in a public instrument. Such public instrument, in order to be valid and enforceable under Spanish law, must be drafted in Spanish and executed by all parties before a Spanish Notary Public.

The possibility of executing the transfer document in a foreign jurisdiction will depend on whether the formalization in a public instrument is required. If no formalization in a public instrument is required, the transfer of receivables may be formalized abroad in a public or private document.

Should a public deed be granted in order to assign a receivable, such public deed will have to comply with the aforementioned formal requirements.

c) Specification of Receivables. Regardless of the form of the agreement, in order to provide legal certainty regarding the object of the transfer it is necessary to include a complete description of the receivables with reasonable detail, including references to the contractual parties, due date and subject or purpose of the agreement. In this respect, the validity of the contract could be challenged by any party with a legitimate interest in the contract (e. g., debtor) on the basis of the uncertainty of the object of the contract.

Therefore, and although there is no legal requirement to attach schedules or lists of receivables to the transfer agreement, in order to obtain more certainty on the object of the contract it is customary to cross-reference an attached schedule or list of receivables.

2. Administrative, Corporate and Other Approvals

As a general rule, the assignment of a receivable does not require special governmental or administrative approvals, except for transactions that affect receivables related to air transport, radio, minerals, mineral raw materials of strategic interest and mining rights, television, gambling and telecommunications. The legal consequences in case such approvals are not granted are determined on a case-by-case basis.

The execution of the transfer agreement must be authorized by the corporate bodies of the relevant entities in accordance with Spanish corporate law and by-laws.

The approval of the debtor is not required. Nevertheless, the assignment will not have effects vis-à-vis the debtor or any third parties unless such assignment is duly notified or it is evidenced that the debtor or such third party was aware of such assignment or should have been aware.

Until the moment the debtor is duly notified of the assignment it will be entitled to fulfill its obligation by paying the claim to the assignor, while the latter will not be able to object to such payment and then be liable for such amount vis-à-vis the assignee.

3. Filing Requirements

No filing is required in order to assign receivables. The validity of the transfer of a receivable does not require notification to the debtor. In case such notification is not completed (or the knowledge of the debtor is not evidenced otherwise), the debtor will be entitled to fulfill its obligation by paying the claim to the assignor, while the latter will not be able to object to such payment and then be liable for such amount vis-à-vis the assignee.

On the other hand, should the notification be completed (or the knowledge of the debtor evidenced otherwise) the assignee is fully subrogated in the position of the assignor, except for those rights and obligations that deal specifically with the personal conditions of the assignor.

G. Liabilities

1. Characteristics as to:

a) Language of Documentation. As a general rule, the assignment agreement by means of which a liability is transferred can be drafted in Spanish or in any foreign language agreed upon by the parties. In addition, such documents can be drafted, for example, in English or bilingually.

However, the assignment of any receivables arising from transactions that have been formalized in a public deed should be executed in a public instrument.

Such public instrument, in order to be valid and enforceable under Spanish law, must be drafted in Spanish and executed by all parties, either personally or duly represented, before a Spanish Notary Public. In such case, the private document of transfer could be drafted in Spanish or in any foreign language agreed upon by the parties and then attached into a Spanish public instrument.

b) Form of Documentation. It is not compulsory, although highly recommended, for both the seller and the purchaser, to enter into a transfer agreement in written form, in order to evidence the terms and conditions of the transfer agreement.

Although liabilities can be assigned with no mandatory formal requirements, as stated above, the law foresees that the assignment of any right arising from acts that have been formalized in a public deed should be executed in a public instrument. The public instrument must be drafted in Spanish and executed by all parties before a Spanish Notary Public.

The possibility of executing the transfer document in a foreign jurisdiction will depend on whether or not formalization in a public instrument is required. If no formalization in a public instrument is required, the transfer of receivables may be formalized abroad in a public or private document.

Should a public deed be granted in order to assign a receivable, such public deed will have to comply with the aforementioned formal requirements.

c) Specification of Liabilities. Regardless of the form of the agreement, in order to provide legal certainty regarding the object of the transfer it is necessary to include a complete description of the liabilities in reasonable detail, including references to the contractual parties, due date and object or purpose of the agreement. In this respect, the validity of the contract could be challenged by any party with a legitimate interest in the contract (e. g., debtor) on the basis of the uncertainty of the object of the contract.

Therefore, and although there is no legal requirement to attach schedules or lists of receivables to the transfer agreement, in order to obtain more certainty on the object of the contract it is customary to cross-reference an attached schedule or list of receivables.

2. Administrative, Corporate and Other Approvals

As a general rule, the assignment of a liability does not require special governmental or administrative approvals, except for transactions that affect receivables related to air transport, radio, minerals, mineral raw materials of strategic interest and mining rights, television, gambling and telecommunications. The legal consequences where such approvals are not granted are determined on a case-by-case basis.

The execution of the transfer agreement must be authorized by the corporate bodies of the relevant entities in accordance to Spanish corporate law and by-laws.

The assignment of a liability is not deemed effective until the creditor has given its consent to such assignment.

3. Filing Requirements

If the assigned liabilities are related to obligations in which any public authorities or governmental bodies act in their capacity as creditors, such assignment will not have legal effect until such consent is given. The assignment of a liability is not deemed effective until the creditor has given its consent to such assignment.

4. Purchaser's Liability for:

a) Tax Obligations. As a general rule, upon the purchase of an entire business or business unit (*rama de actividad*), the purchaser will be held liable, jointly and severally (*solidariamente*) with the seller, for any tax obligations incurred by the seller from the operation of such business. Such liability will extend to any obligations arising from the non-payment of any withholdings made or that should have been made.

In this respect, note that the purchaser of an entire business or a business unit can request from the relevant Spanish tax authorities, with the seller's consent, a certificate detailing the tax debts, fines and liabilities arising from such business. If such certificate is obtained, the liability of the purchaser will be limited to the debts, fines and liabilities contained in it. When no such certificate is obtained, the liability of the purchaser will also extend to any fines imposed or to be imposed on such business. However, note that the referred certificate is not customary in Spain since it must be jointly requested by the seller and the purchaser, and the former normally requests that the latter to carry out a due diligence on tax matters regarding the transferred assets.

b) Environmental Contamination. The same general rules apply. However, note that the statute of limitations for environmental contamination in Spain varies depending on the seriousness of the offense (which can be rated very serious, serious or minor) and the type of asset affected by the environmental contamination (e. g., waters, land, waste, etc.). Under Spanish law, the general statute of limitations for

- very serious offenses with respect to the environment is three (3) years;
- serious offenses with respect to the environment is two (2) years; and

- minor offenses with respect to the environment is six (6) months, except otherwise stated in specific legislation.

c) Products Sold or Services Rendered by the Seller to Third Parties. Under Spanish law, the purchaser is not responsible for any liabilities regarding products sold or services rendered by the seller to third parties prior to the acquisition.

5. Automatic Transfer of Other Liabilities

As a general rule, the purchaser will not automatically acquire the liabilities of the seller due to the acquisition of assets.

6. Contractual Protection as to 4 and 5 above

It is customary to include special provisions (e. g., indemnifications) regarding the issues mentioned above under G, 4 and 5 above in the asset sale and/or transfer agreement.

H. Employees

1. Transfer of Employees

Provided that the assets transferred constitute a *"entidad económica"* (basically a business unit), the relevant employment agreements will be automatically transferred to the purchaser, maintaining the same terms and conditions as to the underlying labor relationship.

2. Approval of Works Council, Trade Union or Other Institutions

The transfer is not subject to approval of any works council, labor agency, trade union or other institution. However, notice of the transfer to the employee representatives (if existing) or to each of the employees will need to be served before the transfer is completed.

3. Contractual Protection as to Labor Issues

It is customary to include special provisions (e. g., indemnifications guarantees) as to labor law issues into the asset sale and/or transfer agreement.

I. Tax Implications

1. Value Added Tax

As a general rule, the purchase of an asset is taxed under VAT (at the standard rate of 16% or other reduced rates applicable in certain circumstances), which is deductible for the purchaser if it is entitled to such deduction under Spanish VAT regulations, and stamp duty tax (at a rate varying from 0.5% to 1%). However, the purchase of an entire business or a business unit (*rama de actividad*) is exempt under VAT and taxed under transfer tax at the rates mentioned above.

In addition, the purchase of shares is tax exempt unless the value of the company's real estate assets is higher than 50% of the overall asset value. In such case, the transfer will be taxed at a rate ranging from 6% to 7% over the purchase price (transfer tax) prorated to the effective ownership transferred.

That said, there are specific VAT rules applicable to the transfer of real property. Broadly speaking, the purchase of real property directly from a land or building developer (unless the developer has used the real estate continuously during the last two years) is subject to VAT irrespective of the condition of the seller as a company or a businessperson. The standard VAT rate is 16% for commercial assets and a reduced 7% rate applies to residential real property.

Subsequent purchases are VAT exempt but subject to transfer tax at a rate that currently varies from 6% to 7% depending on the Autonomous Community (*Comunidad Autónoma*) where the property is located. However, the seller can waive this exemption and charge VAT on the sale if the purchaser is a businessman or professional (i.e. a taxable person) and is entitled to deduct all the VAT. Transfer Tax is imposed on the purchaser and is not a recoverable tax.

The transfer of properties that are subject to VAT are also subject to stamp duty tax at a rate that varies generally from 0.5% up to 1.5% depending again on the Autonomous Community (*Comunidad Autónoma*) where the property is located.

2. Real Property Transfer Tax

Whenever urban land is transferred, the seller must pay tax on the increase of the value of that urban land. The tax base is calculated as an annual percentage of the cadastral (official) value of the real property in question at the time of transfer. The tax rate applicable varies depending on the municipality and ranges from 10% and 30%.

3. Other Tax Issues

The purchaser normally pays the transfer taxes, except the tax on the increase in value of urban land, which is paid by the seller.

J. Bankruptcy Law

1. Challenge of Asset Transfer in Case of Insolvency

As a general rule, an asset transfer may be subject to a claw-back action in the event

- it damages the bankrupt's estate, and
- was carried out within two years prior to the insolvency's declaration ruled by the applicable courts. Creditors may challenge those transactions too in the event the

receiver has not challenged them within an initial two-month period following the request of the creditor to do it.

In this respect, there are three legal presumptions on damage to the bankrupt's estate that could affect an asset transfer:

- the asset transfer was entered into for lucrative title (*título gratuito*), in which case the damage to the bankrupt's estate is presumed and no proof is admitted to the contrary; or
- the asset transfer was entered into for valuable consideration (*título oneroso*) with any related party (as defined by Spanish insolvency law) to the insolvent entity, in which case the damage to the bankrupt's estate is presumed, and proof to the contrary is admitted. If not presumed, the damage to the bankrupt estate must be established by whoever exercises the claw-back action.

2. Acquisition of Assets that are Subject to Insolvency Proceedings

There are specific rules on transfer of assets that apply in the event the seller is declared bankrupt, ranging from an enhanced involvement of the insolvency court in the decision-making process of the seller to certain rules about how the transfer is executed and effective. Such rules are quite complex and extensive and can be found in Spanish insolvency laws, which are of general application.

K. Timing and Costs

1. Timeframe of Asset Transfer

To the extent that the transfer of assets is not registered with any Spanish registry, the acquisition can be completed in the same day, provided that the drafting and execution of

- the relevant transfer agreement
- any corporate authorizations; or
- any mandatory third-party consents or notices can be completed within such timeframe. The notarization can be carried out simultaneously.

Note that the registration of a transfer of assets filed in any Spanish registry (e.g., Spanish real property registry (*Registro de la Propiedad*) and Spanish movable property registry (*Registro de Bienes Muebles*)) takes between ten (10) to fifteen (15) business days in Spain.

In addition, note that in the event the purchaser or the seller belongs to any country deemed a tax haven for Spanish law purposes, such investment must be notified beforehand to Spanish authorities.

2. Costs of Asset Transfer

When notarization is required, notary fees are set by law and the final amount as to a specific transaction will depend on the declared value of the purchased assets and the number of clauses in the deeds.

Notary fees range from 0.1% of the declared price of the assets (for assets of EUR 400,000 or more) to around 0.4% (for assets valued under EUR 100,000). Note that in the event the declared price of the asset is over EUR 6,000,000 the notary public is free to negotiate with purchaser and seller the amount of the fees.

Spanish real property registry (*Registro de la Propiedad*) and the Spanish movable assets registry (*Registro de Bienes Muebles*) usually charge about 42% of the notary's fees.

In addition, unless otherwise agreed, note that the seller is responsible for the payment of the notarial fees relating to the deed of transfer, while the purchaser pays any fees relating to the issuance of first copy of the public deed and other expenses subsequent to the transfer.

L. Miscellaneous

1. Choice of Foreign Law

The sale and/or transfer agreement can be made subject to foreign law.

2. (International) Arbitration, Choice of Venue

Both international and domestic arbitrations are possible.

Only issues that are disposable by the parties pursuant to law can be subject to arbitration. Issues that cannot be arbitrated are those where a final judicial resolution has been rendered, matters joined with others of which the parties may not make free disposition, and issues in which the attorney general (*Ministerio Fiscal*) must intervene in the representation of those who are unable to act on their behalf.

An arbitration procedure may be institutional or ad hoc, "at law" or "in equity."

3. Other Distinctions, Characteristics

Spanish law does not provide for any other relevant distinctions or unusual characteristics noteworthy in connection with a customary asset deal.

M. Literature

International Business Publications (US), Spain Investment and Trade Laws and Regulations Handbook, 1st Edition, 2008

Elena Merino-Blanco, Spanish Law and Legal System, 1st Edition, 2006

Antoni Vager and *Sjef Van Erp*, Introduction to Spanish Patrimonial Law, 1st Edition, 2006

Switzerland

By *Eva-Maria Strobel* and *Matthias Maurer*

A. General Aspects

1. Asset Deal vs. Share Deal: Essential Consideration

Businesses in Switzerland may be acquired by a purchase of either shares or assets. When deliberating about the appropriate transaction structure, essential considerations for sellers and purchasers of assets are examined:

An asset deal permits the sale/purchase of specific assets or entire business units. In a share deal, an interest in a company is acquired. A purchaser must decide whether separate management of the acquired assets is feasible.

In contrast to a share deal, an asset deal will not effect any changes to the shareholder structure.

An asset deal is more complex with regard to the object of the contract since it requires the schedules of the assets to be included. This is the case even though the legislative body has attempted to simplify the asset deal by introducing the asset deal pursuant to the Swiss Merger Act ("**MA**").

As a consequence of the introduction of the MA in Switzerland, there are two ways to structure an asset deal. An asset deal may be executed by an enumeration of all assets and liabilities transferred ("traditional asset deal"). Alternatively, an asset deal may be structured as a transfer of assets and liabilities of an entity, a business or a branch uno actu pursuant to the relevant articles of MA.

The new regime introduced by the MA, allows for the transfer of assets and liabilities in one single deed of transfer; the single deed of transfer is sufficient for the assets and liabilities to transfer by operation of law as opposed to a traditional asset deal structured as a transfer of certain clearly defined assets and liabilities, in which the transfer of each and every asset and liability must be made in the form prescribed by the Swiss Civil Code. However, in practice, for the purpose of legal certainty, general descriptions of the assets to be transferred in an MA asset deal are included. The advantage of single transfers is that the purchaser acquires only the liabilities listed in the agreement and transferred in such transactions. As single transfers, unlike the transfer of assets and liabilities under the MA, are not announced to the public, the creditors of the seller cannot claim that, on the basis of the publication of the notice dealing with the transfer of assets and liabilities in the Federal Commercial Gazette, they are entitled to assume that the purchaser has also assumed liability for their claims.

The liability of the seller may vary depending on which transaction structure is used. In the case of a share deal, the seller will only be liable for physical or legal defects affecting the shares. There is no statutory implied warranty with respect to the assets owned by the company itself. In the case of an asset deal, liability is more of an issue. Notably, joint liability in an asset deal pursuant to the MA must be kept in mind.

Publicity may also be of concern to the transacting parties. Contrary to a share deal and a traditional asset deal, an asset deal carried out under the MA must be registered with the Commercial Register, requiring disclosure of central elements of the transaction.

The financing of a share deal may be less attractive to creditors, as, for example, in the case of bankruptcy, creditors of the target company prevail over creditors of the shareholders holding the shares in the target company as security. Conversely, in the case of an asset deal, assets may be used as security.

In the case of a share deal, the person acting as seller may acquire tax-free capital gains. In order to do so, shares have to be part of the seller's private assets and the transaction must not qualify as partial settlement (*Teilliquidation*).

For the purchaser, an asset deal may be more attractive since goodwill on the acquired assets and financing costs are tax deductible.

In the case of a share deal, carry-forward of losses is secured.

Contrary to a share deal, an asset deal may trigger VAT.

2. Distinction between Sale and Transfer in Rem

Swiss law distinguishes between the obligation to transfer ("signing") and the fulfillment of this obligation ("closing"). It is possible to provide for the sale and the transfer in rem in separate documents.

3. Regional Differences

Switzerland is a federal state, where power is divided amongst its constituent parts, the Cantons. While federal law regulates most of the civil law, there are regional differences with regards to the legal requirements for the transfer of assets. For instance, the taxation scheme, or registration and notarization requirements, may vary significantly from one Canton to the other. As such, the remainder of this text will focus exclusively on the situation in the Canton of Zurich.

4. Acquisition by Foreigners

There may be distinctions with regard to the acquisition of assets by foreigners or foreign entities, but only insofar as transactions in real estate are concerned.

The Federal "Lex Koller" Act provides for an authorization requirement for certain Swiss real property transactions by non-resident foreigners. The definition of non-resident foreigners includes legal entities domiciled abroad and foreign-controlled companies domiciled in Switzerland. Not only the acquisition of formal ownership of real property is subject to the limitations of the Lex Koller, but any transaction leading to the beneficial ownership of a foreign company over Swiss real property (e. g., the purchase of shares in a company holding Swiss real property), including fiduciary transactions and transactions conveying an owner-like status (e. g., options, pre-emption rights, long-term lease agreements).

No authorization is generally necessary for transactions regarding real property used for business purposes, such as manufacturing premises, warehouse facilities, offices, shopping centers, retail premises and hotels. In such cases, it is irrelevant whether the foreign owner purchases the real property for investment purposes, for its own use or with the aim of renting the real estate out to a third party.

Acquisitions of residential real property are generally prohibited and subject to authorization. Foreign-registered or foreign-controlled entities may only acquire residential real property without authorization if such real property is part of (and needed by) its permanent business, or if it is impossible or unreasonable to separate the living space from the business premises. If this is not the case, non-resident entities can only purchase residential real property (such as holiday apartments) if they are in possession of a valid authorization from the respective Cantonal authorities.

Unless a transaction subject to the Lex Koller has obtained authorization from the competent Cantonal authority, no entry in the Commercial Register is possible and other transactions not requiring the entry in the register can not be completed. A transaction completed in violation of the authorization requirement is null and void and the violators are personally sanctioned by criminal law.

Despite these general rules, in many cases it is difficult to determine whether an authorization is required or not because of the complexity of the rules and exceptions. If the purchaser cannot immediately rule out the possibility of an authorization requirement, he must apply to the appropriate authority for a declaration that no authorization is required. Because of the severe consequences of a violation of the Lex Koller, the authorization requirement should be verified with regard to any real property transaction involving a foreign company (including a Swiss company controlled by a foreign shareholder).

5. Public Registers, Records and Databases

The Commercial Register holds the most important information regarding businesses in Switzerland. It contains all important information on Swiss companies and makes the information accessible to the public. Anyone who sets up a business must have it recorded in the Commercial Register.

Besides the Commercial Register, the real property registers are important databases for obtaining information with regard to assets if real property is concerned. Several real property registries operate in Switzerland. The most important land register is the Swiss Federal Land Register ("*Eidgenössisches Grundbuch*"). Despite its name, it is managed by the cantons and the cantons are liable for damages arising from the keeping of the land register.

The Swiss Federal Land Register provides comprehensive information about property rights in real estate because all land must be registered, and all property rights outlined above (ownership and restricted property rights) must be registered in order to become legally effective. The register is public, and includes the description, ownership and restricted rights of the property, the description of the property, name and identification of the owner, type of ownership and date of acquisition. Upon demonstration of a plausible interest (e. g., by producing a draft of preliminary agreement), further information contained in the main register book, the plans, the supporting documents and the journal may be accessed.

The fact that the land register is public has two material legal consequences: First, nobody can object not to have known of the existence of a property right (e. g., an existing encumbrance on the property). Second, the acquirer of piece of real estate acting in good faith is fully protected in his reliance on the legal status of the property as shown in the land register. If, for example, the legal title of the seller in the property is defective (because, for example, the contract by which the seller himself acquired the property was invalid) but the commercial register showed full legal title of the seller, the acquirer acting in good faith can rely on the title as shown in the register and acquire the property. If, however, the acquirer is acting in bad faith, because he knew or should have known about the legal flaws of the registration, he can not rely on the (incorrect) registration.

Furthermore, information regarding intellectual property rights, in particular trademarks and patents and ownership of domain names are available on the website of the Swiss Institute for Intellectual Property (www.ige.ch and www.swissreg.ch) and the Central Registry for the Top Level Domains ".ch" and ".li" (www.switch.ch). There is, however, no register for copyrights or know-how information in Switzerland.

Lastly, there are registers for specific assets such as aircraft or sea vessels.

6. Purchase Price Requirements

In general, there are no restrictions with regarding the purchase price. Additionally, there are no legal requirements regarding the allocation of the purchase price to groups of assets or individual assets. Allocating the price in the agreement may, however, be recommended for tax and accounting purposes.

The parties are free to choose the currency of the purchase price. There are no special rules requiring a minimum price. Notwithstanding, if the price is found to be abusive under the Swiss Code of Obligations, it may be reduced.

B. Tangible/Movable Assets

1. Characteristics as to:

a) Language of Documentation. Aside from documents that are filed with governmental authorities, there are no language requirements. Documents may be drafted in any language chosen by the parties and may be executed bilingually. Documents that are filed with federal governmental authorities must be submitted in one of the four official Swiss languages (German, French, Italian, Rhaeto-Romanic). Documents to be filed with Cantonal governmental authorities are to be drafted in an official language of the respective Canton (e. g., German and French in the Canton of Bern; German in the Canton of Zurich; Italian in the Canton of Tessin).

b) Form of Documentation. In the case of an MA asset deal, the written form is mandatory.

Where a traditional asset transfer is planned, no requirements of form apply. However, transfer of special assets may call for special requirements of form (e. g., real property). For evidentiary reasons, the written form is, however, recommended and common.

Documents may be executed outside Switzerland.

Parties observe written form if not jointly signing the same document. Each party may sign in counterpart, as long as documents are exchanged afterwards. If telegram, telex or fax is used, the written form is even deemed to be observed if no exchange of documents after signing has taken place.

For the transfer in rem of tangible assets, seller and purchaser must be in agreement regarding the transfer, and possession of the assets must be transferred to the purchaser. This means that, in general, the purchaser must secure physical control over the tangible assets transferred. The physical taking over of possession, i.e. physical delivery of the tangible assets to the purchaser, can be substituted. If tangible assets are, for instance, located in a warehouse with a third party, possession can be transferred by ordering the owner of the warehouse to hold the property at the request of the purchaser. The tangible assets may also remain in possession of the seller if a special agreement is concluded (e. g., the seller sells a tangible asset and leases it at the same time).

c) Specification of Assets. In the case of an MA asset deal, schedules listing all assets and liabilities to be transferred must be drafted. The relevant provision of the MA requires the schedules to contain a clear description of all assets and liabilities to be transferred; real estate, securities and intangible assets, such as, for instance, IP Rights, must be itemized.

According to the common practice of the Commercial Registers, the degree of specification depends on the circumstances of each individual transaction. Parties shall define the scope of the agreement appropriately. Hence, except for the formerly listed assets, generic descriptions of the assets and liabilities, e.g., "all assets located in warehouse" are considered to be sufficient. The principle of identification ("*Bestimmt-*

heitsgebot") must be observed, though. In other words, the assets that the parties intend to transfer must be identifiable. A third party must be capable of distinguishing between the transferred assets and non-transferred assets.

In the Canton of Zurich, in the case of a purchase of a business unit, filing of a balance sheet meets the requirements of the MA.

In the case of a traditional asset deal, contracting parties need to define the asset to be transferred in accordance with the principle of identification. In order to ensure transfer of the intended assets and liabilities, it is recommended that a detailed description be provided. Depending on the circumstances of the deal and the types of assets and liabilities, parties should provide for generic or individual descriptions.

2. Administrative, Corporate and Other Approvals

It is necessary to distinguish between the different kinds of approval, and whether the transfer is being made by way of an MA or a traditional asset deal.

Approval by Administrative Bodies

In the case of an MA asset deal, the Commercial Register ensures legal compliance of the sale and purchase agreement. If it is not satisfied with the schedules provided, it will deny registration in the Commercial Register. In the absence of an entry in the Commercial Register, the transaction does not become legally effective.

The transfer of tangible assets by way of a traditional asset deal does not require special governmental or administrative approval. Exceptions may apply in exceptional cases. Governmental approval may be required for certain regulated industries, in particular banks, or with regard to specific categories of assets, e. g., weapons.

Approval by Corporate Bodies

In the case of an MA and a traditional asset deal, the board of directors decides whether the sale and purchase agreement is concluded or not. Approval by other corporate bodies is not required, unless stipulated in the parties' articles of association. However, there are exceptions to this rule. If a transaction violates the purpose of the corporation and/or is deemed equivalent to liquidation, approval of other corporate bodies is required (in a corporation, approval by the shareholder meeting). If no approval is provided, the transfer is invalid.

Approval by Creditors

If selling a tangible asset, the seller must be able to transfer in rem. Where a tangible asset is encumbered, either the creditor or a third person on behalf of the creditor retains possession of it. Therefore, the contracting party cannot transfer the good itself, but only a substitute to the purchaser. However, the transfer is only binding for the if notice is given to him.

3. Filing Requirements

Depending on the structure, disclosure requirements and relevant registers will vary.

In the case of an MA asset deal, disclosure of the asset deal in the Commercial Register is obligatory. An MA asset deal must be published in the Commercial Register of the respective Canton and in the Federal Commercial Gazette. The Commercial Register as well as the Federal Commercial Gazette are published on the internet: www.zefix.ch and www.shab.ch.

The transfer is legally binding and effective upon entry in the Commercial Register only. In addition, all entries in the Commercial Registers of Switzerland are published in the Federal Commercial Gazette. Also, the sale and purchase agreement must be submitted to the Commercial Register. If the sale and purchase agreement was not signed by all members of the board, excerpts from the minutes of the board meetings of the contracting parties, at which the decision to conclude the sale and purchase agreement was taken, must be filed.

The publication in the Commercial Register contains inter alia the following data:

- the name, registered office and legal type of entities involved;
- the date of the sale and purchase agreement;
- the total value of the assets and liabilities to be transferred;
- the consideration to be received.

In the case of a traditional asset deal, disclosure is not required.

4. Automatic Transfer of Encumbrances

Subject to B, 2 above, as a general rule, encumbrances regarding tangible assets automatically transfer to the purchaser. In particular, pledged assets remain pledged. However, this is not applicable where the purchaser acquires the assets in good faith ("bona fide principle").

C. Real Property

1. Characteristics as to:

Language of Documentation

Documents may be drafted in any language. However, any documents to be filed with federal authorities must be drafted in one of the official Swiss languages (German, French, Italian, Rhaeto-Romanic) and any documents to be filed with Cantonal authorities must be drafted in one of the official languages of the respective Canton (e. g., German and French in the Canton of Bern; German in the Canton of Zurich; Italian in the Canton of Tessin).

In the case of a transfer of real property, the notarization and notification of the Land Register are obligatory. Both are subject to the law of the Canton in which the property is located. Depending on the regulation of the Canton, notably its official languages, documents have to be notarized and/or filed in a specific language or need to be translated upon request.

Bilingual documents are permitted.

Form of Documentation

In the case of an MA asset deal, the part of the sale and purchase agreement providing for the transfer of real property must be notarized. However, defining the parts to be notarized may prove to be difficult. Thus, it has become common practice to notarize the whole sale and purchase agreement. Nevertheless, addenda not related to the transfer of real property may be exempted. Where parties conclude a separate agreement for real property, only such agreement needs to be notarized. A single act of notarization is sufficient, even if properties are located in different Cantons. The notary public at the seat of the transferring party is competent.

In a traditional asset deal, the transfer of property must be notarized at the place where the property is located. Since sale and purchase agreements often comprise property in different communities and Cantons, transfer of property must be notarized separately in every community concerned.

Execution outside Switzerland

The rules regarding competence of the notary public are deemed to be mandatory.

Although Swiss law does not impose restrictions on the choice of governing law, formal requirements and transfer in rem are subject to the law of the place where the respective property is located.

The Cantons regulate the process of notarization. Thus, Cantonal law may declare signing of different documents to be permissible. However, it is common practice to notarize a single document containing signatures of both parties. In any case, both parties must appear before the notary public.

Specification of Assets

In the case of an MA as well as a traditional asset deal, neither general nor generic descriptions are permissible. Individual descriptions of the real property concerned is mandatory. If in doubt, please refer to the respective Land Register (see D, 1, c below).

2. Administrative, Corporate and Other Approvals

Approval by Administrative Bodies

In the case of an MA asset deal, the Commercial Register ensures compliance of the sale and purchase agreement with the law (see B, 2 above). In addition, if real property is transferred, the Land Register will only register the transfer of property, after having assessed the formal validity of the sale and purchase agreement (notarization, competence, etc.). Real property is not transferred in rem until the Land Register has made a corresponding the entry.

For Swiss real property transactions by non-resident foreigners, please see A, 4 above.

Approval by Corporate Bodies

In general, the board of directors decides whether the sale and purchase agreement has been concluded or not. Approval by other corporate bodies is not required, unless provided for in the seller's and/or purchaser's articles of association. See B, 2 above.

Approval by Creditors

In the event that real property is encumbered, the purchaser of the property must be aware that the property remains encumbered after the transaction. The Land Register informs the creditor about the transfer, though his/her approval is not required.

Where the purchaser acquires the real property and the secured liability, the creditor is entitled to prevent relief of the seller. Upon this event, the Land Register shall notify the creditor of the offer by the purchaser to assume the underlying liability. The creditor must exercise his/her right to deny relief of the seller within a year following the issuance of the offer.

If such a situation arises in the context of an MA asset deal, it should be noted that in the case of an MA asset deal, the seller shall remain jointly liable with the purchaser for all liabilities transferred for a term of three years after the purchase.

3. Filing Requirements

Please see B, 3 above. In addition, transfer of real property must be registered in the Land Register (see C, 2 above). Authorization is required in case of an acquisition of Swiss real property by foreigners (please see A, 4 above). Without registration, the transfer is not valid. The filings must be made with the competent notary public.

4. Automatic Transfer of Encumbrances

Encumbrances on real property automatically transfer to the purchaser (see C, 2 above). A waiver of encumbrances must be in writing. It is not valid until the encumbrance has been deleted from the Land Register.

5. Automatic Transfer of Lease Agreements

In the case of an asset deal, lease agreements regarding the respective real estate automatically transfer to the purchaser. Regarding residence or office space, the purchaser may only terminate the lease agreements where he/she requires occupation of the property for his/her own use. As regards to other types of leasing, the purchaser is entitled to terminate the lease agreements observing the regular legal term. Neither the purchaser nor the tenant has an extraordinary right to terminate the lease agreement as a result of the transfer.

D. Contracts

1. Characteristics as to:

a) Language of Documentation. The sale and transfer documents may be executed in any language. Bilingual documents are permitted. Since there is no obligation to file the documents with public authorities, a translation is not required (see B, 1, a above).

b) Form of Documentation. While the transfer of documents does not require a specific form (except in case of an MA asset deal), the written form is recommended for evidentiary purposes.

The sale and transfer documents may be executed outside Switzerland.

Signing in counterparts is permissible (see B, 1, b above).

c) Specification of Contracts. In the case of an MA asset deal, schedules of the assets and liabilities to be transferred must be drafted. The MA requires the schedules to contain a clear description of the contracts to be transferred. According to the Commercial Register, the degree of specification depends on the circumstances of each individual transaction. Parties shall define the scope of the agreement appropriately. According to the practice of the Commercial Register of Zurich, schedules must outline the names of the contracting parties, the date of conclusion and a description of the content. The use of abbreviations and/or numbers is not accepted. If contracts are transferred as part of the purchase of a business unit, generic descriptions may be appropriate. However, schedules must enable third parties to determine which contracts are assigned.

In the case of a traditional asset deal, contracting parties need to define the contracts to be transferred. In order to ensure transfer, contracts have to be sufficiently specified. Depending on the circumstances surrounding the deal and the type of contract that is used, parties should provide generic or individual descriptions. See also B, 1, c above.

2. Administrative, Corporate and Other Approvals

The transfer of contracts by way of a traditional asset deal does not require special governmental or administrative approval.

In the case of an MA and a traditional asset deal, it is up to the board of directors to decide whether or not the sale and purchase agreement is concluded. For more details on governmental, administrative or corporate approval, please refer to B, 2 above.

In the case of a traditional asset deal, transfer of contracts is subject to approval of the other parties. As a rule, a contract may be transferred only if the other party agrees to the transfer. Exceptions apply with regard to lease agreements and employment agreements, as well as insurance agreements (for the latter see D, 3 below, for employment agreements see H below).

Where the transferring party is the tenant of a property, it may also transfer the lease contract. However, the landlord must give its consent in writing, but may refuse the transfer of the lease contract for material reasons only. Only circumstances to the extreme detriment of the landlord qualify as material reasons. Moreover, the former and new tenants of the transferred property are jointly liable until the end of the regular lease term.

In the case of an MA asset deal, it remains unclear whether in the event of a transfer of assets and liabilities there is an automatic transfer of related contracts to the purchaser, or whether approval of the other contracting parties to a transfer must be obtained. According to the practice of the Commercial Register of Zurich, the consent of the other contracting parties is not needed. However, entry in the Commercial Register is refused for obvious reasons (e. g., because the contract is concluded with an administrative body).

3. Automatic Transfer of Contracts (Other than Lease and Employment Agreements)

In addition to lease contracts related to a property transferred and employment contracts related to a business or a branch transferred, some asset-related insurance contracts are automatically assigned to the purchaser. While, in general, insurances are automatically terminated in the case of a change of ownership, two exemptions apply: one with regard to vehicles, and one with regard to real property. In both cases, Swiss law provides for an automatic transfer of the compulsory automotive third party liability and the building insurance agreement to the purchaser. Special termination rights follow the completion of the transfer, though.

4. Filing Requirements

There are no special filing requirements for contracts. In general, an MA asset deal must be published in the Commercial Register of the respective Canton and the Federal Gazette of Commerce. However, where a traditional asset deal is chosen, disclosure is not required. For further information, please see A, 5 above.

5. Treatment of Existing Contractual Claims and Obligations

All claims arising out of or in connection with contracts that have been validly transferred are deemed to have been transferred.

The legal consequences with regard to claims that have arisen out of or in connection with contracts before their transfer depend on the type of asset deal. In the case of an MA asset deal, these claims are transferred automatically. Nevertheless, it is recommended that the debtor be notified.

If the respective contract provides for a prohibition of transfer ("pactum de non cedendo"), claims arising out of or in connection with this contract may not be transferred. However, where an entire business unit is transferred, such claims may be considered part of the transaction.

In the case of a traditional asset deal, a specific transfer of the claims that have arisen out of or in connection with contracts before their transfer must be transferred explicitly. While the agreement to transfer a claim (obligation to transfer) may be concluded orally, the agreement to transfer in rem must be in writing. Although the consent of the debtor is not required, it is recommended that the debtor be notified of the agreement. If the respective contract provides for a prohibition of transfer ("pactum de non cedendo"), claims arising out of or in connection with this contract may not be transferred.

6. Warranty Claims Resulting from Events prior to Transfer

As a general rule, all claims and obligations are transferred once a contract is transferred. This also applies to warranty claims resulting from events prior to the transfer of the assets affected, if not otherwise provided for in the transfer agreement. The potential exposure is usually covered by representations and warranties and/or indemnifications (see also D, 5 above).

E. IP Rights

1. Characteristics of Intellectual Property Rights (e. g., Trade Marks, Patents, Utility Models, Domain Names) ("*IP Rights*"), as to:

a) Language of Documentation. The formalities that have to be observed when transferring intellectual property rights depend on the specific right involved. In general, documents relating to the sale and/or transfer of IP Rights, such as trademarks, trademark applications, geographic indications, patents, patent applications, utility models, designs, topographies, and so forth, can be drafted in any language.

It is nevertheless advisable to adopt one of the official languages in Switzerland when dealing with registered IP Rights. The registration of IP Rights, i.e. patents, patent applications, utility designs, trademarks, trademark applications, topographies and designs must be recorded with the Federal Institute of Intellectual Property (*Eidgenössisches Institut für Geistiges Eigentum* – "**IGE**"). While the recording of the registration is serves a declaratory purpose only, the timely recording of a change of ownership is critical to the protection of the ongoing validity and enforcement of IP Rights for several reasons:

If not recorded, legal claims may be brought against the assignor, and the transfer of the registered IP Right does not become effective against third parties acting in good faith.

If the purchaser wants to maintain and/or enforce transferred registered IP Rights, prosecute infringements, file oppositions or attend to renewals or annuity payments, and if the assignment has not yet been recorded with the IGE, it must submit to the court the relevant documentation proving transfer of the respective right and, if the documentation is not provided in one of the official languages, a translation thereof. If prompt injunctive relief is required, an undesired delay may result from the necessity to record the transfer of rights and/or provide the required documentation.

If a change of ownership is not promptly recorded, a misconception can arise in the marketplace as to the identity of the actual owner, leading to a possible loss of rights where a trademark no longer functions as an indication of origin.

It should be noted however, that there are no fines or penalties assessed for late recording of a transfer.

The purchaser can apply for the recording either by himself or jointly with the seller. In the former case, the purchaser who files the application for recording has to provide the IGE with a copy of the sale and transfer documents; these then have to be translated into one of the official languages. In the latter case, the seller and the purchaser jointly apply for recording of the registered IP Rights and execute their respective forms, which must be filed in one of the official languages in Switzerland. As such, there is no need to submit the sale and transfer documentation. It is, therefore, advisable to execute an application for recording when closing the transaction.

Trade secrets, know-how and goodwill can not be registered. These IP Rights are transferable without any formal requirement, e. g., by written transfer agreement entered into and completed by handing over the relevant documents and records.

Copyright can be assigned in Switzerland without observing any formal requirements. There is no copyright register in Switzerland. Morale rights are not transferable, though.

b) Form of Documentation. Except in an MA asset deal, the transfer of IP Rights does not require any specific form. While oral agreements would be sufficient from a legal point of view, written documentation is recommended. To effect recording of the transfer of registered IP Rights, documentary evidence on the transfer or a joint application for the recordal must be submitted to the IGE.

Under Swiss law, IP Rights can be co-owned by several parties. As a general principle, any co-owner may independently dispose of his portion of the IP Right. It should be noted, however, that in the case of co-owned patents, the IGE requests the express consent of all co-inventors for the transfer of a share in a patent, insofar as the owner of this share cannot give evidence that all co-owners have the unrestricted right to transfer the rights on their shares.

Transfer documents are generally executed separately and apart from the acquisition agreement for the purpose of affecting the sale. The IP Rights will either be specifically mentioned in the acquisition agreement or become the subject of a separate bill of sales. If registered IP Rights are concerned, it is advisable to execute a separate document that can be submitted to the IGE in order to avoid having to disclose all terms and conditions of the sale and purchase agreement.

The documents can be executed outside Switzerland. Signing in counterparts is permissible.

c) Specification of IP Rights. As a general rule, the IP Rights to be transferred must be specified in the transfer agreement to the extent that a third party would be able to distinguish the assets from any other non-transferred rights. In order to comply with this principle, we recommend using lists or schedules identifying the IP Rights in question, although this is not mandatory in a traditional asset deal. Schedules of all IP Rights to be transferred are mandatory in an MA asset deal.

If registered IP Rights are concerned, we recommend listing at least the country of origin and the application and/or registration numbers. A specification by category, or language such as of "all IP Rights related to the business" or "all trademarks related to the logistics division" is sufficient for a traditional asset deal, provided that identification is possible without recourse to any legal valuation or discretion.

2. Administrative, Corporate and Other Approvals

The transfer of IP Rights does not require special governmental or administrative approval.

Unless provided for in the seller's and/or purchaser's articles of association or partnership agreement, the approval of corporate bodies is not required by Swiss law.

IP Rights can be pledged or assigned for security purposes in Switzerland. Such assignment or pledging must be entered into the register in order for it to be binding on third parties. In the event that the IP Rights are encumbered, for instance, in pledge, the approval of security holders is not required. If a third party has become owner of the assets (for instance in case of security assignment), the transfer is invalid.

3. Filing Requirements

If and to the extent that the IP Rights to be transferred are registered in public registers, the change of ownership should be filed with the IGE. However, such registration is merely of declaratory nature and does not affect the validity of the transfer. Please see above under E, 1, a with regard to the advantages of immediately recording a transfer. Besides this, the transfer of IP Rights does not require filings with public authorities or registrations, except to indicate that the deal is structured as an MA asset deal.

4. Applicable International (Multilateral) Agreements or Treaties

Switzerland is a party to the TRIPS Agreement and to the Paris Convention for Protection of Industrial Property. It has signed the Madrid Agreement and the Madrid Protocol regarding trademarks. It is also a party to the European Patent Convention.
Besides this, Switzerland is subject to a number of bi-lateral treaties with other countries concerning IP Rights.

F. Receivables

1. Characteristics as to:

a) Language of Documentation. The sale and transfer documents regarding receivables can be drafted in any language.

Bilingual documents are permitted (see B, 1, a above).

b) Form of Documentation. Except in case of an MA asset deal, transfer of receivables does not require a special form. Oral agreements are permissible. The documents can be executed outside Switzerland. Signing in counterparts is permissible (see B, 1, b above).

c) Specification of Receivables. In case of an MA asset deal, all receivables must be listed. In case of a traditional asset deal, the receivables transferred must be described in depth (or stated explicitly) (see B, 1, c above). For evidence purposes, it is recommended to list the receivables in schedules to specify the underlying legal relationships, and to indicate the outstanding amount of the receivables.

2. Administrative, Corporate and Other Approvals

The transfer of receivables by way of a traditional asset deal does not require special governmental or administrative approval.

In both an MA and a traditional asset deal, the board of directors decides whether or not the sale and purchase agreement has been concluded. For more details on governmental, administrative or corporate approvals, please be referred to B. 2 above.

If receivables are transferred by MA or traditional asset deal, the approval of the debtor is not required. However, if he is unaware of the change in creditor, the debtor still fulfills his obligation by making a payment to the former creditor. Therefore, it is advisable to notify the debtor.

It is only when a contract provides for a prohibition of transfer ("pactum de non cedendo") that the consent of the debtor is required in order to effect the transfer of the receivables that have arisen out of or in connection with the contract. Nevertheless, if an entire business unit is transferred in the course of an MA asset deal, such claims may be considered part of the transaction.

3. Filing Requirements

Except in an MA asset deal, the transfer of receivables does not require filings with public authorities or registration into public registers or databases. Although the notification of the transfer to the debtor is not required, it is recommended.

G. Liabilities

1. Characteristics as to:

a) Language of Documentation. The sale and transfer documents regarding liabilities may be drafted in every

language. Use of the local language is not mandatory. Only documents to be filed with public authorities in an MA asset deal must be drafted in one of the official local languages.

Bilingual documents are permitted.

b) Form of Documentation. The transfer of liabilities in the course of an asset deal under the MA requires written form.

The transfer of liabilities in the course of a traditional asset deal does not require a special form; oral agreements are valid. For evidentiary purposes, the written form is recommendable.

The sale and transfer documents may be executed outside Switzerland.

Signing in counterparts is permissible.

c) Specification of Liabilities. In the case of an MA asset deal, schedules listing all liabilities to be transferred must be drafted. The description contained in the schedules must be clear. As long as the liabilities are clearly identifiable, the use of general and/or generic descriptions is sufficient.

While there is no need to itemize all liabilities in the case of a traditional asset deal, it is advisable to do so, specifying the underlying legal relationships and the outstanding amount of the relevant liabilities.

2. Administrative, Corporate and Other Approvals

The transfer of liabilities does not require special governmental or administrative approvals, except if the deal is structured as an MA asset deal.

The approval of corporate bodies is basically not required unless otherwise stipulated in the seller's and/or purchaser's articles of association or partnership agreement.

With regards to liabilities and the creditor's approval, one has to distinguish between the internal assumption of liabilities between seller and purchaser, whereby the purchaser assumes the obligation to satisfy the liability concerned and to hold the seller harmless from claims of third party creditors, and the external assumption of liabilities. In the latter case, the approval of the creditors is obligatory. Without such approval, the transfer is deemed invalid vis-à-vis third parties.

In the case of an MA asset deal, it remains unclear whether in the event of a transfer of liabilities there is an automatic transfer to the purchaser, or whether approval of the other parties must be obtained. According to the practice of the Commercial Register of Zurich, as a general rule the consent of the other parties is not needed.

3. Filing Requirements

The transfer of liabilities does not require any filings with public authorities or registrations into public registers or databases, unless the asset deal is structured as an MA asset deal.

As the transfer is subject to the creditors' approval, the creditors must be informed of the transfer. In an MA asset deal, registration in the Commercial Register must take place. In the latter case, no (additional) notification to the creditors in a specific form is required in the Canton of Zurich. Please see also G, 2 above.

4. Purchaser's Liability for:

a) Tax Obligations. If the purchaser acquires assets by way of an asset deal, it usually assumes only those liabilities that are expressly provided for in the asset purchase agreement. In an asset deal, the tax subject is not transferred. Therefore, as a general rule, the purchaser is not liable for tax obligations related to the acquired assets for periods prior to the acquisition.

However, specific attention should be paid with respect to VAT-related issues. Under Swiss law, the purchaser is liable for VAT due for periods prior to the acquisition if the entire business with all its assets and liabilities are transferred. Whether all assets and liabilities are eventually transferred is dispositive for these purposes. If this is the case, the seller and purchaser are jointly liable for tax liabilities for a period of two years prior to the acquisition.

The purchaser may also be held liable for social security claims relating to the transfer of employees. If real property is transferred, the purchaser should consider that some Cantons provide for liens on taxes payable. It is, therefore, important to conduct a tax due diligence.

b) Environmental Contamination. As mentioned above, if the purchaser acquires assets such as real property by way of an asset acquisition, it usually assumes only liabilities that are expressly provided for in the asset purchase agreement. Usually, the liability of the seller for any default affecting the real estate is excluded in the agreement, provided, however, that the seller has not intentionally concealed the default from the purchaser. As a consequence, the purchaser may, e. g., be held liable for the costs of decontamination of the acquired assets for periods prior to the acquisition, unless he has specifically reserved in the deed of sale that such liability shall remain with the seller. It is advisable to use clear language in the sale and purchase agreement in order to avoid misinterpretation regarding the scope of liabilities transferred.

c) Products Sold or Services Rendered by the Seller to Third Parties. In the case of an asset deal, there are generally no specific liability risks for the purchaser for products sold or services rendered by the seller to third parties prior to the effective date of the acquisition. According to Swiss law, product liability ties in with the legal person or entity acting as seller, producer, importer or supplier of the infringing goods, rather than the business (unit). Product liability is thus generally not automatically transferred in the case of an asset deal, even if the entire business is acquired by the purchaser. However, if the sale and purchase agreement provide for a transfer of "all liabilities," courts may consider that this also covers product liability claims that accrued prior to the acquisition. It is, therefore, recommended to use clear language in the sale and purchase agreement in order to avoid misinterpretation regarding the scope of liabilities transferred.

5. Automatic Transfer of Other Liabilities

As mentioned before, the liabilities transferred in the case of an asset deal must be specified. Under Swiss law, there is, generally, no automatic transfer of liabilities due to the acquisition of assets. However, if the sale and purchase agreement provide for a transfer of "all liabilities," this wording may also cover liabilities and, according to Swiss law, these liabilities would remain with the seller.

6. Contractual Protection as to 4 and 5 above

It is customary to include both representations and warranties and indemnifications regarding the issues mentioned above under G, 4 and 5 above into the agreement. For instance, as Swiss environmental laws have become significantly stricter in recent years, the purchaser will usually ask that the seller to warrant that the assets sold have not violated environmental laws regarding air, water, and soil pollution.

H. Employees

1. Transfer of Employees

Both the MA and the relevant provision in the Swiss Code of Obligations applicable to the traditional asset deal provide for an automatic transfer of the employees of a distinct entity or a distinct business unit that is transferred to the purchaser. Although there is a presumption that all employment relationships are transferred with the business (unit), the purchaser may, by express agreement, exclude some employees from the transfer.

Prior to a transfer of the entity or business unit, the seller or the purchaser has to inform the employees affected in written form on, inter alia, the transfer, the reasons for the transfer and the legal, economic and social consequences of the transfer for the employees. If, due to the transfer, measures likely to affect the employment conditions are contemplated, the works councils (or, if there are none, all employees of both the transferring and acquiring companies) must be informed of these changes sufficiently in advance so as to offer them the opportunity to make comments on the proposed changes. The consultation procedure must be contemplated before the binding decision of the competent corporate body is taken. Although the MA does not provide any indication regarding the duration of the consultation procedure, it is advisable to allow a period of approximately 15 days based on the relevant case law on collective dismissal.

If an employee opposes the transfer of his/her employment contract, the employment relationship is automatically terminated upon the expiration of the legal term of notice (which ranges from one to three months, depending on the duration of the employment relationship), irrespective of any longer term of notice that may be fixed in the employment agreement. If the purchaser is interested in a particular (group of) employee(s), it should obtain the employee's prior consent to the transfer.

Upon transfer of the employment agreement, the purchaser (new employer) assumes all liabilities (including those outstanding prior to the transfer date) vis-à-vis the employees, but the former employer remains jointly and severally liable for any claims of the employees that are due and payable prior to the date of transfer, until the time at which the employment agreement can be legally terminated or is actually terminated as a result of the opposition of the employee. The employee's previous period of service will count when calculating his or her seniority. This is decisive in determining the required period of notice of termination, the obligation to pay the employee's salary in case of sickness, and,payment of compensation, if any, in case of a termination of the employment agreement.

In Switzerland, it is possible to dismiss employees without seeking special approval by giving them a notice provided for either by law or by the employment agreement. However, special requirements will apply in the case of a collective dismissal that satisfies one of the three requirements stated in Art. 335d Swiss Code of Obligations (where the dismissal concerns more than ten employees in a business that employs more than 20 but less than 100 employees, or that concerns 10% of the total number of employees in a business that employs at least 100 but less than 300 employees, or that concerns thirty employees in a business that employs at least 300 employees), special requirements apply. Any employer contemplating a collective dismissal must consult with the representatives of the employees and give them at least the opportunity to present proposals concerning measures to avoid or limit the number of dismissals and limit their consequences. The employer must also inform the employees and the Cantonal employment office of the reasons for the collective dismissal and the details thereof. If the employer does not meet these requirements, the termination is deemed abusive and the employer must pay an indemnity to the employees concerned.

Under Swiss law, the social benefits of the employees are not covered by the companies themselves but by pension plans generally constituted in the form of foundations. As a result, the transfer of a business does not directly affect the pension benefits of the employees under the pension plan since the latter is legally and financially independent from the business transferred.

However, in a situation where only a business unit is transferred to a new entity, the transaction will generally also affect the pension plan. As a rule, if a number of employees leave the pension plan to be covered by the plan set up by the purchasing entity, a partial liquidation of the foundation is necessary. An amount corresponding to the personal accumulated capital of each employee together with a proportionate share of the pension plan's free reserves will be transferred into the pension plan of the purchaser.

2. Approval of Works council, Trade Union or Other Institutions

If a works council exists, the statutory consultation procedure must be observed. Although the employer is not obliged to accept proposals made by the works council, he is obliged to explain why a specific proposal is rejected. The MA entitles the work council (or, in its absence, each single employee) to request the court at the seller's registered seat to prohibit the registration of a merger, spin-off or transfer of business in the register of commerce. Should the court prohibit the registration of the transfer, the company transferred must go through a new consultation procedure. In view of these sanctions, it is recommended to fully comply with the information and consultation requirements.

3. Contractual Protection as to Labor Issues

It is customary to include both representations and warranties and indemnifications, in particular regarding the transfer of employees, consultations with trade unions, redundancies, wrongful dismissals, negotiations regarding the terms and conditions of the employments, the seller's discharge of obligations, and/or pension, bonus and retirement benefits schemes, into the sale and purchase agreement.

I. Tax Implications

1. Value Added Tax

As regards VAT, traditional and MA asset deals are treated equally. The sale of assets, as a general rule, is subject to VAT at a rate of 7.6%, but if the purchaser is also subject to VAT, it may either obtain a deduction of the VAT as input VAT or obtain a refund.

If a business is transferred between two VAT payers, the parties have to apply a special declaration procedure and be thus relieved from charging the VAT and then applying for the deduction or refund of such VAT as input VAT.

2. Real Property Transfer Tax

All charges regarding transfer of real property are levied at the level of the Canton. Thus, in each Canton, different rates of charges and taxes are applicable.

A charge is initially levied by the notary public for the notarization of the sale and purchase agreement. In the case of a traditional asset deal, if several properties form the object of the sales and purchase agreement, it may cover them all, provided all properties are situated in the same canton or district. Whether a notary public is entitled to notarize agreements regarding properties that are situated in the same canton or only in the same district (e. g., Zurich) depends on the applicable Cantonal regulation. If properties from different cantons or districts are concerned, each property must be dealt with in a separate purchase agreement which will then be notarized by the competent cantonal public notary. Because agreements on the acquisition of real estate are public deeds, they must be drawn up in the official cantonal language. In addition, each notary public will insist on inserting certain language in order to comply with cantonal particularities. The requirement of notarizing agreements in each canton my lead to a "Tour de Suisse," where representatives of both the seller and the purchaser sign and notarize different agreements in different Cantons on the same day, or – in case of multiple, dispersed portfolios – on several days. It is important in this case that the agreements are contractually linked with each other: if one agreement is not duly executed and subsequently closed, all agreements become null and void.

The charge for the notary public is subject to VAT.

Secondly, a Land Register fee is levied.

Thirdly, in certain Cantons, the capital gain on the transfer of real property is subject to a separate tax. Many Swiss Cantons apply a real estate transfer tax.

In the Canton of Zurich, notarial charges of 0.1% of the purchase price (plus VAT), a Land Register fee of 0.25% and special property income taxes, but no transfer taxes apply.

A more favorable tax regime applies to MA asset deals. Currently, in most of Swiss cantons reduced charges and taxes for MA asset deals apply. In addition, MA asset deals are exempt from social property income tax. Beginning July 1st, 2009, no more transfer taxes will be levied.

In the Canton of Zurich, in comparison to a traditional asset deal, an MA asset deal is exempt from special property income tax.

3. Other Tax Issues

From the seller's point of view, the transfer of business assets is a taxable event. The seller is required to recognize a taxable gain corresponding to the difference between the net book value of the assets sold and the transfer price. The gain is subject to ordinary cantonal and federal income taxes, unless the Swiss company benefits from a special tax regime or is able to offset the gain against carried forward losses.

The costs to finance the acquisition are fully tax deductible.

As regards income taxes, different tax regimes apply to a traditional and an MA asset deal. An MA asset deal may be tax exempted if

(i) the purchaser is liable for Swiss income tax purposes; and

(ii) the transaction does not cause a change in valuation of the transferred assets; and

(iii) an entire business is transferred; and

(iv) the purchase does not transfer the acquired assets in the following five years.

Depending on the deal structure, withholding and turnover taxes may be an issue. There is, however, as a general rule, no transaction tax on transfer of assets, except for real estate.

J. Bankruptcy Law

1. Challenge of Asset Transfer in Case of Insolvency

In the event of a bankruptcy, all assets owned by the debtor constitute the bankruptcy estate. Swiss law provides creditors in bankruptcy proceedings with the legal tool to challenge transactions entered into by a debtor prior to the opening of bankruptcy proceedings, provided that the transaction impairs the realization of assets in favor of the creditors.

According to the Federal Act on Debt Enforcement and Bankruptcies, the following items can be voided: gifts that were made, collateral that was given for existing obligations that the debtor was not bound to secure, due debts settled by means other than payment and immature debts paid in the year prior to the opening of bankruptcy proceedings. Further, any transaction made within five years prior to the opening of the bankruptcy proceedings can be challenged and will eventually be declared void, if the debtor executed them with the apparent intention of disadvantaging its creditors or favoring certain creditors to the disadvantage of others. According to Swiss case law, wrongful intent can be established if the debtor could have realized that the effect – if not the intent – of the transaction could be detrimental to some of its creditors.

2. Acquisition of Assets that are Subject to Insolvency Proceedings

If insolvency proceedings have already commenced, either in the form of a creditor moratorium and liquidation or bankruptcy, several limitations with regard to the transfer of assets apply. A company in insolvency can no longer freely dispose of or divest its assets.

In the case of bankruptcy, the administrator may sell specific assets or the entire business by auction or in a private transaction upon approval of the creditors' meeting.

In the case of a creditor moratorium, assets may be transferred and assigned in part or in their entirety to a third party pursuant to a reorganization agreement negotiated by the administrator on behalf of the company. The agreement is subject to the creditors' approval.

If necessary, in order to maintain and safeguard the value of a business that may be able to survive under new ownership, the administrator is entitled to dispose of, or divest part of, the assets even before the company is formally liquidated or a reorganization agreement has been reached. Any such transaction must, however, be approved by the court.

When purchasing a business from a reorganization or bankruptcy estate, the purchaser usually would like to exclude certain liabilities and undesired contracts. Employees who are active in the acquired business are automatically transferred to the purchaser (see H, 1 above). However, in the case of an asset purchase from a bankruptcy estate, in contrast to the general rule set forth above, the purchaser is not liable for transferring employees' claims that relate to the period prior to the purchase.

K. Timing and Costs

1. Timeframe of Asset Transfer

Depending on the complexity and type of asset deal, duration of a transaction may vary considerably. Notably, official notification/registration duties have a major impact on the timing. Thus, registration requirements with MA asset deals as well as real estate deals must be taken into account.

2. Costs of Asset Transfer

A general estimation of costs associated with an asset transfer is impossible to render. At first, costs depend essentially on the type of assets transferred. Moreover, notarization and registration charges as well as taxes vary according to the law of the concerned Canton(s).

L. Miscellaneous

1. Choice of Foreign Law

As regards traditional asset deals, choice of foreign law is possible. However, mandatory legal provisions must be observed. Notably, dealings in Swiss property are subject to Swiss law.

An MA asset deal is an institution that exists under Swiss law. Thus, it can only be executed under Swiss law.

2. (International) Arbitration, Choice of Venue

Arbitration is available as means of dispute settlement. There are no restrictions as to the venue and rules to be followed.

3. Other Distinctions, Characteristics

There are no other noteworthy distinctions or characteristics as to the transfer of assets under Swiss law.

M. Literature

Lukas Glanzmann, Umstrukturierungen (Reorganizations), 2nd Edition, 2008

Rudolf Tschäni, M&A-Transaktionen nach Schweizer Recht (M&A Transactions under Swiss Law), 1st Edition, 2003

Nedim Peter Vogt, *Ralph Malacrida* and *Rolf Watter*, Mergers, Acquisitions and Corporate Restructuring, 1st Edition 2005

Taiwan (ROC)

By *Jackie S.J. Lin* and *Yvonne C.Y. Liu*

A. General Aspects

1. Asset Deal vs. Share Deal: Essential Considerations

There are many aspects worth considering in determining which deal structure to use in the territory of ROC. The following points, among others, should be noted:

Tax Implications

The asset purchase deal and the share purchase deal may be subject to different tax treatments. In an asset deal, in general, the purchaser and the seller may be subject to title transfer taxes, value-added tax and capital tax (which may be up to 40% depending on the taxpayer's total income status) and relevant registration fees applicable to each asset to be transferred from the seller unless the deal structure meets the tax benefits/exemptions qualifications under relevant financial laws and regulations, e. g., Merger and Acquisition Law or The Financial Institution Merger Act. The seller in the share acquisition deal, on the other hand, will only be subject to 0.3% securities exchange tax and the capital gains of the share disposal are exempt from income tax. In addition, in an asset deal, the tax benefit enjoyed by the seller may not be transferred to the purchaser of the asset. Since tax rulings in the ROC are quite complicated, it is strongly advised that tax advisers be consulted when the investors structure the deal.

Financial Standing of the Seller

The other factor that may affect the deal structure is the financial standing of the seller. According to Taiwanese laws and regulations, if the purchaser acquires all of the shares of the seller, all of the debts and obligations pertaining to the seller in the target company and any encumbrances over the shares, if any, will be assumed by the purchaser to the extent of its investment in the target company or the shares acquired.

License Permits

Foreign persons or entities are required to set up a local presence to own and carry on business, so in an asset deal, a foreign purchaser would need to establish this local entity in order to close the deal, whereas in a share deal, foreign persons or entities can own shares of a local company directly. In addition, the Taiwan government has published a negative list under which foreigners are prohibited altogether from investing in certain industries or are subject to investment ceilings. Therefore, the share deal would be more complicated than the asset deal in structuring the investment in such restricted industries.

2. Distinction between Sale and Transfer in Rem

There is no clear distinction between the sale (obligation to transfer) and the transfer in rem (fulfillment of the obligation to transfer). In general, once the sales agreement is executed by the seller and the purchaser, the seller is bound by the agreement and bears the obligation to transfer the assets as agreed.

3. Regional Differences

Most of the legal requirements are the same or similar in all regions in our jurisdiction. However, there might be a few minor differences in each county in relation to the title registration process for the real estate and the application for factory assignment or application for the business enterprises license, etc.

4. Acquisition by Foreigners

Regarding distinctions with regard to the acquisition of assets by foreigners or foreign entities, there are certain investment restrictions and requirements imposed on the foreigners or foreign entities. For example, there are certain types of industries where foreigners or foreign entities are prohibited altogether from investing or their investments are subject to certain investment ceiling. In such circumstances, special approvals from the competent authorities are required for the investment by the foreigners.

Further, the ROC government allows foreigners or foreign entities to own or invest in the real property on a basis of reciprocity.

5. Public Registers, Records and Databases

In general, the following information is available to the public and could be obtained from the online databases in connection with an asset transfer:

General corporate information (e. g., company name, tax ID number, the identity of the chairman of the board of directors, the directors and supervisors, establishment date of the company, authorized and paid-in capital, business scope, etc.) could be found on the database maintained by the Ministry of Economic Affairs ("**MOEA**") at http://www.moea.gov.tw/.

Title searches, including the mortgage details, for the real estate could be made through the online database at http://land.hinet.net/or through the land service agent in each regional government for more details.

Chattel lien could be searched through the online database at http://www.cto.moea.gov.tw/04/01.asp maintained by the MOEA or at each regional government.

A search for factory information could be made through the online database at http://gcis.nat.gov.tw/open_system_2_fact.htm maintained by the MOEA or at each regional government.

For the company whose shares are listed in or traded through the Taiwan Stock Exchange or the Gre-Tai Market, more detailed information, e. g., financial statements, shareholdings of each director and supervisor, etc., as required to be published under the laws and regulations.

Information in relation to trademarks and patents could be obtained from the online database maintained by the Intellectual Property Office at http://www.tipo.gov.tw/.

In addition, most of the court judgments already rendered could be searched through the online database maintained by the Ministry of Justice at http://law.moj.gov.tw/.

6. Purchase Price Requirements

Public companies must follow the Regulations Governing the Acquisition and Disposal of Assets by Public Companies (the **"Regulations"**) for the acquisition or disposal of the shares, tangible and intangible assets. For example, in a deal of merger, de-merger, acquisition, or transfer of shares, the public company must engage a CPA, attorney, or securities underwriter to give a fairness opinion on the share exchange ratio, acquisition price, or considerations, and then submit it to the board of directors for resolution. And, under the Regulations, if a public company acquires or disposes real estate where the purchase price reaches 20% of the paid-in capital of the company or more than NTD 300 million, an evaluation report issued by a professional appraisal company is required. Further, if the purchase price of the real property is more than NTD 1,000 million, two evaluation reports from two professional appraisal companies are required, and if there is a difference of 20% or more in the assessment result and the actual purchase price, or if there is a difference of 20% or more between the results of the two appraisal reports, a fairness opinion issued by a CPA on the purchase price is also required. For the acquisition or disposal of intangible assets by public company, a fairness opinion issued by a CPA is required if the purchase price is more than 20% of the company's paid-in capital or more than NTD 300 million.

There are no analogous laws and regulations governing the non-public companies in this regard. However, under the Company Act, the chairman, directors and supervisors owe royalty and fiduciary duties to the company. Hence, if the purchase price is obviously much lower than a reasonable price without justifiable cause, the chairman, directors and/or supervisors may be held, jointly and severally, liable for the loss suffered by the company and they may also be subject to criminal punishment if applicable.

B. Tangible/Movable Assets

1. Characteristics as to:

a) Language of Documentation. Documentation drafted in English is fine and acceptable. However, if any disputes are brought to court or applications are required to be made with relevant competent authorities, a Chinese translation of the documents is required.

The documents can be executed bilingually. However, in general if there is any discrepancy in the English and Chinese versions and no clear indication of the governing language in the document, the Chinese language would govern.

b) Form of Documentation. In general, both oral and written agreements are legally binding and recognized under the Civil Code. However, if the agreement is in relation to the rights in rem or real estate, only a written agreement with due notarization will be legally binding upon the seller and the purchaser. The documents can be executed outside of our jurisdiction and, in practice, certain kinds of documents, e. g., monetary receipts, are commonly executed outside of Taiwan to avoid the stamp duty payable. The signing of counterparts is permissible, and the exchange of the executed pages completes the execution.

c) Specification of Assets. In general, a general description of assets is acceptable if such description is sufficient to identify the assets to be transferred. The attachment of schedules or lists of assets to the transfer agreement is not statutorily required. However, in practice, it is quite common to attach schedules or lists identifying the assets to be transferred for identification and closing purposes.

2. Administrative, Corporate and Other Approvals

As indicated above, there are certain industries that foreigners are not allowed to make investments in or in which they are subject to investment restrictions. In addition, there are certain restrictions on procuring real estate applicable to foreigners. In such case, a special governmental approval is required. Further, a prior approval from the Central Bank of the Republic of China (the "**CBC**") may be required prior to the remittance of the purchase price into Taiwan for closing purposes.

In general, approval of the board of directors is required for an asset deal. And, if the assets to be sold are all or the major assets of the Taiwan corporate seller or if the Taiwan corporate purchaser procures all business or assets from the seller, approval of shareholders is required as well. In general, the assignment of the underlying assets will not affect the security holders' interest over the underlying assets. Hence, there is no need to obtain such security holders' consent for the transfer of the underlying assets.

Failure to obtain the required approval from the board of directors and/or shareholders may cause the transaction to be invalid. Further, without obtaining the required governmental approval, the asset transfer may be invalidated and/or not be allowed to be registered with the competent authority to effectuate the title transfer of the assets.

3. Filing Requirements

If the assets to be transferred are real estate assets, the transfer must be registered and filed with the government to effectuate the title transfer. The competent authorities would digitalize the information in relation to the real property to make the information available to the public.

In addition, the title transfer, creation of lien or leasehold on certain other tangible assets, e. g., vessels, aircraft, farms, fishing rights, etc. are required to be registered with the competent authorities for administration purposes. Such information is not available to the public and can only be procured through an application by the interested party with the competent authorities.

4. Automatic Transfer of Encumbrances

In case the assets are subject to encumbrances (e. g., pledges, retention of title), the purchaser will be subject to the encumbrances, which will be automatically transferred with the assets to be sold.

C. Real Property

1. Characteristics as to:

a) Language of Documentation. Documents drafted in English are fine and acceptable. However, if any disputes are brought to court or applications are required to be made with relevant competent authorities, a Chinese translation thereof is required.

The documents can be executed bilingually. However, if there is any discrepancy between the English and the Chinese version and no clear indication as to the governing language, the Chinese language, in general, will govern.

b) Form of Documentation. According to the Civil Code and relevant registration rulings, agreements in relation to the sale of real property and any other rights in rem are required to be made in writing and such written agreement must be duly notarized. The documents can be executed outside of our jurisdiction and, in practice, it is preferable that such real property purchase agreement be executed outside of Taiwan to avoid the stamp duty that is payable. Signing in counterparts is permitted, with the exchange of the execution pages completing the execution of the agreement.

c) Specification of Assets. A general description typically will be acceptable if such description is sufficient to identify the real property to be sold. However, in practice, each parcel of land and building should have been assigned with a land/building number by the government for identification purposes. It is common practice to refer to such identification number for a sale or purchase of the real property.

2. Administrative, Corporate and Other Approvals

Regarding governmental or administrative approvals, in general no prior governmental approval is required, except for certain real properties, e.g., swamps, forests, etc., which are prohibited or subject to transfer restrictions for foreigners.

In general, the approval of the board of directors is required for corporate governance purposes. And, in certain circumstances, e.g., where the assets to be sold are all or major assets of the Taiwan corporate seller, the approval of the shareholders is required as well. In general, the assignment of the underlying assets will not affect the security holders' interest over the underlying assets. Hence, there is no need to obtain such security holders' consent for the transfer of the underlying assets.

Failure to obtain the required approval of board of directors and/or shareholders may cause the transaction to be invalid. Further, without obtaining the required governmental approval, the asset transfer may be invalidated and not be allowed to be registered with the competent authority to effectuate the title transfer of the assets.

3. Filing Requirements

Under the Civil Code and relevant land laws and regulations, the title transfer must be registered with the land authority for registration of the real property to effectuate the transfer.

4. Automatic Transfer of Encumbrances

In case the real property is subject to encumbrances, the purchaser will be subject to the encumbrances, which will be automatically transferred with the real property to be sold. The security holder may waive the security right by signing the agreement and standard written form and filing with the land registration authority to remove the security registration. Such agreement shall be notarized by a public notary.

5. Automatic Transfer of Lease Agreements

If the real property is subject to lease agreements that are executed prior to the asset transfer, the lease agreements will be transferred to the purchaser by operation of law. However, this does not apply to lease agreements in which the term is longer than five years or where there is no definite term period, as well as where the agreement is not notarized by public notary when executed.

D. Contracts

1. Characteristics as to:

a) Language of Documentation. Documents drafted in English are fine and acceptable. However, if disputes are brought to court or if applications are required to be made with the relevant competent authorities, a Chinese translation of the documents is required.

The documents can be executed bilingually. However, if there is any discrepancy between the English and the Chinese versions and no clear indication in the document as to the governing language, the Chinese language, in general, will govern.

b) Form of Documentation. According to the Civil Code, a general contract, without rights in rem involved, can be made orally or in writing and, except for certain special cases, notarization is not required. The documents can be executed outside of our jurisdiction and, in practice, with respect to certain kinds of documents, e. g., monetary receipt or chattel sales agreement, execution outside of Taiwan is preferable to avoid the stamp duty. Signing in counterparts is permissible, with the exchange of execution pages completing the execution of the contract.

c) Specification of Contracts. A general description is typically acceptable if such description is sufficient to identify the contracts to be transferred. The attachment of schedules or lists of contracts to the transfer agreement is not required. However, in practice, it is quite common and recommended to attach a schedule or list identifying the contracts to be transferred for identification and closing purposes and to avoid future disputes.

2. Administrative, Corporate and Other Approvals

As indicated above, certain business industries are subject to foreign investment restrictions or prohibitions. In addition, remittance of foreign currency into Taiwan for a closing may need the approval of the Central Bank of the Republic of China. In this case, governmental approval is required.

In general, the approval of the board of directors is required for corporate governance purposes unless the Chairman has the full authorization to transfer the contract without the approval of the board meeting. And in certain circumstances, e. g., if the assets to be sold are all or the major assets of the Taiwan corporate seller, the approval of the shareholders is required as well.

Further, according to the Civil Code, an assignment of contracts requires the consent of the other party.

Without the required governmental approval or the other parties' consent, the assignment of such contracts may be challenged by the other party and, as a result, cannot bind the other party. In such a case, such party can still claim its rights under the contracts assigned to the purchaser.

3. Automatic Transfer of Contracts (Other than Lease and Employment Agreements)

Contracts, including any insurance contracts specifically identifying the seller as the insured beneficiary, will not be transferred automatically to the other party without its consent, unless the deal structure meets the qualifications under the M&A law or other relevant laws and regulations.

4. Filing Requirements

The transfer of a contract does not need to be filed with any public authorities or registered in a register.

5. Treatment of Existing Contractual Claims and Obligations

If the sold contracts are not fulfilled or only partially fulfilled, it is generally the case that the rights and/or obligations, whether fully completed or not, will be assumed by the purchaser of the sold contract. The seller and purchaser may have different agreements as to the rights and/or obligation allocation in the transfer agreement. It is common to request that the seller give a representation and warranty that unless disclosed in the schedules of the contract, the obligations under the contracts have been completely fulfilled. If a violation of the representations and warranties occurs, the seller may be subject to a default payment or an indemnification as prescribed under the asset sale and/or transfer agreement.

6. Warranty Claims Resulting from Events prior to Transfer

Under the Civil Code, the purchaser will assume all rights and liabilities pertaining to the sold contracts. Hence, unless agreed otherwise in the agreement, the purchaser is liable for any underlying obligations, including warranty claims, in relation to the assigned contracts. In general, the purchaser will request that the seller disclose any pending or potential liabilities in the agreement. If such warranty claims have been disclosed in the agreement, the purchase price will generally reflect such potential risk. However, the default payment or indemnification clause may be included in the transfer agreement to punish the seller if the representations and warranties given are false or misleading.

E. IP Rights

1. Characteristics of Intellectual Property Rights (e. g., Trademarks, Patents, Utility Models, Domain Names) ("*IP Rights*") as to:

a) Language of Documentation. Documents drafted in English are fine and acceptable. However, if disputes are brought to court or if applications are required to be made with the relevant competent authorities, a Chinese translation of the documents is required.

The documents can be executed bilingually. However, if there is any discrepancy between the English and the Chinese version of a document and no clear indication as to the governing language was set forth in the document, the Chinese version of the document, in general, will govern.

b) Form of Documentation. To apply for the title transfer of patent or trademark rights, an application form must be submitted as published by the competent authority, i.e. Intellectual Property Office of the Ministry of Economic Affairs (**"IPO"**), along with other documents, e. g., one original copy of the assignment agreement. There is no statutory requirement regarding the notarization of the submitted documents. The application form must be submitted in Chinese, and if the assignment agreement is not prescribed in Chinese, a Chinese translation is also required to be submitted. The assignment agreement may be executed outside of ROC (Taiwan) and countersigning is permitted, with the exchange of the signature pages completing the execution of the assignment agreement.

c) Specification of IP Rights. Generally speaking, a description in general may be acceptable if the description is sufficient to identify the IP Rights to be assigned. However, it is advisable to clearly identify the IP numbers granted by the IPO in the assignment agreement because the assigned IP numbers must be specifically identified in the assignment application form.

2. Administrative, Corporate and Other Approvals

In general, the transfer of IP Rights does not require any special governmental or administrative approvals. Furthermore, the transfer of IP Rights does not require the approval of any security holders of such IP Rights because their security interests in such encumbered IP Rights will not be affected. Besides, if the assigned IP Rights are all or the major assets of the Seller, such assignment, according to the Company Act, shall be approved by the seller's shareholders' meeting. If the shareholders' approval is not obtained, the assignment agreement may be invalidated by the court when the dispute is brought to court.

3. Filing Requirements

According to the Trademark Act and Patent Act, transfer of IP Rights is required to be registered with the IPO. The IPO will digitalize the registered details of such IP Rights on the database to be available to the public. Without completing the registration procedure with the IPO, the IP Rights assignee can not assert his patent or trademark rights against any third party.

4. Applicable International (Multilateral) Agreements or Treaties

So far, the only international treaty that the ROC has entered into is the TRIPS. In addition, the Taiwan government also entered into the following bilateral agreements on IP rights with other countries:

(1) Memorandum of Understanding Between the Intellectual Property Office of Ministry of Economic Affairs in Taiwan and the Australian Commerce and Industry Office on Cooperation in Industrial Property;

(2) Agreement on Protection of Industrial Property rights Between the National Institute for Industrial Property of France and the Intellectual Property Office of Taiwan;

(3) Agreement on the Development and Protection of Intellectual Property Rights Between the Republic of China and Republic of Nicaragua;

(4) Agreement on the Development and Protection of Intellectual Property Rights Between the Republic of China and Republic of Guatemala;

(5) Agreement on the Development and Protection of Intellectual Property Rights Between the Republic of China and Republic of Costa Rica;

(6) Memorándum de Entendimiento Entre el Ministerio de Economía en Santiago Y el Ministerio de Asuntos Económicos en Taipei;

(7) Memorandum über gegenseitiges Einverständnis über die Ergebnisse der Gespräche zwischen Herrn Ming-Bang Chen Generaldirektor des Intellectual Property Office, MOEA, Taipei und Dr. Jürgen Schade Präsident des Deutschen Patent-und Markenamts am 16.11.2001 in München;

(8) Agreement on the Mutual Granting of Patent Priority Right between the Taipei Representative Office in the Netherlands and the Netherlands Trade and Investment Office;

(9) Agreement on the Mutual Protection of Intellectual Property Rights between the Republic of China and the Republic of El Salvador;

(10) Acuerdo sobre Proteccion mutual de los derechos de la Propiedad Intelectual entre la Republica de China y la Republica del Paraguay;

(11) Announcement: the mutual recognition of patent and trademark priority rights effected on 15 June 2000 between Chinese Taipei and Austria;

(12) Arrangement on Cooperation Concerning Mutual Recognition of Intellectual Property Rights Between the Taipei Representative Office in the United Kingdom and the British Trade and Cultural Office in Taipei;

(13) Memorandum of Understanding between the Intellectual Property Office in Taipei and the Office for Harmonization in the Internal Market (Trademarks and Designs) in Alicante on the Exchange of Information Relating to the Protection of Trade Mark Rights;

(14) Arrangement for the Protection of Industrial Property Rights between the Taipei Economic & Cultural Office in New Zealand and the New Zealand Commerce and Industry Office;

(15) Exchange of Letters between Ministry of Economic Affairs and European Communities concerning Trademark Priority Claims;

(16) Arrangement between the New Zealand Commerce and Industry Office and the Taipei Economic & Cultural Office, New Zealand on the Reciprocal Protection and Enforcement of Copyright;

(17) Exchange of Letters between National Bureau of Standards, Ministry of Economic Affairs in Taipei and Federal Intellectual Property Office in Bern concerning the Recognition of Priority Rights in Patent Applications for the Territory of the Principality of Liechtenstein;

(18) Exchange of Letters between National Bureau of Standards, Ministry of Economic Affairs in Taipei and National Institute for Industrial Property in Paris concerning the Mutual Granting of a Priority Right as Regards Patents, Designs and Trademarks and Cooperation;

(19) Memorandum of Understanding between the Taipei Economic and Cultural Representative Office in the United States and the American Institute in Taiwan;

(20) Exchange of Announcements between National Bureau of Standards, Ministry of Economic Affairs in Taipei and Japanese Patent Office concerning the Mutual Recognition of Patent Priority Right;

(21) Exchange of Letters on Mutual Recognition of Patent Priority Rights Between the Federal Intellectual Property Office (FIPO) in Bern and National Bureau of Standards in Taipei;

(22) Announcement: the mutual recognition of priority right on utility model patent between Chinese Taipei and Germany;

(23) Announcement: the mutual recognition of priority right on patent of invention between Chinese Taipei and Germany;

(24) Memorandum of Understanding between the National Bureau of Standards in Taipei and the Australian Commerce and Industry Office on the Protection of Industrial Property;

(25) Agreement for the Protection of Copyright Between the Coordination Council for North American Affairs and the American Institute in Taiwan;

(26) Memorandum of Understanding Regarding Institutional Cooperation between Taiwan Intellectual Property Office (TIPO) and the Spanish Patent and Trademark Offices; and

(27) Memorandum of Understanding on Intellectual Property Cooperation between the Taipei Economic and Cultural Office in the Philippines and the Manila Economic and Cultural Office.

F. Receivables

1. Characteristics as to:

a) Language of Documentation. There is no statutory language restriction on the documents for the transfer of receivables. The documents can be drafted in any foreign language agreed on by the parties, but a Chinese translation thereof is required to be submitted if any disputes arising therefrom are brought to court or if an application with the competent authority is required. The documents can be executed bilingually. However, if there is any discrepancy between the Chinese and the English version, the Chinese version may govern if no specific prescription in this regard is set forth in the agreement.

b) Form of Documentation. An agreement on the transfer of receivables can be made orally or in writing, and notarization is not statutorily required. However, it is required under the Civil Code to notify the debtors of such transferred receivables, otherwise the transferee cannot make any claim against the debtors to collect the receivables. The documents can be executed outside of Taiwan and it is permissible that each party signs on a separate document and then exchanges the signing pages to complete the execution of the documents.

c) Specification of Receivables. The law or regulations are silent on the description of the receivables to effectuate the transfer. However, the description shall be sufficient to identify the receivables to be transferred. It is not statutorily required to attach schedules or lists of receivables to the transfer agreement. Nevertheless, it is common practice to attach schedules or list of receivables to the transfer agreement to identify the receivables to be transferred.

2. Administrative, Corporate and Other Approvals

In general, the transfer of receivables does not require special governmental or administrative approvals. If the assigned receivables are all or the major assets of the seller, such assignment shall be approved by the seller's shareholders' meeting. In such case, without obtaining the shareholders' approval, the assignment agreement may be invalidated by a court if a dispute is brought to court. In addition, there is no need to obtain the debtors' approval but a notice must be served on the debtors for such assignment, otherwise the transferee of such receivables cannot make any claims against such debtors.

3. Filing Requirements

No special filings with public authorities or registrations are required. However, according to the Civil Code, notice must be served on the debtors for such receivables transfer. Absent notification of the debtors, the transferee cannot claim against such debtors to collect the receivables transferred.

G. Liabilities

1. Characteristics as to:

a) Language of Documentation. The documents can be drafted in English or any other foreign language agreed on by the parties. The documents can be executed bilingually but if there is any discrepancy in the different versions, the Chinese language will govern unless agreed otherwise in the documents.

b) Form of Documentation. The transfer of liabilities can be made orally or in writing. Notarization is not statutorily required. Signing in counterparts is permissible.

c) Specification of Liabilities. The law and regulations are silent on the description of the liabilities for the purpose of effectuating the transfer of liabilities. However, the description shall be sufficient to identify the liabilities agreed to be transferred. It is not a statutory requirement to attach schedules or lists of liabilities to the transfer agreement. Nevertheless, it is common practice to attach schedules or lists of liabilities to the transfer agreement to identify the liabilities to be transferred.

2. Administrative, Corporate and Other Approvals

In general, the transfer of liabilities does not require special governmental or administrative approvals. The transfer of liabilities may require the approval of the seller's board meeting for corporate governance purposes but does not require shareholder approval. However, the transfer of liabilities requires the creditors' approval. In the absence of the creditors' approval, the transfer cannot bind the creditor. The creditor can still claim against seller for the liabilities.

3. Filing Requirements

Special filings with public authorities or registrations into registers are not required for the transfer of liabilities. However, it is required to obtain the creditor's approval on the transfer of liabilities.

4. Purchaser's Liability for:

a) Tax Obligations. Generally speaking, tax obligations in relation to the acquired assets for periods prior to the acquisition shall be borne by the Seller unless agreed otherwise by the parties.

b) Environmental Contamination. According to the Soil and Groundwater Pollution Remediation Act, the Purchaser, though it may not be the party responsible for environmental contamination, will be held liable, jointly and severally, for the costs required to remediate the contamination if the contamination is not removed or controlled due to purchaser's gross negligence. Further, the purchaser may be held liable, jointly and severally with the seller, for the damages claimed by a third party who suffered from the contamination if such damages have arisen due to the purchaser's gross negligence.

c) Products Sold or Services Rendered by the Seller to Third Parties. The product or service warranty liability will be allocated in accordance with the agreement between the seller and the purchaser. In general, if the purchaser buys the whole department or business concerned, the product warranty liability and after-sale service in relation to the transferred department or business shall be borne by the Purchaser unless agreed otherwise in the transfer agreement.

5. Automatic Transfer of Other Liabilities

There is no clear rule or guideline regulating which liabilities of the seller will be automatically transferred to the purchaser due to the acquisition of assets. In general, if the liabilities of and interests with respect to the purchased assets are accrued prior to the acquisition, such liabilities and interests may be borne or enjoyed by the seller unless otherwise prescribed under the laws and regulation or agreed otherwise in the agreement by the parties.

6. Contractual Protection as to 4 and 5 above

According to the Soil and Groundwater Pollution Remediation Act, the purchaser who is not the actual party responsible for the contamination but pays the damages suffered by a third party is statutorily allowed to make a claim against the seller to recover the amount of the damages if the seller is the actual wrongdoer with respect to the contamination. It is customary to include the indemnification clause on environmental pollution in the asset sale and purchase agreement. It might not be customary to include the indemnification clause in the asset sale agreement for the liabilities of taxes, the products warranty or the after-sale liabilities if such liabilities have been fully disclosed in the transfer agreement for the purchaser's evaluation. However, the purchaser may claim against the seller for the default payment or indemnification for the false or misleading representation or warranties in this regard.

H. Employees

1. Transfer of Employees

Employees of the seller will not automatically transfer to the purchaser along with the asset transfer. According to the Labor Standard Law, the seller must serve notice to all of its employees who will be retained by the purchaser after the acquisition. For those employees whom the purchaser will not retain after the acquisition, the seller must notify such employees of employment termination prior to a specific period of time as prescribed under the Labor Standard Law. The seller is also liable for the severance pay or pension at the amount payable under the relevant labor laws and regulations to the employees who did not receive an offer from the purchaser or who received an offer from the purchaser but refused to accept it.

2. Approval of Works Council, Trade Union or Other Institutions

The asset transfer does not require the approval of the works council, labor agency, trade union or other institution. However, if the termination of the employment will trigger the thresholds set forth in the Protective Act for Mass Redundancy of Employees, the statutory procedures for the termination of the employment shall be followed. In such case, negotiation with the representative of the work union may be required. An administrative fine will be imposed successively on the seller if it did not follow the statutory procedure for the redundancy as set forth in the Protective Act for Mass Redundancy of Employees.

3. Contractual Protection as to Labor Issues

If the employee liabilities have been disclosed in the transfer agreement for evaluation, it is not customary to include indemnifications into the transfer agreement in this regard. However, it is customary to request the seller to pay any agreed upon default payments or indemnification if the seller makes false or misleading representations and warranties in relation to the employee liabilities.

I. Tax Implications

1. Value Added Tax

The value of the movable assets in the asset transfer will be subject to the VAT, at the current rate of 5%. However, if the asset transfer qualifies under the requirements as prescribed in the Merger & Acquisition Law, such VAT may be exempt by operation of law.

2. Real Property Transfer Tax

The land transfer tax is payable for each land transfer. The land agencies will publish annually the land value, which may be lower or higher (unusual) than the current market price. Based on such public announced land value, land transfer tax will be charged annually. The floor percentage rate is 1% of the announced value and may be subject to additional 1.5%–5.5% of the announced value when it exceeds a certain threshold of announced land value.

In addition, the land-value-increase tax will be imposed on the land transfer. The local land agency will publish current land value annually. If a transfer of land title takes place, land-value-increase tax will be imposed on seller at the percentage from 20%-40% of the value increased (compared to the land value announced in the year of sale and that announced in the year of the initial purchase).

Under certain circumstances set forth in the Merger and Acquisition Act or the Financial Institutions Merger Act, the land transfer tax may be exempt and the land-value-increase tax may be allowed for the deferred payment until the subsequent transfer by the purchaser in the future.

3. Other Tax Issues

In addition to the VAT, land transfer tax, land-value-increase tax, stamp duty, deed tax, securities transaction tax and income tax, etc. may be imposed, as the case may be, in an asset transfer deal.

J. Bankruptcy Law

1. Challenge of Asset Transfer in Case of Insolvency

According to the Civil Code, the creditor may file with the court to invalidate the asset transfer if the debtor, i.e. the seller, is fully aware that such transfer will damage the interests of the creditor and the purchaser has knowledge of this The statute of limitation for such invalidation appeal right is one year after acknowledgment of the creditor or ten years after the transfer was made. Further, according to the Bankruptcy Act, the receiver must request that the court invalidate the transfer if the aforementioned circumstances exist before the bankruptcy was announced by the court.

2. Acquisition of Assets that are Subject to Insolvency Proceedings

Once the bankruptcy is announced, the receiver will take over to manage the assets of the seller and no transfer is allowed to be made unless approved by the receiver under the bankruptcy procedures.

K. Timing and Costs

1. Timeframe of Asset Transfer

In general, it is estimated that it may take around three to six months to complete the title transfer in an asset deal. However, if it is an extraordinary circumstance or if the assets to be transferred are in large volumes or have complicated ownership conditions, it will take longer to complete the registration of the title transfer.

2. Costs of Asset Transfer

In addition to the tax, fees or costs indicated above, the following cost or fees, other than costs payable to advisors, may be payable in the asset purchase deal:

Patent registration fee: between NTD 6,500 and NTD 15,000 for each registration.

Trademark registration fee: between NTD 5,500 and NTD 11,500 for each registration.

Notarization fee: The ROC government published a table of notarization fee indicating the standard notarization fee payable depending on the contract price, the notarized matters in nature, etc. The minimum notarization fee is NTD 1,000.

Land registration fee: 0.1% of the contract price or 0.1% of the land value announced by the government.

Deed tax: 6% of the contract price payable by the purchaser. However, in the area where the land-value-increase tax is imposed, the deed tax will be exempted.

Stamp Duty: 0.1% of the contract price payable by the parties executing the contract. The stamp duty is payable to monetary receipt and property sales agreements made within the territory of ROC.

L. Miscellaneous

1. Choice of Foreign Law

The sale and/or transfer agreement may be subject to foreign law. However, as to the procedure for title registration of real property in Taiwan, Taiwan law will govern even though the agreement prescribes otherwise.

2. (International) Arbitration, Choice of Venue

International arbitration is allowed. In general, there are no restrictions as to the choice of venue as long as such choice is mutually agreed upon by the parties in writing and does not violate the public policy of Taiwan.

3. Other Distinctions, Characteristics

In Taiwan, it is quite common to engage land service counsel in each region to handle the title registrations of the rights in rem. Generally, they would charge their service fee on each parcel of land and building to be transferred.

United Arab Emirates

By *Florian Amereller* and *Jochen Murach*

A. General Aspects

1. Asset Deal vs. Share Deal: Essential Considerations

When structuring a transaction, a foreign investor should keep in mind that it is only permitted to hold an equity ownership in United Arab Emirates ("U.A.E.") onshore companies of up to 49%, as at least 51% of the equity must be held at all times by U.A.E. nationals. Only the free zones (see below) allow for 100% foreign ownership, but conducting business in the U.A.E. market itself is, at least in general, prohibited. Therefore, the acquisition of shares in a U.A.E. onshore company is per se subject to a ceiling of 49% for a foreign purchaser. It should also be noted that there is currently an ongoing legislative discussion as to whether this maximum statutory threshold for foreign shareholdings should be further increased.

In general, tax considerations are less relevant under the laws of the U.A.E. when structuring a transaction as an asset deal in contrast to a share deal. Corporate income tax regulations have been enacted in various Emirates but they generally are not being implemented, except for branches of foreign banks and companies active in the petroleum and gas business. In addition, there is no property, property transfer or any other asset tax that might become relevant in a share or asset deal, except for a stamp duty and registration fee in case of real estate transactions.

In practice, however, share deals might be easier to handle due to general considerations. Under U.A.E. law, most relevant permits and licenses are attached to the owner (rather than to the assets of the business), so that in an asset deal, the new owner will have to apply for the required permits and licenses in order to operate the business, while in a share deal the entity owning the assets will remain the same and can continue operating under the terms and conditions of the existing licenses.

2. Distinction between Sale and Transfer in Rem

The general rule is that ownership of the goods to be sold shall be transferred to the purchaser as soon as the sale agreement is executed. However, the law itself does provide for certain exceptions and also allows for contractual agreements deviating from the rule. For example, the Civil Code explicitly allows for the reservation of ownership (i.e. that the transfer of ownership to the purchaser be suspended) until the whole purchase price has been paid, notwithstanding that the goods have been delivered. It is therefore permitted by law, and also not unusual in practice, to execute a sale and purchase agreement determining the rights and obligations of the parties and the agreed procedure regarding the transfer of the assets while the actual transfer of assets itself is then subject to the relevant procedure as agreed under specific transfer agreements. The advantage of such separation is that local particularities under the respective laws can be properly addressed under the specific transfer agreements.

3. Regional Differences

For the purpose of this overview, it should be noted that the federal constitution of the U.A.E. apportions powers between the federal government and the seven constituent Emirates. The provisions relevant for the sale and transfer of assets are part of the federal law (Civil Code, Commercial Transactions Code), so that there are no regional differences as regards the legal requirements in connection with the transfer of assets as such. However, certain issues that might become relevant for a transfer of assets (for example, transactions regarding natural resources within each Emirate, licenses or registrations) are governed by the specific laws of the respective Emirate.

In addition, certain aspects relevant with respect to the transfer of assets, such as aspects of land ownership or the grant and enforcement of mortgages, have not been regulated under formal federal laws on land ownership. In these cases, the rules of conflict of laws between U.A.E. federal and local legislation allow individual Emirates to legislate in areas in which the federal government has not exercised its legislative powers. Accordingly, the individual Emirates have power to legislate in matters relating to real estate until such time as federal legislation is adopted. As a result, there might be regional differences among the Emirates with regard to the transfer of real estate.

Finally, free zones in the U.A.E. have been granted authority to self-legislate in civil and commercial areas which means that there might be differences between the mainland and the various free zones.

In view of the scope of this publication and due to Dubai's economic importance, this outline will focus on the legal situation in the Emirate of Dubai, unless stated otherwise.

4. Acquisition by Foreigners

With regard to the acquisition of assets by foreigners, certain restrictions under companies and real estate law should be considered.

A foreign company can establish a presence in the U.A.E. by setting up a branch or a representative office or by forming/acquiring a local company. A branch or a representative office of a foreign company is required to have a U.A.E. national sponsor. A U.A.E. company is required to be at least 51% owned by U.A.E. nationals or U.A.E. companies fully owned by U.A.E. nationals, although shareholders agreements and corporate documents can in principle be structured so that the foreign investor would have (at least) equal control of the company, management and profit distribution rights. (However, foreign companies are permitted to establish wholly-owned branches or incorporate wholly-owned subsidiaries in each of the free zones, without the need to appoint a U.A.E. national sponsor or have any U.A.E. national ownership.) For activities of national interest, such as those relating to telecommunications or petroleum, there may be restrictions on foreign ownership and/or additional licensing requirements. In addition, certain industries face heightened regulation, such as banking, insurance and investment.

With regard to real property, the U.A.E. federal law does not prohibit land ownership by non-U.A.E. nationals. Until recently, however, all Emirates had restricted land ownership to nationals of the U.A.E. and other Gulf Cooperation Council ("**GCC**") member states. Dubai was the first Emirate to permit the sale of freehold real estate to expatriates of other nationalities by allowing expatriates to acquire freehold interest, a right of usufruct or a long lease of up to 99 years in "designated areas" as approved by the government. Certain Emirates have since followed Dubai's example, whereby the rules may deviate (for example, in some Emirates, the foreigner can only own the building or unit (in the designated area) but not the underlying land; some Emirates may also differentiate further between the rights of U.A.E. nationals, GCC nationals and other foreigners). However, the legislation in the various Emirates is still fairly recent and requires further guidance and clarity by implementing rules as well as by development of the related jurisprudence.

5. Public Registers, Records and Databases

The U.A.E. has not established an umbrella organization holding all relevant public registers, records, or databases with information relevant to an asset transfer. Instead, there are a number of institutions, each responsible for different information whereby some exist on the federal and some on the Emirate level. Corporate details about the seller and the purchaser can be obtained from the public commercial registers at the Department of Economic Development of each Emirate and the Dubai Chamber of Commerce. The Federal Ministry of Economy holds the relevant information with respect to registered trademarks, and the Department of Industrial Property, Design and Patents at the Ministry of Finance and Industry administers information regarding patents. Information as to real property including, for example, freehold ownership, rights of usufruct or mortgages, can be obtained from the Lands Department on the respective Emirate level. Finally, private credit agencies (e. g., Dun & Bradstreet) might provide relevant financial information (regarding the creditworthiness) of either party to the deal.

6. Purchase Price Requirements

As a general rule under the Civil Code, the parties are free to agree on the purchase price, whether it is greater or less than the true value of the assets, and are free to select the currency in which the purchase price shall be payable. If, however, the contracting parties declare a price contrary to their true agreement, the true price shall be taken to be the valid one.

The purchase price for real property or any encumbrance thereon becomes, for example, relevant as the basis for calculation of the fees to be paid to the Land Department for registration.

B. Tangible/Movable Assets

1. Characteristics as to:

a) Language of Documentation. The official language in the U.A.E. is Arabic, although English is widely spoken. As a general rule, it is sufficient to draft the contract documents in the English language. However, depending on the respective assets to be transferred, it might be advisable to draft the relevant documents bilingually to enable registration with the relevant authorities without the need for lengthy translation, certification and legalization proceedings. Documentation for transactions in free zones can be drafted in English only.

Generally, specific rules might apply with regard to securities, where the document certifying such right is considered a tangible asset, while the certified right itself is transferred as a right. However, the following outline focuses on the general rules with regard to movable property under U.A.E. law.

b) Form of Documentation. In general, a contract may be made in writing or orally and may be executed at any place. For reasons of evidence, however, it is always advisable to execute a written contract. The written form might also be mandatory under the law in certain cases. For example, the transfer of ownership of a "commercial business" (under U.A.E. law, this is defined as a group of tangible assets, such as goods, equipment, tools, machines, etc., and intangible assets, such as customer contacts, goodwill, trade name, patents, licenses, etc., that cover the necessary elements for the practice of a commercial activity, whereby real property is explicitly excluded from the definition) or the creation of a real right thereon shall not be valid as between the contracting parties and with regard to third parties, unless it is attested and authenticated by a notary public and entered into the commercial register and a summary thereof is published in two local Arabic daily newspapers.

Finally, the written form might not be legally required for the transfer as such to be valid, but for administrative and practical reasons (e. g., registration of a motor vehicle; application for license to operate certain assets).

c) Specification of Assets. In principle, the parties to a contract shall agree on the essential elements of the transfer and the assets must be specified so that they are defined or at least capable of being defined, i.e. identified and distinguished from other assets (requirement of specification). Such identification can take various forms, e. g., by way of reference to detailed annexes, by way of indication of location or by way of description in the contract documents.

With regard to the transfer of ownership of a "commercial business", U.A.E. law explicitly requires that the written contract indicate all elements agreed upon to be included in the sale, with prices of the tangible and intangible elements. Also, the transfer of a "commercial business" shall not include the trade name, unless the documents explicitly or implicitly provide for such transfer of trade name.

2. Administrative, Corporate and Other Approvals

The transfer of tangible assets usually does not require special governmental or administrative approvals. However, regarding certain assets that are subject to special rules for reasons of safety or national interest, the approval(s) from the Ministry of Health, the Federal Environment Authority, the Ministry of Interior, the Supreme Petroleum Council, and/or the Central Bank or other regulating authorities might be required, as the case may be. The respective transfer might be null and void if the parties have not acted in accordance with the relevant provisions. In this context, it is to be noted that the transfer might also be subject to certain international (e. g., United Nations) or foreign national (e. g., U.S.) embargo restrictions if the relevant assets are ultimately delivered to embargoed countries, even if the transaction takes place in the U.A.E.

An approval by corporate bodies of either party is generally not required, but might be necessary, notably in case of the transfer of core elements of a company's commercial business, or if so provided in the party's articles of association.

The general rule regarding commercial mortgages (defined as a pledge on moveable property in security of a commercial debt) is that the pledge is not effective against the debtor or a third party unless possession of the pledged property is transferred to the pledgee or to such other person as is appointed by the contracting parties. In other words, in order for the pledge to be valid, the pledged property must remain in the hands of the pledgee or the appointed person until the debt is satisfied. The Civil Code stipulates for any possessory pledge that the pledgor may not dispose of the goods pledged save with the consent of the pledgee or (under certain conditions) with the permission of the court. It is to be noted, however, that special rules apply to pledges on a "commercial business" (which might also include tangible assets).

3. Filing Requirements

In general, the transfer of tangible assets does not require special filings with public authorities or registrations in public registers or databases. However, special rules might apply with respect to certain categories of assets (such as, for example, the sale of cars, certain kind of heavy equipment, aircraft, etc.).

4. Automatic Transfer of Encumbrances

As outlined above, in the case of a commercial mortgage on tangible assets (as well as with regard to other possessory pledges), such securities are only effective against the debtor and third parties as long as the pledged property remains in the hands of the pledgee or the appointed third party until the debt is satisfied (whereby it is to be noted that pledges on a "commercial business" are not possessory pledges), and the pledgor may not dispose of the goods pledged without the consent of the pledgee. As a general rule (regarding possessory pledges), any transfer of the pledged good by the pledgor to a third person shall not affect the rights of the pledgee to detain the property pledged until such time as the debt is discharged.

In case the ownership of a moveable item (sold in the course of a commercial transaction) is retained by the seller pending the payment of the full purchase price, the condition related to the retention of title may not apply towards the third party unless agreed to in writing. The purchaser may not dispose of the item (sold under retention of title) before settlement of all installments, save where the seller agrees otherwise in writing. Any disposal by the purchaser in violation of this shall not apply to the seller, unless the third party proves his good faith, in which case the remaining installments shall become due.

As a general rule, if a thing hired is sold without the consent of the lessee, the sale shall be effective between the seller and the purchaser, but shall not affect the rights of the lessee. If the lessee consents to or affirms the sale, the sale shall be effective as against him, and he shall be bound to deliver the leased property, unless he has paid the rent in advance, in which case he has the right to retain it until he recovers the equivalent of the rent in respect of the balance of the period for which he has not had the enjoyment of the leased property.

C. Real Property

1. Characteristics as to:

a) Language of Documentation. Regarding the transfer of real property, the sale and purchase agreement may be drafted in English or any other language or bilingually. However, since the purchase agreement/transfer deed must be registered with the Land Department of the respective Emirate and such registry only accepts documents in the Arabic language, the original document must either be drafted in Arabic or bilingually, or, if in any other language, translated by a certified local Arabic translator, such translation to be subject to attestation by the Ministry of Justice.

b) Form of Documentation. Unlike in other jurisdictions, the sale and purchase agreement regarding real estate does not necessarily require a specific form under the law of the U.A.E. In practice, a written agreement is sufficient to bind both parties.

However, for the transfer of the real estate to be effective vis-à-vis third parties, the transfer then has to be registered with the Land Department of the respective Emirate, which then records the title. Execution of the sale and purchase agreement outside the U.A.E. as well as signing in counterparts is, in practice, possible, provided they are notarized and legalized by the U.A.E. embassy in the country of origin and attested by the U.A.E. Ministry of Foreign Affairs.

c) Specification of Assets. The real estate to be transferred must be adequately specified in the documents, either by way of detailed description or reference to an Annex or to the respective register title in the Land Department.

2. Administrative, Corporate and Other Approvals

The transfer of real property does, in general, not require any special governmental or administrative approvals under U.A.E. law. However, as mentioned earlier, the rights of foreign (other than U.A.E. or GCC) companies or individuals to acquire real estate might be subject to restrictions: They are granted the right to own a freehold interest, a right of usufruct or a long-term lease of up to 99 years only in certain specifically designated freehold areas. It should be noted that even companies incorporated in the U.A.E. or in any other GCC country that have foreign shareholders will not be considered a U.A.E. or GCC national for the purpose of owning real property outside the freehold areas.

In addition, special rules might apply in case the respective real estate is of public interest (e. g., strategic location, or certain resources, such as gas or oil), though these properties – at least in most cases – can only be owned by U.A.E. citizens anyway.

An approval by corporate bodies of either party is generally not required, but might be necessary, notably in the case the transferred real estate represents the core asset of a company's business, or if so provided in the party's articles of association.

In case the real property is subject to a pledge by way of security (mortgage), the pledgor may dispose of his real property that is pledged without the same affecting the rights of the pledgee.

3. Filing Requirements

The transfer of any real property requires registration with the Land Department of the respective Emirate in which the real estate object is located. The purchase and sale agreement typically provides for the seller to file for the registration of the transfer of freehold title to the purchaser with the Land Department, upon receipt of the last installment of the purchase price. Under the current regulations, the Department charges a fee of 1% of the purchase price from each party.

Special rules can apply in case of the sale and purchase of real estate units that are still under construction ("off plan"). In Dubai, for example, a recent law regulating the Interim Real Estate Register in the Emirate of Dubai (2008), as amended (2009), provides for formal requirements (e. g., registration of any disposal off-plan with the Interim Real Estate Register maintained by the Land Department, otherwise such disposal shall be void), and stipulates specific rights and obligations of the parties (e. g., detailed rules on the termination and compensation rights of developers in case of default of purchaser).

As a general remark, the system of freehold property was enacted in Dubai in 2006. Since then, it has been continuously supplemented. Nonetheless, the regulations are still not conclusive and sometimes fairly ambiguous. So far, they cannot be considered as a comprehensive legal basis for the multiple issues arising in the context of freehold ownership. As such, there are a number of grey areas where definite answers cannot be provided. In view of this new ownership model, one needs to bear in mind that neither the government and its executive bodies nor the local courts have been able to establish a common registration practice yet. It remains to be seen how the authorities will eventually deal with the practical and legal issues related to the freehold system. Such uncertainty must always be taken into consideration.

4. Automatic Transfer of Encumbrances

Although freehold owners are considered absolute owners, their rights will often be restricted by covenants or easements designed to protect the rights of neighbors and the public interest. These rights are not necessarily registered with the Land Department and, depending on their nature, e. g., whether they are open and evident or whether they have been created by simple permission, they might (not) remain if the real estate is being transferred to other owners without any alteration of their condition.

In addition, real estate may be subject to encumbrances (third parties' rights in rem), whereby the pledge by way of security (mortgage) is the most common form.

As between pledgee and pledgor, a pledgor may dispose of his real property that is pledged by way of security without it affecting the rights of the pledgee. In relation to non-contracting parties, a pledge shall only be effective as from the date of registration of the deed of pledge with the Land Department.

Neither an assignment of a pledge by way of security nor a waiver of the pledge are effective against third parties unless this is noted on the original pledge deed giving rise to the pledge, and the pledge is registered with the Land Department. Any pledge registered by way of security remains valid after the transfer of the real estate, and the pledgee will have the right to follow the pledged property as it is transferred and to obtain satisfaction of his debt, upon maturity, from whoever may be in possession of the property. However, the person in possession of the real estate pledged has, under certain conditions, the right to pay the debt covered by the pledge, to disencumber the property and to intervene in any sale by auction.

The U.A.E. Civil Code lists a number of events in which a pledge by way of security shall expire (e. g. if the pledgee waives the same). However, once the mortgage is registered and recorded with the Land Department, it will not be lifted unless the pledgee makes a formal application to deregister the mortgage. A recent law concerning mortgages in the Emirate of Dubai, for example, provides that the mortgage remains registered and recorded until full repayment of the underlying debt.

5. Automatic Transfer of Lease Agreements

With regard to real estate, the same rule applies as with regard to tangible assets (see above, under B, 4). Therefore, if the real property is sold without the consent of the lessee, the sale shall be effective between the seller and the purchaser, but shall not affect the rights of the lessee. If the lessee consents or affirms to the sale, the sale shall be effective as against him, and he shall be bound to deliver the thing hired, unless he has paid the rent in advance, in which case he has the right to retain the thing hired until he recovers the equivalent of the rent in respect of the balance of the period for which he has not had the enjoyment of the thing hired. Neither the purchaser nor the tenant is granted an extra-ordinary termination right under law due to the transfer.

It should be noted that, in certain Emirates, including the Emirate of Dubai, for a long-term lease on real property to be effective, the lease agreement will also have to be registered with the Land Department. Similarly, certain Emirates require that any lease agreement for private and commercial properties must be registered with the Lands Department. For example, the Dubai Tenancy Law (2007) applies to all leased properties in Dubai (for commercial, professional or residential purposes, with limited exceptions) and requires that all lease agreements shall be in writing and registered with the Real Estate Regulatory Agency (at the Dubai Land Department). Judicial bodies and governmental entities shall not consider any matter arising from a lease agreement that has not been registered in accordance with the law.

D. Contracts

1. Characteristics as to:

a) Language of Documentation. Regarding the transfer of contracts, the law (which only stipulates rules regarding the assumption of debts) does not explicitly provide for such possibility. However, in practice, such transfers have been executed in the past and been held valid and enforceable, provided that the other party to the respective contracts consents to the transfer and the transfer agreements comply with the general provisions regarding contracts.

The transfer documents may be drafted in every language (also bilingually), whereby English and Arabic are certainly preferable. Unless there is a specific need for registration with a local authority (such as transfer of (long term) lease agreements regarding real property with the Land Department), there is no need for a (certified) Arabic translation.

b) Form of Documentation. The transfer of contracts may be made in writing or orally and may be executed at any place. For reasons of evidence, however, it is always advisable to execute a written transfer agreement. A specific form will also be required if the (transferred) contract is subject to a specific form or registration requirement, such as, for example, transfer of a (long-term) lease agreement (registration and written form). Signing in counterparts is generally possible.

c) Specification of Contracts. The requirement of specification also applies to the transfer of contracts, i.e. the parties to the transfer agreement shall agree on the essential elements of the transfer and the contracts must be specified so that they are defined or at least capable of being defined. A general description is only sufficient, if the subject of transfer under the contract can be clearly identified and distinguished from other contracts. It is therefore advisable to create and refer to annexes to the transfer agreement that either enclose the respective contracts in copy or that describe the respective contracts in detail, specifying parties, date and subject of the contract.

2. Administrative, Corporate and Other Approvals

The transfer of contracts generally does not require special governmental or administrative approvals. In accordance with the general rule – see below - the assignment of contracts involving governmental authorities (e. g., public tenders) nearly always requires the approval of the government. The approval of any corporate bodies regarding the seller and/or purchaser is generally not required, unless, for example, such condition is provided in the respective party's articles of association, or the affected contracts can be deemed core assets of the company's business.

The general rule regarding the transfer of debts under U.A.E. law also applies to contracts. The transfer is not valid unless the other party of the contract consents to it. With respect to transfer of ownership of a "commercial business," the law has simplified the procedure of seeking the consent of every third party that is party to contracts that relate to the "commercial business" by stipulating a transfer by virtue of law and a right of every party to such contracts to request cancellation (of such disposal) within a certain period, and provided he has reason to justify such cancellation and follows the statutory rules to effect it.

In practice, the third party's consent becomes particularly relevant as regards the transfer of employees or lease contracts: In most cases, the consent of the former employer is required in order to obtain the statutory employment permits and residence visa; and the transfer of a lease requires the consent of the landlord.

3. Automatic Transfer of Contracts (Other than Lease and Employment Agreements)

Notwithstanding special rules regarding the transfer of trade names, in the case of the transfer of ownership of a "commercial business", the purchaser shall, by virtue of law, subrogate the seller in all the rights and obligations arising from the contracts related to the "commercial business", unless agreed otherwise or unless the respective contract is entered into on the basis of personal considerations. However, any third person who is party to these contracts may request the cancellation of the disposal within a certain time period and provided he has reason to justify such cancellation. Also, insurance contracts may automatically transfer to the purchaser unless such insurance contract was based on personal consideration.

4. Filing Requirements

In cases when the contract has to be filed with public authorities (e. g., Land Department) or notified to any other agency, the transfer of such contract is generally also subject to such filing, registration or notification obligation.

5. Treatment of Existing Contractual Claims and Obligations

In the event of an assigned contract, the respective claims and/or obligations under such contract do automatically transfer to the new party (purchaser) even if such contract is not or not completely fulfilled on the part of the seller, subject always, however, to the required consent of the other party of the contract (see above), except where the transfer agreement provides otherwise. It is therefore advisable for the purchaser and customary in practice to address the issue of contracts that might not or not fully be fulfilled on the part of the seller in the respective transfer agreements, subject to negotiation, e. g., through adjustment of the purchase price, indemnification clause, representations and warranties, etc.

In case of the transfer of ownership of a "commercial business" (notwithstanding special rules as for the transfer of trade name) regarding any debts arising prior to the notification of the disposal, the purchaser shall fix a date for the creditors to submit a statement of their debts for settlement. The purchaser shall then remain liable for those debts, for which the creditors submit a statement within a certain period, and shall be released of any debts regarding which the creditors do not produce such statement in due time. The seller shall in any case remain liable for the debts related to the commercial business that have accrued prior to the notification of the disposal unless he is discharged therefrom by the creditors.

6. Warranty Claims Resulting from Events prior to Transfer

In principle, the transfer of a contract also comprises the transfer of any secondary rights and obligations under such contract due to a breach of contract, even if such breach occurred prior to the transfer of the assets affected. Therefore, if the consent of the other party is not limited in this regard and if the transfer agreements do not provide otherwise, the other party to the contract has the right and obligation to raise any warranty claims resulting from deficiencies of goods or services, even if these have been delivered before the transfer, against the new party (i. e. purchaser). Usually, such issue is dealt with in the transfer agreements, whereby the solution might take different forms (see above). In the case of the transfer of a "commercial business", as outlined above, it should be noted that the purchaser shall become liable for the debts if the creditors of such debts submit a statement thereof within a certain period, and the seller shall remain liable for the debts related to the commercial business that have arisen prior to the notification of the disposal to the creditors of such debt, unless he is discharged hereof by the creditors.

E. IP Rights

1. Characteristic of Intellectual Property Rights (e. g., Trademarks, Patents, Utility Models, Domain Names) ("*IP Rights*") as to:

a) Language of Documentation. The sale and transfer documents regarding IP Rights may be drafted in every language. In case of registered IP Rights (e.g., trademarks, patents, design patents, domain names) a certified Arabic translation and notarization by a notary public in the U.A.E. or, in the case of a notarization by a foreign notary public, legalization by the competent U.A.E. embassy and the U.A.E. Ministry of Foreign Affairs are required. Bilingual documents are permitted.

b) Form of Documentation. The transfer of IP Rights should be in writing and attested to by a notary public and should show details of the applicable period, purpose and territory. The sale and transfer documents may be executed outside the U.A.E., provided they are notarized and legalized (see E, 1, a above). Signing in counterparts is possible, but a joint signing on the same document is advisable. Certain applications might require the use of a specific pre-printed form (as issued by the respective authority).

Transfer of ownership of a "commercial business" might be deemed to include those intellectual property rights of the seller that can be considered necessary elements for the commercial activity (unless the parties specifically agree otherwise). Nevertheless, for the transfer to be effective vis-à-vis third parties, the parties have to file the relevant registrations. However, regarding the trade name of the seller, the law provides that, unless the parties agree otherwise, the transfer of a "commercial business" shall not include the transfer of the trade name.

c) Specification of IP Rights. Considering that the transfer of IP Rights is subject to certain registration requirements and each transfer of trademarks, etc., has to be filed separately with the authorities (see below E, 3), it is preferable to have a separate agreement for each IP Right with a distinct description of the specific right. In practice, the filing of a general sale and transfer agreement, including all relevant IP Rights, might prove difficult.

2. Administrative, Corporate and Other Approvals

Apart from registration requirements (see below E, 3), the transfer of IP Rights as such does not require special governmental or administrative approvals. An approval by corporate bodies of either party is generally not required, but might be necessary, notably in the event the transferred IP Rights represent core assets of the company's business, or if so provided in the party's articles of association. In case the IP Rights are subject to registration requirements, a pledge thereon has to be registered as well to be effective vis-à-vis third parties. Therefore, the pledgor may dispose of his registered IP Right which is pledged, however, without the same affecting the rights of the pledgee.

3. Filing Requirements

The change of ownership requires filing with the relevant public registers, for instance, in case of trademarks with the Department of Commercial Registration at the Ministry of Economy, and, in case of patents, with the Department of Industrial Property and Design Patents at the Ministry of Finance and Industry. The transfer will only be effective towards third parties from the date of entry into the register.

Unlike trademarks and patents, the protection of a copyright does not require any deposit with the authorities. However, such registration with the relevant authorities would facilitate the burden of proof in the case of dispute and legal proceedings. Also, only registered material can be printed, published and circulated on a commercial basis.

4. Applicable International (Multilateral) Agreements or Treaties

As a member of the World Trade Organization (**"WTO"**), the U.A.E. is obliged to comply with the Agreement on Trade-Related Aspects of Intellectual Property Rights (**"TRIPS"**), stipulating the minimum standards for the protection of intellectual property for all WTO signatories.

The U.A.E. is also member of the World Intellectual Property Organization (**"WIPO"**) and contracting party to the following WIPO-administered international treaties:

- The Berne Convention for the Protection of Literary and Artistic Works (2004)
- The Paris Convention for the Protection of Industrial Property (1996)
- The Patent Cooperation Treaty (PCT) (1999)
- The Rome Convention for the Protection of Performers, Producers of Phonograms and Broadcasting Organizations (2005)
- The WIPO Copyright Treaty (2004)
- The WIPO Performances and Phonograms Treaty (2005)

F. Receivables

1. Characteristics as to:

a) Language of Documentation. The Civil Code generally does not explicitly provide for the possibility to assign any obligatory rights vis-à-vis third parties. However, in practice, such assignment has been executed and been held valid, provided that the debtor consents hereto (see below).

The transfer documents regarding receivables may be drafted in English, bilingual or any other language. Unless there is a specific registration requirement, there is no need for an Arabic translation.

Generally, special rules might apply to securities with regard to the rights as certified in the securities documents. However, the following outline focuses on the general rules with regards to receivables under U.A.E. law.

b) Form of Documentation. In general, the transfer of receivables may be made in writing or orally and may be executed at any place. For evidentiary purposes, however, it is always advisable to execute a written transfer agreement. A specific form will also be required if the (transferred) receivable is subject to a specific form or registration requirement (see F, 3 below).

c) Specification of Receivables. The general requirement of specification also applies to the transfer of receivables, which means that the parties of the transfer agreement will agree on the essential elements of the transfer and the receivables must be specified so that they are defined or at least capable of being defined. A general description is only sufficient if the respective receivables subject of transfer can thereby be clearly identified and distinguished from other receivables. It is therefore advisable to refer and create annexes to the transfer agreement that either enclose the documents proving the receivables in copy or that list and describe the respective receivables in detail, specifying parties, the subject matter and the outstanding amount of the receivables.

2. Administrative, Corporate and Other Approvals

The transfer of receivables generally does not require special governmental or administrative approvals, or the approval of any corporate bodies with respect to the seller and/or purchaser, unless provided in the respective party's articles of association. However, the assignment of receivables accrued under contracts involving public authorities requires the consent of the competent governmental bodies.

The general rule regarding the transfer of debts under U.A.E. law is also applied to the transfer of receivables, which means that such transfer is not valid unless the other party to the contract consents hereto (in this case the debtor). Without such consent, the transfer is invalid. To the extent that the receivables can be considered a right arising from contracts related to a "commercial business", the rules regarding the transfer of contracts within the transfer of ownership of a commercial business apply.

In case of certain types of receivables, the transfer might also have to be registered with certain authorities.

3. Filing Requirements

Where the document giving rise to the receivable has to be filed, notified or registered with public authorities, the transfer of such receivable is generally also subject to such filing, registration or notification obligation.

G. Liabilities

1. Characteristics as to:

a) Language of Documentation. The transfer documents regarding liabilities may be drafted in English, bilingually or in any other language. Unless there is a specific need for registration, notification or filing with any public authority or agency, a (certified) Arabic translation is not required.

b) Form of Documentation. In general, the transfer of liabilities may be made in writing or orally and may be executed at any place. For reasons of evidence, however, it is always advisable to execute a written transfer agreement. A specific form will also be required if the (transferred) liability is subject to a specific form or registration requirement. Signing in counterparts is possible.

c) Specification of Liabilities. In addition to the general rule of specification (see above), the U.A.E. Civil Code stipulates certain conditions for an assignment of a debt to be valid. Among others, the law requires that the property transferred must be a known debt capable of being satisfied; an assignment must not be dependent on a condition other than an appropriate or customary condition, nor must any future contract be dependent on it; the performance (of the assignment) must not be deferred to an unknown future date; and it (the assignment) must be limited in time to a specific time limit.

2. Administrative, Corporate and Other Approvals

In general, the assignment of a debt requires an agreement between transferor and transferee and the consent of the creditor. The assignment shall be void if one of the necessary conditions is not present and the debt shall revert back to the transferor.

Otherwise, the transfer of liabilities does not require special governmental or administrative approvals, and the approval of any corporate bodies regarding the seller and/or purchaser is generally not required.

In case of the transfer of ownership of a "commercial business", the procedure to notify and receive consent from the creditors has been simplified by law: in principle, the purchaser shall, by virtue of the law, subrogate the seller in all the rights and obligations arising from the contracts related to the "commercial business" (unless agreed otherwise or unless the respective contract is entered into on the basis of personal considerations). However, any third person who is party to these contracts may request the cancellation of the disposal within a certain time period and provided he has reason to justify such cancellation. As regards debts of the seller that have arisen prior to the notification of the disposal, the purchaser shall only be liable for those debts related to the business for which the respective creditors submitted a statement within the prescribed period upon notification of the sale in two Arabic daily newspapers, and shall be released of any debts regarding which the creditors do not produce a statement within such period. In any case, the seller shall remain liable for the debts related to the "commercial business" and that have accrued prior to the notification of the disposal (unless discharged by the creditors). If the trade name, however, is transferred as well, any person to whom the ownership of a trade name is transferred, following the transfer of the title to a "commercial business", shall subrogate his predecessor in the rights and obligations accrued under the said trade name. An agreement to the contrary shall not apply to third parties, except from the date of its entry in the commercial register and the notice served to the concerned parties to that effect.

3. Filing Requirements

In general, the transfer of liabilities does not per se require special filings with public authorities or registers or databases. However, in cases when the document giving rise to the liability has to be filed, notified or registered with public authorities, the transfer of such liability will generally also be subject to such filing, registration or notification obligation. In addition to the rules regarding the consent of the creditor (see above), generally, the creditor shall be notified of the actual transfer; for example, the transfer of debt resulting from a loan would have to be filed with the bank.

4. Purchaser's Liability for:

a) Tax Obligations. To the rather limited extent that U.A.E. law does impose taxes on assets, for example, a stamp duty on transfer of freehold property, the purchaser of the respective assets is rather unlikely to be held liable for those tax obligations related to the assets for periods prior to the acquisition, though, in practice, the authorities may decide otherwise.

b) Environmental Contamination. Environmental legislation in the U.A.E. is still relatively weak though its practical importance is expected to increase. There is no law on the transfer of liabilities from one owner of the real estate to the next with regard to contaminated land. However, as a general rule, if land is purchased, environmental liabilities usually pass with the land (even if they relate to periods prior to the acquisition), although a new owner may have the right to file claims against an old owner under the general provisions of law. It is, however, possible to use an environmental indemnity clause in a contract to limit exposure for actual or potential environment-related liabilities. Vis-à-vis the authorities, such contractual clause is, however, irrelevant. The authorities may hold the new owner liable, although, in certain cases, more than one person (the owner as well as the polluter) can be held responsible for contamination under U.A.E. public law.

c) Products Sold or Services Rendered by the Seller to Third Parties. The liability of the purchaser for products sold or services rendered by the seller to third parties depends on the structure and subject of the actual acquisition. If the acquisition takes the form of a share deal, the entity that delivered the goods or performed the services remains the same and is, as such, liable for any defects and deficiencies. In case of an asset deal, the purchaser will only become liable vis-à-vis a third party to the extent that the respective contract with the third party or the respective liabilities are validly being transferred from the seller to the purchaser. As a general rule, the valid transfer of a contract also extends to the secondary duties even if the respective performance or delivery relates to a period before the acquisition. However, if the acquisition does not comprise the transfer of the contract or the specific liability, the purchaser does not become liable only due to the fact that he acquired assets from the seller that were involved in the delivery of deficient goods or performance of deficient services. Such liability then remains obligatory between the contracting parties, unless the purchaser himself becomes liable under the general provisions of the civil law for any breach of law or contract. Special rules apply to the transfer of ownership of a "commercial business" regarding the transfer of contracts and the seller's and purchaser's (possibly joint) liability for debts accrued prior to the notification of the disposal (see above).

5. Automatic Transfer of Other Liabilities

As outlined under G, 2 above, in case of the transfer of ownership of a "commercial business" as defined under U.A.E. law, the seller shall remain liable for any debts related to the "commercial business" that have arisen before notification of the transfer (unless he is discharged by the creditors), and the purchaser shall be (jointly) liable for those debts, regarding which the creditors submitted a statement within the prescribed period after notification. The purchaser shall not become liable for the obligations of his predecessor if the transfer of title of "commercial business" does not include the trade name, unless there is an agreement to the contrary entered into the commercial register. However, any person to whom the ownership of a trade name is transferred, following the transfer of the title to a "commercial business", shall subrogate his predecessor in the rights and obligations accrued under such trade name. Any agreement to the contrary shall not apply to third parties, except when entered into the commercial register and a notice is served to the concerned parties to that effect. Regarding the automatic transfer of contracts in case of the transfer of ownership of "commercial business", please see above.

6. Contractual Protection as to 4 and 5 above

U.A.E. law does, in general, allow for the contractual agreement of indemnification clauses. Such clauses may not reduce the rights of a third party or the public sector, so that the contractual agreement may stipulate a right of recourse of the purchaser against the seller or the claim of the purchaser that the seller shall hold him harmless. However, such clause cannot limit the liability claims of the third party (private and/or public) according to the general rules.

H. Employees

1. Transfer of Employees

U.A.E. law does not regulate the specific case of transfer of employment agreements in an asset transfer. However, the general rules with regard to the automatic transfer of contracts in case of transfer of "commercial business" can, in principle, also apply with respect to employment agreements. In other words, to the extent that the respective employment agreements can be considered "contracts related to the commercial business", the employment agreement will automatically be transfered from the seller to the purchaser and bind the purchaser to the same terms and conditions, unless it was agreed otherwise or unless the respective employment agreement was entered into on basis of personal considerations. It may be assumed that certain service agreements with managers might qualify as entered into on the basis of personal considerations, so that, in these cases, there will not be an automatic transfer, though this will have to be examined on a case by case basis. However, according to the general rule regarding the transfer of "commercial business", the employees, as the second party to these contracts, have a right of cancellation of the disposal within a certain time period, provided they have reason to justify such cancellation. The jurisprudence in the U.A.E. on the application of these general rules on employment agreements has not been clearly developed yet, so that it is difficult to predict what may be considered as sufficient in this regard.

Regarding any outstanding debts vis-à-vis the employees at the time of the disposal of the "commercial business", the general rule applies such that the purchaser shall become (jointly) liable for those debts related to the business for which the respective creditors (employees in this case) submitted a statement within the prescribed period upon notification of the sale in two Arabic daily newspapers, and shall be released of any debts regarding which the creditors (here: employees) do not produce a statement within such period, whereby, if the trade name is transferred as well, special rules might apply.

In practice, in case of any transfer of employment agreements from seller to purchaser (whether by virtue of law or by the parties' agreement), it is important to ensure (also with the relevant authorities) that the residence visa and employment permits (which are usually tied to a specific employer) are validly being transferred to the new employer.

2. Approval of Works Council, Trade Union or Other Institutions

U.A.E. labor law does not provide for any works councils, labor agencies, trade unions or other institutions.

3. Contractual Protection as to Labor Issues

Due to the current specialized work force shortage in the U.A.E., it might be in the purchaser's interest to insist in contractual guarantees that the relevant staff be transferred and to reserve cancellation (or other) rights if this will not be the case (for example, due to the employee's cancellation in case of automatic transfer under the rules regarding the transfer of "commercial business", or due to the lack of the employee's consent as required under the general rules of the Civil Code).

I. Tax Implications

1. Value Added Tax

Dubai, and some other Emirates, impose taxes on some goods and services (including sales of alcoholic beverages, hotel and restaurant bills, and residential leases). However, there is no general sales tax in the U.A.E., although there are legislative plans to introduce a VAT in the near future.

2. Real Property Transfer Tax

The U.A.E. does not impose tax on acquisitions, sales or transfers of real estate, nor does it impose any other real estate or other property tax, incremental value tax, tax on sale profits, or tax on transactions.

However, the Land Department of the respective Emirate where the real property is located charges certain registration fees for the respective transfer (approximately 1% of the purchase price for seller and purchaser each).

3. Other Tax Issues

In practice, the U.A.E. does not impose any personal income taxes, nor does it require any social security contributions for non-U.A.E. national employees. No corporate income tax is imposed on the Federal or Emirate level, except for branches of foreign banks and petrochemical/gas industry. Though tax laws are in place, they are momentarily not enforced. The U.A.E. does not impose taxes on dividends (paid or received), interest payments or royalty payments.

It is also to be noted that the U.A.E. is party to over 40 tax treaties.

J. Bankruptcy Law

1. Challenge of Asset Transfer in Case of Insolvency

According to the U.A.E. bankruptcy rules for traders or other persons who carry out commercial activities, it is only upon issuance of the bankruptcy judgment that the bankrupt entity shall be prevented from operating and disposing of its properties, but without prejudice to its right to take all necessary precautions to preserve and protect its money or property. Any disposals made by it on the day on which the bankruptcy statement has been rendered shall be deemed to have occurred thereafter, except for taking necessary measures to safeguard rights and except as applicable to certain groups of properties.

However, all acts of disposal by the bankrupt entity (if such acts are done by the debtor after suspension of payment), may be adjudged inexecutable against the group of creditors, if such act is harmful to them, and if the disposee was aware at the time of its occurrence that the bankrupt entity has stopped payment. In this case, the group of creditors may file a case for redemption. Also, the rights of mortgage or lien, levied on the debtor's property may be adjudged invalid against the group of creditors if a record thereof has been made after the date of payment stopping.

If an act of disposal is adjudged to be invalid towards the group of creditors, the disposee is obliged to return to the bankrupt entity what was obtained under the disposal, and has the right to claim back what was given to the bankrupt entity or (if that does not exist anymore in the bankruptcy) to make a claim against the group of creditors for the benefit which has accrued from such disposal, and shall join the bankruptcy as an ordinary creditor with respect to any excess thereof. The trustee in bankruptcy shall only apply for the invalidity of the debtor's disposal towards the group of creditors if the disposal occurs before the bankruptcy judgment has been issued, in accordance with the rules set forth in the respective law. It follows from the judgment of invalidity of the disposal that it shall be rendered ineffective for all the creditors whether their rights have been ensued before or after the disposal. A case brought by the trustee against a third party shall not be heard after six months from the day when the bankruptcy judgment becomes effective. In general, actions arising from implementing the rules (as set out above) shall not be heard after the lapse of two years from the bankruptcy judgment.

In general, any person may recover from the bankruptcy particular things to which his title is established at the time when the bankruptcy is declared. If a sale contract is terminated either by judgment or in accordance with the contract before the purchaser's declaration of bankruptcy has been adjudicated, the seller may recover the goods. If the purchaser is declared bankrupt before the payment of the price, and the goods are still held with the seller, the latter may retain them. In all cases, however, the trustee (with the court's permission) has the right to fully implement the sales contract, and demand the goods to be delivered, provided he pays to the seller the agreed upon price. Except where it is a "commercial business" transfer, if the purchaser is declared bankrupt before the payment of the price and after the goods are taken into his stores, the seller may not apply for termination of the sale or recovery of the goods, and his right of lien shall be forfeited.

In general, the declaration of bankruptcy shall not lead to the termination of the contracts binding on both sides, of which the bankrupt is a party, except where they are based on personal considerations. If the trustee in bankruptcy fails to perform the contract, the other party may apply for termination (whereby any decision taken by the trustee in respect of the contract shall be brought before the judge), and the contracting party may join the bankruptcy proceedings as an ordinary creditor in the compensation resulting from the termination.

2. Acquisition of Assets that are Subject to Insolvency Proceedings

The properties of the bankruptcy may not be sold during the period of "preliminary proceedings". However, upon request of the trustee in special cases, the judge of bankruptcy may permit the sale, whereby the controller must be notified or his opinion needs to be obtained before such permission can be issued. The sale of movables shall be affected as indicated by the judge. The sale of real property shall follow the proceedings under the Civil Procedures Law. Special rules apply for the continuing operation of a trading store by a person appointed by the trustee.

K. Timing and Costs

1. Timeframe of Asset Transfer

The timeframes applicable to the sale/acquisition of a business by way of an asset deal (taking into account the proceedings for registration, authorization, notarization, etc.) can vary widely depending on the kind of assets, the structure of the deal, the parties' identities and nationalities, the specific contract documents, and the scope of closing procedures. In general, there are no statutory rules for certain (minimum/maximum) periods.

2. Costs of Asset Transfer

Apart from the fee to be paid to the Land Department (see above) which is calculated on the basis of the purchase price of the real property, fees for notarization of certain documents are relatively low (for example, the notarization of a contract is charged at a rate of 0.25% of the value of the contract, whereby the fee may not be more than a maximum of AED 10,000) and therefore do not constitute a major issue from an economic perspective.

L. Miscellaneous

1. Choice of Foreign Law

U.A.E. law provides for certain limitations regarding the agreement on the governing law of a contract. Legally speaking, if the parties are residents in of the same state, form and substance of the contractual obligations shall be governed by the law of the state in which they are both residents (despite any other contractual agreement). If they are residents in different states, however, the parties may agree on the governing law. In the absence of such (explicit or implicit agreement), the governing law shall be the law of the state in which the contract was concluded. However, such contractual agreement on the governing law does not affect (i) contracts over real property, which (by virtue of law) are governed by the law of the place in which the real property is situated, nor (ii) the question of possession, ownership or any other rights over property as well as the question whether the property is moveable or real property, which (by virtue of law) shall be governed by the lex situs (i.e. the law of the state in which the property is located in case of real property) or the law of the place in which the property is located at the time when the cause resulting in the acquisition or loss of possession, ownership or any other right over the property arose in case of movables).

In addition to the above limitations to selecting a governing law, the collision rules under U.A.E. law stipulate further restrictions, among others, U.A.E. courts shall not apply the provisions of any foreign law if such provisions are contrary to the Islamic *Shari'a*, public order or morals in the United Arab Emirates. Since the principles of *Shari'a* and the public order might be subject to interpretation by the courts, it is difficult to predict in certain cases whether a U.A.E. court will in effect apply a specific foreign provision.

2. (International) Arbitration, Choice of Venue

According to the U.A.E. Civil Procedure Code, parties to a contract may generally stipulate that any dispute arising between them in respect of the performance of a particular contract shall be referred to arbitration, in which case no suit may be filed before the courts. If, however, one of the parties files a suit, irrespective of the arbitration provision, and the other party does not object to such filing at the first hearing, the suit may be considered, and in such case, the arbitration provision shall be deemed cancelled.

In addition, the United Arab Emirates ratified in 2006 its accession to the New York Convention on the Recognition and Enforcement of Foreign Arbitral Awards (1958) ("**New York Convention**"). As such, the U.A.E. courts, when seized of an action in a matter in respect of which the parties have made an agreement on arbitration, shall (at the request of one of the parties) refer the parties to arbitration (unless the court finds the agreement null and void, inoperative or incapable of being performed). Also, under the New York Convention, the U.A.E. courts are obliged to recognize any arbitral awards made in any state as binding and enforce them in accordance with the rules of procedure of the territory where the award is relied upon, under the conditions as laid down in the Convention.

However, it has not yet been clearly developed by U.A.E. jurisdiction whether a U.A.E. court facing an enforcement request will directly apply the New York Convention (and make enforcement proceedings of foreign arbitral awards in the U.A.E. much easier) or whether it will continue applying the enforcement rules under the U.A.E. Civil Procedure Law, which might, in practice, complicate the proceedings: though the Civil Procedure Code stipulates, in theory, that foreign judgments (from certain jurisdictions) and foreign arbitral awards are enforceable in the U.A.E., it also requires that in order for an award to be enforced in the U.A.E. the court would have to determine that the original dispute was not subject to U.A.E. state court jurisdiction, whereby the Civil Procedures Law basically provides that the U.A.E. courts have competence to hear any actions filed against U.A.E. parties or against foreigners with domicile in the U.A.E. In addition, the U.A.E. Civil Procedure Code sets out that enforcement of an award is possible only if a U.A.E. award is equally enforceable in the country of origin of the award.

3. Other Distinctions, Characteristics

Particularly the current restrictions with regard to foreigners acquiring certain assets are noteworthy under U.A.E. law, which may be summarized as follows: a foreign company may only acquire up to 49% of shares in a mainland company in the U.A.E., and non-U.A.E. respectively non-GCC nationals may acquire freehold interest in real property only in specific designated areas, whereby the rules may vary from Emirate to Emirate.

M. Literature

Sabah M.A. Mahmoud, UAE Company Law and Practice, 3rd Edition, 1997

Mohamed Mahmoud, Commentary to the UAE Civil Transactions Act, 2nd Edition, 2005

Mohamed Mahmoud, Commentary to the UAE Commercial Transactions Act, 1st Edition, 2002

Nuri Khater Hamad, Rules of intellectual property – a comparative study between the Jordanian, UAE, and French law, 1st Edition, 2005

Adnan al-Sarhan, Commentary to the provisions of contracts in the UAE Civil Transactions Act. The first part: The Sales Contract. A comparative study between the Islamic jurisprudence and some civil laws (French, Egyptian, Iraqi, Jordanian), 1st Edition, 2005

United States of America

By *Marcel Valenta*

A. General Aspects

1. Asset Deal vs. Share Deal: Essential Considerations

The answer regarding the essential considerations for an asset deal versus a share deal obviously pertains to a scenario where a purchaser pursues the acquisition of all or substantially all of a selling entity's assets (as opposed to the acquisition of just a few specific assets), i.e., where the sale is not in the usual and regular course of the selling entity's business and where the transaction would have the same, or at least a similar, basic economic result as a statutory merger or a purchase of stocks.

Whether an asset acquisition is preferable over a merger or a stock sale depends in almost every case on the business objectives sought to be accomplished with the transaction - the legal form then follows the business substance.

If the selling entity is supposed to stay in business and to be left intact, the deal will almost always be structured as a reverse subsidiary merger or, sometimes, if the selling entity has only a few stockholders, as a stock sale. In a reverse subsidiary merger, the acquiring parent company P forms a merger subsidiary S which is merged into target T with T surviving the merger and continuing its legal existence as a subsidiary of P. T's stockholders will become stockholders of P and, typically regardless of the type of consideration used, the transaction will in all likelihood qualify as a tax-free reorganization under Section 368 of the Internal Revenue Code of 1986, as amended (the "**Code**"). No third-party consents to the transaction are generally necessary (although, on occasion, non-assignment language in third-party contracts is drafted to encompass reverse subsidiary mergers) and T continues to do business as T.

There are scenarios, however, where an asset acquisition is the superior choice of structure. From a corporate law perspective and the purchaser's point of view, the two main reasons to structure a transaction as an asset sale are the purchaser's wish to (i) avoid certain liabilities of the selling entity and "cherry-pick" its assets and/or (ii) avoid possible stockholder disapproval and the expense involved in providing notice to stockholders.

As for "cherry-picking" assets and the avoidance of liabilities, an asset acquisition allows the acquiring corporation a certain amount of freedom in tailoring the transaction according to its needs. It may not include some of the selling entity's assets in the acquisition and may contractually limit the liabilities it is willing to assume. Business reasons will be the key driver to these decisions and almost always will the selling entity's liabilities play the most important role in the structuring decision. If the selling entity has considerable unknown, contingent or undisclosed liabilities, an asset acquisition is generally the most efficient structure to shelter the acquiring corporation from such liabilities. There are limitations, however, to the purchaser's freedom to refuse taking on the selling entity's liabilities. Certain state tax laws, for example, allow authorities to follow assets to recover taxes owed by the seller even post-acquisition, i.e., when such assets already are in possession of and, by all legal means, owned by the purchaser. To give another example, certain state environmental laws may subject a purchaser to remediation obligations with respect to activities of a prior owner of real property even if the purchaser had nothing to do with such previous activities. In addition, there are also limitations to a purchaser's freedom to "cherry-pick" and exclude unwanted assets from the deal. To qualify as a tax-free reorganization under Section 368 of the Code, among other things, a purchaser will have to purchase "all or substantially all" of the selling entity's assets. The term has special meaning in tax law. As a rule of thumb and, as always, subject to possible future changes, the Internal Revenue Service has stated in advance rulings that the "all or substantially all" requirement is fulfilled if the purchaser ends up with 90% of the value of the selling entity's net assets and 70% of its gross assets upon consummation of the transaction.

The avoidance of possible stockholder disapproval is another reason why a purchaser might want to structure a deal as an asset acquisition. A merger or consolidation may require stockholder approval of each participating corporation. If a minority of the stockholders dissents, the dissenters may have dissenters' rights and may demand that the corporation exchanges their shares of stock for fair value. In an acquisition of all or substantially all of the selling entity's assets, generally, the stockholder approval of only the selling entity, but not of the purchaser, is required. On the purchaser's side, the consent of the purchaser's board of directors is generally sufficient. If it is not, and stockholder consent is also required for the acquiring corporation, the percentage necessary for the approval of an asset acquisition, at least in some states, is lower than the percentage necessary for the approval of a merger. Moreover, if the purchaser's consideration in an asset acquisition consists solely of cash and the net proceeds are distributed to selling entity's stockholders within a year of the consummation of the transaction, then some states deny dissenting minority stockholders the dissenters' rights they might otherwise have if the transaction were to be structured as a merger. But again, there are exceptions. Under the „de-facto merger doctrine" an asset sale is treated, for all legal purposes, like a statutory merger, and, accordingly, courts grant the selling entity's stockholders dissenters' rights, provided the economic and legal result of the contemplated asset sale would be more or less identical to the result that would be accomplished if the transaction were structured as a merger. Most often this will be the case, if the selling entity sells all or substantially all of its assets to the purchaser and then promptly dissolves upon the consummation of the transaction. However, there is a wide array of case law conditioning the applicability of the "de-facto merger doctrine" on different requirements. Therefore, if the parties wish to avoid having an asset sale treated as a "de-facto merger" a careful assessment of the circumstances underlying the contemplated transaction will be necessary.

This leaves the question why a seller would want to structure a deal as an asset acquisition. Rarely are sellers pressing to have the sale of an entire company consummated in form of an asset sale for pure corporate law reasons. Almost always would they be left behind having to deal with liabilities the purchaser did not agree to assume. From a selling stockholder's perspective, at least when the sale of an entire company is contemplated, a merger or a stock sale simply provides a cleaner cut; no liabilities are retained (except for possible indemnification rights which typically expire 12 to 18 months after closing of a transaction) and the business as a whole changes hands with nothing left back for the seller to be concerned about. The few instances where a seller might choose an asset sale as the preferred structure of choice are cases where it desires to retain and, possibly, continue to run a small portion of the selling entity's business upon consummation of the transaction or where it intends to rid itself of one of its business units or subsidiaries but driver for structuring such deals as asset sales are business reasons, not legal advantages inherent in the structure of an asset deal.

2. Distinction between Sale and Transfer in Rem

U.S. law does not distinguish between the obligation to transfer (sale) and the transfer itself with the same dogmatic rigor as some Continental European jurisdictions tend to do. This is not to say that U.S. law does not distinguish between an agreement to sell assets and the actual transfer of assets. The practical legal implications of how assets are sold in the U.S. and in Europe may be more similar then, than people initially would assume. In the simplest of transactions, an asset sale in the U.S. will be accomplished by three documents: (i) an asset purchase agreement ("**APA**") memorializing the parties' understanding of the terms and conditions based on which seller promises to sell and purchaser promises to purchase certain specified assets, (ii) a bill of sale conveying the selling entity's assets (items that would typically be shown on a balance sheet as having value, but not, for example contractual obligations) to purchaser in exchange for the purchase price at closing, and (iii) an assignment and assumption agreement assigning to purchaser seller's rights and obligations under those contracts that purchaser agreed to take on in the deal.

The process, thus, is bifurcated and consists of a signing and a subsequent closing (both can fall on the same date and can happen simultaneously if this is practical under the circumstances and the parties so wish). Consistent with this bifurcated approach, it is possible in the U.S. to consummate a large multi-jurisdictional asset transaction by memorializing the parties' basic understanding of the framework of the contemplated deal in the APA, while the transfer of specific assets is accomplished through separate local agreements in addition to the various other documents necessary for factually transferring the assets over to purchaser.

3. Regional Differences

Corporate law and, accordingly, the law governing asset acquisitions are matters of state law in the U.S. Throughout the last few decades, the corporate law of the State of Delaware has proven to be the most dominant and most influential body of corporate law among all fifty states. There are a number of reasons for this. Delaware corporate law is extraordinarily well-established and tends to be business-friendly. In addition, the most famous court in U.S. corporate law, Delaware's Chancery Court, focuses exclusively on corporate matters and is known for its speedy, consistent and well-argued decisions of high-profile corporate cases. Most of America's Fortune 500 companies are incorporated in Delaware and chances are better than not that an acquisition of the assets of a U.S. seller will be governed by Delaware law.

But despite Delaware's undisputable influence on U.S. corporate law in general, notable differences exist from state to state and, particularly, California and New York State are known for their elaborate and distinctive bodies of corporate law. Accordingly, the answers given here attempt to provide a general overview over U.S. law and are not specific to any state.

The foremost concern of state law distinctions in the context of asset sales probably is the question if and, if so, to which extent, a state has enacted so-called "bulk sales" laws. "Bulk sales" laws, once upon a time the law of the land in most states, were intended to prevent a seller from defrauding or evading creditors by transferring all or substantially all of its assets to another entity. "Bulk sales" laws in their strongest form, i.e., those which gave creditors far-reaching rights to pursue the purchaser of a debtor's assets, have been abolished in almost all of the states as a hindrance of the free flow of goods in a free market system. However, "bulk sales" laws remain in effect in some states, even if only in lesser forms. Under the Uniform Commercial Code ("**UCC**"), for example, which has been adopted in most states, a debtor must generally notify its creditors of a planned sale of all or substantially all of its assets. How "bulk sales" laws and creditor's rights impact a proposed asset transaction depends on the case in issue and may differ from state to state. Suffice it to say that it is almost always time well spent to carefully work through these issues before committing to an agreement for the sale of assets that in one way or another may be subject to the reach of the seller's creditors.

4. Acquisition by Foreigners

Generally, U.S. law does not impose restrictions on foreign entities contemplating to acquire assets in the U.S. The few exceptions are industry specific. Airlines operating out of the U.S., for example, cannot be under foreign control. The limitations imposed have recently come under political scrutiny and may become less stringent in the future, but currently, law forbids foreign citizens to own more than 25% of a U.S. domestic airline's voting stock, and operations must be under the "actual control" of U.S. citizens. Similar and, in most cases, more far-reaching restrictions exist for companies engaged with the U.S. military or if the transaction is otherwise a concern of national security. The so-called Exon-Florio Act, as amended, grants the President authority to block or suspend a merger, acquisition or takeover by a foreign entity if there is "credible evidence" that a "foreign interest exercising control might take action that threatens to impair the national security" and existing provisions of law do not provide "adequate and appropriate authority for the President to protect the national security in the matter before the President". The President has delegated this review process largely to the Committee on Foreign Investment in the United States, an inter-agency committee chaired by the Secretary of Treasury. An example for matters of national security rising to prominence as a national security debate and eventually preventing a transaction with a foreign entity is the DP World controversy which began in February 2006. The port management businesses in six major U.S. seaports were supposed to be sold to a company based in the United Arab Emirates, DP World. The deal, although initially consummated, was eventually reversed when DP World succumbed to the political pressure asserted by Congress selling the business to U.S. controlled American International Group.

5. Public Registers, Records and Databases

The United States does not have a central company register similar to the German *Handelsregister*, but there are other ways to obtain reliable information about a potential target company in the U.S., particularly if it is publicly-traded.

Publicly-traded companies are subject to an expansive disclosure regime. Under the oversight of the Securities and Exchange Commission ("**SEC**"), publicly-traded companies have to update and disclose detailed information about the business, including financial statements, periodically and need to report material new information as it arises. If a publicly-traded company, one of its business units or any of its subsidiaries is targeted for an asset acquisition, the information gathering process should always start at the SEC's webpage which features EDGAR, an Electronic Data-Gathering, Analysis, and Retrieval system. EDGAR contains every public filing of every publicly-traded company in the U.S. from 1996 through today and expands at the rate of more than 3,000 company filings per day (see: http://www.sec.gov/edgar/searchedgar/webusers.htm).

For private companies, there are a number of service providers offering "snapshots" or company profiles of almost every privately-held U.S.-company. Unlike the SEC's EDGAR which is for free, these services almost always come at a charge. A company may voluntarily provide information to these service providers and, depending on whether a company has in fact done so, the requested report may be more or less detailed and more or less helpful. Dun and Bradstreet at http://www.dnb.com/us/is one of the more well-known services in the U.S.

In addition to these sources for general information on a target business, there also are specialty databases from which to obtain specific information on a target. Legal counsel to a purchaser will routinely conduct lien searches and request a so-called "good standing certificate" from the Secretary of State of the target's state of incorporation. A lien search (also called a "UCC Search" because the law of secured transactions is governed by the UCC), while often helpful, does not have to be accurate. Creditors are free to publicly file a financing statement indicating that they have taken a lien on all or certain specified assets of a debtor as collateral. UCC filings are purely for notification purposes and, almost always, are obtained by a purchaser in the initial stages of a transaction to sort out if there are any potential red flags involving the target's ownership of the assets it purports to own and intends to sell. Whether the circumstances described in a filing are true, however, and whether a creditor has in fact a valid secured interest in the assets of a debtor is a different story and has to be assessed by requesting from the selling entity and reviewing the underlying documentation establishing the debt and the security interest during the due diligence process leading up to the transaction.

In response to a representation by selling entity that it is "in good standing" which is customarily included in almost every APA, legal counsel to a purchaser will typically request from the selling entity a "good standing certificate" issued by the Secretary of State of the selling entity's state of incorporation. But, again, the value of a good standing certificate is limited. Other than verifying that a company is properly in existence, that its articles of incorporation (called "certificate of incorporation" in Delaware) are properly filed and that its annual franchise taxes are properly paid (a minimum fee to maintain the good-standing status every year), it does not provide any further details or additional information.

6. Purchase Price Requirements

To determine the adequacy of a purchase price general contract law principles apply. Unlike in Continental Europe where offer and acceptance are sufficient to form a contract, under common law, in addition, both sides must provide consideration, i.e., they must incur a legal benefit as well as a legal detriment as a result of their bargained-for exchange. But courts will generally not inquire into the adequacy of the agreed-upon consideration and a "peppercorn," as a famous quote from old English jurisprudence states, may be enough. As such, the parties are free to agree on a price that they find mutually acceptable, bearing in mind that it at least should be worth a "peppercorn." Accordingly, peppercorn payments are sometimes used when a struggling company is sold. A failing company's liabilities will often exceed its assets and, as a result, its net worth will be negative. If a purchaser agrees to take over such a negative net-worth entity, the seller, in return, may agree to pay purchaser for taking on the company's excess liabilities. But, under common law, the purchaser must still make some payment, even if that payment is only one dollar, in order to establish that both sides have given consideration. In this sense then, there is a minimum purchase price requirement in the U.S., even if the required consideration need not be worth more than a peppercorn.

The freedom contract law provides is curtailed, however, by corporate law principles. In a sale of assets, as well as in any other corporate dealings, the board of directors and the majority stockholders must act in good faith, with fairness and for the benefit of the corporation. The majority stockholders of the selling entity must negotiate a fair price for the assets to be sold. If they do not, minority stockholders may seek the protection of federal and state courts, demand fair value for their shares and halt the closing of the transaction. This is particularly true, if majority stockholders stand to reap personal benefits from the transaction or otherwise oppress or "freeze out" minority interests.

Furthermore, U.S. tax law requires a proper allocation of the purchase price. From a federal tax perspective, a sale of the assets of a business is treated like a number of sales of individual assets. The purpose of adding a purchase price allocation provision to an APA is to assure that both purchaser and seller are consistent in their reporting of the transaction for tax purposes. In most asset transactions involving the sale of an entire business, the parties will have to comply with Section 1060 of the Code. Section 1060 requires both, purchaser and seller, to file IRS Form 8594, generally describing the allocation with their returns for the year in which there was a transfer of assets.

Allocating the purchase price often is an area of dispute between the parties because of the different tax effects an allocation may have. From a seller's perspective, the allocation determines how much gain, loss or income the seller will recognize as a result of the asset sale. For the purchaser, in contrast, the allocation will determine what value the assets will have on its books for tax and financial statement purposes, and this determination will affect if and how it can depreciate and amortize the purchase price against its income. In addition, other consequences may give rise to controversy. A substantial allocation to land to be sold, for example, may give rise to material real estate transfer taxes and may affect future ad valorem property taxes. Despite possible disputes though, the parties often file identical forms to decrease the likelihood that the IRS will scrutinize the transaction.

B. Tangible/Movable Assets

1. Characteristics as to:

a) Language of Documentation. It would be highly unlikely to have the sale of assets of a U.S. company in the U.S. be governed by anything other than an agreement in English just as it would be highly unlikely that courts in any of the fifty states would accept and defer to a legal document that is not drafted in English. To avoid any complications and not to jeopardize the enforceability of a contemplated transaction, the agreements for a U.S. asset sale should always be in English. It is possible to prepare legal documents in two or more languages with the caveat, however, that it should be explicitly provided that the English version governs the APA and other transfer documents exclusively.

b) Form of Documentation. Generally under the UCC, agreements for the sale of goods worth more than USD 500 or involving the sale of real estate, among others, are required to be in writing. Overall though, U.S. law is comparatively liberal in its requirements to form. Notarization typically is not necessary for the execution of the APA; it can be executed in a foreign jurisdiction and, if the parties so wish and provide, may be executed in counterparts. Specific conveyance documents for tangible assets do generally not require notarization.

c) Specification of Assets. U.S. law allows for a wide leverage in describing the assets to be transferred. From purely a legal perspective, general or generic descriptions work just as well as specifically listing the assets on schedules. In reality, however, both seller and purchaser will have a strong interest in precisely identifying the assets to be transferred and the assets excluded from the transaction.

Identifying the assets to be transferred and the liabilities to be assumed is not surprisingly then at the heart of almost every asset purchase transaction. The APA and the schedule of exceptions work in unison and serve as the tools for identifying the assets the purchaser will acquire. How these tools are used depends, among other things, on the amount of detail the parties desire, the nature of the assets involved and the status of the purchaser's due diligence at the time the APA is finalized.

A typical APA initially describes the assets to be acquired in a general way, followed by a categorization into various groupings, such as "all real property", "all inventories", "all accounts receivable", "all tangible personal property", etc. This general description is then further supplemented, to the extent appropriate, by reference to the schedule of exceptions to list or describe particular items within certain groupings. This method works well when the purchaser's due diligence is well under way at the time the APA is finalized and allows the parties to specify, for example, which particular contracts purchaser will acquire.

Alternatively, the parties might omit any specific identification or description and describe the acquired assets only by categorizing them into general groupings. However, if the parties choose such a general description for the acquired assets, they should pay particularly close attention to the definition of "Excluded Assets" and detail, preferably in specific lists, which assets are not going to be part of the deal.

The interplay between the section that lists acquired assets and the section that lists the excluded assets also requires close attention when drafting the APA. Customarily, APAs specifically provide that the listing of "Excluded Assets" takes priority over the listing of „Assets". Again then, particular care needs to be given to the listing of excluded assets because that list will control in any situation in which a particular asset could be both an asset and an excluded asset.

No matter what general approach is chosen, if there are specific assets that are of significant importance to the purchaser, the purchaser should always insist on specifically listing those assets instead of relying on an introductory "catchall" phrase or any "including" clause that lists assets of a similar type.

2. Administrative, Corporate and Other Approvals

The need for special governmental authorization typically arises in the context of an asset acquisition because immediate ownership of the assets changes hands (as opposed to ownership of the entity holding the assets changing hands, as would be the case in a reverse subsidiary merger or a stock sale). One of the representations and warranties in the APA will call for the selling entity's compliance with legal requirements and will require the selling entity to list all approvals and permits necessary to run the selling entity's business. The list of required governmental authorizations for the transaction and permits to run the selling entity's business varies from industry to industry and from business to business and can range from a simple local business permit to antitrust approval. Similarly, the required action can range from not having to do anything, to simply notifying a public authority of the transaction, to obtaining a specific consent from a public authority.

Obtaining antitrust approval under the Hart-Scott-Rodino Antitrust Improvements Act of 1976, as amended (so-called "HSR Filing"), frequently is the most critical of the required government authorizations. Companies are generally required to notify the Federal Trade Commission and the U.S. Department of Justice before completing transactions such as mergers and acquisitions, if the transaction affects commerce and if certain thresholds are met or exceeded. As of 2009, for example, a pre-filing is required if (1) (a) one of the parties has sales each year or assets of USD 130.3 million or more and the other party has sales or assets of USD 13 million or more and (b) the transaction is valued at USD 65.2 million or more; or (2) the value of the transaction is USD 260.7 million or more. Generally, after the pre-filing a 30-day waiting period ensues during which the authorities can require additional information and the transaction cannot be closed. The parties can request early termination of the 30-day period which typically is granted if the case at hand is fairly straightforward and on its face does not trigger any antitrust concerns.

As initially mentioned, on the seller side, the sale of all or substantially all of the assets of a selling entity typically requires approval of the selling entity's board of directors and its stockholders. The thresholds required for a quorum may vary, as may the thresholds for the votes necessary to approve a matter: generally though the majority of all shares outstanding and the majority of the members of the board will constitute a quorum, while the votes cast for a matter must outnumber the votes cast against it for approval. On the purchaser side, in most cases only the approval of the board of directors is necessary. However, depending on the applicable state laws, the size of the transaction and its implications for the purchaser, stockholder approval may, in addition, be necessary.

If either the selling or the acquiring company is publicly listed in the U.S. and depending on the size of the deal, both companies may also have to report the transaction with the SEC by filing a so-called Form 8-K on EDGAR.

Whether the approval of creditors is necessary to properly transfer encumbered assets, generally depends on the underlying contractual arrangement between the creditor and the debtor. Most often, a creditor will insist that its consent is necessary for encumbered assets to be transferred. Even if a creditor's consent was required but not obtained, the purchaser still takes ownership over the asset subject to the creditor's lien (or other encumbrance). In this scenario, a creditor would not only have a right against the asset now held by the purchaser, but also, on a contractual basis, against the breaching seller who promised to obtain a creditor's consent without then following through on that contractual promise.

In practice the parties will routinely address the problem of encumbered assets at the outset of a transaction by arranging that liens are paid off and removed prior to closing (unless the purchaser is assuming the related loans). The purchaser then receives the assets free and clear of any encumbrance. In addition, in a customary APA, a seller will have to represent and warrant that all assets sold and transferred are in fact free and clear of any encumbrance. Assets that are not will have to be listed on a schedule of exceptions. That way, the purchaser will have a clear picture of the seller's level of ownership over its assets and the extent to which there are encumbrances. If the seller breaches this representation, it will typically have to indemnify the purchaser for such a breach. However, the purchaser should be weary of a selling entity dissolving right after the sale of all or substantially all of its assets – with the selling entity gone or stripped of all its assets, the purchaser's indemnification rights may be worth little. An escrow arrangement will often be the proper way to address this problem.

3. Filing Requirements

The transfer of tangible assets does typically not require special filings with public authorities or registrations into public registers or databases.

4. Automatic Transfer of Encumbrances

The law of secured transactions is governed by Article 9 of the UCC. Article 9 disfavors the legal construct of retention of title on the theory that it hinders the free flow of goods in a free market. Instead, a creditor seller will have to step through the formal process of obtaining a security interest in the goods sold; yet, ownership of such goods, even if subject to an encumbrance, will transfer to the purchaser. Generally, encumbrances follow the assets automatically; however, a bona fide purchaser for value, i.e., someone who pays for the goods in the good-faith belief they were unencumbered, will take an asset free of the encumbrance. Yet, good faith cannot simply be claimed; it is negated by notice. Notice can be actual, if the seller informs the purchaser about the encumbrance, based on inquiry, if the purchaser finds out about the encumbrance during the due diligence process, or constructive, if seller's creditor has publicly filed a UCC-1 Financing Statement with the UCC Office or, depending on the state, the County Clerk in the state where the debtor is located. Most of the time will a purchaser be on notice of an encumbrance and almost never, in the context of acquisitions of companies which generally deal with sophisticated creditors, will a purchaser be able to claim bona fide purchaser status.

But again, in practice the parties will routinely address this problem at the outset of a transaction and make sure that liens are paid off and removed prior to closing.

C. Real Property

1. Characteristics as to:

a) Language of Documentation. Please refer to B, 1, a above. It is highly unlikely that U.S. courts would accept transfer documentation for real estate located in the U.S. in a language other than English. Accordingly, transfer documents should always be drafted in English. If bilingual agreements are used, it should be explicitly stated that the arrangement is exclusively governed by the English version.

b) Form of Documentation. Documents providing for the transfer of interests in real estate, except for the assignment of a lease of less than one year duration, need to be in written form. In addition, most of the documents will have to be notarized. In a typical asset deal involving real estate, the purchaser will ask the seller to provide a warranty deed to purchaser for each piece of real estate to be transferred.

A warranty deed contains a number of seller promises (that there are no encumbrances, other than those that have been previously disclosed; that seller will do whatever is necessary to pass title to purchaser, if seller omitted something required to pass valid title; that seller will protect the purchaser against anyone who comes along later and claims paramount title to the property, etc.); yet, at its core seller warrants to purchaser in a warranty deed that seller has good and valid title in the piece of property to be transferred. This is in contrast to a so-called "quitclaim deed" which does not profess that the seller has any title to the transferred estate. Thus, a purchaser will frequently request from seller a proper warranty deed. The warranty deed has to be notarized and is, upon delivery to purchaser at closing, recorded at the appropriate county clerk office in the state where the transferred property is located. Although recording the deed is technically not necessary to convey title, a diligent purchaser will always do so, if only to put the public on notice that it now owns the property.

In addition to a warranty deed, a purchaser will in most cases ask seller to also obtain a title insurance protecting the purchaser against any defects in the title that seller conveyed to purchaser. The purpose of the insurance is to provide purchaser with the possibility of recourse, particularly if defects surface subsequent to seller's dissolution which renders seller's promises in a warranty deed practically meaningless.

If real estate is subject to a mortgage, purchaser will frequently request that seller satisfy the mortgage and provide proof of satisfaction. The mortgagee, typically a bank, will execute a form called Satisfaction of Mortgage which will have to be notarized.

The transfer documents mentioned here, other than the APA (which can be executed in counterparts, if the parties so provide), are executed by the seller only. If executed outside the U.S. the required notarization will need to be legalized.

c) Specification of Assets. Like tangible assets, real estate can be described in general terms in the APA. The parties will want to assure, however, that there is no ambiguity as to which pieces of property are conveyed as part of the deal and, accordingly, typically press for a specific identification. Whether the APA itself should identify the real estate with specificity, is left to the parties. They may also defer to the warranty deeds to be delivered at closing as warranty deeds need to be sufficiently specific to unambiguously describe the real estate to be transferred.

2. Administrative, Corporate and Other Approvals

As long as the transfer of real estate is part of a sale of all or substantially all of a selling entity's assets, the answer to B, 2 above is fully applicable.

The transfer of a piece of real estate itself is generally not subject to governmental or administrative approvals (an example of an exception would again be the above-mentioned transfer of U.S. ports to a foreign-controlled entity). If the sale does not constitute a sale of all or substantially all of the business (as may be the case for a real estate investment company), stockholder approval will likely not be required on either the seller side or the purchaser side. Whether board approval is necessary depends on the respective parties' bylaws. Generally, if a transaction is below a certain threshold, officers are allowed to enter into the underlying agreements without board approval.

3. Filing Requirements

As mentioned, to accomplish the transfer of real estate, purchaser will request from seller a warranty deed. The warranty deed will have to be notarized and will, upon delivery to purchaser at closing, be recorded at the appropriate county clerk office in the state where the transferred property is located. Although recording the deed is technically not necessary to convey title, a diligent purchaser will always do so, if only to put the public on notice that it now owns the property.

4. Automatic Transfer of Encumbrances

A creditor's consent will frequently be necessary for the transfer of encumbered real estate. However, the lack of consent will not invalidate the transfer. If real estate is transferred without a creditor's required consent, the debtor will still be liable to the creditor on basis of its breach of its contractual obligation to obtain consent, while the purchaser will be liable to the creditor on the terms of the encumbrance having taken the property subject to it.

Automatic Transfer of Lease Agreements

Whether an automatic transfer of a lease agreement takes place depends mostly on what the relevant lease in issue provides. It would not be common, but legally possible, for a lessee and a landlord to agree that a lease terminates upon the sale of the building. Absent such an arrangement, the lease remains in effect as between the lessee and the old landlord and, like any other contract, would need to be specifically assigned to, and assumed by, the new landlord to be binding between the new landlord and the lessee. However, the new landlord is not entitled to simply force a lessee out. Instead, the lessee can enforce the terms of the lease against the new landlord on a principle called privity of estate. Even if there is no contract between the new landlord and the lessee, there is a relationship between the two based on the common, yet divergent, interests they share in a building. The law recognizes the existence of these common, yet divergent, interests and sides with the lessee when resolving them. In addition, a lessee who has unlawfully been forced out by the new landlord, may also sue its old landlord for breach of contract, provided the lease had not been assigned to the new landlord.

D. Contracts

1. Characteristics as to:

a) Language of Documentation. Please refer to B, 1, a above. It is highly unlikely that U.S. courts would accept documentation for the transfer and assignment of contracts in the U.S. in a language other than English. Accordingly, transfer documents should always be drafted in English. If bilingual agreements are used, it should be explicitly stated that the arrangement is exclusively governed by the English version.

b) Form of Documentation. As with all other assets to be purchased in an asset deal, the agreement that the seller transfers its contracts to the purchaser is set forth in the APA. The actual assignment of rights under the contracts to be transferred from the seller to the purchaser as well as the assumption of liabilities and/or obligations under these contracts by the purchaser is accomplished by the bill of sale and the assignment and assumption agreement. The bill of sale will be executed and delivered by the seller at closing, while the assignment and assumption agreement is executed and delivered by both parties. Both documents do not require notarization and, generally, can be executed abroad. If the parties so wish and provide in the APA (and they almost always will), the assignment and assumption agreement can be signed in counterparts.

c) Specification of Contracts. As has been outlined above in B, 1, c, U.S. law allows for a wide leverage in describing assets in an asset deal. Accordingly, contracts may be described generally or by means of generic descriptions. Much will depend on the circumstances of the transaction in issue. If the selling entity has entered into a large number of fairly standard contracts pertaining to a specific aspect of its business activities, a generic description may be appropriate. For key contracts, however, both parties will naturally be interested in specifically identifying them. Again, the representations and warranties in unison with the schedule of exceptions will be helpful tools to identify material contracts to the extent they have not been brought to the purchaser's attention during initial discussions between the business people or during the due diligence process.

2. Administrative, Corporate and Other Approvals

The answer depends on the type of contract involved. If, for example, the selling entity has a number of third-party contracts with the U.S. military, special governmental approval may be necessary before these contracts can be assigned to the purchaser, particularly if the purchaser is under foreign control. Moreover, many government contracts cannot be assigned at all and require a novation with the purchaser after the transaction is consummated, i.e., the purchaser and the relevant government entity will have to negotiate and commit to an entirely new agreement.

Whether board or stockholder approval is necessary for the assignment of a specific contract depends on the selling entity's charter and bylaws and the importance of the assigned contract relative to the selling entity's entire business. Stockholder approval will normally not be required, unless the assignment of a number of contracts amounts to the sale of the selling entity's entire business. Even board consent will often not be required, if the officers under the company's bylaws are empowered to enter into, terminate and assign contracts of a certain value (and the assigned contract happens to be below the threshold set forth in the bylaws).

Often contracts cannot be assigned without the consent of other parties. The most common examples are leases that require consent of the lessor and joint ventures or strategic alliances that require consent of the joint venturer or partner. The attempted assignment will not be valid absent such a required consent, exposing the seller to breach of contract claims from the counterparty to the contract and to indemnification claims from the purchaser who paid a purchase price based on the assumption that it would succeed the seller under the contract and benefit from it.

3. Automatic Transfer of Contracts (Other than Lease and Employment Agreements)

Typically, contractual rights do not automatically transfer to the purchaser. In certain instances, however, a party may seek to enforce an existing contract against the successor of its counterparty. These cases often arise in the context of bankruptcies or secured party asset sales made under Section 9–504 of the UCC, and to the extent that there is a prior relationship between the selling entity and the purchaser prior to the bankruptcy filing or the forced asset sale. Under the doctrine of successor liability (see below) courts in the U.S. may hold a purchaser liable under a contract that was not specifically assigned to it; in this regard, the obligations under this contract "automatically" follow the purchaser.

In a typical APA, the assets to be sold will specifically include insurance benefits, including proceeds, arising from or relating to the assets and assumed liabilities prior to the closing date. Although standard form insurance policies preclude assignment without the insurer's consent, U.S. courts have held that an assignment without consent may nevertheless be effective when the injury or damage takes place during the policy period (including before closing). Generally, though, the purchaser will seek a partial assignment of the seller's policies or inclusion as an additional insured to these policies to eliminate any question of coverage.

4. Filing Requirements

Generally, no special filings with public authorities or registrations into registers are required for the transfer of contracts.

5. Treatment of Existing Contractual Claims and Obligations

With the exception of any successor liability issues (see below) which may encompass liability under old seller contracts, a seller's unfulfilled obligations under assigned contracts are generally not automatically transferred to the purchaser. Typically, a purchaser will assume those liabilities that arise under the assigned seller contracts after the effective time of the transaction (provided such liability does not relate to a breach by the seller prior to the effective time in which case seller will be liable for it), while the seller will retain any liabilities relating to assigned contracts that arose prior to the acquisition. Indemnification provisions in the APA will follow this delineation and provide for indemnity to the benefit of the purchaser if the purchaser incurs damages stemming from, or is otherwise held responsible for, liabilities that the seller agreed to retain.

6. Warranty Claims Resulting from Events prior to Transfer

It is typical for the purchaser to assume any liability to seller's customers arising under written warranty agreements that the seller gave to its customers in the ordinary course of business prior to the effective time of the asset acquisition (provided that the liability does not relate to a breach by the seller prior to the effective date and, obviously also, that those customer contracts are part of the acquired assets in the first place). All other warranty obligations are to be retained by the seller and the APA will typically provide for indemnification to the benefit of the purchaser against any warranty claims which were not assumed by purchaser.

E. IP Rights

1. Characteristics of Intellectual Property Rights (e.g., Trade Marks, Patents, Utility Models, Domain Names) ("*IP Rights*") as to:

a) Language of Documentation. Please refer to B, 1, a above. It is highly unlikely that U.S. courts would accept documentation for the transfer of intellectual property rights in a language other than English. Accordingly, transfer documents should always be drafted in English. If bilingual agreements are used, it should be explicitly stated that the arrangement is exclusively governed by the English version.

b) Form of Documentation. The terms of the bill of sale are sufficient to convey title to purchaser to any and all of seller's copyrights, patents and trademarks. Still, purchaser's counsel will generally ask seller to also provide separate assignment forms for seller's intellectual property. The separate forms are useful to record the transfer of the relevant intellectual property on the records of the United States Patent and Trademark Office or, as the case may be, the United States Copyright Office. Assignment of copyrights, patents, or trademarks forms require notarization, a process far easier and significantly less formal in the U.S. than, for example, the notarization procedures in Germany. However, if the forms would be executed outside the U.S. the foreign notarization of the respective jurisdiction would need to be legalized to be effective in the U.S. The U.S. has been part of the 1961 Hague Convention abolishing the Requirement of Legalization for Foreign Public Documents and simplifying the legalization process for legal documents from jurisdictions which also are part of the Hague Convention.

c) Specification of IP Rights. As has been outlined above in B, 1, c, U.S. law allows for a wide leverage in describing assets in an asset deal. Accordingly, in the APA, IP Rights may be described generally or by means of generic descriptions. However, because the purchaser will want to file evidence of the acquisition of IP Rights with the United States Patent and Trademark Office or, as the case may be, the United States Copyright Office the parties will regularly specifically identify the IP Rights to be transferred.

2. Administrative, Corporate and Other Approvals

Special governmental or administrative approvals are normally not required to transfer IP Rights. The purchaser will want to make sure, however, that the transfer is reported to the United States Patent and Trademark Office or, as the case may be, the United States Copyright Office to assure that its status as rightful owner of the transferred IP Rights is properly documented in public records.

Whether board or stockholder approval is necessary for the assignment of a specific IP Right, again, depends on the selling entity's charter and bylaws and the importance of the assigned right relative to the selling entity's entire business. Stockholder approval will normally not be required, unless the assignment of a number of IP Rights amounts to the sale of the selling entity's entire business. Since IP Rights generally are key to a business, board consent will frequently be required to transfer them to an unaffiliated third-party. Again though, the selling entity's bylaws should be consulted to assess if the officers of the company are empowered to assign certain IP Rights.

Although it is possible to acquire an IP Right subject to an encumbrance, the purchaser will frequently demand that the encumbrance is removed prior to closing. Which consequences not obtaining a secured party's consent may have, depends on the underlying contractual arrangement between the selling entity and secured party that set up the security interest. Generally, a transfer to the purchaser will not be invalidated but the purchaser will take the IP right subject to the encumbrance and the seller may be liable to the secured party for breach of contract.

3. Filing Requirements

The transfer of intellectual property should be filed with and recorded by the United States Patent and Trademark Office or, as the case may be, the United States Copyright Office to verify purchaser's status as the new owner of the assigned intellectual property. Not filing evidence of the transfer could subsequently cast doubt on purchaser's proper ownership (it does not negate the validity of the transfer between seller and purchaser) and should therefore be avoided.

4. Applicable International (Multilateral) Agreements or Treaties

The United States is a party to the Trade-Related Aspects of Intellectual Property Rights and a member of the Paris Convention for the Protection of Industrial Property. It also is a member of the World Intellectual Property Organization.

The United States along with the European Union, Japan, and Switzerland is currently spearheading an effort to create a new global standard for intellectual property rights enforcement, under the so-called "Anti-Counterfeiting Trade Agreement".

F. Receivables

1. Characteristics as to:

a) Language of Documentation. Please refer to B, 1, a above. It is highly unlikely that U.S. courts would accept documentation for the transfer of accounts receivable in a language other than English. Accordingly, transfer documents should always be drafted in English. If bilingual agreements are used, it should be explicitly stated that the arrangement is exclusively governed by the English version.

b) Form of Documentation. As with all other assets to be purchased in an asset deal, the agreement that the seller transfers its accounts receivable to the purchaser is memorialized in the APA. The actual assignment is accomplished by the bill of sale and the assignment and assumption agreement. The bill of sale will be executed and delivered by the seller at closing, while the assignment and assumption agreement is executed and delivered by both parties. Both documents do not require notarization and, generally, can be executed abroad. If the parties so wish and provide in the APA (and they almost always will), the assignment and assumption agreement can be signed in counterparts.

c) Specification of Receivables. As has been outlined above in B, 1, c, U.S. law allows for a wide leverage in describing assets in an asset deal. Accordingly, in the APA, accounts receivable may be described generally, by means of generic descriptions or, if the parties so wish, with specificity.

2. Administrative, Corporate and Other Approvals

Special governmental or administrative approvals will generally not be necessary for the transfer of accounts receivable.

Also, stockholder approval will normally not be required for the transfer of specific accounts receivable. Whether board consent is necessary, depends on the selling entity's bylaws. If a transfer stays below a certain materiality threshold, the officers of a selling entity may well be empowered to facilitate it without board approval. As mentioned before, however, if the accounts receivable are transferred as part of a sale of all or substantially all of the selling entity's assets, board and stockholder approval of the selling entity will frequently be necessary.

Whether the transfer of accounts receivable requires a debtor's consent depends on the corresponding underlying contractual arrangement between the selling entity and the debtor. Generally, accounts receivable are freely transferable and do not require the debtor's consent. The purchaser will nevertheless want to make sure that the debtor is properly notified of the transfer, so as to avoid post-transfer payments to the seller which the purchaser then would have to recoup from the seller.

3. Filing Requirements

Generally, no special filings with public authorities or registrations into registers are required for the transfer of accounts receivable. As mentioned above, however, the purchaser will want to make sure that the debtor is properly notified of the transfer, so as to avoid post-transfer payments to the seller which the purchaser then would have to recoup from the seller.

G. Liabilities

1. Characteristics as to:

a) Language of Documentation. Please refer to B, 1, a above. It is highly unlikely that U.S. courts would accept documentation for the assumption of liabilities in a language other than English. Accordingly, the underlying documents providing for the purchaser's assumption of liabilities should always be drafted in English. If bilingual agreements are used, it should be explicitly stated that the arrangement is exclusively governed by the English version.

b) Form of Documentation. The assumption of specified liabilities by the purchaser as well as the retention of specified liabilities by the seller is provided for in the APA as well as in the assignment and assumption agreement that the purchaser and the seller execute and deliver at closing. Both documents do not require notarization and, generally, can be executed abroad. If the parties so wish and provide in the APA (and they almost always will), both, the APA and the assignment and assumption agreement, can be signed in counterparts.

c) Specification of Liabilities. Again, U.S. law provides for a fairly wide leverage as to how the parties may identify and describe assumed and retained liabilities. However, the assumption and retention of liabilities is typically a heavily negotiated issue. Most purchasers will wish to identify the liabilities they will assume with sufficient specificity as is necessary to minimize the risk of unanticipated exposure and controversy. Accordingly, a typical APA will list groupings of types of liabilities to be assumed by the purchaser and to be retained by the seller and be very precise in delineating when and how liabilities must have arisen (before or after the effective time of the transaction; because of seller's breach or not) to be assumed or to be retained. But a typical APA will often go further than identifying liabilities in groupings and add exhibits which specifically list individual liabilities to be assumed or to be retained.

2. Administrative, Corporate and Other Approvals

Special governmental or administrative approvals will generally not be necessary for the assignment and assumption of liabilities.

Also, stockholder approval will normally not be required. Whether board consent is necessary, depends on the selling entity's bylaws. If the assignment and assumption of specific liabilities in the context of the acquisition of assets stays below a certain materiality threshold, the officers of a selling entity may well be empowered to facilitate the assignment without board approval. As mentioned before, however, if an assignment and assumption of liabilities occurs as part of a sale of all or substantially all of the selling entity's assets, board and stockholder approval of the selling entity will frequently be necessary.

Whether the assignment of liabilities requires a creditor's consent depends on the corresponding underlying arrangement between the selling entity and the creditor giving rise to the liability. The consequences of not obtaining a required consent will typically also be set forth in the corresponding underlying arrangement giving rise to the liability and can range from invalidating the assignment to the creditor being entitled to seek recourse against both, the selling entity and the purchaser.

3. Filing Requirements

Generally, the assignment of liabilities does not require special filings with public authorities or registrations into registers or databases. Whether the assignment requires the notification of a creditor depends on the corresponding underlying arrangement between the selling entity and the creditor giving rise to the liability. In many cases though, a notification will be required.

4. Purchaser's Liability for:

a) Tax Obligations. The selling entity will typically be asked and agree to retain any liability for taxes, including (i) any taxes arising as a result of seller's operation of its business or ownership of the acquired assets prior to the effective time of the acquisition, (ii) any taxes that will arise as a result of the sale of the assets pursuant to the contemplated asset acquisition and (iii) any deferred taxes of any nature. However, there are limitations to a purchaser's ability to shelter itself from a seller's tax liabilities. Certain state tax laws, for example, allow authorities to follow assets to recover taxes owed by the seller even post-acquisition, i.e., when such assets already are in possession of and, by all legal means, owned by the purchaser. Accordingly, a purchaser will want to assure that it is not exposed to such a risk and will seek appropriate indemnification rights from the seller.

b) Environmental Contamination. The selling entity will typically be asked and agree to retain any environmental, health and safety liabilities arising out of or relating to the operation of seller's business or seller's leasing, ownership or operation of real property. Again, there are limitations to a purchaser's ability to shelter itself from seller's environmental liabilities. In 1980 the federal superfund law was enacted, the Comprehensive Environmental Response, Compensation And Liability Act Of 1980 (**"CERCLA"**). In the years since the enactment of that statute, environmental issues have become a central feature of acquisitions. Under CERCLA, the current owner will be liable for the costs of cleaning up contamination caused by a prior owner, effectively preempting the ability of a purchaser to refuse to accept liability for the activities of the seller or the seller's predecessors. CERCLA determined that every purchaser would be liable for certain environmental liabilities regardless of the provisions of any APA or any common law doctrines or state statutes. In addition, certain state environmental laws may similarly hold a current owner liable for contamination caused by the seller or the seller's predecessors.

c) Products Sold or Services Rendered by the Seller to Third Parties. The risk for the purchaser to be held liable for seller's old liabilities is particularly relevant in the context of product liability. As product liability law has evolved since the early 1960s in the U.S., U.S. courts increasingly have determined that injured consumers who otherwise lack a remedy should be able to recover against successors of the manufacturer of a product. Justice, so the argument goes, would not be promoted if a successor was liable in a merger or de facto merger, but not in a sale of assets for cash, when the needs and objectives of the parties are the same in all three instances. Accordingly, a purchaser should be aware of the inherent limitations of attempting to avoid liability for products manufactured by the seller before the closing and should (as purchasers frequently do) seek indemnity from seller for liability arising from products manufactured pre-closing.

5. Automatic Transfer of Other Liabilities

Traditionally, the well settled rule of successor liability was that "where one company sells or transfers all of its assets to another, the second entity does not become liable for the debts and liabilities" of the transferor. In recent years, however, the theory of successor liability has been significantly expanded and an extensive body of law has been established based on which a purchaser of assets may be held liable for a seller's wrongdoings.

There are nine basic theories pursuant to which a predecessor's liabilities could be imposed upon a successor:

(i) express or implied agreement to assume;

(ii) de facto merger;

(iii) mere continuation;

(iv) fraud;

(v) continuity of enterprise;

(vi) product line;

(vii) duty to warn;

(viii) inadequate consideration for the transfer, coupled with the failure to make provision for the transferor's creditors; and

(ix) liability imposed by statute.

Some of these points have previously been discussed (such as the successor liability imposed by statute for environmental or tax liabilities, the treatment of an asset sale as a „de facto merger" with its implication of treating the purchaser factually as the successor of the seller, or the successor liability for seller's defective products), however, probably the key issue in this context is fraudulent conveyances.

An asset transfer will successfully be challenged if a plaintiff creditor can show fraud on part of the purchaser, the selling entity, its stockholders or all three. The fraud exception to disqualifying an asset deal arises from the judicial doctrine that transactions entered into in order to escape liability should not be permitted. The exception covers various cases, such as where the consideration for the assets was fictitious or inadequate or where there is a demonstrable intent to defraud creditors, i.e., where the selling entity engages in a fire sale to rid itself of its assets before being rendered insolvent leaving its creditors empty handed. The exception has also been applied in the more difficult situations where the transfer of assets, although perfectly legitimate, is done (at least in part) to avoid liability, e.g., by transferring assets to an entity which subsequently files for bankruptcy. In all these cases, a U.S. court will invalidate the transfer and hold the defrauding party liable.

In addition to the case law, this area is governed by the Uniform Fraudulent Transfer Act (**"UFTA"**), which has been enacted in most states. The purpose of UFTA is to limit a debtor's ability to transfer assets if doing so puts them out of reach of its creditors at a time when the debtor's financial condition is, or would be, precarious. UFTA provides that a "transfer" is voidable by a creditor if (a) the transfer is made with actual intent to hinder, delay or defraud a creditor, or (b) the transfer leaves the debtor insolvent or undercapitalized and is not made in exchange for reasonably equivalent value. If a transaction is determined by a court to constitute a fraudulent transfer under UFTA, the court can order any appropriate equitable relief, such as voiding or enjoining the transfer in whole or to the extent necessary to satisfy creditors' claims, attaching the transferred assets or appointing a receiver to take control of the transferred assets.

As a bottom line, a purchaser should take away from this section that (i) it cannot simply step in the shoes of the seller without incurring the risk that certain liabilities will also remain with a business that, before the transaction, more or less looked the same as it does after the transaction, (ii) it may be difficult to avoid liability in certain areas, such as environmental, tax and product liability law, and (iii) the transfer may not be structured in a way that curtails the rights of the selling entity's creditors. All three points have in common that a great emphasis should be given to due diligence to get as complete a picture of these issues at as early a stage in the transaction as possible. Not all of these points can be addressed to the purchaser's satisfaction, not even in generous and well-drafted indemnification provisions.

6. Contractual Protection as to 4 and 5 above

A purchaser will routinely request to be indemnified against risks stemming from environmental, tax or product liability issues. The purchaser should make sure, however, that its indemnification rights are effective. Key issues will be the survival of the indemnification rights, a monetary cap and, depending on whether or not the selling entity plans to dissolve post-transaction, the feasibility and terms of an escrow.

H. Employees

1. Transfer of Employees

Determining whether or not an employee will transfer from seller to purchaser in an asset sale will generally be a matter of contract between the parties and will be addressed in the APA. The APA will generally discuss when and how any employees of the seller will transfer to the purchaser. If some or all of the employees are transferred from seller to purchaser, the seller should be aware of any potential notice and other obligations or liabilities that may arise under any existing employment agreements or policies as well as by operation of law, such as the notice and reporting obligations that may be required under the Worker Adjustment and Retraining Notification Act ("**WARN**") or any similar state or local law. For example, in some cases, the APA will require the seller to terminate some or all employees prior to the closing. In this instance, all such employees will be deemed terminated by the seller (even if they are later rehired by the purchaser), which may trigger, among other things, notice or severance obligations under agreements with the employees or notice and reporting obligations under WARN for those employees who have suffered an "employment loss" (depending on the total number of employees and other factors considered under the statute). The seller would also be required to provide any other termination payments required by law, which will generally include the final payment of salary, accrued but unused vacation pay, and any earned, but unpaid incentive compensation.

2. Approval of Works Council, Trade Union or Other Institutions

With respect to U.S. employees, this will largely be a matter of contract. In situations where some or all of the seller's workforce is represented by a labor organization or "union" in the U.S., there will generally be a Collective Bargaining Agreement ("**CBA**") between the seller and the union. Each CBA is individually negotiated by the parties and would contain any relevant provisions regarding approvals necessary for the transfer of employees in an asset sale or otherwise. Therefore, in any asset deal, it is critical that the seller be familiar with the terms of any applicable CBA in advance of negotiating the APA, and that the purchaser request and carefully review the terms of any such agreement in connection with the due diligence process. In the event a CBA does require approval of the union and the seller fails to seek or achieve such approval, seller would be in breach of the CBA and would be subject to the various damages under common law and as may be expressly provided by the agreement, including possible injunctive relief to prohibit the transfer.

3. Contractual Protection as to Labor Issues

In the U.S., employment-related liabilities often remain with the seller and are a retained liability, as determined by the APA. Thus, it is less common to include special indemnifications regarding employment-related liabilities in the APA.

I. Tax Implications

1. Value Added Tax

Except for the State of Michigan, the United States do not have a value-added tax. Many state and local jurisdictions impose sales, documentary or similar transfer taxes on the sale of certain categories of assets, however. For example, a sales tax (ranging from 0% to 13% in all 50 states) might apply to the sale of tangible personal property, other than inventory held for resale, or a documentary tax might be required for recording a deed for the transfer of real property. In most cases, these taxes can be avoided if the transaction is structured as a sale of stock or a statutory merger. Responsibility for payment of these taxes is negotiable, but normally the seller will remain primarily liable for the tax (while the purchaser may have successor liability for them).

2. Real Property Transfer Tax

Real estate transfer taxes in the U.S. may be imposed by states, counties, or municipalities on transfers of real property within the jurisdiction. Total transfer taxes are levied against the assessed value of the property (which may be reassessed in connection with the transaction) and range from small percentages (for example, 0.01% in Colorado) to relatively large percentages (2.2% in the District of Columbia). In addition, a documentary tax might be required for recording a deed for the transfer of real property.

3. Other Tax Issues

In most acquisitions, the income tax consequences to the purchaser and to the seller and its stockholders are among the most important factors in determining the structure of the transaction.

In a taxable asset purchase, the purchaser's tax basis in the purchased assets will be equal to the purchase price (including the assumed liabilities). A purchaser may allocate the purchase price among the purchased assets on an asset-by-asset basis to reflect their fair market value, often increasing the tax basis from that of the seller. This step-up in basis can allow the purchaser greater depreciation and amortization deductions in the future and less gain (or greater loss) on subsequent disposition of those assets.

On the seller side, a different tax treatment follows the selling entity's status as an "S" corporation or a "C" corporation. A "C" corporation is a corporation that, for federal income tax purposes, is taxed under 26 U.S.C. § 11 and Subchapter C of Chapter 1 of the Code. Most major companies (and many smaller companies) are treated as "C" corporations for federal income tax purposes. Income of a "C" corporation is taxed on a corporate level and then again, if dividend payments are made to its stockholders, on a stockholder level. An "S" corporation, in contrast, for federal income tax purposes, is a corporation that makes a valid election to be taxed under Subchapter "S" of Chapter 1 of the Code. In general, "S" Corporations do not pay any income taxes. Instead, the corporation's income or losses are divided among and passed through to its stockholders. The stockholders must then report the income or loss on their own individual income tax returns.

If the seller in an asset acquisition is a "C" corporation and liquidates post-transaction, it will recognize gain or loss on an asset-by-asset basis, which will be treated as ordinary income or loss or capital gain or loss, depending on the character of each asset. However, corporations do not receive the benefit of a lower rate on long-term capital gains, and the gains can be taxed at a rate as high as 35%. Its stockholders then will be taxed as if they had sold their stock for the proceeds received in liquidation (after reduction by the seller's corporate tax liability). Gain or loss to the stockholders is measured by the difference between the fair market value of the cash or other assets received and the tax basis of the stockholders' stock.

The tax treatment to the seller and its stockholders in an "S" corporation's sale of assets will depend upon the form of consideration, the relationship of the tax basis in the seller's assets (the inside basis) to the tax basis of its stockholders in their stock (the outside basis), whether there is built-in gain (i.e. fair market value of assets in excess of tax basis at the effective date of the "S" corporation election), and whether the seller's "S" status will terminate. Generally, the amount and character of the gain or loss at the corporate level will pass through to the stockholders and be taken into account on their individual tax returns, thereby avoiding a double tax. However, the purchase price will be allocated among the "S" corporation's assets and, depending on the relationship of the inside basis and the outside basis, the amount of the gain or loss passed through to the stockholders for tax purposes may be more or less than if the same price had been paid for the stock of the "S" corporation.

J. Bankruptcy Law

1. Challenge of Asset Transfer in Case of Insolvency

The two basic paths into bankruptcy for an enterprise in the U.S. are outlined in Chapter 7 and Chapter 11 of the Bankruptcy Code. A Chapter 7 case leads to the dissolution of the enterprise, while a Chapter 11 case is entered into in an attempt to successfully reorganize the enterprise for it to emerge from bankruptcy as a profitable stand-alone business.

In both, Chapter 7 and Chapter 11 cases, an automatic stay is ordered, meaning that for a period of time all judgments, collection activities, foreclosures, and repossessions of property are suspended and may not be pursued by the creditors on any debt or claim that arose before the filing of the bankruptcy petition.

Moreover, in a Chapter 11 case a debtor in possession or a trustee is appointed, who has what are called "avoiding" powers. These powers may be used to undo a transfer of money or property made during a certain period of time before the filing of the bankruptcy petition. By avoiding a particular transfer of property, the debtor in possession can cancel the transaction and force the return or "disgorgement" of the payments or property, which then are available to pay all creditors. Generally, and subject to various defenses, the power to avoid transfers is effective against transfers made by the debtor within 90 days before filing the petition. However, transfers to "insiders" (i.e. relatives, general partners, and directors or officers of the debtor) made up to a year before filing may be voided. The trustee is also authorized to void transfers under applicable state law, which often provides for longer time periods. Voiding powers prevent unfair prepetition payments to one creditor at the expense of all other creditors.

In addition to pursuing a debtor under bankruptcy laws, a creditor who believes to have been defrauded by an insolvent debtor's conveyance of assets to a third party can also seek to invalidate such a transfer under the fraudulent conveyance laws discussed in G, 5 above.

2. Acquisition of Assets that are Subject to Insolvency Proceedings

Assets of a bankrupt entity may only be acquired in accordance with the rules set out in Chapter 7 and Chapter 11 of the Bankruptcy Code. In a Chapter 7 case, generally, the debtor has insufficient assets to satisfy all of its creditors' claims, so it is unlikely that a non-creditor purchaser will ever be confronted with the option to buy assets from a Chapter 7 debtor. In a Chapter 11 case, the debtor files a so-called plan of reorganization which, in an elaborate proceeding, must be accepted by the various classes of creditors. Any asset sale to a non-creditor purchaser, if at all admissible under the plan, will have to adhere to the terms of the plan.

K. Timing and Costs

1. Timeframe of Asset Transfer

Except for the 30-day waiting period in connection with the pre-merger notification under the HSR Act (which may be abbreviated upon request), typically, delays are not caused by registration, authorization or notarization procedures. However, an asset deal will often require a detailed due diligence and will be more work intensive than a merger or a stock deal due to the effort required in specifically identifying the assets to be transferred and the liabilities to be assumed as well as thereafter accomplishing the transfer of the different assets (real estate, IP Rights, tangible assets etc.). Hence, an asset deal will routinely take two to three months and, depending on the size of the deal, may often take longer.

2. Costs of Asset Transfer

The most costly expense in an acquisition in the U.S. (other than advisors' fees) will likely be the costs related to the possibly required HSR filing. The costs, unless the parties agree otherwise, are typically borne by the purchaser. For transactions valued in excess of USD 50 million (as adjusted) but less than USD 100 million (as adjusted), the filing fee is USD 45,000. For transactions with values ranging from USD 100 million (as adjusted) to less than USD 500 million (as adjusted), the filing fee is USD 125,000. And, for transactions with values equal to or exceeding USD 500 million (as adjusted) the filing fee is USD 280,000. The currently applicable adjusted thresholds can be found on the webpage of the Federal Trade Commission at www.ftc.gov and, for 2009, are referenced in B, 2 above.

Other than the HSR filing fees and the real estate transfer fees (see I, 2 above) already mentioned, there may be certain local fees which, however, will likely be minimal.

Also, notarization costs, if any, are negligible. Notarization in the U.S. serves a very different purpose than it does in other jurisdictions, particularly in Continental Europe. In the U.S., it is simply meant to verify the identity of a person signing the document and, in most cases, is gratuitous.

L. Miscellaneous

1. Choice of Foreign Law

For a few reasons, it is generally recommendable for an asset sale in the U.S. to also be subject to U.S. law. First of all, a purchaser will often find that U.S. law, in many respects, is more flexible and more "business-friendly" than the purchaser's own local law. Secondly, a purchaser will have to assess if it is able to avoid the long arm of U.S. courts with respect to certain key issues by choosing a different law. In important areas, such as environmental liability, product liability, tax, employment law etc. U.S. courts will likely find that they have jurisdictions to adjudicate issues arising in these areas as a result of an asset sale. Hence, a purchaser should carefully assess if, and if so, which advantages there would be in choosing a foreign law to govern the APA.

2. (International) Arbitration, Choice of Venue

The parties may agree on arbitration, on a domestic as well as an international level. As far as the choice of venue is concerned, any venue is possible, as long as either party has any sort of nexus to the venue.

3. Other Distinctions, Characteristics

U.S. law is reflective of the free market philosophy that has formed the U.S. from the days of its founding fathers. It is, from a European viewpoint at least, libertarian and meant to facilitate and promote the free flow of goods in a free market. Accordingly, there are few obstacles to consummating an asset deal in this country and there should be few, if any, negative surprises for a purchaser doing business in the U.S.

M. Literature

Martin D. Ginsburg and *Jack S. Levin*, Mergers, Acquisitions and Buyouts, 2009

Vietnam

By *Matthias Dühn* and *Christoph Angerbauer*

A. General Aspects

1. Asset Deal vs. Share Deal: Essential Considerations

Share deals currently account for the vast majority of M&A transactions in Vietnam, whereas asset deals are rather uncommon. In Vietnam, the share deal is a predictable, quick and (relatively) calculable means to acquire a business entity in Vietnam, whereas the asset deal as such has not yet become an established category of M&A transactions. Accordingly, there is generally a great tendency to structure deals as share deals in Vietnam.

The main considerations when structuring a deal in Vietnam are similar to in other countries. Whether an acquisition of a company is structured as a share or an asset deal is mainly driven by legal-, tax- and commercial considerations. With respect to legal considerations, Vietnam has recently implemented specific legislation with regard to share deals, so that M&A transactions can now be structured in a more reliable and calculable way than before. This is also true for the taxation of share deals, where clear rules exist. Regarding the commercial considerations, a share deal in Vietnam – like in other jurisdictions – in particular presents the risk of assumption of undisclosed liabilities. Therefore, the purchaser is usually advised to perform an extensive due diligence before negotiating the share purchase agreement.

An asset deal, on the other hand, is usually more time-consuming as all the assets have to be clearly and individually identified and inventoried. One of the biggest advantages is that – due to individual identification – in most cases there is no danger of "hidden" liabilities to be transferred to the purchaser. Some general points have to be taken into consideration when planning an asset deal in Vietnam:

Scope of Business

Any purchaser who wishes to take over the business of an entity in Vietnam by way of an asset deal must set up a new legal entity in Vietnam that is licensed to engage in the same business operations as the seller's company. Otherwise, a foreign individual or a foreign entity (which has no subsidiary in Vietnam) would not be permitted to continue running the same business operations as the seller of the assets. In other words: The targeted assets have to be transferred into a Vietnamese (acquisition) entity that is itself licensed to engage in the same scope of business as the seller's business. One must thoroughly examine whether setting up a (100%) foreign-owned enterprise in the specific business sector is permitted under Vietnamese regulations (although entering into WTO, some restrictions for specified sectors still persist) and whether this can be done in the required timeframe (setting up of a company in Vietnam usually takes between two to four months, but may also take much longer). Alternatively, an existing foreign-owned Vietnamese enterprise – permitted for the same scope of business – may act as a purchaser and acquire the targeted assets.

Land Ownership

In Vietnam, land cannot be owned by private entities or individuals, but is owned collectively by the people and administered by the state of Vietnam. Full private ownership of land is therefore not possible, neither for Vietnamese, nor for foreigners. Only so-called Land Use Rights can be granted and assigned by the state. Only Vietnamese individuals or organizations can have Land Use Rights; they are not available to foreign individuals or entities. In practice, if a foreign investor wishes to acquire a piece of land from a Vietnamese individual or company for implementation of their projects in Vietnam, they will negotiate with such Vietnamese individual or entity about the compensation for the return of such land to the state, and the state will then recover such land and lease out to the foreign investor with the lease term being in accordance with the duration of the investment project provided in the investment certificate (usually for a maximum of 50 years, and in exceptional cases, for up to 70 years). The ownership structures of Land Use Rights are often unclear and should therefore be examined very carefully. Buildings, factories or construction works, on the other hand, which are attached to the land, can be owned by foreign invested enterprises in Vietnam.

Tax Considerations

Where a target company has accumulated losses carried forward and the purchaser wishes to preserve the losses, it will have to acquire the business via a share deal, as there are no provisions to transfer losses via an asset deal from one company to another. Also, if a target company has been granted tax incentives, the purchaser will have to acquire the company via a share deal structure if it wants to preserve and continue taking advantage of the incentives.

2. Distinction between Sale and Transfer in Rem

Vietnamese laws and regulations do not formally distinguish between the sale (obligation) and the transfer in rem (fulfillment of the obligation to transfer). Generally, the purchaser will acquire ownership directly upon entering into the sales contract. Only where Vietnamese laws explicitly require the ownership rights of certain assets to be registered with the relevant authorities do the ownership rights pass to the purchaser upon completion of the procedures for registration of ownership rights. In these cases, the purchaser will typically try to oblige the seller to cooperate and guarantee completion of the procedures for registration of the ownership rights of such assets before making the final payment to the seller. In all other cases, where registration of ownership rights is not required, the purchaser will directly become the owner of the sold asset and accordingly has the right to require the seller to immediately deliver the sold asset. Equally, the seller has the right to require the purchaser as the immediate owner to receive the sold asset at any time (with reasonable notice). Regarding share sales, a share sale changes the ownership required to be registered/notified to the licensing authority. Upon registration, such sale is complete.

3. Regional Differences

There are no regional differences regarding the legal requirements in connection with the transfer of assets. However, practically speaking, different legal requirements may be applied by different authorities in different provinces for setting up a company in Vietnam as a precondition for purchasing assets in Vietnam (see above) or in notification procedures.

4. Acquisition by Foreigners

There are generally no distinctions with regard to the acquisition of assets (other than land/real estate) by foreigners or foreign entities, as the new "Law on Enterprises" has replaced the old "Law on Foreign Investment" and thereby eliminated prior distinctions between foreign and domestic investors.

5. Public Registers, Records and Databases

In Vietnam, only very limited information is available in central or public registers, records, or (online) databases and such information may or may not be reliable or updated:

Corporate information about the seller (such as scope of business and other business registration contents, copy of business registration certificate, certificate on the change of business registration contents, etc.) can be obtained for a fee from the local business registration offices or their websites. However, the business registration offices may not update such corporate information regularly. Accordingly, the information obtained may be outdated or differ in scope and quality and therefore be unreliable for due diligence purposes.

Information as to real property (such as ownership rights and encumbrance status, etc.) may be obtained from the relevant authorities, such as land registration offices under the Service of Natural Resources and Environment or the land registration offices under the Department of Natural Resources and Environment or the People's Committees of the hamlets, wards, townships. In Ho Chi Minh City, real property information can be either obtained from the Land Registries or through the website of the Center for Information on Natural Resources & Environment and Registration of Lands and Houses of Ho Chi Minh City (http://www.nhadattphcm.gov.vn). This Center is under the control of the Service of Natural Resources and Environment of Ho Chi Minh City.

Information with regard to the financial status of both the seller and purchaser is only publicly available for joint stock companies, in which the shareholders are entitled to request such information from the joint stock company, and any individuals or organizations are entitled to request such information from the competent business registration offices. However, transparency standards are not yet comparable to other jurisdictions. In all other cases, financial information has to be carefully double-checked, as accounting and bookkeeping standards in domestic companies do not yet reach international standards. Also, keeping different sets of financial information for different purposes is not uncommon for domestic companies in Vietnam.

6. Purchase Price Requirements

The purchase price is freely negotiable between the parties. The purchase price must be agreed on in Vietnamese Dong, but may – for practical reasons – be negotiated in US dollars or any other foreign currency. An exception applies for transactions with credit institutions and payments made via intermediaries, including authorized collection, entrustment, agency and other necessary cases permitted by the Prime Minister. In these cases the purchase price may directly be agreed upon in US dollars or any other foreign currency.

State minimum price mechanisms do not affect the free negotiability of sale and purchase contracts. That is, the sale/purchase price can be lower than the minimum price. However, when registering the assets with relevant authorities the State will base its fee calculation on the minimum price if the purchase price is lower than the minimum price or will base the calculation on the purchase price if such purchase price is higher than the minimum price. Minimum prices are set for important goods such as land, water, natural resources; State properties (houses, national reservation goods, etc.); the State's exclusive goods (electricity, air transportation services, telecommunication services, etc.); important consumption goods (such as oil and gas, water, bus transportation, some types of medicines, etc.); price stabilized goods (such as oil and gas, cement, iron, steel, fertilizers, rice, coffee, salt, etc.); and some imported goods (motorcycles, wines, etc.), for the purposes of economic management and taxation.

B. Tangible/Movable Assets

1. Characteristics as to:

a) Language of Documentation. The sale and transfer documents regarding tangible assets may be drafted in every language and English/bilingual documents are permitted and recommended if there is a foreign element to the contract. In practice, if a party to the sale agreement is a foreign party, the sales agreement will usually be bilingual in Vietnamese and English. The English version may prevail for the purpose of interpretation. The Vietnamese version should only prevail if the purchased asset is required to be registered to effect the ownership rights associated with the asset. In this case, a Vietnamese version of the agreement is necessary for the purpose of submission to the authorities for certification of such ownership rights, since the Vietnamese authorities only refer to the Vietnamese version. The most important assets that require registration of ownership rights are land use rights, houses, buildings, construction works and road, air, sea transportation vehicles (including automobiles).

In practice, if a dispute arises from the sales agreement and if such dispute is to be settled by the competent courts of Vietnam, the courts of Vietnam would only refer to the Vietnamese version for settlement of the dispute. Therefore, it is useful to sign contracts in both English (other foreign language) and Vietnamese, with the English prevailing. Further, it is recommended that there be an agreement in the sales contract as to arbitration, in which the English version will at all times prevail if agreed on by both parties. Even where arbitration is still new in Vietnam, it is usually a better alternative than relying on the Vietnamese court system that has not yet reached international/western standards. For the avoidance of doubt, parties to commercial disputes may chose arbitration outside Vietnam, e.g., in Singapore (Singapore International Arbitration Centre, SIAC).

b) Form of Documentation. Legally, sale and purchase agreements need not be made in writing. However, for purposes of documentation and evidence, sale and purchase agreements will usually be entered into in writing. However, they are not required to be notarized/certified or registered. Signing in counterparts is possible, the documents do not have to be jointly signed by the parties; however in this case, the time at which the written contract is entered into shall be the time when the last party signs the contract.

The place of entry into an agreement shall be as agreed by the parties and if there is no agreement on place of entry into an agreement, such place shall be the residence of the individual or the head office of the legal entity that has made the offer to enter into the contract. In case of entry into a contract in absentia, the determination of the place where the contract was entered into must comply with the law of the country of residence of the individual or the head office of the legal entity who requested the contract to be entered into.

Registration of ownership rights is required for the transfer of certain assets. The most important assets that require registration of ownership rights are land use rights, houses, buildings, construction works and road, air, sea transportation vehicles (including automobiles).

c) Specification of Assets. All assets must be clearly identifiable. Therefore, subject to the agreements of the parties, a description or a list of assets may be provided in the sales agreement or the appendix that is attached to the sales agreement. In practice, it is highly recommended that such lists be as detailed as possible to avoid any discrepancies.

2. Administrative, Corporate and Other Approvals

- The transfer of tangible assets does not require special governmental or administrative approvals. It is only required to be notarized/certified or registered if such assets are subject to the registration of ownership rights.
- Except for private enterprises, the sale of assets amounting to 50% or more of the total assets in a company must be approved by the Members' Council (if it is a limited

liability company with more than two members), the Owner (if it is a single limited liability company) or the shareholder's general meeting (if it is a joint stock company), unless otherwise indicated in the company's charter.

- In case of the sale of encumbered tangible assets, the seller is only entitled to sell such encumbered assets if the security holder agrees thereto.

The transfer of assets is invalid without the above approvals. Such invalid transaction shall not give rise to civil rights and obligations of the parties as from the time the transaction is entered into. Rather, the parties shall restore everything to its original state and shall return to each other what they have received.

Assets may be acquired in good faith (bona fide principle) if such assets are moveable property that is not required to be registered for ownership and has already been transferred to the bona fide possessor. In such circumstances, the owner can only claim back the assets if the possessor received the assets without consideration or they have been stolen or lost.

Moveable property that has to have its ownership registered (especially automobiles) generally cannot be acquired in good faith. The owner usually has the entire right to reclaim the real property from the bona fide possessor. A bona fide acquisition is only possible if the third person received the property by way of an auction or pursuant to a judgment or decision of an authorized State body.

3. Filing Requirements

The transfer of tangible assets does not require special filings with public authorities or registration with public registers or databases, except if the tangible assets are subject to the registration of ownership rights.

4. Automatic Transfer of Encumbrances

The sale of encumbered assets is only permitted if the security holder agrees to the sale. If the security holder does not agree, the sale is invalid with the abovementioned consequences. Encumbrances do not automatically transfer to the purchaser. In practice, the security holder will therefore only allow the sale if she/he is given a different asset as security or the debt is otherwise settled.

C. Real Property

1. Characteristics as to:

a) Language of Documentation. The sale and transfer documents regarding real property may be drafted in every language and bilingual documents are permitted, if there is a foreign element to the transaction. However, Vietnamese laws require that real property documents be notarized/certified and ownership rights be registered. Accordingly, the transfer documents must (also) be drafted in Vietnamese.

b) Form of Documentation. Real property documentation must be in writing and notarized before a notary. Also, ownership rights have to be registered with the relevant authorities. Transactions involving real property are governed exclusively by the laws of Vietnam and documents regarding transfer of real property cannot be executed outside of Vietnam. Documents must be jointly signed on the same document.

c) Specification of Assets. Detailed description of the real property in the transfer documents is required. In case of land, the particulars such as category, class, area, location, symbol boundaries, status of the land and term of land use rights, must be described. In case of assets annexed to the land, the detailed description such as area and location of houses, buildings or construction works and any other related information are required. In addition, documents proving the seller's ownership rights over such real property must be indicated.

2. Administrative, Corporate and Other Approvals

- The transfer of real property does not require special governmental or administrative approvals. It must be notarized and the ownership rights must be registered with the relevant authorities.
- Except for private enterprises, the sale of assets amounting to 50% or more of the total assets in a company must have the approval of the members' council (if it is a limited liability company with more than two members), approval of the owner (if it is a single limited liability company) or approval of the shareholder's general meeting (if it is a joint stock company), unless otherwise stated in the company charter.
- In case of the sale of encumbered real property, the seller is only entitled to sell such encumbered real property if the security holder agrees thereto.

The transfer of assets is invalid without the above approvals. An invalid transaction does not give rise to civil rights and obligations of the parties as from the time the transaction is entered into. In this case, the parties will restore everything to its original state and return to each other what they have received from one another.

Immovable property can generally not be acquired in good faith. A good faith (bona fide) acquisition is only possible if the third person received the property by way of an auction or pursuant to a judgment or decision of an authorized state body.

3. Filing Requirements

The transfer of real property requires special filings with the authorities. With respect to land use rights, a transfer agreement must be notarized at the relevant Notary Public Offices or the relevant People's Committees where the land is located. Thereafter, the procedures for the issuance of land use rights certificates shall be carried out at the relevant People's Committees (through the relevant Land Registries).

Like land use rights, the transfer of real property that constitutes assets annexed to the land (houses, buildings or construction) is also required to be notarized/certified at the relevant Notary Public Offices or the relevant People's Committees. In case the seller is an organization licensed to do business in real estate, such notarization or certification is not required, but the registration of ownership rights of such assets must be carried out at the relevant Service of Constructions or the relevant People's Committees.

4. Automatic Transfer of Encumbrances

The sale of encumbered real estate is only allowed if the security holder agrees to the sale. Encumbrances will not automatically transfer to the purchaser. If the obligation is fulfilled by the obligor, a waiver of encumbrance must be filed at the relevant Land Registries where the encumbrance of such assets was previously registered. Accordingly, the security holder and/or the seller will have to submit a request for a waiver of any encumbrance and any documents relating to the encumbered real property. Thereafter, the Land Registries will issue certification on such waiver of encumbrance to the security holder and/or the seller.

5. Automatic Transfer of Lease Agreements

Lease agreements will automatically be transferred to the purchaser. In case the purchaser purchases real property (for instance, a house) that is subject to a lease agreement, the purchaser must guarantee the rights and interests of the lessee which are provided in the lease agreement. Further, the lessee, as provided by laws, has the right to continue to lease such house with the same terms and conditions agreed upon in the lease agreement in case of change of the house's owner. There is no extraordinary right to terminate the lease agreement due to the sale.

D. Contracts

1. Characteristics as to:

a) Language of Documentation. The sale and transfer documents may be drafted in every language and English/bilingual documents are permitted and recommended if a foreign element is involved. In practice, if a party to the sale agreement is a foreign party, the sales agreement will usually be bilingual in Vietnamese and English. The English version may prevail for the purpose of interpretation.

b) Form of Documentation. Sale and purchase agreements need not necessarily be made in writing. Although, for purposes of documentation and evidence, sale and purchase agreements will usually be entered into in writing. However, they are not required to be notarized/certified or registered.

Signing in counterparts is permissable, such that the documents need not be jointly signed by the parties; however, in this case, the time when the written contract is entered into shall be the time when the last party to the agreement signs the contract.

c) Specification of Contracts. All contracts must be clearly identifiable. Therefore, subject to the agreement of the parties, a description or list of contracts may be provided in the sale agreement or an appendix that is attached to the sale agreement. To avoid discrepancies, all contracts should be described in as much detail as possible.

2. Administrative, Corporate and Other Approvals

- The transfer of a contract does not generally require special governmental or administrative approvals.
- Except for private enterprises, the sale of assets amounting to 50% or more of the total assets in a company must have the approval of the members' council (if it is a limited liability company with more than two members), approval of the owner (if it is a single limited liability company) or approval of the shareholder's general meeting (if it is a joint stock company), unless otherwise stated in the company charter.
- In the event the rights in such contract are encumbered, the transferor of such rights is only entitled to transfer the encumbered rights if the security holder so agrees.

The transfer of contracts is invalid without the above approvals and, unless so approved, will not give rise to civil rights and obligations of the parties. In such circumstances, the parties must restore everything to its original state and shall return to each other what they have received.

3. Automatic Transfer of Contracts (Other than Lease and Employment Agreements)

In a contract transfer, if the rights in the contract are secured by an asset (for instance, an automobile), the security will automatically be transferred to the purchaser. If the secured automobile is insured by an insurer, the insurance premium follows the secured assets. Therefore, if a party (for example, a bank) transfers its rights (to request repayment) and obligations (to provide a loan to a borrower) in a loan/mortgage agreement to another bank and such loan was secured by an automobile that was insured by an insurer, the purchaser (new bank) will have the same rights and obligations as the initial bank together with the secured car that is insured by an insurer. However, this is usually only because banks contractually allow themselves to transfer security. If the borrower does not make a repayment to the new bank (purchaser), the new bank has the right to claim the secured automobile. If any insured event occurs, the new bank has the right to receive the insurance proceeds. In order to secure a loan, banks will usually request that the insurer issue an endorsement indicating that the bank is a named beneficiary to the insurance policy.

4. Filing Requirements

This depends on the type of rights or obligations in the contract to be transferred. For instance, if there is a transfer of rights to collect debts that were incurred from loan agreements (e. g., sale and purchase agreements, asset lease agreements, service agreements), such transfer of rights must be registered with the competent authority. Please note that the registration of the transaction for this transfer is not compulsory, but if such transfer is registered, the payment priority (of the transferee or mortgagee) will be determined based on the priority of registration.

5. Treatment of Existing Contractual Claims and Obligations

The seller is responsible for providing full and necessary information regarding the contract to be transferred, if the representations, warranties, etc. require this. Technically, it would be possible to make the sale on an "as is" basis, offering no representation or warranty in relation to the contracts, provided that no misrepresentation is made. In the case of insufficient information, the seller must only compensate the purchaser on the basis of the contract if he violated any such representations, warranties, etc. and thereby caused the purchaser to incur damages. Upon transfer, the seller shall not be responsible if the sold contracts are not or not completely fulfilled by the obligor, unless otherwise agreed upon by both parties.

6. Warranty Claims Resulting from Events prior to Transfer

As a general rule, the transfer of a contract also includes the transfer of any claims and any obligations related to such contract, since the required consent of the other party to the contract usually also covers such claims and obligations. This also applies to warranty claims resulting from events prior to the transfer of such contract if not otherwise provided for in the asset sale and/or transfer agreement. The potential exposure resulting therefrom is customarily covered by representations and warranties and/or indemnifications.

E. IP Rights

1. Characteristics of Intellectual Property Rights (e.g., Trademarks, Patents, Utility Models, Domain Names) ("*IP Rights*") as to:

a) Language of Documentation. The sale and transfer documents regarding IP Rights, excluding copyright, may be drafted in any language and bilingual documents are permitted. The English version may prevail for the purpose of interpretation. However, if the transfer of IP Rights requires registration, it will need to be drafted bilingually in Vietnamese and English or translated into Vietnamese.

b) Form of Documentation. All documents regarding the transfer of IP Rights must be in writing. The transfer of IP Rights must be registered if required by law. The place of entry into an agreement shall be as agreed by the parties and if there is no agreement on place of entry into an agreement, such place shall be the residence of the individual or the head office of the legal entity that has made the offer to enter into the contract. In case of entry into a contract in absentia, the determination of the place where the contract was entered into must comply with the law of the country of residence of the individual or the head office of the legal entity who requested the contract to be entered into. Signing in counterparts is possible, the documents need not necessarily be jointly signed by the parties.

c) Specification of IP Rights. As discussed above, the subject of an agreement must be described clearly. In this case, the subject of the transfer agreement is the IP Right, therefore the right must be described accordingly.

2. Administrative, Corporate and Other Approvals

- The transfer of IP Rights does not require special governmental or administrative approvals, but they may require registration with the National Office of Intellectual Property (NOIP), which, in practice, is similar to an approval.
- Except for private enterprises, the sale of assets amounting to 50% or more of the total assets in a company must be approved by the members' council (if it is a limited liability company with more than two members), approved by the Owner (if it is a single member limited liability company) or approved by the shareholder's general meeting (if it is a joint stock company), unless otherwise stated in the company charter.
- If IP Rights are encumbered, the transferor of such IP Rights is only entitled to transfer the encumbered IP Rights if the security holder agrees.

The transfer of IP Rights is invalid without the above approvals. Any invalid transaction will not give rise to civil rights and obligations of the parties. In such circumstances, the parties must restore everything to its original state and return to each other what they have received.

3. Filing Requirements

The transfer of IP Rights must be registered if such IP Rights were established on the basis of registration.

4. Applicable International (Multilateral) Agreements or Treaties

Vietnam is subject to the TRIPS Agreement and the Paris Convention for the Protection of Industrial Property. In addition, Vietnam has signed the Madrid Agreement and the Madrid Protocol regarding trademarks. Finally, Vietnam participates in the Berne Convention, Stockholm Convention, Rome Convention, Brussels Convention, Geneva Convention, Lahay convention, UPOV and the international cooperation agreement on patent rights.

F. Receivables

1. Characteristics as to:

a) Language of Documentation. The sale and transfer documents regarding receivables (such as the right to claim for debts, right to receive payments from selling assets, right to receive loan repayment, right to receive monthly house/office rental or monthly land lease, etc.) may be drafted in any language and bilingual documents are permitted. The English version may prevail for the purpose of interpretation.

b) Form of Documentation. The transfer of receivables has no prescribed form, but will usually be memorialized in writing. Place of entry into the transfer agreement can be as agreed by the parties and in the absence of an agreement, such place shall be the residence of the individual or the head office of the legal entity who has made the offer to enter into the contract. Signing in counterparts is possible, and the documents need not necessarily be jointly signed by the parties; however, in this case, the time when the written contract is entered into shall be the time when the last party to the agreement signs the contract.

c) Specification of Receivables. All receivables must be clearly identifiable. Therefore, subject to the agreements of the parties, description or list of receivables may be provided in the sale agreement or an appendix which is attached to the sale agreement. To avoid discrepancies, all outstanding receivables contracts should be described therein in as much detail as possible.

2. Administrative, Corporate and Other Approvals

- The transfer of receivables does not require special governmental or administrative approvals.
- Except for private enterprises, the sale of assets amounting to 50% or more of the total assets in a company must be approved by the Members' Council (if it is a limited liability company with more than two members), approved by the owner (if it is a single member limited liability company) or approved by the shareholder's general meeting (if it is a joint stock company), unless stated otherwise in the charter.
- The approval of debtors is generally not required, but the transferor must inform the debtors accordingly.

Transfer of receivables is invalid without the above approvals. An invalid transaction will fail to give rise to civil rights and obligations of the parties. In such circumstances, the parties must restore everything to its original state and return to each other what they have received.

3. Filing Requirements

The transfer of receivables does not have to be filed with the authorities, but notification to the debtors is required.

G. Liabilities

1. Characteristics as to:

a) Language of Documentation. The transfer of liabilities (such as tax obligations, environmental issues, etc., prior to the acquisition of the liabilities) may be drafted in any language, and bilingual documents are permitted. The English version may prevail for the purpose of interpretation. However, the transfer of liabilities is only permissible with the consent of the party that is owed the liability.

b) Form of Documentation. The transfer of liabilities has no prescribed form, but will usually be made in writing. Place of entry into the transfer agreement can be as agreed by the parties and if there is no agreement on the place of entry into an agreement, such place shall be the residence of the individual or the head office of the legal entity who has made the offer to enter into the contract. Signing in counterparts is possible, and the documents need not be jointly signed by the parties.

c) Specification of Liabilities. All liabilities must be clearly identifiable. Therefore, subject to the agreements of the parties, description or list of liabilities may be provided in the sale agreement or an appendix attached to the sale agreement.

2. Administrative, Corporate and Other Approvals

- The transfer of liabilities does not require special governmental or administrative approvals.
- Except for private enterprises, the sale of assets amounting to 50% or more of the total assets in a company must be approved by the Members' Council (if it is a limited liability company with more than two members), approved by the owner (if it is a single member limited liability company) or approved by the shareholder's general meeting (if it is a joint stock company), unless otherwise provided in the company charter.
- The transfer must be approved by the creditor.

The transfer of liabilities is invalid without the above approvals. An invalid transaction will fail to give rise to civil rights and obligations of the parties. In such circumstances, the parties must restore everything to its original state and return to each other what they have received.

3. Filing Requirements

The transfer of liabilities does not require special filings with the authorities but does require the approval of the creditor.

4. Purchaser's Liability for:

a) Tax Obligations. In principal, tax obligations related to the acquired asset for periods prior to the acquisition are borne by the seller, except as otherwise agreed by the parties. The purchaser can assume the liability (i.e. agree to pay it or indemnify the seller for it) but the seller will still be liable to the tax authority.

b) Environmental Contamination. In principal, the seller is responsible for environmental contamination related to the acquired assets for periods prior to the acquisition, except as otherwise agreed by the parties. The purchaser can assume the liability (i.e. agree to pay it or indemnify the seller for it) but the seller will still be liable.

c) Products Sold or Services Rendered by the Seller to Third Parties. Products sold or services rendered by the seller to third parties prior to the acquisition are the possession/responsibility of such third parties. In case the products or services are under warranty term, such warranty responsibility shall be borne by the seller.

5. Automatic Transfer of Other Liabilities

Subject to the agreements between the parties, the purchaser is only responsible for the liabilities agreed to be transferred by the parties.

H. Employees

1. Transfer of Employees

Vietnamese labor laws and regulations are unclear about automatic transfer of employees in an asset transfer. If the seller transfers the right to use all or the major assets of the seller, the purchaser shall continue to implement the labor contracts with the employees. In order to implement the labor contracts with the employees, the authorities usually require the contract between the seller and the employees to be terminated and the seller subsequently must settle all benefits (salary, severance allowance, social insurance and any other benefits) that are enjoyed by the employees. The purchaser then must enter into new labor contracts with the employees, subject to the employees' acceptance; there cannot be a simple "transfer" of employment from one entity to another.

2. Approval of Works Council, Trade Union or Other Institutions

The "transfer of employees" does not require the approval of a works council, labor agency, trade union or other institution, but it does require the approval of the employee.

3. Contractual Protection as to Labor Issues

In general, the parties are free to agree on most matters, provided that minimum employee benefits stated in the labor code are met and such agreements are not contrary to law.

I. Tax Implications

1. Value Added Tax

Most asset transfers will trigger VAT issues. Goods and services used for production, business and consumption in Vietnam are all subject to VAT, with only few exceptions, such as, most importantly, transfer of Land Use Rights and technology. The current VAT rate is 0%, 5% and 10%, depending on the types of goods and services, with 10% as the most common rate applied to goods.

2. Real Property Transfer Tax

Where there is a transfer of real property, the following taxes/fees shall be applicable:

- Land use rights transfer tax (applied to individuals and organizations who transfer land use rights): 4% for residential land and 2% for agricultural land, based on the land price issued annually by the State; land use rights transfer tax (applied to non-business organizations who transfer land use rights); 4% for residential land and 2% for agricultural land based on the land price issued annually by the State;
- Personal income tax (applied to individuals who transfer real property): 2% on the transfer price or the price issued annually by the State, whichever is higher, or 25% on net gain upon showing proper supporting documents;
- Corporate income tax (applied to business organizations who transfer real property): 25% on the income gained from the transfer of real property;
- VAT (applied to the purchaser who purchases the assets annexed to the land such as houses, buildings or construction works): the purchaser shall bear the VAT rate of 10% when purchasing assets annexed to the land;
- Registration fee (applied to the purchaser who has to pay the registration fee before registering ownership rights of the land or assets annexed to the land): 0.5% on the purchase price, if such purchase price is not lower then the annual land price determined by the State.

3. Other Tax Issues

Transfer of an asset shall be subject to the following tax: VAT, which shall be borne by the purchaser; Corporate Income Tax, which shall be borne by the seller as organization; Import/Export Tax (where applicable), which shall be borne by the purchaser as importer or exporter.

J. Bankruptcy Law

1. Challenge of Asset Transfer in Case of Insolvency

In the event of insolvency of the seller, there is a risk for the purchaser that creditors of the seller would challenge the transfer if it were conducted by the seller within three months prior to the date on which a court accepted jurisdiction over a petition to commence bankruptcy procedures. An asset transfer within these three months might be regarded by Vietnamese laws as an invalid "other transaction for the purpose of disposing of assets of the enterprise," as described above.

2. Acquisition of Assets that are Subject to Bankruptcy Proceedings

After a court decision to commence bankruptcy proceedings, all activities of the enterprise shall continue to be conducted as normal, but shall be subject to the supervision of the bankruptcy judge. From the date the enterprise receives the judge's decision to commence bankruptcy procedures, the following acts may only be undertaken with the written consent of the judge: (i) the pledge, mortgage, assignment, sale, donation or lease of any asset; (ii) receipt of assets from a contract assigning them; (iii) termination of the performance of an effective contract; (iv) borrowing; (v) sale or conversion of shares or transfer of ownership rights in any assets; and (vi) payment of any new debt arising from the business activities of the enterprise and payment of wages of the employees of the enterprise. From the date the enterprise receives the judge's decision to commence bankruptcy procedures, it may not (i) conceal or dispose of any asset; (ii) pay any unsecured debt; (iii) abandon or reduce any right to claim a debt; and (iv) convert unsecured debts into debts secured by assets of the enterprise.

K. Timing and Costs

1. Timeframe of Asset Transfer

The timeframe for the sale/acquisition of a business by way of an asset deal depends on the size of the deal. Taking into account that usually a new entity must be set up to take over the assets in Vietnam, the transfer of assets may take from three months to over one year. Normally, the following factors will affect the timing and cost of the deal: due diligence on the assets being sold/purchased, including ensuring that all assets have proper documents of title (where required) prior to sale; structuring the purchasing entity (i.e. establishment of a company in Vietnam through a stand-alone offshore investment vehicle); negotiation with the seller and contract drafting.

2. Costs of Asset Transfer

There is no stamp duty in Vietnam although the sale of certain assets (i.e. real property, shares, etc.) will trigger certain taxes. Other notarization and registration fees are generally low in Vietnam and the major cost will be legal due diligence for a purchaser.

L. Miscellaneous

1. Choice of Foreign Law

If the contract is entered into in Vietnam and performed entirely in Vietnam, the laws of Vietnam will apply. With respect to Vietnamese real property, the laws of Vietnam must always be applied. Parties to a contract with a foreign element are free to choose foreign law, provided that it is not contrary to basic principles of Vietnamese law. While Vietnamese law will apply to any registrations or approvals required as a result of the sale, the parties can choose foreign law to apply to the contract.

2. (International) Arbitration, Choice of Venue

International arbitration is permissible and recommended for dispute settlement if the disputes are commercial in nature. There are no restrictions as to the choice of venue for settlement of disputes by arbitration. Additionally, Vietnam is a signatory to the 1958 New York Convention on the Recognition and Enforcement of Foreign Arbitral Awards.

However, pursuant to the Civil Procedure Code of Vietnam, a party wishing to enforce a foreign arbitral award in Vietnam cannot do so unless it submits an application to the Ministry of Justice for a review of the award by the relevant Vietnamese Court and such application is accepted. Vietnamese law will not recognize and enforce a foreign arbitral award that is contrary to Vietnamese law principles. Therefore, there can effectively be a re-hearing in the Vietnamese courts of any foreign arbitral award, and this has been the practice to date.

3. Other Distinctions, Characteristics

There are no further noteworthy distinctions and/or characteristics as to the transfer of assets under Vietnamese law.

FSC
www.fsc.org
MIX
Papier | Fördert gute Waldnutzung
FSC® C083411

Kolibri 360 GmbH
Ferdinand-Jühlke-Straße 7
99095 Erfurt, Deutschland
produktsicherheit@kolibri360.de